P9-DUR-829

THE CRUCIBLE OF CHRISTIANITY

EDITED BY

ARNOLD TOYNBEE

THE
OF

ABRAHAM SCHALIT

KURT SCHUBERT

A.H.M. JONES

A. NICHOLAS SHERWIN-WHITE

J.-G. GAGÉ

JOCELYN M.C. TOYNBEE

A. HILARY ARMSTRONG

DAVID FLUSSER

M.J. VERMASEREN

CARDINAL DANIÉLOU

HARRY A. WOLFSON

ROBERT M. GRANT

G.E.M. DE STE. CROIX

556 illustrations

158 in colour

398 photographs,

drawings, maps and plans

Picture adviser : J.M.C. Toynbee

CRUCIBLE CHRISTIANITY

JUDAISM, HELLENISM AND THE HISTORICAL BACKGROUND TO THE CHRISTIAN FAITH

WORLD PUBLISHING COMPANY

New York and Cleveland

Designed and produced by Thames and Hudson, London
Managing Editor: Ian Sutton BA
Art Editor: Ruth Rosenberg PH D
House Editor: Brian Graham MA
Research: Imogen Bright, Georgina Bruckner MA, Gloria Wood BA
Special Drawings: Trevor Hodgson M DES RCA
Plans and Drawings: Paula Brown DIP AD
Maps: Edgar Holloway
Index: H. V. Molesworth-Roberts
Special Photography: C. Bibbey, Françoise Foliot, Ronald Sheridan, John Webb
Illustrations reproduced by: Klischeewerkstätten der Industriedienst, Wiesbaden, Germany
Photosetting: Keyspools Ltd, Golborne, England
Printed in Germany by Universitätsdruckerei H. Stürtz AG, Würzburg
Paper: Woodfree white art paper supplied by Gerald Judd Ltd, London. Grey text paper supplied by Mühlebach AG, Brugg, Switzerland
Bound in Germany by Hollmann KG, Darmstadt

Library of Congress Catalog Card Number: 75–86917

CONTENTS

INTRODUCTION

ARNOLD TOYNBEE

THE SUBJECT OF THIS BOOK is the place and time in which Christianity made its appearance in the world. The place is the western end of the Old World; within this, the Mediterranean basin; and, within that, the eastern part of it, known in the Romance languages as the Levant. The time is a span of approximately four centuries in all, *i.e.* the last two centuries before the beginning of the Christian era and the first two after it.

The word 'approximately' must be stressed; for the reader will find that each chapter of the book has its own time-span. This is determined by the character of the particular human activity with which a particular chapter is concerned. It is true that all human activities interact with each other and that therefore all facets of human life are interdependent. But it is also true that each activity has its own distinctive pace and rhythm, and this means that the period covered in this book does not either begin or end at exactly the same date in all the various transactions with which the book deals. 'Periods' are, at best, arbitrary though unavoidable cuts across the continuous flow of history. This artificial dissection of what in truth is a unity is an unavoidable intellectual operation, simply because the human mind is an imperfect instrument and, to handle its objects, it has to break them up into units that are manageable at the cost of being artificial.

As for the practice of reckoning chronology in terms of the Christian era (*i.e.* counting forwards and backwards from the supposed date of Jesus' birth), this was started in Western Christendom in the 6th century of this era and has now become a world-wide usage, as a result of the recent world-wide predominance of the Western civilization. In the Western world itself, two attempts to substitute new eras, dating respectively from the outbreak of the French Revolution and from the Fascist seizure of power in Italy, have both been ludicrous failures; and today the adoption of the Christian era has become practically world-wide. It has now been adopted not only in Eastern Christendom, but also by the vast non-Christian majority of the human race. It has, in fact, become the 'the Common Era', as it is called in present-day Jewish parlance.

A drama in three acts

The place and time covered in this book take the shape of a drama in three acts. The first act is an age of agony; the second is a breathing-space during which the Mediterranean world enjoys a spell of comparative orderliness and peace. In the third act the agony recurs.

The first act opens in 218 BC with the outbreak of the second of the three wars between Rome and Carthage. In this war, Hannibal brought the Roman Commonwealth in Italy to the verge of destruction, and left to Italy, which he had just failed to liberate from Roman rule, a legacy of social dislocation. The sequel was the extension of Rome's military and political ascendancy from Italy to the whole perimeter of the Mediterranean; the cold-blooded destruction by Rome of Carthage and Corinth, two of the largest and most important cities of the Mediterranean world; and the outbreak, in 133 BC, of a domestic revolution in the Roman body politic which lasted, off and on, for a century and engulfed the whole of the huge area that had now come to be at Rome's mercy.

The second act began with the establishment of the *Pax Romana* by Augustus. (A convenient conventional date is 31 BC, the year of Augustus' decisive victory over Antony and Cleopatra.)

For the purpose of this book, the third act opens with the first of the successive breakdowns of the Roman Peace. After the attainment of an apparent, but illusory, peak of material prosperity during the first two-thirds of the 2nd century AD, ominous symptoms of economic and social and spiritual *malaise* began to appear before the death of the Emperor Marcus Aurelius in AD 180. The spiritual *malaise* is documented in Marcus' own private note-book. The *malaise* in all sides of life erupted into a fresh bout of agony after the murder of the Emperor Alexander Severus in AD 235; but the subsequent half-century of anarchy did not wreck the *Pax Romana* irretrievably. At a heavy cost in terms of regimentation and taxation, the Roman Imperial régime was re-established by Diocletian, and, as reorganized under this more authoritarian régime, the Roman Empire survived till after the beginning of the 7th century in the Levant, with its high Hellenic culture and relatively sound economic basis, while, even in the backward West, the Empire survived till after the beginning of the 5th century.

The reader will notice that this third act is followed up to different points in different chapters. In Chapter XIII, for instance, Professor Wolfson, whose subject is the impact of Greek philosophy, first on Judaism and then on Christianity, has had to carry his story down to the 7th century AD, which saw, in the controversy over Monotheletism, the last of the Christian Church's domestic dissensions that was conducted in Greek philosophic terms. In Chapter VII, Dr J. M. C. Toynbee's subject is the art and architecture of the Graeco-Roman world and particularly those elements and aspects of it that lent themselves to Christianity's purposes; to tell this story adequately, she has had to carry it down to the 5th century of the Christian era. For Chapter XII, whose subject is Christianity as a missionary religion, and likewise for Chapter XV, which deals with Christianity's encounter with the Roman Imperial government, Cardinal Daniélou and Mr de Sainte-Croix have had to carry their stories down to AD 311 (the year of the Emperor Galerius' grudging edict of toleration), AD 312 (the year of the Emperor Constantine's adoption of Christianity), and AD 313 (the year of Constantine's 'Edict of Milan', to which his eastern colleague Licinius adhered). Galerius' and Constantine's edicts rescinded the previous official ban on Christianity without imposing a ban on the other religions represented within the Roman Empire's frontiers, whose adherents, in the aggregate, greatly outnumbered the Christians at this date. The tables were turned in the last two decades of the 4th century, when, after a brief spell of religious toleration for all religions alike, all the non-Christian religions and philosophies were penalized, as Christianity had been till AD 311. This carries Professor Vermaseren in Chapter X almost to the close of the 4th century, if not to AD 529, the year in which the four institutes of philosophy at Athens were closed by the Emperor Justinian. By contrast, the time-span of Chapter XI, which deals with Christianity as a Jewish sect, is short, though its shortness does not give the measure of this subject's intrinsic importance. At the opposite end of the scale, Professor A. H. M. Jones, in Chapter IV, on Hellenism in Syria and Palestine, has had to start with the overthrow of the Persian Empire by Alexander the Great in 334–330 BC, and at even earlier dates for the beginnings of the Hellenization of the Phoenician and Philistine cities and for the Greek colonization of the lowland eastern half of Cilicia, which included the city of Tarsus, St Paul's Greek home-town.

Four centuries of the Roman Peace

It has been mentioned that, in the relatively backward half of the Roman Empire, the effective duration of the Roman Peace was little more than four centuries long. Seen through the eyes of modern Westerners who, since the Renaissance, have reinitiated themselves into an intimate acquaintance with Ancient Greek literature, art, and history, those four centuries look, in retrospect, like an intermediate period of abnormal unity and peace between two ages – the post-Roman age of the Western world and the pre-Roman age of the Ancient Greek world – in which the normal state of affairs has been a society that, in spite of having a common religion and culture, is split up politically among a number of local sovereign independent states that habitually go to war with each other. It is significant that, in the technical terminology of our Egyptologists, 'intermediate periods', in the sense of periods that are exceptional and abnormal, mean, not periods of unity and peace, such as was the brief spell of the Roman Peace in the West, but periods of disunity and strife, of the kind that has been normal in the Western world since the liquidation of the Roman Empire in the West and that was likewise normal in the Ancient Greek world before the Roman Peace was imposed on it. By contrast, unity and peace were normal in the three-thousand-years-long history of Ancient Egypt after its political unification *c.* 3000 BC, and the same blessings have been normal in China as well since her political unification in

221 BC, in spite of the fact that Chinese history, like Ancient Egyptian history, has been punctuated by occasional 'intermediate periods' of disunity and strife.

It is also significant that, before Egypt had been united with Palestine, Syria, Anatolia and the other countries round the perimeter of the Mediterranean Sea by their common inclusion in the Roman Empire, the same four regions had once been united, for more than two centuries, with each other and with the regions to the east of them, as far as the Indus basin inclusive, by their common inclusion in the Persian Empire. On the other hand, during the three centuries that had elapsed between the destruction of the Persian Peace by Alexander and the establishment of the Roman Peace by Augustus, Syria-Palestine had been painfully disrupted, and this in two ways. Politically, it had been partitioned between the Persian Empire's Ptolemaic and Seleucid Greek successor-states. In language, culture, and religion, the region had been partitioned between a sprinkling of colonial Greek city-states and Hellenized Phoenician and Philistine city-states on the one hand and, confronting and opposing them, the anti-Hellenic faction in the Palestinian Jewish and Samaritan communities, which not only suppressed the Philhellene faction of their own countrymen, but successfully resisted the Seleucid government's subsequent attempts to Hellenize them by force. When the Palestinian Jews afterwards attempted to defy the Roman Empire, which took over, in the Levant, the defunct Seleucid Empire's cultural policy together with its political heritage, the Jews were eventually crushed militarily and politically; yet, even then, Judaism survived. It is a living religion today, after the last shadowy vestiges of the Roman Empire have disappeared.

Births cost pangs, and, conversely, times and places in which agony abounds are likely to be prolific. Christianity was not the only live institution that came to birth round about the beginning of the Common Era. The same time and place saw the birth of Pharisaic (*i.e.* modern) Judaism, and of the contemporary oriental missionary religions (*e.g.* the worships of Cybele, Isis, Jupiter Dolichenus, and Mithras) which, like Christianity, adopted an Hellenic dress to equip them for competing for the conversion of the population of the Roman Empire. The Roman Peace, which opened up the Mediterranean world as a field for competitive missionary enterprise, as well as for competitive trade, was likewise established at the same epoch-making date.

The spiritual seed-bed

The Mediterranean world under the régime of the *Pax Romana* may be thought of as being a spiritual seed-bed. The ground had been harrowed and furrowed by the tribulations of the two centuries of agony that had been brought to an end by the Emperor Augustus, in whose reign Jesus had been born. On this spiritually receptive soil, Pharisaic Judaism and gentile Christianity were only two among the many seeds that were sown: but, in this epoch of the history of the Mediterranean world, as in the parable of the sower, a majority of the seeds that were sown wilted before they had produced a crop. Out of all the seeds sown in the Mediterranean world round about the beginning of the Christian era, only gentile Christianity and Pharisaic Judaism are alive today. Jewish Christianity had a short life, and the missionary religions that competed with Christianity are also now extinct, except in so far as Christianity has incorporated in itself some of their constituent elements, such as the Isiac and Cybelene forms of the worship of the Great Mother and the Mithraic and Dolichenian ideal of the Church Militant. As for the Roman Empire, this would-be world-state has become 'ancient history' long ago – unlike its elder brother the Chinese Empire, which is still a going concern, and is now competing with the Soviet Union and the United States for the role of becoming a literally world-wide world-power.

Conflict and tragedy

The ground from which Christianity and Pharisaic Judaism sprang was not only a seed-bed; it was also an arena. It was the scene of a series of dramatic encounters, each of which, in turn, developed into a conflict and ended as a tragedy.

One of these tragic conflicts arose out of the encounter, recorded, on the political plane, by Professor Schalit in Chapter II, between Hellenism and Judaism. An historian whose vision can soar 'above the battle' will discern, in this conflict, not a righteous war of light (whether Jewish light or Greek light) against darkness, but a tragic war between light and light – a war between two ideals, both of them high, which clashed.

The Hellenic ideal was to enable mankind to grow together into something like a single family through the universal reception of an oecumenical common culture. Whether or not Alexander the Great had been the first Greek to conceive of this ideal, he had certainly been energetic in putting it into practice. After having wrested from the Persians their historic role of being the privileged imperial people, Alexander had sought to reconcile them to the catastrophic change in their political fortunes by establishing a Graeco-Iranian partnership. He had drafted Iranians into the *corps d'élite* of his army, had staged a festival of reconciliation, and had coaxed his soldiers, from marshals downwards to privates, into following his own example by marrying Iranian wives. The original framework of this new world-community was to be Greek, but Alexander's intention had been to enrich his oecumenical Hellenic culture by incorporating in it the choicest elements in the cultures of all peoples.

Alexander had died prematurely and suddenly, but his ideal had not died with him; and, among his successors, the most sincere and active exponents of this ideal of unification had been the Seleucids. Seleucus I Nicator had been the only one of Alexander's marshals who, after Alexander's death, had not repudiated his Iranian wife, and, during the three-centuries-long interval between the destruction of the Persian Peace and the establishment of the Roman Peace, the Seleucid Empire had been the leading embodiment, at the western end of the Old World, of the Alexandrine ideal of a world-state. Moreover, Greek culture had been readily, and in some cases enthusiastically, adopted by non-Greek peoples – *e.g.* the Bithynians – who had successfully resisted being subjected to Greek rule, as French culture, though not French rule, has been welcomed, in our day, by the Vietnamese. Even in the Palestinian Jewish community, the Hellenizers had been in the ascendant for a few years in the third and fourth decades of the 2nd century BC before they had been overwhelmed by the anti-Hellenic reaction led by the Hasmonaeans; and the Hasmonaeans themselves, after they had come into power, had gone far towards conforming to the standard contemporary type of Greek or Hellenized parochial princes.

The parallel between this Hellenization of the Mediterranean world and the current Westernization of the whole of the present-day world is both unmistakable and striking, and Alexander's premature death is an accident whose historical consequences, so far from having become 'ancient history', are one of the pertinent facts in atomic-age man's present precarious situation. If Alexander had lived to attain the average of the ages that were actually attained by his marshals, he might have imposed a lasting political unity on the whole of the civilized zone of the Old World, from India and China to Carthage and Rome inclusive; and, in that event, mankind would have rid itself of the cancerous institution of war before it had discovered how to tap the potentially annihilating force of atomic energy.

The Hellenic ideal of world-unity was noble and enlightened; the opposing Jewish ideal was noble and conscientious. The Jews believed that they had been chosen, for being entrusted with a special religious mission, by a god who, besides being their private national god, was the only god who truly existed, and who was, moreover, the creator and sustainer of the whole universe. The Jews' ideal was to remain faithful, at all costs, to their special trust; their prescription for keeping themselves unspotted from the world was to practise separateness.

Herod the Great, statesman and monster

As between the Jews and the Hellenes themselves, a harmonization of their respective ideals was never achieved. If any statesman could have achieved it – and, in achieving it, could have averted the catastrophic consequences of the actual failure – this benefactor of mankind would have been Herod the Great. Herod was neither a Greek nor a Jew; he was an Idumaean; and the Idumaeans had been conquered and been forcibly converted to Judaism by the Hasmonaean prince John Hyrcanus (reigned 135–105/4 BC). As a result of thus incorporating Idumaea in Judaea by force of arms, the Jews had caught a Tatar, as the French did when they bought the island of Corsica from the Genoese Bank of St George over the islanders' heads, and the Russians did when they annexed Georgia and Ossetia. The French caught their Corsican Napoleon, the Russians caught their Osseto-Georgian Stalin; the Jews caught their Idumaean Herod.

In his private life, Herod the Great was a monster. Peter the Great put to death only one son, and Constantine the Great only one son and a wife; Herod the Great put to death two sons and a wife, besides liquidating all the rest of the Hasmonaean family in addition to his Hasmonaean wife Mariamne, whom he had married with a view to legitimizing his own usurpation of the Judaean throne. By comparison with Herod the Great's private career, Stalin's and Hitler's records were innocent – even supposing that the massacre of all male infants at Bethlehem, the crime that has made Herod's name notorious, has to be written off as an unsubstantiated legend. Yet, like Constantine and Peter, Herod justly earned his title 'the Great' in virtue of his prowess in statesmanship.

The Idumaean statesman Herod realized in advance a hard political fact that the Roman historian Tacitus noted retrospectively. Herod realized that the Palestinian Jews had not seen the last of Hellenism when, under Hasmonaean leadership, they had succeeded in shaking off the domination of their tottering Seleucid Greek sovereigns. The Seleucid Empire had been tottering because, twenty-two years before Judas Maccabaeus's revolt, the Seleucid Empire had been struck a stunning blow by Rome; the Seleucids had eventually collapsed because the Romans had seen to it that they should not recover; and one of the

Roman devices for weakening the Seleucids had been to encourage and support the Palestinian Jewish resistance movement. By Herod's time, however, the Romans' short-sighted policy of persistently undermining the Seleucids' power had caught the Romans out. They had improvidently created a political vacuum which they had then found themselves compelled to fill, and, in stepping into the fallen Seleucids' shoes, the Romans had taken over the Seleucids' policy of Hellenization. In this new situation, the Palestinian Jews would have to reckon with Rome in future, and Rome's military power surpassed that of the former Macedonian Greek colonial powers to the degree in which the present military power of the United States surpasses that of the former West European colonial powers.

The Herodian compromise

Herod perceived that, now that there was this new Roman factor to be reckoned with, the incompatibility between Jewish separateness and Hellenic oecumenicalism could be resolved, if at all, only by a compromise; and his solution was to be liberally Hellenic in his dealings with Greeks and Romans, while taking care to be strictly Jewish in his dealings with Jews. On the political plane this dual policy was feasible, since, for the Pharisees, who, by this date, were setting the tone for Palestinian Jewish public opinion, religious liberty took precedence over political independence as a Jewish national objective. But Herod comprehended that a political compromise would be unstable unless it could be underpinned by a cultural one, and accordingly he practised Antiochus IV's munificence and Solomon's munificence simultaneously. Like Antiochus IV, Herod gave generous gifts to historic Greek cities and founded new Greek cities in his own dominions. (Herod's Greek foundations were Sebaste on the site of Samaria and Caesarea on the site of Strato's Tower.) At the same time, Herod, like Solomon, built a temple for Yahweh in Jerusalem; and Herod's temple outshone Solomon's, as well as the pathetic little post-Exilic temple which Herod was replacing. It may be mentioned in passing that the excellence of the masonry of Herod's buildings has won the admiration of our modern archaeologists.

Christianity's appeal

Herod's failure, though perhaps inevitable, was undeserved. The catastrophe that he had striven to avert descended upon Palestinian Jewry several years after his death, at the outbreak, in AD 66, of the first Romano-Jewish war. It was left for Christianity – the new religion that had sprung out of the unresolved Helleno-Jewish conflict – to succeed, to some extent, in getting the best of both worlds, after the Jews had suffered their catastrophe. Christianity made Jewish monotheism acceptable to Greek and Roman polytheists, who were already feeling their way doubtfully towards monotheism, by diluting this with a tincture of polytheism in the doctrine of the Trinity, with a tincture of Graeco-Roman man-worship in the deification of Jesus; and, no doubt, this was one of the causes of Christianity's sensational success in converting the great non-Jewish majority of the population of the Roman Empire. Christianity's appeal was, in fact, not unlike that of the new religions, pullulating today in Japan, that have suffused elements drawn from Shintoism and Buddhism with a glow of Judaic monotheism.

Conflicts within Judaism

There were also two contemporary tragic conflicts within the bosom of Judaism: one between Sadducees and Pharisees; the other, within the Pharisaic sect itself, between methodical Pharisees and Jesus.

Between 168 BC (the date of the Hasmonaean insurrection against the Seleucid régime) and AD 70 (the date of the destruction of Jerusalem, including the Temple, by the Romans), the Sadducees represented, in the Palestinian Jewish community, what, in Britain and the United States today, is called pejoratively 'the Establishment'. The Sadducees may have derived their name from Zadok, who had been appointed high priest by Solomon, as a reward for his loyalty to the House of David, in place of Abiathar, whom Solomon had deposed as a punishment for his having supported Solomon's discomfited competitor Adonijah. An alternative possible origin of the Sadducees' name is the Hebrew word *sedaqa*, meaning uprightness in the sense of correctness, as contrasted with the Pharisees' excessiveness. In any case, the Sadducees were the party of the hereditary priesthood of the House of Aaron; and, in the reign of the Hasmonaean prince John Hyrcanus, the Sadducees and the Hasmonaean dynasty, which was itself of Aaronic descent, had made common cause against the Pharisees. The Hasmonaeans and the Sadducees were attracted to each other, not only by their common social origin, but also by a common religious outlook. Doctrinally, the Sadducees were conservative, though not so conservative as the Samaritans. The Samaritans recognized only the Pentateuch as being canonical. The Sadducees also recognized the whole of what has since become the canonical corpus of the Torah, including the

Books of the Prophets – which is surprising, considering how revolutionary-minded this Israelite and Judahite prophetical literature is.

As against the Sadducees, the Pharisees were dissenters – and this both in the Sadducees' eyes and in their own. Besides recognizing the canonicity of all the written Mosaic Law that was accepted by the Sadducees, the Pharisees believed that Yahweh had also imparted to Moses an unwritten law that had been handed down orally from Moses to the Pharisees themselves. The Pharisees interpreted the written law in the light of this alleged oral tradition, and they were accused by the Sadducees of interpreting parts, at least, of the written law with a freedom that was tantamount to abrogation. The Sadducees' stronghold was the Temple at Jerusalem. The Pharisees' strongholds were the synagogues that they had organized wherever they had spread. When the Temple was destroyed in AD 70, the Sadducees disappeared with it, leaving the Pharisees in possession of the long disputed field of contention for the mastery over the future of Judaism.

The elusive historical Jesus

The issue between the methodical Pharisees and Jesus seems to have been not either theological or ethical or political, but to have been a difference of opinion over method. The historical Jesus, unlike the historical Muhammed, is difficult to discern, because he has been overlaid by the 'image' of him that the Church began to build up immediately after his death. However, there is evidence in the Gospels themselves that Jesus was a monotheist in the straitlaced Jewish and Muslim sense. One of the sayings that are attributed to Jesus is: 'Why callest thou me good? There is none good but one, that is, God.' Another of Jesus' reported sayings is: 'My God, my God, why hast Thou forsaken me?' Since these two sayings were denials, out of Jesus' own mouth, of the divinity that his followers attributed to him, they would surely have been expurgated if they had not been notoriously authentic. On the ethical issue, Claude Montefiore has reckoned up that the Gospels and the Talmud have ninety per cent of their ethical precepts in common. On the political issue of separateness versus oecumenicalism, Jesus said – this, too on the evidence of the Gospels – 'I am not sent but unto the lost people of the House of Israel,' and his reported instructions to his apostles were on the same lines. 'Go not into the way of the gentiles, and into any city of the Samaritans enter ye not; but go rather to the lost sheep of the House of Israel.' These two sayings, too, must surely have been notoriously authentic, or they would not have been retained in the scriptures of a Christian Church that rapidly became overwhelmingly non-Jewish in its membership. What then was this orthodox Pharisee Jesus' offence in his fellow Pharisees' eyes?

In the eyes of Judaean Pharisees, a minor offence of Jesus was that he was a Galilaean; for, in Judaean Jewish eyes, Galilaean Jews were suspect. 'Galilee of the Gentiles' had been converted to Judaism only a century before the probable date of Jesus' birth. We do not know whether the Galilaeans had been voluntary converts or had been converted forcibly, like the Idumaeans and the Ituraeans. In any case, the Galilaeans tended to run to two opposite extremes, both of which were obnoxious to Judaean Jews. If a Galilaean Jew became a Pharisee, he tended also to become a Zealot, *i.e.* a militant political nationalist and, as such, an embarrassment to Pharisees of the majoritarian school whose policy was to be politically obedient to any government, Jewish or gentile, that left them free to practise their religion according to their own lights. At the opposite extreme, Galilaeans were suspected of being prone to relapse into paganism, as the high priest Caiaphas evidently assumed that Jesus was relapsing when Jesus declared: 'Hereafter shall ye see the Son of Man sitting on the right hand of power and coming in the clouds of heaven' – appearing, in fact, in the guise of the Canaanite storm-god Baal-Hadad.

Jesus' major offence in the eyes of his fellow Pharisees, however, was that he taught the people 'as one having authority, and not as the scribes'. This astonished Jesus' audiences, because the regular Pharisees were methodists in the sense that a conventional-minded rabbi would refrain from promulgating a novel interpretation of the Mosaic Law until he was satisfied that he had secured for it an informal consensus among his brethren. Pharisaic Jewish interpretations of the Mosaic Law, like Muslim interpretations of the Muhammadan Law, were established by consensus. Jesus ignored this rabbinical convention, and this was, we may guess, his unpardonable offence in rabbinical eyes – unpardonable, because it undermined the whole of the laboriously constructed basis for the development of the Pharisaic oral law.

All the same, Jesus was a Pharisee, though an unconventional one, and the two living religions that are the surviving fruits of the seeds sown in the Levant in the centuries immediately before and after the starting-date of the Common Era are, both of them, Pharisaic in origin. Rabbi Johanan ben Zakkai did for the mainstream of Pharisaic Judaism, inside the Jewish fold, what St Paul did for the Christian side-stream of Judaism outside the Jewish fold, in the vast Graeco-Roman world. Each of these two great souls gave his religion a new orientation, and, with it, a new lease of life.

Why is it that, within the Jewish fold, the Pharisees eventually prevailed, not only over the uninspiring Sadducees, but over such an inspiring though recalcitrant member of their own sect as Jesus was? Why is it that modern Jewry is Pharisaic Jewry, and that Jesus has not left his mark on it, any more that the Sadducees have left theirs?

The Pharisees' triumph

This question presents itself because the Pharisees did their worst to make themselves unpopular, and this not only with the Hasmonaean and Sadducaean 'Establishment', but also with the unsophisticated mass of the Palestinian Jewish common people. While on the one hand the Pharisees dissented from the worldly-minded Hasmonaeans and Sadducees, on the other hand they practised a puritanical separateness as against the Jewish common people, thus creating an inner circle of segregation within the common Jewish separateness as against the gentiles. The Pharisees' motive for setting up this double-fenced separateness was an obsessive anxiety to make sure of keeping their own ultra-conscientious observance of the Mosaic Law uncontaminated, and they advertised their consequent aloofness from the masses (the Pharisees themselves were a tiny minority) by branding ordinary Jews–among them, Jesus, no doubt–as 'natives' ('*am ha'aretz*, meaning literally 'the people of the land'). This term was as opprobrious as the English word 'natives' is in its modern usage, and it was also fraught with several offensive historical reminiscences: the contempt shown by the Babylonian Jewish purists of Nehemiah's and Ezra's day for the laxity of the undeported Palestinian Jews' descendants; and the contempt of the original Israelite barbarian invaders of Palestine for the more highly civilized but militarily weaker Canaanite natives whom the invaders had evicted or exterminated.

Moreover, the Pharisees, in their own practice of Judaism, laid themselves open to attack on two fronts. On the one side the Sadducees found the Pharisees' 'enthusiasm' (in the derogatory 18th-century meaning of this English word) as distasteful as Bishop Butler found John Wesley's. On the other side, Jesus was shocked by the pedantry that betrayed the Pharisees into sinning against the spirit of the Mosaic Law in their preoccupation with the observance of the letter of it, down to the last jot and title. The vast corpus of the Talmud perhaps justifies Jesus' indictment, though nothing can justify the animus with which this indictment is presented in the Christian scriptures, especially in the Gospel according to St Matthew.

Why, then, did the Pharisees eventually prevail nevertheless? They prevailed on the strength of virtues that outshone their glaring faults: the noble virtues of sincerity, disinterestedness, wholeheartedness, and readiness to expose themselves to persecution for the sake of abiding by their convictions. For instance, they had been enthusiastic freedom-fighters in the ranks of the Hasmonaean resistance movement, so long as the Hasmonaeans had been in the wilderness. The Pharisees then went into opposition to the Hasmonaeans at their peril, as soon as the Hasmonaeans' military and political success corrupted these former patriots into becoming worldlings. Thereafter, when Palestine had fallen under Roman domination, the Pharisees refused to pander to Jewish political nationalism. They disliked Roman domination no less than the Zealots did. At the same time, they disapproved of the Zealots' reckless militancy, and they proclaimed their disapproval at their peril, once again. In this, the Pharisees were in agreement with Herod, who did his best to hold the Zealots in leash, because he foresaw that, if ever the Zealots were to break loose, they would involve the whole of Palestinian Jewry in a disastrous collision with Rome.

As for the Pharisees' and Herod's relations with each other, these were notable for the two incongruous parties' mutual forbearance. The Pharisees strongly disapproved of Herod's Philhellenism, yet they tolerated it, under protest, because Herod, for his part, was careful not to interfere with the Pharisees' practice of their religion. No doubt Herod found the Pharisees' criticism of his policy irritating, particularly when it was outspoken, as it was on more than one occasion. Yet he usually kept his temper and refrained from taking reprisals, because he was aware that, so long as he respected the Pharisees' religious liberty, their own principles would inhibit them from carrying their opposition to him to the point of following up words by action.

The Pharisees' disinterested devotion to the obligations of Judaism, as they saw these, overawed the Sadducees whom they denounced, and won the hearts of the 'natives' whom they despised. In consequence, the Pharisees' virtues won them the guerdon on which their hearts were set. It is the Pharisees' stamp, not the Sadducees' or Jesus', that modern Judaism bears.

Issues for today

This topic and the others that are dealt with in this book are expounded, in successive chapters, by scholars each of whom speaks with authority in his own field, though his authority may not be backed, in every case, by a consensus of his colleagues. The whole subject of the book is so complex, and some of it also so contentious, that it requires a learned and skilled specialist to cope with each single part of it. At the same time, the subject is so important that it is a matter of absorbing interest for all intellectually cultivated men and women, while, for those of them, and they are many, who are spiritually alert, the subject is also a matter of concern in the deeper meaning of the word 'concern' that it has acquired thanks to the special usage of it among members of the Society of Friends.

Why did Christianity and Pharisaic (*i.e.* modern) Judaism make their appearance in the world when and where they did? This is an historical question about events that happened some two thousand years ago. Two millennia are no more than the twinkling of an eye, of course, on the geological and, *a fortiori*, on the astronomical time-scale. Moreover, the question is not just a matter of academic interest. It is so clearly one of the clues to human destiny that it is a major concern, not only for Jews, Christians, and Muslims, who worship, all alike, the god of the Jews, but also for a Christian-educated religious-minded agnostic, like the writer of this preface, as well as for Hindus, Buddhists, Confucians, Taoists, Shintoists, and adherents of other religions and philosophies of Indian and East Asian origin. This is, in fact, a concern for all human beings, of all races, civilizations, and nationalities, who are intellectually and spiritually awake.

What is this wide-awake public to whom this book is addressed? 'It is like a grain of mustard seed which a man took and cast into his garden; and it grew, and waxed a great tree.' The earliest time and place at which we catch sight of it is at the turn of the 13th and 14th centuries in Florence. As it is revealed to us by Dante in his *Vita Nuova*, it is still a tiny Florentine coterie. When, two hundred years later, the Renaissance burst the bounds of Central and Northern Italy and spread far and wide over Transalpine Europe, it awoke to consciousness one fresh contingent of this public after another, *pari passu* with its own onward march. Today, when seven centuries have passed since the birth of Dante and his Florentine contemporaries, the cultivated public has become literally world-wide in its distribution, and at the same time, with the increasing diffusion of higher education, it has incorporated progressively one social class after another which had previously been left sitting in darkness.

The countries in which the cultivated public extends today over the widest gamut of income-groups do not coincide with the countries that are foremost in point of affluence. In Scotland, Finland, and Iceland today, this cultivated public embraces fishermen and shepherds and mechanics, as well as members of the liberal professions. Every Englishman who visits Scotland is aware of this remarkable phenomenon there, and the writer of this preface has observed it at first hand in Finland and in Iceland as well. In England, too, he has watched this intellectually and spiritually awakened public growing in numbers, and spreading from one profession and one walk of life to another, during his thirty-three years' service as Director of Studies at the Royal Institute of International Affairs.

A humanistic understanding

An increasing number of people in responsible positions in the business world, for instance, have been realizing that they need a humanistic understanding of life if they are to do their professional work as it ought to be done; and, beyond this utilitarian consideration, they find themselves wanting to acquire this increased understanding for its own sake, because they are aware that they are responsible human beings living at a critical time in human history. Other important constituents of this same public are the first-rate scientists and technicians, many of whom likewise realize their need for a humane education to balance their technical one. Another important section of the non-specialist intellectual élite is the growing body of civil servants – both those who serve national governments and the increasing number who are now serving the whole human race by working in international agencies.

This non-academic cultivated public is not only able and serious-minded. It also has a concern for the future of mankind. In fact, this is the salt of the earth, and, in the time in which we live – the age in which man's acquisition of a mastery over atomic energy has now brought it within mankind's power to destroy itself – the responsibility for saving mankind from itself rests on the shoulders of this portion of the human race – a portion of it that is still a minority, though happily it is now a rapidly growing one.

This is the public for which Dante and Petrarch and the 18th-century French philosophers and Adam Smith and Hume and Gibbon and Goethe and Renan were all writing, each for his own generation, but each also for posterity. Today, 'the harvest truly is plenteous, but the labourers are few'. Since Renan's generation, a disconcerting gap has yawned open between the cultivated public and the cultivated writer. Down to Goethe's day, at any rate, there was no foretaste, in the Republic of Letters, of the distinction, which has now come to loom so large, between 'academic' and 'non-academic', 'professional' and 'amateur', 'specialist' and 'layman'. By contrast, in our time the enormous increase in the amount of things that there are to know has conspired with the comparably great increase in the exactingness, in every profession, of the demands on the practitioner's time and strength to drive a wedge between the general cultivated public and the specialists in the increasing number of smaller and smaller patches into which the broadening field of knowledge has now been broken up. We are in danger of relapsing into the pre-Renaissance condition of Western Christendom in which the 'clerks' possessed an esoteric knowledge which was beyond the laity's reach – a state of affairs in which some clerks abused the privilege of their benefit of clergy by keeping their knowledge to themselves.

Scholars and the public

Today there is a tendency for scholars to write, not for the cultivated public, but for each other. This is a loss for both parties, and it also threatens to impoverish culture itself. It is a loss for the academic scholar when he insulates himself from intellectual intercourse with fellow human beings whose minds are no less able than his, and who may have had a wider experience of life. Conversely, it is a loss for cultivated men and women, whose intellectual interest and whose social and moral concern is as actively alive as it has ever been, when they are not given the opportunity of sharing in the results of the researches and reflections of scholars who have devoted themselves to the study of some particular topic and consequently have, on this point, a wealth of knowledge and understanding to offer which, under the strenuous conditions of modern life, cannot any longer be acquired, unaided, by intellectual equals of theirs whose work happens to carry them into some other field. If the divorce between the specialists and the public were to go to further extremes, the achievement of the Renaissance might be undone; the Republic of Letters might dissolve; and culture might come to be in danger of dying from a plethora of uncommunicated and therefore unutilized knowledge.

It is an auspicious feature of the present book that France is admirably represented among the contributors to it. For, in France, a gap has never opened between the professional scholar and the other members of the cultural élite. These have taken up non-academic professions, but they have remained capable, nevertheless, of meeting the scholar on equal intellectual terms. It is no accident that the latest of the immortals on my list was a Frenchman. As a scholar, Renan could hold his own against anyone in the world in his generation; yet, at the same time, Renan, like Gibbon and like Dante, was himself a member of the public for which he wrote. This abiding solidarity between the academic and the non-academic members of the Republic of Letters in France is, no doubt, one of the reasons why French culture has been so continuously full of vitality and so continuously pre-eminent.

French scholars who have become famous among their confrères, at home and abroad, for full-length works of technical scholarship have not felt it beneath their dignity also to write works of the kind that, in French, are called, with characteristic French irony, '*oeuvres de vulgarisation*', on the principle of *lucus a non lucendo*. They have written works of this kind with zest, because they have found here an opportunity for putting forth their highest intellectual and artistic prowess. They have judged right; for what intellectual exercise could be more exacting, more stimulating, or more rewarding than to expound, in short compass, an important but intricate subject to receptive and appreciative minds? The publishers and the editor of this book are grateful to the writers, French and others, who have accepted the invitation to contribute because they have realized the value of the service that they have been invited to perform. It is a service that is of mutual benefit; for it is a service to the writers as well as to their readers – a public who will be, we may predict, considerably more numerous than the narrower circle of each writer's own fellow specialists.

Acknowledgements

The publishers would like to thank Mr Jerry O'Dell and Miss Emily Lane, the translators respectively of Chapter III and Chapters VI, XI and XII.

The illustrations-sections have been the responsibility of the publishers, who take this opportunity of thanking, first our picture adviser, Professor Jocelyn Toynbee, second Professor M. J. Vermaseren, who supplied from his own archive the majority of the illustrations for Chapter X, third all the authors for their patient advice over the wording of the captions, and also the following individuals and institutions for their generous help in providing photographs and advice:

John Allegro; Museum of Art, Amman; Allard Pierson Museum, Amsterdam; Fred Anderegg; Museum of Antiquities, Antioch; Miss Diana Ashcroft; Father P. B. Bagatti, Studium Biblicum Fransciscanum, Jerusalem; Mrs Pauline Baines; Bardo Museum; Chester Beatty Library, Dublin; National Museum, Belgrade; French Institute of Archaeology, Beirut; Benedettine di Priscilla; Roloff Beny; Bollingen Foundation; Rheinisches Landesmuseum, Bonn; Museum of Fine Arts, Boston; Departments of British and Mediaeval Antiquities, Coins and Medals, Egyptian Antiquities, Greek and Roman Antiquities and Western Asiatic Antiquities of the British Museum; Brooklyn Museum; Museo Provinziale Campano, Capua; Peter Clayton; Celeia Museum; Dumbarton Oaks Collection; German Archaeological Institute; Giraudon; Dr A. E. Gordon, University of California; Department of Archaeology, The Hebrew University, Jerusalem; Commissioners of Public Buildings in Ireland; Israel Department of Antiquities and Museums; Israel Government Press Office; Israel National Museum; Archaeological Museum, Istanbul; Italian Air Ministry; Dr Renate Jacques, Gewebesammlung der Ingenieurschule für Textilwesen, Krefeld; Professor A. H. M. Jones; Badisches Landesmuseum, Karlsruhe; Dr Kathleen Kenyon; Libyan Department of Antiquities; Mansell Collection; Associazione Turistica pro Melfi; Metropolitan Museum, New York; Ministry of Public Building and Works; Dr E. Nash and Fototeca Unione; Kunsthistorish Instituut, Nijmegen; The Observer and Mr Ronald Harker; Palestine Exploration Fund and Miss P. M. Saul; Museo Archeologico, Perugia; Peterborough Museum; the authorities of the Petit Palais, Paris, and Mme Adéline Cacan; Museo di San Vitale, Ravenna; Ikonenmuseum, Recklingshausen; Museum der Stadt Regensburg; Royal Commission on Historical Monuments; John Rylands Library, Manchester; Sadea S.p.a. and Miss M. Giachetti; Scala; Professor J. B. Segal; Mrs Miriam Shaked; Mrs Miriam Shalem; Edwin Smith; Professor M. Floriani Squarciapino; Syrian Department of Antiquities and Museums; Professor John C. Trever; Rheinisches Landesmuseum, Trier; Unesco; Wadsworth Atheneum; Warburg Institute; Wellcome Foundation; Bradford Welles; Städtisches Museum, Wiesbaden; Roger Wood; Professor Yigael Yadin and the Masada Expedition; Yale University Art Gallery.

I

THE MEDITERRANEAN WORLD'S AGE OF AGONY

THE HISTORICAL ANTECEDENTS

ARNOLD TOYNBEE

'Learning comes through suffering'

AESCHYLUS

Twin roots

determined the character and moulded the history of Christianity – the Jewish and the Graeco-Roman. Both formed an essential part of the spiritual synthesis of the new religion, and without either it could not have achieved the universality of appeal which led to its eventual triumph. To Greece it owed its theological formulation, and Roman practice in statecraft was increasingly drawn upon when the Kingdom of Heaven began to take on the lineaments of an earthly empire. But, in the purity of religious impulse which has made Christianity, in its better periods, one of the supreme religions of mankind, we detect the influence of the East. At an astoundingly early date Judaism had freed itself from the primitive and bloodthirsty elements characteristic of so many early religions. Even the cardinal tenets of Jesus' mission, such as love of one's neighbour and the so-called 'Golden Rule', had been substantially anticipated by post-Exilic rabbis.

Who were the Jews? The unsettled conditions at the eastern end of the Mediterranean in the 13th and 12th centuries BC, among which and as a result of which the Jews first come on to the stage of history, make answers to this question always tentative. The most that can be said is that, about 1200 BC, there were considerable migratory movements of Aramaean tribes emanating from the Arabian peninsula and reaching Palestine, among other countries. Of these tribes, some, including the twelve known as the 'children of Israel', reached the 'land of Canaan', and absorbed much of the indigenous Canaanites' highly developed culture, which was a combination of the two dominant cultures of the area, the Sumerian-Akkadian and the Egyptian. In Abraham's migration from 'Ur of the Chaldees', one may perhaps see a folk-memory of the troubled period in Sumerian-Akkadian history consequent upon the Amorite invasions at the beginning of the 2nd millennium, while Jacob's 'descent' into Egypt may be connected with the Hyksos domination that ended about the middle of the 16th century BC.

Having successfully resisted the 'People of the Sea', especially the Philistines, who were also on the move at this time, the tribes of Israel were united under the Judahite King David — a period of prosperity which was as brief as it was striking: in particular, the temple built at Jerusalem by David's son Solomon was one of the wonders of the ancient world.

After Solomon the tribes divided again into two kingdoms: Israel (in the north) and Judah (in the south). Israel was conquered by the Assyrians, Judah subsequently by the Babylonians, and the élites of both communities suffered deportation. Unlike the deportees from Israel, those from Judah preserved their identity, and after the Persian conquest some of them returned to Judaea.

It was after the Jewish exiles' return that the great work began of compiling what is known to us as the Old Testament (part of our difficulty with the early period lies in the fact that the history of Israel, which except in the short Davidic period was the more powerful and sophisticated of the kingdoms, is seen through later Judahite eyes). Israel now becomes an alternative name for the progenitor Jacob, with Judah as one of his twelve sons. Their supposed descendants, the 'twelve tribes', are seen, each in his booth, in this fresco from the Dura Europus synagogue, which has as its subject Moses' miraculous provision of water. 'And the Lord said unto Moses, Go on before the people, and take with thee of the elders of Israel; and thy rod, wherewith thou smotest the river, take in thine hand and go. Behold, I will stand before thee there upon the rock in Horeb; and thou shalt smite the rock, and there shall come water out of it, that the people may drink. And Moses did so in the sight of the elders of Israel.' Here the miraculous spring is shown as a well, from which the water flows in twelve streams. At the back stands the Ark, represented (anachronistically) by the Menorah, incense-burners and Table of the Shewbread in a Hellenistic temple. In the well some archaeologists have discerned fishes – living creatures in the Water of Life. (1)

Three mighty empires confront us, almost at the dawn of civilization, in Iraq. The first was founded by Sargon of Agade *c.* 2300 BC. An impressive bronze of an Akkadian king (above, left) is sometimes thought to be Sargon. Above right: Naram-Sin, fourth of the dynasty, leads his warriors to the top of a high wooded mountain, perhaps to defeat the Lullubi. (2, 3)

Ur-Nammu reunited the Sumerian-Akkadian world *c.* 2100 BC (Third Dynasty of Ur). Below left: the moon god Nana confers upon him the rod and line symbolic of right and justice. Ur was finally sacked by invading Amorites *c.* 1900 BC. Abraham's departure with his flocks and all he possessed may be connected with this event, and it must have resembled this scene from the Royal Standard of Ur (below, right), commemorating the successes of the First Dynasty, and probably showing captured booty. (4, 5)

Hammurabi of Babylon (below) extended Amorite rule over much of Mesopotamia. His famous law code shows considerable parallels with the Mosaic Law, particularly in the *lex talionis*. (6)

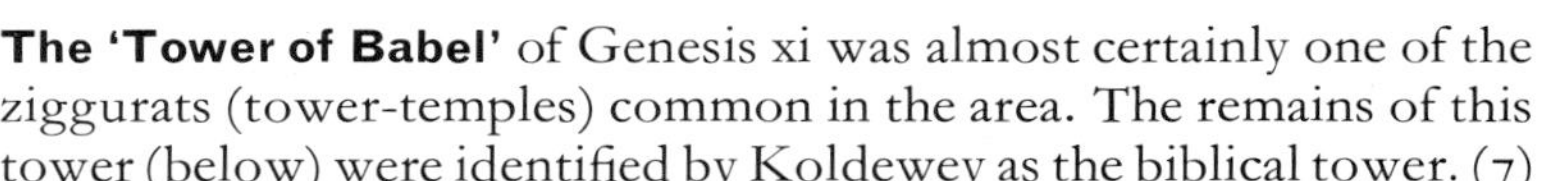

The 'Tower of Babel' of Genesis xi was almost certainly one of the ziggurats (tower-temples) common in the area. The remains of this tower (below) were identified by Koldewey as the biblical tower. (7)

'Israel is ravaged and has no offspring.' The name of Israel is first mentioned among other conquered Palestinian peoples on the stele of Pharaoh Merneptah (above), dating from about 1230 BC. (8)

The Kassites were dominant in Babylonia following the collapse of the first Babylonian empire. Their reticulated temple architecture, exemplified in that at Uruk (below), decorated with the Tigris and Euphrates, was widely imitated, notably in Herod's temple. (9)

'Habiru', a word used in documents in the Akkadian language to mean intruders, make their appearance in the Amarna age (14th century BC), when Palestine was in a state of anarchy as a result of Egyptian weakness and of pressure from the north. Many scholars have identified them with the Hebrews, but this identification is controversial. In a letter (above) the ruler of Gezer complains of their incursions. (10)

All peoples tend at first to see themselves as the centre of the universe; the Chinese view of their country as 'the Middle Kingdom' has its counterpart in the Greek and Jewish dichotomies of mankind into Greeks and barbarians and into Jews and gentiles. In this map drawn to illustrate the campaigns of Sargon of Agade (right, above), Babylon, the hub of the universe, is the horizontal bar in the middle. The Euphrates flows down from the hills (the semicircle at the top) to the Persian Gulf (the horn shape in the bottom right-hand corner). Seven islands near the surrounding ocean represent remote peoples. Due north of Babylon (two o'clock on our picture) is a land where the sun is never seen. Assyria is to the north-east. (11)

'The Holy City of Jerusalem' seems to have been the centre of the mosaic map of Palestine at Madaba in Transjordan, a motif repeated in many mediaeval 'T and O' maps. Constructed in the 6th century AD, the mosaic remained intact beneath the ruins of the church when it was destroyed by the Moslems. In 1890, however, when a new church was built on the site, a local builder destroyed the greater part of the map. To judge by what remains, it was an incalculable loss. Each of the villages is portrayed in a different way, and colours are used to evoke the beauties of the Palestinian countryside. The size of the towns corresponds to their importance, Jerusalem (above, far right) being particularly large. One can recognize the colonnaded main street (*cardo maximus*) running north and south, with the Basilica of the Ascension and Church of the Holy Sepulchre to the west of it. To the right of the picture is Bethlehem Ephrata and Nicopolis. (13)

Delphi was, for the Greeks, the 'navel' of the universe, and the stone which was thought to be the actual navel (*omphalos*) still survives. On this 4th-century BC crater (right, below), Orestes takes refuge at the *omphalos*; the net carved on it can be clearly distinguished. To the left, Apollo warns off the Fury. To the right is Artemis. (12)

'All roads lead to Rome.' Our subject takes us from Iraq to Jerusalem, where it comes under Greek influence, and thence to Rome. The 'Tabula Peutingeriana' (below, far right) is a 13th-century copy of a Roman road map, showing Rome in the centre. (14)

Η ΑΓΙΑ ΠΟΛΙΣ ΙΕΡΟΥΣΑ
ΚΛΗΡ
ΒΕΝΙΑΜΙΝ
ΕΦΡΑΘΑ
ΒΕΘΩΡΩΝ
ΑΚΕΛ
ΔΑΜΑ
ΝΙΚΟΠ

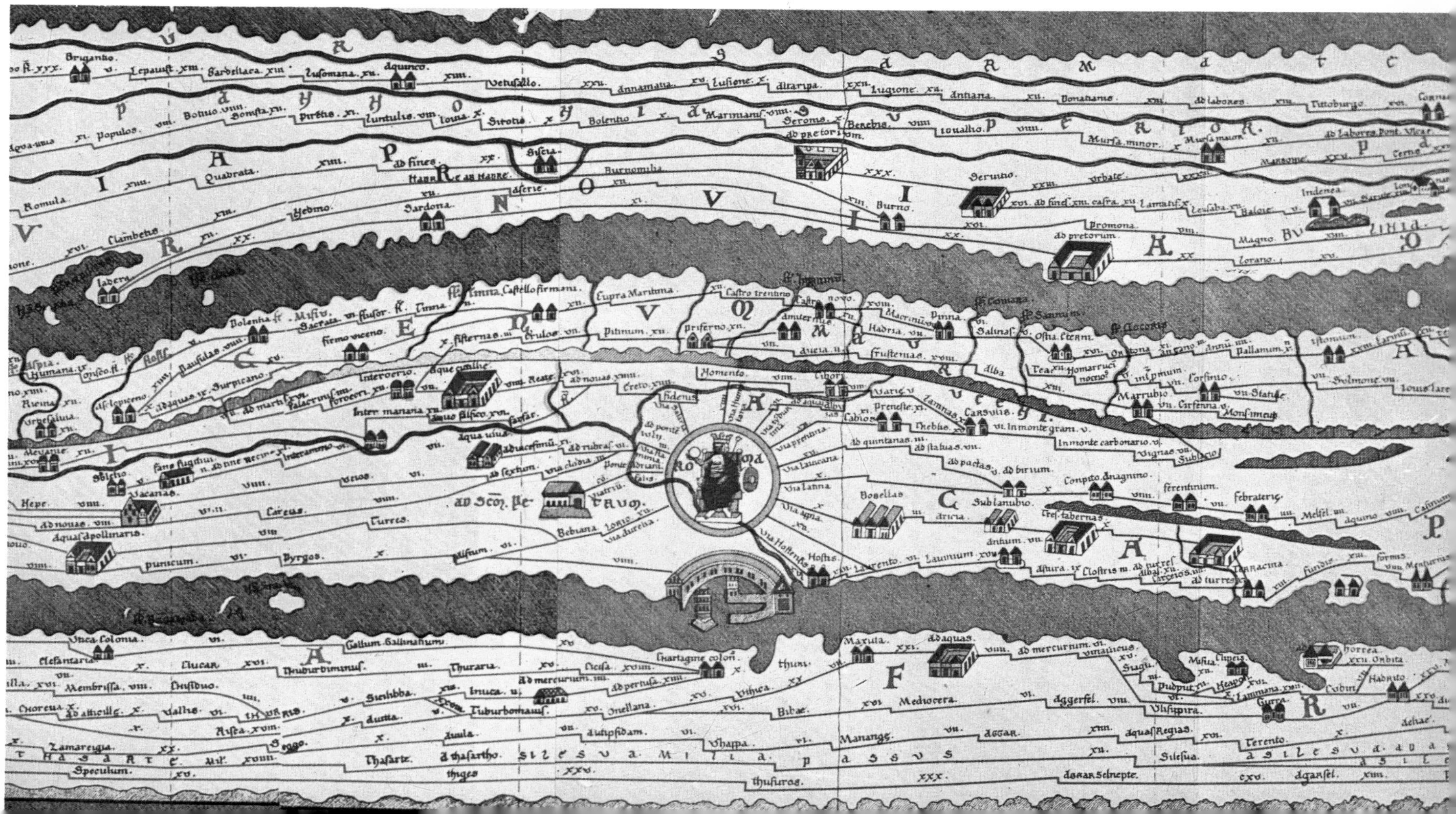

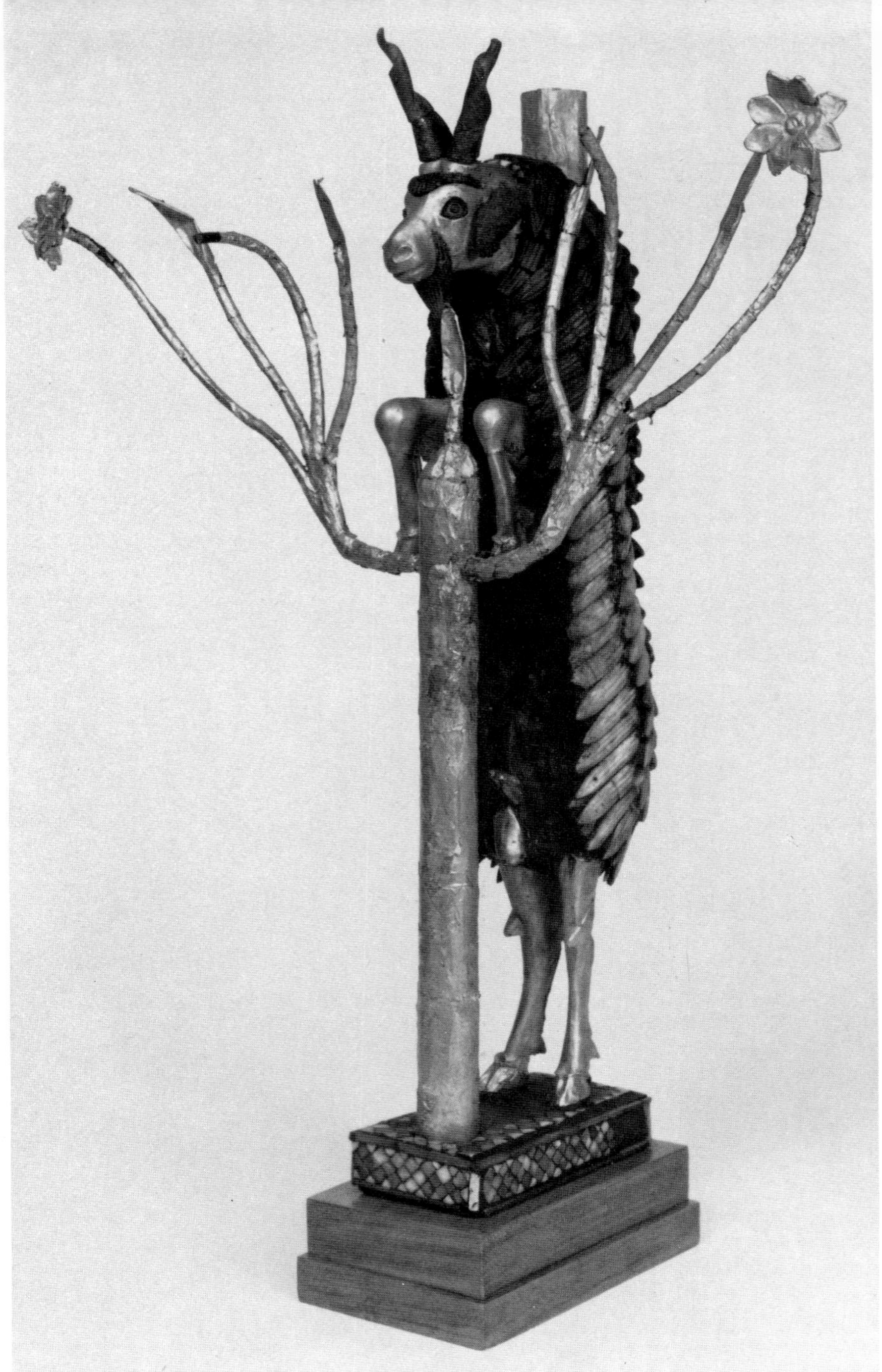

In contradiction with the Bible recent archaeological discoveries have confirmed that 'the peoples round about' had a strong influence on Judaism.

The Sumerian-Akkadian world (present-day Iraq): the account of creation at the beginning of the Book of Genesis has several features in common with the Assyrian Epic of Creation. The most probable explanation of these similarities is that both stories go back to a common source. Angels as emanations of the divine are also characteristic of Babylonian thought, and the cult figure (above) discovered in the Royal Graves at Ur recalls the 'ram caught in a thicket' of Abraham's sacrifice. (15)

Egypt: the 'cherubim' mentioned in many passages in the Old Testament were almost certainly representations of a winged figure, with a lion's body and a woman's head, which the Greeks called a sphinx. This Phoenician ivory (right) belongs, on a smaller scale, to the same family as the two great cherubim, their wings outstretched and touching at the tips, which guarded the approach to the Holy of Holies in Solomon's temple. (17)

Canaan: references in the Old Testament to the 'horns' of the altar inform us that the Israelites took over the common Canaanite form of altar (above, centre left). The 'idols', probably of Astarte, are another Canaanite element in Israel's culture. Cult figures, such as that found at Bethlehem (above, centre right), are reproduced in numerous terracotta plaques, many of them found in levels deposited by Israelite occupants. (16, 18–22)

Phoenicia: 'passing the children through the fire of Moloch' – child-sacrifice – was a custom that several kings of Israel and Judah practised in common with other peoples in Canaan. This vase (left) found at Carthage contains the remains of one such sacrifice. (23)

A hard country exacted habits of self-discipline and application from its inhabitants, the results of which can still be seen in the Jewish character. Only with assiduous effort can a living be wrested from the unpromising soil, and the modern Israeli's achievement of making the desert 'blossom as the rose' with the help of irrigation has its counterpart in the carefully maintained terracing near Jerusalem (above), looking today very much as it must have looked in biblical times. Most of nature's gifts have fallen to Northern Syria (in the broad geographical sense of the word). The southern part of the country 'from Dan to Beersheba',

where the history of Israel was worked out, is a land of many contrasts. Only the plain of Jezreel, the coastal plain, and some oases (*e.g.* Jericho) in the Jordan valley to the north of the Dead Sea are favourable for agriculture; the remainder of the country consists mostly of upland pastures, providing sufficient grazing for sheep and goats. Nevertheless difficult material conditions have proved a spur to invention. The Phoenicians were perhaps the most skilful traders the world has known so far; while it is also to the Syrian peoples that we owe the inventions of watertight cisterns, the alphabet, and monotheism. (24)

'Thou shalt not make unto thee any graven image, or any likeness of any thing that is in heaven above, or that is in the earth beneath, or that is in the water under the earth.' Researches by Cecil Roth, Michael Avi-Yonah and others suggest that the Second Commandment was not always observed in its full rigour. When the Israelite kingdoms were flourishing, great latitude was allowed in practice; in times of political or social stress, the art of Israel and Judah tended to become aniconic.

Proto-Aeolic capitals, common in the Near East at this time, have been found in Israel (above). Though deriving ultimately from the Egyptian lotus capital, the Israelite capitals follow intermediate Cypro-Phoenician models. (25)

Pottery models of horsemen (below, right) and chariots, and of tables, beds and chairs (below, left) have been found, dating from the period of the Monarchy. Much more common are the figurines of Astarte, shown on a previous page. (26, 27)

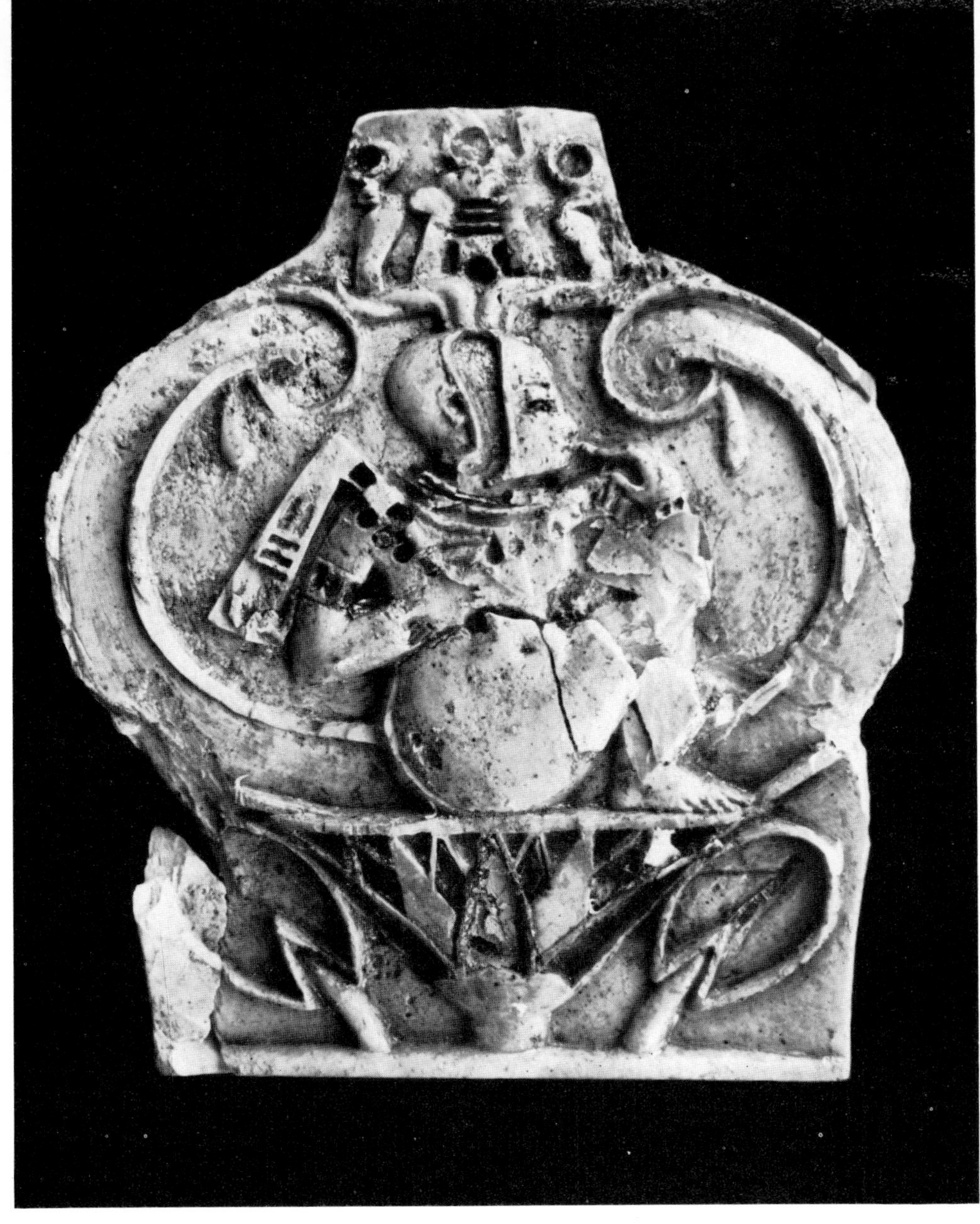

Numerous Israelite seals have survived from the period *c.* 800–600 BC. This seal (below), from Tell Duweir, shows a cult act. (29)

Phoenician workmanship was highly prized in Israel. This ivory plaque (above), showing Horus seated upon a lotus, was probably part of Ahab's 'ivory house'. Below: an incense stand from Megiddo, showing priests making offerings to seated deities. (28, 30)

Amoz the scribe owned this cornaline seal (below), which again shows a cult act. In the Bible, Isaiah's father is named as Amoz. (31)

As the Assyrian threat grew, aniconism asserted itself in Israelite art. Here (below), the artistic effect is gained by finely spaced lettering. (32)

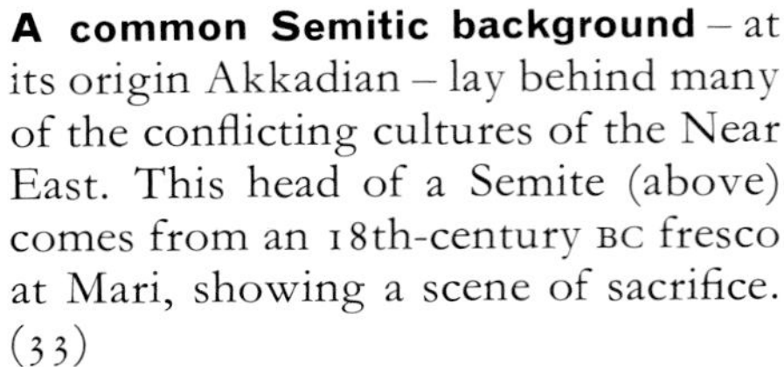

A common Semitic background – at its origin Akkadian – lay behind many of the conflicting cultures of the Near East. This head of a Semite (above) comes from an 18th-century BC fresco at Mari, showing a scene of sacrifice. (33)

The Kassites, probably Sanskrit-speaking Eurasian nomads, disrupted the old order in Iraq. This terracotta (above) is one of their rare monuments, but a lack of documents makes it uncertain who is represented. (34)

'And the Canaanite was then in the land.' A highly developed culture flourished in Canaan at the time of the Patriarchs *c.* 1800 BC, as at the time of the Exodus. A 16th- or 15th-century BC potsherd from Bethshean (far right) provides a striking likeness of an unknown Canaanite. (37)

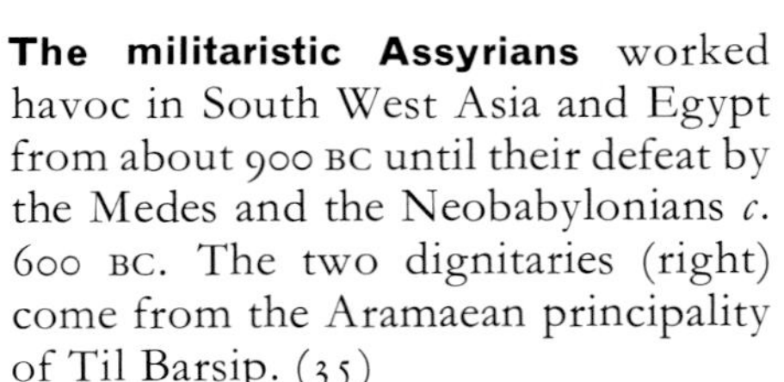

The militaristic Assyrians worked havoc in South West Asia and Egypt from about 900 BC until their defeat by the Medes and the Neobabylonians *c.* 600 BC. The two dignitaries (right) come from the Aramaean principality of Til Barsip. (35)

The Philistines were the most vigorous of the miscellaneous army of freebooters that made up the 'Peoples of the Sea', and, after settling in Palestine, they caused Israel constant trouble. From Tell Yahudiyeh comes a Philistine coffin-lid (above). (36)

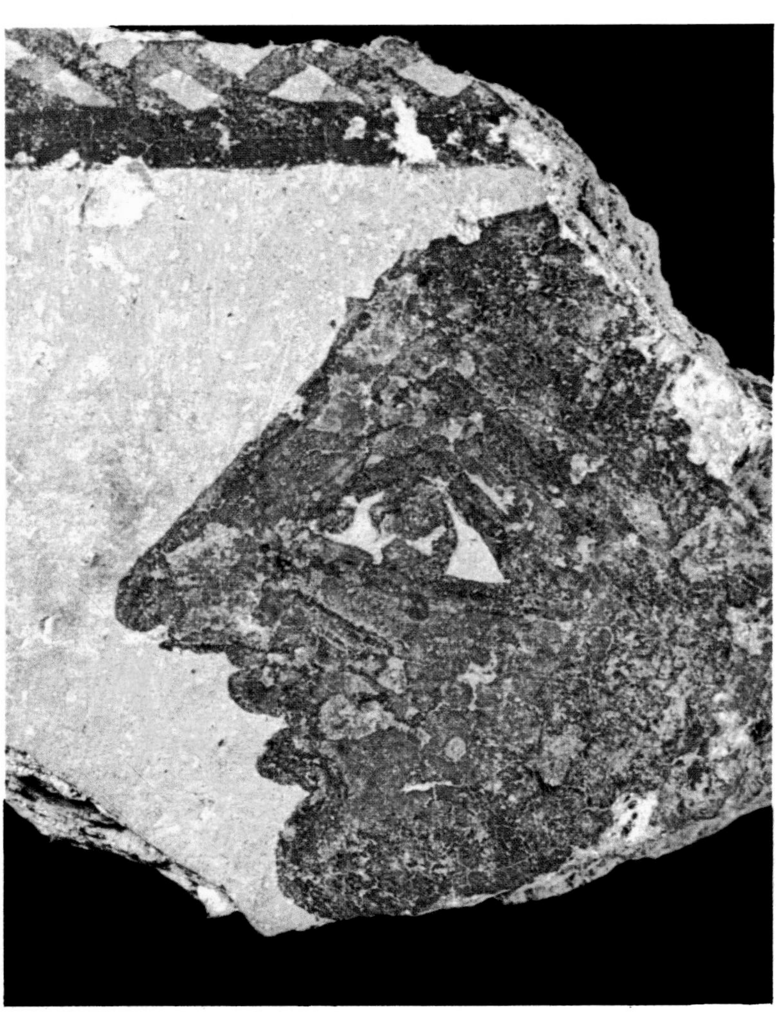

The Persians conquered the Assyrian Empire's Neobabylonian successor-state and restored captive peoples to their homes. On a frieze of tiles from Susa (above) are depicted the Persian Royal Guard, known as the 'Immortals'. (38)

Assyrian militarism, more brutal than any previous, is displayed in representations of beheadings and impalings, like this scene (above) from the gates of Balawat. Israel first encountered Assyria in 853 BC, when the army of a coalition organized against Shalmaneser III included a contingent from Ahab son of Omri. (39)

Hezekiah, having lost many cities, was saved by an outbreak of plague in Sennacherib's army (700 BC). The inscription (left) records the cutting of a tunnel at Jerusalem during his reign to secure water in a siege. (40)

Sennacherib reviews the plunder of Lachish on a relief from Nineveh. (41)

Jehu, a usurper, broke Israel's alliances with Phoenicia and Judah and submitted to Shalmaneser (above). Our picture, the earliest of an Israelite, shows the king wearing western Semitic dress, *i.e.* low turban and long over-garment. The inscription reads: 'The tribute of Jehu, son of Omri [*i.e.* of Omri's dynasty, or ruler of Omri's land], I received from him silver, gold, a golden bowl, a golden vase with pointed bottom, golden tumblers, golden buckets, tin, a staff for a king and *purukhti* fruits.' (42)

To break the spirit of conquered peoples, the Assyrians carried out a policy of compulsory exchanges of the key parts of populations (*i.e.* the 'establishment' and the skilled workers). In 722 BC Sargon II of Assyria (right) defeated Israel. 'The King of Assyria took Samaria and carried Israel away into Assyria and placed them in Halah and in Habor on the river of Gozan and in the cities of the Medes.' (43)

Provisions granted to 'Jehoiachin, King of Judah' in captivity at Babylon are recorded on this tablet (below). (44)

Nehemiah rebuilt the walls of Jerusalem after the return from exile. Part of his wall still survives (below). (45)

After the return of some of the Jewish deportees from exile, measures which had been devised in Babylonia to preserve national identity, such as the institution of synagogues and strict observance of the Mosaic Law, were imposed on Judaea by Babylonian Jews. Ezra and Nehemiah proscribed mixed marriages and so gave the Jewish community the exclusionary character which it has retained ever since.

As part of the same process, the Old Testament, the written foundation of Judaism, underwent its final recasting, and the Jews became (in the words of the Prophet Muhammed) 'the people of the Book'. There is little doubt that this whole development would have been impossible had it not been for the invention, some centuries previously, of the alphabet, which greatly simplified the written word, as against the cumbersome hieroglyphic or syllabic systems. This relief, from the palace of King Tigath-Pileser III at Nimrud, shows two scribes, one writing on a clay tablet with a stylus in cuneiform script, the other with a pen on a roll of parchment or leather in Aramaic. (46)

THE HISTORICAL ANTECEDENTS

ARNOLD TOYNBEE

THE SUBJECT of this book is an event, and the setting in which it occurred. The event is the emergence of a new religion, Christianity. The setting – the 'crucible' – is the contemporary experiences of the people who were concerned in this event in various ways and in different degrees. This setting has many aspects, and the most relevant and most important of these are described and expounded in the following chapters by the scholars who have co-operated in the writing of this book.

p 24–5 (11–14) The geographical field and the social setting of the emergence of Christianity is the region that the Greeks, in the age inaugurated by Alexander the Great, had come to think of, and to write of, as the *oikoumenē*. The literal meaning of this Greek word is 'the inhabited part of the world'; but its range was tacitly limited to as much of the world as was known to the Greeks, in so far as this was inhabited by the Greeks themselves and by non-Greek peoples whom the Greeks recognized, not perhaps as being quite their own cultural equals, but at least as being culturally superior to the barbarians and savages in the civilized world's penumbra. In this usage of the word, the *oikoumenē*, at the beginning of the Christian era, extended westwards to the westernmost Greek and Phoenician colonies and Roman military outposts, and eastwards to the easternmost of the Greek principalities and trading-stations in India. Of course, this was, in truth, little more than half of the whole civilized world of the day. The Chinese, who had stumbled on the north-eastern fringe of the Greek *oikoumenē* in the course of the later decades of the 2nd century BC, had been surprised and impressed to find that they themselves were not the only civilized inhabitants of the earth's surface; but they would have been riled – if they had not been amused – at a geographical definition of the civilized world that left out China, which, in Chinese eyes, was the civilized world's centre – 'the Middle Kingdom' that was suzerain over 'all that is under Heaven'. The Greeks' erroneous geographical limitation of the civilized world will, however, serve the purpose of this book, since the geographical matrix of Christianity falls within these Greek-set limits. At the same time the limits tell us that the emergence of Christianity was an historic event for only about half the civilized world of the day. India's concern in the event was minimal, China's concern was nil, and it was quite beyond the ken of the nascent civilizations in Middle America and Peru. From the historic moment when Paul first addressed himself to non-Jews, Christianity aspired, like Buddhism before it and Islam after it, to convert the whole of mankind, but none of the three historic missionary religions has attained their identical objective. All three coexist in the present-day world.

In human terms, the crucible of Christianity has as many facets as human life itself. It can be regarded from the military, the political, the economic, the cultural, the psychological, and the spiritual point of view. Each of these ways of looking at the human setting of the emergence of Christianity is illuminating and is therefore indispensable. This book attempts to cover all these aspects in some form. Human life, like all life, is perpetually on the move. It has always proved impossible to freeze it when the attempt has been made. Within the circle of the worshippers of Yahweh, the Sadducees, who were the 'establishment' in the post-Exilic Jewish community in Judaea, tried to pin down the revelation received from Yahweh by Israel and Judah to the texts of a set of scriptures. The Samaritans, who were the surviving remnant of the population of the Kingdom of Israel, restricted the written revelation to a smaller set of scriptures than the Sadducees. But the Pharisees kept Judaism moving by innovating in the role of champions of tradition. The Pharisees maintained that, besides the written law, there was an oral transmission of which the Pharisees were the depositories. As for the Christians, they moved, under Paul's impulsion, so radically and so far that Christianity, which had started as one of the numerous contemporary sects of Judaism, eventually broke right out of its original Jewish framework, to become a separate religion – though the integrally Jewish opening chapter of the history of Christianity was longer and more important than the 'pagano-Christian' tradition presents it as having been. (See the first of the two chapters that Father Jean Daniélou has contributed to this book.)

Thus, like persons, events and movements and institutions have to be observed on the move through time in order to be comprehended. Their situation at any particular moment in time is not intelligible if we do not view it against the background of its historical antecedents. All the chapters of this book are inevitably historical in their approach to their respective subjects. The purpose of the present introductory chapter is, in broad outline, to follow the antecedents of Christianity's emergence rather farther back into the past than is feasible in chapters that deal in detail with the immediate setting of the event.

'Learning comes through suffering'

This longer historical perspective brings out an historical fact that goes to the heart of the study of the emergence of a new religion. Paul Tillich has defined religion as being man's 'ultimate concern' – a total concern with the ultimate reality which is 'the ground of being'. (This formula covers non-theistic and theistic religions alike.) To have this concern is of the essence of being human. We have it when we are unconscious of having it; we have it still, even if we deny that we have it at all. There are, however, different degrees of sensitivity to the ultimate 'ground of being'. A prophet or a saint will be more intensely and more frequently sensitive to it than 'the average sensual man', and everyone's relative awareness or unawareness of the ultimate is also affected by his experience. Even the most insensitive human soul awakens to 'ultimate concern' when it is confronted with some extreme personal crisis; and the most potent of all kinds of awakening experiences is suffering.

This truth has been expressed by the Athenian poet Aeschylus in the two Greek words *pathei mathos*, which can be translated 'suffering is the price of learning' or, conversely, 'learning comes through suffering'. A survey of the historical antecedents of the emergence of Christianity shows that the peoples out of whose midst Christianity arose had experienced sufferings that were exceptionally agonizing. They were agonizing to a degree that distinguishes these particular bouts of agony from the suffering that is the common human lot. These exceptional sufferings had afflicted the whole of the *oikoumenē* (within the Greek limitations of the meaning of the word) for about three quarters of a millennium before Christianity made its appearance.

The sufferings had been most intense, and had recurred most frequently, in the nucleus of the *oikoumenē* – its nucleus, that is to say, in its role as the region that brought Christianity to birth. This nuclear region is the segment of the South West Asian 'Fertile Crescent' that extends from the north-east border of Egypt to the north-west border of Babylonia (the present-day Iraq). It includes the territories of Israel and Judah, two suffering peoples whose common tribal god Yahweh has become the God of Judaism, Christianity, and Islam. It had been the field of activity of the pre-Exilic prophets of Israel and Judah. It contains Jesus' home, p 218 Nazareth, in Galilee; his reputed birthplace, Bethlehem, in Judaea; (2–3) Jerusalem, the holy city of Judaism which became the holy city of p 112 (34) Christianity too because Jesus was put to death there; and Antioch, p 114–5 a Greek colonial city and the ex-capital of the defunct Seleucid (39, 40) Greek successor-state of the Persian Empire, which was the place where Christians first came to be called by that name. East of the River Euphrates, the nuclear region also embraces Osrhoëne, a little Aramaic successor-state of the Greek Seleucid Empire that p 277 was the first state in the Greek world – forestalling Armenia and (f 2) the Roman Empire – to adopt Christianity as its religion.

In the course of the three-quarters of a millennium ending in the establishment of the Roman Peace round the perimeter of the p 160 Mediterranean as a result of Augustus' victory at Actium in 31 BC, (34–6) the region between Egypt and Babylonia had experienced two bouts of agony. The first bout had lasted – in terms of conventional p 36 (46) dates – from 747 BC, the accession year of King Tiglath-pileser III of Assyria, who had keyed up Assyrian militarism to a demonic pitch, to 522 BC, the year in which the Persian Emperor Darius I had re-established the Persian Empire on a firm enough basis to give relative peace to South West Asia for the best part of two centuries. The region between Egypt and Babylonia had shared the time of troubles that ended in 522 BC with these two neighbours. The second bout of agony had begun in 221 BC with the first of an accelerating series of sporadic local wars that had grown and spread till they had coalesced into a single great war which had engulfed the whole basin of the Mediterranean and had continued, almost without interruption, till 189 BC. This devastating great war had had a no less calamitous aftermath of further wars and of economic and social and political revolutions that had not come to an end till 31 BC. The nuclear region between Egypt and Babylonia had shared this second time of troubles with the Greek world, which had escaped the worst horrors of the first bout thanks to its geographical good fortune in having lain beyond the range of Assyrian arms, except for the outlying Greek city-states on the island of Cyprus. In the second bout, on the other hand, the Greek world as a whole had suffered as cruelly as the region between Egypt and Babylonia, which had been incorporated in the Greek world, and been partially assimilated by it, by that date.

It was assuredly no accident that two societies which had been subjected to these ordeals should have made the two major contributions to the genesis of Christianity. Nor was it an accident that the greater contribution should have been made by the society that had suffered the most severely. Though Christianity is unimaginable without its Greek, as well as its Jewish, component, the Jewish component was the dominant one at the start and it has retained this dominance, so far, through all the successive changes that Christianity has undergone and in all the sects into which the Christian Church has been fractured.

Eclipse of the 'great powers'

These two societies whose respective birth-places were the region between Egypt and Babylonia and the perimeter of the Aegean Sea were coeval with each other. Both had sprung up among the ruins of older societies that had been wrecked in the 13th and 12th century BC by a destructive *Völkerwanderung* (a relatively short German word for a mass-migration of barbarian invaders of the civilized world and of civilized victims of the invaders who have been driven to seek and win new homes in place of their old homes from which they have been evicted). On the cultural plane the effect of this catastrophe had been a temporary retrogression. In the Aegean world, for instance, the art of writing seems to have been totally lost for about 400 years, and, when it was recovered, perhaps about 800 BC, the new script was not a revival of the lost native script (a variety of this had survived in Cyprus alone); the p 36 (46) new script was borrowed from the Phoenician members of the contemporary society that had arisen between Egypt and Babylonia. In this region there had not been so extreme a break in the continuity of the cultural tradition, though the displacement and replacement of populations through invasion and conquest had been as drastic there as it had been round the Aegean.

One general political effect of the 12th-century BC *Völkerwanderung* had been the temporary effacement of 'great powers' – the kind of states that, in the preceding epoch, had dominated the political arena. Two of the pre-*Völkerwanderung* great powers – the loose association of Achaean principalities in Greece and the rather more closely-knit Hittite Empire in Anatolia – had been annihilated. The New Empire of Egypt – which in its heyday in the 15th century BC had expanded northwards to the right bank of the westward elbow of the Euphrates and southwards up the Nile beyond Napata (the present-day Merawi) in the Northern Sudan – had just succeeded in beating off the invaders who had assaulted it first from the western side of the Nile Delta and then, in a final and still more formidable attack, from the East. But, though the Egyptian f 1 Empire had thus managed to preserve its independence in the Nile p 33 (3 valley, the almost superhuman effort by which this had been achieved had left Egypt permanently enfeebled. Successive native Egyptian régimes succeeded in maintaining or recovering Egypt's independence within her original bounds between the First Cataract of the Nile and the coast of the Delta, but no native Egyptian régime ever again succeeded in re-erecting Egypt to great-power political stature.

Egypt had achieved political unity at the dawn of her civilization, probably not much later than 3000 BC. In what is now South-eastern Iraq, civilization had dawned a few centuries earlier than in Egypt; and, when the curtain rises on the first act of the drama in this region, it reveals a society fractured politically into a number of sovereign local city-states, which were not inhibited from going to war with each other by the cultural bond of their common civilization. In this Sumerian society, in contrast to Egypt, political unity had been achieved tardily and also at a high cost in the toll taken by destructive warfare, and, each time that unity had been established, it had been short-lived. The Akkadian Semitic Empire p 22–3 of Agade, the Sumerian Empire of the Third Dynasty of the city- (2–10) state of Ur, and the Amorite Semitic Empire of Babylon had, each p 32 in turn, been ephemeral. The feeble successors of the Amorite (33–4) Babylonian empire-builder Hammurabi had been supplanted by f 2 sluggish barbarian Kassites about half-way through the 2nd millennium BC, and in the 12th century BC the native Babylonian régime that had superseded the Kassites had been less successful than the contemporary native régime in Egypt in stemming the flood of the *Völkerwanderung*. South-eastern Babylonia had been overrun and been permanently occupied by Chaldaean barbarian invaders from Arabia, and even some parts of Babylonia to the east of the lower Tigris had been encroached upon by bands of Aramaeans – the most adventurous of all the barbarian peoples that, in the 12th century BC, had erupted into the western end of the civilized world out of Arabia on the one side and out of South-eastern Europe on the other.

This eclipse of the great powers in and after the 12th century BC had left the field open for states of a smaller calibre – states on the scale of the Sumerian city-states that had originally divided up politically the region that had since become Babylonia. The two regions at the western end of the civilized world in which new constellations of small sovereign states loomed up after the dust raised by the *Völkerwanderung* had settled were the basin of the Aegean Sea and the area between Egypt and Babylonia that became the nucleus of the geographical matrix of Christianity.

Hard countries

In both these regions, political fragmentation into a large number of small local sovereign states is favoured by the permanent configuration of the physical landscape, as it had been favoured by the original configuration of it in Babylonia. Here the patches of drained and irrigated alluvial soil that had been the agricultural bases of the economic life of the original Sumerian city-states had been insulated from each other, at first, by wildernesses of still unreclaimed jungle-swamp. But, when these residual intervening no-man's-lands had been tamed in their turn and the expanding Sumerian city-states had collided and conflicted with each other, the opportunity – and necessity – of unifying the local networks of water-control had made political unification as imperative in

Babylonia as in Egypt. By contrast, the physical obstacles to political unification in the intervening section of the 'Fertile Crescent' and in the Aegean basin were permanent. They were mountains, and, in the Aegean basin, stretches of 'estranging sea' as well. In these two regions, therefore, the political fragmentation that was the sequel to the destruction of the Achaean Confederacy and recession of the Egyptian Empire were in consonance with the permanent structure of the local physical environment.

The Greek and Syrian[1] societies of the last millennium BC could not vie with Egypt and Babylonia in economic productivity. Before the beginning of the mechanization of the processes of manufacture about two centuries ago, the most productive form of economic activity was the systematic cultivation of extensive irrigated alluvial soils, and the political decline of Egypt and Babylonia had left the efficiency of their irrigation networks unimpaired. The irrigational agriculture of Egypt has continued to be a going concern, without a break, from the date of its organization on a pan-Egyptian scale down to the present day. The first unrepaired dislocation of part of the Babylonian network seems not to have occurred till the last days of the Persian Empire about half way through the 4th century BC, and thereafter Babylonia continued to be the granary of successive South West Asian empires until the last remnant of the Abbasid Caliphate was snuffed out by the Mongols in AD 1258. In Syria, irrigated soils,
p 28–9 such as the oasis of Jericho, are rare patches, and the arable lands
(24) in which cultivation is dependent on rainfall are not extensive either, though some of them, too, are fertile, especially those in the north, round Aleppo.

However, 'a land flowing with milk and honey', which looked like an economic paradise to the spies sent ahead by pastoral
23 (10) nomad invaders from the North Arabian steppe, would have sounded unattractive in the ears of an Egyptian or Babylonian peasant. Palestine is, in truth, a land of few fields, of mountain pastures which Swiss herdsmen would find too meagre for their cows, and of scrub that even the goats might be glad to abandon to the bees. Greece is, from the economic point of view, a replica of Palestine. Greece flows penuriously with milk and honey just because it does not stand thick with corn. If the inhabitants of Greece and of Syria (in the broad geographical sense of the name) were not to remain poverty-stricken, they had to live by their wits, and they did. In both regions, the parsimony of nature has been a permanent stimulus to human ingenuity. The economic prowess of their inhabitants in the last millennium BC has been emulated by the present-day Greeks, Lebanese, Palestinians, and Israelis.

'Temperate contests'

In the last millennium BC a second stimulus was provided by the political fragmentation that had been a sequel to the 12th-century BC *Völkerwanderung*.

The stimulating effect of political fragmentation has been pointed out by two famous 18th-century Western historians: Hume in his essay 'Of the Rise and Progress of the Arts and Sciences' and Gibbon in his 'General Observations on the Fall of the Roman Empire in the West'. Thinking in terms of the Western world of their own time, these two eminent students of human affairs were alive to the dynamism generated by competition between a large number of small local units that are independent of each other politically while all participating in a common culture. Multiplicity opens the way for variety; emulation encourages progress. Gibbon (writing on the eve of Britain's defeat in the American War of Independence) carried this doctrine to the length of booking even the institution of war on the credit side of society's account, on the assumption that wars between states whose peoples have a common civilization will be (in Gibbon's words) 'temperate contests'. As negative evidence in support of their identical thesis, Gibbon cites the Roman Empire, and Hume the Chinese Empire, for proof that the price of political unity has been cultural uniformity and consequent sluggishness and dullness. This thesis can be supported by a comparison of the history of Egypt during the last three millennia BC with the history of Babylonia during the same period and with the histories of the Syrian and the Greek society in the last millennium BC. Like the Roman and the Chinese Empire, the Egyptian Empire did purchase political unity's gifts of peace and stability at the price of cultural rigidity and immobility. Iknaton's abortive attempts at all-round revolution is the exception that proves the rule. The relative turbulence of contemporary Babylonian history paid dividends in greater flexibility and greater dynamism. The still more turbulent Syrian and Greek societies were also still more dynamic and still more creative than the Babylonian society had been.

So far, so good. But Hume's and Gibbon's thesis ignores the maxim *respice finem* that is attributed to Solon, a 6th-century BC Athenian who was better qualified to pass judgment on human affairs, since he combined a philosopher's reasoning with a businessman's and a statesman's experience. In the Hume–Gibbon thesis the weak point is the essential condition implied in Gibbon's word 'temperate'; and the history of the first five thousand years of so-called 'civilization' provides ample evidence that, in a society that is fragmented into a number of sovereign local states, contests between these do not remain temperate, even if, by tacit agreement, they have been kept within bounds in their earlier stages. Gibbon himself lived to see the limited warfare of the 18th-century Western world ended abruptly, and this for ever, by the French *levée en masse* in 1792; and the histories of the Sumerian, Syrian, and Greek societies, of which we know the whole story, turned out to be tragedies. The cultural profits originally earned by political disunity were gradually eroded by social losses until, in the end, fratricidal warfare became such an intolerable scourge that its

The 'People of the Sea', an alliance including Achaeans and Philistines, ravaged the eastern Mediterranean until their defeat at the Battle of the Nile c. 1188 BC by Ramses III – the gigantic figure seen in this drawing of the reliefs at Medinet Habu trampling his foes, with the hawk goddess Nekbet, the whisk of victory in her talons, hovering above. However the Philistines were still strong enough to establish themselves in the Gaza strip, and the history of their conflict with the Hebrews during the next two centuries is described in the Old Testament. (1)

victims, who were at the same time its perpetrators, resigned themselves to forcible unification at alien hands. The Sumerian statelets were united by Akkadian empire-builders, the Greek statelets by Roman empire-builders, and the Syrian statelets by Assyrian, Babylonian, Persian, and Roman empire-builders in succession. Before this admission of political bankruptcy, the members of the Syrian and the Greek society had lived through centuries of agony, individual as well as collective.

In these two politically fragmented societies the period of achievement was inevitably as brief as it was brilliant – and it was brilliant in a number of fields.

Lebensraum

Both societies made their economic fortune by an imaginative and enterprising *tour de force*. They made up for what their barren homelands denied them by taking to the sea. Each society commanded advantages for maritime enterprise which the other lacked. The coastal communities of Syria – the seafaring Canaanites whom the Greeks called 'Phoenicians' – had a short coastline and poor natural harbours, but their location was ideal for trading. Phoenicia lay at one end of the portages between the Mediterranean and the heads of the Red Sea and the Persian Gulf, which are inlets of the Indian Ocean, and the Phoenician city-states were also strung along the land-bridge between Egypt and Babylonia, the two most productive regions in the western half of the contemporary civilized world. The Greeks were less close than the Phoenicians were to Egypt, and they were debarred, by the Phoenicians' intervening presence, from trading direct with Babylonia. In compensation, the Greeks were closer than the Phoenicians were to the previously unexploited western basin of the Mediterranean, and their intervening presence debarred the Phoenicians from trading direct with another potentially lucrative unexploited area: the basin of the Black Sea, with its fisheries and the cornlands in its northern hinterland.

In the race for the control of the western basin of the Mediterranean the Phoenicians forestalled the Greeks, in spite of this region's being more distant from the Phoenicians' home-ports. The competition here was a drawn battle. The Greeks established themselves in force in South-eastern Italy and Sicily and along the French Riviera. The Phoenicians controlled the straits between the western tip of Sicily and the north-easternmost corner of North West Africa, and they also controlled the narrower straits between the western basin of the Mediterranean and the Atlantic. They monopolized the trade with the hinterlands of the Mediterranean coasts of North West Africa and Spain, and they debarred the Greeks from sailing through the Straits of Gibraltar (between 'the Pillars of Hercules') into the ocean. The Massiliot Greek settlers on the Riviera countered by gaining access to the Cornish tin mines by a short cut overland across Gaul; but the colonial Phoenicians' commercial ascendancy in the western Mediterranean and the Atlantic was safeguarded by their naval predominance there, and this was founded on a political union under the leadership of Carthage. The colonial Phoenician monopoly here was not broken till the western colonial Greeks, in their turn, were united politically with each other and with the non-Greek occupants of the major part of peninsular Italy under the leadership of Rome.

The Greeks eked out their agricultural resources – which were inadequate for feeding a population that was on the increase from the 8th to the 2nd century BC – by changing over from subsistence farming to specialization in crops for sale abroad, particularly vines and olives. Wine and oil were easy to pack and ship; their value was high in proportion to their bulk and weight; and they were in demand in accessible countries with climates that ruled out local production. This Greek agricultural revolution was copied by the colonial Phoenicians and by the Romans after them; but the colonial Phoenicians did not follow the Greeks in making an industrial revolution as well. They continued to confine their economic activities to trade – wherever possible, as monopolist middlemen. All the same, the Phoenicians did not do badly in their economic competition with the Greeks, considering that they lacked two great natural advantages: the weight of numbers and the abundance of good harbours along a coastline that was vastly longer and more sinuous than Phoenicia's.

Cultural achievements

In intellectual achievement the two societies were on a par, though in this field their prowess took different forms. The Phoenicians p 36 (46 performed the extraordinary analytic mental feat of dissecting the sounds of human speech into an irreducible minimum number of elementary constituents. Since this number is small, a phonetic script conveying these elementary sounds will run to only something between twenty and thirty letters, and the Phoenicians' invention of this elemental notation, the alphabet, made the art of reading and writing potentially accessible to everybody, in contrast to the Sumerian and Egyptian and Chinese scripts, which are composed of an irrational mixture of syllabic phonemes with ideograms, and which therefore require such a multitude of separate signs that the mastery of these is a life's work and has consequently been the esoteric mystery of a handful of full-time specialists. The merits of the alphabet are so obvious and unquestionable that, since its invention by the Phoenicians in the course of the second half of the 2nd millennium BC, it has been adopted for conveying one foreign language after another until today it is current in its Aramaic form as far east as Mongolia and Manchuria and in its Greek form as far west as California and Vietnam. The Phoenicians had overdone the process of reduction; they had provided letters for the consonants only, not for the vowels. The Aramaeans used some of the Phoenician consonantal letters to convey vowel sounds; the Greeks went further in making the same improvement. Our so-called 'Latin' alphabet is the West-Greek variety of the Greek improvement on the original Phoenician alphabet.

Though the alphabet had been invented to convey a language of the Semitic family, in which the vocabulary is built of sets of three consonants, it proved, with the Greek addition of a gamut of vowels, to convey the sounds of Greek – an Indo-European language – far more precisely than the syllabic script known to us as 'Linear B' which, in the Mycenaean Age, had been adapted for conveying Greek from the 'Linear A' that had been invented in Crete for conveying the language (still undeciphered) of the pre-Greek Minoans. The Greek intellectual feats that were of the same magnitude as the Phoenician invention of the alphabet were, first, the 'demythologizing' of man's traditional religious approach to the universe by the reduction of natural phenomena to their physical elements, and, second, the analysis of the operations of human thought. The Greeks were the inventors of the two sciences of physics and logic. (In their scientific exploration of the human psyche, the Greeks did not probe below the level of consciousness. The scientific exploration of the subconscious abyss was not started till our own day, though, of course, from time immemorial, the subconscious has been constantly welling up from below the psyche's conscious surface to express itself in the utterances of seers and poets.)

Politics and religion

However, these performances in the fields of economics and thought, impressive though they are, are not the chief way in which either the Greeks of the last millennium BC or their contemporaries in Syria have made their mark on the history of the western half of the habitable surface of our planet. The Greek achievements that are the most influential today are those in the fields of art and politics; the corresponding contemporary Syrian achievements are in the field of religion.

The Greeks' political achievement was confined within the limits of the domestic politics of a single sovereign state. In their conduct of inter-state relations, the Greeks failed as disastrously as their Syrian contemporaries and Sumerian predecessors. The masters in this more important and more difficult department of politics, in which the only solution is unification, have been the Egyptians, the Chinese, and, in a lesser degree, the Romans. The Greeks' political invention was constitutional self-government inside a local sovereign state. The Carthaginians followed the Greeks in this and surpassed them in the more difficult art of political unification; but, in general, the Greeks' Syrian contemporaries were politically conservative and unenterprising. Most of them never got beyond the monarchical régime which most Greek states were leaving behind them already as early as the 8th century BC.

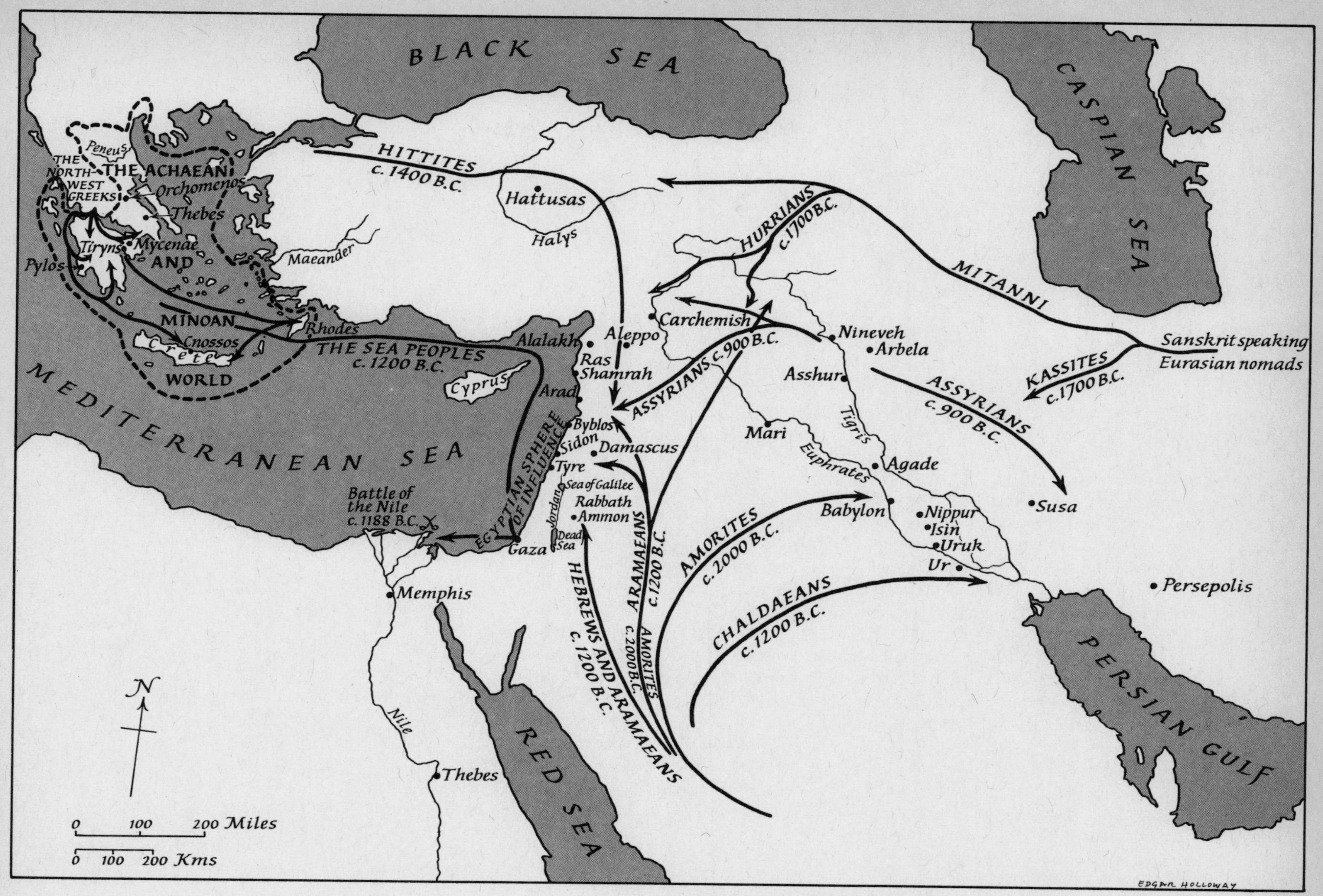

This map portrays in simplified form events in the Near East during the period covered by Chapter I. Dates, especially in the early period, must be taken as approximate. In 480 BC, before the Greek resurgence, the Persians occupied almost the whole of the area with the exception of mainland Greece south of the River Peneus. (2)

Conversely, the Greeks were crude and backward, compared to their Syrian contemporaries, in the field of religion. In and after the 6th century BC, Greek thought outgrew Greek religion progressively, and, for Greek thinkers, the moral, even more than the intellectual, inadequacy of their ancestral religion became a scandal. But the Greeks found themselves unable to produce out of their own spiritual resources a religion that was worthy of their achievements in other fields. When the Greeks came across the religions of
37–52 their eastern neighbours – Anatolia, Egypt, Syria, Iran – they
(1–51) recognized the spiritual superiority of these religions and opened their hearts to them. After they had tasted a number of them, they eventually adopted Christianity – a religion that had started as a sectarian form of the spiritually dynamic and creative national religion of one of the Syrian peoples, the Jews. The Greeks did not, however, adopt this originally Jewish religion without infusing into it some characteristically Greek elements. They diluted Jewish monotheism with a tincture of Greek polytheism; they supplemented the Jewish worship of a transcendent God with the deification of a human being; and they defined the elusive tenets that were implied in this syncretism in terms of Greek logic. In Greek eyes this partial Hellenization of Christianity had transformed it from a variant of Judaism into an oecumenical religion with a message for all mankind. In Jewish eyes the Greeks had contaminated Judaism with the paganism that Judaism had cast off, and the sensational success, as a missionary religion, of the 'pagano-Christianity' to which all inhabitants of the Roman Empire except the Jews and the Samaritans were eventually converted was, in the Jews' judgment, a facile triumph won by contemptible concessions to expediency. As the Jews saw it, the price of Christianity's worldly success was a precipitate fall from the spiritual heights that Judaism had attained as the reward for centuries of spiritual travail. Yet Christianity's apparent deviation from Judaism had some antecedents in Judaism itself, as Professor Flusser shows in his chapter on Jesus in the context of history.

From child-sacrifice to a transcendent god

The spiritual ascent of the Jewish people's national religion had indeed been not only steep but rapid. The Greeks first began to meet the Jews in the seventh and eighth decades of the 4th century
BC, after Alexander the Great had destroyed the Persian Empire, p 102–3
and after Alexander's generals had carved up the Persian Empire's (5–7)
former dominions into a number of Greek-ruled successor-states. Judaea – the district corresponding to the territory of the former Kingdom of Judah – was taken by Ptolemy, who had made himself master of Egypt, and a Jewish community was soon installed in
the Egyptian Alexandria, a new city that Alexander had laid out p 112
as the capital for his projected world-empire, but which actually (33)
became the capital of the Ptolemaic dynasty. The older Jewish community in Babylonia – descended from the Judahites who had been deported by the destroyer of the Kingdom of Judah, Nebuchadnezzar, and who had not returned to Judaea when Cyrus the p 35 (44)
Persian conqueror of the Neobabylonian Empire had given them p 33 (38)
leave – now fell under the rule of another Greek dynasty, the Seleucidae. By this time the Jews were worshipping their national god as 'God' – the only true god, lord and creator not only of the Jewish people but of all mankind and the whole universe.

In the absoluteness of their monotheism the Jews had become singular by this date, but their own records show that they had become absolute monotheists only recently, and this through a long process of spiritual enlightenment and at the cost of repeated struggles. Yahweh's synonym 'Elohim' tells us that there had been a time when the people of Judah had worshipped, not 'God' but 'the gods', like the other peoples of Syria and, indeed, like all other peoples everywhere whose early religious history has been preserved. When, about 1000 BC, the Judahite war-lord David had annexed the Jebusite city-state of Jerusalem to Judah and had made Jerusalem Judah's capital, Judah – a rural community that dated back only to the 12th-century BC *Völkerwanderung* – must have been p 33 (37) captivated by the older culture of the Canaanite urban community that it had now incorporated.

In the field of religion, Jerusalem's ascendency over Judah had reached its culmination when, in the 7th century BC, King Josiah had centralized all public worship in Jerusalem and had suppressed it everywhere else in the kingdom. But, till immediately before Josiah's accession, the temple at Jerusalem, like its contemporary counterparts at Tyre and Carthage and Ephesus and Corinth, had been associated with polytheism and with rites that latterday Jewish orthodoxy repudiated in retrospect. This polytheistic kind of religion, which had been the normal kind of its day, had been practised by Josiah's father Amon, by his grandfather Manasseh and by his great-great-grandfather Ahaz, and Kings Ahaz and Manasseh of Judah had both burned their sons alive – presumably as a sacrifice to their national god Yahweh, as, in the 9th century BC, King Mesha of Moab had sacrificed his son to his national god Chemosh and as the Carthaginians sacrificed their children to Baal p 27 (23) Hammon throughout their history. It had not been till the centralization of public worship at Jerusalem by Amon's son Josiah that the practices of ritual prostitution in the temple there and of burning children alive in the neighbouring valley of Hinnom had been banned, and that the worship of all gods except Yahweh had been abolished in the temple itself and at other points in Jerusalem, and the worship of Yahweh himself everywhere else throughout the kingdom. Retrospectively, latterday orthodox Judaism represented Ahaz, Manasseh, and Amon as having been impious innovators, p 34 (40) and Josiah and his great-grandfather Hezekiah as having been pious restorers of a pristine religious purity. It is perhaps more probable that the posthumously stigmatized kings of Judah had been conventional conservatives, and the posthumously hallowed kings high-handed revolutionaries.

Covering up the traces

The exponents of the form of Judaism that eventually became orthodox managed to monopolize the writing of the history not only of Judah but of Israel and all the other communities that constituted, collectively, the Syrian society of the last millennium BC. Thus posterity is shown the history of this society in this age as it was seen subsequently by Jewish eyes; and, for believing Jews, Christians, and Muslims, the historical books of the Old Testament are not fallible works of human authors, like the works of the Athenian historians who have similarly monopolized the writing of the history of the whole of the contemporary Greek world; Jewish scripture has been held to be divinely inspired – to be the Word of God Himself – and, as such, it has commanded an assent that has been emotional and uncritical. It is only in our time that archaeological research has begun to recover evidence about the neighbours of Judah in the last millennium BC that is direct and p 26–7 independent. This evidence informs us that 'the peoples round (15–23) about' did make important contributions to the progressive spiritual elevation of the religion of Judah. We have learnt of the debt of Jewish 'wisdom' literature to Egyptian prototypes, and of the affinity of Jewish mythology and poetry with the Phoenician literature inscribed on 14th-century BC clay tablets at Ras Shamrah, a northerly Phoenician city that was overwhelmed in the 13th- and 12th-century BC *Völkerwanderung*.

Yet, when this has been said, it has also to be said that the spiritual progress achieved by the people of Judah within a time-span of only two centuries – the time-interval between Isaiah's generation and Deutero-Isaiah's – was prodigious; that this spiritual achievement accounts for the survival of the worship of Judah's god Yahweh down to the present day; and that this, in turn, accounts for the survival of the descendants of the people of Judah, as a community with a continuous history, 2556 years after the destruction of the Kingdom of Judah by the Neobabylonian Emperor Nebuchadnezzar and 1834 years after the eviction of the Jews from all Palestine except Galilee by the Roman Emperor Hadrian. Today, Chemosh and Milkom have no worshippers, whereas Yahweh is still being worshipped not only by the Jews and the Samaritans but also by the Christians and the Muslims, and the followers of these religions amount collectively to nearly half of the living generation of mankind. Today, likewise, there are no identifiable representatives of the peoples of Moab and Ammon, whereas the people of the Kingdom of Judah are still represented by the Jews, and the 'lost' people of the Kingdom of Israel by a small surviving remnant of the Samaritans.

The struggle for survival

The spiritual progress of the religion of Judah between the 8th and the 6th centuries BC is accounted for by Aeschylus' already quoted dictum 'learning comes through suffering'. These two centuries, within which the people of Judah moved from polytheism to monotheism and in which the prophets of Judah and Israel delivered their startlingly radical messages, are the centuries in which Syria suffered the first of its two bouts of agony. The survival of the Jews as a distinct community is accounted for, in turn, by their spiritual progress during those two agonizing centuries. By the time when the leaders of Judah were faced by the ordeal of their deportation to Babylon with the risk of losing their p 35 (4 national identity – a loss to which most of their fellow deportees resigned themselves – the Jews had come to feel that they had been entrusted by God with a unique spiritual treasure which it was their duty to preserve and to hand on. Evidently they could not preserve it without also preserving the identity of their own community, since the community was the bearer of the treasure; and this compulsive demand on the Jews stimulated them to devise a novel way of maintaining the existence of a community and a religion in exile and in dispersion, without a foothold in their ancestral country and without access to the temple which, for the Jews, had become the only legitimate place for the ritual worship of their God. The deported Jews devised a substitute for the temple ritual in the new institution of synagogues, and a substitute for their lost roots in the soil of Judah in the bond of the Mosaic Law.

The agony out of which monotheistic Judaism was born between the 8th and 6th centuries BC was threefold. There was a domestic economic and social crisis which widened the gulf between rich and poor and raised the question of social justice acutely. There was an intensification of the fratricidal warfare between the local sovereign states of the Syrian world; and there was the emergence above the northern horizon of a new great power, Assyria, which was a threat to the Syrian society's life in all its aspects. The first two of these afflictions were shared with the Syrian world by the contemporary Greek world in full measure. The menace from an aggressive great power bore less heavily on the Greek world at this stage.

In the last and worst phase of Assyrian militarism, which opened p 34– in 747 BC, Judah was comparatively fortunate. She and Moab were (39–4 the only two states in the Syrian world that the Assyrians did not p 32 (wipe out. Moab was saved by her remoteness; Judah by the unexpected withdrawal of an Assyrian army that had laid Jerusalem under siege. However, the Assyrian Empire's Neobabylonian successor-state completed Assyria's unfinished levelling work. The Kingdom of Judah was destroyed and its notables were deported. For the Jews the replacement of Babylonian rule by Persian rule in p 33 (538 BC spelled the end of two centuries of agony. For the Greeks, *f 3* on the other hand, the Persians' previous conquest of the Lydian Empire, and of the Asian Greek city-states, formerly subject to Lydia, along the west coast of Anatolia, spelled a menace.

The Persian Emperors Darius I and Xerxes were right in their reckoning that, in order to retain their hold on this eastern fringe of the Greek world, they would have to go on to conquer the rest of it, including the Greek colonial settlements along the west and north shores of the Black Sea and to the west of the Straits of Otranto. In this ambitious enterprise the Persians came within an

Under Persia's tolerant rule, the province of Judah minted coins proudly bearing its name in Aramaic, and with figural decoration such as the male head and deity seated upon a wheel shown here. (3)

ace of success, but the outcome showed that they had miscalculated – not the requirements of Persian policy, but Persian capacity for meeting these requirements. The conquest of the entire Greek world was beyond even the mighty Persian Empire's strength. The unsubjugated major part of this world was too distant from the Persians' economic and military bases, too far-flung, too populous, and, above all, too high-spirited.

The Persians' failure in 480–479 BC to conquer continental European Greece was followed immediately by a Greek counter-attack, in which the subject Asian Greek communities were liberated, and, from then onwards, it was evident that the free Greeks now had it in their power to proceed to conquer the rest of the Persian Empire sooner or later. This possibility, however, depended on the fulfilment of one condition. The unison that had saved the Greek world in 480–479 BC must be maintained, or, if not maintained, it must be re-established. It was not maintained; Athens and Sparta, the two leading continental European Greek powers of the day, parted company as soon as the Persian menace receded; and Greece was not reunited till King Philip II of Macedon established the Corinthian League in 338 BC.

'Be ye separate'

The miserable failure of Athens and Sparta to rise to the occasion that had been presented to them gave the Persian Empire a reprieve that lasted for 144 years; this century and a half during which the Jews continued to live under the easy-going Persian régime was the period within which two emissaries of the Jewish community
5 (45) in Babylonia, Nehemiah and Ezra, succeeded – whatever the precise dates of their missions may have been – in inducing the Jewish community in Judaea to conform to the practices that had been worked out in Babylonia by the deportees for preserving the Jewish community's separate identity in adverse circumstances. One key practice was the punctilious observance of the Mosaic Law; another was strict social segregation – above all, abstention from mixed marriages, since intermarriage is the sovereign means of overcoming the traditional barriers – racial, political, cultural, and, of course, also the religious barrier – that stand in the way of the unification of the human race into something like a single family.

Ezra's policy was the logical, and perhaps indispensable, means of attaining his objective; and his ruthless enforcement of it was crowned – though it may not have been justified – by success. In Ezra's strait-jacket the Jewish community in Judaea did maintain its separate identity, whereas the latitudinarian-minded 5th-century BC Jewish garrison in Persian service in the Egyptian frontier fortress at Elephantine lost its identity, like (eventually) the majority of the Jews' fellow Yahweh-worshippers who were descendants of the population of the former Kingdom of Israel. However, the Jews' successful self-segregation cost a high price in terms of human relations. It bred alienation and hostility between the Jews and their neighbours, and, from Ezra's day to ours, this mutual aloofness has repeatedly rankled into conflicts that have brought lamentable suffering on both parties. The Jews' conflict with the Greeks and Romans, which was the prelude to the birth of 'pagano-Christianity', is the subject of Professor Schalit's chapter in this book.

The Assyrians' 'methods of barbarism' by which they built their p 34 (39)
empire were more brutal than those of any previous empire- p 32 (35)
builders of whose misdeeds we have a record. The Assyrians in Syria, like the Persians subsequently in Greece, were confronted by spirited peoples who had enjoyed local sovereignty for centuries. In order to subjugate them, they had to break their spirit by destroying their states and obliterating their national identities, and they found an effective means for accomplishing this. They carried out compulsory exchanges of populations, in which communities – or at any rate their élites – were uprooted and were p 35 (44)
transplanted to alien territories with which they had no historic sentimental associations and where they found themselves intermingled geographically with other human flotsam and jetsam. The Assyrians' aim had been self-interested and negative, but it had had one result that was positive and propitious for the future of the human race. The Assyrians' uprooted and intermingled victims were moved by their common sufferings to fraternize with each other.

Already in the pre-Assyrian days of local national sovereignty in Syria, fratricidal wars had not inhibited economic and cultural intercourse. The Israelite prophet Elisha was welcome in the Aramaean Kingdom of Damascus, and each local capital harboured settlements of foreign traders. The Assyrians' reduction of the former national sovereign states to the status of subject provinces with cosmopolitan populations had given an impetus to this process of social fusion. Under the post-Assyrian and post-Babylonian Persian régime in Syria, intermarriage between members of the débris of the historic local communities had become frequent, according to the Jewish accounts in the Books of Ezra and Nehemiah. The Jewish deportees who had returned to Judaea had had a friendly reception from their neighbours there. They had responded in kind, and they too – and particularly their leading notables – had participated in the intermarriage that was fusing the fragments of uprooted peoples together into an oecumenical community. Ezra succeeded in reversing this process of social amalgamation as far as the Judaean Jews were concerned. In the name of religion he was able to exert a moral pressure that compelled Judaean Jews who had contracted mixed marriages to break them off.

The pattern sets

This deliberate act of resegregation was inhumane, besides being at variance with the general spirit of the times. It permanently poisoned the relations between the Judaean Jews and their local neighbours, including their fellow Yahweh-worshippers the Samaritans. For the time being, the Judaean Jews could make this break with their neighbours with impunity. The Persian peace kept *f 3*
physical conflicts between Persian subjects within bounds, and the Jews, like their neighbours the Phoenicians, could count on the Persian Imperial government's benevolence. The Persians had saddled themselves with formidable recalcitrant subjects in the Babylonians and the Egyptians, so they valued and wooed the loyalty of the Babylonians' Phoenician and Jewish ex-victims, and there was nothing in the Persians' general policy that would antagonize either of these two Syrian subject peoples of theirs. The

Jews' paramount concern was to be free to practise their religion, with all the social implications of this, and religious toleration was a cardinal principle of Persian statesmanship. The Phoenicians' paramount concern was trade, and their incorporation in the Persian Empire promoted this. The Persians did not covet the Phoenicians' commercial business for themselves, so they fostered it as a counterpoise to the commercial prowess of their recalcitrant Anatolian Greek subjects. Under the Persian régime the Phoenicians prospered. The Persian Empire gave them a continental hinterland that stretched from the Mediterranean to the Jaxartes and the Indus. This invaluable hinterland had been forfeited by the Anatolian Greeks when they had been liberated politically in 479 BC.

In Syria, Persian rule was replaced by Macedonian Greek rule in 332 BC. By that date the self-segregation of the Judaean Jewish community, which Ezra had inaugurated, had had time to set hard; but the change of régime did not produce any immediate change in the Judaean Jewish community's fortunes. Though the p 103 (7) Persian Empire's local Ptolemaic Greek successor-state was not specially well disposed towards the Jews, as the Persian authorities had been, it was not specially hostile to them either. The Ptolemies' concern with their subjects was fiscal, not religious, and, in general, the new Greek masters of South West Asia and Egypt were as tolerant of their subjects' religions as their Persian predecessors had been. Indeed, religious intolerance was less of a temptation for the Greeks than it might have been for the Persians. In Zoroastrianism the Iranians had a native religion of their own which p 248–52 (32–51) had attained as high a spiritual level as Judaism. The Greeks' native religion was a rather disreputable one; sophisticated Greeks had lost all belief in it; and, so far from being hostile to oriental religions, they were attracted by them in the hope that they might serve to fill the painful spiritual vacuum from which Greek souls had been suffering since the 5th century BC.

Hellenism

The Greeks in the age of Alexander and his successors did differ from their Persian predecessors in their attitude to the capital question of the social and cultural unification of mankind. The Persians had inadvertently created or maintained the conditions that would make this possible; the Greeks – taught by their own disastrous persistence in political particularism from 478 to 338 BC – had now embraced oecumenicalism as a positive ideal and as a desirable objective. Like present day Westerners, the Greeks assumed that mankind's coming common civilization would, as a matter of course, be theirs. They resented and resisted Alexander's attempt to impose an amalgam of the Greek and the Iranian ways of life on the conquered and the conquerors alike. Alexander's generals objected to mixed marriages as decidedly as Ezra did. After Alexander's death, all of them, with the one notable exception p 103 (6) of Seleucus, repudiated the Iranian wives whom Alexander had wished on to them. On the other hand, none of Alexander's successors except the one Seleucid Emperor Antiochus IV ever sought to impose the Greek way of life on his non-Greek subjects by force. The Greeks had no temptation to be coercive; for they were confident that Hellenism was so superior to all other ways of life, and therefore so attractive, that it would be adopted voluntarily, sooner or later, by all non-Greeks who had the good fortune to have access to it.

Any non-Greek who did effectively Hellenize himself was accepted generously by born Greeks as one of themselves – and effective Hellenization did not require the abandonment of the cultural convert's ancestral religion. At the most it involved the nominal identification of his gods with their Greek counterparts – and a refusal of even this perfunctory form of Hellenization in the field of religion was not held against those peoples to whom this minimum concession too was unacceptable – as it was to Iranians and Egyptians, as well as to Jews. Resistance to Hellenization was exceptional at the start. Even the Persians (*i.e.* the people of Persis, the present-day Fars), who had not only been deposed from their imperial dominion over other peoples but had been reduced to being a subject people themselves, were mollified when their first Macedonian Greek governor, Peucestas, took the trouble to learn their language and tactfully put on their national dress. The Persians' fellow Iranians, the Parni, who conquered from the Seleucidae first Parthia and eventually the rest of the former Seleucid dominions east of the Euphrates, were not being insincere when they styled themselves 'Philhellenes'. After 198 BC, when Judaea finally passed out of the Ptolemies' into the Seleucids' hands, there was a Hellenizing movement there which must have made Ezra p 50–5 turn in his grave; and, when the Hellenizing faction of the Judaean (2–16) Jews had been eliminated, and Judaea had liberated itself from Seleucid rule by force of arms, the Pharisees, who had taken part in the resistance for religion's sake, fell foul of the Hasmonaean kings of the Seleucid Empire's Judaean successor-state. The Pharisees justly accused these military leaders and political beneficiaries of the successful revolt of having transformed themselves into Hellenistic-style princes – reproductions, on a petty scale, of the Greek Seleucidae whom they had ousted from Judaea with the Pharisees' help.

The Judaean Jewish reaction against Hellenization was the biggest with historic consequences. Its success was an enabling condition for the genesis of Christianity through a mating of Hellenism with Judaism. This was, however, neither the only anti-Hellenic reaction nor the earliest. Persis had shaken off Hellenism, as well as Seleucid rule, as far back as about half way through the 3rd century BC. In Egypt, the victory of an Egyptian phalanx, raised by the Ptolemies, over the Seleucids' Greek phalanx at Raphia in 217 BC had given the Egyptian people the self-confidence to start a series of nationalist revolts against Ptolemaic Greek rule which might have eliminated Hellenism from Egypt if Augustus had not annexed Egypt to the Roman Empire in 31 BC. The Roman Empire was a far mightier power than any of the Greek successor-states of the Persian Empire that Rome replaced; Rome took over from them the championship of Hellenism; and, west of the Euphrates, Rome's intervention gave Hellenism in Egypt and South West Asia a reprieve that lasted for half a millennium. The decisive anti-Hellenic reaction was postponed, even in Iran, till the 3rd century of the Christian era, and till the 5th century in Syria and Egypt, and meanwhile Hellenism had resumed its advance. The Roman Emperor Hadrian had built a Graeco-Roman city, Aelia Capitolina, on the site of Jerusalem, p 75 which had been derelict since AD 70. At an early date in the 3rd (*f 6*) century of the Christian era, the local capitals of the departments ('nomes') of Egypt were given municipal self-government on Greek lines. This Roman reprieve of Hellenism gave time for the 'pagano-Christian' Church, which had sprung from Hellenism's encounter with Judaism, to become the Roman Empire's official religion.

Collision course

From 168 BC onwards the relations between Hellenism and Judaism degenerated into a conflict, but it may be questioned whether this unhappy turn of affairs was inevitable. The Seleucid Emperor Antiochus IV's attempt to stamp out Judaism – of all religions – by force was not only morally indefensible; it was also patently impolitic and, in principle, un-Hellenic. If the Greek handling of Judaea in the fourth decade of the 2nd century BC had been the responsibility of a statesman with Alexander's vision and with Peucestas' tact, the fateful clash might perhaps have been avoided. Mainly, it would seem, through the personal fault of Antiochus IV, the conflict was not escaped, and, once started, it ran its terrible course to its climax and conclusion in AD 135. It was not a clear-cut issue between right, either Jewish or Greek, and wrong, either Greek or Jewish. It was a tragic collision between two ideals: the Jewish ideal of preserving monotheism intact and the Greek ideal of uniting mankind into a single family by the bond of a common culture. Both ideals were noble; each of them was, and is, of immeasurable value; and the collision between them was tragic because they were not, and are not, intrinsically irreconcilable.

The collision between Hellenism and Judaism was a tragedy in two acts. In the first act the political protagonist on the Hellenic side was the Seleucid Empire; in the second it was the Roman Empire. Herod the Great foreboded the second act, and he p 52– managed to postpone it, though he could not avert it. During the (14–2 interlude that Herod's statesmanship prolonged, Christianity came to birth. The first act in the Jewish-Hellenic tragedy was one incident in the bout of agony which afflicted the whole Hellenic world, extending to the Atlantic coast of Europe and to North-western India, from 221 BC to 31 BC.

Sparta and Athens, which had been the two leading city-states in continental European Greece at the time of the Persian invasion in 480–479 BC, and which had saved Greece in that crisis by their brief co-operation, had not only quickly parted company again but had ruined themselves and the rest of the Greek world by failing to rise above a self-centred pursuit of their respective national interests, conceived of by each power in narrow-hearted and short-sighted terms. They had fallen into two devastating wars with each other, and they had exploited and oppressed their allies. This portentous political failure of the Greek society in its so-called 'classical' age has to be booked on the debit side of Hellenism's account against the credit for its superb contemporary achievements in architecture, the visual arts, drama, philosophy, historical literature, oratory, and some departments of physical science.

After Athens and Sparta and Thebes in turn had gone bankrupt militarily and politically, there were some apparently promising symptoms of a moral rally. The chronic warfare between the Greek city-states was temporarily arrested in continental European Greece by King Philip II of Macedon (359–336 BC) and in Sicily by Timoleon (344–337 BC). Alexander the Great (336–323 BC),
02 (5) after destroying the Persian Empire, set out to replace it by a world-state that was to embrace all mankind – Greeks and non-Greeks – on a footing of equality with each other; and Alexander might have succeeded in giving a new and better turn to the whole course of mankind's subsequent history if he had lived for half a
03 (7) century longer, to die – as two of his generals, Ptolemy and Antigonus, did die – as an octogenarian.

Symptoms of a rally

The Greek world suffered a cruel set-back from the wild scramble for the territorial spoils of the Persian Empire among Alexander's generals that followed Alexander's own sudden premature death. Yet symptoms of a rally continued to appear. The ideal of a world-
06 (5) community was kept alive by Zeno, the Cypriot Phoenician founder of the Stoic school of Greek philosophy. Zeno's Samian contemporary Epicurus restored to private life the rightful role of which it had been starved by the Greek city-state's exorbitant demands on its citizens' services. Women and slaves recovered some of the human rights that had been grudged to them since the close of the Homeric Age. There were even some constructive achievements in the field of inter-state politics in which the Greek society had come to grief. Though Alexander's world-state had been a flash in the pan, and Zeno's remained an unfulfilled ideal, the century beginning with Alexander's crossing of the Hellespont in 334 BC did see the construction of four effective associations of city-states on a regional, though not on a world-wide, scale: the Seleucid Empire in Asia, the Aetolian and Achaean Confederacies in continental European Greece, and the Roman Commonwealth in peninsular Italy. There were also two local attempts – one at Sparta by Kings Agis IV and Cleomenes III, and the other in Roman Italy by the brothers Tiberius and Gaius Gracchus – to remedy glaring social injustices by a radical redistribution of agricultural land, the basic factor in the economy of the world of that age. There was even a temporary alleviation of the atrociousness of war. Alexander's successors put back into circulation the defunct Persian Imperial government's accumulated treasure by
7 (17) hiring hosts of mercenaries to serve in their wars with each other;
(f 3) but (if an Aetolian statesman was telling the truth in 197 BC) they
0–13 won and lost their battles in the open field, and they tried to avoid
9–38) the destruction of cities; indeed, they founded many new ones.

Cumulatively these symptoms of a rally looked auspicious, but unhappily these appearances proved illusory. Alexander's incorporation of the entire Persian Empire in the Greek world had vastly increased the Greek world's scale, but his subsequent premature death had denied him the opportunity of converting a politically fractured society into a united world-community. The sudden increase in scale had not been accompanied by any change in political structure. The post-Alexandrine, like the pre-Alexandrine, Greek world was still a world partitioned among a number of contending local states. On the political plane nothing had changed except the scale on which states were built and wars were waged, and this change aggravated the havoc wrought by the great war of 221–189 BC, a war which opened with the Seleucid Emperor Antiochus III's probe of the Ptolemaic Empire's barrier fortresses, and which lasted till the eviction of the Seleucid Empire from its possessions to the north-west of the Taurus Range. The destructive effects of this world war and its long drawn out aftermath of consequent wars and revolutions can be gauged by the two facts that in 221 BC there were five great powers at the western end of the *oikoumenē* and that in 167 BC there was only one. The five great powers had been the Seleucid empire, the Ptolemaic empire, the Kingdom of Macedon, the Carthaginian empire, and the Roman Commonwealth. By 167 BC Rome alone was still standing. The Macedonian monarchy had been liquidated and the kingdom had been broken up; the Carthaginian and Seleucid empires had been crippled by being disarmed and being mulcted of strategically important territory; the once far-ramifying Ptolemaic empire had shrunk to within the confines of Egypt, and it was surviving, even within these reduced limits, only thanks to Rome's fiat.

Rome's abuse of her victory

In the great war of 221–189 BC, Rome and Carthage had been the protagonists, and the principal action had been Hannibal's invasion of Italy. Hannibal did not succeed either in disrupting the Roman Commonwealth or in capturing Rome itself, but he was posthumously victorious. South-eastern Italy never recovered from the devastation that it had suffered while it had been Hannibal's war-zone. The peasantry of those parts of peninsular Italy that had escaped physical devastation was uprooted by long-term military service in distant theatres – a burden from which it was not relieved by Carthage's capitulation in 201 BC. Worst of all, the Roman nobility, which virtually monopolized the government of the Roman body politic, was thrown off its balance.

The political unification of peninsular Italy through the building of the Roman Commonwealth had been the Roman nobility's work. In its politically creative prime this 'establishment' had displayed a persistence tempered by moderation and a daring held in leash by good judgment; and its virtues had benefited not only the Roman nobility itself but the Roman people as a whole and the other peoples of peninsular Italy who had been induced or constrained to submit to Rome's hegemony. Rome had been generous in conferring Roman citizenship on alien communities, and tactful in the terms on which she had received the rest of the peninsular Italians into her Commonwealth as her lightly burdened and respectfully treated allies. But the Roman 'establishment's' virtues, which had borne this fine political fruit, did not survive the harrowing ordeal of the Hannibalic war. The 'establishment' emerged more powerful than ever. By 167 BC the whole basin of the Mediterranean was at its mercy; throughout Rome's vast newly acquired subject territories and only nominally independent satellite states, the Roman 'establishment' had a free hand; it now abused the power that had been so greatly extended and enhanced; and this was a terrible fate for the western end of the *oikoumenē* which the Roman nobles now dominated. Their temper had undergone a sinister change. They had become vindictive and they had lost their nerve.

Their loss of nerve was shown in an inability to tolerate the survival, within striking distance of Italy, of any other great power or, indeed, of any ex-great power that might conceivably recover some of its former strength. Carthage, after her capitulation in 201 BC, demonstrated by her consistently submissive conduct during the next half century that she had reconciled herself to her drastically reduced circumstances and now wanted simply to lead a quiet life as one of Rome's satellites. Yet in 149–146 BC the Romans destroyed Carthage, and exterminated the Carthaginian people, in cold blood. The Roman nobility's pathological anxiety was displayed still more gratuitously in their treatment of the Seleucid Empire. In the campaigns of 192–190 BC this colossus had proved to have feet of clay. Antiochus III had been no Hannibal; he had not even known how to make use of Hannibal's services. Yet Rome continued to harass the stricken giant. She encouraged the Judaean Jewish resistance movement and, as late as 161 BC she sent commissioners to Apamea-above-Orontes to implement the disarmament clauses of the Romano-Seleucid peace treaty of 188 BC. In thus continuing to torment the Seleucid Empire, Rome was throwing away her chance of salvaging Babylonia – the Asian counterpart of Egypt – for Hellenism and for herself, and she was also condemning herself to solve, at her own cost, the Seleucids' problem of Judaean Jewish nationalism. Babylonia, as well as Media, was occupied and annexed by the Arsacids (the Parnian masters of Parthia) in 141 BC, and two Seleucid attempts, and half a dozen subsequent Roman attempts, to recover these valuable lost dominions all ended in failure. As for Rome's encouragement, in the 2nd century BC, of the Judaean Jewish resistance movement against the Seleucid Empire, this brought upon both the Romans and the Jews the nemesis of the fearful Romano-Jewish wars of AD 66–70 and 131–5.

The political bankruptcy of the Roman 'establishment'

The Roman nobility's post-Hannibalic vindictiveness found vent in a brutal treatment of minor allies. When, in the third and most hard fought of the four Romano-Macedonian wars – the war of 171–168 BC – Rome's victory hung fire, Rhodes offered her good offices for mediation and Pergamum was suspected by the Romans of intending to do the same. In revenge, Rome deliberately ruined Rhodes commercially by giving Delos to Athens on condition that it was to be a free port, and she deliberately humiliated Pergamum. In ruining Rhodes, which had previously policed the seas of the Levant, Rome gave an opening for piracy to prey on Mediterranean maritime commerce till this evil became so acute that Rome herself had to suppress piracy in 67 BC after having allowed it to take its toll for a century. In humiliating Pergamum, Rome laid up for herself three wars (88–85, 84–82, and 74–63 BC) with another of her Anatolian satellite states, Pontic Cappadocia, in the reign of its Philhellene but Romanophobe Iranian King Mithradates VI Eupator. The Achaean Confederacy, which had gone to war with Rome in 147 BC in a fit of aberration after having been Rome's ally since 198 BC, was punished by the destruction of Corinth in the same year as Carthage and just half a century after Corinth had been ostentatiously liberated by Rome from Macedonian rule.

Macedon was the one prostrated great power towards whom Rome showed some consideration and even generosity. In 167 BC the loot required for rewarding the Roman army that had defeated the Macedonians in the preceding year was taken, not from Macedon herself, but from the Molossian Epirots who had sided with her. After the Molossians had capitulated, seventy towns of theirs were sacked and their inhabitants were enslaved. Rome's relative indulgence to Macedon is surprising, considering that Macedon's resistance had been more stubborn than that of any of her fellow-victims. Were the Romans moved by the gallantry of a martial people which was a match for the Romans in valour, man for man, and which, though crushingly outnumbered, 'faced fearful odds' in trying conclusions with Rome again and again? This favourable explanation of Rome's comparative leniency towards Macedon is impugned by the odiousness of Rome's treatment of Numantia – an opponent that was far punier than Macedon and was, if possible, still more gallant.

In this pre-Augustan age of agony, the scourge of war was aggravated by the scourge of revolution – economic, social, and political. The free port of Delos became the market for a slave-trade by which ranches and plantations in the devastated areas of
p 158–9 Italy and Sicily were stocked with slave herdsmen and slave
(27–9, 31) plantation hands exported from the remnant of the Seleucid Empire. These were ex-freemen – some of them well-educated – who had fallen into slavery in large numbers in the anarchy of the Seleucid Empire's death-throes. These victims of Rome's political malice and economic cupidity made their protests in the Sicilian slave-revolts of 135–131 and 104–100 BC. The conversion of the Kingdom of Pergamum into a Roman province in 133 BC provoked a similar revolt there under the leadership of a claimant to the vacant throne, Aristonicus.

Among the victims of the Roman 'establishment's' moral débâcle was the 'establishment' itself. In 133 BC Tiberius Gracchus, a Roman noble, who had carried through some imperatively necessary legislation for long-overdue agrarian reform, was lynched by his peers – and these senators. Down to that day, Roman domestic politics had been conducted constitutionally for perhaps about 230 years. Tiberius' blood was the first that had been shed in Rome's domestic political arena within that period of nearly a quarter of a millennium. This murder of a Roman public officer by members of the governing body of the Roman state condemned the Roman body politic to a century of chronic political revolution and intermittent civil war. The representatives of an 'establishment' cannot take to behaving like gangsters with impunity. In opening the flood-gates for anarchy, the ring of Roman noble families that had first built the Roman Commonwealth in Italy but had then wrecked the western half of the *oikoumenē* had manifestly forfeited its mandate. Reconstruction could not be started until the Roman nobility had been deprived of the power that they had shown themselves no longer fit to wield; but before they were justly deposed they had made havoc.

Augustus – a saviour?

The fundamental reason why the two centuries ending in 31 BC had been agonizing for all the peoples – the Roman people among the rest – that had been at the Roman nobility's mercy was that, in the antisocial state of mind (the antithesis of the spirit of their forbears) in which the Roman nobles had emerged from the Hannibalic War, they had shattered all states and other public institutions within their reach, including the Roman constitution itself, without being willing to take responsibility for filling the vacuum which they themselves had wantonly created. The vacuum was filled at last by a Roman who was a noble by adoption and a demi-noble by birth, but a bourgeois on his father's side.

Augustus won his way to unchallengeable supreme power in the p 16
Graeco-Roman world as a war-lord – the victor in the last of a series of rounds between rival war-lords that had started with the duel between Marius and Sulla. But the veterans of Augustus' adoptive father Caesar, whose swords had carried Augustus into p 12
power, were not the people who kept him in power till his death forty-four years after his decisive victory at Actium. It has been said, truly as well as wittily, that you can do everything with bayonets except sit on them, and, before bayonets were invented, this was, of course, just as true of swords' points. In any case, one man cannot administer half the world single-handed. The form of ability that is the surest test of fitness to rule is the ability to pick out able assistants and to inspire them to serve their employer loyally and energetically. Augustus made a show of partially reinstating the deposed nobility as his partners; but he and his successors drew their most effective coadjutors and executants from two sources outside the circle of the previous Roman 'establishment'. One of their sources of recruitment was the class of Roman businessmen who had accumulated capital in taking up government contracts for military equipment and had invested the proceeds in tax-farming and usury. These *nouveaux riches* had behaved no better than the nobility, but their predatory business operations had given them valuable experience in large-scale administration. Corporation-men are potential civil servants. A wolf-cub can be transformed into a sheep-dog if he is assured of a high enough salary to make it worth his while to look after the sheep instead of preying on them. Augustus' second source of recruitment was the staff of educated slaves which had become an indispensable part of the personnel of every corporation of contractors and every noble politician's private household. An educated slave has the highest conceivable incentive for giving satisfaction to his master. This is his only prospect of earning his manumission. Thus, in the building of a Roman world-state, the soldiers played a less important part than the sheep-dogs; but the sheep-dogs counted for less than the sheep themselves. The ultimate sanction for Augustus' authority was the relief and gratitude of the population of a world that was in desperate need of peace and order after its outrageous maltreatment by Augustus' predecessors, the unworthy scions of the once estimable Roman nobility.

The date of the Battle of Actium was perhaps about twenty-six years earlier than the date of Jesus's birth. At this second historic date, Augustus was still alive, in power, and at work with about eighteen more years of life, power, and work awaiting him.

II

A CLASH OF IDEOLOGIES

PALESTINE UNDER THE SELEUCIDS AND ROMANS

A. SCHALIT

'The anger of the Romans was aggravated because the Jews alone had not given way.'

TACITUS 'HISTORIES V'

The tenacious survival of the Jewish people, its original culture intact and its spiritual integrity uncompromised, is a story unique in history. It was made possible by a unique religion. In the course of three thousand years Judaism has changed and developed but it has never surrendered its Law, its single-mindedness and its absolute faith in its own mission. It was Judaism, not any racial features, which gave the Jews their separate identity and it is Judaism that has kept them a separate identifiable people until today. It involved far more, of course, than merely religious observances, as understood by the Greeks and Romans. It governed every aspect of society; it regulated daily life; it controlled contact with other nations. It enabled the Jews to survive conquest and deportation on the one hand and the more subtle pressures of cultural coexistence on the other. Even the ultimate disaster of the head-on clash with Rome, the destruction of the Temple and the dispersion of the Jews throughout the known world, seem only to have strengthened their spiritual resources.

This gold glass (opposite) from the Jewish catacombs at Rome, dates from the 4th century AD. In symbolic language it sums up the ritual that held the Jewish people together, that was, and is, a dialogue between Yahweh and his chosen. At the top is the Torah shrine, containing in nine scrolls the Law set out in the first five books of the Bible. Beneath it stands the burning Menorah, the Seven-Branched Candlestick which stood in the Temple and which had been carried off to Rome by Titus. Beside the shrine two birds stand on globes, and at the bottom are two guardian lions (carved lions were actually set up in synagogues). The other objects are the amphora with oil for the Menorah, the *ethrog* (citrus-fruit, used during the Feast of Tabernacles), the *shofar* (ram's horn, blown to announce the New Year on the Feast of Rosh Hashanah) and the *lulab* (palm-branch, symbol of Judaea, the forbidden homeland). (1)

The impact of Hellenism was felt in Judaea as elsewhere in the lands which came under Greek control as a result of Alexander's conquest. The leading families had definite views on which of the successor dynasties should be their overlords, one party siding with the Ptolemies, the other with the Seleucids, who eventually won Palestine at the Battle of Paneion (200/198 BC). Young aristocrats practised Greek athletics in the nude – a custom deeply distasteful to most orientals – while in certain of the later books of the Bible, notably in Jonah, something of the Greek oecumenical spirit may be felt. The mass of the people resisted this development, seeing in it only time-serving on the part of the rich to the detriment of the poor.

Even before the Greek conquest, while still under Persian rule, the province of Yehud (Judah) had minted coins bearing its name, in imitation of the Athenian drachma (above, left); and the earliest Hasmonaean rulers readily took over the common Hellenistic good-luck symbols of stars and anchors (below). An interesting lesson in the Hellenization of Palestine is provided by a comparison of a coin of the Seleucid Alexander II with one of John Hyrcanus (below, right). The double cornucopiae are retained on the Jewish coin (at the bottom), but the *caduceus*, symbol of the Greek god Hermes, is replaced by a 'neutral' pomegranate. The head is replaced by an inscription with the ruler's name. (2, 3, 5–8, 10, 11)

Herod the Great, a man of deep contradictions, part statesman, part monster, saw, in contrast with the more short-sighted of his contemporaries, that it was necessary to reach a *modus vivendi* with the Roman state, but was utterly ruthless in his methods. Unlike the early Hasmonaeans, he minted coins bearing overtly pagan symbols, the *caduceus* of Hermes and the tripod of Apollo (below). Above: the rock-cut Herodian tombs of 'Absalom' (left) and 'Zechariah' in the Kidron valley combine the Classical orders with oriental features such as the pyramidal roof (*nefesh*) on top. Above right: a tomb popularly believed to be the communal grave of the seventy-one members of the Great Synhedrion, Jerusalem. (4, 12–15)

The common Hellenistic idiom was adopted by Queen Helena of Adiabene when, upon her and her two sons' conversion to Judaism (AD 35–40), she laid out a family vault in Jerusalem (right), decorated with a classical but 'neutral' frieze of acanthus and grapes (opposite, below far left). (9, 16)

Herod changed the face of Jerusalem. His greatest, and best remembered, architectural achievement was the rebuilding of the Temple, illustrated in the next chapter. He also built a huge palace, or castle, for himself in the north-west corner of the Upper City of Jerusalem (right – some of the drafted blocks in the bottom five courses are Herodian). It rested on foundations going back to Hasmonaean times, and was defended by high ramparts and three dominating towers which he named Phasael, Hippicus and Mariamne after his brother, friend and wife. After Herod's death this citadel was the residence of his successors and of the Roman procurators. In AD 66 it was occupied by the rebels and in AD 70 held out alone for a month when the rest of Jerusalem had fallen. (20)

Herod's seaport was Caesarea (left), named after his patron Caesar Augustus. Originally a Phoenician settlement (Strato's Tower), it was rebuilt by Herod, grew rapidly during his reign and remained a leading city during the subsequent Roman period. After AD 70 it became the administrative capital of the Roman province. Here we see a large public building, flanked by two over life-size statues, one in marble (an Emperor?), the other in porphyry (Roma?). (17)

As a place of retreat both from the cares of state and from the menace of his enemies, Herod built his luxurious palace at Masada (above and right). It was built on three terraces overhanging the sheer drop at the northern end of the fortress plateau. The topmost part of the palace was a small dwelling-house facing a semicircular terrace, from which steps led down to a strange circular platform, the purpose of which is unknown. From here a further flight of steps led to the heart of the palace, a square courtyard surrounded by a corridor with columns standing against the walls. The base of these walls was richly painted in imitation of marble veneer. The whole complex, designed to function as a unit for Herod and a small entourage, illustrates not only the enterprise and daring of Herodian architecture, but also the king's wealth, power and pride. (18, 19)

The resistance to the Roman rule in Judaea which Herod had suppressed with an iron hand during his reign exploded more than sixty years after his death – years of mounting tension and bloodshed – in the great revolt of AD 66. Jerusalem enjoyed its precarious freedom for four years. But in AD 70 a large army under Titus, son of the Emperor Vespasian, besieged and captured it, destroyed the Temple and levelled the city with the ground.

For the Romans it was a major war, and their victory was celebrated by coins and a triumphal arch in Rome. Left: the coin 'Judaea Capta', with a captive Jewish man (standing) and woman (seated) under a palm-tree. Below: the famous relief from the Arch of Titus showing the Seven-Branched Candlestick, the Table of the Shewbread (?) and the sacred trumpets from the Temple being brought to Rome. The other objects being carried aloft may be placards describing the war.

After the fall of Jerusalem the last remnant of the Jewish patriots, the Sicarii under Eleazar Son of Ya'ir, held out in Herod's great fortress of Masada for three years. (21, 22)

A broken potsherd with the name Ben Ya'ir scratched upon it may be a relic of Masada's last hours. (23)

The epic story of Masada's resistance to the military might of Rome, told by the contemporary Jewish historian Josephus, is outlined on the next page. During recent excavations many poignant remains have been discovered, shedding fresh light on the heroism and tragic fate of the defenders. Top: stone missiles from Roman war-machines, each about the size of an orange. Somewhat larger patriot missiles, each weighing about 100 lb, were also discovered. Centre: bones and skulls, found in a cave near the top of the southern cliff – perhaps the skeletons of Sicarii thrown there by the Romans. Right: one of the most amazing finds was the skeleton of a young woman, with her scalp preserved owing to the dryness of the climate, and her dark hair, beautifully plaited, still attached to it. (24–6)

The rock of Masada lies about 40 miles south-east of Jerusalem in the barren country close to the Dead Sea. Its flat top is surrounded on three sides by steep cliffs, making it a natural fortress with only one drawback – lack of water. Herod's engineers had brilliantly overcome this by constructing vast cisterns in the rock and ensuring that they were filled by the rare heavy downpours of rain. It was Herod too who built the line of walls round the summit, the storehouse and barracks, and the luxurious 'hanging palace' perched on the northern spur (right, in the foreground) and descending in three levels over the edge of the precipice.

This was the stronghold seized by the rebels in AD 66 and held by them under Eleazar ben Ya'ir after the fall of Jerusalem in AD 70. Silva, the Roman commander, established eight camps round it and built a wall over two miles long and six feet thick to prevent its defenders escaping. He then had to reach the top for the assault, and for this purpose built an earth ramp on the western side, still plainly visible today (on the right of the photograph) and forming one of the most amazing feats of Roman military engineering. It is 215 yards long. On top of it a strong stone platform was constructed (now vanished) on which the Romans placed their catapults and battering ram. The ramparts were finally breached at this point, and a wooden palisade behind them burnt. The Sicarii faced certain defeat, and chose death rather than captivity. On the night before the last attack 960 men, women and children committed suicide. When the Romans came they found only the corpses and smoking ruins. 'Nor could they do other than wonder at the courage of their resolution,' writes Josephus, 'and at the immovable contempt of death which so great a number of them had shown, when they performed such an action as that.'

As revealed by excavation, Masada contains a number of buildings beside the palace and fortifications, some dating from Herod's time, some from that of the Sicarii and some from later periods, when a Byzantine monastery was built on the rock. This building (below) is perhaps the most interesting of all. Built by Herod and altered by the Sicarii, it is thought to have been a synagogue. The pillars belong to the first building, the stepped benches to the second. (27, 28)

The second revolt in AD 132 under Simon bar Kokhba was again ruthlessly crushed by the Romans. By the orders of Hadrian vast numbers of Jews were deported from Judaea and sold into slavery so that there could no longer be a centre of resistance or a national home.

A remnant was left in the north, headed by the Synhedrion under the leadership of the house of Hillel. From the 2nd century AD onwards major synagogues were established all over Galilee and round the Sea of Galilee. Above: a capital with the Menorah from Caesarea. Below: part of the ruins of the synagogue at Beth Shearim. Left: a figure supporting the Menorah on his head, from the catacombs at Beth Shearim. (29–31)

A new beginning was made during these years, when the Talmudic oral traditions began to be written down and codified. The synagogues where the rabbis taught are Hellenistic in their architecture and decoration, showing how far Jewish art, at least, had been affected by the prevailing Imperial style. The synagogue of Capernaum (above) was founded soon after the Bar Kokhba revolt. Synagogues were always erected with the façades pointing towards Jerusalem; they were basilican in plan, often with the roof supported on Corinthian pillars. There might even be figure-carving, for the Mosaic prohibition of images was not always strictly imposed. The inscriptions, too, are often in Greek. The synagogue of Kfar Bira'm (below) lies further north in the mountains, close to the border of modern Lebanon. The façade has the usual triple entrance, probably a legacy from Syrian temples. (32, 33)

Abraham and Isaac, identified by name, are represented on the mosaic floor of the synagogue of Beth Alpha, dating from the 6th century AD (above). The third inscription reads: 'Lay not (thine hand upon the lad).' The style is unsophisticated, the work of local craftsmen. Right: pavement at Huldah, showing *lulab*, *ethrog*, incense-shovel, Menorah and *shofar*. The oddly spelt Greek inscription appears to mean: 'Praise (the Lord), ye people.' (34, 35)

The most splendid of these Talmudic-period mosaics to survive is that of Ma'on, of which a small section is shown here. The complete floor consisted of 55 medallions linked by the curling tendrils of a very stylized vine, and containing pictures of symbolic objects, plants and animals. The workmanship is far more accomplished than that of Beth Alpha, and the pavement was probably laid by Byzantine craftsmen. At the top is the Menorah, guarded by lions. Beneath the branches of the candlestick are the *shofar*, the *lulab* and the *ethrog*. Two palm trees are flanked by doves. The bird in the cage perhaps symbolizes the soul imprisoned in the body. The animals are portrayed with singular charm, and the hen has laid an egg in a bowl. (36)

The Diaspora made its mark all over Europe and the Near East, leaving impressive symbols of unity among the scattered Jewish colonies, as also of the partial integration of Jew and non-Jew at a social and artistic level. It was this partial integration that paved the way for what appeared at first to be a Jewish sect – Christianity – eventually to conquer the gentile world.

Galilee and Italy: the tomb of Marinos and Justa his wife at Beth Shearim (right) records their names in Greek, along with the Menorah, flanked by *shofar*, *lulab* and incense-shovel. An inscription on another tombstone in South Italy (far right) retains Aramaic. (37, 38)

Rome: a sarcophagus from the Vigna Rondanini catacomb (opposite, above) shows the Menorah held by classical Victories, with Cupids representing the seasons (only Winter is left) and little figures treading grapes. (41)

Tunisia: the mosaic floor of the synagogue at Hamman Lif, near Tunis (opposite, below), displays striking combinations of Jewish and pagan motifs. Amid the many animals which appear in the mosaic is a lion that may or may not stand for the Lion of Judah. The mosaic was provided, according to the inscription, by Juliana, a proselyte. (42)

Rome: the Menorah and other familiar symbols appear scratched on the walls of the Jewish catacomb of Vigna Rondanini (below). (40)

Alexandria: a lamp with the handle in the form of the Menorah also comprises the *shofar*, *lulab* and *ethrog* in its decoration. A Christian lamp with the Cross in place of the Menorah has been discovered at Bethshean, and further variations on the theme may be seen on p. 338–9. (39)

Exiled again as in the days of the Old Testament, the Jews of the Diaspora seemed once more to be following the Ark of the Covenant (now represented by the Torah shrine in their synagogues) as it travelled from land to land. This fresco, of the captured Ark leaving the Philistine city of Ekron after it had devastated the Temple of Dagon, comes from the synagogue of Dura Europus on the Euphrates, where a powerful Jewish community was established. Titus, according to Sulpicius Severus, had said that once Jewish power had been torn up by the roots (Jerusalem) 'the trunk too will perish'. History has proved him wrong. (43)

PALESTINE UNDER THE SELEUCIDS AND ROMANS

ABRAHAM SCHALIT

DURING THE CENTURY that elapsed after the Battle of Ipsus (301 p 103 (6, 7) BC) the Ptolemies and the Seleucids fought each other no less than five times for the possession of Southern Syria, called Coele (Whole) Syria in the Seleucid Empire, *i.e.* Palestine, Phoenicia, and Syria south of the River Eleutherus (the Nahr-al-Kabir). The final stage in this struggle was reached in the Battle of Paneion near the sources of the Jordan (200/198 BC), when the victory of Antiochus III decided the issue in favour of the Seleucids. Coele Syria ceased to be under the Ptolemies. Nor did it revert to them again. In this way the Jewish people in Judaea came under Seleucid rule.

This change of masters in Judaea was not effected without some participation by the people in the development of events. Of this there are several evidences. The Book of Daniel hints at it,[1] while the Church Father Jerome relates[2] that, in the years preceding the war, the people in Judaea were divided into two parties, the one siding with the Ptolemies and their rule of the country, the other favouring the Seleucids. This division is strikingly illustrated by the breach within the family of the Tobiads. Joseph the son of Tobiah, the head of the family, and his sons in Jerusalem adhered f 1 to the Seleucid party, whereas the youngest son, Hyrcanus, who had established himself in a semi-independent principality in Transjordan, had close economic and political ties with the Ptolemies.[3] Thanks to the victory of Antiochus, the Seleucid party gained the upper hand in Jerusalem. There the King was welcomed by his supporters, who, together with the people, helped him to drive the Egyptian garrison from the Baris (Hebrew: Birah = citadel). In recognition of the support that he had received, Antiochus issued two proclamations, the one in favour of the Temple and its ministers, and the other in favour of the Jewish religion.

In his letter to the governor Ptolemy,[4] the King commanded that the damage done to the Temple during the fighting should be repaired at the expense of the royal treasury, and that animals, salt, wine, and fine flour should be provided for the sacrifices; that the priests and the various ministers of the Temple, as well as the members of the Judaean council of elders, should be exempted from the payment of taxes; that the people should be relieved of a third of the crown-tax and of the salt-tax; that exemption from all taxes should be granted for a period of three years to the entire people and also to the refugees who returned before a specified date; and that all who had been captured and enslaved up to the time of the conquest should be set free.

The second order (a 'πρόγραμμα') forbade the bringing of unclean animals into Jerusalem. Its purpose was to keep any suspicion of Levitical uncleanness away from the Temple and its vicinity. Nor was there anything unusual in Antiochus' conduct towards his Jewish subjects; this was the traditional policy of the Seleucid kings towards every religion and every temple-city under their rule.[5] These orders were undoubtedly issued at the request of the members of the council of elders, and they actually gave an 9 (1) official stamp to the Torah as the constitution of the temple-city of Jerusalem – a constitution that would be binding on all the people of Judaea,[6] which was this temple-city's territory.

The Judaean Jewish council of elders which had obtained these privileges from Antiochus was an aristocratic body composed of the representatives of the noble and wealthy families of two social classes, the lay and the priestly, the former headed by the Tobiads. It was presided over by the high priest, who was originally vested with a twofold authority. He was the head of the nation (in the sources this authority is called προστασία τοῦ λαοῦ: *cf.* Josephus, *Antiquitates Judaicae* XII 161), and in this capacity he negotiated with the foreign paramount power and was responsible for the regular payment of the country's taxes, thus performing, as regards external relations, the functions of a secular prince. In addition to this he performed a religious function as the head of the Temple, and in this role he also discharged the duties of chief justice, exercising his jurisdiction in accordance with the law embodied in the Torah.

At the end of Ptolemy III's reign or at the beginning of Ptolemy IV's, a significant change had taken place in Judaea. Joseph, one of the Tobiads, had secured from the King in Alexandria the contract for the farming of the taxes of Ptolemaic Syria and Phoenicia, and he had also supplanted the high priest as the secular head of the people.[7] The farming of the taxes had laid the foundations of the Tobiad family's vast wealth, while the leadership of the nation had given political supremacy to Joseph and the rest of the Tobiads. This new situation had not, however, led to a split among the Jerusalem nobility on the lines of priests against laymen. On the contrary, the assumption of national leadership by a layman had created a balance of forces in the aristocratic council which had increased the social solidarity between the council's two component classes. Moreover, the two groups were linked with each other by economic as well as by family ties; for, besides the great wealth acquired through commerce and the farming of the taxes by at least some lay families, such as the Tobiads, and undoubtedly also by others whose names are unknown, both groups were landowners, and this basic economic factor, which was common to them both, united them as a class against the tenants. The existence of family ties between laymen and the aristocratic priesthood is illustrated by the case of Joseph the son of Tobiah himself. His mother was the sister of the high priest Onias II. A further bond uniting the priestly and the lay nobility was their close ties with the foreign paramount power – the priests in virtue of their association with the Temple service, the laymen for economic and political reasons.

Hebraism and Hellenism

This was the internal situation in Judaea down to the close of the period of Ptolemaic rule. Nor did the Seleucid conquest alter the position. Antiochus III maintained his Ptolemaic predecessors' traditional policy, attracting to himself the wealthy and aristocratic classes and thereby cementing the ties between them and himself. The Seleucids, like the Ptolemies, represented an alien culture, and this led to a transformation of values among the people of Judaea, the historical significance of which cannot be exaggerated. For the first time in the period of the Second Temple since the days of Ezra and Nehemiah, an influential social class of Jews, looking beyond the confines of its own culture, discovered an unknown world – a p 50–51 (2–16) discovery which exerted a profound spiritual and material influence on them. In feeling the attractiveness of Hellenism, and in succumbing to it partially and temporarily, the Judaean Jews were going the same way as most other peoples in Coele Syria.

The spiritual influence of Hellenism can be seen in certain books of the Bible in which there is a freer mood – a mood opposed to the rigidity of thought and attitude that were characteristic of the party of Ezra among the people. Mention need only be made of the Book of Jonah with its all-embracing humanity, its concern for the distress of man as such, its complete ignoring of any distinction between Jew and non-Jew. To the sailors, Jonah confesses that he fears 'the Lord, the God of Heaven, who hath made the sea and the dry land' (i 9). Here is expressed a cosmopolitan approach to man and his destiny, of which the Scriptures reveal no trace before the Book of Jonah (which dates, apparently, from the first half or the middle of the 3rd century BC). This broad approach presumably made its appearance among the Jews under the influence, at least to some extent, of the spiritual culture of the Hellenistic world. No less characteristic are certain psalms which are likewise hymns to the spirit of man as man.

These new horizons among some circles of the Jewish nation in Palestine are strikingly revealed in the Book of Ecclesiastes. Even if the view is accepted that there is no direct connection between Hellenistic philosophical thought and the spiritual outlook of the author of Ecclesiastes, the mere fact that such philosophical thought and scepticism found expression, and that the problem of life's ultimate purpose was propounded, is undoubtedly due to the new wind that was blowing in Judaea as a result of the impact of Hellenistic culture on certain circles there in the 3rd century BC. The Greek language, too, penetrated all aspects of life in Judaea. The extent of this can be gauged from the numerous Greek words that are to be found in the Mishnah and that, from the 3rd century onwards, gave the Hebrew language a new character. At about the same time, Greek names were adopted by Jews. It is significant that Antigonos of Socho – he lived apparently in the 3rd century BC and was one of the 'pairs', the earliest transmitters of the Halakhah – had a Greek name. There is no clear evidence of the influence of Greek literature at the time. But is it mere coincidence that Sirach in one passage (xiv 19–22) expresses an idea that is wholly reminiscent of Glaucus' remarks to Diomedes (*Iliad* VI 145–9) on the transitory nature of man's life on earth?

The material influence which contact with the world of Hellenism exerted on aristocratic circles in Judaea is apparent in every sphere of daily existence, from the pleasures of life, food and drink,
p 50–51 to housing and the external habits of life, social customs, and forms
(2–16) of speech.[8] Now, for the first time, Jewish society discovered the
f 1 musical arts, to which it was drawn as if by magic. However, this Hellenizing trend was opposed by the overwhelming majority of the Judaean Jewish people; for the spiritual enterprise that was engrossing this majority's attention and concern was the laying of the foundations of the Halakhah.[9]

Thus, within the bosom of the Judaean Jewish community at the time of the Seleucids' take-over of Coele Syria from the Ptolemies, there was ideological and religious conflict. There was also bitter social strife. The rich and noble class was opposed by the masses of tenant farmers who tilled the lands of the aristocracy and of the foreign paramount authorities for a trifling share of the produce. The opposition also included the artisans in the towns, the sages and the scribes, who lived in penury.[10] The antagonism grew more acute; for the rich Judaean Jews and the foreign paramount power alike oppressed the lower classes in Judaea both economically and in the field of law – economically by the landowners' exploitation of the tenants and by the exaction from these of compulsory labour on behalf of the King, and in the field of law by perverting justice in favour of the wealthy and the powerful. This state of affairs, which prevailed in Palestine before the
f 2 Maccabaean revolt, is very clearly reflected in Ecclesiasticus, whose author, Sirach, lived at the end of the 3rd and the beginning of the 2nd century BC. Sirach, who belonged to the well-to-do but not the wealthy class, observes with penetrating, realistic eyes what is taking place in society, and he despairs of the lot of the poor. He arrives at the conclusion that the common people cannot hope for a change of heart on the part of the rich and of the authorities, and he advises the poor to bear their burden patiently, for the rulers will always side with those who are powerful and wealthy. Between the rich and the poor there is an unbridgeable gulf. It is evident that in circumstances such as these the people would vent their anger in a crisis not only against the foreign power but also against the wealthy and the aristocracy, since both combined to oppress the masses. This is just what happened.

The retribution of intrigue

The spark that started the conflagration came from the Hellenizers. As previously mentioned, Joseph the son of Tobiah had ousted the high priest from the secular leadership some thirty years before the Seleucid conquest. Antiochus III did not remove Joseph from this position, and he probably continued to occupy it until his death, when the role apparently reverted to the high priest – on this occasion to Simon II, the successor of Onias II. This change was not resisted by Joseph's sons, for Simon was valuable to them as an
ally against their mortal enemy, their brother Hyrcanus, who was *f 1*
waiting in Transjordan for a favourable opportunity to seize power in Jerusalem. When Simon died round about the time of Seleucus IV's accession (187 BC) – that is, approximately between 187 and 185 BC – and when Simon's son Onias III became high priest, the accord between the Jerusalem Tobiads and the high priest ended. Onias was a friend of Hyrcanus,[11] and thus the Cisjordanian Tobiads had every reason to supplant him in the leadership of the nation, the position previously held by their father Joseph. The time was also opportune for such a move, since the standing of Onias had been impaired by reason of a dispute that had broken out between him and the head of the Temple, Simon of the family of the Sons of Bilgah, as a result of which Onias was constrained to go to Antioch to vindicate himself before the King.[12]

Hopes of drastic changes in Jerusalem ran high, particularly on the accession of Antiochus IV Epiphanes after the murder of Seleucus IV (175 BC). Onias was obliged to stay in Antioch, and Hyrcanus, the dangerous Transjordanian rival of the Tobiads, also disappeared from the scene. He preferred, when hard pressed by Antiochus Epiphanes, to die by his own hand.[13] The Cisjordanian Tobiads now decided to seize control of Jerusalem, while they attempted at the same time to accommodate their ambitions to the new policy of the King, who was known for his admiration of Hellenic culture and for his eagerness to propagate it.[14] With the intention of putting an end in Jerusalem to family strife with the Oniads, and of cultivating a party policy that would be in keeping with the cultural designs espoused by the King, the Tobiads succeeded in attracting to their side the high priest Onias' brother Jesus, who had changed his name to Jason. Jason now proposed that the King should appoint him high priest in exchange for a sum of money, should register the population of Jerusalem as Antiochians, thereby transforming the city into the *polis* of 'Antiocheia', and should build in it a gymnasium and an ephebeion.[15] To this Antiochus agreed, and thus, with the help of Jason, who became the high priest, the Tobiads gained control of Jerusalem and ruled over the new *polis*.

Beyond this the Tobiads did not aspire, nor did they have any intention of introducing changes in the Jewish form of worship. All the same, the very establishment of the institutions of the new 'Antiochian' *polis*, together with Greek physical training of the aristocratic priestly youth and their captivation by the way of life of a Hellenistic city, had the effect of weakening the Jewish religious tradition and relegating it to the background. Henceforth the position of supreme importance in the life of the young priests was no longer occupied by religion and the Temple service, but by gymnastic exercises in the palaestra and by the desire to become integrated with the Greeks by concealing their circumcision.[16]

For three years Jason was high priest. But his compact with the Tobiads was not successful. The extremists in that party, led apparently by the priest Menelaus, the brother of Simon the head of the Temple, supplanted Jason by offering the King a still larger sum for the high priesthood. Thereupon, Jason fled to Transjordan and was succeeded by Menelaus. In order to secure himself against the return of Onias, who was then still in Antioch, Menelaus had Onias assassinated.[17]

The violence of Menelaus and his brother Lysimachus produced chaos in Jerusalem. Finally civil war broke out, in which Lysimachus was killed.[18] In the meantime Antiochus marched against Egypt with the intention of conquering it, but, when he was on his second campaign there (in 168 BC), an embassy from the Roman Senate forced him to renounce his conquests and to evacuate Egypt.[19] This reverse of Antiochus generated a rumour in Jerusalem that the King had died. Jason thereupon returned from Transjordan with an armed force, penetrated to Jerusalem, and

The powerful Jewish family of the Tobiads split into two parties, one supporting the Ptolemies, the other the Seleucids. Both branches, however, were steeped in Hellenistic culture; in the castle at Araq el-Emir (shown here in a conjectural reconstruction), which is probably identical with the Tobiad Hyrcanus' castle of Tyrus in Transjordan mentioned by Josephus, the lion frieze is a particularly Greek motif. (1)

slaughtered his adversaries, the members of Menelaus' party. Menelaus himself succeeded in escaping to the Baris (citadel). Jason found himself unable to hold out for long in the city, and he withdrew; but Antiochus, having learnt of what had taken place and believing that a revolt had broken out against him, advanced on Jerusalem at the head of his army and took the city by storm. The opponents of Menelaus were massacred; the Temple treasury was plundered; and a new citadel (*acra*) was built and was occupied by a garrison of Seleucid troops. Apparently Antiochus saw the cause of the events in Jerusalem, and the opposition to Menelaus, in the existence of the Jewish religion. He came to the conclusion that the implementation of Menelaus' plan, which was his own, necessitated the suppression of the worship and religion of the contending Jewish parties. Thus began, in 168 BC, the religious persecutions of Judaism under Antiochus IV.[20]

Events followed one another in quick succession. At the King's command the observance of the Sabbath and circumcision were prohibited, and the Jews were forced to eat forbidden foods. Anyone found in possession of a scroll of the Torah was executed. The Temple was desecrated. Ritual prostitution, as practised in Syrian fertility cults, was introduced within its precincts. On Kislev 15, 167 BC, the supreme desecration took place. On the old altar there was erected one dedicated to the Olympian Zeus, on which swine were sacrificed.[21]

The torch of the Maccabees

Some Jews complied with the King's orders. Many preferred, however, to die rather than transgress the commandments of their religion. For instance, a thousand men, women, and children refused to profane the Sabbath, offered no resistance, and were put to death (I Maccabees ii 29–35). The first opposition encountered *f 2* by the King's officers came from the family of Mattathias of Modin, the son of the priest Hasmon. This was the spark that set the flame of revolt ablaze in Judaea. Joined by a company of Assidaeans (puritanically strict observers of the Torah), who were 'mighty men of Israel', Mattathias took the momentous decision to permit fighting on the Sabbath.[22] Under his leadership guerrilla war was waged for an entire year against the Seleucid forces and their collaborators among the Judaean Jews. On Mattathias' death his son Judas, known as Maccabaeus, took over the command, whereupon the rebels assumed the offensive and repeatedly defeated the Seleucid armies. The peak of their success was the securing of a truce that opened the way for the purification of the Temple in Jerusalem from pagan worship, its rededication on Kislev 25, December 165 BC, and the institution of Hanukkah, the Festival of Lights.[23]

The war continued with varying fortunes. In 163/2 BC both sides found it necessary to arrive at a compromise by which the Seleucid government re-conceded religious liberty to the Jews in exchange for the Jews' re-submission to the government's political authority. The revolt had in fact been suppressed, but the young King Antiochus V Eupator, the son of Antiochus IV Epiphanes, who had died in 163 BC, during an expedition into the eastern regions of his empire, together with the regent Lysias, revoked the decrees of the late king against the Jewish religion. To signalize this reversal of Seleucid policy, Menelaus, the author of the turmoil, was executed. From that time on, the Seleucid government consistently refrained from reverting to Antiochus IV's policy of religious persecution. Religious tolerance was, after all, the normal practice of the Seleucid, Ptolemaic, and other Greek or Hellenized successor-states of the tolerant Persian Empire.

Now that the Judaeans who had joined Mattathias in defence of their religion had achieved their objective, the Assidaeans no longer saw any need to continue the fight. On the other hand, the sons of Mattathias and their party persisted in their military struggle against Seleucid rule. This decision of Judas Maccabaeus was not necessarily the outcome of a lust for political power or secular rule. The first clear indications of a secular political tendency in the public life of Judaea, with the foundation of a regular state as the ultimate goal of the struggle, emerge only in the days of Jonathan. Judas, like his father, was a genuine fighter for religious freedom even when he decided to continue the struggle despite the fact that the Seleucid government had given in by revoking Antiochus Epiphanes' orders to persecute the Jews and by reassuring them that their religious freedom would not again be infringed. The true reason for Judas' continuation of the war is to be seen in his deep distrust of the rulers of the Seleucid Empire even after the death of Antiochus Epiphanes. For it was by no means clear what the future would have in store and what would be the attitude of the new men in power to the Jewish religion in general, despite all their assurances of peace. First of all, the Jews felt themselves threatened not only from the territories bordering on Judaea but also in Galilee and even in remote parts of Transjordan such as Batanaea, Auranitis, Galaaditis and Trachonitis. It was not the opposition of the Jews to Hellenization that aroused the anger and ill-will of the gentiles against their Jewish neighbours, but the fact that there was a deep-rooted enmity of long standing between the gentiles, who had settled in p 106–7 various parts of Palestine after the Kingdoms of Israel and Judah (13) had disappeared, and those Jews who had returned from their p 34–5 exile and had tried to infiltrate with more or less success into the (39–45) homeland of the exiles from both kingdoms, but had met with enmity and hatred on the part of the new masters of the country.[24]

The anti-Jewish animosity in many circles of the Seleucid administration in Judaea and Samaria as well as in other regions of the Seleucid Empire spread like a fire over the areas of Cis- and Transjordan and gave to all enemies of the Jews a stimulus to get rid of them by massacre. Judas and his brothers answered the call of the threatened Jewish communities in Galilee and in Transjordan and saved them partly by defeating their enemies and partly by repatriating them to Judaea. But the main problem which Judas faced was the attitude of the Seleucid Empire to the Jewish religion despite the compromise reached in 164/3, or more exactly in spring 163 BC. After a short regency of Lysias on behalf of the infant-king Antiochus V Eupator, the son of Antiochus Epiphanes, Antiochus V and Lysias were both put to death by Demetrius, the son of Seleucus IV Eupator, who had been in Rome as a hostage and had secretly fled to Antioch in order to win the throne of his father, which had been usurped first by his uncle Antiochus Epiphanes and then, after Epiphanes' death, by his son. The first steps as regards Jewish matters taken by Demetrius, an energetic but gloomy and hard-natured man, may have deepened the distrust harboured by Judas. He therefore arrived at the conclusion that there would be no religious security for the Jews without a complete rupture of relations between Judaea and the Seleucid Empire.

Judas realized that, to reach this end, there was need for help from some great power that was not on friendly terms with the Seleucid Empire and was looking for every possible opportunity to harm and weaken it by encouraging the centrifugal elements in it. Such a power was Rome, about which the Jews had information that was, perhaps, not exact, but that was enough to convince them that the great western power would lend a sympathetic ear to their proposals. In addition, Judas was well aware of the circumstances under which Demetrius had left Rome; that he had left not only without the consent of the Roman Senate, but even against its will and its policy in the East. Demetrius on the Seleucid throne was *persona non grata* for the Roman Senate, and for a long time the Senate was reluctant to give its approbation to Demetrius' accession to the throne. On the other hand the Romans had already been active in Judaea in helping to bring about the agreement of 164/3 BC (*cf.* II Macc. ii 34–8). All this was enough to encourage the Judaean rebels to turn to the Roman Senate for help. In 161 BC Judas sent an embassy to Rome, and his envoy was granted by the Senate a *foedus aequum* (*i.e.* a treaty on terms of equality) – a rare privilege for any foreign community to receive from Rome at this stage of Rome's history. But Demetrius was alert to the danger from the western power. Immediately after the defeat of Nicanor at Adasa (Adar 13, about March 161 BC) he sent a huge army under the experienced general Bacchides, who defeated and killed Judas in a battle near Alasa or Elasa not later than about two months after Nicanor's defeat, *i.e.* about April 161, even before the Jewish embassy had returned home.

High priest and commonwealth

All seemed lost for the Maccabaean cause after the death of Judas. His brother Jonathan, who had been elected his successor by the rebels, was in fact a guerrilla fighter who could only harass but not seriously harm the Seleucid forces in Judaea. But the situation changed rapidly with the appearance of a rival king on the Syrian scene, the pseudo-Seleucid Alexander Balas. In order to win the support of the Maccabaean rebels against his rival Demetrius, the pretender appointed Jonathan high priest of the Jews. Jonathan was, then, the first Hasmonaean to be invested with the high-priesthood and to inaugurate the lineage of the Hasmonaean high priests which lasted for 116 years (153–37 BC), or 117 years, if we add Aristobulus III, the brother of Queen Mariamne, Herod's wife, who held the office of high priest for less than a year (from about December 37 till about October 36 BC).

The appointment of Jonathan as high priest precipitated events. To win over the newly appointed Hasmonaean high priest, Demetrius made many extravagant promises to him. Jonathan was of course clever enough not to trust Demetrius, even when he promised to add the three districts of Aphaerema, Lydda, and Ramathaim to the territory of the Jews. The reason for this promise was the demographic fact that, although the districts were attached to Samaria, they had for long been inhabited mostly by Jews. They were finally attached to the territory of the Jews by a formal declaration made by Demetrius II Nicator (I Macc. xi 34).

There was now no doubt about the general course that was being taken by the Hasmonaean rulers. The final goal was the foundation of an independent state under their leadership. In 142 BC Simon, the brother and successor of Jonathan after his assassination by Tryphon, demanded and was granted by Demetrius II Nicator immunity from Seleucid taxation as well as confirmation of his possession of all fortresses that were in his hands. This was correctly interpreted by Simon as the actual confirmation of the independence of Judaea, and he gave formal expression to this fact by introducing a new era, which started from the year 170 of the Seleucid era, *i.e.* 142 BC. In this year, says the author of I Maccabees (xiii 41–2), 'was the yoke of the heathen taken away from Israel. And the people of Israel began to write in their instruments and contracts: "In the first year of Simon the great high priest etc." '

In the same year, 142 BC, Simon took Gazara, the Seleucid fortress on the road between Jerusalem and the coast, and also the coastal cities Jamnia and Joppa. He evicted the inhabitants of Gazara and Joppa, and replaced them by – as the author of I Maccabees (xiii 48) put it – 'men who observed the Law'. In 141 BC the Seleucid garrison of the citadel of Jerusalem capitulated. When, however, in 138 BC, Antiochus VII Sidetes reunited what was still left of the Seleucid empire, the Seleucid power still proved more than a match for the Hasmonaeans. In one of the next years – the date is controversial – Antiochus VII besieged Jerusalem and compelled the reigning Hasmonaean prince and high priest, John p 50
Hyrcanus, to make peace on Antiochus' terms, which were (10, 1
generous politically (he demanded no retrocessions of territory) and were scrupulously tolerant in the delicate matter of religion. In 130 BC John Hyrcanus had to bring a contingent to join his suzerain Antiochus VII's expeditionary force on a campaign for the reconquest, from the Parthians, of the Seleucids' lost dominions east of the River Euphrates. In 129 BC the whole Seleucid expeditionary force except the Jewish contingent was destroyed in Media, and Antiochus VII lost his life. John Hyrcanus alone succeeded in making his way back home with his Jewish troops. The Seleucid monarchy was now in its death-agony, and John Hyrcanus and his successors on the Hasmonaean throne had a free hand from 129 BC till 63 BC, when Pompey annexed Syria and the Hasmonaean p 126
state to the Roman Empire.

A 'robber state'

During this interval the Hasmonaeans made sweeping conquests of ex-Seleucid territories, in emulation of the Ituraean principality in the Baqa' and the Nabataean principality which had its nucleus at Petra. An even more disastrous fate was meted out to the Samaritans and their country. John Hyrcanus destroyed the Samaritans' temple[25] on Mount Gerizim*, levelled the Hellenized city of Samaria with the ground, and enslaved the inhabitants.[26] Galilee, too, must have been conquered in the reign of John Hyrcanus, presumably by his sons Aristobulus and Antigonus. It is improbable that Galilee was annexed by Aristobulus when he was high priest. His reign – if he did reign – was brief, and for most of the time he was a sick man.[27] The Ituraeans of Galilee, like the Idumaeans, were forced to undergo circumcision. But not the whole of Galilee was inhabited by gentiles at this date. It has been demonstrated by many scholars[28] that the country was already Judaized to a great extent when it was conquered by the Hasmonaeans. John Hyrcanus conquered Idumaea and forcibly p 106
circumcised its inhabitants.[29] Alexander Jannaeus (102–76/5 BC) (13)
conquered the Peraea (a strip of territory along the east bank of the p 50
River Jordan) and made it Jewish. In Transjordan he also con- (5, 6)
quered the Hellenized cities Abila, Seleucia-in-Gaulanitis, Hippos, p 110
Pella, Gadara, Gerasa, Dium. Here only Philadelphia (Rabbath (30, 3
Ammon) maintained its independence.[30] Alexander Jannaeus p 110
destroyed this Seleucia,[31] and also Philoteria on the Sea of Galilee.[32] On the coast, where the Hasmonaeans already held Joppa and Jamnia, Alexander Jannaeus conquered every other city, from Dora to Rhinocoloura inclusive, except Ascalon.[33] By the year

* *Editor's footnote:* The temples on Mount Gerizim and in Jerusalem were dedicated to the same God.

63 BC, in which Coele Syria was annexed to the Roman Empire by Pompey, the whole of it had been partitioned between the Hasmonaean, Nabataean, and Ituraean principalities except for Philadelphia, Ascalon, Ptolemais, Tyre, Sidon, Berytus, Byblos, Tripolis, Orthosia.[34]

f 2 These sweeping conquests caused anger and bewilderment everywhere amongst the gentiles round about Judaea. The newly born state of the Hasmonaean conquerors was regarded as a robber state, which had fallen on the legitimate inhabitants of the coastal and Transjordanian cities, had seized them without any shadow of right and justification, and had driven out their autochthonous population who had refused to undergo circumcision and to accept the Jewish Law. These feelings produced furious disputes between the Jews and the gentiles, the echoes of which are still to be heard in the surviving Midrashic literature as well as in the Apocrypha and Pseudepigrapha of the Old Testament. The gentiles were evidently the plaintiffs and the Jews the defendants. The Midrash keeps true to form in reproducing the plaintiffs' arguments, *e.g.* in a passage in Gen. rabba I, 3, where we read:

> Why did God reveal to Israel what was created on the first day and the second day? in order that the gentiles might not sneer at Israel and say: 'You are a people of robbers' and that Israel might answer them: 'The world and what is in it is God's. By His will the land was given to you, and by His will it was taken away from you and given to us.' This is the meaning of the words of the Scriptures: 'The might of His creations He has revealed to His people, to give them the inheritance of the gentiles.'

This is, of course, a homiletic way of expressing a social and political situation. But the arguments, as they had certainly been propounded, in the bitter dispute between the parties, by the Jews in general and especially by the Hasmonaeans, who were the spokesmen of the Jewish case in the time of the expansion of the new Jewish state, are revealed to us with sufficient clarity in a historically very important passage in I Maccabees xv 18–31, 33–5. The Hasmonaean court historian gives the following report:

> And he [*i.e.* King Antiochus Sidetes] sent unto him [*i.e.* unto Simon] Athenobius, one of his friends, to commune with him, saying: 'Ye hold possession of Joppa and Gazara, and the citadel that is in Jerusalem, cities of my kingdom. The borders thereof have ye wasted, and done great hurt in the land, and have got the dominion of many places in my kingdom. Now, therefore, deliver up the cities which ye have taken, and the tributes of the places whereof ye have gotten dominion outside of the borders of Judaea; or else give me for them five hundred talents of silver; and for the harm that ye have done, and the tributes of the cities, other five hundred talents; otherwise we will come and make war upon you.' And Athenobius . . . reported to him the King's words. And Simon answered and said unto him: '*We have neither taken other men's land, nor have possession of that which appertaineth to others, but of the inheritance of our fathers; howbeit, it was had in possession of our enemies wrongly for a certain time. But we, having (taken) the opportunity, hold fast the inheritance of our fathers.* Nevertheless, as touching Joppa and Gazara, which thou demandest, – (though it was) they that did great harm among the people and in our land – we will give a hundred talents for them.'

The position of both sides, then, is quite clear. Both insist on their right, the gentiles as the present owners of the land, who had been driven out and dispossessed because they refused to accept the Jewish Law with all its implications, a Law which was not theirs and which they despised; and the Jews, who regarded the land as the inheritance of their fathers, which had been taken from them by violence and had been occupied by strangers and newcomers, who had no right whatsoever to claim ownership of it and who at the first available opportunity had been justly dispossessed by the lawful owners of the property of which they had been robbed. There was, in fact, a confrontation between two irreconcilable points of view. Each party was pleading from a different legal standpoint. In the eyes of the Jews, the gentile inhabitants of the coastal plain and of Transjordan were intruders, who claimed

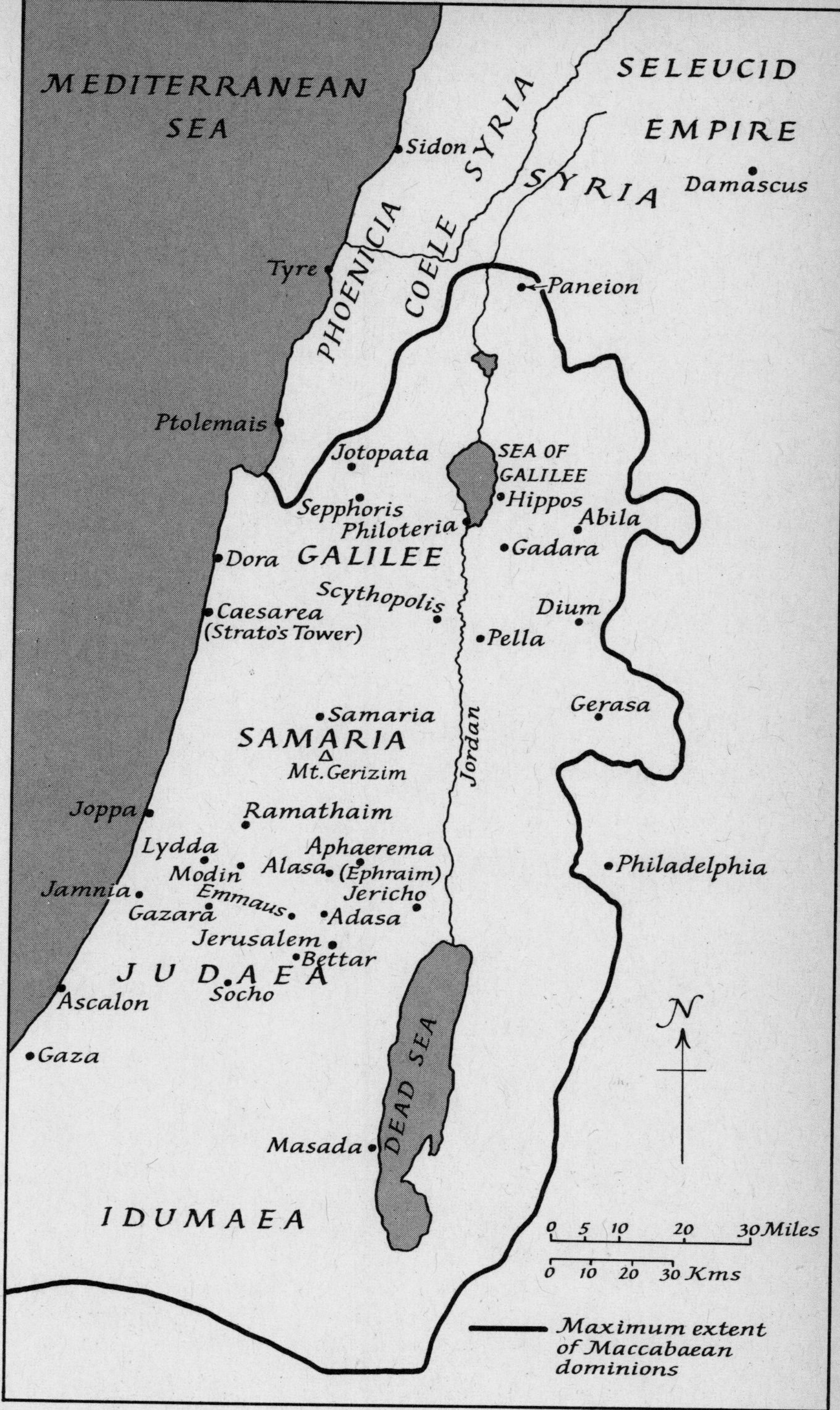

Palestine in the 2nd century BC. Modin was the home of the family which freed Judaea from Seleucid rule, the Hasmonaeans, descended from Mattathias, son of the priest Hasmon. Members of the family subsequently conquered Western Palestine, as well as parts of Transjordan. (2)

ownership of a land which was legally and justly not theirs, while the conquered gentiles, who had been stripped of their property by the Hasmonaeans, regarded the Jewish conquerors as robbers who had asserted themselves simply by violence. In order to understand Simon the Hasmonaean's conduct towards the inhabitants of Gazara and Alexander Jannaeus' ruthlessness against Gaza and other cities, account has to be taken of their point of view. In their eyes the Jews settled by them in place of the expelled gentiles were not 'colonists',* *i.e.* strangers and newcomers, and the removal of the intruders was only the restoration of the original lawful situation.[35]

* *Editor's footnote:* On their own premises, however, the Hasmonaeans were surely on weak ground in extending their territorial claims to places which had never been inhabited or been ruled by Jews, *e.g.* the Philistine city of Gaza and the Samaritis. The Samaritans were descended in the main from the people of the former Northern Kingdom (the Ten Tribes).

Internal contradictions

Such was the attitude of the Hasmonaeans and their followers to the conquest of the land of the gentiles, within – and, in Philistia, beyond – the borders of the historical Land of Israel. But, as the Hasmonaean state expanded, its internal problems mounted. Now the inner contradiction was fully exposed between the Hasmonaeans and their party on the one hand and on the other hand the traditionalists and strict observers of the Law, for whom the very *raison d'être* of the Jewish people lay in its being a chosen people set apart from the gentile world and awaiting its redemption at the End of Days.

The first signs of the breach had already appeared under Judas Maccabaeus when the war for religious freedom had been fought and won, and the Assidaeans saw no reason to continue the struggle for political freedom. The Assidaeans were willing to acquiesce in being under foreign rule so long as their foreign rulers allowed them liberty of worship. They were the spiritual heirs of Ezra and Nehemiah, and, against this historical background, the fact that the Hasmonaeans were Jews – and were also members of the first class of priests, the class Jojarib – did not count for righteousness in the Assidaeans' eyes when the Hasmonaeans behaved in ways that drew on them the Assidaeans' disapproval.

The Messianic Kingdom was the dispensation for which the Assidaeans yearned, and the life of their community was centred on it. According to the outlook of these eschatologists, the Jewish people were not concerned with this world, which was the world of the gentiles and the arena of their illusory glory. But the gentiles' glory will pass away, together with this world, at the coming of the Kingdom of God which is bound up with the Kingdom of the Messiah. Then the 'Ancient of Days' will sit on his throne and 'one like the son of man' will come to him with the clouds of heaven and will receive from his hand everlasting dominion. Then the earth will witness the concrete fulfilment of the vision on high: the King Messiah, who is a human king, will receive into his hand 'dominion and glory and a kingdom . . . his dominion is an everlasting dominion, which shall not pass away, and his kingdom that which shall not be destroyed'.[36] This, in the Assidaeans' eyes, is the true Kingdom of Israel, not the kingdom established by the Hasmonaeans. These had recruited an army of foreign mercenaries and had introduced the uncleanness of the gentiles into the Holy Land; they had imposed taxes on the people and had multiplied weapons of war in order to shed blood for the greater glory of their house and their party. They had arrogantly occupied a throne which was not theirs and which had been promised to David and to his seed for ever. They had surrounded themselves with violent men who pursued worldly pleasures, and they had presumptuously distorted the image of the nation and the purpose of its existence. What had they and theirs in common with the Kingdom of Israel?

The rigorous observers of the Torah fell out with John Hyrcanus and with Alexander Jannaeus, and apparently it was in the course of this conflict that they became a self-conscious political party:
p 80 (2) the Pharisees. There was a Pharisaic insurrection against John Hyrcanus,[37] and a riot against Alexander Jannaeus in the Temple of Jerusalem at one of the annual celebrations of the Feast of Tabernacles. Six thousand of the demonstrators are said to have been massacred within the Temple precincts by Alexander's Pisidian and Cilician guard. This incident was followed by a six-years-long civil war in the Hasmonaean state.[38] The insurgents were not labelled Pharisees; and indeed militancy was contrary to Pharisaic principles. But the Pharisees were the beneficiaries of this upheaval. Alexander's widow and successor Salome Alexandra (75/4–67/6 BC) capitulated to them.

The sun of the Hasmonaeans began to set after Queen Salome Alexandra's death. Her two sons, Hyrcanus, the elder and the successor to the high priesthood and the kingship, and Aristobulus, the younger, fought each other for supremacy. When, in 63 BC, the Roman war-lord Pompey appeared on the scene, conquered Judaea, and captured the Temple Mount after besieging there Aristobulus and the Sadducaean priests who supported him, the fate of the Kingdom and of the Hasmonaean dynasty was sealed. Pompey put an end to the Hasmonaean Kingdom, banished Aristobulus and his sons to Rome, and confirmed Hyrcanus as high priest – but this without the royal title or any political authority to speak of.

Pompey and his lieutenant and local successor Gabinius liberated p 126
the Hellenized cities along the coast and in the interior that had been conquered by the Hasmonaeans, and Pompey also reconstituted Seleucia-in-Gaulanitis, though not Philoteria. The liberated cities in Transjordan, together with Scythopolis, were now grouped in an association, the Decapolis.[39] The liberated communities were grateful to the Romans; for they had found Hasmonaean rule oppressive. Like the Hasmonaean Simon in 142 BC, the Decapolitan cities celebrated their liberation by inaugurating a new era. The Hasmonaean state – now confined to districts inhabited by Jewish majorities – was made tributary to Rome and was given the juridical-political status of a *civitas stipendiaria* within the Roman Empire. This was an intermediate stage on the road to the complete Roman provincial administration of a later period.[40] In all these events a significant part was played by Antipater the Idumaean, a friend of Hyrcanus, his adviser in his dispute with Aristobulus, and his intermediary in negotiations with Pompey and with the other Roman rulers who followed one another in Judaea.

Pompey's action marked the first beginnings of Rome's subjugation of Judaea. The second stage came in the days of Gabinius. The increasing frequency of the revolts instigated by Aristobulus' eldest son Alexander, who had escaped on the journey to Rome and had returned to Judaea, led Gabinius, the Roman governor of Syria in 57–55 BC, to divide Judaea into five 'councils' (*synhedria*):
Sepphoris, Jerusalem, Gadora (or, if another reading is adopted, p 51
Adora, that is, Adoraim in Idumaea), Jericho, and Amathus.[41] The Roman administration's motive for this division was probably an intention to dismember the country – as Rome had dismembered Macedonia[42] – into separate sections, between which there would be no commercial or legal transactions, nor perhaps even intermarriage. In this way Gabinius intended to weaken the national power of the Jews and so prevent any further uprising on their part. Gabinius also appointed Antipater governor of the country and charged him with the supervision of law and order.

For ten years, until the arrival of Julius Caesar in 47 BC, these p 126
momentous changes remained in force. Caesar reversed them, restored to Hyrcanus much of the authority of which he had been deprived by Pompey and Gabinius, and even to some extent re-enlarged the territory of Judaea. Antipater, however, who had served Pompey and Gabinius, not only retained his position by order of Caesar but was commended by him and was granted Roman citizenship and exemption from taxes as a reward for his having fought in Egypt on Caesar's side.[43] Aristobulus' other son Antigonus, who had escaped from Rome, appeared before Caesar and demanded that he should be appointed ruler in consideration of the fact that his father had lost his life on Caesar's account. (He had been poisoned in Rome by Pompey's adherents on the eve of the Battle of Pharsalus, while his brother Alexander had been executed in Judaea by order of Pompey's father-in-law.) However, Antigonus failed to supplant Antipater in Caesar's esteem. Antipater was confirmed as governor of Judaea. To consolidate his position, he appointed his two sons Phasael and Herod to important offices, the former as ruler of Jerusalem and the latter as *stratēgos* of Galilee.

The rise of the House of Antipater

Herod's appointment made itself felt immediately in a deed that foreshadowed subsequent events. He seized and executed without trial many Galilaean Jewish 'bandits' who had been attacking Syrian villages. These were not bandits in the literal sense. Their objective was political. They were actually 'freedom-fighters' in a resistance-movement against the deposition of the Hasmonaean dynasty and the introduction of a Roman administration. Herod's action enraged the Synhedrion in Jerusalem, and he was summoned to stand trial on a capital charge. Unable to prevent his aggressive son's trial from being held, Antipater secretly advised him not to appear without an armed guard. However, Hyrcanus had been warned by Sextus Caesar, the governor of Syria and a friend of Herod, that no harm was to befall Herod. So Herod showed arrogant self-confidence when he presented himself before his judges. He came wearing fine clothes, instead of dressing in the humble style customary for a defendant who was facing the death penalty. The judges were intimidated and remained silent. Only one member of the Synhedrion, apparently Shammai the Elder, demanded that the accused should be judged with the utmost stringency of the law and warned his colleagues that they would eventually suffer death at Herod's hands. Hyrcanus, however, remembering Sextus Caesar's warning and fearing that Herod might be sentenced to death, gave Herod an opportunity of slipping out of the city. But Herod was not content with this; he returned to Jerusalem with an armed force, intending to wreak vengeance on his judges. It was with difficulty that his father and brother managed to dissuade him from carrying out his intention.

This incident was a warning to Hyrcanus' supporters and to the aristocracy of Jerusalem of what the future held in store for them. It was clear that a new power had emerged in Judaea – a man who, openly relying on the might of Rome, treated the supreme domestic authority in Judaea with contempt. Hyrcanus was warned not to underestimate the rising power of the House of Antipater; already effective authority was in their hands, whereas Hyrcanus had only the trappings of a title. The warning was of no avail. Antipater and his sons enlarged their power and not only maintained but even consolidated their position, in spite of the great changes that were taking place in the Roman Empire in general and in its eastern regions in particular.

126 (2) After the assassination of Julius Caesar (44 BC), Cassius, one of the leading conspirators, came to Syria, and Antipater and his sons immediately went over to his side. In Judaea the tension grew day by day, until Antipater's enemies, setting a trap for him, poisoned him at a banquet in the belief that, with his disappearance, his sons too would disappear from the scene. But these hopes were disappointed. The sons, following in the footsteps of their father, served each and every Roman ruler in turn, no matter what his party might be; and when, after the Battle of Philippi (42 BC), p 160 (35) Antony came to the East, Phasael and Herod unhesitatingly sided with him. Antony rejected the accusations levelled against the brothers by a deputation of their enemies. He preferred Herod and Herod's money. Subsequent attempts to incite Antony against the Antipatrids likewise proved unavailing and even led to several of the envoys being executed. Herod and Phasael were raised to the rank of tetrarchs.

When Antigonus the Hasmonaean tried to invade Galilee, he was successfully repulsed by Herod. The threatening danger provoked by this son of Aristobulus led to a reconciliation between Hyrcanus, who feared the vengeance of his murdered brother's son, and the Antipatrids. To strengthen the bonds between them, Hyrcanus and his daughter Alexandra agreed to the betrothal of Herod to Mariamne, the daughter of Alexandra and of Alexander the son of Aristobulus – a betrothal that was eventually to prove calamitous for both parties. Antigonus took refuge with his brother-in-law Ptolemy the son of Mennaeus, the Ituraean ruler of Chalcis in the Baqa' (now in the Lebanese Republic), and waited for a favourable opportunity of recapturing his father's throne. The chance came in 40 BC, when the Parthian armies overran Syria. Having obtained the support of the Parthian general for his plan, or at least his agreement not to obstruct it, Antigonus hastened to Jerusalem with a troop of cavalry, recruited from all parts of Judaea, and besieged the Antipatrid brothers. These had fortified themselves in the Hasmonaean palace, and they defended themselves there resolutely. Antigonus' men, on their side, were reinforced by a large number of pilgrims who had come to Jerusalem to celebrate the Festival of Pentecost.

Meanwhile the Parthians had marched on Jerusalem with a small force. They pretended that they had come in peace, and they tried to capture the Antipatrids by trickery. They proposed to them that they should leave their stronghold, go to the Parthian camp in Galilee, and there enter into peace negotiations. Phasael was taken in and went with Hyrcanus, though Herod, who realized that the Parthians' overtures were not sincere, had refused to go and had warned his brother against going. Either by his own hand or in battle Phasael lost his life, and Hyrcanus was mutilated by Antigonus or by the Parthians to incapacitate him for holding the priesthood, and was carried away captive beyond the Euphrates. Herod now succeeded in escaping from the besieged palace together with the members of his household, including his mother and his Hasmonaean fiancée and her mother. Herod took them to his stronghold at Masada and then hastened to Rome to seek p 52–3
Antony's help. The triumvir referred the case to the Senate; and (18, 19)
the Senate, acting on his advice, declared Herod King of Judaea p 56–7
and disqualified Antigonus, who, as an ally of the Parthians, was (27, 28)
proclaimed an enemy of Rome. Herod had undoubtedly come to Rome with a prearranged plan; so there is no substance in Josephus' statement that Herod was surprised at the decision taken by the Senate because he had gone to Rome to persuade Antony to give the Judaean crown to Aristobulus, the younger brother of Herod's fiancée Mariamne. Josephus' source may well have been memoirs in which Herod tried to exonerate himself from responsibility for the Hasmonaeans' overthrow.

Survival of the fittest

The Senate gave Herod its mandate but no military help, since the Roman army in the East was then engaged in repulsing the Parthian invasion, and for three years Herod was unable to defeat his Hasmonaean adversary, who was supported by the majority of the people. After the passing of the Parthian danger, Antony despatched a large army to Herod's assistance, and Antigonus was defeated after a bloody war in Judaea, culminating in 37 BC in the capture of Jerusalem by Herod after a stubborn siege. At Herod's request the Hasmonaean captive was beheaded, or was crucified according to one source.[44] With the death of Antigonus the Hasmonaean dynasty came to an end and was succeeded by the Idumaean Herod of the House of Antipater.[45] The death-agony of the Hasmonaean dynasty lasted for some years after Herod's conquest of Jerusalem in 37 BC. The fortress Hyrcania was one of the last cells of opposition. A sister of Antigonus held out there until about 32 BC. The Hasmonaean dynasty had a last gleam of hope after the overthrow of Herod's Roman patron Antony at the Battle of Actium (31 BC). Herod's position then seemed to everyone, including himself, to be hopeless. However, he weathered this crisis and emerged from it secure on his throne. He continued to occupy it till his death in 4 BC.

Herod's survival was a remarkable achievement; for he, like his father Antipater before him, had been confronted with almost insuperable political difficulties by the bout of Roman civil wars that had started in 49 BC. Members of the House of Antipater had twice found themselves on the losing Roman side: first in 47 BC after the overthrow of their Roman patron Pompey by Caesar, and
then in 31 BC, after the overthrow of their next Roman patron, p 127
Antony, by Octavian (the subsequent Emperor Augustus). Yet in (25)
47 BC Antipater, and in 31 BC Herod, had been pardoned and been p 160
left in power by the Roman victor. (34)

They had owed their survival partly to their own exceptional ability as politicians, but mainly to the clear-sightedness of the successive masters of the Roman Empire in appreciating the facts that Judaea was an exceptionally difficult country for Rome to control and that Antipater and Herod were indispensable local instruments of Roman policy. They were indispensable because they were both political realists and effective men of action. They realized that it would be a forlorn hope for the Palestinian Jewish people to challenge Rome's overwhelmingly superior military might; they were willing to serve as Rome's agents for holding the Palestinian Jews on leash; and they had the political ability required for carrying out this arduous and invidious task.

The son's task was far more difficult than the father's. True, both pursued a policy of unconditional, cringing obedience to Rome and her representatives in the East and in Judaea. But, whereas Antipater acted more behind the scenes and under cover of his suzerain the high priest Hyrcanus, Herod, from the very beginning of his political career, chose to serve as a deliberate and willing representative of the Roman conqueror. Accordingly, the difficulties which faced him in his relations with his Jewish subjects mounted year by year.

Although the disparaging appellation of an 'Idumaean slave' (*sc.* of Rome), which according to many modern scholars had allegedly been attached to him by the people, is not found in any of the surviving Jewish and non-Jewish sources, the fact remains that Herod was looked upon as the representative of the Roman order in Judaea, who had undertaken to stamp out the last traces of Jewish self-government and to pave the way for the total subjugation of Judaea. In the relations between Herod and his Jewish subjects, Herod's Idumaean origin was of minor importance. In the first place, according to the Pharisaic Halakhah, he was regarded as a full Jew, since he was the third-generation descendant of a proselyte family – and it has to be emphasized that there was no juridical difference between a voluntary proselyte and one who had been converted to Judaism by force. Secondly, the good relations between the Pharisees and apparently the whole Jewish f 5 people on the one hand and Herod Agrippa I on the other, of which we are told in the Mishnah (Sotah 7, 8), were by no means affected by the fact that Agrippa was of Idumaean origin. Thirdly, in the Jews' great war against the Romans in AD 66–70, the descendants of the Idumaean proselytes were the most fanatical fighters for the freedom of Jerusalem – a clear proof of the assimilation, in the course of a few generations, of the Idumaeans who had originally been made Jews by force.

If, then, Herod was hated by the Jews, the reason for this was first and foremost his position as someone who had been appointed king in order to accomplish the final subjugation of Judaea and to wipe out the last centres of resistance to the Roman new order. The resistance against Herod and his Roman overlords was maintained by a movement that was kept alive by daring individuals. Herod reacted against their acts of sabotage with his customary vigour and grim cruelty. He sold them into permanent slavery abroad on the basis of a special law which he issued in violation of the Mosaic Law. The Romans referred to them disparagingly as 'brigands' and 'bandits', but presumably they were freedom-fighters who refused to accept the rule of Antipater's House in Judaea and accordingly undertook individual action against Herod and his collaborators among the Jews. They were the spiritual predecessors of the Zealots and the Sicarii of the years before, during, and after the great war against the Romans. The opprobrious official Roman terminology was adopted by Herod in his law against disturbers of the order which he had been appointed by the Roman Senate and People to preserve. So, to maintain this Roman order, Herod instituted a reign of terror in the country. Unbeknown to the public, the King and his council sentenced suspects or wealthy men to death and confiscated their possessions. The condemned were taken by the secret police to fortresses, such as Hyrcania, which served as prisons, and there all trace of them disappeared.[46] This shedding of innocent blood extended to some of the members of the King's family. Those of them who were murdered were Aristobulus the high priest and young brother of Queen Mariamne the Hasmonaean, Mariamne herself, Hyrcanus her grandfather, Alexandra her mother, the sons of Baba who were related to the Hasmonaeans, and finally Herod's own two sons by Mariamne, Alexander and Aristobulus.

Herod the statesman

It would, however, be a mistake to see in Herod only a bloody ruthless tyrant. Herod was first and foremost a statesman, and as such we cannot but acknowledge the acumen of his political insight and judgement, as well as his imaginativeness in trying to establish a secure place for his kingdom and for the Jewish people within the framework of the Augustan Roman Empire. His admirable capacity for grasping what was possible and impossible in a political situation may be illustrated by citing his judgement on the situation of Antony after the Battle of Actium and the brutally logical conclusion that he drew from this judgement. He was also a realist on the question of the possibility of the existence of independent nations in the age of Augustus and of the Roman dominion over the *oikoumenē*. He was deeply convinced – and this conviction had governed his father's policy too – that there was no room for national independence now that Rome had extended her supremacy over the whole ambit of the known world, and that the only way to exist in a tolerable, nay even in an honourable, way was to come to terms with the Roman power on the basis of absolute political obedience. His train of thought was as follows: the Augustan Roman Empire signifies, not tyranny, but justice and security for p 126– all the peoples of the civilized world, especially for the small and (5, 6) weak peoples, whose survival depends on the existence of the Roman Empire. Even lunatics would not wish for the fall of the Roman Empire, which is the shelter and the hope of all mankind.[47] Herod applied this reasoning to the Jewish people. If the Jewish people wishes to survive, it can do so only within the ambit of the Roman Empire. Rebellion against this hard fact means suicide. And Herod drew the full consequences of this political judgement of his. He held the reins of government with an iron hand, mercilessly suppressing every sign of disobedience and rebelliousness.

In pursuit of this objective, he enacted his harsh law against the so-called 'bandits', employed his well-organized secret police and military forces, and used the many fortresses which he had built all over the country. By eliminating all subversive elements in the land, Herod hoped to lead the Jews in Palestine to accept the salutary conclusion that peace with Rome and with himself was worth while and that an honourable *modus vivendi* within the framework of the Roman Empire was not only possible but was also desirable and was in the Jewish people's own best interests. Herod's view was that the Jewish people was an integral part of the Roman-ruled world. The reality of its existence lay within, and not outside, this Roman world. The Jewish people was only one of the many peoples subdued by Rome, and it had, like other subdued peoples, to pay due regard to this basic fact. Moreover, Herod took the initiative in showing that the way to live in this one world was not to practise isolation and national exclusiveness, but to open the doors to foreign cultural influences and to mutual understanding. He pursued this policy in his grandiose Hellenistic way by spending fabulous sums of money on a number of Greek cities. He equipped p 52– them munificently with huge public buildings: markets, theatres, (17, 2 aqueducts, promenades, and other public works of social consequence. He introduced Greek artists and men of letters into his dominions and founded musical festivals and public games, to which many foreign non-Jewish guests were invited, even in Jerusalem, the centre of Jewish exclusiveness. In a word: Herod

The 'Theodotos inscription', dating before AD 70, is the only remnant of the numerous synagogues that stood in Jerusalem prior to the Roman destruction. Theodotos, who is described as coming from a family of synagogue rulers, built a synagogue, guest-house, and ritual bath complex. (3)

Traces of what is apparently a form of Herod-worship have been discovered in the Temple of Zeus Baalshamin at Si'a in the Hauran, seen here in De Vogüé's reconstruction. Herod's statue is third from the left; the other statues are of Zeus (?) and the builders of the Temple, Maleichat and his grandson of the same name. The base of Herod's statue with the right foot attached was seen in the middle of last century, but has since been lost. (4)

tried, if only partially, to remove the fence with which, under the guidance of the Pharisees, the Jewish religion had surrounded the Jewish people. He tried to integrate the Jews in the Hellenistic-Roman *oikoumenē* as one of the many peoples which made their contribution to the common welfare – a welfare which was also their own.

In this Imperial context Herod also saw himself as one of the minor 'aides' of Augustus in his great work of redemption on behalf of the reborn Roman Empire. Consequently Herod would have wished to be honoured like Augustus, as Josephus explicitly assures us, with statues and temples. In other words: he wished to see the Hellenistic-Roman ruler-cult applied to him. There are, indeed,
f 4 apparent traces of a Herod-cult in Si'a in Transjordan.[48] However, such a cult, if it was actually established in Herod's kingdom, could have been introduced only in that part of the kingdom in which the majority of the population was non-Jewish.* In the Jewish part of it, ruler-worship was utterly unthinkable, as Herod himself was well aware. But, since the field of Herod's activity as King lay mainly within the habitat of the Jewish people in Judaea, and since the introduction of ruler-worship there was incompatible with the Jewish religion, Herod conceived the daring idea of having himself honoured in the Jewish region of his kingdom, if not as a God, then as the King Messiah, whose coming, in due course, had been predicted by the ancient prophets of Israel. According to the prophets, the Messiah was to redeem God's people and to establish his Messianic Kingdom. To this end Herodian propaganda tried to suggest to the Jews of Judaea that Herod was of Davidic stock and that in his days all the prophecies of the prophets had been realized: Herod's kingdom was nearly as extensive as that of David and Solomon, and Herod was the man who had restored Solomon's
80–81 temple in an even more splendid form than the original.[49] But the
, 6–9) people of Judaea were not in the least deceived by this political
p 90 propaganda. Herod was regarded as being of foreign stock, despite
(f 2) the fact that he was a third-generation proselyte. Did not Herod advocate the integration of the Jewish people in the gentile world – that world whose glory is illusory and is destined to pass away with the coming of the Messiah of the House of David at the time which God had appointed when He had created the world?

Such was the outlook of the Pharisees; but these, living, as they did, by their implicit belief and faith in the coming of the Messianic Kingdom, did not oppose Herod actively. There were, however, other Jews who had once openly fought against Herod and had since gone underground in a secret movement of rebellion. Like the Pharisees, they too awaited the coming of the Messiah the son of David, but nevertheless advocated active opposition. These activists recognized that it was impossible to wage an offensive war against the Romans and against their tool Herod, but they felt that, all the same, it was better to undertake individual action than to sit and wait passively. They held that it was preferable to hasten the Messiah's coming.

'Divide and rule'

While Herod was alive, he suppressed all active Jewish opposition with an iron hand, and a tense peace reigned; but on his death the revolt immediately broke out. Even before Herod's will had been confirmed by Augustus, the Palestinian Jewish people had risen against the Herodian dynasty, and it was only after the arrival of Publius Quintilius Varus, the governor of Syria, that the revolt was finally crushed, at the cost of much bloodshed (4 BC). The agitation continued, however, and increased from year to year.

Herod's sons (by other wives than Mariamne) were assigned different sections of the Herodian kingdom. Archelaus was appointed ethnarch of Judaea and Samaria, while Herod Antipas (Antipater) and Philip were made tetrarchs, Antipas of Galilee and the Jewish part of Transjordan (the Peraea), and Philip of Gaulanitis, Trachonitis, Batanaea, and the city of Panias (Paneion). No action was taken by them to calm the widespread feeling of resentment. The situation deteriorated yet further when, in AD 6/7, Archelaus was deposed by the Roman government at his Jewish subjects' request and Judaea was placed under the rule of a Roman procurator. Some procurators of Judaea were cruel, corrupt, and unconscientious, and few, if any, of them had a proper understanding of the special ideology of the Jewish population.

Virgil's famous line '*parcere subiectis et debellare superbos*' accurately sums up the Romans' policy, and, in summing it up, it reveals the policy's limitations. It was a negative policy under both its heads. The Romans were, in truth, lenient to subjects of theirs who were submissive, but – in Judaea, at any rate – it seems not to have

* *Editor's footnote:* The Romans did not give Herod possession of the Decapolis or of Ascalon, but his kingdom came to include all other Greek or Hellenized cities in Coele Syria to the south of Phoenicia, the Ituraean principality, and Damascus. In contrast to his Hasmonaean predecessors, Herod treated his non-Jewish subjects well. In this non-Jewish part of his dominions, Herod converted Strato's Tower into a magnificent port-city and renamed it Caesarea. He also rebuilt Samaria; peopled it with new non-Jewish colonists to replace the Macedonian Greek colony there which had been destroyed by John Hyrcanus; renamed the place Sebaste; and crowned the highest point of the hill with a temple dedicated to Augustus.

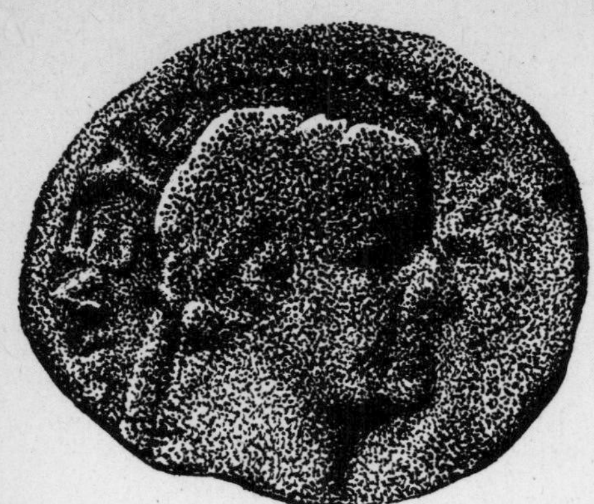

Agrippa I (AD 37–44), the grandson of Herod the Great, was installed as King of Judaea by the Romans. He has always remained one of the most popular Jewish Kings, even though he minted coins bearing his own portrait (left), as well as that of the Roman Emperor. (5)

occurred to the Romans to seek their submissive subjects' positive co-operation for trying to win over their recalcitrant subjects to an acquiescence in Roman rule, or, short of that, for trying to dissuade a wavering majority from rallying to the militants.

The Roman administration in Judaea failed to recognize that, in order to get the better of the rebellious elements, it must rely p 80 (2) primarily on the Pharisees, who had enormous religious and moral influence over the Palestinian Jewish people and who were, moreover, opposed to violence for ideological reasons. The Pharisees had disapproved of both the Hasmonaeans and the House of Antipater, but they had put up with these two pre-Roman dynasties, because, under them, they had been free to live according to the Jewish Law. They were free to do so under the Roman régime too; and the Romans ought to have had the sense to reap the potential benefits of their religious tolerance. However, the Pharisees had no effective contacts with the local Roman administrative authorities in Judaea. This is indicated by all the existing sources. The procurators concentrated all their attention and efforts on combating the militants. These were actually in a minority, as is the case always and everywhere in revolutionary disturbances. But, because they were the target of the procurators' hostility, these militants gained increasing sympathy among the mass of the Jewish population.

Thus Judaea was moving nearer and nearer towards the abyss. Yet, instead of being, as they were, years of suffering foreshadowing the end, the intervening years between Herod's death and the first Romano-Jewish war (AD 66–70) could have seen a solution of the grave crisis towards which the people of Judaea were heading as a result of the Roman conquest. A positive solution could have been found in either of two ways.

One way would have been to restore the rule of local satellite princes acceptable to the Jewish people. This course was open to *f 4* Rome, as is shown by the short episode of Herod Agrippa I's reign (AD 37–44). Agrippa's domain was extended progressively by the Roman government till it became approximately coextensive with Herod I's. According to the available information, this was an interlude of peace and a respite for the Palestinian Jewish people. (Agrippa had a Hasmonaean grandmother: his grandfather Herod I's murdered wife Mariamne.) Herod Agrippa I did succeed in giving satisfaction to both his Jewish subjects and his Roman suzerains, but he was less successful in winning his non-Jewish subjects' goodwill. The Roman Imperial government regarded it as impossible to place Herod Agrippa I's young son and heir, Herod Agrippa II, in charge of more than a fragment of his father's kingdom, namely the former domain of Herod I's son, the tetrarch Philip, in North-eastern Palestine, augmented by some districts of Peraea.[50] In the war of AD 66–70, Herod Agrippa II fought on the Roman side, and he retained his principality till his death.

The alternative course – the one which Herod followed and which was the redeeming feature of his harsh and unpopular rule – was to seek a *modus vivendi* with the Roman Empire through integration within the edifice reared by Augustus. That the Jewish people invariably revolted against any attempt to incorporate it into the structure of the great powers that ruled over the country is a mistaken idea. Against such a view there is striking proof offered by the empires of Persia, of the Ptolemies, and of the Seleucids, despite Antiochus Epiphanes, who was an exception to the general rule.

Incorporation within the Roman Empire – the solution which was espoused by Herod – would under no circumstances have led to the Jewish people's being engulfed by the Hellenistic-Roman civilization. In the days of Augustus the Jewish people was strong not only by reason of natural increase but also – and this is of prime significance – by reason of its resolute character. The Jews were unquestionably the one people unaffected by all those factors which gave to most of the peoples conquered by the Roman Empire a uniform way of life and transformed them into a colourless, homogeneous maelstrom, an aggregation devoid of any special cultural significance. Had the Jewish people made peace with the Roman Empire, they would undoubtedly have remained what they were: a nation preserving its independence and its specific character. Acquiescence in the political rule of Rome would not have submerged the Jewish people in the quagmire of the cosmopolitan civilization of the Roman Empire, if for no other reason than that their national centre in Judaea would not have been destroyed. The spiritual concession which such acquiescence would undoubtedly have entailed would have been nothing compared to the enormous advantage that would have flowed from it, which would have been none other than the continued possession of the land of its forefathers by the nation and the continued existence of the nation in it.

An opportunity wasted

If the Pharisees bear any responsibility for what happened during the last two generations before the destruction of Jerusalem in AD 70, their responsibility lies in their failure to recognize that the Messianic belief and the hope of a future Jewish kingdom did not warrant their ignoring the obvious present fact of the overwhelming might of Rome – a fact that Herod had perceived so clearly. There was no room for the illusion that, even though the Palestinian Jewish people was to all intents and purposes subject to Roman rule, Israel had no connection with the Roman Empire and that Jewish life could be pursued without regard to this political reality. The Pharisees ought to have opened the eyes of the people to the necessity of adopting a realistic attitude towards the Roman Empire. They could have done this without renouncing any essential features of the Jewish religion and way of life. Such a policy was possible within the Roman Empire, considering that the Roman government never attempted to impose its Imperial ideology upon the conquered nations. Unfortunately the Pharisees did not rise to the occasion. They went on living in an ideal world of their own, and they abandoned the political arena to the militants.

The continuing presence of the Jewish people in Palestine through a compromise with the Roman Empire would have given the course of Jewish history, and of world history too, a different turn that might have had incalculable consequences. It is doubtful, for example, whether, in that event, Pauline Christianity would have achieved the success that it did achieve after the destruction of Jerusalem. An indispensable prerequisite of that success was the deracination of the Jewish people from Palestine and its subsequent final dispersion – a twofold catastrophe which was p 62–
the inevitable result of the persistent rebelliousness that was the (37–4
reaction of one element in the Palestinian Jewish population towards Rome from the moment when the Jewish and Roman worlds first met.

Increasingly, the Roman authorities, both in Judaea and at Rome itself, came to realize that the centre of Jewish power in Jerusalem had to be destroyed in order to put an end once for all to Jewish uprisings. 'The anger of the Romans was aggravated because the Jews alone had not given way.'[51] Josephus ascribes to Titus the explicit and apparently authentic statement that it would have been better if Vespasian and he had immediately attacked and destroyed Jerusalem. The Romans granted to the Jews extensive privileges throughout the Roman Empire, but the Jews were not reconciled by this to Roman rule. The Jews were the enemies of the Empire from the day on which Pompey conquered their country.[52] The prevalent attitude of the Roman civil and military authorities is revealed in the view that is said to have been expressed in Titus' camp before the Temple was burnt. The witness for this is not Josephus but Sulpicius Severus, the 4th-century Christian writer, who was probably following Tacitus. According to Sulpicius Severus, Titus declared that Jewish power must be torn up by its roots, and that then the trunk too would perish.[53]

The Romans were at fault in not wishing or trying to understand that the problem of Judaea might call for something other than the routine procedures of Roman provincial administration. If they had been in touch with the Pharisees, they would have learnt from them that the Jewish revolutionary movement was different from the usual pattern of the rebelliousness of other conquered peoples, inasmuch as it was based on a special religious ideology. This was the ideology of the Pharisees as well as the 'zealots', but the Pharisees differed from the 'zealots' in believing that their religion did not require them to take up arms against a foreign government that respected their conscience and did not violate their religious liberty. A greater understanding of the religious motives underlying the revolutionary movement would perhaps have produced a more acceptable system of government and a different approach to the rebellious Jewish faction in Palestine, and this might have opened the door to a Roman policy that would have led to some agreement between the two sides. Instead, the Romans merely adopted the routine provincial procedure of 'pacification' by military subjugation (*debellare*) almost immediately after a direct provincial administration had been instituted in Judaea upon the banishment of Archelaus in AD 6/7.

Judaea capta

p 224 (9) During and after the governorship of Pontius Pilate there was an uninterrupted series of acts of violence and bloodshed on both sides. The nearer that events moved towards the outbreak of the first war between the Jews and the Romans, the worse the position *f 4* became. The reign of Agrippa I (AD 37–44) was only a passing episode, and, though it was congenial to the Palestinian Jews, it was not congenial to the non-Jewish section of the population. As against the Pharisees, who did not believe in the imminent advent of the Redeemer, the revolutionary parties, and the masses incited by them, believed that a miracle would occur. God would descend from Heaven with His armies and would come to the help of His people for the destruction of the evil Roman Empire.[54] The inflammable material accumulated, and it needed only a spark to set it ablaze. In the summer of AD 66 the explosion came. During the procuratorship of Gessius Florus there was an outbreak of violence in Jerusalem which led to the intervention of Cestius Gallus, the governor of Syria. Gallus' defeat broke down the last barrier to the outbreak of the first Romano-Jewish war. An entire Imperial p 335 (5) army was despatched to Palestine by Nero under the command of his ablest general, Titus Flavius Vespasianus.

In AD 67 the war began in Galilee, the defence of which was directed by the Jerusalem priest Josephus. At the fall of the fortress of Jotapata, Josephus surrendered to the Romans and went over to their side, first and foremost because he fully realized that it would be impossible to achieve the liberation of Judaea and that there was no alternative to making peace with the Romans. Josephus was an eyewitness of the war, and especially of the destruction of Jerusalem, and we are indebted to his first-hand account for our information about these events.

During the second year of the war (AD 68), down to the date of Nero's death (June 9th, AD 68), Vespasian succeeded in conquering virtually the whole country except for Jerusalem and its environs. Suddenly, because of a revolt in Rome, the war stopped. Vespasian waited expectantly, but the appearance of Simon bar Gioras compelled him to tighten the cordon round Jerusalem (until June AD 69). From July 1st, AD 69, the day on which Vespasian was proclaimed Emperor, fighting ceased outside Jerusalem, but inside it a terrible civil war raged until Titus began to besiege the city several days before Passover, AD 70. The siege lasted for about five 54–5 (21, 22) months and ended in the destruction of Jerusalem and the Temple. Three years later Masada, the last stronghold of the rebels, fell, 55–7 (23–8) and its fall brought to an end a war in which Jerusalem had been destroyed and Judaea had been extensively damaged. The other regions of Palestine recovered after years of tribulation. Nor was the Jewish national strength in Palestine seriously diminished by this war. The proof of this is Bar Kokhba's revolt in AD 132. p 93 (*f 3*) Apparently Bar Kokhba raised a very large force, and this indicates that the Jewish population in Palestine had recovered its numerical strength within two generations.[55]

It is clear that after the war of AD 66–70 the Roman administration obstructed the progress of the Jews to a very considerable extent with an eye to preventing the outbreak of another revolt. Judaea was made into a separate province with a senatorial governor of its own and a garrison consisting of a legion with its complement of auxiliary troops. Jewish land was confiscated for the Imperial treasury, and the position of Jewish farmers was seriously impaired. The destruction of Jerusalem brought with it the liquidation of its wealthy class, and high taxation added yet further to the economic distress. With a view to maintaining peace, Vespasian established a military colony in Judaea at Emmaus. The Roman colony of Flavia Neapolis was planted at Samaria, and this new foundation increased the power of the non-Jewish element in Palestine. In these circumstances, large sections of the Jewish people became embittered. This bitterness is reflected in IV Esdras, whose author is perplexed at the grim punishment visited upon Israel and at the inexplicable success of Rome, who stands, in his eyes, for wickedness. After the murder of Domitian (AD 96) and the accession of Nerva there was some alleviation of the agony which the Flavians had inflicted upon the Jews.

In or about the years AD 115–7 – years in which the Roman Empire's military and economic resources were being strained p 335 (6) almost to breaking-point by the Emperor Trajan's over-ambitious war of aggression to the east of the River Euphrates – there were Jewish revolts against Roman rule in Cyrenaïca, Cyprus, and Egypt.[56] It looks as if, in Cyprus and Cyrenaïca, the Jewish element in the local population had been numerically strong enough to attempt to exterminate the non-Jewish element and thus to monopolize the possession of the island. (Cyrenaïca is virtually an island, since, on the landward side, it is insulated by the Libyan desert.) In Cyrenaïca 'the whole countryside was ravaged and the cities seriously depopulated. Hadrian had to introduce settlers from other parts of the Empire'.[57] In Cyprus

> the Jews . . . are said to have perpetrated unspeakable outrages . . . It is said that the dead in Cyprus numbered 240,000, and that Salamis was utterly destroyed and the non-Jewish population exterminated. . . . As a result of this outbreak, no Jew was allowed to set foot in the island, and even those who were driven there by adverse winds were put to death.[58]

In Egypt the local Jews were reinforced by the Cyrenaïcan Jewish army, and for a time the Roman army lost control of the countryside and was hard put to it to retain a foothold even in Alexandria.

The reprisals in which these Jewish revolts were crushed were also savage, and the figure of 240,000 for the number of lives taken in Cyprus may include the Jews who lost their lives, as well as the Jews' non-Jewish victims.

Trajan ordered his particularly brutal Mauretanian cavalry general, Lusius Quietus, to move to Palestine – where the Emperor expected trouble – from the Parthian front. In order to forestall a possible Jewish insurrection in Mesopotamia, Quietus massacred the Jewish diaspora there *en route*. We do not know whether Quietus reached Palestine before he was put to death by the Emperor Hadrian, who succeeded Trajan on August 11th, AD 117, and immediately evacuated the territories beyond the Euphrates that Trajan had occupied.

Hadrian's plan to rebuild Jerusalem as the Hellenistic colony of Aelia Capitolina was the signal for the start of the Second Revolt of AD 132–5. Here Hadrian draws the line of the city walls with a ploughshare. (6)

The last rebellion

The new Emperor rejected Trajan's policy of expansion by conquest and devoted himself to the works of peace. In Judaea there were hopes of improvement, and an exchange of views apparently took place between Hadrian and the Jewish sages, either in Rome or in the East during the Emperor's stay there (AD 129/30). But these hopes were soon dashed to the ground. Hadrian set himself to rehabilitate the provinces of the Empire and to raise their standard of living. Hadrian aimed at revitalizing Hellenism, which was the cultural basis of the Roman Empire, as it had been the basis of the Seleucid Empire. Hadrian included Judaea within the compass of his activities, and accordingly he proposed to *f 6* rebuild Jerusalem from its ruins as a Hellenistic city, to be called Aelia Capitolina. A start was probably made on this work immediately after Hadrian left the East. This – together with the prohibition of circumcision, which was not aimed specifically against the Jews (these were not the only people in the Empire who practised circumcision), but was rather an inseparable part of the Emperor's 'Hellenizing' policy – infuriated the Jews of Judaea and precipitated a revolt. It cannot, however, be maintained that, had Hadrian acted otherwise, there would have been no uprising. The Bar Kokhba war was presumably part and parcel of a general conflict that had been continuing since AD 115, throughout the Roman Empire, between the Jews on the one side and the government and the non-Jewish population on the other side. The interval between the end of the revolt in Trajan's reign and the outbreak of the Bar Kokhba war had been merely a breathing-space during which the Jews had been making the necessary preparations for a fresh uprising.

According to the new documents discovered in the Judaean desert, the years following the fall of the Flavian dynasty had been, in Judaea, years of economic revival. In Southern Judaea the economy was now flourishing. Of this we had earlier known nothing. The later literary tradition about the Bar Kokhba war, especially that preserved in rabbinical literature, had hitherto given no grounds for assuming that the first years of Hadrian's reign were marked by a relative economic prosperity, at least in certain regions of the country and probably to some extent in others as well. This prosperity may have provided the economic basis for making the preparations for the revolt – preparations which undoubtedly took many years.

The destruction of Jerusalem had not extinguished the flame of the militant Messianic movement. Its centre of gravity had first passed to the Diaspora and from there had returned to Judaea. The p 62–(37–4 suppression of the movement in Egypt, Cyrenaïca, Cyprus, and other countries on the one hand and the accession of Hadrian on the other postponed the revolt in Judaea. The Judaean Jews had entertained exaggerated hopes of Hadrian's intentions. When their expectations were disappointed, they awaited only the signal for launching a revolt for which everything was ready. The signal was given by the building of a Hellenistic city on the site of Jerusalem and by the prohibition of circumcision. The rebels defeated the armies of the Roman governor of Judaea and Syria; Bar Kokhba captured Jerusalem; and steps were apparently taken for rebuilding the Temple. Hadrian despatched a large army under the command p 93 (*f 3*) of Iulius Severus, who had been transferred from Britain. The war was hard and bloody; for both sides fought fanatically. The Romans had to reconquer Judaea step by step, and the struggle continued for two and a half years until it ended with the fall of Bettar, the last stronghold of the rebels, and the death of Bar Kokhba in battle.[59]

The Roman losses were heavy, but the losses suffered by the Palestinian Jewish people were many times more severe. They were more terrible even than those suffered by them in the war of AD 66–70. Judaea was now denuded of its Jewish inhabitants. Many hundreds of thousands had fallen in battle or had died of hunger or disease; tens of thousands were sold as slaves or were sent to their deaths in circuses. The rest, fleeing from the country, dispersed in all directions. Under pain of death, it was prohibited for Jews to set foot in Jerusalem. The name 'Judaea' was suppressed, and the province was renamed Syria Palaestina. The colonization of Judaea by non-Jews was now carried out systematically. This significant fact is reported by Eusebius, the historian of the Christian Church. He remarks that, for the first time in its annals, the See of Jerusalem was now occupied by a bishop who was not a Judaeo-Christian.

After the Bar Kokhba war it finally and definitely became clear that between Judaism and Christianity there was an unbridgeable gulf. The Jewish people were reduced to a dispersed nation without p 64 a centre in its own land, while Christianity launched a campaign of expansion probably unparalleled in the history of the world. Judaism retired within itself, leaving the field of action to the daughter religion. In the 2nd and 3rd centuries AD Christianity ploughed the soil deeply, and it reaped the harvest in the days of Constantine. These subjects are dealt with more fully in Chapters XI and XII.

Additional Note by the Editor

The recovery of the numerical strength of the Jewish population in Palestine between the years AD 70 and 132 brings out a demographical fact that is of prime importance for an understanding of the passage of history that is the subject of this chapter. The liquidation of the Kingdom of Judah in 587 BC had been followed by a Jewish population-explosion that is comparable to the Greek population-explosion which had begun in the 8th century BC and to the Italian one which had begun in the 5th century BC. The Greek population-explosion subsided in the 2nd century BC, and the Italian in the course of the last two centuries BC, but in the second century of the Christian era the Jewish population-explosion was evidently still continuing. In fact, in the age of the Roman Principate the Jewish community in the Roman Empire was probably increasing at a considerably faster rate than any other.

This long sustained post-Exilic Jewish population-explosion is a remarkable social phenomenon, considering that the Kingdom of Judah, so long as it existed, had been one of the smallest, and presumably also one of the least populous, of the states in the region between Egypt and Assyria. When the Assyrian King Sargon liquidated the Kingdom of Israel in 722 BC, he records that he deported 27,290 of its people; when the Kingdom of Judah was liquidated by the Babylonian king Nebuchadnezzar, the aggregate number of its people who were deported successively in 597, 586, and 581 BC amounted to no more than 4600 (Jer. lii 28–30). If we may assume that, in each case, the persons selected for deportation were the notables and the skilled workers, these two figures give the approximate ratios in which the total populations of the two kingdoms stood to each other while they were both still in existence. Israel will have been nearly six times as populous as Judah, approximately equal to the populations of the Kingdoms of Damascus and Hamath.

The population of Judah (a rural country) may have been smaller than that of the tiny commercial island of Tyre with its tight-packed 'high-rise' houses. Yet, by 200–198 BC, the date of the take-over of Coele Syria from the Ptolemaic Empire by the Seleucid Empire, the Jews had not only repopulated Judaea but had spread far beyond its narrow bounds. There was a Jewish diaspora in Babylonia, descended from Nebuchadnezzar's deportees; there was another in Egypt, whose original nucleus had been formed by the Jewish refugees from the Babylonian invasion and conquest of Judah. By 200 BC the Egyptian Jews had become strong enough numerically in Alexandria to be able to hold their own against the city's Greek population. There was also a Jewish diaspora in Coele Syria, outside the bounds of Judaea, as we know from the record of the repatriation of the survivors of this diaspora *c.* 163 BC. By the time, about half way through the first century of the Christian era, when Paul was making his missionary journeys, there were Jewish congregations in every important city of the Graeco-Roman world, at least as far westward as the city of Rome itself.

The causes of this Jewish population-explosion are not known. We may guess that one cause was the high moral standard of Jewish family life; that another cause was the Jews' abhorrence of the Greek vice of sodomy; and that the most potent cause of all was the Jewish people's determination to maintain its identity as a community dedicated to the observance of the Torah. Whatever the causes, the post-Exilic Jewish population-explosion is an historical fact, and an important one.

Among other things, it is one of the keys to an understanding of the terrible episode in the history of the relations between the Jews and the non-Jewish population of the Roman Empire in or about the years AD 115–7, in the interval between the two Romano-Jewish wars of AD 66–70 and AD 132–5 in Palestine.

III

A DIVIDED FAITH

JEWISH RELIGIOUS PARTIES AND SECTS

KURT SCHUBERT

'Among the Jews there are three schools of thought, whose adherents are called Pharisees, Sadducees, and Essenes respectively.'

JOSEPHUS 'DE BELLO JUDAICO'

Rival sects vigorously disputed the heart and mind of Judaism from the 2nd century BC until, with the destruction of the Temple by the Romans in AD 70, only one group remained, the Pharisees. During the period when the Jews came under Seleucid rule, the Pharisees were satisfied with limited objectives – religious autonomy and freedom to worship in the Temple. They repudiated both the militaristic Hasmonaeans and the apocalyptic Assidaeans, who saw the Maccabaean war merely as a prelude to the eschatological cataclysm, in which the Jews would sweep the nations of the earth before them and establish the worship of the one true God over all mankind. But they were equally opposed to the Sadducees, the aristocratic 'official' party that combined liberalism in religion with a desire for peaceful coexistence with the occupying powers. In spite of, or perhaps because of, Roman support, the Sadducees were unable to retain control. The final disaster of AD 70 left the Pharisees in possession of the field, and it was Pharisaism which developed into the normative form of Judaism down to the present day.

Aaron, the brother of Moses, and Israel's first high priest, symbolizes the hieratic aspect of Judaism, the subject of such conflicting interpretations by Sadducees, Pharisees and Essenes. In this fresco from the Dura Europus synagogue, his princely status is indicated by his red caftan and white trousers, Parthian royal dress. The only vestige of the high priest's garments in Exodus xxviii is the chequered lining of the caftan. He stands in the Temple compound, which is entered through three doors, the middle one half-concealed by a blue curtain with pink lining, and contains a burning golden Menorah, two incense-burners and an altar with the sacrificial animal upon it. In the background is the Temple proper with the Ark of the Covenant; by a familiar convention it is to be taken as concealed behind the curtain which here forms its background. (1)

ΑΡΩΝ

'The Scribes and the Pharisees sit in Moses' seat: All therefore whatsoever they bid you observe, that observe and do; but do not ye after their works: for they say and do not.' Since the Gospels, the Pharisees have had a bad press. Yet they had a subtle and differentiated approach to ethico-theological problems. The 'Seat of Moses', set up in synagogues like that of Chorazin (above), was reserved for such teachers of the Law. The party in control of the Temple, however, was the Sadducees, who had to tread a difficult path between co-operation with the Romans and the demands of extremists, such as the Zealots, who regarded any compromise as blasphemy. (2)

'Simon who built the Temple': a limestone ossuary perhaps containing the bones of one of the Temple architects. Herod began his rebuilding almost as soon as he ascended the throne, partly in order to appease those Jews who were scandalized by the pagan temples which he had allowed to be erected in his kingdom. (3)

The giant substructure (below), erected as a platform for the Temple by Herod's engineers, is now all that is left of his great achievement. 'Where the ground was lowest,' says Josephus, 'it had to be built up by 450 feet.' As the 'Wailing Wall' it is known and venerated by Jews throughout the world. (6)

The symbolic Temple (above, also from Dura Europus) was an apocalyptic idea that gained currency after the destruction of the actual Temple. Below: the Ark of the Covenant, from the Capernaum synagogue. By returning to pre-Temple concepts the Pharisees were able to formulate a post-Temple Judaism. (4, 5)

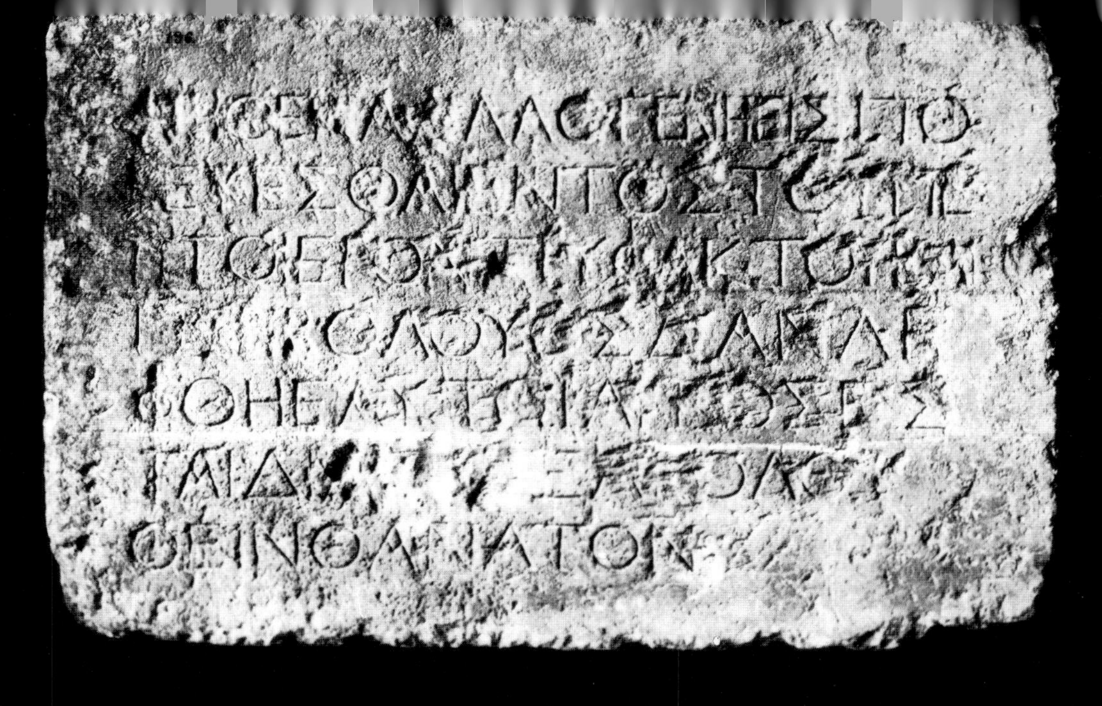

Nicanor, an Alexandrian Jew, supplied magnificent bronze gates for the Temple, giving access to the Inner Court. The Talmud records a story that they were brought by sea to Joppa and only saved from sinking in a storm by a miracle. The ossuary (above) containing Nicanor's bones has been discovered in Jerusalem. (7)

'No foreigner was allowed to enter the Sacred Precinct,' says Josephus, and in fact stones inscribed in Greek have been found forbidding entry by non-Jews into the Inner Court on pain of death. This rule was upheld by the Roman governors. Gentiles were, however, allowed into the spacious Outer Court. (8)

'He who has not set eyes upon the structure of Herod has not seen a structure of beauty in his life.' This verdict, reported in the Talmud, comes from one of the rabbinical sages usually virulently hostile to the 'Idumaean slave'. It was a vast undertaking, built of blocks of white limestone with the ornamental parts gilded. From a distance 'it appeared like a mountain covered with snow'. A reconstruction model is shown here (below). We are looking west. On the right is the Sanctuary, approached from the 'Court of Women' by the Gates of Nicanor. Beyond this is the Outer Court (or Court of Gentiles) surrounded by a double colonnade. (9)

'Son of man, can these bones live?' Ezekiel's vision in the valley of the dry bones, symbolic of the national restoration for which the Jewish sects hoped and worked, covers the full width of the north wall at Dura, perhaps the *chef d'oeuvre* of the master 'philosopher' who seems to have supervised this cycle. Our picture opens with the mountain of transition, on the left, which is surmounted by trees and divided into two halves. To the left are the disjointed members, shown not as 'dry bones' but as covered already with flesh and hair. In the other half they have come together to form three corpses. This half of the mountain also engulfs a castle in its fall. In the central section, Ezekiel in Parthian dress watches as the corpses are given breath. Four females in the guise of the Greek figure *pneuma* may be the four winds upon whom he called; or, more dramatically (see below), they may represent one *pneuma* and the souls of the three corpses. To the right of this scene Ezekiel has changed into Greek dress, no doubt signifying a change in his spiritual state. Next stand ten small figures probably representing the restored ten 'lost' tribes of Israel. Above all broods the hand of God.

From the 4th century BC onwards Palestine had lain under Greek influence; and among other manifestations of Greek culture came Greek ideas on the soul. In the Old Testament man had been regarded as a psycho-physical unity. The Greeks, on the other hand, especially after Plato, regarded man as a compound of two distinct entities, a body and a soul. With the growth in Judaism of a belief in life after death, a dichotomy may be observed in the treatment of this belief. The Essenes, for example, continued to maintain that it was the psycho-physical unity which was resurrected, while to the Pharisees the Last Judgement involved a reuniting of the independent soul with the body. If the second interpretation of our picture is correct, it would seem to reflect the Pharisaic conception. (10)

The Essenes, the third of the main Jewish religious sects, were for long the most mysterious, known almost entirely through second-hand and unsympathetic accounts. This situation was dramatically changed by the discovery of the Dead Sea Scrolls, now considered with fair certainty to be the library of an Essene community living at Qumran, on the shores of the Dead Sea. Archaeological evidence shows that it was founded towards the end of the 2nd century BC and destroyed by the Romans in AD 68. Before the destruction, members of the community managed to hide their manuscripts in caves nearby, where they remained until 1947.

Above: the beginning of the 'Manual of Discipline', which gives details of the community's organization, rules of entry, 'degrees of purity', regulations for property and daily routine.

Right: the Isaiah Scroll, the longest and best preserved of all the Dead Sea Scrolls. It is 24 feet long and contains in 54 columns practically the entire text of Isaiah. This section runs from the end of chapter 38 to the beginning of chapter 40.

Below: tables reconstructed from fragments found at Qumran, and thought by some archaeologists to be desks from the *scriptorium*. Contemporary illustrations of men writing, however, always show them resting the scroll or tablet on their knee. (11–13)

Scrolls were placed in jars, about two feet in height and made at the monastery, before being hidden in the caves where they were found. (14)

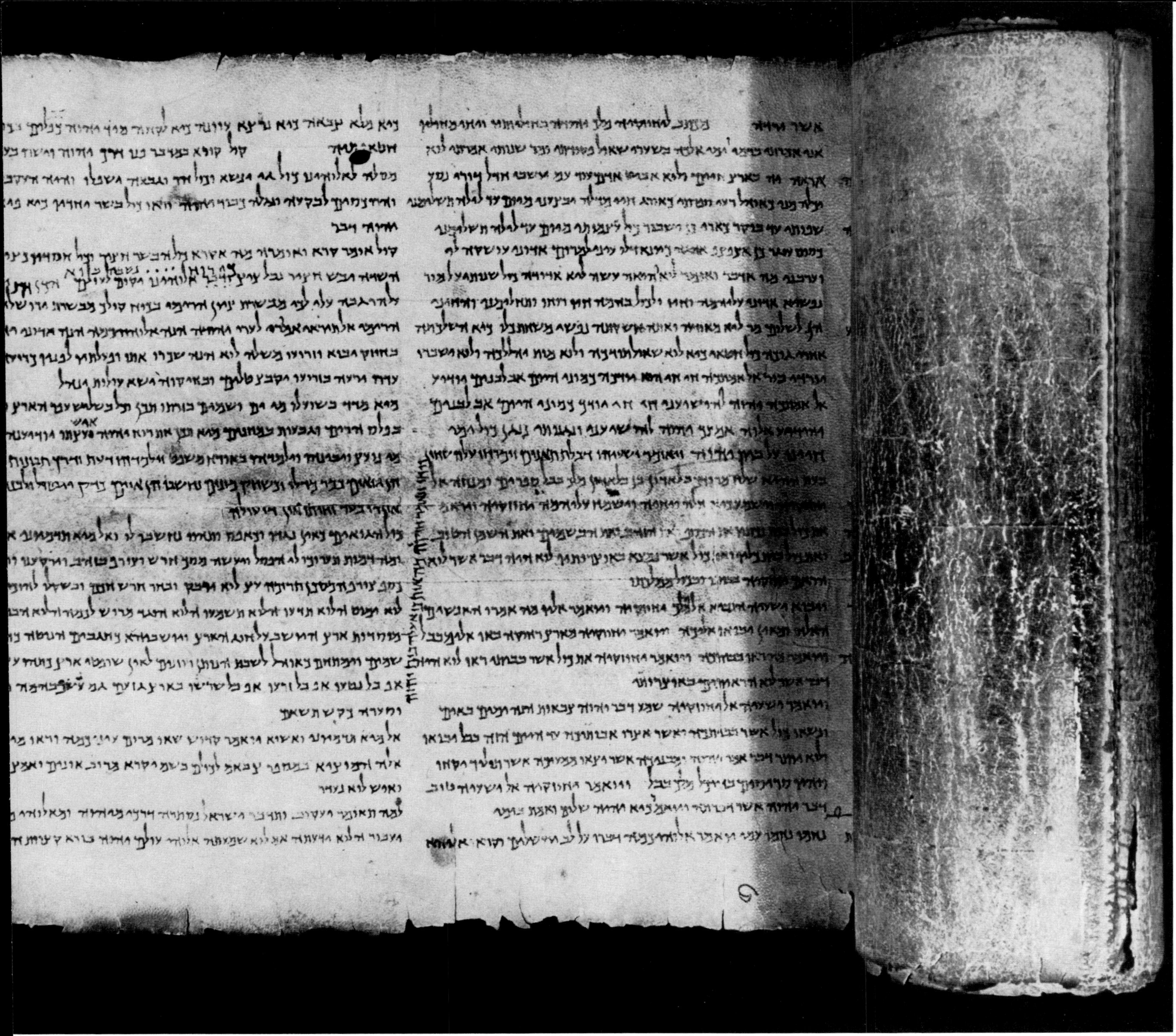

The Hebrew alphabet was found written on this broken potsherd (below), apparently for practice or to try out the pen. Next to it is an inkwell from Qumran – a Roman type of 'non-spill' inkwell known also from Italy and Egypt. (15)

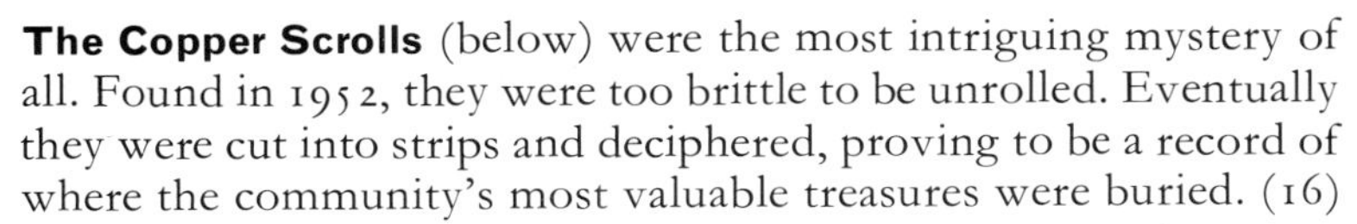

The Copper Scrolls (below) were the most intriguing mystery of all. Found in 1952, they were too brittle to be unrolled. Eventually they were cut into strips and deciphered, proving to be a record of where the community's most valuable treasures were buried. (16)

On a plateau between the sea and the cliffs, near the small watercourse of Wadi Qumran, the Essenes of the 2nd century BC built their desert monastery. It was substantially enlarged *c.* 4 BC–AD 6 until it consisted of several groups of buildings, with meeting-rooms, halls and cisterns for water. Two of the latter are visible in this view (left), which shows the western part of the ruins, looking west. The Essenes almost certainly joined in the rebellion against Rome in AD 66 and one of their apocalyptic books, 'The War of the Sons of Light and the Sons of Darkness', seems clearly to cast the Roman army in the role of the Sons of Darkness. Whatever the facts of the case, it is certain that the monastic buildings were all burnt to the ground when Vespasian and the 10th Legion passed along the Dead Sea coast on their way from Caesarea to Jericho. (17)

The barren caves where the Essenes hid their precious books lie high up in the cliffs overlooking the Dead Sea. Here several of the most important caves can be seen burrowing into the bastion-like formations that project from the hill. (18)

JEWISH RELIGIOUS PARTIES AND SECTS

KURT SCHUBERT

THE JEWISH religious parties at the time of Jesus can be understood only in the light of their earlier histories. Unfortunately we are not so well informed about Israel's post-Exilic history as we are about the previous period, but this observation applies only to her mundane history, not to her cultural history. Many of the historical sources dealing with the pre-Exilic period underwent their final redaction only after the 6th century BC. Cases in point are the great Deuteronomic history, the so-called Priestly Document and the work of the Chronicler. From the point of view of cultural and religious history, therefore, these sources largely reflect the Exilic and post-Exilic situation, in spite of their subject matter's being pre-Exilic history. For this reason they can be used as legitimate sources for charting the spiritual currents within Judaism during the period between 587 and *c.* 250 BC. Although, admittedly, few of the prophetic books originated in the post-Exilic period, numerous passages, short and long, inserted into the works of the prophets after 539 BC tended to up-date their contents. To such passages belong, in particular, those that speak of a new creation, a new heaven and a new earth, or of the resurrection of the dead, *i.e.* passages in which the expectation of the *eschaton* has a tone of special urgency. Thus many of the ultra-messianic passages in the older prophetic books originate from the period of *c.* 550–250 BC. When one of the older prophetic texts, for example Amos ix 13–15, deals with the ingathering of the exiles, it is a clear sign that the Babylonian exile in the 6th century BC is already implied, and consequently that the passage in question has been interpolated *ex post facto* into an earlier text. Even older passages, such as Psalm ii 7 and Psalm cx 1, which originally applied to the contemporary ruling king from the House of David, were interpreted as referring to an eschatological Son of David. Thus the word *mashiah* ('anointed'), which originally designated each king after he had been anointed at his enthronement, became the technical term for the monarchical leader in the eschatological act of salvation—the Messiah.

Towards the end of the 4th century BC, at the latest, the canon of the Torah (the Pentateuch) and – about 200 BC – that of the Books of the Prophets were already fixed. Only the canon of the *Hagiographa*, the so-called 'Writings', was fixed later. This is the reason why the Book of Daniel, which received its final form in the first half of the 2nd century BC, was listed, notwithstanding the prophetic-apocalyptic character of its contents, among the *Hagiographa* rather than among the Books of the Prophets.

There are a number of texts from the 2nd century BC which were not accepted into the canon of the Hebrew Bible and which are commonly designated apocryphal in Catholic literature and pseudepigraphal in Protestant. These texts are datable to the first two-thirds of the 2nd century BC by the fact that they are included
ɔ 84–6 among the literature of the Essene community at Qumran, which,
1–18) as has been convincingly shown by archaeology, was founded between 140 and 130 BC. The Qumran literature can be divided into three broad groups: (1) books of the Old Testament, (2) apocryphal and pseudepigraphical books already known through secondary translations, and (3) books peculiar to the Qumran community which were never copied or translated and were therefore unknown before the discovery of the Dead Sea Scrolls. The reason why this third group, unlike the first and second, was confined to Qumran is clear enough from the esoteric character of the texts.

The other two groups, however, seem to comprise books which the Qumran Essenes regarded as part of their heritage and which they brought with them to the desert when they founded their community. The second group – the apocryphal and pseudepigraphical texts – does indeed exhibit many parallels with the doctrines and views of the specifically Qumran group, but the likelihood is that these doctrines and views derive from the Assidaean movement; from this common source we must trace not only the liberal Pharisees but the much more radical Qumran Essenes and indeed many other groups connected with the Essenes but not sharing their separatist and esoteric tendencies – a conclusion supported by the fact that the texts in question were so widely translated into other languages. The texts are as follows: the Ethiopic *Book of Enoch* (with the exception of the Book of Parables, chapters 37–71, concerning the messianic Son of Man), the *Book of Jubilees* and the basic Jewish source-strata of the *Testament of Twelve Patriarchs*. Together they provide a valuable source of information on Jewish religious and cultural history in the half-century before the Essenes founded their settlement at Qumran.

A further source, that is not however to be taken uncritically, is the works of the Jewish historian Josephus. He wrote primarily for Greeks and Romans, not for Jews. His pro-Roman political attitude is especially evident in those passages in which he describes the Jewish revolt against Rome. Moreover, in order to be understood by his pagan readers, he was forced to describe Jewish religious beliefs in terms of pagan concepts which were incapable of rendering adequately the original contents. P 54–7 (21–8) *f 3*

The post-biblical Hebrew and Aramaic sources must also be taken into account. These consist of two groups which, in respect of their origins, are basically different: the Qumran texts and the rabbinical texts of the Talmud and Mishnah. The Qumran texts are of Essene origin, the rabbinical texts derive from the Pharisees. The Essenes radicalized the concepts of their Assidaean predecessors, the Pharisees liberalized them. In both cases account should be taken of the particular literary genre of the respective groups of texts. This also holds good for another text-group, the New Testament. Here special attention should be paid to the fact that the Gospels, for example, represent the end-product of an oral and literary tradition with a time-span of some 40 to 70 years, and that they therefore reflect not only the situation at the time of Jesus but the situation at the time of the Evangelists as well. Of no less importance for the period are the Books of the Maccabees, which originated in circles close to the high-priestly and royal family of the Hasmonaeans. P 50 (5–6, 10–11)

All these sources, taken together with the findings of the archaeologists, enable us to draw the following picture of the religious-political groups in Judaism at the time of Jesus.

Early divisions

The later Jewish religious parties – the Pharisees, Sadducees and Essenes – for which our earliest evidence dates from about the middle of the 2nd century BC, have an earlier history that stretches far back. Let us begin with the party of the Sadducees. As their name indicates, the governing stratum of this party stems from the high-priestly aristocracy. A priest by the name of Zadok served under David and Solomon, and, according to Ezekiel xl 46 and xliv 15, descent by birth from the line of Zadok was a prerequisite for legitimate priesthood. Since the establishment of the post-Exilic community in 539 BC, the Sons of Zadok had held the office of high priest. This office not only had a prominent function in the sphere of public worship; it was an embodiment of political power as well. The high priest was the representative of intra-Jewish – or better, intra-Judaic – autonomy. Because of this fact, however, the Zadokite priestly families, as the rulers of the land, were particularly well-disposed to the idea of political co-operation with the people bordering on Judaea. But, at that time, p 108–9 political co-operation also implied religious syncretism. It was (19–28) therefore these highest religious officials who were especially susceptible to syncretic tendencies. As early as the period of p 43 (*f3*) Persian rule in Palestine, in the two centuries running from the p 50 (3) establishment of the post-Exilic community in the year 539 BC to p 102–3 the time of Alexander the Great, the high-priestly families were (5) disposed to maintain friendly relations with their pagan or p 106–7 syncretist neighbours. These were the tendencies against which the p 35 (45) reforms of Ezra and Nehemiah were directed in the second half of the 5th century BC (we shall not go into the difficult question of the relative dates of these two reforms). These reforms, though they caused far-reaching changes in Judaea, made no lasting impression on the high-priestly family.

The Sons of Zadok lived on excellent terms with the Hellenized sections of society during the 3rd century BC, when Judaea lay p 103 (7) under Ptolemaic rule. Members of the Hellenized Tobiad family p 106–7 intermarried with that of the high priests. In fact, as we have seen (13) in the previous chapter, this was a period of increasing p 50–51 Hellenization in Palestine, and it would certainly have gone on unhindered (2–16) had it not been for the fact that, after the conquest of Judaea by p 67 (*f1*) the Syrian Seleucids around 200 BC, it acquired alien political p 103 (6) overtones. Hellenists like the Sons of Zadok were regarded as quislings.

p 69 (*f2*) The success of the Maccabaean revolt in 168–164 BC and the subsequent government of the Maccabees accordingly spelt the downfall of the main Zadokite line. After 152 BC the office of high priest passed to the Hasmonaeans, a family related to the Zadokites only by a collateral branch. The old Zadokite families, however, soon came to terms with them, and the Hasmonaeans themselves moved away from the conservative circles to which they owed their rise, and formed links with the Sadducees. The tendency at the upper, high-priestly, levels reverted to cultural p 50 assimilation and political nationalism. The best proof of this is (5–6, the support they gave to John Hyrcanus (134–104 BC) and 10–11) Alexander Jannaeus (103–76 BC).

The opposition to creeping, as well as to forcible, Hellenization grew out of the movement of the 'pious' (as we must translate the Greek word *Asidaioi*, which is a transliteration, with a Greek ending, of the Hebrew word *hasidim*, 'the pious [people]'). The fact that these Assidaeans were already in existence at the time of the outbreak of the Maccabaean revolt in 167 BC is clearly attested by I Maccabees ii 42, which says: 'At that time they were joined (5, 6) by a company of Assidaeans, warlike Israelites, every one a volunteer for the Law.' Thus the Assidaeans existed even before the Maccabaean revolt, probably as early as the beginning of the 2nd century BC. That they have an even longer prehistory is, for a number of reasons, highly probable.

As we have seen, some of the Qumran texts (group 2) very probably originated in Assidaean circles. These dissident, apocalyptic priests looked with disfavour on the official worship conducted in the Temple, which they believed was celebrated according to an erroneous calendar – their own calendar of 364 days being the only true one. Since they considered the old Temple to have been completely profaned, they were working for a new Temple, which was going to descend from heaven, together with a heavenly Jerusalem. For a time (168–164 BC) the Assidaeans made common cause with the Maccabees (this is reflected in the Book of Daniel), but parted company with them because they found their objectives were too limited. The Maccabees were satisfied with seeing freedom of worship restored, with political and military guarantees, but did not share the Assidaeans' crusading urge to bring about a new world-era. They were accordingly labelled as 'hypocrites' by the Assidaeans. What is mere freedom of worship when it is compared with the eschatological kingdom of God!

On the basis of what we can ascertain from our source material, the Assidaean movement must have been a catchment-area for several apocalyptic groups and sects, all of which certainly applied Isaiah lx 21 to themselves. The 'righteousness of the poor or p 31(humble', in Trito-Isaiah's presentation of it – a theological concept p 84– that certainly did not derive from priestly circles – left an indelible (12) mark on the ideology of the Assidaeans right down to the Essenes and to the New Testament community. Within the Assidaean movement there were both dissident priestly elements and a strong lay group.

The communal consciousness of the Assidaeans was characterized by a radical dualism. This is most evident in passages dealing with the Last Judgement or with the Resurrection. Thus Daniel xii 2 says: 'Many of those who sleep in the dust of the earth shall awake, some to everlasting life, and others to shame and everlasting contempt.' All those Jews who did not belong to the sole chosen community, namely that of the Assidaeans, were reckoned to be among the damned.

After 160 BC at the very latest, since the death of Judas Maccabaeus had eclipsed the eschatological hopes aroused by the Maccabaean revolt, one group withdrew from the Assidaean catchment-area, a group which – sobered by experience – had abandoned the apocalyptic radical-dualistic outlook. This group was the Pharisees, and we shall now turn our attention to them.

The Pharisees: moderation and compromise

First, the meaning of the name Pharisee. It goes back to the p 80(Hebrew word *perushim*, which means literally 'the separated'. The general connotation of this concept derives from the Pharisees' ideal of ritual purity. They were the people who held themselves apart from, and refused to associate with, the *'am ha'aretz*, the simple common folk who were not very meticulous in their observance of the Law. Nevertheless, the interpretation of the term Pharisee as 'the separated', solely on the basis of their exclusiveness over against people who did not take the ritual laws very seriously, seems to be inadequate. First, the term *'am ha'aretz* itself is ambiguous. Occasionally it is used not only of people who were not strict in their observance of the Law, but also of people who, in their observance of the Law, followed different precepts from those of the Pharisees. Among the *'am ha'aretz* were groups which differed from the Pharisees in their interpretation of the Law. It is not beyond the bounds of possibility that apocalyptic groups may have been stigmatized as being *'am ha'aretz*. Moreover, it seems probable that the term *perushim*, 'the separated', had a political connotation as well. Politically the term Pharisee signifies a dissident or a secessionist. In contrast with the apocalyptic groups, the Pharisees sought to achieve the Kingdom of God in the present world; they did not agree that it must absolutely be postponed to the world to come. After the Pharisees had seceded from the apocalyptic Assidaeans, this realistic attitude undoubtedly won them much goodwill and many followers.

The Pharisees are mentioned as a distinct group for the first time under the Hasmonaean Jonathan (160–143 BC). This accurately reflects the historical situation. They are mentioned by Josephus in *Antiquitates Judaicae* XIII 5, 9 together with the Sadducees and Essenes (the mention of the Essenes appears to be somewhat premature for the time of Jonathan). In the time of John Hyrcanus (134–104 BC), probably towards the end of his reign, a conflict broke out between the Pharisees and the Hasmonaeans which reached its peak under Alexander Jannaeus (103–76 BC). Although p 50 the Hasmonaeans did not belong to any legitimate high-priestly (5, 6) family, since 152 BC they had been discharging the duties of the high-priestly office, an office that had been entrusted to them by a Syrian (Seleucid) king. The apocalyptic Assidaeans, as becomes clear later from the Essene Qumran texts, reacted to this much more violently than the Pharisees did.

In the opinion of the Pharisees a division of power between the high priest and the king would have sufficed. As the high priest had become the representative of intra-Jewish autonomy and self-government in the post-Exilic period, such a division of power would have made the Hasmonaean king subservient to the Zadokite high priest. It is clear that the Hasmonaeans would not agree to be thus quietly stripped of their power.

The conflict between the Pharisees and the Hasmonaeans was resolved after the death of Alexander Jannaeus. Under the wise rule of Salome Alexandra (76–67) peace was made. This period saw the beginning of the decisive influence of the Pharisees in
p 51 the Synhedrion, the highest Jewish authority, which is called the
(13) 'high council' in the Gospels. The appearance of Rome on the political horizon of Judaea shortly after the death of Salome Alexandra created a new situation in which the Hasmonaeans were stripped of their power step by step. The Pharisees, however, at first found it attractive to live in the shadow of Rome, because the importance of the Synhedrion as the authority for intra-Jewish self-government was thereby greatly enhanced. The realistic temperament of the Pharisees helped them not only to survive
p 51–3 the reign of Herod the Great (40–4 BC) and the administration of
(14–20) the country by the Roman procurators, but also to make the most
p 79–81 of the catastrophe of AD 70, the destruction of the Temple. After
(1–9) this period neither the Sadducees, who by virtue of their sacerdotal
f 2 office were centred on the Temple, nor the priestly and other apocalyptic groups, who were ideologically orientated towards the Temple or towards political power in Jerusalem, had any support. Through this development *Pharisaism* was promoted to the status of being *the standard form of Judaism*. A group that had originally been secessionists now became the sole preservers and protectors of Judaism. For a proper understanding of Pharisaism, the fact cannot be too strongly stressed that *it grew out of an opposition to the continued ultra-eschatological expectations of Assidaean apocalyptic circles.*

It is still a widely held belief that until AD 70 the Pharisees, or at least some of them, sympathized with apocalyptic sects and themselves adopted an apocalyptic outlook, but that after the year 70 they abandoned such views and dissociated themselves firmly from them. The truth is exactly the reverse. Before 70 there is hardly any evidence (apart from a few hints in Josephus) that the Pharisees were at all concerned with ultra-eschatological and apocalyptic speculations. After 70 such evidence is plentiful. Not that one should build too much on this. After AD 70, in fact, Pharisaism had to embrace whatever apocalyptic tendencies there were, since, as we have just seen, Pharisaism had become practically synonymous with Judaism.

How did this misconception about the Pharisees arise? The old accounts of Jewish religious parties in the last two centuries of the Second Temple rested on the following assumption. The two parties represented in the Synhedrion were the Sadducees and the Pharisees. The groups outside the Synhedrion were not important and had few adherents. All non-Sadducaean doctrines were therefore regarded as Pharisaic. Since the Pharisees clearly and demonstrably shared many of the typical apocalyptic views, for instance
p 82–3 the doctrine of the resurrection of the dead, they were considered
(10) as a group which originally, *i.e.* before AD 70, did not differ in
f 1 any essential respect from apocalyptic circles. As the Saduccees were, in spite of the influence they exercised, only a relatively small group, the Pharisees were regarded as the popular party, which united within itself practically all non-Sadducaean elements. The obvious and remarkable fact that there is not a single ultra-messianic or apocalyptic utterance in the early Pharisaic parts of the Talmud and the Midrash, which originated in the period before AD 70, was explained away by arguments which are now – especially since the discovery of the Qumran texts – seen to be thoroughly specious.

If we abandon, then, the theory that all non-Sadducaean texts have to be Pharisaic we can postulate an indeterminate number of minor groups more radical than the Pharisees though not so extreme as the Qumran community. To them can be assigned such works as the *Psalms of Solomon*, dating from around the middle of the 1st century BC, which shows in its last two Psalms (17 and 18) a deep longing for the Davidic Messiah; and those parts of the Ethiopic *Book of Enoch* (chapters 37–71) which allude to the messianic Son of Man. It was also through them, no doubt, that the earlier Assidaean texts, such as the older strata of *Enoch*, the *Book of Jubilees* and the original elements of the *Testaments of the Twelve Patriarchs*, passed in translation into other ancient languages. None of these books is Pharisaic; indeed one of them – the *Psalms of Solomon* – seems to be directed *against* the Pharisees.

The Pharisees, following Greek conceptions, believed that at the Resurrection the independent soul is reunited with the body. These strange shapes from the catacombs at Beth Shearim are thought to represent souls. (1)

The theory that the Pharisees were dissident Assidaeans who opposed the apocalyptic outlook of their former brethren is borne out by a number of considerations:

(1) The Book of Daniel, which came into being *c.* 165 BC while the Maccabaean revolt was still active, is the only Assidaean-apocalyptic work that was accepted into the Pharisaic canon of the Old Testament. This book, with perhaps the exception of a few glosses, was given its final shape before the Pharisees broke with the Assidaeans *c.* 160–150 BC. Those Assidaean works that were given their final shape after 160 BC – despite several older sections such as those in the Ethiopic *Book of Enoch*, in the *Book of Jubilees* and in the basic Jewish stratum of the *Testaments of the Twelve Patriarchs* – did not gain admittance into the Pharisaic canon. The canon of the Books of the Prophets, including the twelve minor prophets, was already fixed by about 200 BC, as is evident from the Wisdom of Sirach xlix 10. For this reason, the Book of Daniel was not listed among the prophetic books of the Old Testament, but was accorded a place among the *Hagiographa*, the so-called 'Writings'.

(2) There is a saying from the Tannaitic period, probably from the time of early Pharisaism, according to which the Holy Spirit, *i.e.* the gift of prophecy, departed from Israel after the last three minor prophets – Haggai, Zechariah and Malachi (Tos. Sotah 13, 2 etc.). This saying is evidently a polemical barb aimed at the apocryphal writings (popular in apocalyptic circles) which claimed to reveal divine mysteries. Among these mysteries were calculations about the end of the world, which was supposed to be imminent, and about the coming messianic era. The allusion to the end of prophecy also implies a rejection of apocalyptic eschatological expectations.

(3) The term 'apostates' in the Habakkuk Commentary of Qumran almost certainly refers to the Pharisees. It is not improbable that this term was a polemical play on the name by which the Pharisees referred to themselves, *viz.* 'secessionists'.

(4) The earliest messianic pronouncement from Pharisaic circles is attributed to Johanan ben Zakkai on his death-bed, about AD 80.

According to B. Berakhoth 28b, he is supposed to have said: 'Prepare a throne for Hezekiah, King of Judah, who is coming.' That Hezekiah is here an appellation of the messianic Son of David needs no special proof.

(5) The sceptical attitude of the Pharisees towards messianic movements is exemplified by the speech of Gamaliel before the Synhedrion (Acts v 34–9), even when Luke's recasting of this speech is taken into account.

(6) The time of Herod the Great, about a generation before Jesus, is the date of a saying of Hillel's which is recorded in Aboth 2, 7: 'He who has acquired for himself words of the Torah has acquired life in the coming world.' When this straightforward call of Hillel's to study and observe the Law is compared to the brightly coloured visions of the apocalyptists or to the sayings, filled with ultra-messianic longing, of the rabbinnical sages of the 2nd century AD, an acute difference is immediately apparent between the moderate attitude of early Pharisaism and the apocalyptic eschatological hope which, favoured by external circumstances, gained a following among the rabbinical sages towards the end of the 1st century AD. For Hillel, life, based on the Torah, was to be lived in the present era and in the present world; the apocalyptists, in contrast, sought to transcend the present era and the present world.

(7) At the base of the apocalyptic outlook was a radical dualism. All the forces in the universe were either on the side of light or on the side of darkness. The postulation of a middle category, which was accepted even by the strict Shammaites, led to an abandonment of dualism, which, for the apocalyptists, was essential. Among people, such as the Qumran Essenes, who wanted to bring about forcibly the (for them imminent) advent of the messianic era through a rigorous observance of the Law, there was no place for moderates. But even among the strict Shammaites, the basic position of Pharisaism was maintained – through a life based on the Torah, a Kingdom of God must be established in the present era, regardless of when the present age would reach its ultimate eschatological goal, a goal that even the Pharisees never lost sight of.

In contrast to the various apocalyptic groups, which disappeared from the historical scene because they foundered on the problem of the unfulfilled Kingdom of God, and in contrast to those who became assimilated, despairing of Judaism's destiny, because of their scepticism about the realization of eschatological expectations, the Pharisees were *sceptics without being resigned*. They lived by this hope, even though it was not to be realized in their generation. Thus they laid the foundation for the historical survival of Judaism.

In several of the Qumran texts the Pharisees are called 'hypocrites' or 'teachers of hypocrisy'. This is particularly clear in 4Q P. Nahum 1, 2: 'Here is meant Demetrius King of Jawan, who, following the advice of the "teachers of hypocrisy", wanted to march against Jerusalem.' This evidently refers to the Seleucid Demetrius III Eukairos, with whom the Pharisees had entered p 50 (5, 6) into an alliance against the Hasmonaean King Alexander Jannaeus, and with whose help they gained a decisive victory over the hated king near Sichem in 88 BC. But, as this text indicates, Demetrius' further aim seems to have been the conquest of Jerusalem, and for this reason some of Alexander's enemies apparently went over to his side, and thus saved the situation for him. As early as Daniel xi 34 the Assidaean authors of this passage had accused the Maccabees of 'hypocrisy' because, unlike the Assidaeans themselves, they did not fight for the realization of the eschatological kingdom of God, but only for political and religious liberty. Evidently those who were sceptical about ultra-eschatological speculations and expectations were liable to be labelled 'hypocrites' in apocalyptic circles. When the Pharisees are called 'hypocrites' in the Gospels, the term must be understood against this background.

The nature of the Law

p 80 (2) Both the Pharisees and the apocalyptists held the Torah, the Law of Moses, in the highest reverence, but the difference between their respective conceptions of the Law becomes evident when the Qumran Essenes' interpretation is compared with the Pharisees'. At Qumran an authoritarian understanding of the Law was taken for granted. Only one interpretation – more extreme than the biblical – was considered valid. It was completely different in Pharisaism. The Pharisaic relationship to the Law could be described as being democratic. A number of different interpretations could be put forward. The conception of the Law that prevailed in rabbinical literature permitted a discussion about the proper interpretation; at Qumran the interpretation was authoritatively fixed. The relation of the Pharisees to the Law has been aptly described as eternal discussion about the Eternal. The difference between the attitude of the married Essenes and the New Testament community, on the one hand, and that of the Pharisees, on the other, to the problem of divorce illustrates the contrast between the liberal approach of the Pharisees and the authoritarianism of the other groups. In the Damascus Document, which belongs to the milieu of the Qumran Essenes, it is stated in 4, 20f.: 'They are ensnared by two things: by the lewdness of taking two wives during their lifetime, although the basis of creation is: male and female created he them [Gen. i 27].' This polemic is probably directed against polygamy as well as against divorce. In the latter context this polemic recalls the dispute be-

Herod's Temple, begun in 20 BC to replace the modest post-Exilic structure, is seen in the Comte de Vogüé's reconstruction which is very impressive, although the most modern reconstruction is now that of Professor M. Avi-Yonah in the grounds of the Holyland Hotel, Jerusalem (see plate 9). In the foreground is the south-east corner of the Temple platform, here built up about 150 ft above the floor of the Kidron valley. The platform itself is about 400 by 300 yds, forming the 'Court of the Gentiles'. It was entirely surrounded by colonnades, and the southern colonnade, known as the Royal Colonnade, was particularly impressive, with 162 monolithic Corinthian columns. Beneath it were at least two entrances, the 'Gates of Huldah', one double, the other triple. A gate in the eastern side of the central complex gave access to the Court of the Women, from which fifteen semicircular steps led through the Gates of Nicanor to the Courts of the Israelites and the Priests, the Altar Court and the Sanctuary. In the north-west corner is the Antonia fortress, so built as to overlook the Temple with a view to detecting any signs of trouble. One of the bridges which led to the upper city, the remains of which are now known as 'Robinson's arch', can be seen behind the south-west corner. (2)

tween Jesus and the Pharisees in Mark x 2–9 and Matthew xix 3–8. Jesus also refers to Genesis i 27 and expresses the opinion that Moses permitted divorce only because of the people's hardness of heart. The Pharisees of this period were also eager to restrict divorce, but they did not think it possible to declare it forbidden on the basis of Genesis i 27, since, in Deuteronomy xxiv 1, it is expressly permitted. They sought to make divorce more difficult by imposing conditions in the realm of the law of property. The well-known Pharisaic sage Simeon ben Shetah, who lived in the first decade of the 1st century BC, was the originator of a reform of Jewish marriage law that is still in force today. The ruling that the sum fixed in the marriage licence (*ketuba*) was to be a general mortgage on the entire property of the married man and on his estate not only made divorce considerably more difficult, but also protected the widow, after the death of her husband, from the greed of the other heirs. It is obvious why such an agreement was viewed as a compromise by the radical apocalyptists. In this instance, where the Qumran Essenes and Jesus commanded, the Pharisees sought to settle the matter by argument. Most probably the Qumran and New Testament term 'hypocrite' for the Pharisees is to be understood in this light as well.

The apocalyptic groups such as the Qumran Essenes (here Jesus and his followers were not in accord with the other apocalyptic groups) unrelentingly subjected human nature to the Law in all its severity, whereas the Pharisees attempted to adapt the Law to the human condition. The Pharisees, too, were thinking in terms of the Law, but the Law of God would have lost all meaning for them if it had been directed against man and his real needs.

The emphasis placed by the Essenes and Pharisees on observing the Sabbath is based on the Old Testament, which was fundamental for both sects. According to I Maccabees ii 29–38, at the beginning of Antiochus IV's persecution (169/7 BC) a group of Assidaeans let themselves be killed rather than profane the Sabbath, as they thought, by resistance; and the Essenes, according to the Damascus Document 11, 16 etc. believed that it was better to let a man drown on the Sabbath than to fish him out of the water by using an implement. The Pharisaic rule in Joma 8, 6, on the other hand, says quite simply: 'Danger to life supersedes the Sabbath.' Similarly in Shabbat 2, 5 it is said:

> He who extinguishes a light on the Sabbath because he fears pagans or robbers or an evil ghost, and he who does so for the sake of a sick person, so that he may sleep better, that man is

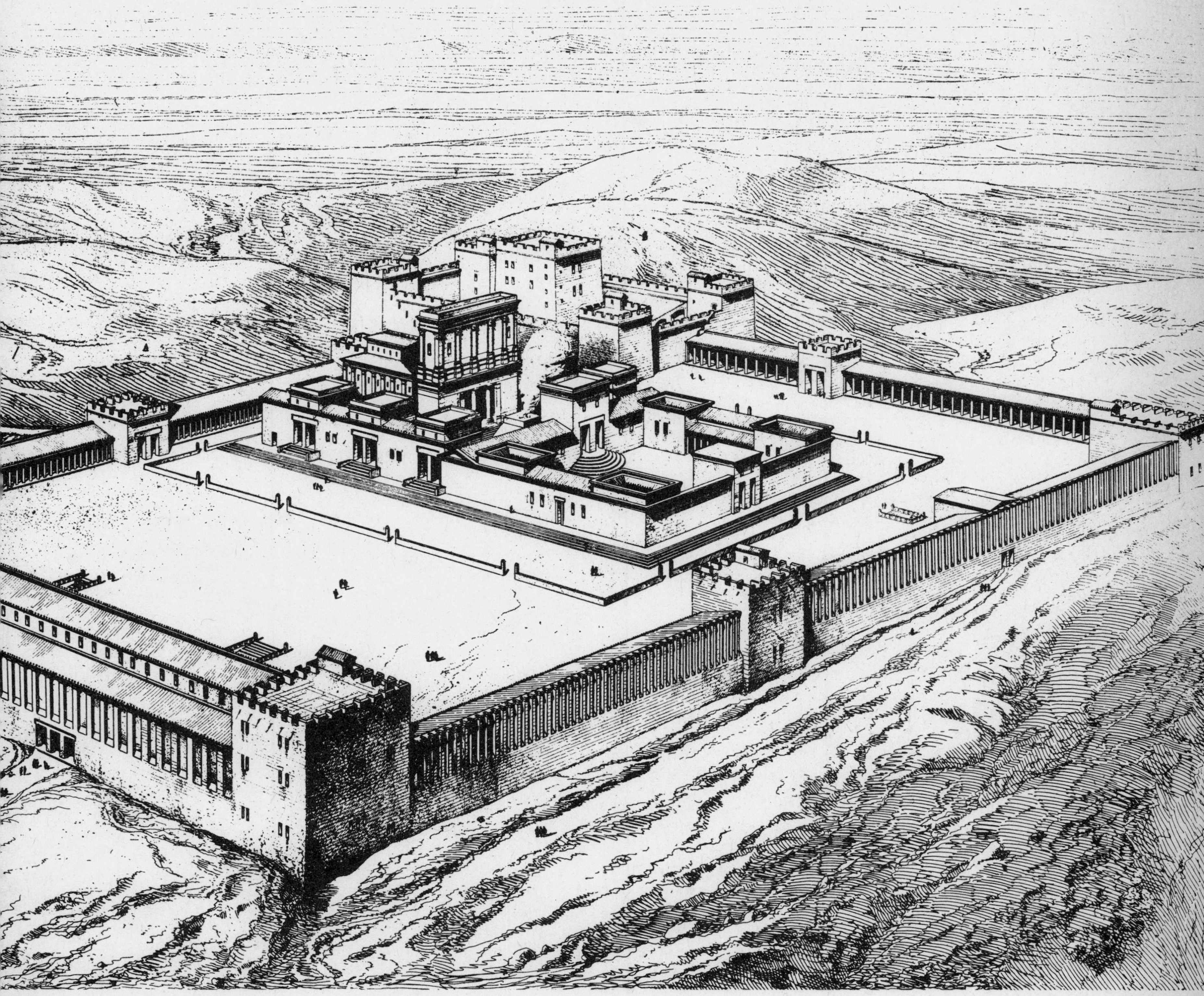

free from guilt. But if he wishes only to preserve the lamp or save the oil and the wick, he is guilty.

Even the work of clearing debris, which is otherwise forbidden on the Sabbath, must be done if it is necessary to save a life:

> If a building collapses on a man and there is any doubt about whether he is still lying under it or not, or whether he is alive or not, and likewise if there is any doubt about whether he is a stranger or an Israelite, one must clear away what is lying on him. If he is found alive one must care for him. If he is already dead, one leaves him there (Joma 8, 7).

And the Sabbath must yield not only to man but also to animals. A comparison between the Damascus Document 11, 13 and Shabbat 18, 3 is very instructive. In the Damascus Document it is said: 'On the Sabbath one must not help an animal to give birth.' But the Mishnah adds to this (referring to a feast-day): '. . . but one must care for it'. The respective attitude of the two sects towards the Sabbath again makes it clear why the Essenes, as apocalyptic extremists, saw in the realism of the Pharisees only hypocrisy and a failure of obedience to the faith.

The Pharisaic rabbinical tradition distinguishes between a written Torah and an oral Torah. The written Torah is the Pentateuch, the five books of Moses; the oral Torah is the elaboration, in the tradition, of the legal precepts contained in the written Torah. According to rabbinical tradition, the oral Torah was the legal heir of prophecy. Thus Aboth 1, 1 says: 'Moses received the Torah at Sinai and passed it on to Joshua, Joshua gave it to the elders, the elders to the prophets, and the prophets passed it on p 51 (13) to the men of the Great Synhedrion.' The concept of the oral law created for the rabbinical sages a direct line, a continuity, between Moses and themselves. Even their own interpretations and elaborations of the Law were supposed to have been given orally to Moses by God at Sinai. This conception of the 'oral Torah' made possible and legitimized the development and application of the biblical laws by the Pharisaic rabbis in the first centuries of the Christian era. The oral Law was therefore, for the rabbis, a necessary complement of the written Law. Thus the famous Palestinian sage, Johanan bar Nappaha, who lived in the middle years of the 3rd century AD, said, according to B. Gittin 60b: 'The Holy One, blessed be He, made the covenant with Israel solely because of the oral tradition.'

This concept of an oral Torah, which embraced and included everything that the Pharisaic rabbis discussed about the written Law, its implications and applications, made it possible for them to regard as legitimate their liberal conception of the Law, as opposed to that of the apocalyptic groups. Moreover, on the basis of this conception, they were able to develop an ethic of brotherly concern that stood in sharp contrast to the views of the apocalyptists. In consequence of the basic dualism of their thinking, the apocalyptists divided mankind into the righteous and sinners. It was the firm conviction of the apocalyptists that the righteous comprised solely and exclusively the members of their own special community. All others, whether Jews or gentiles, were counted as lost or even as instruments of the devil that had to be mercilessly fought. These convictions led the Qumran Essenes, as it had their Assidaean predecessors, to preach an eschatological war of revenge. They were to be the executors of God's judgement on their own and on God's enemies. Hence hatred of all enemies, *i.e.* of all outsiders, was considered a fitting preparation for the eschatological war of revenge. The Qumran Canon of Sects (105, 9–11), contains the relevant precept for the members of the community: '. . . to love all the sons of light, each according to his lot as ordained by God, and to hate all the sons of darkness, each according to his guilt before the wrath of God'.

Such a concept would have been inconceivable in Pharisaism. Once again it was the 'hypocrisy' of the Pharisees that made it possible for them to be much less harsh in their judgements of an outsider. The great Pharisee Hillel, who lived about a generation before the birth of Christ, is the source of the so-called Golden Rule, which is a development of Leviticus xix 18, 34: 'Do not unto others that which you would not have them do unto you' (B. Shabbat 31a). It is clear from the context that the reference to 'others' does not apply solely to Jews. According to Joshua ben Hananiah in Tos. Sanhedrin 13, 2, the 'righteous among the people of the world', *i.e.* the righteous non-Jews, would have a place in the world to come, as Israel would. The very assumption that there were righteous men among the gentiles would have seemed absurd to the members of the apocalyptic groups. This opinion of Rabbi Joshua's is called the 'opinion of our Mishnah' in B. Sanhedrin 105a. It has prevailed throughout later, medieval and modern, Judaism. It is reflected in the Mishnah commentary of Moses Maimonides to Sanhedrin 10, 2 and in the letter of Moses Mendelsohn to the Zürich theologian Lavater. Although several passages in the rabbinical tradition, for example Lev. rabba 2, 9, state that gentiles, if they do not wish to be eternally damned, must be converted to Judaism for their salvation, there are other passages such as B. Baba Kamma 38a: 'Rabbi Meir [middle and second half of the 2nd century AD] said: "Even a gentile who devotes himself to the Torah is like unto the high priest."' This variety of opinions is characteristic of Pharisaism, which, as already mentioned, differed in this respect from the apocalyptic groups.

The Pharisees also believed that the observance of the Law had an eschatological function, and that whoever sinned delayed the advent of eschatological salvation. It is in the light of this belief that a number of sayings in rabbinical literature are to be explained.

According to Pharisaic belief, the fate of the world and the fate of Israel are interwoven. There is no eschatological salvation without Israel having proved herself, and Israel's conduct, interpreted in the light of the Law, is relevant, not only to her, but to the whole world. It is in this sense that the comment in B. Sanhedrin 97b is to be understood, namely that every generation must have at least 36 righteous men.

The belief that Israel's observance of the Law has an influence on the salvation of the world must be understood in connection with the Pharisaic doctrine that the Torah is God's instrument of creation. This belief arose out of a development of the Old Testament wisdom-doctrine, and was influenced by the Stoic-Platonic popular philosophy. Especially in Hellenistic Judaism – for example, Philo in his *De Opificio Mundi* – this led to the conclusion that a Jew lived according to the law of nature because he lived according to the laws that regulated nature itself. Within the Pharisaic-rabbinical sphere, Rabbi Akiba, in the first half of the 2nd century AD, emphasized in the Sayings of the Fathers, Aboth 2, 14, that the great advantage of Israel was that, with the Law of the Torah, she had been given the instrument with which God had created the world. The fact that the rudimentary basis of this teaching already appears in the Wisdom of Sirach xxiv, where the wisdom at work in the Creation is equated with the Torah, would seem to indicate that this teaching was prevalent in Pharisaism before the time of Rabbi Akiba.

In the time of Jesus, when Old Testament Judaism was being exposed to various Hellenistic influences, the problem of the relationship of Divine guidance to man's free will came to the fore. On this topic, Josephus writes in *AJ* XIII 5, 9: 'The Pharisees say that some actions, but not all, are the work of fate, and some of them are in our own power.' This account is confirmed by a saying of Rabbi Akiba's dating from the first half of the 2nd century AD: 'Everything is foreseen and freedom of will is given' (Aboth 3, 15). The same line is followed in the opinion of Hanina bar Hama, dating from the first half of the 3rd century AD, which is expressed in B. Berakhoth 33b: 'Everything is in God's hands except the fear of God.' Such apparently paradoxical sayings are typical of the spirit and form of expression of Pharisaism.

After the destruction of the Temple in AD 70 ultra-messianic and pointedly eschatological sayings began to appear in Pharisaic-rabbinical texts too. After the first half of the 2nd century AD there developed something akin to a Pharisaic-rabbinical type of apocalyptic. To this apocalyptic belong, for example, all the speculations about the 'messianic birthpangs', *i.e.* the birthpangs of the world immediately preceding the messianic era, and about the 'generation in which the Son of David will come', the duration of the messianic kingdom and the date of the End of Days.

A number of sayings of Pharisaic-rabbinical sages dating from the second third of the 2nd century AD adapted older apocalyptic themes to the actual contemporary scene. The period of tribulations immediately preceding the messianic era – a favourite theme in these texts – was already mentioned in the Assidaean texts of the 2nd century BC. The historical events reflected in the rabbinical p 75 ultra-messianic sayings, Hadrian's persecution of the Jews and (f 6) the following decade, were among the factors that led to the revolt f 3 of Bar Kokhba in AD 132–5. Thus, according to Sanhedrin 98ab, Jose ben Kisma, who lived during the Hadrianic persecution of the Jews, is supposed to have said in his last hours: 'Sink my coffin deep in the earth, for there is not one palm tree in Babylon to which a Persian horse will not be tethered, nor one coffin in Palestine out of which a Median horse will not eat hay.' A similar saying by Simeon bar Yohai, a student of Rabbi Akiba and a younger contemporary of Jose ben Kisma, is contained in Midrash, Cant. rabba 8, 11: 'When you see Persian horses tethered to the tombstones in the land of Israel, then hope for the coming of the Messiah.' It is possible that this saying of Simeon bar Yohai belongs historically to the year AD 161, for at the outset of the p 335 reign of Marcus Aurelius the Roman-Parthian war had broken (7) out anew and the Parthians won an impressive series of initial victories. Apparently several of the rabbis saw in the Parthians a messianic instrument, just as Deutero-Isaiah had seen one in the Persian king Cyrus.

Like the apocalyptists before them, the Pharisees had to face the problem of the delay of the messianic era. Jose ben Halaphta warned against the messianic enthusiasm typified in the saying of his contemporary, Simeon bar Yohai, quoted above. According to Derekh Eretz rabba 11, he is reported to have said: 'Whoever makes calculations about the end has no place in the world to come.' The old Pharisaic scepticism about ultra-messianic expectations reawakened at the very time when these expectations had reached a fever pitch among the pupils of Rabbi Akiba. The anti-ultra-eschatological trend once again became predominant in the last decade of the 2nd century AD. The redactor of the Mishnah, Judah ha-Nasi, was as decidedly opposed to apocalyptic speculation as had been the rabbis of the period before AD 70. He stood firmly on the ground of realism, and he knew that the Halakhah, the law pertaining to daily life, was the best guarantee for the survival of Judaism, and that Judaism could only be endangered by ultra-eschatological expectations.

Life after death

Like the apocalyptic groups also, the Pharisees believed in the physical resurrection of the dead. The hope of resurrection developed under various influences only during the last centuries of Old Testament Israel. Clear and defined formulations of the hope of resurrection are to be found in the apocalyptic literature only after the end of the 3rd century BC. When the Pharisees broke away from the Assidaeans, about half-way through the 2nd century BC, the belief in resurrection was already so clearly defined, so completely unquestioned, that the Pharisees accepted it and made it one of the keystones of their eschatological expectations. In Mishnah, Sanhedrin 10, 1–3 and in other numerous passages, this belief is expressed with unmistakable clarity. Connected with a belief in resurrection is the expectation of a last judgement at which the righteous are to be separated from the sinners. The Pharisaic belief in resurrection is also the outcome of a lengthy development. The Old Testament belief, and the belief which was generally accepted throughout the Ancient East, was that, after a human being's death, his entire psycho-physical being sank into a nether world, the 'land of no return'. With the development of the belief in resurrection in late Old Testament times, it was again the entire psycho-physical substance of human nature that was to awake to new life. The nether world was no longer the 'land of no return'. The place which, according to older beliefs, was the domicile of all the dead thus became more and more a place of punishment for sinners, *i.e.* hell.

Ever since the confrontation between Judaism and Greek culture, which began towards the end of the 4th century BC, Judaism had been under the influence of a quite differently structured, Greek philosophical (especially Platonic), conception of human nature according to which man was not a unity of body f 1 and soul but was a being that consisted of two distinct and separate elements, a body and a soul. This influence can be seen in texts,

The reconstructed Temple appears on the coins of the Second Revolt (AD 132–5) as a symbol of the renascence of Judaea. Between the two central columns of the Temple façade is the Ark of the Covenant. (3)

dating back to as early as the 2nd century BC, where, for that part of man which continues to exist in the nether world, the terms *psychē* 'soul' and *pneuma* 'spirit' are used. At first, these terms were merely appropriated, for the condition of the souls and spirits of the dead was thought to be similar to the shadow existence of the dead in the nether world, as previously believed. It is not until the post-Christian era that the influence of Greek ideas about the nature of man becomes manifest in the texts. According to the conception expressed in these texts, only the body is interred while the soul wanders about in the air. At the end of time, these souls are to be reunited with their revitalized bodies. It will only be then that the complete eschatological life will be achieved. The concept of an independent life of the soul after death derives from Greek thought, but the belief that these souls can enjoy actual life only when they are reunited with their bodies at the Last Judgement is an Old Testament Jewish contribution. Several later Talmudic texts stress the fact that at the final judgement it is essential for this reunion to take place, since neither soul nor body alone can be held responsible for sins committed during life. A fresco at Dura Europus, showing the resurrection of the dead p 82–3 according to Ezekiel xxxvii, illustrates this. The souls are shown (10) with little butterfly wings flying down to their respective bodies. Besides the Greek philosophical concept of the further existence of the soul after death which the Pharisees had adopted, they were also aware not only of the concept of a last judgement at the end of days, but also of the concept of an individual personal judgement immediately after death.

From an historical point of view the Pharisees were a group which had seceded from the Assidaeans about half-way through the 2nd century BC, but which on the other hand was consistent in following out a path that had been blazed in the pre-Exilic and post-Exilic periods. The Pharisees held to the general programme of basing their conception of their own function firmly on the Law, a programme that had been formative for Judaism since the time of the 6th-century BC Exilic and post-Exilic community. In this sense Pharisaism can be said to have been the continuation of a tradition that had been embodied in the Priestly Document for the post-Exilic community, but that had had a pre-Exilic overture in Deuteronomy, with its ideas about the Covenant and the Law. Pharisaism, and the rabbinical tradition that grew out of it, cannot be understood properly if they are not taken as a continuation, a consistent continuation, of a development which was firmly rooted in the Old Testament.

The Law, the Torah, was a sign of divine election for the Pharisees. By living according to the Torah, Israel could experience her uniqueness and feel the hand of God that hovered over her. This feeling that had sustained Judaism throughout the centuries was, for the Pharisees, the ground of their existence. Pharisaism was the only Jewish religious party that – at the time of Jesus – thought in terms of the situations and the implications p 62–3 of the world-wide Jewish diaspora. The Pharisaic ideal of piety – (37–42) based, as it was, on the study, interpretation and transmission of the Law as a rule for everyday life – required no sanctuary other than man himself, and therefore made the continuance of Judaism p 80 independent of the possession of a local sanctuary. Thus, according (4, 5) to Aboth de'Rabbi Nathan 4, the great Johanan ben Zakkai could tell his student Joshua ben Hananiah, who was distressed by the spectacle of the ruins of the Temple: 'My son, be not distressed! We have another atonement as effective as this – acts of loving-kindness, as it is said [Hosea vi 6]: "For I desire mercy and not sacrifice."'

The Sadducees: a priestly aristocracy

The early history of the Sadducees has already been briefly noted. In Jesus' time they were an important religious party – though not in the sense of being a well-organized community – but much less is known about them than about the Pharisees and Essenes. There would also be little information about the Pharisees in Jesus' time if the rabbinical tradition of the following centuries had not transmitted the Pharisaic teachings. The Sadducees, however, who disappeared from the historical scene after the destruction of the Second Temple, had no successors to preserve their teachings for later generations. The reports about the Sadducees in the New Testament and in rabbinical literature originated within groups that were anti-Sadducee and whose reports were therefore of a polemical nature. Like the Qumran priests, the Sadducees derived their name from the priestly family of Zadok. But the Qumran priests were apocalyptic radicals, whereas the Sadducees were an upper-class, nationalistic liberal party. Because of the assimilationist tendencies, the nationalistic elements in Sadducaeism are often overlooked. Thus the Sadducees are generally held to be simply the party of those members of the Jewish community who collaborated with the Roman occupying power in order to serve their own financial interests. This was only one aspect of the Sadducaean party, however. The Sadducees also co-operated with the Hasmonaean high priests from John Hyrcanus to Aristobulus II, and these followed a pronounced Jewish nationalistic policy. One should also bear in mind that, according to Josephus in *De Bello Judaico* II 17, 2, the governor of the Temple, Cleopas, who was the son of Ananias the high priest and was thus apparently a Sadducee, was the person who persuaded the priests officiating at the Temple not to accept sacrifices from a gentile. This implied a rejection of Caesar's sacrifice, and this act was tantamount to a signal, given by a large part of the official Sadducee Temple priests, for the revolt against Rome.

The teachings of the Sadducees are reported in negative form p 82–3 in Acts xxiii 8: 'For the Sadducees say that there is no resurrection, (10) neither angels, nor spirits.' Josephus describes the Sadducaean *f 1* rejection of the resurrection in the words: 'They also deny the belief in the survival of the soul, and in the punishments and rewards in the Nether World.' It should be patent that, in this passage, Josephus is simply trying to explain, in terms that would be comprehensible to his Greek readers, the Sadducaean rejection of the concept of the resurrection that had been accepted in apocalyptic circles. In this context there is also a clear anti-Sadducaean polemic in the Pharisaic saying in B. Sanhedrin 90a: 'He who denies the resurrection of the dead shall have no part in the resurrection.' A repudiation of the Sadducaean denial of the resurrection is also to be found in the gospel tradition (Mark xii 18–27; Matt. xxii 23–33; Luke xx 27–40), according to which a Sadducee sought to ridicule the hope of resurrection by asking to whom a woman who had married seven brothers, one after the other, would belong after the resurrection.

The Sadducees also denied the doctrine, which enjoyed great popularity in apocalyptic circles, of good and evil spirits and the dualistic outlook implicit in such a doctrine. Among all the Jewish groups, the Sadducees were the most emphatic in their denial of any predestination of man's action. In their opinion, man is an entirely free agent and is therefore fully responsible for his acts. This was a nationalistic-liberal party which rejected all those innovations that were of the utmost importance to a believer in a time of personal trial; it was also a party which was characterized by severity and whose members were primarily upper-class. Such a party could not be expected to have a long existence. The disappearance of the Sadducaean party after the destruction of Jerusalem in AD 70 was therefore merely the logical consequence of beliefs which appear to have been rigidly held by the Sadducees.

The Essenes: a 'Sanctuary for Israel'

The Essenes, like the Pharisees, were products of the movement p 84–6 of the apocalyptic Assidaeans. The Essenes were a continuation (11–18 of the Assidaeans in a radical form. It is virtually certain on archaeological grounds that the Qumran community, whose settlement and texts were discovered near the north-west shore of the Dead Sea in 1947, is identical with the party of the Essenes mentioned by ancient writers. Although other theories have been advanced regarding the identification of the Qumran community, a thorough investigation of all the facts would seem to lend credence to the Essene theory as being the only acceptable one. We shall therefore draw both on ancient reports about the Essenes and on the Qumran texts and the results of archaeological excavations at Qumran in our presentation of Essenism.

The founder of the Qumran-Essene community was a priest who went by the title of a 'Teacher of Righteousness' and who apparently was held to be the prophet of the last days by his followers. In any event, his appearance and the establishment of the community settlement at Qumran led to a vigorous flaring-up again of ultra-eschatological hopes, as is shown by a number of Qumran texts, especially the Habakkuk Commentary. The Teacher of Righteousness was at work in the second half of the 2nd century BC and probably also at the beginning of the 1st. Archaeological excavation at Qumran has revealed the history of the community there. The following strata were unearthed in the course of the excavation:

(1a) The communal home was erected, probably under John *f 4* Hyrcanus (134–104 BC), on ancient foundations dating from the 8th century BC. At the time when the building was erected, the community was apparently obliged to live in an extremely modest style.

(1b) During the reign of Alexander Jannaeus (103–76 BC) the community enjoyed great prosperity; this entire period is to be regarded as its zenith. In 31 BC the building was severely damaged by an earthquake and was subsequently abandoned.

(2) It was not until the reign of Herod Archelaus (4 BC–AD 6) that the structure was rebuilt by the members of the same community. This building stood until AD 68, when Vespasian marched with the 10th Roman Legion from Caesarea to Jericho, skirting the Dead Sea *en route*. On this occasion the Essene settlement at Qumran was destroyed.

This is the historical framework within which we have to fit all the texts that are Qumran texts specifically, *i.e.* all those texts which had not been simply taken over by the Qumran Essenes from their predecessors.

Most scholars follow Josephus (*BJ* II 8, 2–13; *AJ* XVIII 1, 5) and Pliny (*Natural History* v 17), in drawing a distinction between 'monastic' and 'married' Essenes; and the Qumran texts themselves show that this distinction is, in principle, correct. The Manual of p 84 Discipline contains, for example, rules and regulations for the (11) members of the community who lived what was practically a 'monastic' life, whereas the Damascus Document and the Rule of the Congregation take for granted the existence of married members of the community. If we are to believe Josephus and the Qumran texts themselves, the community at Qumran was by no means the sole settlement of the Essenes; it was only the centre, or perhaps one of the centres, of this party. The Manual of Discipline (6, 2) speaks of 'all their places of habitation'. The Damascus Document (7, 6a–7) also presupposes the existence of a number of settlements belonging to this community, settlements whose members are here expressly said to be married people. It is also stated in *BJ* II 8, 4, that 'there were many of them in the population of every city'.

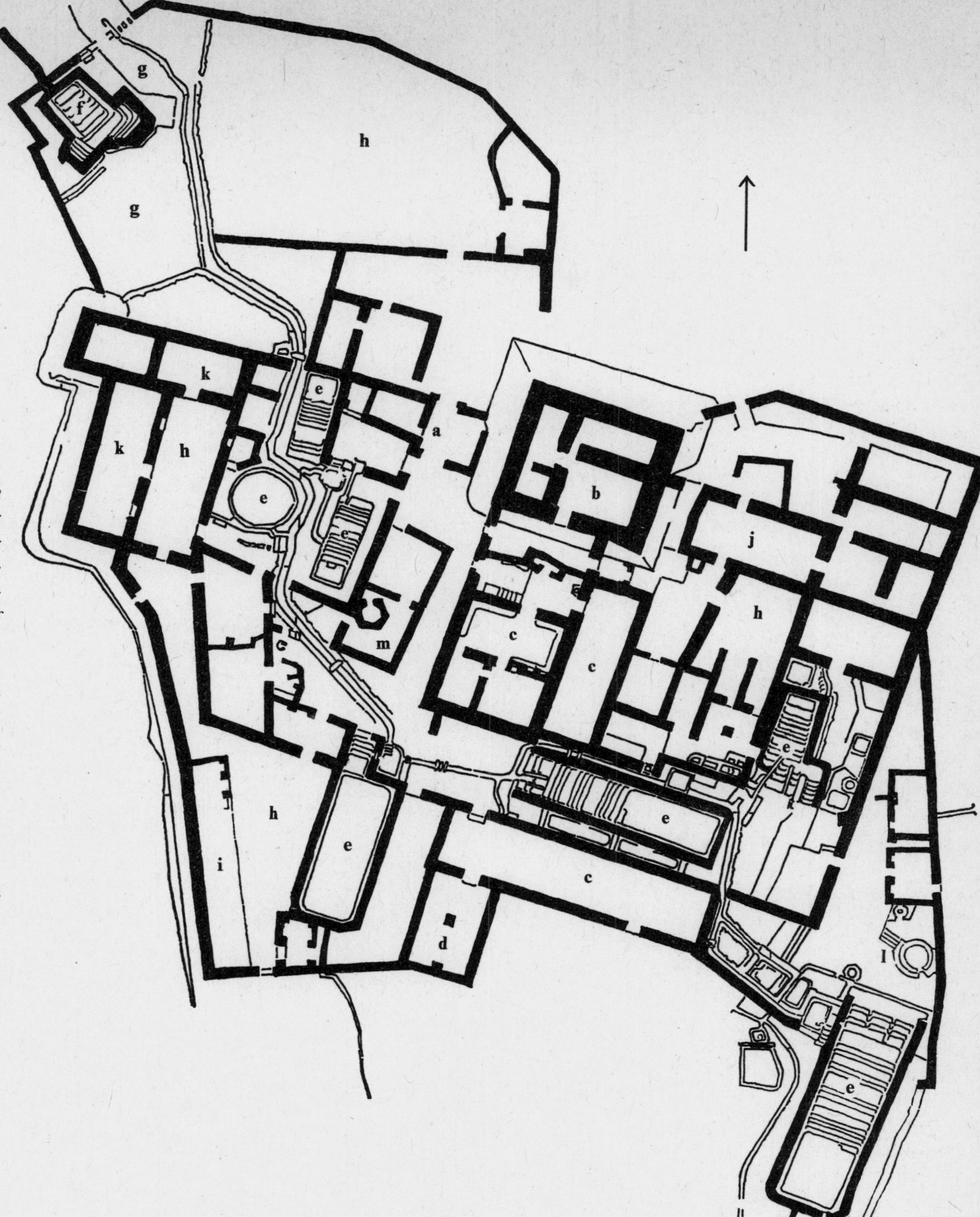

The 'monastery' at Khirbet Qumran on the north-west shore of the Dead Sea was founded during the reign of John Hyrcanus (134–104 BC) on Israelite foundations going back to the 8th century BC. It was considerably extended during the reign of Alexander Jannaeus (103–76 BC), abandoned after an earthquake in 31 BC, reoccupied during the reign of Herod Archelaus (4 BC–AD 6) and finally destroyed by Vespasian in AD 68. The entrance is at (a), (b) is a tower, (c) are meeting rooms, and a complete table service of over 1000 pieces was found at (d), suggestive of the communal ritual meals which the Essenes are known to have celebrated. The most striking feature of the plan is the number of cisterns (e), which seems to indicate that the water-supply at Qumran was geared not only to the life of a sizable community in the desert but also to a rigorous programme of ritual baths; and (f) is in fact a bath. (g) is a filtering basin. Courtyards are at (h), (i) is probably a stable, (j) the kitchen and (k) perhaps store-rooms. At (l) is an oven for making pottery and at (m) one for baking bread. (4)

To a large extent the 'monastic' Essenes practised a communal ownership of goods and lived in celibacy, characteristics that are emphasized by Josephus and Pliny in the above-mentioned passages. But it was not the ideal of celibacy in the Christian sense, but rather considerations of a sacerdotal and ritual character, that led the Essenes of Qumran to adopt this particular mode of life. The disciples of the Teacher of Righteousness retired to the seclusion of Qumran because they believed that public worship at Jerusalem was being conducted according to an erroneous calendar and by unworthy priests.

79–81 In all probability their communal life served the Qumran
(1–9) Essenes as a substitute for the worship at Jerusalem. It has even
f2 been suggested that the Qumran community might have had something like a substitute temple in which they offered blood sacrifices. The heart of the Qumran Essenes' communal life was a course of ritual lustrations and a ritual meal, presided over by priests. These rites, with or without sacrifices in a substitute temple, served the members of the community as a substitute for the rites of the public worship at Jerusalem until such time as their priests, at the End of Days, could officiate at the cleansed sanctuary in Jerusalem according to their own precepts. Participation in this community meant practically that one had to be celibate and to practise communal ownership of goods, for the apparently daily lustration and ritual meals necessitated a life of this kind. Thus, although from the point of view of its sacerdotal structure the Qumran Community may quite properly be called an 'order', this 'order'-like structure was not the reflection of an ascetic ideal comparable to that of Christian monasticism.

Nor should the prizing of poverty as a virtue be interpreted in terms of the Christian monastic ideal of poverty. It is true that, on the strength of Isaiah lxi 1; lxii 2, poverty was held to be a sign of faithfulness to the Covenant and to be an eschatological virtue. As early as Trito-Isaiah (Isa. lxvi 2), in a text dating from the second half of the 6th century BC, the favoured of God were called 'poor and contrite in spirit'. This term continued in use, though in abbreviated form, as 'poor in spirit', in the community of Qumran, where it was used as one of the names for the members of the community. Thus in the War Scroll 14, 6f., for example, it says: 'And he (God) gives a firm stance to the weak-kneed and strength to the loins of those whose necks are accustomed to blows; and through the poor in spirit . . . the stubborn-hearted; and through those of perfect conduct all the people of wickedness shall be destroyed.' Even though the predicate applying to the 'poor in spirit' can no longer be determined, owing to a lacuna in the manuscript, it is evident from the context that the 'poor in spirit' are to execute judgement on the stubborn-hearted (apparently Israelites) and that they are synonymous with those of perfect conduct who are to execute divine vengeance on the pagan people. Thus the 'poor' is also the 'chosen' or 'elect'. In this sense, only those Israelites are 'poor' who belong to the proper congregation.

The Qumran community

It was not the ideal of poverty that led to the quasi-monastic life in the Qumran Essene centre, but rather – as already noted – sacerdotal and ritual considerations. The sacerdotal character of the Qumran community is also clear from the facts that, according to the Manual of Discipline 8, 5f., they believed themselves to be p 79 (1) the 'sanctuary for Israel and the Holy of Holies for Aaron', that their most important offices were reserved for priests, and that in their messianic doctrine the priestly Messiah stood on a higher level in the hierarchy than the lay Messiah from the House of David. Communal ownership of goods and sexual abstinence were not ends in themselves; they were consequences of the sacerdotal structure of the Qumran community. This is attested by an investigation of the names relating not only to the quasi-monastic Essenes but also to the married members of the groups. The most important source on this question is the Rule of the Congregation (1, 25–7), where it is said that the members of the community must consecrate themselves for three days when there is to be a convocation for judgement, a common consultation, or a convocation for war. This three-day consecration can only mean sexual abstinence, as is clear from Exodus xix 14f.

While the communal ownership of goods was adhered to by the 'monastic' members of the community so strictly that, according to the Manual of Discipline 5, 16f., they could not even accept food or drink from non-members if it had not been purchased by the community, the married members of the community were allowed to possess private property. This is proved beyond doubt by the Damascus Document. In this (14, 12–14), the full members are required to contribute a minimum of two days' wages a month for social welfare purposes. The prohibition in the Damascus Document 11, 12 against making one's servant, maid or hired hand work on the Sabbath takes for granted, not only private ownership, but also the general social structure of the day, with master and servant, as being valid for the married members of the community. Private property and apparently also non-monastic conditions are presupposed in a text from cave 4 (4Q Ordinances) in which the poor are permitted to take grain for themselves and their families from other people's stores. From the standpoint of the community's priestly ideal of ritual cleanliness, it is easy to understand why those who lived 'worldly' lives had to consecrate themselves for special occasions, and why those who wanted to live continuously in a state of consecration had to renounce the worldly order, including marriage and private property.

The lay-out of the cemeteries found near Khirbet Qumran makes it evident that it was the priestly ideal of ritual cleanliness and not an ideal of virginal chastity which led to the quasi-monastic structure of the Qumran Essene centre. The large cemetery to the east of Qumran contains, with a single exception, only graves laid out on a north–south axis; here only male skeletons were found, and no gifts of any kind were in the grave. The only grave within this cemetery which can be said with certainty to have contained a woman's body is not laid out along the usual axis and is of another type. Farther to the east another cemetery was found, and here the graves were laid out more carelessly and not on any particular axis. Here the graves of women and children were found, and, in two of the female graves, gifts were discovered. North and south of Qumran other cemeteries were discovered in which women and children had been buried, and here too, in one of the female graves, gifts were found. These discoveries make it clear that, in the large cemetery to the east of Qumran, the quasi-monastic full members of the community were buried. Those who had not yet been accepted into full membership, and perhaps also the married members of the community who had not separated from their wives, were buried apart. The graves of the women and children may also be those of former family relations of the full members. These women and children were separated from their husbands and fathers when the men became full members of the community, and the Qumran Essene congregations had to look after the women and children.

A central feature of Essene communal life was the communal ritual meal which has already been mentioned. It was presided over by a priest and, at it, bread and wine played a special role; occasionally meat, too, was eaten. This communal meal has often been compared to the Last Supper of Jesus or to the early Christian *agapē*. Nevertheless a distinction must be drawn between the true nature and purpose of the Qumran meal and the Christian Eucharist, for in the Qumran meal there is neither a transformation of the bread and wine nor the establishment of a new covenant; neither is there a commemoration of any kind of salvational event.

Josephus reports in *BJ* II 8, 5, that the Essenes took special purifying baths in cold water before their meals. The ritual nature of these baths is attested by the archaeological finds as well as by the Manual of Discipline 5, 13f., where the baths are deemed to be worthless without a corresponding spirit of repentance. The penitential nature of these baths immediately suggests a comparison with the baptism of John, but John rejected at least the p 220 (6) exclusiveness of the Qumran community. Although in all probability a close religious-historical relation existed between John the Baptist and the Qumran community, this hypothetical relation should not, on the other hand, be overestimated. The baptism of John was a single and unique act of conversion, and therefore basically different from the apparently daily ritual baths of the Essenes, even though these Essene baths had a penitential aspect. Moreover, the baptism of John, in contrast to the ritual baths of the Essenes, was performed by John on penitents and not on his own person. This fact may have led to John's epithet, 'the Baptist'. In contrast to Qumran, neither the teachings nor the baptism of John had an esoteric character.

The dualistic doctrine, according to which everything in the cosmos and in man occurs according to a plan of creation that provides for two equally strong forces of light and darkness, was also typical of Qumran. The continuous conflict between these two forces will be terminated only at the End of Days by a victory of the forces of light. Over these two forces stands the one God. Despite the dualistic character of the Qumran Essene outlook, biblical monotheism was never questioned. This dualistic structure, however, together with the esoteric element in the Qumran community and the belief in the participation of the angels in the p 266– (7–11) communal life of the group, reveals, no doubt, a Gnosticizing tendency – though, in contrast to non-Jewish Gnosticism, there p 278– (*f 3, 4*) was not here any division of the godhead into a transcosmic good god of light and an evil, world-creator god. Since, as is said in the p 319– (1–10) Manual of Discipline 4, 18f., God 'at the appointed time of his visitation will exterminate evil for ever', eschatology assumes an p 268– (12–19 especially important place in the doctrines of the Qumran Essenes. They stood, as has already been pointed out, in the direct line of succession of the apocalyptically-oriented Assidaeans, and they remained undaunted in their expectation of the imminent advent of the end, despite the long period of delay. This conviction found expression in the terminology of the community, in which the contemporary age was called the 'Rule of Belial' or the 'End Period of Wickedness'. The Assidaeans, despite their conviction that the final decision rested solely with God, believed that they would play an active role in the final drama; the Qumran Essenes clearly expected an eschatological war of vengeance in which they would be the instrument of God in crushing his and their enemies. The most explicit documentary evidence for this is the so-called War Scroll, but in other Qumran texts too there are clear and irrefutable evidences of the idea of a war of vengeance and of hatred for the enemy, as consequences of an eschatological ideology.

As for the belief in a resurrection that had been developed in earlier apocalyptic circles, this expectation took on a more concrete form among the Assidaeans and the Qumran Essenes. Their hope was for a resurrection, at the eschatological judgement, of the entire human being, as a psycho-physical entity. The fate of the sinner is not always the same in the various texts, and apparently non-Israelites (gentiles) were originally not even considered. In the Qumran texts themselves there are surprisingly few allusions that can be related directly to the belief in a resurrection. The reason is that the Qumran people thought themselves to be members, during their lifetime, of a community which included embodied heavenly beings, the angels, so that resurrection did not represent any enhancement of what they believed themselves to possess during their life here on earth. It would be erroneous, however, on the basis of the paucity of allusions to a belief in a resurrection in the Qumran texts, to deny the existence of such a belief among the Essenes. This doctrine, which originated in the apocalyptic circles of the late Old Testament period, became, on the whole, more explicit and definite in the course of time.

On a coin of Mattathias Antigonus (40–37 BC) the Seven-Branched Candlestick is shown together with an object which appears to be the Table of the Shewbread. (5)

The messianic doctrine of Qumran knew of three messianic functions, as is evident, for example, in the Manual of Discipline 9, 10f., where it says: 'They shall be judged by the earlier judgements by which the men of the community began to be disciplined, *until there shall come a prophet and the Messiahs of Aaron and Israel*.' The Qumran people most probably thought that the expectation of an eschatological prophet (in connection with Deut. xviii 15, 18) had been fulfilled by their priestly Teacher of Righteousness. For them, this was a super-prophet who knew everything that had been hidden from the prophets before him.

Of the two specifically messianic figures, the priestly Messiah was given a higher place in the hierarchy than the Messiah of Israel, who was *ex officio* a layman. This corresponds exactly to the structure of the Qumran community, which was composed basically of priests and laymen in such a way that the priests enjoyed certain distinct privileges. The expectation of a Messiah from the House of David, which was adopted from the Old Testament, was connected in Qumran with the person of the Messiah of Israel, so that the two messianic figures were to be a priest and a man of Davidic descent.

Messianic hopes

The expectation of a heavenly Son of Man is a special variation on the general form of early Jewish apocalyptic. The Son of Man first appears in Daniel vii 13f., in a passage which apparently dates from the period of religious persecution by Antiochus IV Epiphanes and the Maccabaean revolt of 168–164 BC. Undoubtedly the Son of Man was originally a mythological figure that was adapted, as far as this was practicable, to Jewish messianic doctrine. In any case it does not appear probable that the concept of the Son of Man is to be traced to the Iranian concept of the first or original man. On the basis of the almost indisputable fact that
26–7 (16, 8–22)
ancient Canaanite concepts, transmitted through ritual observances, continued to exist in modified form in Jewish apocalyptic, it would seem more probable that the figure of the Son of Man is to be traced back to Canaanite mythology. Thus it has been suggested that one should see in Daniel vii 9–10 and 13–14 an adaptation of a myth that originally had to do with two deities, namely the El and the Baal of the Ugaritic texts. The enthronement, described in Daniel vii 13f., of the Son of Man by the Ancient of Days derives, according to this theory, from a Canaanite belief that Baal was enthroned by El in similar fashion.

Taken within the context of Daniel vii, the introduction of the figure of the Son of Man undoubtedly has an eschatological
p 231 (*f 3*)
character; for it is said of the enthroned Son of Man (Dan. vii 14): 'And there was given to him dominion, and glory, and a kingdom, that all people, and nations, and languages should serve him; his dominion is an everlasting dominion which shall not pass away, and his kingdom that which shall not be destroyed.' This heavenly figure of the Son of Man who came 'with the clouds of the heaven' can, however, be taken only *mutatis mutandis*, as a messianic figure. In the present context of Daniel vii the Son of Man is depersonalized and is made to represent the true Israel, the 'saints of the Most High', who, according to the intention of the final editor, were apparently the Assidaeans. Over against this, it is only of secondary importance that, in an older version of Daniel vii, the 'saints of the Highest' were understood to be angels who belonged to the court of the Ancient of Days and the enthroned Son of Man. Both in the inter-testamental Pseudepigrapha and in the Qumran texts the term 'saints' can refer to angels as well as to the members of the community; in some passages of the Qumran texts, it may have had both meanings simultaneously.

In later Jewish tradition the concept of the Son of Man took on the character of a transcendental redeemer figure. In this connection it is unimportant whether the description of the Son of Man in the Parables of the Ethiopic *Book of Enoch* (chapters 37–71), in IV Ezra (the apocalyptic Ezra), and in the fifth book of the Sibylline Oracles represents a direct development of the concepts of Daniel vii, as it is based on a different stratum, of which there is no surviving record. The Parables make partial reference to Daniel vii, but there the Son of Man executes judgement himself and takes his seat on the throne of God. He represented either a pre-worldly heavenly being or Enoch, who had been taken up into heaven.

The author of IV Ezra xiii 26, dating from the period *c.* AD 100, shared the belief, expressed in the Parables, that the Son of Man was 'he whom the Most High has held in reserve for many ages and through whom He will redeem His creation'. During a storm he came up from the heart of the sea and flew with the clouds of heaven. According to Daniel vii, the Son of Man was apparently on the heavenly clouds from the beginning, in contrast to the four beasts, symbolizing the worldly kingdoms, which arose from the sea. From the four corners of the earth there approached an innumerable multitude to do battle with him. With a fiery stream from his mouth he destroyed them all. Then he called to another, peaceful, multitude to join him, and this multitude is identified with the returning ten 'lost' tribes of Israel. In a slightly modified p 82–3 (10)
form the Son of Man also appears in the fifth (Jewish) book of the Sibylline Oracles 414f. Here he is called a blessed man who comes from the vault of heaven bearing in his hands a sceptre which God has given him. According to Justin *Dialogue* 32, 1, Trypho, too, was familiar with the messianic connotations of the

term Son of Man, but he refused to recognize the crucified Jesus of Nazareth as the Son of Man whom the Jews expected to come 'in glory and power'.

In rabbinical literature the expectation of a Messiah, identical with the Son of Man of Daniel vii 13, rarely appears, probably for the polemical reason that the Gospels recognize Jesus as the messianic Son of Man. The single notable exception is a statement in B. Sanhedrin 98a:

> Rabbi Joshua ben Levi [a Palestinian sage whose date is the first half of the 3rd century BC] pointed out a contradiction. It is written: 'And lo! with the clouds of heaven comes one like a Son of Man [Dan. vii 13],' and further it is written: p 265 (6) 'Humble, and riding upon an ass [Zech. ix 9].' When they [the Israelites] are worthy, then he will come 'with the clouds of heaven', but, if they are unworthy, then 'humble, and riding upon an ass'.

It is extremely difficult to attribute the concepts concerning the Son of Man to a definite group within the Judaism of the intertestamental period. It is certainly probable that these concepts were known to a number of apocalyptic groups. The fact that the Son of Man in *Enoch* 48, 4f. also has certain Davidic Messiah attributes would appear to prove that the heavenly figure of the Son of Man was somehow related to the earthly political messianic hope. It is striking that, although several Enoch manuscripts have been found in the caves of Qumran, the Parables (*Enoch* 37–71) that deal with the Son of Man Messiah are missing so far. This can hardly be due to chance. Again, in the texts that are specifically Qumran texts, there is not one allusion to a messianic Son of Man.

The crusade against Rome

p 54–7 (21–8) *f 3* It is difficult to bring the Jewish groups that revolted against Rome under a common denominator, for they fought not only against Rome but against one another as well. There were various messianic concepts among the groups which expected the imminent advent of the end. This is already clear from the Qumran texts. In these texts the expectations of a priestly and of a Davidic Messiah are to be found side by side, as has already been mentioned. The coexistence of these two messianic concepts was probably responsible for the many differences between the insurrectionary groups in their war against Rome in the years AD 66–70. The only thing that they had in common was their wish to establish by force the absolute rule of God in their own land against the Romans.

It is striking that Josephus, who is our most important source of information about the various groups which fought against Rome and about their ideologies, designated all these groups as 'brigands', a word for which 'partisans' is the only translation that fits the facts. Two other terms, 'Zealots' and 'Sicarii', are used by Josephus in very specific senses, so that we must not mistake the one for the other.

The Zealots of Josephus were in all probability one of the p 79–81 (1–9) *f 2* priestly apocalyptic groups centred on the Temple of Jerusalem. The term 'Zealot' is used by Josephus only after the outbreak of the war against Rome, but in Mishnah, Sanhedrin 9, 6 it probably refers to the period before AD 66. Josephus, in describing the outbreak of the revolt in Jerusalem, states that the governor of the Temple, Eleazar, son of the high priest Ananias, persuaded his priestly colleagues not to accept any sacrifice from a non-Jew. This, however, implied a rejection of Caesar's sacrifice and thereby also the beginning of the revolt. Apparently the Zealots thought that the cleansing of the Temple from all illegitimate practices was a prerequisite for the realization of the Kingdom of God. In the light of Josephus's remark in *BJ* IV 3, 8, it is to be understood that the high priest who was elected after the outbreak of the revolt called himself Pinchas. According to Numbers xxv 7–13 Pinchas, with spear in hand, zealously executed the divine Law.

Another group is called by Josephus 'Sicarii', *i.e.* 'dagger-men', radicals who saw the guerrilla warfare against Rome as the prelude for later large-scale operations with which the messianic era was to be ushered in. According to *BJ* II 8, 1, and *AJ* XVIII 1, 1, 6, the Sicarii derive from Judas the Galilaean. Judas was most probably the son of the so-called 'robber chieftain' Hezekiah, who had made an abortive attempt to revolt under Herod. According to *BJ* II 8, 1, the group founded by Judas the Galilaean was independent and was not associated with any other group, but in *AJ* XVIII 1, 16, Josephus describes it as a fourth 'philosophical school' alongside of the Pharisees, Sadducees, and Essenes, but related to the Pharisees; a Pharisee by the name of Zadok was supposed to have participated in the founding of the group.

Though the Pharisees were drawn into the great insurrectionary movement, they sought still to maintain an orderly administration, in spite of the turbulence of the times, and they soon dissociated themselves from the ultra-messianic fanaticism of the insurgents. The behaviour of Josephus in Galilee, and, even more significant, that of the famous Pharisee leader Johanan ben Zakkai, who fled from besieged Jerusalem to negotiate with the Romans about the future destiny of Judaism after the destruction of Jerusalem, are clear proofs that the spiritual assumptions of the anti-Roman partisans and of the Jewish combatants in the Great War of AD 66–70 did not emanate from the ranks of the Pharisees.

The Sicarii were a group that fought against Rome for more than a century – apparently under the leadership of a single family. It has been noted already that Judas the Galilaean was probably the son of the anti-Roman partisan leader Hezekiah, who was a contemporary of Herod. Judas took up arms in AD 6 when Palestine was officially incorporated in the Roman provincial system. According to *BJ* VII 8, 1, the insurgents in Masada, who defended p 55– (23–8 this fortress in the south of Judaea against the Romans until AD 73, were also led by a descendant of this Judas called Eleazar. This Eleazar was thus a relative of the leader of the Sicarii Menachem, who is described as being the son of Judas the Galilaean in *BJ* II 17, 8.

This Menachem and the priestly Zealots at Jerusalem had several bloody conflicts with each other. These conflicts were caused by the fact that, as can be seen from *BJ* II 17, 8f., Menachem made messianic claims for himself which the Zealots did not accept. After Menachem had made a royal progress into the Temple, the henchmen of the Temple governor Eleazar, son of Ananias, who had instigated the rejection of Caesar's sacrifice, were so incensed with Menachem that they attacked him in the Temple and killed him. After this incident the Sicarii apparently retired from Jerusalem and barricaded themselves in Herod's old fortress, Masada, where they succeeded in resisting the Romans until AD 73, three years after the fall of Jerusalem.

The Zealots, then, were a priestly-nationalistic party which, according to Josephus, did not become politically active till AD 66, at the outbreak of the war against Rome. Alongside of these groups there were several others, the most important of which was probably the one that had been founded by Judas the Galilaean in AD 6 and that remained under the leadership of his family until AD 73. All these groups were fired with an active zeal for vindicating the purity of the Holy Land against all foreign influences. Thus their passionate combativeness was directed, not solely against Rome, but even more against Jewish collaborators with Rome. The statement in Mishnah, Sanhedrin 9, 6 to the effect that the Zealots killed anyone who entered into marital relations with a pagan woman calls to mind the zeal of the priest Pinchas in Numbers xxv 7–13. This passage of the Mishnah deals explicitly with the priestly Zealots, as is clear from the context. It would seem to indicate that the Zealots existed even before the outbreak of the Jewish war against Rome in AD 66.

Thus, the Zealots, the Sicarii and the other insurrectionary groups all belonged to those elements of the Jewish population that drew political conclusions from the apocalyptic outlook. The ideological background for the anti-Roman insurrectionary parties was thus apocalypticism, not Pharisaism.

IV

A TASTE FOR THINGS GREEK

HELLENISM IN SYRIA AND PALESTINE

A. H. M. JONES

'Not setting-by the honours of their fathers, but liking the glory of the Grecians best of all.'

'SECOND BOOK OF MACCABEES'

Greek cultural supremacy
in Asia Minor had a long history, beginning with the founding of the Ionian cities on the east coast of the Aegean early in the 1st millennium. By the 6th century BC Greek colonies were established not only round the Anatolian seaboard, but as far away as Southern Russia, Sicily, Southern Italy, Southern France and Spain. There were very few Greek colonies in Cilicia and Syria, and cultural contacts were limited to a few places like Sidon.

This situation was transformed by Alexander's sudden destruction of the Persian Empire. Although politically divided after his death, the whole Eastern Mediterranean world now belonged culturally to Greece, and she made the most of it. Traders, soldiers and other immigrants flocked to the new areas. By the early years of the 1st century BC and with few exceptions (notably the Jews), they had largely succeeded in forging the whole area into a broad unity.

From the 2nd century BC onward, Rome began increasingly to impinge on the Greek world, and the wars of Sulla, Lucullus and Pompey successively subjected it to Roman hegemony. Nevertheless on the cultural plane Rome was herself the pupil of Greece and in many cases hastened the process of Hellenization, so that in the Roman period Greek civilization was even more dominant than before. This can be seen in the sphere of religion, of language, of thought and of the arts. The so-called 'Aleppo Mask' (opposite) is a parade helmet which belonged to the Samsigerami, a family of Hellenized Arabs ruling Emesa under Roman patronage in the 1st century AD. The face is definitely a portrait of the wearer, his Asiatic features distinguishing him sharply from the Greek type of face familiar from Hellenistic sculpture. But the artistic conventions – the very naturalism which enables us to recognize him – are entirely Greek. The helmet, which was probably used only for ceremonial purposes, though it is sturdy enough for battle, is made of iron covered with silver and in parts gilded. The face hinges upwards from the brow and is secured at the neck by a complicated arrangement of hooks and rings. (1)

Alexander's victories at the Issus and at Gaugamela brought the vast Persian Empire under his personal rule. The famous mosaic found at Pompeii is probably based on a lost painting; it is not certain which of the two battles is represented, but the contrast between the young Macedonian's fierce determination to conquer and Darius' distress and bewilderment is shown with superb economy and skill. Alexander saw himself as the ruler of a universal empire, combining the best elements of Greek and Persian civilization and maintained by an enlightened despotism. It was a prophetic foretaste of the Roman Empire, and, had Alexander died – as two of his generals, Ptolemy and Antigonus, did die – as an octogenarian, the history of the world might well have been different. As it was, most of his reign was occupied by laborious military expeditions. (5)

Before Alexander, under Persia's tolerant rule, the Greek cities of Cilicia were able to maintain much of the Greek way of life, and minted coins bearing their names in Greek. On the coin of Mallus (far left) Demeter holds a lighted torch and an ear of barley. That of Soli (centre) shows an owl and a bunch of grapes, symbol of Baal's close connection with agricultural fertility. The third coin, of Tarsus, has a girl playing knucklebones; to her left, a rose. (2, 3, 4)

After Alexander had died at the age of 33 it took nearly half a century of warfare for his successors to hammer out their respective spheres of influence. Eventually two dominant leaders emerged – Seleucus (right) ruling in Babylonia and Ptolemy (far right) in Egypt. Both, however, were Macedonians and both belonged to the same Hellenistic world. Alexander's dream of a union of peoples within one culture was thus in part achieved. (6, 7)

The Kings of Sidon, always noted Philhellenes and proud of Sidon's place in Greek mythology – Agenor, a mythical King of Sidon, was claimed as the founder of Thebes – employed Greek artists to carve their splendid sarcophagi, which reveal very clearly the growing Hellenization of Syria. The earliest phase, before the coming of the Greeks, is represented by the sarcophagus of King Tabuit (left), carved in black basalt and probably imported from Egypt. Dating from the late-6th century, this is in the common Egyptian anthropomorphic idiom, Phoenicia at this time being under Egyptian cultural domination. (8)

Greek artists were first employed on the late-5th century 'Satrap' sarcophagus (right), though the custom of burial must have seemed strange to them, since the Greeks burned their dead. Its chest-shaped form and the Archaic style of the sculpture betrays its early date. The Satrap is shown hunting, feasting and watching a chariot race. Beyond it (far right) is an example of a sarcophagus made to resemble a miniature temple. It is known as the 'Mourning Women' sarcophagus from the figures between the columns. The frieze on the top shows the funeral cortège of the occupant, King Abdastart I (374–362 BC) who took the Greek name of Strato. (10, 11)

Memories of the East still linger on the 'Lycian' sarcophagus (left), of the mid-4th century, so called from the fact that its lid, as high as the body of the sarcophagus and shaped like a Gothic barrel-vault, has the same form as the tombs often found in Lycia. The ends of the lid are guarded by sphinxes; the sides show mythological scenes. (9)

The 'Alexander' sarcophagus (right) marks the culmination of Greek influence. It dates from after Alexander's conquest, and some have seen in the frieze a representation of his victory over the Persians. Suffice to say that there is a central figure in Greek dress and distinguished by a diadem, in combat with figures in Persian dress. Another wearing Persian clothes appears no less than four times, always in close proximity to the central figure. He has been interpreted as the occupant of the tomb, probably Abdalonymus, one of Alexander's favourites. The far side of the sarcophagus shows a hunt staged in a Persian game reserve, whose original Persian name 'Paradeisos' survives in our 'Paradise'. (12)

By settlement and by trade more than by conquest Greek habits of mind and style of living were carried all over the Eastern Mediterranean. Above: a hunting scene with Greek inscription from a hypogeum at Marissa, in Idumaea, a Ptolemaic stronghold. It was probably built by Sesmaios, a Phoenician, for himself and his family in the 3rd century BC. His son Apollophanes (note his Greek name) who was for 33 years 'archon of the Sidonians of Marissa' and several members of his family were buried there. In later years it was a burial place for several families of the same ethnic background. (13)

From an Egyptian tomb in the Nile Delta come the Greek terracotta figurine and the clay vases (right), dating from the late-4th century BC. Vases were imported as much for their contents as for themselves. Some of those found in this tomb probably came from Greece, some from South Italy; but the forms and techniques were soon being copied so faithfully by local workmen that the products are often indistinguishable. The figurine may likewise have been made by a Greek craftsman working in Egypt. (14–16)

A mercenary soldier buried at Sidon was commemorated by this stele. He wears Greek *chitōn*, cuirass and crested helmet. (17)

'O Artemidorus, farewell!' This mummy-case (right) of a Greek settler in Egypt in the 2nd century AD is a vivid illustration of how Greek and oriental ideas came to be combined. (18)

ZEUS (19) BAAL (20)

HERAKLES (23) MELKART (24)

ARTEMIS (25)

Gods with similar characters and attributes were accepted as the same by both Greeks and their Semitic neighbours. On this page a few such relationships are illustrated in a simple iconographical way, but the examples differ widely in date and are not meant to show any stylistic connection.

Baal, literally 'lord' or 'master', was the name by which every Phoenician city called its own god. This soon merged with the Greek idea of Zeus, supreme 'lord of the sky'. (19, 20)

Reshef, god of lightning and light, became Apollo, who shot his arrows like rays and brought sudden death from afar, as did Reshef. (21, 22)

Melkart was the chief god of Tyre. Seen as the protector of men and personification of strength, he became identified with Herakles. (23, 24)

Tanit, goddess of crops and (sometimes) of the moon, found a natural equivalent in the Greek Artemis. On her stele she raises both hands, holding a *caduceus* and an ear of corn. (25, 26)

Astarte – or Ashtoreth – figures largely in the history of idolatry in ancient Israel. King Solomon built a sanctuary in her honour. Like Aphrodite she personified fertility and sexual love. (27, 28)

APOLLO (21)

RESHEF (22)

TANIT (26)

APHRODITE (27)

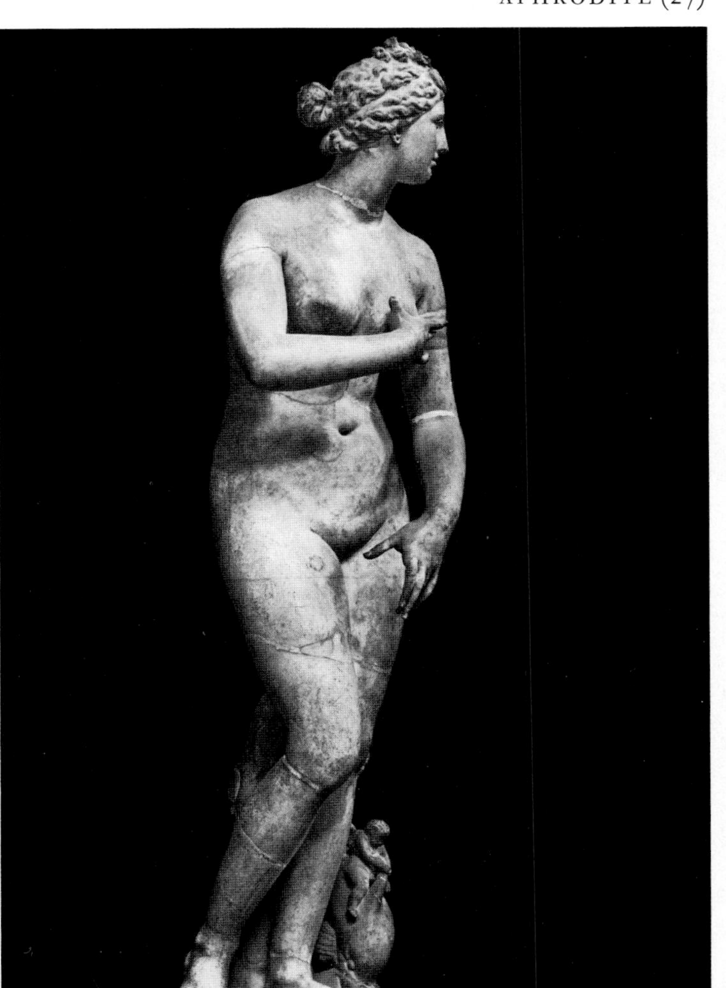

ASTARTE (28)

On the eastern fringe of the Mediterranean world, Greek cities reached out to the civilizations of Arabia, Parthia, India and even China, and were the channels by which eastern luxuries came to the West.

Amman, the ancient biblical city of Rabbath Ammon, was renamed Philadelphia by Ptolemy II Philadelphus (283–246 BC). Little excavation has been possible since, when archaeologists first started exploring the area, Amman was already rapidly growing into the capital of Jordan. We know, however, that the main street was partly laid upon vaults spanning the river bed and was embellished with porticos, public buildings and triumphal arches. The fine theatre seating 6000 on the side of the acropolis (left) is a solitary reminder of the former prosperity of the ancient city. (29)

Palmyra, the biblical Tadmor, was ideally situated for the Persian trade routes. However in early Hellenistic times, with most of Palestine in Ptolemaic hands, the Seleucids preferred a more northerly line, and Palmyra remained obscure. The period of her amazing expansion runs from the 1st century AD until the end of the 3rd century, when Queen Zenobia could challenge Aurelian's Rome. The ruins of Palmyra, the magnificent colonnaded streets and the strange asymmetrical Temple of Bel, have always exercised a peculiar fascination over those who have seen them. Less well known is the delightful and almost perfectly preserved Temple of Baal Samin, who in Roman times became Bel's rival (right). Overlooking it is the Turkish citadel. (31)

Gerasa was developed by Antiochus III or IV to draw the Arabian caravan trade generated by Petra away from Alexandria to the Phoenician ports of Tyre, Sidon and Ascalon. Its period of greatest prosperity was in the first two centuries AD. As one approached from the south, skirting a hill with a temple and a theatre, which had formed the acropolis of the Hellenistic city, one came first upon a pear-shaped forum (right) where the caravans unloaded and their attendants washed and dressed before going into the city proper. Proceeding further north along the colonnaded main street in which these cities prided themselves, one passed on one's left-hand side a monumental fountain, a temple to which the male consort of Artemis, all-powerful ruler of Gerasa, could withdraw, the Temple of Artemis herself, and another smaller theatre (left). Interspersed between these buildings were some fine two-storied shops. In the Early Christian period Gerasa enjoyed a modest revival (30, 32)

The two capitals of the Hellenistic world were Alexandria and Antioch. Alexandria was personified (above) as a beautiful but stern-looking goddess, wearing an elephant scalp and carrying a variety of symbols recalling her Greek and Egyptian origins: *uraeus*-snake (Egyptian royal power), she-panther (Dionysus), lion, club, bar and quiver (Herakles) and cornucopia (the flourishing wealth of Alexandria). Antioch was represented (below) seated on her river, the Orontes. In her right hand she holds a bunch of ears of corn, symbol of fertility. Founded by Seleucus I, the city was enlarged by his successors. (33, 34)

Palmyra was protected by her Tyche ('Fortune'), seated here also on her river with the lion of Atargatis (above). Palmyra's main street (right) has a sharp bend, necessitated by the location of the ancient Temple of Bel. To the left of the tetrapylon which disguised this bend is a caravanserai and a theatre; to the right, the Temple of Baal Samin. (35, 37)

The 'Gad' of Dura Europus, Zeus Baalshamin (above), watches over his city on the banks of the Euphrates (right). Dura was an important Roman frontier post after it was recaptured in AD 164 from the Parthians, to whom the Seleucids had eventually lost it. (36, 38)

Life in ancient Antioch is shown in fascinating detail round the edge of a large mosaic dating from the 5th century AD, where real buildings of the city are represented with their names. Right: in front of the 'Villa of Leontius' a servant, his status indicated by his short tunic, is carrying parcels. Next to him is the 'Public Bath', with a figure which may be an honorific statue of the donor. A man sells refreshments from a table outside 'The Covered Walk', a public place of recreation which affords, among other things, an opportunity for a game resembling checkers or dominoes. Far right: the first building is the 'workshops of the Martyrion' where souvenirs were made for pilgrims to the shrine of St Babylas. In front of it reclines Markellinos, the manager, accompanied by his dog, while his servant Chalkonas brings him refreshments. A group composed of a man and two women seems to pause to the left of 'The Olympic Stadium' which has a tower and a monumental entrance gate. Finally, beside the rider, there is a servant carrying a basket. (39, 40)

Birds of the Nile were never portrayed with such naturalism until Hellenistic art had become rooted in Egypt. From there these 'Nilotic' scenes spread back to other parts of the Near East and to Italy. This mosaic (right) is from the Church of the Loaves and Fishes, Tabge, Israel. (41)

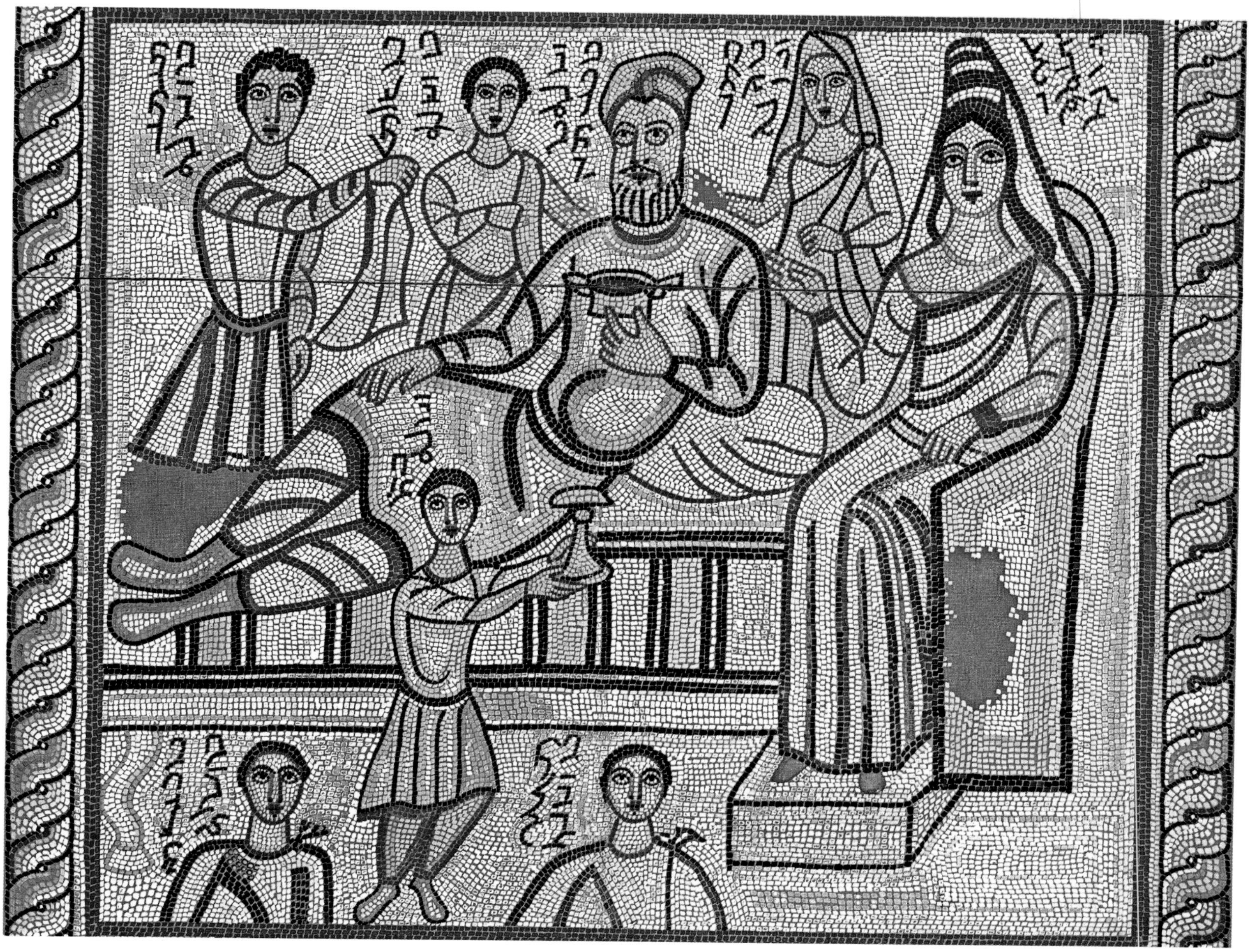

The first kingdom to adopt Christianity as the state religion was Edessa (modern Urfa), renowned for its worship of the still multitudinous sacred fish. The blending of Greek and oriental are plain in the 'Funerary Couch' mosaic (above), made in AD 227–8. The father and his sons wear the Greek *chitōn*, the wife and daughter a high Parthian head-dress. (42)

Superstition was rife in the Hellenistic age – the vulgar equivalent, in some ways, of the mystery cults which were simultaneously bringing oriental religion to the more sophisticated (see Chapter x). This mosaic (left) is a collection of good luck symbols – a hunchback, the magic eye, a raven, trident, sword, scorpion, serpent, dog, centipede and panther. The inscription reads, 'And you too.' (43)

'In the year 343 (AD 32) this stele was erected by Bar'atch ... to the god Baalshamin.' The inscription is carved in Palmyrene Aramaic and in Greek, the Greek version reading 'Zeus' for 'Baalshamin'. Another blending of East and West, an Aramaean god interpreted by Greek philosophy, eventually ruled in this part of the world until, and in some cases after, the advent of the Moslems. (44)

HELLENISM IN SYRIA AND PALESTINE

A. H. M. JONES

GREEK-SPEAKING peoples appear to have settled in the plain of Cilicia in the great migrations which followed the Trojan war. According to legends already known to Hesiod and Callinus, Mopsus, the son of Teiresias, and Amphilochus, the son of Amphiaraus, led their followers to Cilicia, and Mopsuestia and Mallus later claimed these heroes as their founders, while Soli boasted its 'Argive' or 'Achaean' origin; the Hellenism of Soli was later reinforced by Dorian colonists from Lindus in Rhodes. Not all of the Cilician cities were Greek in origin. Tarsus, despite later claims that it was founded by Perseus, Herakles or Triptolemus, was probably a native town, and Myriandus was a Phoenician colony. But the whole area seems to have been already Hellenized p 102 (2–4) in the days of the Persian Empire, when not only Mallus and Soli but also Tarsus and Issus issued coins inscribed in Greek.

There was an overspill from this migration into Northern Syria; Poseideïum, some twenty miles south of the mouth of the Orontes, was according to Herodotus a foundation of Amphilochus. But otherwise there is no reliable evidence of Greek settlement south *f 1* of the Amanus. Trade flourished between Greece and Syria in the second quarter of the 4th century BC. Phoenician merchants settled at Athens, and Athenian merchants in the Phoenician ports. Upper-class Phoenicians were attracted by Greek art. Abdastart, King of Sidon (known to the Greeks as Strato), imported Greek 104–5 (8–12) dancing and singing girls to enliven his guests, and the later kings of Sidon employed Greek artists to carve their splendid sarcophagi. 102–3 (5) But before Alexander's day contacts between Greece and Syria seem to have been superficial.

After Alexander's death Syria was disputed between Ptolemy, satrap of Egypt, and Antigonus, whose ambition it was to take Alexander's place. On Antigonus' fall in 301 BC, Ptolemy occupied p 103 (6, 7) Palestine and Phoenicia up to the river Eleutheros, and Seleucus, satrap of Babylon, occupied Northern Syria and Cilicia. Despite a number of wars, this partition remained substantially unaltered until in 198 BC Antiochus the Great, the great-great-grandson of Seleucus, defeated the generals of Ptolemy Epiphanes, the great-great-grandson of Ptolemy Soter, and annexed Phoenicia and Palestine.

Both the Ptolemies and the Seleucids, if they were to survive in their ruthless internecine struggles, needed Greek, and above all Macedonian, soldiers by the thousand. They could and did employ p 107 (17) mercenaries on a large scale, both as standing garrison troops and as temporary reinforcements in important campaigns, but they did *f 3* not wish to be completely dependent on the Greek mercenary market, from which they might be cut off, and mercenaries were not trustworthy in case of a major defeat. What the kings wanted to do was to create a home supply of Greeks and Macedonians, and this they did by settling soldiers – or any other Greeks whom they could persuade to emigrate – on the land. The settlers were sometimes organized in cities on the Greek model, sometimes planted in country-towns, sometimes scattered over the country-side. The Seleucids on the whole favoured the first two alternatives, the Ptolemies the last.

A home supply of Greeks

Egypt was the heart of the Ptolemaic kingdom, and Southern Syria a frontier province. It was therefore naturally in Egypt that the Ptolemies planted their Greek and Macedonian settlers. Half a dozen towns in Syria received Ptolemaic names, but of them only Ptolemais (the old Phoenician city of Ace) and Philadelphia (the chief town of the Ammonites, Rabbath Ammon) outlived the p 110 (29) Ptolemaic supremacy, and there is no evidence that the new names signified any change of substance. For the Seleucids, on the other hand, Northern Syria, with the adjacent areas of Cilicia and North-west Mesopotamia, was the nucleus of their far-flung empire, which extended westwards to the Aegean and eastwards to Bactria, and it was in this area that they concentrated their European settlers. Seleucus seems to have endeavoured to convert this area into a new Macedonia, renaming the Orontes the Axius, p 112 (34) the mountainous coastal strip Pieria, the rolling plains of the interior Chalcidice, Cyrrhestice, Anthemusias and Mygdonia. He named a dozen or more towns after Macedonian or more rarely Greek cities – Aegae in Cilicia, Apollonia, Arethusa, Beroea, Chalcis, Cyrrhus, Europus, Larisa and Pella in Syria, Amphipolis, Anthemus, Edessa, another Europus and Ichnae in Mesopotamia. p 115 (42) The places so named were often old native towns, but can be proved in many cases to have received substantial bodies of European settlers. Larisa contained, we are told, a group of Thessalians, appropriately to its name, and, at the Europus founded at Dura, p 112–3 (36, 38) parchments and inscriptions of the Roman period show that the leading families still proudly bore Macedonian names. In addition to these settlements, which were not juridically cities, Seleucus probably founded some ten cities, which usually bore dynastic names. These were mostly, so far as we know, new settlements on virgin sites, and were peopled with substantial bodies of European settlers. For his capital, Antioch, Seleucus made use of Mace- p 112 (34) donians and Athenians, numbering, according to a very late but not ill-informed authority, John Malalas, 5400, collected by p 114–5 (39, 40) Antigonus for the royal capital he was building in the same area. Apamea, the chief military base of the empire, was an expansion of the earlier Macedonian settlement of Pella, and Laodicea seems to have been a Macedonian town; the members of the city council bore the curious Macedonian title of 'Peliganes'. We do not know the origins of the population of Seleucia-in-Pieria, which numbered 6000 in 217 BC, but it may have come in part from a nearer source; the old Greek city of Poseideïum, twenty miles away, was in 246 BC a mere fort. It is also suspicious that two old cities about ten miles to the north and west of Alexandria, Issus and Myriandus, disappear from the map.

The cities then would seem to have numbered 5–6000 adult males each. The towns with Macedonian names were probably much smaller, perhaps 1000 each, the strength of a regiment. The total number of new settlers could hardly have been less than 50,000 adult males. We have no means of telling how many of these brought their wives and children with them. We know that many of Alexander's Macedonians married Asiatic wives and were indeed encouraged by him to do so, *f 3* but many of the Ptolemaic soldiers were married to Greek women, and it seems unlikely that Athens would have sent a contingent of settlers who were all bachelors.

Even if the European settlers, men, women and children, in North Syria and North-west Mesopotamia numbered a quarter of a million, which seems unlikely, they can hardly have amounted to ten per cent or even eight per cent of the native population, which is likely to have exceeded the present figure of about 3½ millions. Some immigration no doubt continued after the initial settlement *f 1* by Seleucus Nicator, but on a diminishing scale, and with the defeat of Antiochus the Great by the Romans in 190 BC it must have ceased altogether. Antiochus gave a home to refugees from the Aetolians and Euboeans, who had taken his side when he invaded Greece, and to Cretans, no doubt mercenaries hired for his western campaigns, peopling with them a new quarter of Antioch which Seleucus Callinicus had begun on the island and which he completed. By the Treaty of Apamea (188 BC) he was forbidden henceforth to raise mercenaries or to receive deserters from west of the Taurus.

In the south there were few, if any, European settlers. The only recorded settlements – and they are mentioned only by late authorities of dubious value – were made before the Ptolemaic occupation by Alexander himself, whose general Perdiccas had to suppress a rebellion of Samaritans and, it would appear, of the people of Gilead across the Jordan. To him are attributed settle-
p 110–1 ments of Macedonian veterans at Samaria and at Gerasa and
(30, 32) perhaps Dium and Abila, and at the city that, in the Roman age, came to be called Capitolias. Apart from these, the only Greeks in the Ptolemaic zone would have been the mercenary garrisons established at key points and the officials who administered the interior of the country. On the coastal plain the Ptolemies practised 'indirect rule', allowing the Phoenician and Philistine cities to govern themselves, though they apparently farmed the taxes at Alexandria. In the interior they applied the same system of centralized bureaucratic rule which prevailed in Egypt. The general outline can be reconstructed from the records of the Seleucid, Hasmonaean and Herodian kingdoms, under which it survived with minor modifications. The area appears to have been divided into a series of large circumscriptions known as 'hyparchies' or *merides*, which were subdivided into 'nomes' or 'toparchies', which consisted of a group of villages. The 'toparchies' were quite small areas and correspondingly numerous. Over twenty can be traced in the
p 106–7 belt of fertile country stretching from Galilee to Idumaea between
(13) the coastal plain and the larger toparchies of Gaulanitis, Galaaditis, Ammonitis and Essebonitis. The village officials were doubtless, as in Egypt, natives, but those of the *merides* would have been predominantly Greek.

In the north, Macedonians and Greeks were much thicker on the ground, but they were perhaps more segregated from the natives. The citizens of the cities and the military settlers of the towns owned allotments of land, but they were absentee landlords, residing in the towns and letting their lots to native tenants. In the towns there was more mixture of population. Many of the settlements, whether cities or military colonies, were planted in existing native towns, and when they were built on open sites natives were compelled or encouraged to move into them to provide the artisans and shopkeepers needed to supply the citizens' needs. At Antioch itself the first quarter to be built, by Seleucus Nicator himself, accommodated the Macedonians and Athenians moved from Antigoneia. The third quarter was built by Seleucus Callinicus and Antiochus the Great for the Aetolians, Euboeans and Cretans. The second quarter, which boasted no royal founder, was, it may be conjectured, the native quarter. Antiochus Epiphanes added the fourth, which must have been also peopled with miscellaneous immigrants, including natives.

Trade was one of the instruments of the Hellenization of Syria. This merchant ship comes from a 6th-century BC black-figure cup. (1)

Greek and the vernacular

Some minimal contact there had to be between Greek landlords and officials and the Syrian peasantry whom they employed and administered. In the south a number of enterprising peasants must have learned enough Greek to serve as village officials, law court interpreters, and writers of letters and petitions; for the administrative language was Greek, and Greek officials did not bother to learn foreign languages. This at any rate was the pattern in Egypt, where circumstances were similar. In the north the administration

The linguistic cleavage between the Greek-speaking upper class and the Syriac-speaking peasantry and urban proletariat persisted throughout Hellenistic, Roman and Byzantine times. Syriac has, it is true, left scarcely a trace in Hellenistic and Roman times. It ceased to be a written language save on the extreme fringes of
Syria, at Edessa across the Euphrates, and Palmyra in the depths p 115
of the Syrian desert, and in the Nabataean Kingdom of Petra. All (42)
the surviving written records are in Greek, and it is only from p 116
scattered hints that the survival of Semitic languages can be in- (44)
ferred. f2 Even in the remote villages of Trachonitis and Auranitis the humblest tombstones are in Greek; one inscription reveals that the Roman procurators employed interpreters. The coins and inscriptions of Samosata are all in Greek; but Lucian, its most famous citizen, admits that as a boy – he was of humble origins, apprenticed to a monumental mason – he knew Syriac only.

was looser-knit; the Seleucids seem everywhere to have practised 'indirect rule'. But relations may have been closer between the landlord and his tenants, and between the householder and the shopkeepers with whom he dealt.

With the advent of Christianity we begin to learn more of the common people, and the true state of affairs is revealed. The peasants are all Syriac-speaking. In the mid-4th century AD a certain Publius, a wealthy decurion of Zeugma (Seleucia-on-the-Bridge), founded a monastery in the desert. The first monks were Greek-speaking, but

> the love of this way of life also seized upon those who used the native language, and some of them collected and begged to become members of his flock, and share in his holy teaching. He accepted their request, remembering the Lord's command which he gave to the holy Apostles, saying, 'Go, teach all nations.' And he built another lodging beside the first one and told them to live there. He also built a church in which both groups united morning and evening, so that they could sing matins and vespers together to God, sitting separately and each using his own language.

Between Antioch and Beroea, Theodoret visited a similar double monastery, where 'some hymned their Creator in Greek, and others in the native language'. In AD 387 John Chrysostom urged his urban congregation at Antioch to welcome the peasants who flocked into Antioch on Passion Sunday, 'a people different from us in speech, but agreeing with us in faith'. In the same year the hermit Macedonius (commonly known in Syriac as Guba) tramped into Antioch to intercede for the city with the two Imperial commissioners sent by Theodosius to report on the riot in which his statues had been insulted; 'this he said using the Syriac language, and the interpreter translated it into Greek'.

A contemporary of Macedonius was Maesymas, from the territory of Cyrrhus, 'a Syrian by speech, bred in the country'. In AD 451 Daniel, born in the village of Marathas near Samosata, walked all the way to Constantinople, where he walled himself into a ruined and demon-ridden church in a suburb on the Asiatic side. The local clergy were suspicious and complained to the archbishop: 'Some man, we don't know from where, has walled himself in near us and is attracting people to him, although he is a heretic. He is a Syrian by origin, and so we can't talk to him.' The archbishop tartly replied: 'If you do not understand his language, how do you know that he is a heretic?' and subsequently tested his orthodoxy through an interpreter. In Cilicia, on the other hand, Greek was the language of the people. When Theodoret visited a hermit near Gabala in Northern Phoenicia, he took him for a Syrian (his name was Thalelaeus): 'and he answered in Greek, for he was a Cilician'.

In the towns too the lower classes spoke Syriac, though many no doubt were bilingual or had a smattering of Greek. At Tyre in the

In Hellenistic times Syriac ceased to be a written language except in Petra, Edessa and Palmyra. Aqmat was the wife of one of the prosperous merchants of Palmyra, and the inscription on her tombstone is in Aramaic. (2)

early-4th century AD there lived a philosopher called Meropius with two boys who were related to him – perhaps poor relations – and whom he was educating; the ecclesiastical historian Socrates thinks it worthy of note that they were 'not ignorant of the Greek language'. At Gaza, at that time a celebrated centre of Greek literary studies, the bishop Porphyry had in AD 402 obtained an Imperial order to demolish the principal pagan temple, the Marneum, but it was so solidly built that he was unable to perform the operation. A child told him how to set about it, first in Syriac and then in Greek. The miraculous nature of this intervention became manifest when it was proved that neither he nor his mother knew any Greek. In the cities of Palestine the services were conducted in Greek, but there was a special reader to translate them into Syriac. Procopius, the first martyr of the Diocletianic persecution, held this office at Scythopolis. A western pilgrim who visited Jerusalem in the 4th century AD explains the reason for the practice.

> Since in that province part of the people know both Greek and Syriac, another part Greek by itself, another part Syriac only, so since the bishop – though he may know Syriac – nevertheless always speaks in Greek and never in Syriac, there is always a priest who translates into Syriac as the bishop speaks in Greek.

Social climbers

The Hellenization of the indigenous upper classes was remarkably thorough-going in the three centuries that followed Alexander's conquest. We have only scattered hints of how and why the transformation took place, but by the time of Christ it was complete. There were materialistic motives for which upper-class Syrians and Phoenicians might wish to Hellenize themselves. The king was a Macedonian, his court Macedonian and Greek, and the higher offices of state both at the capital and in the provinces were usually held by Greeks or Macedonians. Greek-speakers, in fact, formed the administrative and social aristocracy. If a native wanted to rise in the world he must first learn the Greek language, and in the second place make himself acceptable to Greek society, which
108–9 meant wearing Greek clothes, adopting Greek table-manners,
9–28) worshipping Greek gods, practising athletic exercises in the nude – a thing deeply distasteful to most orientals – knowing enough Greek poetry to recognize or cap a verse from Homer or Euripides, and finally adopting a Greek name. This was no doubt difficult for the first generation, but many ambitious fathers would send their sons to Greek schools and get them into a Greek sporting-club or gymnasium.

More important perhaps than the materialistic motives was the spontaneous admiration felt for Greek civilization. This was natural, for the Greeks had been supremely successful. A Greek king with a tiny Greek army – orientals did not distinguish between p 102–3
Greeks and Macedonians – had in a few months overthrown the (5)
Great King and his empire, which had endured for two centuries, *f 3*
vast, enormously wealthy, and, despite occasional revolts, invincible. Orientals seem to have taken to heart the contempt evinced by Greeks for barbarians, and resolved to shed their barbarian inferiority by imitating their new masters.

On the Greek side they met with encouragement. The Greeks, it is true, regarded themselves as a master race, and barbarians as inferior beings, but they had no colour bar – and Syrians were not noticeably different in physical type from Greeks – and were quite ready to accept a barbarian intelligent enough to adopt Greek ways; they had none of the Englishman's contempt and dislike of the Europeanized oriental – the 'effendi' or the 'babu'. The Greeks felt no objection to marrying orientals, and seem to have done so freely. In the new cities like Antioch, it is true, this was probably not permitted by law. These cities no doubt, like Alexandria in p 112
Egypt, observed the Athenian rule that a citizen must be of (33)
citizen birth on both sides. But the mixture of Greek and oriental names in the best families of Europus suggests that in the military p 112–3
settlements no such ban existed and that intermarriage was (36, 38)
common; it certainly was so in Egypt, where the papyri provide a number of concrete examples.

Religion was no bar. The Greek immigrants naturally worshipped their own gods and built temples to them. But they acknowledged and venerated the gods of the country. Since the days of Herodotus, moreover, they had identified foreign gods with their own. In Astarte they saw their own Aphrodite, in Tanit p 108–9
their Artemis, Shems was obviously Helios, the Baal who flung (19–28)
thunderbolts was Zeus under another name, Reshef was Apollo, and Melkart of Tyre was their own Herakles. It is difficult to know whether the syncretism of Greek and Semitic religion was more than superficial – the precise blend no doubt varied according to each worshipper. By the Roman period the forms of worship had for the most part been Hellenized, and the native gods were represented by Greek statues, were housed in Greek temples, received sacrifices according to Greek forms, and were honoured in Greek fashion by athletic and musical competitions. As early as 175 BC the Tyrians were celebrating quadrennial games in honour of Herakles, as they now preferred to call Melkart. Many ancient cults continued, the mourning for Adonis at Byblos, the ritual prostitution at Apheca and Heliopolis, the veneration of sacred p 244–5
fish at Hierapolis and the worship of meteoric stones at Emesa and (22)
Doliche (still called by its Syriac name Elagabal at Emesa, but p 244
Hellenized into Zeus Kataibates – Zeus who came down from (20, 21)
heaven – at Doliche). But some of the cults, notably that of Adonis, were adopted into Greek religion – and they were no odder than many indigenous Greek rituals.

Aping the conqueror

Hellenization seems to have begun earliest in the Phoenician cities of the coastal plain where, it may be remarked, there were no Greek settlers and contact with the Greeks was limited to a garrison here and there, a few officials and tax-collectors, and merchants and tourists. In the early-3rd century BC the city of Sidon honoured one of its 'judges' ('sufetes'), Diotimus son of Dionysius, with a statue executed by the Cretan artist Timocharis of Eleuthernae, for the victory of his chariot at the Nemean games, and inscribed the base with the following verses:

> When all the noblest drove their chariots on the courses of Argos with rivalry of charioteers, fair was thy fame, Diotimus, from the land of Phoroneus [an obscure Argive hero], and crowns ever to be remembered were placed on thy head. For the first of our citizens thou didst bring the glory of horses from Hellas to the good home of the sons of Agenor [a mythical king

> of Sidon, father of Europa and Cadmus, the founder of Thebes]. The holy city of Cadmeian Thebes boasts also when she sees her mother-city [Sidon] glorious with victories, and Hellas will offer sacrifice to thy father Dionysius, when she has uttered this loud cry; 'Thou dost not only boast thyself in curved ships but winnest the prize with yoked horses also.'

The citizens of Sidon were not only proud of winning a victory in one of the old games of Greece, but dwell lovingly on their place in Greek mythology and their kinship with the Greek city of Thebes.

It is at Sidon too that we find the earliest examples of the adoption of Greek names by natives. Even before Alexander, King p 105 (11) Abdastart was known at Athens as Strato. Here the Greek name was chosen for its superficial resemblance in sound. More often the Greek name was a translation of a native name. From bilingual inscriptions at Athens we know of an Abdtanit and an Abdshems (slave of Tanit, Shems) who became Artemidorus and Heliodorus respectively, and a Samabaal ('he who obeys Baal') who became, very literally, Diopeithes. The name of the early-3rd-century BC 'sufete', Diotimus, is probably a translation of a Semitic name compounded with Baal. Other Sidonians took common Greek names, often those of kings; thus Shem became Antipater.

By the early-2nd century BC the movement was penetrating the more backward interior. We have in the Second Book of Maccabees a vivid picture of the progressive party among the Jews introducing Greek athletics and founding a sporting-club. In the reign of Antiochus Epiphanes, the high priest Jason

> built gladly a place of exercise under the Tower itself, and brought the chief young men under his subjection, and made them wear a hat. Now such was the height of Greek fashions and increase of heathenish manners, through the exceeding profaneness of Jason, that ungodly wretch and no high priest, that the priests had no courage to serve any more at the altar but, despising the temple and neglecting the sacrifices, hastened to be partakers of the unlawful allowance in the place of exercise, after the game of discus called them forth: not setting-by the honours of their fathers, but liking the glory of the Grecians best of all.

Here too it may be observed that the Hellenizing Jews use Greek names. Jason the high priest was really Jesus; one of his successors Eliakin preferred to be known as Alcimus. These names are, like Strato, chosen for phonetic resemblance. Another, Onias, called himself Menelaus: this Homeric name had perhaps been popularized because Ptolemy Soter's brother was called Menelaus.

Distinguished sons

A number of orientals so imbued themselves with Greek culture that they achieved fame in the Hellenistic world as poets or philosophers. Cilicians were naturally first in the field, since, though they had long been isolated from the Greek world and spoke bad Greek – according to one derivation 'solecism' takes its name from Cilician Soli – they did at least speak Greek by nature. Already in the 3rd century BC two citizens of Soli won academic distinction – Chrysippus as a philosopher, the third head of the Stoa at Athens, and Aratus as a poet, patronized by Antigonus Gonatas, King of Macedon, and by Antiochus I, the son of Seleucus Nicator, and remembered for his surviving didactic epic on astronomy, the *Phenomena*. Chrysippus was succeeded as head p 206 (5) of the Stoa by another Cilician, Zeno of Tarsus, and in the middle of the 2nd century BC another Tarsian, Antipater, held this same post. Crates of Mallus, a distinguished grammarian and literary critic, became head of the Museum at Pergamum under Eumenes II (197–160 BC) and Attalus II (160–139 BC) and visited Rome in 169 BC. At the end of the 1st century BC, Strabo gives a glowing account of the intellectual life of Tarsus.

> There is such an enthusiasm for philosophy among the people here, and for all other university studies, that it excels Athens and Alexandria, and any other place you can mention in which there are philosophical and literary lectures and classes. Tarsus is exceptional in that the students are all local: foreigners do not readily reside there. Not that the Tarsians stay in Tarsus; they travel abroad to finish their education and, having finished it, gladly live abroad, and few come back. The opposite is true of the other cities mentioned, except Alexandria. Large numbers of students go there and they like residing there, but you do not see many of the local people either going abroad for their education or studying on the spot. Both things happen at Alexandria. They receive many foreigners and send out not a few of their own people. At Tarsus they have all kinds of classes in the liberal arts, and in general it is a populous and powerful city, with the title of *metropolis*. Among its citizens are the Stoics Antipater and Archidamus and Nestor, and in addition the two Athenodoruses, one called Cordylion, who lived with Marcus Cato and died by his side [46 BC], the other the son of Sando, sometimes called Cananites from some village, who was Augustus' teacher and received great honour. He returned to his native city when an old man, and overthrew the existing constitution, which was in a corrupt state owing to Boethus amongst others, a bad poet and a bad citizen, who gained power by demagogic measures for the most part. The causes of his success were originally Anthony, who received from him an epic poem on the victory of Philippi, and still more his facility, fashionable among the Tarsians, for speaking impromptu at length on a proposed theme. Anthony promised to be president of the gymnasium at Tarsus and appointed Boethus as his deputy and entrusted the expenditure to him. He was caught peculating the oil amongst other things. And when he was convicted by his accusers before Anthony he appeased his anger by saying, amongst other things, 'As Homer hymned Achilles and Agamemnon and Odysseus, I hymned you. It is not right that I should be slandered before you like this.' His accusers took up his words: 'Homer did not steal oil from Agamemnon or Achilles, but you did, and you will be punished.' But he diverted Anthony's anger by flattery and went on plundering the city none the less until Antony's fall [31 BC]. Athenodorus found the city in this condition, and for a while he tried to remove Boethus and his partners by argument, but, when they committed every conceivable outrage, he made use of the authority given him by Augustus and expelled them, condemning them to exile. At first they chalked up slogans on the walls like this: 'Work from the young, counsel from the middle-aged, farting from old men.' He received this in a humorous way, ordering 'Thunders from old men' to be chalked up alongside. . . . These are the Stoics. The Academic [member of the Platonic School] in our day was Nestor, the tutor of Marcellus, the son of Octavia the sister of Augustus [*ob.* 23 BC]. He too was a leading statesman, succeeding Athenodorus, and continued to be honoured by the Roman governors [of Syria] and in the city. Of the other philosophers 'whom I know well and would relate their fame' there were Plutiades and Diogenes [an Epicurean], who went on lecture tours. Diogenes also composed poems, as if inspired, on any topic proposed, tragic for the most part. The grammarians who have left published work are Artemidorus and Diodorus, and their best known tragedian was Dionysiades, one of the celebrated 'Pleiad' [*i.e.* the seven best tragic poets]. But Rome affords the best proof of the number of literary men who came from Tarsus; it is full of Tarsians and Alexandrians.

This account gives a vivid picture of Tarsus in the days of Paul's father and grandfather, a very Greek city in culture and in politics too. It is notable how many Tarsians were intimate with the great Romans of the day – Cato, Antony, Augustus and his presumptive heir Marcellus.

The tradition takes root

The Phoenician cities, though to their inhabitants Greek was at first a foreign language, did not linger far behind. We hear of Boethus of Sidon, a somewhat unorthodox Stoic who flourished at Athens in the middle of the 2nd century BC, and a little later of Menelaus of Marathus near Aradus, who was a teacher of rhetoric; he went to Rome and became intimate with Gaius Gracchus (tribune of the plebs in 123 and 122 BC), whose speeches he was alleged to have written. About the same time, Sidon produced the

The widespread settlement of solider colonists did much to Hellenize Syria. This late-4th-century BC tomb shows a young officer, almost certainly Macedonian: his servant holds the tail of the horse in the usual oriental fashion. (3)

poet Antipater, seventy-five of whose epigrams survive in the Palatine Anthology. He too went to Rome and was acquainted with Lutatius Catulus, who later became consul in 102 BC. In the 1st century BC Antiochus of Ascalon became head of the Academy at Athens, where Cicero studied under him for six months in 79 BC; he was an eclectic who combined Platonism with Stoicism and formed Cicero's philosophical thought; he also taught Brutus. Another Phoenician philosopher was Antipater of Tyre, who taught Stoicism to young Cato at Rome, and later moved to Athens, where he died about 45 BC. Tyre produced another Stoic, Apollonius, who wrote biographies of the early Stoics. Rather later, another Boethus of Sidon, a Peripatetic philosopher, taught at Athens under Augustus and probably became head of the school; Strabo studied under him and his brother Diodotus.

One inland town achieved extraordinary literary fame, Gadara. It later proudly claimed to be the birthplace of four eminent literary and philosophical figures; Menippus, Meleager, Philodemus and Theodore. Menippus the satirist lived in the early-3rd century BC, but as he was enslaved, probably in boyhood, and sold in the Greek city of Sinope on the Black Sea, he may well have learned his Greek there. Meleager was a poet of the late-2nd century BC and editor of the 'Garland', the first anthology of epigrams which forms the nucleus of the surviving Greek Anthology: in it some 130 of his epigrams survive. He also wrote Menippean satires which are lost. He spent most of his adult life in Tyre and later in Cos. Philodemus was an Epicurean philosopher, who, like so many Syrians, migrated to Rome, where he became tutor to Lucius Calpurnius Piso, later consul in 58 BC. Many of his works survive in the charred papyrus rolls of Herculaneum, where he owned a large villa. He was also a poet, and some of his epigrams survive. Finally Theodore was a teacher of rhetoric who was tutor to the Emperor Tiberius, and wrote a number of influential works, founding a Theodorian school of rhetoric.

The Greek colonies of Syria were surprisingly unproductive of literary men. Antioch could boast of the poet Archias, who wrote epics on Gaius Marius' defeat of the Cimbri and Teutones and on Lucius Licinius Lucullus' victories over Mithradates. He became p 126 (4) a citizen of Heraclea in Italy and consequently a Roman citizen in 89 BC, taking the name of Aulus Licinius Archias from Lucullus. His citizenship was challenged in 62 BC and was successfully defended by Cicero, who hoped he might write an epic on the Catilinarian conspiracy. Apamea produced the great polymath, philosopher, historian and geographer Poseidonius, who profoundly influenced Cicero's generation. He spent his active adult life at Rhodes.

The general impression which one gains is that many cities of Syria provided education up to undergraduate level in Greek literature, rhetoric and philosophy, but that for what would now be called postgraduate studies most Syrians went to some famous centre of learning in Greece like Athens. They rarely returned. The intellectual atmosphere of Syria was no doubt rather provincial, and Athens, Rhodes, Pergamum or Rome afforded a more appreciative audience and greater opportunities for wealth and fame.

Free cities

Hellenization had inevitably its political repercussions. A Phoenician or a Syrian could not be brought up on the Greek poets, orators and philosophers without coming to realize that a free man could lead a good life only as the citizen of an autonomous city, preferably democratic. The Seleucid colonies of the north had from the beginning normal Greek constitutions, with magistrates (mentioned in the middle of the 3rd century BC at Seleucia and Antioch and in 175 BC at Laodicea), councils and popular assemblies: the citizens were divided in Greek fashion into tribes and demes (recorded at Seleucia in 186 BC). Though there was a royal resident in each, their councils and assemblies could, with his concurrence, pass decrees: we possess a decree of the council of Laodicea of 175 BC and of the assembly at Seleucia in 186 BC. The council at Antioch and in many Syrian cities numbered 600, a figure probably taken over from Athens, whose council of 500 was augmented to 600 under Antigonus. He imported Athenian colonists to Syria to found Antigoneia, the precursor of Antioch; and it may be inferred that the constitution was a democracy on the Athenian model.

The Phoenician cities had under the Persians been ruled by the four kings of Arad, Byblos, Tyre and Sidon, each of whom governed a group of towns; their dominions covered the whole coastal plain from Laodicea to Gaza (both exclusive). The dynasties of Sidon, Tyre and Arad came to an end in 278, 274 and 259 BC respectively, and the cities which they had ruled became republics governed by 'judges'. Tyre and Sidon henceforth date their documents according to the 'year of the people' instead of by the regnal year. Arad and her former dependencies Marathus, Simyra and Carne soon began to issue coins using as their era the year 259 BC.

The movement seems to have received a marked impetus in the reign of Antiochus IV Epiphanes (175–163 BC). A large number of cities, both royal colonies like Antioch, Seleucia, Apamea, Laodicea, Alexandria-ad-Issum, Edessa (Antioch-on-the-Callirhoe) and Aegae, and native towns, began to issue coins, evidently with full royal approval, since they bear the King's head and superscription on one side and the city's name and emblem on the other. The native towns include the leading Phoenician cities, Arad, Tyre, Sidon, Byblos, Tripolis, Ptolemais (renamed Antioch-in-Ptolemais), Berytus (Laodicea-in-Phoenice) and Ascalon; four Cilician cities, Tarsus (Antioch-on-the-Cydnus), Adana (Antioch-on-the-Sarus), Mopsuestia (Seleucia-on-the-Pyramus) and Castabala (Hierapolis-on-the-Pyramus); also one inland town in Syria, the holy city of Bambyce (Hierapolis) and another in Mesopotamia, Nisibis (Antioch-in-Mygdonia). The dynastic names indicate royal favour and patronage. Some of them, that of Tarsus for instance, are much older than Epiphanes' reign, but many appear to date from his time. Other cities which did not issue coins received dynastic names, which probably mark the grant of autonomous status on the Greek model; Hamath in Syria, Oeniandus in Cilicia and the town facing Urima across the Euphrates in Mesopotamia were called Epiphaneia and thus must have received their privileges from Antiochus IV; and Urima (Antioch) is likely to be contemporary. Other dynastic titles known from literary and epigraphic sources are Antioch-on-the-Pyramus (Mallus) in Cilicia, Seleucia (Gaza) and, in inland Southern Syria, Nysa (Bethshean, Scythopolis), Antioch-on-the-Chrysorrhoas (Gerasa), Antioch-by-Hippos (Susitha), Seleucia (Abila), another Seleucia in Gaulanitis, Gadara (both Antioch and Seleucia) and Jerusalem (Antioch).

The last case is the only one of which we know the inner history, thanks to the Books of Maccabees. It is evident that the initiative came from below, from the Hellenizing party among the Jews, who obtained a royal licence to establish a gymnasium and to be registered as Antiocheans. Antiochus Epiphanes' part was limited to giving his gracious assent and pocketing a substantial fee, 150 talents. One may suspect that the whole Hellenizing movement was not so much royal policy as a spontaneous movement, wisely patronized by the king to win popularity and to help fill his perennially empty treasury.

The end of the Seleucids

The wars between rival claimants for the Seleucid throne which set in after Epiphanes' death and became endemic weakened the royal power and gave their opportunity to aspiring local dynasts, like the high priests of the Jews and of the Ituraeans, Zeno Tyrant
p 101 (1) of Philadelphia, Samsigeramus priest of Emesa and many other minor figures. The weakness of the royal power also gave an opportunity to the cities to achieve their final goal of freedom, full sovereign independence. Tyre seems to have been first in the field, obtaining its charter in 126 BC. It was followed by Sidon in 111 BC, Seleucia-in-Pieria in 108 and Ascalon in 104.

Not all the cities mentioned maintained their freedom in the troubled period in which the Seleucid monarchy finally dissolved. In the south a large number were conquered by the Hasmonaean p 50 (4, 5, 9) high priests and kings, particularly by Alexander Jannaeus. Elsewhere many fell to local tyrants and dynasts: Pompey seems to have recognized the freedom only of Seleucia-in-Pieria, Tyre, Sidon p 12 and Ascalon. But if he was chary of allowing cities to be fully independent, he encouraged local autonomy, deposing and executing a number of tyrants and freeing many cities from Jewish rule and restoring those which had been destroyed. The coastal plain of Palestine was thus reconstituted as a string of cities, and in the interior he appears to have sponsored and organized a league of ten cities, the Decapolis, which included Scythopolis and the neighbouring towns across the Jordan in Ammanitis and Galaaditis, Auranitis and Gaulanitis, from Philadelphia in the south to Hippos in the north-west and Canatha in the north-east.

Not only did the cities aspire to the constitutional status of Greek cities and to the freedom that was their birthright; they strove where they could to discover or invent a Greek origin for themselves. Sidon, which was lucky enough to have a place in Greek mythology, proudly boasted its kinship with Thebes. Other cities, less lucky, had to invent Greek origins for themselves. The Tarsians, no doubt jealous of Mallus and Mopsuestia, which boasted of Amphilochus and Mopsus, claimed that Herakles or alternatively Perseus or Triptolemus had in the course of their wanderings founded the city. The legend of Perseus and Andromeda was localized at Joppa before Alexander's day, and the pagan Joppans before the city was Judaized treasured the story. We do not know why the Ptolemies called Bethshean Scythopolis, but the Scythopolitans later explained their curious name by the story that Thoas, the king of the Scythians, had sent a party of his subjects to pursue Iphigenia and Orestes and that, having got as far as Palestine, they gave up the chase and settled at Scythopolis. Like individuals, cities also Hellenized their names in various ways. Temple towns like Castabala and Bambyce dropped their barbaric names, calling themselves simply the 'Holy City' (Hierapolis or Hieropolis). Tripolis is presumably a translation of a Phoenician name meaning the Three Cities – it was a joint foundation of Tyre, Sidon and Arad. A curious case is Apollonia on the Palestinian coast. The modern village is called Arsuf, and Reshef was a p 10 Phoenician god equated by the Greeks with Apollo. The name (22) Apollonia is apparently a translation of a Phoenician name derived from Reshef. In other cases phonetic resemblance was exploited. Pella is the name of a famous Macedonian town, and it might be inferred that the city of the Decapolis so called was a Macedonian foundation. But the town is recorded in Egyptian inscriptions with the hieroglyphic signs representing PHR (for PHL, R being regularly substituted in foreign words for an L, a sound which did not exist in Egyptian) and the modern village is called Fahl. It would seem that a Semitic town called PHL tendentiously spelt its name Pella to suggest a Macedonian origin.

It is probable that already in the 2nd century BC Hellenized Syrians and Phoenicians thought of themselves as Greeks. Their neighbours the Jews, who resisted Hellenization, certainly called them Hellenes. When the author of the Second Book of Maccabees, who wrote in the late-2nd or early-1st century BC, speaks of a royal ordinance being sent by the King Antiochus Epiphanes 'to the neighbouring Greek cities', he must mean the cities on the coastal plain of Palestine and east of Jordan, where the population was still purely Semitic by blood.

V

THE EMPIRE OF ROME

THE ROMAN GOVERNMENT
AND THE CHRISTIAN CHURCH

A. NICHOLAS SHERWIN-WHITE

'In those days righteousness flourished and there reigned the fullness of peace which began at His birth. For God had prepared the peoples for His teaching by causing them all to be united under the power of the one Roman Emperor.'

ORIGEN 'CONTRA CELSUM II'

The Roman peace

established by Augustus and maintained by his successors made a political unity of what was practically the whole of the known world. Without this unity, this ease of communication and cultural interpenetration, Christianity could never have spread beyond the narrow Jewish circles that gave it birth.

In the process, the new Church became coloured by some of the traditional Roman values, until by the time of Constantine the idea of a state religion (barely conceivable for the early Christians) could seem natural and even inevitable. VIRTUS, HONOR and IMPERIUM would acquire new meanings, but their old ones would not be altogether forgotten. Constantine and his contemporaries certainly saw the Christian Church as inheriting the legacy of Rome's classical past, and many of the chapters in this book will show that they saw truly.

All this is well caught in the noble fresco of the 'Barberini Roma', dating from the time of Constantine. It used to adorn the Lateran, which was built originally in the time of Nero to serve as the palace of Plautius Lateranus, was restored and extended under Septimius Severus, passed into the Emperors' hands and was given by Constantine in AD 313 to Pope Melchiades to be the papal residence. Although it has been somewhat restored since Constantine's time (the face especially), it still conveys its essential message with its original power. The Goddess Roma is shown as a robust Amazon-like figure, seated on a decorated throne, wearing rich clothes and with a fine helmet on her head, the sceptre in her left hand, and a Victory in the palm of her right hand. The fresco may have formed part of a group which included Constantine and his sons. (1)

VIRTVS · HONOR · IMPERIV

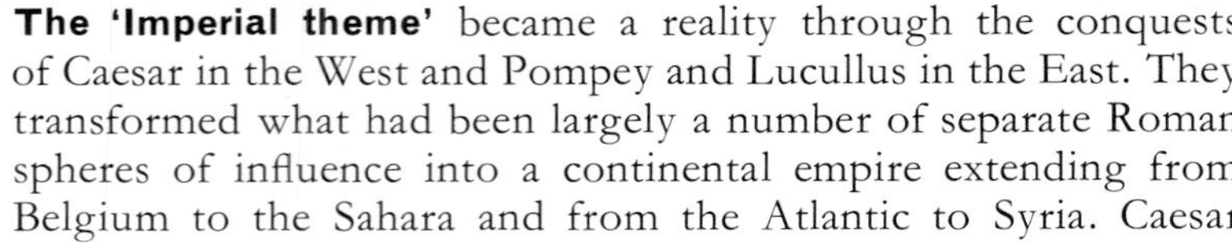

The 'Imperial theme' became a reality through the conquests of Caesar in the West and Pompey and Lucullus in the East. They transformed what had been largely a number of separate Roman spheres of influence into a continental empire extending from Belgium to the Sahara and from the Atlantic to Syria. Caesar

JULIUS CAESAR

POMPEY

LUCULLUS

Rome's far-flung empire is symbolized on reliefs from the Temple of Hadrian, and on coins which he and Trajan issued. Africa wears an elephant scalp, Arabia appears with a camel, Hispania with a rabbit. Sicily is symbolized by the *triskeles*, Achaïa and Gallia are raised by the Emperor as *restitutor*, Asia stands on a prow. Britannia is seated, and Germania is armed. (7–24)

AEGYPTOS

LIBYA

MAURITANIA

PHRYGIA

PARTHIA

VINDELICA

AFRICA

ARABIA

HISPANIA

SICILIA

ACHAIA

wears the laurel wreath of the conqueror. Lucullus minted his coin when he was Sulla's quaestor, hence the letter Q.

The rest of the world accepted Rome because Rome brought peace. This was one of the chief themes of Imperial propaganda. On a coin of Nero (below left) peace is indicated in the traditional Roman manner by the closed doors of the Temple of Janus. On the relief from the Ara Pacis (centre) Mother Earth sits with fruit in her lap and two children on her knees, surrounded by flowers, ears of corn, a bull and a grazing sheep, and the beautiful *Aurae* blowing over the sea and rivers. (2–6)

The first Emperor, Octavian, took the title 'Augustus' which was adopted by all his successors. This figure combines the military qualities of the Emperor with symbols recalling the divine origin of the Julian family. (25)

DACIA

SCYTHIA

ASIA

ITALIA

GALLIA

BRITANNIA

GERMANIA

Most Romans lived by farming. In fact the economy of the western half of the Empire was mainly agricultural, and this was a definite weakness. The estate owners had little interest in industry or commerce so long as they could market their crops and stock.

Country life in the fertile provinces of North Africa meant luxury for the lord and lady and a livelihood for workers on the estate. Here, at a villa near Carthage (left), the living quarters are marked by a handsome loggia running along the whole of the first floor. Beside the house the master is shown hunting, while at the top and bottom the mistress receives the produce of the seasons: in winter (top left) olives, ducks and hens; in summer (top right) sheep and goats; in spring (bottom left) flowers, fish – and jewels from the handmaid's casket; and in autumn (bottom right) fruit and a live hare taken in the vineyard. (26)

The sacrifice to Ceres, a goddess of the corn harvest (below), is one of forty scenes from a mosaic 'calendar' found at Vienne in Southern France. (27)

Threshing is the theme of the mosaic (above) from Zliten in Tripoli. The threshing floor is covered with corn; two men hold a pair of spirited horses, while a third shakes the corn with a fork. The woman sitting under the olive tree is probably the mistress of the villa. (28)

Autumn, crowned with vine leaves (left), also comes from Zliten, symbolizing the harvest for which the rest of the year is preparation. (29)

Horse breeding in North Africa (below). The horses' names are Adorable and Shaggy. (30)

The ploughing scene (below) again comes from Zliten. The Zliten series, which consisted partly of wall mosaics and partly of floor mosaics, is one of the finest of the 1st century AD. (31)

Evolution and change marked Rome's political institutions under the Empire. In Republican times the state was composed of three elements, the Senate, symbolized on the relief opposite by the bearded figure, the people (the young man) and the magistrates, especially the higher or 'curule' magistrates, symbolized by the curule chair (below). By Imperial times the power of the people had become a cypher, and the ancient magistracies tended to become merely honorary; but the Senate always retained some influence. Right: the interior of Diocletian's Senate House, now restored to something like its original state. (32, 33, 38)

Quaestors were Rome's quartermasters, and had managed the treasury (*aerarium*). The coin (upper left) is inscribed 'for the buying of corn', and the relief below it is of one of their assistants, the *viator* ('traveller'). Under the Empire the *aerarium* lost ground to the Imperial *fiscus*. (34, 35)

Praetors formed the old Roman judiciary. The coin (lower far right) commemorates a famous trial of Vestal Virgins for incest, conducted by the praetor Lucius Cassius Longinus Ravilla in 113 BC, although this was not in a normal praetorian court. Shown on the coin are the Temple of Vesta, the urn for voting and the letters A and C for *Absolvo* and *Condemno*: the praetor's powers. From normal decisions of the praetors the citizen had the right of appeal (*provocatio*), as on the third coin. Under the Empire judicial power passed more to the Urban and Praetorian Prefects, and the appeal was to the Emperor. (36, 37)

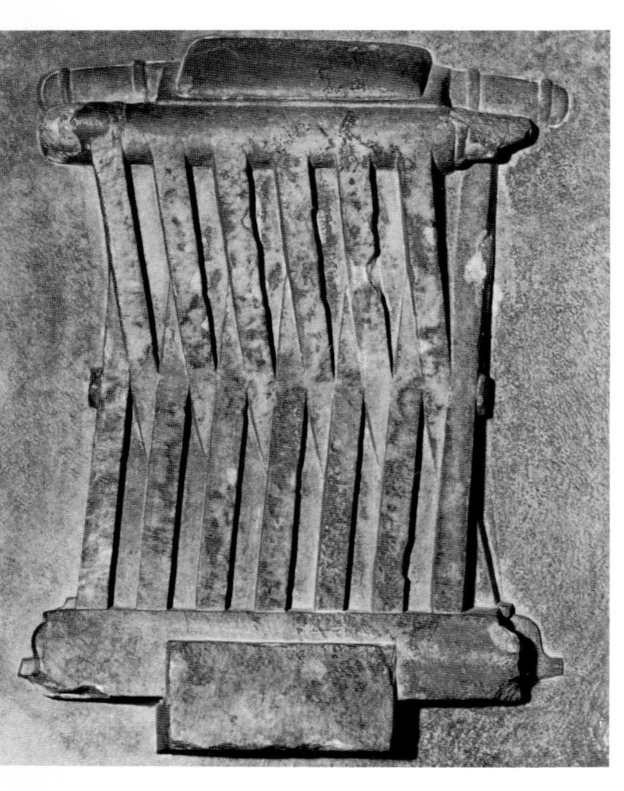

Consuls belonged to two types: the regular consuls, who were solemnly inaugurated on January 1st, often in conjunction with the Emperor as colleague; and 'supplementary consuls', carrying the same authority but holding office for only a few months. The scene (below) from the Ara Pacis is thought to show Augustus with the two consuls of the year. However, the really important posts came to be held by Imperial legates, directly appointed by the Emperor. (39)

Fifty-three thousand miles of road held the Roman Empire together. Administered by the state, the roads were furnished with inns at regular intervals, as well as halting-places where horses could be changed and vehicles repaired. Cuttings were avoided so as to minimize drainage problems. Roman roads were always new routes taking no account of previous paths except in some cases near Rome itself. Their straightness has become proverbial. Armies could be marched from one corner of the Empire to another with a speed that not even Alexander had dreamed of.

Every mile, the Romans placed a milestone, about eight feet high. These are in Jordan. In Republican times they simply recorded distances, later they carried the title of the Emperor who ordered the construction. (40)

The pattern of road-surface varied according to the soil and the terrain. It was usually laid over a foundation of rammed down rubble or flint bound together by sand or gravel. Below: a road near Antioch stretches into the distance. (44)

Across rivers and gorges the roads were carried on bridges, often still in use two thousand years after they were built. The Ponte Grosso (below right) forms part of the Via Flaminia which led from Rimini to Rome. (45)

In towns the roads were composed of flat slabs (above: a section of road at Timgad); elsewhere they might be of roughly shaped stones laid irregularly (right centre: part of the Via Appia). Country tracks were often improved by engineers. Above right: a path in the mountains of Austria. (41–3)

Roman engineering reached its peak in the great aqueducts that brought water into the major cities from hills often 50 miles away. That of Segovia, Spain (below right), built under Augustus, is the most spectacular of them all. (46)

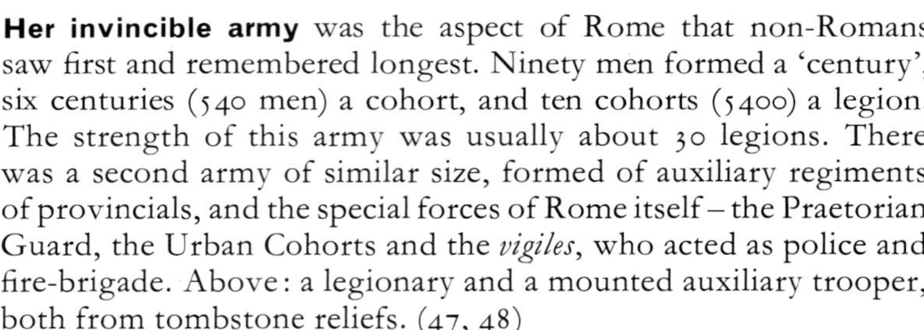

Her invincible army was the aspect of Rome that non-Romans saw first and remembered longest. Ninety men formed a 'century', six centuries (540 men) a cohort, and ten cohorts (5400) a legion. The strength of this army was usually about 30 legions. There was a second army of similar size, formed of auxiliary regiments of provincials, and the special forces of Rome itself – the Praetorian Guard, the Urban Cohorts and the *vigiles*, who acted as police and fire-brigade. Above: a legionary and a mounted auxiliary trooper, both from tombstone reliefs. (47, 48)

Naval warfare was alien to the Roman character, and for long they lagged behind other maritime powers. But Augustus established fleets at Ravenna and Misenum, at Alexandria and in the Black Sea, and this finally solved the problem of piracy in the Mediterranean. Below: a Roman sailor – not often depicted in reliefs; and a warship with crocodile prow, probably an allusion to Egypt and Actium. Two banks of oars are visible at the bottom. The Romans relied exclusively on boarding tactics; hence the large number of marines on board. (52, 53)

The pampered garrison of Rome was the Praetorian Guard (above centre), on whom the Emperor relied for his personal power, but who often took a hand in replacing him. Left and right: two details from the Column of Marcus Aurelius, showing an auxiliary and a group of soldiers with standards. Whereas the regular legionaries wore plate-armour, the auxiliaries had a variety of protective clothing, including chain-mail and scales. The standards, the regimental 'flags' of the Roman army, were held in almost superstitious veneration. (49–51)

A legion's officers were sixty centurions, six military tribunes and a legate of senatorial rank commanding the whole legion. A general would have several legions under him. Below left: a relief showing a centurion. He carries his badge of office, the vine staff, and wears military decorations, one of which is also seen below. Below right: 'discharge papers' – a record of the grant of Roman citizenship, made to troopers in auxiliary regiments, by Trajan to a Spanish veteran called Reburrus serving in Britain with the First Pannonian Cavalry. (54–6)

RISQVE EORVM CIVITATEM DEDIT ET CON
BIVM CVM VXORIBVS QVAS TVNC HABV
SENT CVM EST CIVITAS IIS DATA AVT SI
QVI CAELIBES ESSENT CVM IIS QVAS POSTE
DVXISSENT DVMTAXAT SINGVLI SINGVLAS
A D XIIII K FEBR
M LABERIO MAXIMO II
Q GLITIO ATILIO AGRICOLA II
ALAE I PANNONIORVM TAMPIANAE CVI PRAEST
C VALERIVS CELSVS
DECVRIONI
REBVRRO SEVERI F HISPAN
DESCRIPTVM ET RECOGNITVM EX TABV
LA AENEA QVAE FIXA EST ROMAE

In war the Roman soldier used tough utilitarian equipment, often of leather and iron, of which hardly anything has survived: leather kilts, cuirasses made of strips of metal, bronze helmets, shields of leather over a wooden frame with a metal boss in the centre. The pieces shown on this page were made for ceremonial purposes or tournaments, and are therefore more splendid than working weapons and armour, though similar in form. The bronze cavalry helmet (left) comes from Ribchester in Lancashire and was probably used in jousting. The crown is embossed with battle-scenes and the visor has a 'frieze' of heads, seated figures and sea-monsters. (57)

The ceremonial sword was found at Mainz in Germany. The blade is of iron, the scabbard (right) silver-gilt with reliefs in gilt bronze. These reliefs show Tiberius receiving his nephew Germanicus on the latter's return from Germany in AD 17; a medallion portrait of Tiberius; a temple with a Roman eagle and two standards; and an Amazon armed with a battle-axe.

Below: a bronze parade shield-boss found in the River Tyne, England. The four figures in the corners are the seasons; Mars and a bull stand at the top and bottom; and in the centre is the Roman eagle flanked by standards with the words LEG VIII AUG: 'The Eighth Legion Augusta', whose badge was the bull. (58, 59)

The position of 'First Man' (Princeps – Emperor) was skilfully grafted on to the old Republican constitution by Augustus. In theory he was a permanent magistrate with authority similar to that of a consul. He was also sole commander-in-chief of all the forces and in fact the centre and symbol of the Roman state. Right: the triumph of Tiberius, on a silver cup from Boscoreale. Right centre: Domitian (his head recut as a portrait of Nerva) sets out on an expedition accompanied by Victory, Mars, Minerva and *Virtus*. Below: the ruins of one of the Imperial palaces on the Palatine Hill, Rome. (60, 61, 63)

Torrents of eulogy flowed from all over the Empire to the Emperor in Rome, where they merged into a flood of self-congratulation. Above: an altar relief at Carthage. Rome, seated on a pile of arms, faces a cornucopia, symbol of plenty. The inscription reads: 'To the Imperial Family, P. Perelius Hedulus, priest for life, built the temple at his own expense.'

When the Emperor died he was buried in a magnificent mausoleum (right: Hadrian's Mausoleum, known as the Castel Sant' Angelo). After death he became a god (above left: Claudius as Jupiter). The succession problem was partly solved by 'adoption'. Above right: four 'generations' of Emperors, each of whom adopted his successor – Hadrian, Antoninus Pius, Marcus Aurelius and the child Lucius Verus, who was intended to succeed Marcus Aurelius but died young. (62, 64–6)

The glorified Emperor: in this beautiful sardonyx Tiberius and Livia sit enthroned as Jupiter and Ceres, receiving a young warrior. In the sky above, Germanicus (who died AD 19 in the East) is carried on a winged horse to heaven where Augustus, reclining, awaits him.

Left: in a relief of about AD 40, Augustus is portrayed as a divine hero, garlanded with oak-leaves, sword and sceptre originally in his hands, a globe beneath his foot. The other figures belong to the Imperial family. Germanicus and his mother Antonia, and, left, Drusus, Tiberius' son. (67, 68)

THE ROMAN GOVERNMENT AND THE CHRISTIAN CHURCH

A. NICHOLAS SHERWIN-WHITE

THE CHRISTIAN faith arose in a remote district of Judaea, the smallest and most isolated province of the eastern half of the vast Roman Empire, a land on the road to nowhere, sundered from the main traffic of the ancient world by the deserts to the east and south of it. Christianity's first and most intensive expansion was into the adjacent Roman territories in Syria, Asia Minor and Egypt. Later it spread by the sea routes to the northern coastlands of Africa and inevitably to the capital city of Rome. The faith was born into a world united politically but not yet socially by the military power and the political talent of the Romans. The pattern of administration imposed by Rome on the diverse areas under her rule affected the development of the nascent Christian communities in some measure. Christians conformed to the ordinary rules and usages of civic government, and even in the age of conflict the division between Rome and the Church was confined to a relatively narrow issue. Apart from the strict monotheistic question that arose in the 2nd century AD between Christians and the Roman government, Christians were an essentially conformist people. This appears very clearly in the basic attitude adopted towards Rome by Tertullian in his *Apologia* in about AD 196: 'We too are Romans.'

To understand the conflict it is necessary to understand also the pattern of principles and methods adopted by the Roman government and the Imperial viceroys who ruled the individual provinces. But for the understanding of the quiet growth of the individual
150–1 churches within the Roman provinces it is the local framework and
(2–9) environment that matters. The Roman provincial administration was supervisory; the primary job of proconsuls and legates was to keep the peace by expelling foreign enemies and by quelling major riots. Government as it is understood today, in the sphere of public works and utilities, social services including the maintenance of cults, police and routine jurisdiction, was entirely in the hands of local municipal authorities that enjoyed a large measure of independence. The Roman governor and his satellites were remote beings with whom the ordinary provincial at all levels of society
p 150 had few necessary contacts. So long as he paid his taxes and com-
(4) mitted no major crime, the ordinary tribesman, peasant or man of means lived under the immediate control only of his local community, organized in accordance with ethnic and cultural traditions.

The organization of the Empire

p 126 The conquests of Lucullus and Pompey (74–62 BC) had added
(3, 4) the lands of Asia Minor and Syria to Rome's dominions, while Egypt was annexed by 30 BC. Rome's acquisition of this eastern empire had been completed long before the republican method of government at Rome was replaced finally in 27 BC by the new semi-monarchic system known as the Principate. In Northern Europe
26 (2) the campaigns of Julius Caesar in Gaul (58–50 BC) had added the area of Northern France, Belgium and the Alpine foothills to the coastal lands of North Africa, Spain and Southern France, which were acquired in the 2nd century BC. This had given Rome a
126–7 continental empire in depth: the first Emperor Augustus com-
(7–24) pleted the process by annexing the Alpine and Balkan lands as far as the Danube and the Black Sea (19 BC–AD 12). Hence by the time of Christ's mission all the lands between the three great rivers – Rhine, Danube, Euphrates – and the Syrian and Saharan deserts were within the Roman Empire and were open to the expansion of Christianity, though the development of Early Christianity was not much concerned with the barbarian northern lands.

After the age of great expansion it remained to organize the general government and defence of these lands. The basic system was laid down by Augustus Caesar, the first Emperor or 'Princeps'
(27 BC–AD 14), exploiting methods that were already emerging in p 127
the last generation of the Republic. There was now a nominal divi- (25)
sion of function between the Princeps and the Roman Senate – the aristocratic council formed out of the annually elected magistrates and officials of the former free Republic, who continued to operate under the new order. Border provinces and other areas that required an effective military garrison were in the hands of the Princeps. The prosperous and civilized regions fringing the Mediterranean, which required few or no troops – including the Roman homeland of Italy – were left to the Senate. Such were Baetica (Andalusia), Gallia Narbonensis (Provence in Mediterranean France), Achaïa (Greece), 'Africa' (Tunisia), Bithynia and 'Asia' (western coastlands of Turkey). These were the principal zones of the Early Christian expansion outside Syria, which was an 'Imperial' province.

The Princeps governed his numerous 'Imperial' provinces by means of officials, known as the 'legates of Augustus', who held their posts for several years at a time. They were men of senatorial standing who gained expertise earlier by serving as officers in the Roman legions and by holding the annual senatorial magistracies and 'proconsulships'. The Senate's own 'public' provinces were administered in the old Republican fashion by annual officers drawn from the same senatorial group with the title of proconsul. There was a special category of smaller 'Imperial' provinces managed by 'prefects' and 'procurators' of the Princeps, drawn from the second or 'equestrian' class of Roman society, who had earlier served in the financial administration of the Empire. The technical difference between legates, proconsuls and procurators or prefects made little difference to the provincial subjects. Possibly in the early Empire they were left more to their own devices under proconsular government, though by the 2nd century AD the Princeps had come to supervise 'public' and 'Imperial' provinces alike.

All the provincial governors were responsible for defence and public order, including civil and criminal jurisdiction in cases of major importance such as capital crimes and great property suits. Finance was in the hands of other equestrian officers, also called procurators like the equestrian governors. These managed Imperial expenditure and taxation, though the actual collection of revenue was done on the farming principle by private entrepreneurs (*publicani, conductores*). The procurators also supervised the immense domains owned by the Imperial House throughout the Empire. The receipts from these crown lands formed a great part of the resources of the Imperial treasury or fisc. They constituted a kind of private empire: the villages of the fiscal tenants, largely withdrawn from the jurisdiction of the cities, were under the immediate control of a network of minor Imperial agents, also called procurators, who managed the tenants in a semi-feudal fashion.

In the border provinces, along the great rivers that delimited the Empire, and overseas in Britain (after AD 42), there were stationed the Roman armies that defended the Empire against the outer barbarians. These armies, which were under the command of the most senior of the Imperial legates, were mostly remote from the peaceful, prosperous, central areas in which Christianity spread. In the peaceful provinces Roman soldiery was extremely rare. The governors were rationed to small contingents of troops, seldom exceeding a single battalion, or even a single company, for the suppression of occasional riots. But Syria and Judaea were exceptional. In Northern Syria, a land of ancient civilization, the Roman Empire narrowed to a neck of land between the Mediterranean coast and the Euphrates frontier. Hence a strong legionary force was permanently stationed in Syria to watch the Parthian border, while in the southern province of Judaea several battalions were required to control the unruly Jews. Outside the purely military zones and the fiscal lands, the Roman provincial government was supervisory rather than executive, and, except in Egypt, which had a special régime (see below), the detailed administration was in the hands of local civic governments. Roman administrators were remarkably few in number. The governors had two or three senatorial assessors according to the standing of their province, and equestrian financial procurators were no more numerous. Secretarial bureaux and archives, manned by a small staff of Imperial slaves and soldiery, were kept only at the provincial capitals. The activities of the governors themselves were confined to the capitals, except for an annual or biennial tour of certain larger cities for the holding of judicial assizes. Otherwise the provincials, if they gave no trouble, saw little or nothing of their governors, whose courts were frequented only by notorious criminals and tax defaulters, or magnates involved in great lawsuits. A basic rule reserved all capital crimes for the jurisdiction of the governor, who alone could inflict the death sentence, and this in Roman usage was the penalty for a wide category of crimes. But, so long as the provincials behaved themselves, they and their communities were seldom touched directly by the Imperial governors.

This general quietude was somewhat disturbed by the workings of the Imperial transport system. p 130–1 (40–6) Cities and villages along the great trunk roads were required to provide animals and carriages for Imperial officials. Requisitions were a frequent grievance which Emperors found hard to check. The creation of official supervisors of control posts along the military highways introduced in the 2nd century AD a new form of local Imperial authority which in time greatly altered the pattern of Imperial government and was a factor in the age of the great Christian persecutions.

The governor alone among the administrative officials had the absolute power of action denoted by the Roman term *imperium*, which was limited towards provincials only by certain statute laws that penalized financial extortion and corruption. From this *imperium* was derived the governor's sole power of capital jurisdiction, absolute over ordinary provincials, but limited in the case of Roman citizens, who enjoyed a right of appeal from the capital sentence of a governor to the court of the Princeps at Rome. This privilege was gradually extended in the 2nd century AD to the upper classes and civic aristocracies of the provinces, known as the *honestiores*. Another peculiarity was the absence of an organized system of public prosecution; the initiation of a criminal prosecution normally lay in private hands. The interested parties were expected to act without any official assistance. Though nothing prevented a governor from initiating an inquisition if he wished, p 340 (22) this was not customary. Normally the governors heard criminal cases with the assistance of a panel of assessors, though their advice was not binding. The verdict was the governor's, and in giving sentence on provincial offenders he was not bound by Roman statute law, which properly applied only to Roman citizens. Hence there was an arbitrary element in the criminal jurisdiction, though governors usually followed a mixture of local custom, precedents, and Roman law.

Civic life in East and West

The executive management of the Roman Empire depended upon local self-government through a varied pattern of urban and rural p 128–9 (26–31) or tribal communes. Though the economy of the ancient world was primarily agricultural, the Greek and Roman civilization had evolved a complex system of town life and municipal government. In the civilized lands such as Syria, Asia and Africa, where Christianity developed, public and social life involving dramatic, artistic p 150–1 (2–9) and athletic festivals, religious occasions, and the activity of local administration, was mostly concentrated in cities or townships which formed the centres of rural territories and contained the homes of an artisan and peasant population as well as of the local aristocracy. In the more primitive regions of North West Africa and of the European hinterland there was a more open rural régime, but here too the principle held of local self-government, based here on tribal societies, of which the functions were apt to become centralized. There was a regular transition towards urbanization through the emergence of townships as market sites and traffic centres.

The Greek-speaking and Latin-speaking peoples had evolved distinct forms of civic government in the East and the West respectively, though there was an overall similarity of type. In both, government was in the hands of annual officers or magistrates, elected by an assembly of the free inhabitants of the commune, and of a civic council composed either of ex-magistrates and aldermen or of annually elected councillors. Under Roman influence the aldermanic pattern tended to oust the direct election of such councillors. Office was restricted to the wealthier classes, and effective power was generally restricted to the councils, though in some Greek cities the assemblies retained the power of decision in some matters, and popular feeling could carry much weight. The annual magistrates administered the civic activities, and were competent in jurisdiction in all cases save those reserved for the Roman provincial governor. They also held the local priesthoods and maintained the public worship of the civic gods.

A lively civic life occupied the attention and controlled the activities of the vast majority of the inhabitants of the Empire. The adventures of St Paul in the cities of Greece and Asia Minor show this in some detail. He is perpetually being arrested or imprisoned by civic magistrates or accused before them. At Ephesus, when a riot arises, the chief civic officer harangues the assembly of the people and reminds the enemies of Paul to proceed by due process of law either before the city courts or before the proconsul. At Athens Paul appears before the city council, and at Iconium and Philippi the civic officers expel him from their territory. Since the cities were the basic social and administrative units of the eastern provinces, it is not surprising that the units of Christian organization, the *ecclesiae* or assemblies, came to be based on the cities and to use the same name as the civic assemblies. There are also analogies between the 'elders' or presbyters of the Early Church and the civic aldermen, and between the single 'overseers' or *episcopi* and the civic magistrates of the same city area. But there is a great distinction between them in the manner of appointment.

The active role in city life tended to be reserved for the leisured and wealthy classes. The common man found his outlet in a wide variety of private associations. Some of these were based on membership of trades and crafts, while others were nominally concerned with the practice of a religious cult, but all were principally organized to provide social benefits in the form of regular festivities. Such clubs, which followed the civic pattern in the election of annual officers and informal meetings of their corporate members, covered some activities which were not approved of by the Roman government, and they provided another pattern for the development of the Early Church.

The city governments not only managed the local community and provided the lesser jurisdiction. They also performed a large part of the work of the central government in the field of taxation p 150– (3, 4) and census. The detailed lists of inhabitants, their status and property, on which the system of provincial taxation was based, were drawn up and maintained by the civic magistrates, who thus freed the Roman government from the need to provide a bureaucratic machine for this purpose. Roman officials simply collected and combined the local lists, which then served as the basis for taxation and military conscription. The cities also acted as collectors of direct taxation. The provincial tribute was in most provinces divided up between the various communes, which gathered in their share by farming the collection out to local agents or tax-farmers (*publicani, conductores*). The role of the cities in providing material for the Imperial postal system, together with these other services, spared the central government the expense of maintaining a numerous establishment in the provinces, and reduced the role of the Imperial officials to that of administrative supervision.

In Egypt alone among Roman provinces there was no local self-government, and the country was administered by a full-scale clerical bureaucracy, inherited from the Ptolemaic régime. The province was divided into subdistricts or 'toparchies', of which the basic unit was the village, and districts or 'nomes' with central townships called *metropoleis*, grouped into three 'super-districts' (*epistrategiae*). Each of the administrative divisions from the village upwards had salaried officials appointed by the government. Up to the district officers these were locally recruited and nominated by the Prefect, while the three 'over-officers' of the 'super-districts', and the Prefect and his principal aides, were equestrian Romans appointed by the Emperor. But in the early-3rd century AD the Severan Emperors introduced a measure of municipal government by entrusting to the district townships the local administration of their districts.

The extension of privilege

A man's personal status was that of a citizen of the community to which his parents belonged by birth or legal incorporation. Each community lived according to its own local legal system. In Roman eyes all the non-Roman inhabitants of the Empire were aliens, *peregrini*, living according to alien systems of law. But the Romans in the long course of their historical development in Italy had acquired a habit of incorporating formerly alien communities into the Roman state as Roman municipalities, and also of making personal grants of Roman citizenship to individual aliens who had assisted the Roman state in any way.

With the enlargement of their empire the Romans extended their methods of enfranchisement to the provincial peoples. In the western provinces whole communities came to be incorporated on a generous scale. These were known as 'municipalities of Roman citizens' or as 'municipalities of Latin status'. There were two grades of Roman status that could be given to provincials. The first equated the new citizens in all respects with Roman citizens in Italy. The second grade, the Latin status, which was the commoner grant, equated its holders with Roman citizens in most matters of private law and civic administration. A 'Latin' city received by charter the same style of local government as a full Roman municipality, but as individuals Latin persons lacked the political rights of Romans, so that they could not enter the public services of the Roman state. This did not greatly impede the upper classes, since the full Roman status was conferred automatically upon all persons who held civic office in a Latin municipality.

The Romanization of provincial communities was promoted by the activities of Roman emigrant settlers and itinerant businessmen from Italy in the last century BC. Soldiers of all grades who established themselves in the provinces where they had served, investors in land seeking cheap estates overseas, bankers and moneylenders pursuing profitable openings everywhere, had built up a provincial population of wealthy Roman emigrants in the larger townships. These were apt to combine with any enfranchised elements among the native aristocracy, and to set up as a social élite. From this milieu there were drawn many ambitious provincials of great wealth who entered the service of the Roman state.

In the last century BC there was also a deliberate colonization of the provinces by the formal settlement of Roman legionary veterans on large blocks of farm land as civic colonies, organized like Italian boroughs. Many of the principal cities of the Empire, such as Carthage in Tunisia, Narbonne in Southern France, Cordova and Seville in Spain, were turned by this process into Roman townships. The Mediterranean provinces of France, Spain and Africa were intensively affected by all these types of Roman development. But the Greek-speaking lands, which had an independent and complex culture of their own, did not embrace Romanization wholesale. There was no incorporated native communities of Latin and Roman status in the eastern provinces. But there was an increasing number of individuals of Roman status in the larger Greek cities, enfranchised natives and emigrant Italians, who formed associations like the trade clubs. There had also been a restricted amount of formal military colonization in the eastern provinces during the early Principate. A few great cities like Corinth in Greece, Sinope on the Black Sea coast of Turkey, and Beirut in Lebanese Syria, were Roman civic colonies. But in these, though the Roman colonists formed the local élite, the native population retained much of the land under its own form of civic organization, and eventually the Roman element tended to be overpowered by its predominantly Greek environment.

In the eastern provinces the enfranchised provincial was thus an isolated person, since Roman status was not given to Greek cities, the internal organization of a Greek city being incompatible with Latin usages. Such individuals, like Paul of Tarsus, combined the Roman citizenship as a kind of honorary status with their local franchise. Its practical effects were limited, but it enabled ambitious persons to enter the Roman public service, usually through the Roman army. Men of wealth could secure commissions as senior legionary officers and afterwards gain posts as procurators in the Imperial administration. For proletarians also service in the legions as common soldiers, which was limited to Roman citizens, had advantages. It was well paid relatively to day-labour, and it was rewarded by an endowment on retirement after twenty years service; better still, it led to promotion to the lucrative post of centurion or company-officer. Men of ability could secure advancement from the centurionate to the equestrian service itself. The most exalted provincial personages could push their families through the equestrian service to membership of the Roman Senate, and thence into the highest grades of the Imperial administration. The Roman army thus offered a Roman citizen a ladder of promotion from the bottom to the top of what was otherwise a rigidly stratified class system. The Roman administrative classes were being perpetually renewed in this fashion throughout the first three centuries of the Empire. But the total number of persons promoted in any one generation was not large, and, for humdrum provincials like Paul of Tarsus, the Roman status, apart from personal prestige, was only beneficial in unusual circumstances, when it enabled a man charged with a capital offence to escape from prejudice or corruption in the courts of provincial governors by exercising the right of a Roman citizen to have his trial transferred to a court at Rome. This was secured by a formal appeal to the Princeps (*provocatio ad principem*), which effected a stay of proceed- p 130
ings and the automatic despatch of the prisoner to Rome. This was (37)
the course taken by St Paul when charged with sedition before the procurators Festus and Felix. But later it became customary to despatch such cases to Rome as soon as proceedings were initiated against them.

Military power and its distribution

The Roman army consisted of three main branches. First there was the legionary army, which was maintained at a strength of some thirty legions. These were infantry divisions each with a paper strength of 5400 men, organized in ten 'cohorts' each containing six companies or 'centuries' of 90 men. Then there was a more varied force of independent regiments or auxiliary units (*cohortes*, *alae*, *numeri*) of infantry, cavalry, and special troops such as archers and camel-riders. These units were recruited mostly among the less civilized peoples of the Empire, and they received the Roman p 135
citizenship as a reward on retirement after twenty-five years' (55)
service. Nominally the legions themselves were recruited only from Roman citizens, Italian and provincial, but military service became unpopular in the highly civilized areas, and by the 2nd century AD legionary recruits came largely from the barrack townships that sprang up in the military zones. The third force consisted of three corps stationed at Rome itself: the twelve or (at some periods) sixteen cohorts of the Praetorian Guard, which were the p 135
personal troops of the Emperor, the four Urban Cohorts, which (50)
formed the gendarmerie of the capital, and the six cohorts of *vigiles*, the police and fire-brigade of the city of Rome. The bulk of these long continued to be recruited in Italy. The Praetorian troops were the spoiled favourites of the Emperors, enjoying special rates of pay and terms of service. Being the garrison of the capital, they secured a particular role in the making and breaking of Emperors through the not infrequent palace revolutions, but in the first two centuries AD they seldom saw active service.

Rome was exceptional among the cities of the Empire in housing a large military establishment. The legions and the auxiliary regiments in the first century of the Empire were grouped in corps of three or four legions, supplemented by about the same total strength of auxiliary units, throughout the military provinces of the northern frontier, from Britain to the mouth of the Danube; in the second century, for political reasons, the size of the corps was reduced and the number of such commands was increased. These northern armies saw constant active service. But in the East, where a formal if uneasy peace regulated relations with Parthia, two (later three) army corps were maintained on a peace footing. One of these was in Northern Syria, the second in reserve in Egypt, and the third (after AD 70) lay on the upper Euphrates in Cappadocia (Eastern Turkey). It was only in Syria and Egypt, besides Rome, that a large military presence was a regular element in the life of the civilized provinces and cities. Otherwise one might travel from the Syrian ports to ancient Lisbon (Olisipo) without encountering more than the smallest detachment of soldiery. Likewise in the prosperous and urbanized provinces of Africa the small corps of a single legion with its auxiliaries was moved steadily westwards away from the cities to the tribal borderlands where nomads still gave trouble. The proconsuls and legates of the numerous provinces that had no external frontier normally had no large units at their disposal, though one single cohort was stationed at Lugdunum (Lyons), the largest city in North Gaul, and another at Carthage, while the governors of Bithynia-with-Pontus in Northwest Turkey had a local force of two or three cohorts.

The officers of the Roman army consisted of 'non-commissioned' ratings serving within the companies, the company-officers or
p 135 centurions, and the staff of officers. Each legion had a legate of
(54) senatorial rank as its commanding officer, assisted by a staff of six military tribunes of equestrian or senatorial rank. The auxiliary brigades were officered by equestrian tribunes and prefects. From
p 139 the reign of Claudius (AD 41–54) onwards the staff commissions
(64) attracted not only the Italian gentry but also the Romanized upper classes of the provinces both from the Greek-speaking and from the Latin-speaking zones of the Empire. Imperial service was well paid. Though the amount of the salaries of centurions and military tribunes is not precisely known, at the next stage of promotion the procurators of the civil administration received annual salaries that ranged in the 2nd century AD from an initial 15,000 *denarii* or 'silver shillings' – fifty times the wage of a common soldier – through 25,000 to 75,000 for the topmost grade. The relative value of these salaries is shown by the fact that the nominal capital qualification for membership of the equestrian class was the ownership of property worth 100,000 *denarii*. The senatorial legates and proconsuls were paid on an even ampler scale, rising to an annual quarter of a million *denarii* for the most senior governorships, though the senatorial officials were less continuously employed than the equestrians. The object of these large salaries, which date back to the beginning of the Empire, was to discourage the excessive extortion by which the administrators of the Republican period had enriched themselves. But the creeping inflation of a prosperous age diminished the value of these salaries during the first two centuries AD, while the salary-scale remained static after a single increase of twenty-five per cent in about AD 83.

The administrative class

The administrative career, equestrian and senatorial alike, was based on a rather rigid system of grades and promotions. After a few years' service as a staff-officer the equestrian held a series of procuratorial posts, of which the order was determined not so much by the nature of his duties as by their scale and extent: the financial procuratorships of large provinces were graded above the governorships of small ones. Mixed up with the provincial assignments were the headship of certain ministries at the capital, such as the food office of Rome, the metropolitan police and fire service, the Imperial mint, and the Imperial secretariats, though most of these latter posts were not held by equestrians until the 2nd century AD. The highest grade of this complex system was the nominally military post of the prefecture of the Praetorian Guard: these prefects acted as principal advisers and ministers to the Emperors, and they acquired an increasingly judicial function as their tribunal became during the 2nd century AD one of the great courts of appeal of the Roman system. The grading of these posts was indicated by the salary attached. Promotion was from grade to grade, two or three posts in succession being held in each grade; the order of posts in each grade was not rigidly defined. The building up of this complex system was a gradual process, spread
over the period from the reign of Augustus to that of Hadrian p 127
(27 BC–AD 138), as more and more departments of public life fell (25)
under the direct control of the Emperor, or as existing services p 139
came to be organized more comprehensively. The equestrian (65, 66)
service grew especially by the transfer of offices originally managed by Imperial slaves and freedmen to the control of equestrian procurators. Though the equestrian career had an orderly pattern of seniority, preferment was not bound by any hard and fast rules of age. Equestrians held their military offices at various ages, some when very young men, but others not till their middle thirties. The Emperors were always prepared to promote able men rapidly through the grades, but it was not usual for the most responsible posts to be given to inexperienced favourites even by the more worthless Emperors.

In the first century of the Principate, from 27 BC down to the
reign of Domitian (AD 81–96), a large part of the necessary chores p 138–
of government were managed by a private arrangement. Augustus (61)
and his immediate successors did what the great commanders of the late Republic had done. They used their personal servants, who were slaves and freedmen, to organize the vast amount of secretarial paper-work involved in the government of great provinces, and also to manage particular executive tasks, such as the minting of the coinage required for the great armies, or the oversight of the fiscal estates (see above). Three great secretariats came into existence at Rome, which handled the main part of the Emperor's transactions. These were the bureau of finance and accounts (*a rationibus*), the Imperial Letters (*ab epistulis*), and the Imperial Notes (*a libellis*). The heads of these were really ministers of state, though socially they were merely freed slaves of the Princeps. Each bureau contained a numerous clerical personnel, who likewise were Imperial freedmen or slaves. The 'Household of Caesar', as it came to be called, also supplied the junior personnel of other departments, such as the metropolitan water board and food office, which were under the control of equestrian or senatorial heads. In the provinces also the Imperial procurators and legates were supplied with assistant staff from the Imperial Household. Procurators frequently had a senior Imperial freedman (*libertus Augusti*) as their chief executive aide.

The Imperial Household thus provided the bulk of the junior and intermediate personnel of the administrative machine at the capital, and played a considerable if subordinate role in the provinces, where the governors also used soldiers for executive and clerical work. Certain great posts, such as the headships of the three secretariats, and of departments like the mint, were so important that they were gradually (between the years AD 81–137) transferred from the Household to equestrian procurators of experience. But the total strength of the Household in the lower echelons increased steadily throughout the first three centuries AD, and at Rome the Household, which included the domestic service of the Emperor's palace or court, always had a considerable role. In court society the numerous Imperial freedmen were persons of influence and power, who controlled access to the ear of the Emperor and who enriched themselves accordingly. The obscurer bourgeoisie of Rome did not disdain to marry their free-born daughters to the freedmen of the Emperor, and even to Imperial slaves, whose prospects glittered brightly.

The Household of Caesar had its gradings and its system of preferment. At the head of a complicated pattern of clerks, paymasters, accountants, book-keepers and store-keepers, stood the great figures of the freedmen procurators, assistants and associates of equestrian administrators, and the senior secretaries. The Household was a world of its own.

The survial of Senate and senators

In terms of prestige, though not always of power, the governors and legates of senatorial rank stood high above equestrian and freedmen agents. For the senatorial career enshrined the tradition, and preserved the technicalities, of the governing class of the old Republic. The sons of senators, and young equestrians of high degree seeking promotion to the senatorial order, served as legionary staff-officers (*tribuni militum*) before holding the ancient annual magistracies of the Roman state. These were now restricted increasingly to formal duties at Rome, of which the most important was the presidency of the courts of criminal and civil law, now supplemented by the tribunal of the Princeps. The senior titular › 130–1 (34–9) magistracies, the praetorship and consulship, qualified a senator for advancement to the senatorial grades of the Emperor's service. He chose his legionary commanders and the governors of his non-military provinces from among the ex-praetors, and his army commanders from the ex-consuls. These various praetorian and consular legates held office for several years in each post; most commonly the term was three or four years, but much longer periods were not infrequent. Consular senators might hold three or four army commands, but they were not professional generals in permanent employment. Many years might intervene between posts, and military and civil governorships might alternate. The Imperial service also included some senatorial posts at the capital, such as the prefecture of the state treasury and the curatorship of the metropolitan water supply.

The most ancient, prosperous and civilized provinces, such as Africa, Achaïa and Asia, were not under the control of legates of the Princeps, but were governed by annual proconsuls, appointed by the Senate and selected like the legates from the praetorian and consular senators. The proconsuls were assisted by junior senators p 130 (34) as financial officials (quaestors) and deputy judges, known as 'proconsular legates'. All the various appointments – annual magistracies, Imperial legateships, proconsulships, and curatorships – were combined in one complex career, being graded in a pattern of ascending seniority. Appointments might be spread throughout a man's life. Senators held their military tribunates at the age of eighteen or nineteen, reached the praetorship by the age of thirty, but might still be holding curatorships and army commands when over seventy, since there was no upper age limit.

Central government and its limits

The form of the Roman government was complicated by its historical origins. Out of the institutions of the late Republic the 126–7 (5, 6) genius of Augustus, the first Princeps, who restored peace and order after the civil wars of 49–32 BC in which the Republic finally collapsed, fashioned a dual pattern of government. While he reserved the ultimate power for himself as 'First Man' or Princeps, 130–1 32, 33) he admitted the Roman Senate – the great council of state of the old Republic – to a nominal equality with himself in the administration of the Empire. The Senate's function had always been that of an advisory council to the annual officers – praetors, consuls and proconsuls – of the Roman state. It continued in theory to perform this role both for the Princeps and for the annual magistrates, who were now confined to the administration of Italy and of a number of the most peaceful provinces. But in practice the Princeps dominated the Senate, which only enjoyed such freedom of action as he chose to allow it.

A central government in the modern sense hardly existed. The provincial governors and army commanders were under the *general* authority of the Princeps and of the Senate, but neither of these was in regular routine communication with, or exercising perpetual control over the actions of, the provincial governors. Since proconsuls, legates, and even equestrian prefects all held the *imperium* (above), which gave them unlimited power of action within their respective provinces, they needed no further authority from Rome to do anything, except to open a new war or – rarely – to interfere with some arrangement established by Roman statute law. When the Princeps despatched his legates to their provinces he gave them instructions of a general sort (*mandata*). These might include some specific matters, but were far from being an exhaustive book of rules. Legates were expected to manage for themselves, though they would consult the Emperor about any special problems that arose.

The proconsuls of the senatorial provinces received no regular instructions of any sort in the early Principate, though during the 2nd century AD they were gradually assimilated to the Imperial p 139 5, 66) legates, and came by the time of Hadrian to receive similar *mandata*.

The central government was concerned with crises and special cases rather than with the regular supervision of the whole Empire. When these arose in the sphere under the immediate control of the Emperor, which covered especially the management of defence, foreign policy and the military machine, as well as the administration of territories that comprised some two-thirds of the Empire, he made use of a committee, informal in origin, known as the cabinet or council of the Princeps (*consilium principis*). This was composed of some twenty or thirty of his personal associates, the so-called 'friends of Caesar' (*amici Caesaris*). This title was given to an inner circle of experienced administrators, generals and lawyers, who tended to retain this role from reign to reign, thereby providing an element of continuity in government. This cabinet rather than the Senate was the real centre of power and policy-making. It also acted as the ultimate court of the whole Empire, dealing with such cases as the Princeps accepted for his personal jurisdiction, either on appeal from the ordinary courts of Rome and of the provincial governors, or even in matters of first instance.

For the conduct of his affairs the Princeps also had the help of the secretariat already mentioned, manned mostly by slaves and freedmen. Its organization was remarkably different from that of modern Whitehall. Apart from finance, there were no specific or departmental ministries. The secretary of Accounts (known as *a rationibus*) dealt with the finances of the Imperial provinces, keeping the paper record of receipts and expenditure. But he was not concerned with financial policy or with the management of taxation. The collection of taxes was supervised by the equestrian procurators, while policy was decided in the Imperial cabinet. All other business went through the secretaries of Letters (*ab epistulis*) and Notes (*a libellis*). The business of the governors, army commanders and equestrian procurators was conducted through 'Letters', while that of junior personnel, and also of cities and communes, was managed by 'Notes'. These terms derived from the form of document used in the two cases: only the social equals of the Princeps addressed him by ordinary letter (*epistula*). Thus instead of, for instance, a Ministry of War managing all army administration, matters of pay and supply passed through the Accounts secretariat, strategy and defence were the concern of Letters, while the promotion of officers was divided between Letters and Notes according to the rank of the person.

The Emperor, his function and his image

The Princeps dealt with his business at daily sessions at which he p 138–9 (60–6) gave answers to the questions presented by the 'Letters' and 'Notes' which his secretaries submitted to him. It is doubtful whether any power was delegated to the secretaries to make decisions by themselves, except in the most routine affairs, though they certainly kept files and dossiers (*scrinia*), and provided the Emperor with necessary information. Hence the Emperors were confronted by a great amount of paper-work, which if they were 'bad' or frivolous men like Nero or Commodus they neglected, so p 335 (5) that government ceased to be carried on. They lightened their burden by delegating jurisdiction rather than administration, offloading judicial disputes which they did not want to hear themselves on to the Praetorian Prefect and the City Prefect, whose judicial competence steadily increased.

Rome seen through provincial eyes thus meant the personnel of the Imperial secretariat, the Princeps and his Friends, and the Senate. The formal approach to the Princeps was through the secretariat, who thereby controlled a profitable patronage, though short-cuts were possible if one could secure the support of one of the Friends, such as the governor of one's own province. Access to the Senate usually required a formal deputation to Rome. Provincials soon learned, even in the Senate's own provinces, to prefer the faster route to the ear of the Princeps, who would either settle the matter himself or expedite its despatch by the Senate.

The Princeps had a formal position within the Roman state as a kind of permanent magistrate – with powers similar to those of the Republican consuls, and with authority in his provinces as a permanent proconsul. His actual power, due to his general predominance and his sole control of the armed forces, was very great. Yet there was a nominal and a moral limit to it. Even the worst Emperors refrained from ordering the execution of Roman citizens without formal trial, and the better Emperors employed deprecating formulae in their relations with the Roman Senate, claiming that they were not 'masters' but 'rulers'. But little of this concerned the provincials or was apparent to them. In the eastern provinces, which had been accustomed to the rule of Hellenistic kings before the Roman period, the Princeps was known familiarly as 'king', and his title of *imperator* was rendered into Greek as 'holder of *absolute* power'.

p 139 (62, 64) The distinction between Roman and provincial attitudes comes out in the use of the Imperial Cult. The Hellenistic lands had identified their kings with 'gods' in the limited sense that the term could be given in Greek theology when applied to any being who exercised power. In the Orient this ruler cult was an accepted custom. But it stank in the nostrils of the upper-class Romans, in whose ideology aristocrats were equals, and kings were identified with tyrants. Hence the early Emperors refused to be worshipped during their lifetime as ruler-gods by Roman communities inside or outside Italy. But the ruler cult was encouraged in the eastern provinces, and rather surprisingly was introduced into the barbarian provinces of Northern Europe. In both areas it was thought to provide a bond of loyalty between the provinces and Rome, though it was modified by combining the cult of the ruling monarch with that of the City of Rome. When provincial deputations came to Rome to offer some extensions of the Imperial Cult to the reigning Emperors, these regularly refused or deprecated such offers in public. Even the Emperor Nero refused the offer
p 140 (67, 68) from the Senate itself of his own cult at Rome, with the remark that 'the Princeps does not receive the honour of a god until he has ceased to be among men'. This secondary form of the worship of the dead as divine beings had long been tolerated at Rome as a thing of another order. So the full force of the Princeps' position as an absolute ruler received expression only in the provinces.

Elements of independence

Between the Emperor at Rome or the governor in his provincial capital and the civic communes there was no regular intermediary. But there came into being a form of provincial assembly that partly supplied this lack. By the end of the first century of the Principate each province had a council composed of deputies drawn from the self-governing communes and cities. These were originally created to provide, on the provincials' own request, for the organization of the Imperial Cult. The leading men were encouraged to spend their money lavishly on the ceremonies of the Cult, which were conducted with much pomp, while splendid titles such as Asiarch or Bithyniarch were given to the deputies and their annual presidents, who acted as high priests of the Cult and organized elaborate spectacles of beast-fights and gladiators in connection with it – shows at which in later times persecuted Christians frequently perished. In time the councils took advantage of their position to present complaints against unsatisfactory governors. This involved a regular debate about the conduct of the departing governor, and the despatch of a mission of councillors to prosecute him at Rome. The function of the councils did not develop much further, though they sometimes assisted in the publication of Imperial edicts. But they provided a platform for provincial opinion, even if only of the upper classes, and eventually offered an obvious pattern for the councils of the Early Church.

By no means the whole territory of the Empire in its first century was under the control of Roman governors. The Romans had absorbed their world partly with the co-operation of local dynasts. Many of these retained their dominions under the new order. Beyond the Imperial frontiers also local rulers of tribes and confederations were brought under varying degrees of dependence. Within the Empire the client king was a convenient instrument in areas where the native population was incapable of local self-government or notoriously hostile to alien rulers. The kings had internal autonomy, and kept armies of their own to maintain peace and order, and hence paid no tribute to Rome. Such principalities survived longest in the eastern zone, but after the final provincialization of Judaea and Pontus (AD 41, 63) the remaining kingdoms within the Empire were steadily replaced by direct government. The Empire ceased to be a land of ancient kingdoms, but the idea of kingship was kept in being by the increasing tendency to regard the Princeps as the King of the whole Empire – *Basileus* – though never 'King of Kings'.

Some local city-states that had helped Rome in the age of her conquests long retained full internal independence as 'free states'. Many kept this status under the Principate, especially in the eastern provinces. Such city-states were withdrawn from the jurisdiction of the Roman governors, and received attention from Rome only if their tumults became excessive. Many elements of Greek liberty and democracy survived in the free cities, whereas elsewhere the Romans tended to favour oligarchy. It was by no means an advantage for a Christian community to be established in a 'free state'. The local courts had capital jurisdiction, and there was no indifferent Roman governor to shelter the unpopular Christians from local prejudice. The list of 'free states' included some great cities, famous in Christian history, such as Syrian Antioch, Byzantium, and Athens, though their free status gradually became attenuated in the 2nd century AD.

Roman law

The famous system of law that is commonly regarded as the great legacy of Rome to modern Europe was the civil law concerned with the rules of private property and contracts, its transference and inheritance, and the civic status of individuals. This law regulated the transactions of Roman citizens with one another. It did not operate between aliens, but was the private law of the Roman citizens of Italy and of the Roman boroughs throughout the Empire. Hence it was not the law of the bulk of the provincial inhabitants of the Empire, least of all in the eastern provinces, during the first two centuries AD, before the *Constitutio Antoniniana* formally granted Roman citizenship to all the peoples of the provinces in AD 212, and possibly not even then. Roman governors exercised a double jurisdiction, under Roman civil law for the benefit of Roman litigants, who were numerous enough in the propertied classes of all provinces, and under local law for the non-Roman majority. But inevitably the Roman governors tended to interpret local law by their knowledge of Roman law. Not much is known about the development of provincial jurisdiction outside Egypt, where the papyri show that Hellenistic law continued in use under the Roman régime. But the letters of Pliny the Younger as governor of Bithynia show that in matters of civil law he normally followed local usage, and when in doubt invoked the 'precedents of my predecessors'. When these did not suffice he fell back on his Roman experience. In criminal and administrative jurisdiction the situation was different. Here the governor was dealing with matters affecting public order which were of primary interest to the Roman government. Penalties were at the discretion of the governors, and they tended to follow the rules of Roman criminal law, while in times of crisis the instructions of the central government might disregard all local privileges. When the Emperor
Trajan ordered the abolition of all private associations in Bithynia, p 335
he reluctantly remitted the order for the 'free city' of Amisus, remarking: 'In all other cities which are under the fiat of our rule, this kind of thing must be forbidden.' So the intervention of Roman usage was much more apparent in matters of public order and criminal jurisdiction than in the sphere of civil law, where for the formative generations of Christianity the dominant influences were Hellenistic.

Life was particularly complicated for persons of mixed status, and for aliens sojourning in a commune which was not their native place. The Roman Empire was full of sharp legal differentiations of status. Certain legal transactions could not take place, or could not be enforced, between inhabitants of the same place whose civic status was different. Property could not easily be inherited from a citizen of a Greek city by a son who had acquired the Roman citizenship. Ways were invented to circumvent such difficulties, but personal situations could be awkward for a citizen of Tarsus who happened to be a Roman citizen, and still more awkward when he was also an orthodox Jew.

VI
'THE WORLD'S GREAT AGE'

GRAECO-ROMAN SOCIETY AND CULTURE
31 BC-AD 235

J.-G. GAGÉ

'Greece, the captive, made her savage victor captive, and brought the arts into rustic Latium.'

HORACE 'EPISTLE II'

The Graeco–Roman world-state
was the matrix within which Christianity grew to birth. A vast free-trade area, which has only rarely been equalled either before or since, it could offer a facility of movement which was the enabling condition for the spread of Christianity round the Mediterranean, and a degree of cultural uniformity which, despite local variations, made the growth of the new religion, once it had started upon its course, almost easy. It was this Graeco-Roman society, too, which provided Christianity with the forms of imagination by means of which the earliest Christian thinkers expressed themselves. In architecture, as we shall see in Chapter VII, it provided a blend of Roman concrete construction and Greek decoration which had been worked out over the past three hundred years and which proved particularly suitable for the first official Christian buildings. It even provided the Church with its name, *ecclēsia*, from the democratic assemblies in the Greek East; and with the name of its chief official, the *episkopos*, from the town-clerk.

Mediterranean society might have been very different. If Antony and Cleopatra had been victorious at Actium, they might, so recent research has suggested, have established a world-state centred on Alexandria. Such a state would inevitably have leaned more towards the Orient and, in that event, the Eastern Churches might have predominated over those in the West. As it is, Augustus promoted a blend of the Greek and the Roman which proved remarkably stable, lasting, with Rome as its centre, for over 300 years until, with the establishment of Constantinople as an Imperial seat, the two segments began to drift apart. Symbolic of the unified empire, in which one can discern in embryo so many elements of the emergent Church, is this Greek column capital lying where it fell against a background of the Roman brickwork of the Hadrianic Baths at Leptis Magna. (1)

Civic life in the Graeco–Roman society embraced many of the functions which we associate with central government. Thus, although the Roman Peace was the essential condition for the spread of Christianity, it was the local context which moulded the earliest Christian communities. The relief (above) shows personifications of three Italian, originally Etruscan, towns. (2)

Census was the responsibility of the local authorities. In one interpretation, this relief shows census officials at Rome. (3)

Direct taxation was again managed by the cities. This relief shows German peasants paying their taxes in the form of rents. (4)

The civic year was enlivened by cultural, athletic and religious festivals: a sacrifice in the presence of the Imperial family. (5)

Political activity for the majority was restricted to local government. These local election slogans were found at Pompeii. (6)

Romanization meant urbanization throughout the Empire, and in the frontier lands complete new cities were built on virgin sites. They were equipped with all the necessities for a lively civic life: temple, council-chamber, judgement-hall, theatre or amphitheatre, bath-house or gymnasium. The *basilica* at Timgad in North Africa (above) was probably used for hearing law suits, of which the vast majority were in local jurisdiction. Only exceptionally, as in the case of St Paul, would the decision be referred to Rome.

Much of the business of Empire was undertaken on private initiative. A grave relief (above) commemorates public works of the deceased, which included the management of the corn supply and provision of a gladiatorial show. Below: the bridge over the River Tagus at Alcantara, remarkable for its bold design, was built at the expense of eleven leading citizens of the province of Lusitania. It is 617 feet long and the central arches are nearly 90 feet in diameter. (7–9)

The citizen's loyalty was, above all, to his home town: only secondarily did he think of himself as a 'Roman' or a 'Latin'. When attacked in Jerusalem, St Paul proclaimed: 'I am a Jew of Tarsus, a citizen of no mean city.' Different Emperors naturally favoured those provinces where they had been born, and the Severi took special care for their native North Africa. This temple at Djemila (Cuicul) in the Algerian highlands (above) is dedicated to them. Beside the road stands a tall conical fountain. (10)

Few Roman markets have such an intimate air as that at Leptis (below), presented by Annibal Rufus. One stall has deep grooves, as from the honing of knives. Elsewhere standard weights and measures, another civic responsibility, have been discovered. (11)

Roman Hellenism reached its zenith during the 2nd century AD, when Hadrian made Athens fashionable once more. Dating from this period are some fine structures including a library (below), one wall of which still survives. (12)

Shows and circuses, theatre and amphitheatre, were the amusements of the Graeco–Roman world. Roman theatres differed from the traditional Greek theatre in construction, reflecting the move away from high religious drama to burlesque. The Roman theatre was an enclosed structure, with the *scaenae frons* rising to the full height of the auditorium and joined to it at the sides. As at Orange (above) it was often richly decorated with tiers of colonnaded niches and statuary. (13)

Used as a fort in the Middle Ages and later as the city-gate, the Constantinian Baths at Trier (below), being always exposed to view, may have influenced mediaeval church design in their recessed windows and the disposition of the masses. (14)

The city of Thysdrus, goaded by oppressive taxation, revolted in AD 238 and placed Gordian I, proconsul of Africa, on the Imperial throne. All that remains of this once prosperous city is the great amphitheatre, rivalled only by the Colosseum at Rome. (15)

By sea as well as by land, Roman rule meant security and peaceful development, although here Rome's achievement consisted not so much in innovation as in the protection and fostering of existing trade. Top right: a mosaic from Sousse showing a merchant ship unloading a cargo, probably of metal bars, in a shallow harbour. Two workmen are wading through the shallow water, each carrying one ingot. On the shore two other men are weighing ingots in a large pair of scales. The axis of navigation was the route from the North African cornlands to Ostia, which fed the capital. Centre right: one of the corn ships, the 'Isis Geminiana', on a tomb fresco now in the Vatican. At the stern of the ship stands the captain, Farnaces. In the centre, a porter pours corn from a small sack inscribed *res* (property) into a larger one, in the presence of Abascantus, probably the owner of the ship and of the tomb, and the agent of the state with his tally-stick. On the right, another porter says, '*feci*' (I have done it), while two more carry sacks from the shore. Below: large jars set in the ground at Ostia, used for storing corn or oil. (17, 19, 20)

The system of navigation was remarkably well developed even by modern standards. When St Paul has to undertake a sea-voyage, we understand that this is perfectly normal, although no doubt it was more of an adventure than it would be today. Fleets were posted against pirates at Ravenna, Misenum, Alexandria and in the Black Sea, and, to judge by their remains and their appearances on monuments, lighthouses must have been not uncommon. That at Dover (above), perhaps one of the first structures the Romans built when they came to Britain, was used in the Middle Ages as the belfry for the adjoining church of St Mary-in-the-Castle. Right: the massive stone quayside at Aquileia, now at some distance from the sea. (16, 18)

River transport utilized many small watercourses not now used for this purpose. In the relief (far right) a small barge carrying two barrels of wine is being pulled along a stream in Gaul. Two men tug at the ropes (there must have been three originally), and another steers with an oar. Above stands a row of wine-jars. (21)

FARNACES
MAGISTER
ARASCANTUS
ISISGI
MINIA
NA
RES
FEC

Senators and equestrians formed the 'Imperial aristocracy'. For a senator a property-qualification of a million sesterces was required; for an equestrian, it was 400,000 sesterces. Too many uncertain factors are involved for one to be able to work out a satisfactory modern equivalent, but it is clear that both figures represented considerable amounts. The grandees' magnificent houses have been revealed by excavation and in wall-paintings. The one shown below right must have had the proportions of a Blenheim palace. Even the more modest houses at Pompeii have many attractive features, like this courtyard with a fountain and some rare and important wall-mosaics (below, left). They had all the requirements for gracious living. Left: dinner with music. (22, 23, 25)

Hunting was an increasingly popular recreation among the well-to-do. In this mosaic (right) animals are being captured for the games. To provide a series of wild animal shows was one of the means by which rich men could win popular favour. (24)

Symptoms of decline can be discerned as early as the 2nd century AD when, in order to halt the depopulation of the Italian countryside, Trajan instituted a maintenance scheme for children (above) and destroyed records of debt to the state, events commemorated on companion reliefs in the Roman Forum. Social sickness was increasing, as a consequence of economic sickness. An excess of slaves discouraged the free poor from becoming self-supporting craftsmen. Consequently the municipal bourgeoisie were overloaded and were now becoming exhausted.

The realism of Hellenistic art could show most vividly the horrors of slavery. Below right: this terracotta was suspended from a string for children to whip. Next to it are two Negro slaves, one sleeping against a wine-jar, the other with his hands manacled. Many of the first Christians were slaves. (26–9)

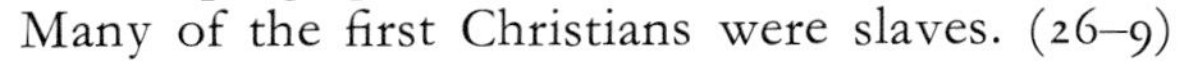

As real military power passed increasingly to professional soldiers, the aristocracy looked back nostalgically to their own glorious past. Here (above) are scenes from the life of a Roman commander of the old school, including his victory celebration, sacrificial offering and marriage. (30)

Bread and circuses were all that the urban proletariat cared for. Some idea of the excitement of the circus may be gained from the relief (below). Economic activity was left to the bourgeoisie, the slaves (left: a slave holding his master's boot) and the freedmen (ex-slaves), some of whom were not ashamed of their humble origins. The freedman Publilius Satur's tombstone (below) shows his sale as a slave, by a Greek dealer, to the Roman who was first his master, then his patron when the slave was freed. (31–3)

It was Augustus who laid down the broad lines which the Graeco-Roman world was to follow for many years and, although he had started out as leader (*dux*) of Italy, his reforms were received no less enthusiastically by a grateful Greek world. Weary of war, it saw him as a saviour who, by his victory at Actium, had inaugurated what was practically a new Golden Age. This bronze from Meroë in the Sudan (right), showing Augustus as an idealized young hero, is Greek rather than Roman in conception. (34)

Antony and Cleopatra (below) stood for a different culture and a different way of life. Had they defeated Augustus at Actium, Alexandria could hardly have eclipsed Rome, but might have built up an independent oriental empire dominating the Near East. There might have been no Roman occupation of Judaea, and no Pontius Pilate. (35, 36)

GRAECO-ROMAN SOCIETY AND CULTURE

31 BC–AD 235

J.-G. GAGÉ

IN THE WATERS OF ACTIUM on September 2nd, 31 BC, it was not
Hellenism that was defeated but rather, if anything, Egypt.
p 127 Octavian had manipulated Italian opinion skilfully; he had made
(25) Antony's collaboration with Cleopatra appear to involve the
p 160 danger of a humiliating subjection of Roman Italy to an oriental
34–6) monarchy. Considering that Antony was still a Roman *imperator*
26 (2) devoted to the memory of Julius Caesar, it is actually very difficult
to say what, in the case of victory, he would have done with the
26–7 former *provinciae*, long since established by Rome, which extended
7–24) from Macedonia to Syria. Studies of Alexandria at this period, in
which distinguished work has been done by learned Hellenistic
scholars such as W. Tarn, have shown that Cleopatra was the
centre of a vigorous propaganda in oracle form, and no doubt a
7–41 number of cults, ranging from Isis to Dionysus, were also enlisted.
1–10) However, these activities cannot be said to have amounted to a
definite political platform, and it would be a mistake to overestimate the success that this propaganda in Antony's and Cleopatra's service had achieved, on the eve of the Battle of Actium, in the lands which were genuinely Greek. Greece itself remained hesitant. Sometimes it showed some partiality towards the republican spirit which had inspired Caesar's assassins; republicanism, after all, had a respectable philosophical ancestry. Even in the province of Asia, where the heavy hand of Rome, represented by authoritarian governors and dishonest tax-farmers, had certainly provoked very serious 'popular' anti-Roman movements, the weariness produced by so many years of struggles between factions played into Augustus' hands. People were concerned with two
54–5 things above all: civic liberties and security for sea-borne trade,
6–21) and the new régime promised to guarantee both. This made the
restoration of Rome's political order almost facile.

An order restored

In 31 BC the Roman Empire was still essentially the political embodiment of a 'Mediterranean' society, in spite of the fact that the great land-mass of the whole of Gaul had been annexed to the Empire by Caesar – Gallic and perhaps even German cavalry of Caesar's had been seen in the streets of Alexandria – and in spite of the further fact that by this date the Danube provinces too were taking shape. The all-important axis of this Mediterranean world
112 was the sea route Alexandria-Puteoli (later Ostia); but we have
(33) also to take account of a number of Aegean ports, and of the
54–5 increasing traffic between Italy and Africa, particularly Carthage,
7, 19, besides the ports of the Iberian peninsula strung along the coast
20) from Tarragona to Cartagena, and indeed to Gades on the Atlantic.
It is possible that Antony and Cleopatra had contemplated making this far-flung society into a political unity centred on Alexandria. However, the indispensable precondition for this was the complete suppression of piracy and the unimpeded exchange of commodities between the various regions; and this was just what the *pax Augusta* was to achieve.

26–7 This programme was preponderantly economic and incidentally
(5, 6) was open to the possibility of economic abuses, such as the
exploitation of Egypt and Africa to provide grain for the population of Rome; yet it was expressed almost spontaneously in formulae of liturgical praise in honour of the quasi-divine hero-saviour to whom this general felicity seemed to be due. This pagan Imperial 'gospel' became more and more vocal under Augustus and his immediate successors. At Alexandria, when Philo castigates Caligula's unworthiness, the gospel swells into a veritable canticle:

> This is the man who ended both the visible wars and the 'invisible' ones in the form of raids by pirates. This is the man who cleared the sea of pirate ships and filled it with merchant ships. This is the man who retrieved the civic liberties of all the cities, who reduced disorder to order, who civilized and
> reconciled all the wild savage tribes, who augmented Greece *f 1*
> by creating many counterparts to her, and who Hellenized the most important parts of the barbarian world. This is the man who safeguarded peace, gave each his due, distributed his favours widely and generously, and never in his whole life withheld any blessing or advantage (*Legatio ad Gaium* 21).

Immediately after the 'miracle' of Actium there was a ban on
things Egyptian, especially the cult of Isis, in Rome and in Italy. p 237–41
This condemnation soon became merely formal; it contrasted (1–10)
strikingly with the position that the Caesars secured for themselves in Egypt itself, where they claimed to be the legitimate descendants of the Pharaohs and the Lagids. Moreover, in Latin literature the Alexandrian style could not be rejected by a Virgil or a Horace, nor could the clock be turned back in painting: paintings in the Egyptian style were already to be found on the walls of the houses of the rich right in the heart of Italy, especially in the towns of Campania. It was fairly easy, and was also politically indispensable, for Augustus' régime to avoid any general demotion of the Greeks, although certain aspects of what one might call the 'nationalistic' restoration promoted by the Princeps ran this risk. In Asia the *Sebastos* very quickly came to be worshipped, in temples expressly dedicated to him, as the champion of the liberties of the people.

In Greek eyes these liberties remained precious, even though they were being exercised within the only narrowing limits of local
self-government. The homage paid by the people of the province p 139
of Asia to the Emperor in Rome brought its reward. They now (62)
felt themselves both completely free to carry on their favourite occupations and also securely protected against misconduct on the part of the senatorial governors, as well as against the greed of the superseded *publicani*. Augustus reorganized the *equites* into an *ordo equester*, a second social class of the Empire which was strictly controlled by the Emperor himself and was remunerated on a
fixed salary scale. This transformed the method of tax-collection. p 150 (4)
It would be optimistic to imagine that the taxes were greatly reduced or that every social class in a tribute-paying province had reason to be satisfied. But, at all levels of Roman administration in the province of Asia, from the residency of the proconsuls (which was sometimes located at Pergamum, the former capital of the Attalids) to the office of the procurators at Ephesus, there were now fewer crying abuses and at any rate more substantial guarantees of a 'redress of grievances' if the provincials appealed to the Senate or to the Emperor.

The problem of the Greeks

Let us consider the problem of the Greeks in the Empire for a moment. The Roman Empire presented itself from the start as administratively bilingual (see the inscription of the *Res Gestae* of Augustus himself at Ancyra). Latin and Greek were the Empire's only two official languages. The vernaculars still spoken in some provinces, Celtic in Gaul, Phoenician or the Libyan dialect of Berber in Africa, etc., were more or less tolerated: they were certainly not suppressed, but they also had no official currency. This use of the two languages manifestly matched the geography of the Empire. From Africa – where the 'Altars of the Philaeni' now separated Tripolitania (included in Africa Proconsularis), which was in course of being Latinized, from Cyrenaïca which was thoroughly Hellenized – to the regions of Macedonia and Thrace, there was an extremely stable division between the Greek and the Latin provinces. However, the official parity between the two languages has, of course, to be distinguished from the Greek p 150–3 (2–15) language's role in cultural life. Similarly 'Romanization' (in the sense of an assimilation of local forms of life and of town-planning to those of Roman Italy) has to be distinguished to some extent from the strictly linguistic process of 'Latinization', which is illustrated so clearly and so perfectly in Spain and Gaul.

It is important to underline these differences before going on to consider the social structure of the Empire, since the consequence was that, in the age of the Antonines for example, towards the middle of the 2nd century AD, there could be something like social equality between a fairly 'blue-blooded' Italian senator, a Gallo-Roman senator, and one from the province of Asia. At the same time their cultural standards would still remain different, and on this plane assimilation was never complete. However it could, and often did, happen – paradoxical though this often was – that it was the Gallo-Roman dignitary who was passionately devoted to p 152 (12) Greece and sought for opportunities of visiting Athens, while the rich *clarissimus* from the province of Asia was just beginning to develop a taste for life at Rome. The Empire was too diverse to allow of unification in any modern sense. On the other hand, people of various social classes, whatever their birthplace, now had reason for travelling from one end of the Empire to the other. The *clarissimi* travelled in the service of the Senate and the Emperor, the *equites* in the Emperor's service only, and to this extent it is correct to speak of an 'Imperial aristocracy', whose titles to this status were becoming more and more independent of the individual's home and of his local connections.

Before considering how and on what terms the upper classes became accessible during the first two centuries AD, first for dignitaries from the Latin West and then for those of the Greek East, it will be as well to define the legal basis which Augustus adopted in regard to the Empire's Greek inhabitants. The recent discovery of inscriptions such as the 'Edicts of Cyrene' has enabled us to revise the former conventional view.

It can be said without inaccuracy that in the period following the Battle of Actium the Roman Empire was threatened by two dangers. In the first place, in so far as Augustus' Principate was based on the corporate feeling of a 'citizen' body, the *cives Romani*, who were still mostly resident in Rome or in the Italian municipalities, there was a danger that, *vis-à-vis* Rome, the provincials might relapse into being merely tributaries – juridically foreigners whose rights did not match their obligations. Second, Augustus reconstructed Italian society on hierarchical – in fact, thoroughly conservative – lines; and, to this extent, he was reversing the policies of Julius Caesar. He was reversing these in depressing the status p 158–9 (27–9, 31–2) of slaves and in limiting both the number of manumissions and the rights of many categories of freedmen. These two policies were not co-ordinated, and accordingly there could be wealthy or aristocratic provincials who were outside the Roman citizen-body or, in other words, were *peregrini*. Augustus also reintroduced a subdivision of the 'Latin Status' which, at the close of the Republican age, had looked as if it were becoming obsolete. Freedmen with restricted rights, known as *Juniani Latini*, were thus assimilated to provincials who were ceasing to be mere *peregrini* on their way towards attaining Roman citizenship.

In the Imperial age the two policies were actually modified or even reversed under the pressure of circumstances or for the furtherance of the Emperor's interests. Augustus had been consistently parsimonious in granting Roman citizenship, but p 139 (64) Claudius, in the words of Seneca's satire, 'swore that he would see all the Gauls in togas'. We shall return to this development later. The point also applies to the position of slaves and the rights of freedmen. Here too the original restrictive measures were not carried to their logical conclusion. So far from that, Augustus himself established a precedent by employing slaves and freedmen in the organization of his own household. In this, Augustus was behaving as a private slave-owner, whose freedom of action was restricted, so far, by only a minimum of protocol. Most of the Caesars followed Augustus in this. To the disgust of the Senate, Claudius made the 'Imperial freedmen' eligible for appointment to posts in the public administration, and subsequently they played a very important part at the summit of the Imperial government in virtue of their being the Princeps' employees. Most of them were of Graeco-oriental origin. In many cases they were highly educated and adept at business. It must be borne in mind that they were playing an active part in the Imperial administration long before the aristocrats of the same provinces were admitted into the senatorial order.

Freedmen who had been emancipated by private owners had the p 159 (32) right of organizing themselves into colleges of *Augustales* – first in the Italian *municipia* and then in those in the Latin provinces. The title *Augustales,* which perhaps involved ritual obligations, enabled its holders to minister publicly to the Emperor's prestige alongside of the 'bourgeois' governing class, the decurions. Certainly actual slaves were too long left at the mercy of their masters' caprice. Slaves were not juridical persons; they had no legal status. Freedmen, however, were assimilated to plebeians whose freedom was absolute, and the freedmen stood for a spirit of initiative and of readiness to take risks. This spirit was marred, all too often, by excessive acquisitiveness; yet it supplied an element that was sadly lacking in a society which in the main persisted in valuing only landed property, and in recognizing and honouring as its aristocracy a class of *latifundiarii* who were insufficiently interested in industry and commerce. The acquisitive *parvenu* type of freedman has been immortalized in Trimalchio, but there must have been many who succeeded in rising above Trimalchio's vulgarity.

The broadening of the state

In the matter of personal statute, Italy was exclusive-minded. She wanted to keep to herself the political and economic profits of Empire which Augustus as 'leader' (*dux*) of all Italy in 32 BC had promised or restored to her. Italy was normally opposed to the extension of grants of the *civitas Romana* in the provinces and later, *a fortiori,* to the admission of provincials, no matter how rich and distinguished, to the Senate at any rate. As reconstructed by p 130 (32. …) Augustus, the Senate was purely Italian, and did not even include many representatives of the Italian *municipia*. The Senate of the Flavians – after Vespasian's great registration of the Senate by act of censorship, in the sequel to a civil war – was, if possible, even more Italian, in the sense that the newcomers came from those parts of Italy which were semi-'provincial', such as the former province of Cisalpine Gaul. As Tacitus put it, they introduced sober virtues into that eminent body. A few Hispano-Romans and Gallo-Romans had already been admitted. The former were already the most Italian of provincials; the latter had been admitted as a result of a celebrated appeal by Claudius; but the progressive opening up of the Senate by the concession of equal opportunities to provincials did not become marked before Trajan's day. Recent work by Lambrechts, Barbieri and others has enabled us to gauge the development of this process in certain regions and to work out percentages, though these are still only provisional.

Thus at the beginning of the Principate there was a danger that most provincials, whether mere subjects of Rome by right of conquest or citizens of nominally 'free' cities, would be for a long time to come in the status of *peregrini*, under a number of legal servitudes, particularly financial ones, in return for a protection accompanied by a minimum of benefits. This was long to be the situation in the western provinces, though collective grants of 'Latin Status' (*ius Latii*) enabled an increasing number of cities there to become autonomous *municipia*. It is known that Vespasian, at one stroke, made a comprehensive grant of the *ius Latii* to all Spanish communities which did not already possess Roman citizenship, and it seems that in many cases they were transformed into *municipia Romana* soon afterwards.[1] This upward movement was unmistakable, and it was alluring for 'Latinized' provincials. Full Roman citizenship made them almost the equals of the Italians.

As one can easily imagine, the problem was different in Graeco-oriental provinces. A decree of Claudius confirms what might anyway have been guessed. A person coming from those parts

The Greek cities in mainland Greece and in Asia Minor were, as allies of Antony, technically enemies, but were always treated with respect by Augustus. Successive Emperors furthered the Hellenization of Asia Minor, and, toward the end of our period, Graeco-orientals came to play an increasing role in the business of Empire. (1)

could not qualify for a senatorial career unless he had a very good knowledge of Latin. Naturally in the early days of the Empire many of Rome's Graeco-oriental subjects must have spoken and written Latin badly. Considering the prestige of Greek, it is not to be expected that dignitaries whose language was Greek would be interested in seeking Roman citizenship or angling for posts for which Roman citizenship was a required qualification. That, I think, is the problem which worried Augustus.

An anecdote relating to his last days, on the occasion of his last visit to Campania, is indicative. Suetonius recounts that the Princeps had just received the homage of some Alexandrian sailors near Puteoli. It is significant, because it is not accidental, that their salutation was made in the quasi-liturgical form that we have already observed in a passage of one of Philo's works: *per illum se vivere, per illum se navigare* (through him they lived, through him they sailed the seas). The victor of Actium, revisiting as an old man a Campania that was steeped in Alexandrian influences, had, so to say, forgiven Egypt. *A fortiori*, he had done justice to Hellenism. In these circumstances he gave to his friends 'in addition to various small gifts, Roman togas and Greek cloaks (*togas . . . et pallia*), with the stipulation that the Romans should adopt the dress and language of the Greeks and the Greeks those of the Romans' (Suetonius *Augustus* 98).

The 'Graeco-Roman man'

49 (1) This ideal of an harmonious symbiosis between Romans and Greeks – this dream of a 'Graeco-Roman man', as one may perhaps put it – can be traced in Augustus' mind and in his political measures. He must have become aware of it during his stay in Samos in the winter of 30–29 BC. During the last century of the Republic the Greek provinces had suffered economically from a certain amount of collusion between the equestrian *publicani*, who farmed the major taxes, and groups of Italian businessmen, *negotiatores Italici*, who had settled in a number of commercial centres, for example Delos and Mytilene. The foundation of Roman colonies on Greek soil confronted the Greeks with a new threat. It must always be remembered that, during the years in which Octavian (or Augustus as he became in January 27 BC) was reorganizing the Greek East, thousands of veterans who were p 135
sworn to loyalty to Caesar and were for the most part proud of (55)
being Italians, were migrating to the settlements assigned to them as rewards. This was the last act of military violence before a partial demobilization. Every province, apart from the Latin ones, tried to escape. As a matter of fact, this time the brutality which had characterized evictions in Italy at the beginning of the triumvirate was avoided, but, even though the ruffianliness of this soldiery had now been toned down, they did not make desirable neighbours. However, it must be admitted that the colonies which were planted in this manner, at Antioch-in-Pisidia for instance, proved to be unaggressive islands of Latinity. The infusion of Italian blood was very slight, and marriage alliances, common business ventures and even common religious associations sprang up so quickly and peacefully between the Roman colonists and the Greek or Hellenized natives that there are cases in which the leading dignitaries of a province, who look like Greeks, were really the actual descendants of Caesar's veterans.[2]

Thus in the Greek and Hellenized provinces groups of Roman citizens, organized in a *conventus*, coexisted with the native communities. Augustus manifestly took this fact into account on at least two occasions which are known to us. Between 29 and 27 BC, he issued directives regulating the worship of his own person which was developing in the province of Asia, and he did this at the risk of producing serious repercussions at Rome. He authorized the cult – and this is remarkable – in different temples and under different forms. At Pergamum and Nicomedia he allowed the 'Greeks' of Asia and Bithynia respectively – those to whom he gave

this name according to Dio Cassius LI 20 – to practise a cult of Rome and of himself, the *Sebastos* (*Augustus*). In other cities, for instance Ephesus and Nicaea, he instructed the 'Romans' to
p 139 worship *divus Julius*, the deified Julius Caesar, and *Roma*. This
(62) distinction is clearly designed to exempt the Italian *cives Romani* from a form of cult which Augustus eschewed in Italy itself. In a way he was treating the 'Greeks' as subjects, and in fact they had long since become used to living under a monarchical régime. The honour of these provincials was saved by their being treated as Greeks.

Later in his reign, Augustus was made cognizant of complaints from Cyrenaïca, which, like Asia, was a senatorial province. In trials in the governors' courts, the Cyrenaïcans were being victimized by the criminal intrigues of Roman citizens domiciled in the province, who were abusing their right to sit as judges in these cases. In the rediscovered edicts, Augustus once again treats the 'Greeks' with consideration. It is not certain that he gave them recognition as a single comprehensive community;[3] but at least he defended their rights, intimated that they might soon sit on juries, and moved the Senate to establish a process for investigating complaints of this kind. All the commentators agree in thinking that it is remarkable that the Cyrenaïcans, in their several cities, should thus have been treated as a collectivity, notwithstanding the presence of a powerful Jewish community in this province. It is also noteworthy that, in the matter of immunities and of mutual obligations of the several cities, the edicts draw a distinction between immigrant *cives Romani* and natives of the province who had been granted citizenship individually.

The main problems were thus recognized in the time of Augustus and were treated with a concern for fairness which moderated the current Roman nationalistic tendencies. Undoubtedly the Emperors of the first two centuries, and especially those of the Julio-Claudian dynasty who were descended from the conqueror of Gaul, saw Romanization as an obligatory task. It was to be carried out initially, and perhaps exclusively, in the western provinces, and the means was to be the linguistic process of Latinization. In Greek-speaking provinces this policy had its manifest counterpart in the renunciation of any major colonization projects, and in a courteous acquiescence in a sort of privileged status among *peregrini* for populations that spoke Greek and that
f 1 also lived in cities with Greek institutions, with traditions of freedom, and with a respectable, though not always distinguished, standard of culture.

Hellenization-Romanization

It is necessary to define the meaning of the terms 'Romanization' and 'Hellenization' if one is to form a balanced judgement on whether, in the first two centuries AD, the societies embraced in the Roman Empire were relatively homogeneous or were decidedly diverse. Except on a strictly linguistic plane, the two terms are not absolutely on all fours with each other. In the western provinces, as we have seen, Romanization presupposed a previous Latinization, the fostering of the exclusive use of Latin among peoples with an Iberian, Celtic or Punic past; but the term 'Romanization' can also be used meaningfully in the case of regions in which, to consolidate her authority or her popularity, Rome acquiesced in employing Greek. In such cases 'Romanization' was almost equivalent to 'Hellenization'. It is known that on the Anatolian plateaux it was Imperial policy over the centuries to foster the creation of autonomous cities, where before there had been only rural townships or villages attached to temples. With the exception of the not inconsiderable Imperial domains administered by procurators, the territory of Anatolia was Hellenized under Rome's direction and the enterprise initiated by Alexander's conquest was thus carried on. This work of civilization, which was already bearing fruit by the middle of the 1st century AD, was conducted behind the line of legionary camps that, from the Flavian age onwards, defended the Euphrates frontier against the Parthians, and this is the best claim that the Roman Emperors had to being, as several of them claimed to be, new Alexanders. This involved only a minimal infusion of Roman blood. This Roman policy no doubt explains the form given by Philo to his laudation of Augustus in words that have already been quoted: 'This is the man who augmented Greece by creating many counterparts to her and who Hellenized the most important parts of the barbarian world.' Rome did still better than that. By the 3rd century AD her achievements in the field of Hellenization were being guarded, in her name, by a Roman army that was now semi-barbarian and that was diluted with some purely oriental contingents.

In the Empire as a whole Romanization meant leading native communities to reshape themselves in a municipal mould. The mould was Italian, and it was of little use in the Greek provinces, even where the cities were recent foundations without a long tradition of independence. However, a standardized form of common institutions was worked out bit by bit, with the result that in the 2nd century AD there was scarcely any difference between the domestic administration of a Latin or Roman *municipium* in Gaul
or Africa and one of these *poleis*. The *curia* and its decuriones in the p 150
Latin West had their counterparts in the *boulē* and its *bouleutai* which (7)
existed, in many cases since an earlier date, in the Greek East. A very similar bourgeois class monopolized the local public offices
and undertook the heavy duties called *leitourgiai* – the *munera* or p 151
curae of Latin towns. There was the same parish-pump vanity, the (8, 9)
same liking for decorations and public inscriptions or statues.

This spirit of rivalry long kept local life going, at least in its urban form, in the Latin provinces, and in Africa longer than anywhere. In the Greek provinces it took the more pretentious form of 'euergetism'. The *euergetai* were the grandees – the dignitaries – who were an ornament to their cities in virtue of their talents, their roles in the Imperial cult, their missions to Rome and, above all, their representation of their respective cities in the official provincial *concilia*, assemblies whose agenda was the maintenance of the cult of Rome and Augustus. *Euergetai* were sometimes paid the same honours as the 'founders' of their cities. We have inscriptional evidence of this for the Gaii Julii in Asia.[4] *Euergetai* presented their cities with statues and treated them to festivals. The Latin provinces had their equivalent in a hierarchy of dignitaries, a series of provincial flamens (priests) and the provinces' *patroni*, usually senators, at Rome. But in a Greek province the abiding influence of ancient traditional forms is more noticeable. In Asia the representatives were usually ex-Asiarchs or in a *neocorus* city (*i.e.* one with an official temple of the Imperial cult) ex-high priests.

Conversely the Emperors more or less supported the Hellenization of life and culture to the west of the linguistic frontier. This Hellenization was more or less successful in gaining ground in the Latin provinces (see the quotation from Favorinus of Arles below).

After Augustus Roman citizenship was granted progressively both to individuals and, in increasing measure, to whole communities throughout the Empire, and this transformed what had originally been the citizenship of one city into a sort of 'citizenship of Empire'. Before Caracalla, in the famous *constitutio Antoniniana* (AD 212), granted Roman citizenship to almost all the inhabitants of the Empire, subject to its being fitted into the framework of their local city franchises, the possession of Roman citizenship made provincials who were natives of an *urbs peregrina* virtually mobile. It opened for them the entry into one of the two upper classes, *i.e.* into careers in public service beyond the limits of their native provinces. However, they were not entirely deracinated from their home-city, and the Emperors found it necessary to see that they were not totally relieved of their local obligations.

Social mobility

How much mobility and how much stability was there in 'Graeco-Roman' society? Changes in social position did not depend solely on changes of economic fortune. The hand of the Emperor was always felt. He might encourage in provincials the ambition to embark on the higher Imperial careers. He was also able at any moment, through caprice or through policy, either to expedite promotion or to break a career.

At the bottom there was always that malady of all ancient
civilizations, an excessive number of slaves; and consequently, p 158–
apart from more direct abuses, there was insufficient inducement (27–9,
for free men at the proletarian level to become craftsmen or 31–2)
industrial workers. It was only at Rome that there was a *plebs frumentaria*, depending on public distributions for the necessities

of life. At Rome the most insignificant pauper citizen theoretically kept his *libertas* with the status which that involved. (Pliny develops this idea in a rather far-fetched way in his *Panegyric* of Trajan.) But p 112 there was an equivalent in such great cities as Antioch and Alexan- 3, 34) dria; and within the narrower framework of municipal institutions, especially in Italy, it was rare for a *plebs urbana* not to be assisted by foundations mostly endowed by rich individuals. We shall see why p 159 these *plebes* were mad about 'spectacles' and why so many distribu- (33) tions of largesse were made during festivals and games.

The number of slaves and the proportion of slaves to free people varied. The proportion was very high at Rome, where the grandees lived. In the provinces – for instance in Asia – the free population, working in the cities and the ports, was certainly more industrious, but the dignitaries continued to surround themselves with a staff of slaves. When the leading members of the family of the Pompeii Macrini, descended from Theophanes of Mytilene, entered the Senate, it is highly probable that they transferred almost their entire household of freedmen and slaves from the Aegean to Rome. An inscription of Tusculum (Vogliano-Cumont) has revealed this family's activity in the 2nd century AD in the cult of Dionysus, and this bond of religion must have given their household a somewhat unusual character. In Rome the senatorial aristocracy lived in 156–7 luxurious mansions and, during the summer, in country houses in 3, 25) Italy. Their income, although spent in town, came chiefly from land. Pliny the Younger was neither of the oldest stock nor of the highest income level, yet there must have been dozens of hundreds of *coloni* cultivating the soil of estates whose revenues paid for Pliny's well-spent periods of retreat in his Laurentine villa (he had cultivated tastes, collected a library, and appreciated landscapes). The possession of extensive estates was not merely an indispensable social qualification for these *clarissimi* – their fortune had to be at p 335 least a million sesterces. From the time of Trajan onwards a (6) provincial could not sit in the Senate unless he had invested at least a third of his fortune in Italian land. Soon there were scarcely any senators, even of Italian origin, who did not also own land in the provinces. The old families of the republican period had mostly vanished and the 'patricians' still required for staffing certain priesthoods were usually artificially ennobled plebeians, but the new aristocracy was determined to remain a class of *latifundiarii*. This was never more noticeable than in the age of the Antonines, p 139 when Antoninus Pius continued to manage his lands and brick- (65) works and when the literary court favourite, Herodes Atticus, drew his fabulous fortune from similar sources – P. Graindor has described him as 'a millionaire of the ancient world'.

The serious economic consequences were not felt for a long time by the Imperial government. Its estates, scattered through all the provinces and managed by an army of procurators, were the *latifundiarii's* competitors and in some respects their accomplices. In the West, the standard of living of the dignitaries who attained senatorial rank was almost the same, though it looks as if there may have been less social mobility and economic activity in the grandees' way of life and standard of living in the West than in Asia and Syria, where income derived from land was apparently not so sharply divorced from income derived from business. The dignitaries of the eastern provinces, several of whom rose to be senators, are known to us from a wealth of inscriptions. They had their own 'peerage', and the existence of free municipal institutions did not prevent the formation of veritable 'dynasties', starting in some cases with equestrian rank. In the 2nd century AD the most popular *euergetai* were typically 'Graeco-Roman' – for example the Vedii Antonini at Ephesus, or Vibius Salutaris, a Roman who was devoted to Ephesus and its Temple of Artemis and showered gifts upon it. From the beginning of the Empire we hear of Ionian aristocrats who had taken up the cult of the *Sebastos* and had set an example to all their cities. It was from this circle, which was still wholly Greek in its traditions, that Caligula recruited the young men[5] whom he wanted to introduce to Rome shortly before his assassination.

Dio of Prusa, known as Chrysostom, who was victimized by 138–9 Domitian and became one of Trajan's advisers, was only a leading (61) bourgeois in his native town in Bithynia. He did not lead a sheltered 335 (6) life: letters exchanged between Pliny and Trajan show that his enemies intrigued against him and accused him of having mis-

One common type of honorific inscription takes the form of a 'cursus honorum'. That of Pompeius Falco (he has fourteen names in all) begins with his highest post, the proconsulship of Asia. (2)

managed the city's finances. The historian Dio Cassius was probably one of his descendants. He was a good writer in literary Greek, with a wonderful appreciation of Roman Imperial policy. Even when he is criticizing the Roman Emperors whom he had to serve, from Commodus to Severus Alexander, he has a fine sense of the traditions and destiny of Roman rule. He came closer than many Italian civil servants to the ancient breed of Roman statesmen who had been devoted to the *respublica*. There is no indication that his personal and provincial interests as a Greek from Bithynia prejudiced him against the Roman world-state – which the Empire virtually was. It is not surprising that two or three generations p 336 after his time, in the reign of Diocletian, an Imperial capital was (12) established in Nicomedia and that the business of the Imperial p 335 court and its departments of state was conducted in Latin there. (*f 5*)

The 'Imperial aristocracy'

Moreover, the son of a father who was already of senatorial rank p 130–1 was already himself a senator *in posse*. At an early age he started his (32, 38) career by holding in succession the ancient public offices, quaestor- p 130–1 ship, tribunate of the people or aedileship (if he was not patrician), (34–9) praetorship and eventually consulship. This was the prelude to *f 2* administrative duties which mostly depended on the Emperor. These posts were by turn civil and military. After he had been praetor he would be the commander of a legion, *legatus propraetore* of an Imperial province, or proconsul of a lesser senatorial province. After he had been consul he might be made governor of a large Imperial province such as Syria. For the provincials he was alternatively the representative of the Senate and of the Emperor; for the soldiers he was a military officer; and if, for instance, he was given charge of the Italian roads or of one of the treasuries he was p 132–3 an administrator. There were two kinds of consulship. The holder (40–46) of the regular consulship took office ceremonially on January 1st, often as the colleague of the Emperor, and this kind carried the greatest prestige with it; but the 'supplementary' *consul suffectus*, whose term of office lasted for only a few months, acquired full consular rights. If our man became a consul of either kind, he might succeed one day to one of the great proconsulates, for example Asia or Africa, or alternatively he might be nominated *f 2* *praefectus Urbi* by the Emperor, a post whose judicial functions were constantly increasing in importance. He would have lived only for a few years in Rome; much more of his life would have been spent outside Rome in administrative work in a number of different provinces which might be far distant from one another.

In the first century of the Empire it was rarer for Greek provincials to study Latin rhetoric and law than it was for Italians and Latin westerners to study Greek, and consequently senators of Greek origin were seldom given administrative posts in Italy or Latin provinces. This distinction disappeared in the 2nd century AD, when bilingualism was improving both in frequency and in standard. The rule of not giving major posts in a province to natives of that province was adopted late in the day. Marcus p 139 (65) Aurelius introduced it after his experience with Avidius Cassius. A senatorial career rarely broke the ties of a *clarissimus* with his home p 335 (7) province. So far from that, it increased his influence there. On the other hand, in consequence of living in several provinces where he was initially a stranger, the senator often formed new ties which lasted, and as 'patron' of a province in which he had served he mediated between the Imperial power proper and the representatives of the cities in the person of its flamens or ambassadors. This comes out in trials for embezzlement in the reigns of Domitian and Trajan which are known to us through Pliny's letters.

In order to enter the equestrian order a more modest fortune, 400,000 sesterces, was required, and in practice it could be entered by licence granted by the Emperor. The *eques* started his career with minor military commands, the *militiae equestres*, as reorganized by Claudius, and these were usually followed by a series of procuratorships, mostly financial. H. G. Pflaum has shown[6] that there was a fairly precise hierarchy of procuratorships with a salary-scale rising grade by grade from 60,000 to 200,000 sesterces, the level of the *procuratores ducenarii*.

The former class of equestrian *publicani*, who had lived on the p 150 (4) profits of tax-farming and had all too often made their fortunes by exploiting provincials, had been transformed into a hierarchy of professional tax-collectors, and the old system of tax-farming been almost entirely superseded. It seems that the salary had certain perquisites attached to it to tempt candidates. If the *eques* made progress in winning the Emperor's favour, he could attain the prefectures, of which the two highest were the posts of *praefectus Aegypto* (*i.e.* viceroy of Alexandria), and Praetorian Prefect, who p 135 (50) was head of the pampered garrison of Rome and also chief of staff, with increasing administrative and judicial functions – an important enough personage to be envied or feared by the senators and, on occasion, to be dangerous to the Emperor himself.

It was possible to become an *eques* at a very early age, but the title was not hereditary, as the rank of *clarissimus* was. Obviously, since the Emperor had a free choice, the Italians were at first more numerous among equestrians than among senators, but, later on, the number of *equites* of provincial origin increased; and the process was more rapid for *equites* than it was for senators. What is important from the social point of view is that, though the son of an equestrian, however eminent, was not guaranteed the same rank, he could normally expect to become a senator. This was ensured by the institution of *adlectio*, whereby the Emperor took an official from the equestrian order and enrolled him in the Senate on some particular rung of the senatorial ladder, with a dispensation from the requirement of holding the quaestorship at any rate, and more often, as time went on, from having to hold the praetorship either. This practice was beneficial on the whole, because it let fresh air into the senatorial order, and it became more and more frequent from the time of the Flavians onwards. By the 2nd century AD it had almost become the rule. As often happened in the history of the Roman Empire, a prerogative of the Princeps which could have been exercised capriciously tended actually to work for the good of his subjects. It was a means of making full use of highly trained or genuinely gifted men. It acted as an effective counterweight to the undesirable policy of turning the Senate into a closed caste which the Senate itself might have been tempted to pursue.

For more than two centuries the senators and the *equites*, the greater and lesser 'Imperial aristocracy', to use modern terms that are not precisely applicable, had divided their time between their city, Rome, and the provinces, and even those of them who distinguished themselves the least would have gained a very full experience of the realities in the life and the administration of the Empire. Though both careers imposed heavy responsibilities, it was impossible to avoid a lingering jealousy between the two orders, and a touchiness on the part of senators over any diminution of their corporate powers. It is a well-known apparent paradox that the growth of 'Caesarism', which sometimes led to a deadly tension between the Emperor and the 'senatorial opposition' at Rome, was not always frowned on by the provincials – the reason being that it sometimes led to an improvement in conditions and a stricter control over the governors by Imperial agents. This is hardly surprising, since, under Nero and again under Domitian, the moving spirits in the opposition were usually senators with a Stoic p 206– (5, 6) background, who were very Roman or Italian in outlook. We realize how little provincial opinion might be impressed by these senators when we read in Tacitus (*Annals* xv 20–21) the summary of Thrasea's speech to the Senate opposing the demand that provincials should be given the right to appear at trials of governors. Actually, Thrasea wanted to prevent provincial intrigues from favouring the hirelings of the Emperor in the Senate, but the tone of his speech was unfortunate:

> So let us face this unprecedented provincial arrogance (*adversus novam provincialem superbiam*) with a measure befitting Roman honour and dignity. Without diminishing our protection of provincials (*tutela sociorum*), we must recover the conviction that a Roman's reputation depends on Romans alone (translation by Michael Grant in the Penguin Classics).

Rhetoric versus philosophy

As has been said, the Roman Empire was administratively bilingual, but this did not reflect the situation in cultural life. In any case the linguistic frontier, which is easy enough to follow on the map, does not give the measure of the limits of the expansion of such a potent civilization as Hellenism was. Let us look at the instruments, the forms and the principal centres of 'Graeco-Roman' culture.

Not all the Emperors were men of letters or philosophers. Nevertheless the Emperors progressively developed something like a court life and so tended to be permanent patrons of the arts. Furthermore the Principate had at the beginning taken effective steps to ensure the good will or at least neutrality of the artists and the philosophers. In the fantasy *The Banquet of the Caesars* which Julian wrote in the 4th century AD in Saturnalian form there is the somewhat surprising picture of the deified Augustus vouched for p 140 (67, 68) on Olympus by Apollo in response to a plea made by Zeno the founder of Stoicism. p 206 This fantasy had its point: the Emperors always tried, wherever possible, to win the blessing of the men of letters. They tried to make the Principate into a philosophical ideal, and from Trajan's reign to Marcus Aurelius', after the quarrel in p 139 (65) the 1st century AD between the tyranny of the Caesars and the schools of philosophy had become ancient history, they largely succeeded. On the whole, the culture of the upper classes in the 2nd century AD was based chiefly on rhetoric, but the brilliant movement known as the Second Sophistic introduced a new ideal. The exponents of this school used the ancient term of *sophistēs* to cover prowess in both rhetoric and philosophy. They certainly showed a capacity for thinking profoundly as well as sincerely, but they were all too prone to making set-speeches in ornate language, and to indulging in frivolous panegyrics.

However, not all cultivated Romans in and after the 1st century AD were dedicated Atticists. This had to wait until the reign of Hadrian and the fashions that he initiated or encouraged. p 152 (12) After Actium the Italian and, in essence, Latin reaction was propitious for the flowering of a great literature in the Latin language. We p 335 may note that Nero, in his theatrical dream of being an Olympic or Pythian victor, was making a complete break with the men who had first influenced him. Seneca and Lucan were Hispano-Romans by origin, and no province was more thoroughly Romanized than Baetica, from Cordova to Seville (Hispalis). The Latin that was spoken and written there was so fine that Greek gained less ground there than elsewhere. Curiously enough, another son of this province on the Atlantic fringe of the Empire, Hadrian, was to be an exception to the rule when he became the great propagandist of Hellenism and the champion of Athens.

In the 1st century AD Rome was an educational centre which was capable of being self-sufficient. It came to be better equipped, and

to receive more official support, under the Flavians, after Vespasian had sponsored the foundation of two professorial chairs for instruction in Greek and in Latin rhetoric respectively. In Quintilian's programme, which was published at this time (see the beginning of the *Institutio Oratoria*), the author is pessimistic about the neglect by many parents of their children's education, and he is almost aggressive in claiming for rhetoric the educational role in which its rival was philosophy. An incident in the dispute was the celebrated 'conversion' of Dio of Prusa, who preferred to live as a philosopher – a choice which entailed not only a *credo* but also a
p 205–7 way of life and practically a style of dress, including a beard! On
(1–4) the whole, it was *de rigueur* for Latin senators like Pliny the Younger and most of his correspondents – Greeks and Hellenized orientals were only just beginning to make their appearance in Italy – to receive an education in public speaking, of the legal even more than the political genre. The standard was high, but experience showed that a knowledge of private and administrative law was insufficient for men who were to serve as judges, administrators, and so on. The resulting specialization of jurists attached to the Emperor and serving in the *consilium principis* organized by Hadrian had a major effect on culture. At the end of the 2nd century AD under the Severi these specialists sometimes held the post of Praetorian Prefect.

In this generation, in which Caracalla's edict was in gestation, the brilliant activities of the Roman lawyers chiefly benefited the Imperial monarchy, and the old aristocracy could not rejoice in it. Legal training became more specialized and more concrete, and it became increasingly attractive to men of mere equestrian rank. This development balanced the fashion for Hellenism, and Latin kept its prestige as the legal language (*e.g.* in the school of law at Berytus) with consequences that we moderns cannot afford to underestimate. In the middle of the 3rd century AD, when it seemed that the barbarians had come to stay and when poetry appeared to be relapsing into being merely a conventional exercise, the successful maintenance of the solid Latin discipline of law prevented a total collapse and kept hope alive for a Latin culture until the Constantinian restoration. It is at first sight strange that at the height of the 3rd-century AD crisis intellectuals, scholars and writers, like Gargilius Martialis who appears to have been Severus Alexander's biographer, concentrated their energies in military careers. This little-known combination of scientific culture with military service had been going on for half a century. Gargilius himself met his death in Numidia while doing battle with some rebellious tribes.

Attic nights

Nevertheless, the period running from the Flavian to the Severan
p 152 age was a *floruit* of Hellenism. Athens became fashionable once
(12) again, and Hadrian enlarged its area by adding a new town. Students of philosophy and even philology went there to study under masters with high reputations, and it was there that Aulus Gellius conceived his *Noctes Atticae*. At the same time the Second Sophistic revived Atticism in language. It was a festival time, although the festiveness was somewhat illusory. One of the
p 139 principal illusions was – to judge from an epic glorifying Lucius
(65) Verus that was satirized by Lucian of Samosata (Πῶς δεῖ ἱστορίαν συγγράφειν – *How to Write History*) – the serious entertainment of the idea that the Roman Emperor would conquer the Parthians (the panegyrist ventured to say 'Persians'). Lucius was hailed as a new Alexander, the champion of Hellenism. But the realities of the situation were different, particularly since the Arsacid kings officially styled themselves Philhellenes. Such was the obsession with the Persian Wars in a Greece that was intoxicated with its own past.

This school of intellectuals achieved exceptional renown in the age of the Antonines. It lured western provincials as well as Roman nobles to Greece. The case of Favorinus of Arles is well known. We now also know that, a generation before his time, a dignitary from Toulouse, Trebellius Rufus, was honoured at Athens and that the Areopagus exchanged letters with the *curia* of Toulouse about him. These Greek honours no doubt built up his prestige in the province of Gallia Narbonensis and he appears to have become the first flamen there. The neighbouring schools of Marseilles could no longer satisfy the curiosity of a Gallo-Roman amateur of this type. All the same, Trebellius Rufus failed to achieve a literary reputation.

Favorinus was probably the author of the *Address to the Corinthians* which has been handed down as Dio Chrysostom's *Oratio XXXVII*. He is probably pleading for the re-erection of his own statues in the Greek cities which had removed them when he had fallen into disgrace with Hadrian. Here is his apologia:

> Well, if someone who is not a Lucanian but a Roman, not one of the masses but of the equestrian order, one who has affected not merely the language but also the thought and manners and dress of the Greeks, and that too with such mastery and manifest success as no one among either the Romans of earlier days or the Greeks of his own time, I must say, has achieved – for while the best of the Greeks over there may be seen inclining towards Roman ways, he inclines towards the Greek and to that is sacrificing both his property and his political standing and absolutely everything, aiming to achieve one thing at the cost of all else, namely not only to seem Greek but to be Greek too – taking all this into consideration, ought he not to have a bronze statue here in Corinth? – Yes and in every city – in yours because, though Roman, he has become thoroughly Hellenized, even as your own city has . . . ; in all cities everywhere, because he pursues the study of wisdom and already has not only roused many of the Greeks to follow that pursuit with him but also attracted even many of the barbarians. Indeed, it seems that he has been equipped by the gods for this express purpose – for the Greeks, so that the natives of that land may have an example before them to show that culture (τό παιδεύεσθαι) is no whit inferior to birth with respect to renown; for the Romans, so that not even those who are wrapped up in their own self-esteem may disregard culture with respect to real esteem; for the Celts, so that no one even of the barbarians may despair of attaining the culture of Greece when he looks upon the man (translation by T. E. Page (and others) in the Loeb Classical Library).

Such extremes outdid, perhaps intentionally, even Hadrian's mania for things Greek – Hadrian, the Princeps who had just broken with Favorinus. It is doubtful whether the orator of Arles ruined himself for this reason, but the infatuation with Greece certainly carried sincere souls away and also stimulated genuine talents. From Hadrian's reign to Marcus Aurelius', the custom of giving Imperial salaries and 'immunities' to the 'sophists' and professors, and the parochial rivalries which brought them invitations from one town to another, especially in the province of Asia, created for this cultural élite, not indeed a well-established status of the modern kind, but at least a semblance of privilege. These talented men, exemplified in Aelius Aristides and Herodes Atticus, rubbed shoulders as equals with the richest senators, even when they were not wealthy senators already, as Herodes was. They also carried on a correspondence with the Emperor. If the letters of Avidius Cassius, quoted in the *Historia Augusta*, which are so hard on Marcus Aurelius, could be accepted as being something more than sheer forgeries, they would prove that at least one man of action, who happened to be the son of a *rhetor* from Cyrrhestica, held this festival to be too expensive a luxury at a time when the Empire was labouring under hard-fought wars and under the plague.

Even when Athens had resumed its historic role, with its 'university' consisting of four endowed chairs of philosophy, the academic world still had more than one centre. It was always possible for a teacher with a high reputation to draw pupils to a small town, as Epictetus drew them to Nicopolis. An inscription at Oenoanda in Lycia, dating from the end of the 2nd century, in which an Epicurean teacher, named as Diogenes, has put his doctrine on record, has provided unexpected evidence of the existence of a school of philosophy in a smallish town. With greater justification, the cities of Asia developed foundations of their own. Smyrna, for example, had a museum as well as one of the finest libraries in the ancient world, and at Aphrodisias there was, we learn from an inscription, a family in which both father and son enjoyed a literary reputation which added to their prestige as priests of the *Sebastoi*.

Gymnasiis indulgent Graeculi

If one considers the domestic life of some single city and picks out
a Greek-type city – though a Latin-type town such as Carthage
would not present a very different picture – it is clear that the
focuses of cultural tradition were the gymnasium and the various
p 153 places of entertainment, the odeon, the theatre and so on. *Gymnasiis*
(13–15) *indulgent Graeculi* ('Greeklings have a weakness for gymnastics'),
as Trajan wrote to Pliny in a letter on the subject of an over-
ambitious building project in a Bithynian city. The gymnasium at
p 112 Alexandria, and to some extent the one in Syrian Antioch too, was
(33, 34) a stronghold of Hellenism which cast a suspicious eye on the local
Jews and was ready to turn against the Romans if the Emperors
appeared to favour the Jews unduly; but not all gymnasia of the
2nd century AD displayed this spirit. Most of them failed to
preserve that balance between athletic training and intellectual
education which characterized the Classical and Hellenistic ages,
though the young continued to pass through them, and most of
these cities (which often had a *gerousia*, a council of old men, besides
their *boulē*) gave careful attention to the training of the *neoi* and the
neaniskoi.

The whole municipal system of training, and the control of the
trainees by benefactors who enjoyed the Imperial favour, did entail
certain risks, but in general the system worked in a peaceful routine.
The high points in the Graeco-Roman cultural year were the
p 151(8) 'spectacles'. The 'madness' of the arena, the circus for races and
p 152 the amphitheatre for gladiatorial combats and wild animal hunts –
(15) all these performances are attested by inscriptions, ruins and the
p 157 protests of the Christians from Italy to Africa, Gaul and the farthest
(24) limits of Spain. The passion for 'sport' in the form of violent
p 159 contests (*agōnistikē*) was an evil which entertained and corrupted
(33) the Empire, particularly when the Emperors themselves yielded
f 3, 4 to it and made spectacles of themselves in order to win the applause
given to their rivals for popularity, the athletes. Logically the
Christians' reaction, on the precedent of Seneca's, would have
been sheer disgust if a tragic obstacle had not inhibited these
dissenters. The exhibition of Christians in the circus, and, still more
p 340 sensationally, their exposure *ad bestias* in the arena, supplied
(25) Christian hagiographical literature with its magnificent vocabulary
for the martyr's combat. Similarly the increasingly military charac-
p 248–52 ter of the persecutions and the competition of Mithraism gave
(32–51) poignancy to the simile of the *militia Christi*.

The bloody spectacles savoured by the Romans such as the
gladiatorial shows were not so repugnant to the Greek world as
used to be thought. The researches of L. Robert have brought to
f 3 light more than one piece of evidence to this effect in the Greek
East. But in the genuinely Greek provinces there was an attempt
to conduct competitive sport (*agōnistikē*) on the lines of the athletic
tradition of Ancient Greece. The documentary evidence, which is
worth collecting, is now very full. We have many inscriptions
celebrating, as heroes, athletes or artists, including musicians, who
had been victors in a series of competitions (*agōnes*). There were
efforts to maintain the most ancient of these, such as the Olympic
Games, and we know that Nero took an interest in these. Many
new games were founded in a number of towns, especially in Asia
Minor, and in many of these cases the founders were private
individuals. The Balbilleia at Ephesus, founded about AD 70–1 by
Nero's former prefect-astrologer, are a curious case. As in Ancient
Greece, the total winner in a major sporting competition brought
glory to his native city, and, for some Bithynian cities, Trajan even
sanctioned, subject to certain reservations, the right of 'iselastic'
entry (*i.e.* by means of a breach made in the walls) for the
p 139–40 returning athletic victor. It was becoming rather rare for these
(64–8) spectacles not to be associated with the Imperial cult.

It was on these occasions that the assiduously itinerant 'sophists'
of the 2nd century AD often gave their popular lectures. One of
their stock conceits was that the town – Corinth, Smyrna, and so
on – was still independent, as it had been in the past – a genre of
fiction that was unlikely to give the Emperor much anxiety. It was
also at Olympia, the site of the Games, that, according to Lucian,
a man called Peregrinus stacked, lit and mounted a 'Heraklean'
pyre, and so burned himself to death. The Latin West had no exact
p 153 equivalent of the gymnasium, but in many towns the baths and
(14) their appurtenances performed the same function. The fugitive

The decadence of Roman amusements is aptly illustrated by this relief from Halicarnassus of the female gladiators 'Amazon' and 'Achillia', now released from service, as the inscription above proclaims. (3)

pieces assembled in Apuleius' *Florida*, the tritest of this highly gifted writer's works, originated in lectures delivered – in many cases in the presence of the proconsul – in the theatre at Carthage. The author, who was styled *philosophus Platonicus* in his home town Madaura, produced *c.* AD 170 a Latin adaptation of the exercises of the sophists. These were brilliant but frivolous.

Marcus Aurelius: the end of the ancient world

The relative stability of this Graeco-Roman society displayed some weaknesses and lapses even as early as the first two centuries AD. Banditry afflicted the countryside in certain provinces, but it was kept within limits and it was no great problem for the towns. The 'picaresque' chapters of Apuleius' novel (*The Golden Ass*) give us some surprising *aperçus* of it. In the reign of Septimius Severus, Bulla's brigand band, reinforced by deserters from the army and by rebellious Imperial employees (the *Caesariani*), made havoc in the heart of Italy. This was an alarming symptom, and indeed it was a sign of the times. In the rising of Maternus in Gaul, which is characterized as being a 'war of the deserters', we can perhaps detect a revolt of social 'outcasts' combined with something like an anti-Roman revival of native social consciousness. The seriousness of these episodes must not be either exaggerated or underestimated. From AD 181 to 235, in the reigns of Commodus, the last of the Antonines, and the Severi, the principal pillars of the Empire's structure remained erect and so far still scarcely shaken. It is customary to attribute to Septimius Severus the introduction of the military régime which eventually repressed and eliminated the senatorial class, but in truth Severus' régime still respected many of the realities and many of the appearances too. The relative positions of the upper classes and the allocation of high office were maintained without any radical change down to the reign of Severus Alexander. Indeed, this Emperor tolerated at least a penchant towards the restoration of a civil régime. The real change came when this weak liberal Princeps was assassinated in AD 235, and the Mainz army group placed on the Imperial throne, for the first time, a soldier from the Danube region, Maximinus, who had not held any of the offices that conferred social prestige and whose only education had been that of the camp.

In fact many innovations were already germinating in the guise of Commodus' whims, and it has seemed legitimate to some distinguished modern historians to reinstate, with a new meaning, an epigram of Ernest Renan's: Marcus Aurelius: the end of the ancient world. Like Renan, they see in Marcus' reign the beginning of a new epoch in ancient history. But was it the beginning of a general decline or the beginning of a renewal in the positive sense of the creation of new forms? Rostovtzeff inclines to the pessimistic

Various types of gladiators provided a varied programme: the 'Samnites', the 'Thracians' who fought the 'mirmillones' in Gallic armour, the 'net men' who sought to entangle the 'secutor'. On this relief from Ravenna two gladiators fight with javelins. (4)

view, whereas Mazzarino descries in it a plan for the 'democratization of the ancient way of life'. In other words this way of life continued to be predominantly Graeco-Roman and was not really being sacrificed but was rather being given a new social basis, and Imperial policy was adjusting itself to the change.

It is impossible to summarize the history of so great a crisis as that of the 3rd century AD, or even its first symptoms, in a few pages. We must be content here with just the following few remarks.

Two crises

In the course of the 2nd and 3rd centuries AD two fundamental crises can be discerned, and both of them are expressions or aggravations of social sickness. First there is the crisis of the municipal bourgeoisie. This class had long supplied the public officers and decurions (or *bouleutai*) in the cities and had contributed to the flowering of the towns. This had been virtually a new phenomenon in the western provinces, which before the Roman conquest had known nothing better than a crude kind of *oppidum*. f 1 In the cities of Asia Minor it had been a fairly ambitious renewal. These bourgeois were city-dwellers who were much attached to their cities and were landowners in their cities' respective territories. By monopolizing the holding of local public offices they had raised their standard of living, and had been able to look forward to seeing their sons and grandsons rise to equestrian or senatorial careers with the aid of a show of loyalty to the Emperors. Through them the upper classes maintained useful links with their respective provinces.

p 158 (26) For various reasons these bourgeois who had supplied many of the benefactors, the *euergetai*, were now showing signs of exhaustion. Their charitable foundations were rapidly disappearing, and this bred discontent among the urban proletariat, since, under the régime of the early Empire, many of the services which we think of as being public responsibilities were dependent on private initiative. The cities' expenses were heavy. The decurion class was now in process of being constrained to undertake the onerous p 151 (8–9) 50 (5) p 152 o, 11) duties which were called 'liturgies' in the Greek East and *munera* in the Latin West, and this was in addition to, or as an alternative to, the holding of the local public offices. The Severi postponed the crisis in their beloved African provinces by acts of favouritism, and they carried the process of municipalization to the limit; but – perhaps originally for convenience's sake rather than out of malice – they imposed on the decurion class the responsibility for the payment of the most important taxes, particularly the tax on which they depended for rewarding an extremely demanding army and civil service, the unpopular *annona militaris*. Neither the stability of the decurion class nor its loyalty to the Emperors could stand up to such pressure for long. The first effect was to make this class perilously unpopular with the local peasants, who had up till then been fairly docile. p 153 (15)

As it happened, the Emperors had at this juncture to step up their military effort on all the frontiers and to introduce progressive changes in the methods of recruiting the army. Up till then, recruitment had been a fairly light burden on civil society and even on the garrisoned provinces – indeed the burden had sometimes been hardly perceptible. Legionary soldiers were recruited among urban plebeians from Italy and later from the provinces which had been the most thoroughly Romanized. The soldiers of the auxiliary corps were drawn from among *peregrini* who were often only very slightly urbanized. On discharge, they had been given Roman citizenship and had in many cases been incorporated in municipal life. p 134 (47) p 134–5 (48. 49) p 135 (55) Hadrian drew the logical conclusion from the growing lack of interest among the Italians. He had made it the general practice to recruit units of the army locally, in the provinces where they were stationed. But Hadrian certainly had not intended to change the social composition of the army. Nevertheless, at the beginning of the 3rd century AD the army was composed more and more of country people and less and less of city dwellers accustomed to urban life. The divergence of interests between the soldiers and the civilian population, especially the decurions, did not start so early and was not so general as Rostovtzeff supposed, but it would be true to say that this tendency had set in before the members of the upper classes, especially the senators, abstained from or lost interest in appointment to the chief military commands. In my opinion the régime of the Severi cannot fairly be described as being a military one. The civil hierarchies were not seriously affected. But in the recruitment of officers and civil servants there is already evidence of a decided increase in the numbers drawn from the army – evidence in fact of the formation of a new 'military class', disguised as an expansion of the equestrian order.

Decay or rebirth?

It is still more misleading to speak of a military régime apropos of Commodus than it is apropos of Septimius Severus. Commodus' fantasies derived from the 'craze for athleticism' which unfortunately had spread and induced a sort of low complicity among the people. Commodus was not actuated by any hostility in principle to the civil hierarchies. We must leave to others the task of describing the curious religious movements which took advantage of Commodus' régime – in some cases paradoxically. The striking fact is that this last of the Antonines broke the tacit compact between the 2nd-century Principate and the senatorial aristocracy of large-scale landowners who were also liberals, at least in their culture. Here again, as always, we are only speaking of pagan circles. Commodus neither invented nor deliberately propagated a 'new culture'. But since the Imperial autocracy was assuming a more and more superstitious complexion, since the proletariat was condemned to credulity by its lack of education (the means of acquiring culture which we have been describing were almost confined to the upper classes), the pagan cultural ideal of these classes was seriously threatened. How could it have remained unimpaired? After AD 212 almost all the inhabitants of the Empire had the status of *cives Romani*, and among them were tens of thousands who had only a veneer of Hellenization, and as many who had been Latinized only by the army. The respective positions of the two languages hardly changed on the map; but, if Hellenism was to have a future in the West, it would have to make a new synthesis of the elements of the high pagan culture, since this was now less relevant to the professional techniques of Roman statecraft.

Rodenwaldt has drawn attention to a phenomenon which reveals its significance earliest in the history of art. In the evolution of the Roman bas-relief and the decoration of fine sarcophagi we can trace p 190 (33) the development of a new sense of pathos in the second half of the 2nd century AD. The serial themes of the reliefs on these sarcophagi p 186 (24) are taken from the legends of the Labours of Hercules or of Achilles. There is one variety which recounts a Roman's life in an idealizing idiom, starting not later than his marriage and proceeding to his exploits in hunting and war. p 159 (30) The resemblance to the themes of Imperial art is striking. It is as if the grandees wanted to imitate the Imperial virtues or to recapture them from the Emperor. These sculptured biographies of well-to-do or public personages have a social significance. They give food for thought, and what they suggest is that there was at least some nostalgia for the heroic way of life and for military achievement among this upper class which was soon going to be ousted from posts of actual military command. In real life the Emperor was now going to monopolize this style. He was going to be less of a 'philosopher' than he had been.

It is naturally likely that these movements corresponded to some modifications or transferences in the actual content of culture. The primacy suddenly given to Syria by the Severi demonstrates this. f 5 To all appearance the Imperial court continued to favour Hellenism. However, the Second Sophistic is running dry and new tendencies are germinating in philosophical thought, while Athens has manifestly ceased to play the leading role, and the Atticism of the purists is fading out in the works of the new Graeco-Syrian virtuosos. The jurists write in Latin which is almost military in character. Men of letters who are also courtiers are intrigued by the oriental mysteries. There was no longer room in the entourage of the Severi for Graeco-Roman culture as this had been understood and patronized by their predecessors.

By contrast with the traditional claims of the old Roman aristocracy (see plate 30), real power was increasingly held by orientals. The columns and three-dimensional lid, on which reclines the deceased, identify this sacrophagus from Melfi as Asiatic; the other figures are Apollo, a hero, Persephone (?), a male deity and Hades (?). (5)

VII
AWAY FROM SHEER BEAUTY

ARCHITECTURE AND ART IN THE GRAECO-ROMAN WORLD
31 BC–AD 390

JOCELYN M.C. TOYNBEE

'When he perceives those shapes of grace that show in body, let him not pursue: he must know them for copies, vestiges, shadows, and hasten away towards That they tell of.'

PLOTINUS 'ENNEAD I'

Roman and Christian art
are two episodes in the same story. Christianity was a movement that took place within the Roman Empire, and the art of the Christians inevitably rested upon the repertory of techniques – and often of actual imagery – of contemporary pagan art. The same artists would be commissioned now by pagan now by Christian clients. This is as true in architecture (where the basilica can be traced to Roman audience halls, *thermae*, and the shrines of the mystery cults) as of painting (where the catacombs are decorated in exactly the same impressionistic style as the houses of Pompeii, Herculaneum and Stabiae). Not until after 400, in frescos in Italy and in Coptic paintings for example, does a formal, clear-cut, specifically Christian style appear.

Many examples of the adaptation and sometimes literal re-use by Christians of pagan themes will be found in the succeeding pages. In the 4th-century mosaic from a room in a country house at Hinton St Mary in Dorset, England, discovered on September 12th, 1963, the figure of Bellerophon slaying the Chimaera symbolized Christ defeating the powers of evil; and four figures at four corners, the descendants of the figures of the four winds found on many pagan mosaics, could represent the Evangelists. (Writing *c.* AD 185 Irenaeus had compared the Evangelists to the winds, their message going out to the four corners of the earth.)

The central roundel of the mosaic is shown here. There has been a vigorous debate about whether the head can represent Christ. If it does, it would have the distinction of being the earliest portrait of Christ found in Britain. In favour of this hypothesis is the fact that the Chi-Rho monogram is found backing several other portraits (for example in the vault mosaic of the Capella di Sant'Aquilino in San Lorenzo, Milan) which are certainly of Christ, and that it would hardly be placed unexplained behind anyone else. Against: it is unlikely that a portrait of Christ would be set in the floor where it might be trodden upon. However, a decree of Theodosius II and Valentinianus III of AD 427 forbids the representation of the *signum Christi* on floors *(Corpus Iuris Civilis* II, *Codex Iustinianus* I 8), and this implies that the Cross or Chi-Rho, and so perhaps the figure of Christ also, had previously appeared in that position. The pomegranates on either side of the main figure are symbols of eternal life and the tree below is probably the Tree of Life. (1)

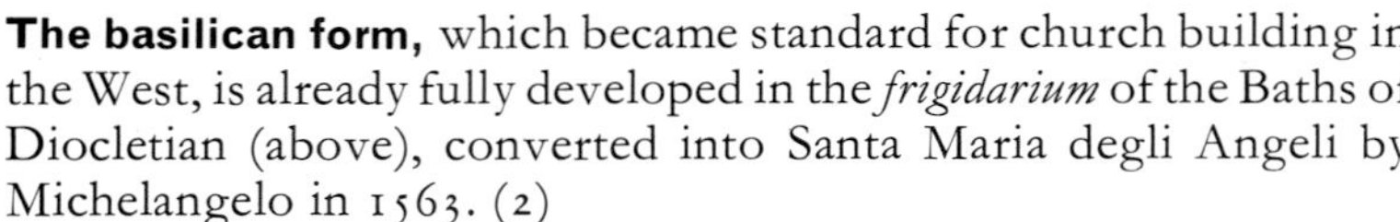

The basilican form, which became standard for church building in the West, is already fully developed in the *frigidarium* of the Baths of Diocletian (above), converted into Santa Maria degli Angeli by Michelangelo in 1563. (2)

Underground shrines followed the same basilican plan. This one, near Porta Maggiore, Rome, was probably used by a 'mystic' sect. Concrete was poured into prepared trenches, the earth between dug away, and the roof vaulted. (3)

The new concrete construction, by giving buildings a rigid, almost unbreakable fabric, enabled vast areas to be spanned by solid vaults. Roman vaulting was not exploited in the West until Romanesque times, but Byzantine architects learnt its lessons and applied them in their own way. Below: the most impressive of Roman basilicas, that of Maxentius and Constantine, built early in the 4th century AD. The three arches opened into a 'nave', of which only fragments survive, and its bays were roofed by enormous groin-vaults of concrete. A detail of one of the subsidiary vaults (right) shows its brick and mortar construction and deep coffers. (4, 5)

The Severan basilica, Leptis Magna. (6)

Former Imperial audience-hall, Trier. (7)

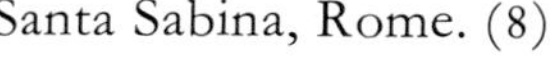

Santa Sabina, Rome. (8)

The ruined basilica (opposite page) of the Severan Emperors at their native town of Leptis Magna, North Africa, still displays its fine colonnade of Corinthian columns The building, originally over 100 feet high, was later converted into a Christian church with a nave and two aisles. The apse where the magistrate sat became the place of the altar. The same thing happened at many other places – for instance at Trier, where Constantine's basilica of about AD 300 (opposite, bottom left) is now the Evangelical church. Next to it (opposite, bottom right) is the 5th-century church of Santa Sabina in Rome, showing how closely Christian architects followed their pagan models. Except for the aisles they are almost twin buildings. (6, 7, 8)

Roman aesthetic sense adapted itself surprisingly easily to Christian values. Left: a pilaster from inside the basilica at Leptis, showing the story of Hercules and Dionysus. The emphasis on the interior as opposed to the exterior of a building was partly dictated by concrete construction. The extreme example is the 'Hunting Baths' at Leptis (below), an ugly collection of concrete shapes from outside, housing interiors bright with fresco and mosaic. But it also fitted in well with the Christian ethos, in which the inner life was supreme, and entry into the church symbolized entry into the heavenly kingdom. (9, 10)

Detail from the Severan basilica, Leptis Magna. (9)

'Hunting Baths', Leptis Magna. (10)

The central plan, either round or polygonal, which found its Christian apotheosis in churches like San Stefano Rotondo in Rome or San Vitale in Ravenna, had been fully exploited by Roman architects. It was used for tombs (*e.g.* the mausolea of Augustus and of Hadrian, or the smaller tomb of Caecilia Metella on the Via Appia), in *thermae* and palaces, and in some cases for temples. Those by the Tiber in Rome and at Tivoli were round, but small in scale. The masterpiece in this form is the Pantheon, of crucial importance for its influence on Byzantine architecture.

From pagan mausoleum to Christian church: Santa Costanza in Rome (below) was begun as a pagan tomb but finished after the official conversion of the Empire to Christianity as a memorial to Constantine's daughters Constantina and Helena. The circular or octagonal plan became popular for Christian *martyria* and baptisteries. The originality of Santa Constanza lies in the fact that its central dome rests on a drum borne on an arcade of twelve pairs of columns. The wall of the drum rises with clerestory windows above the roof of a barrel-vaulted ambulatory which runs round the central rotunda, buttressing the dome. There is again a marked contrast between the undistinguished exterior and the fine interior with its annular mosaics – still with pagan themes – seen here in Piranesi's engraving. (14, 15)

Dedicated to 'all the gods' by Hadrian in AD 126, the Pantheon has been called 'perhaps the first major monument to be composed entirely as an interior'. The cylindrical base is of brick, the dome chiefly of concrete, so that the thrust is vertical (left: a Renaissance drawing showing the construction and original interior elevation). The exterior is extremely simple, being merely divided into three bands by cornices, although it would originally have been covered by stucco and tiles. On the picture (above, left) one can just make out the retaining arches within the wall. The interior consists, on the ground floor, of seven marble-lined niches, alternately apsidal and rectangular, and an attic storey of architectural motifs, crowned by the vast hemispherical dome (above), its five concentric rings of coffering climbing up to the 'eye', which is the only source of light for the whole building. The trabeated portico, impressive as it is, is a concession to tradition that adds nothing to the essential grandeur of the design. (11, 12, 13)

The glowing interiors which, as we have seen, were so appropriately given a religious significance once the Christians began to build on a large scale, had developed in the Roman Empire both through individual and official patronage. Marble veneer, stucco, fresco and mosaic were used lavishly in the *thermae*, in private houses, in mausolea, and in the semi-private shrines associated with the mystery religions. This detail (left) from the Stabian Baths at Pompeii gives some idea of its exquisite quality. (16)

The favourite Roman images of a happy after-life were taken over along with the architectural forms to which they belonged. Left: a detail from the Santa Costanza mosaics, showing the vine-scrolls associated with Bacchus. Birds are another symbol of paradise, and Cupids and wingless *putti*, like the one at the right-hand edge of the picture, stand for the souls of the departed. Renaissance drawings of the lost wall and dome mosaics suggest that at some slightly later date biblical scenes were added to counterbalance more definitely Bacchic mosaics now known to us only from other drawings. (17)

To please the departed, who were conceived of as in some sense dwelling in the tomb, the walls of tombs belonging to the well-to-do were frequently decorated in a bright, almost gay style. St Peter's is built over such a pagan cemetery, and even here the dichotomy between exterior and interior is apparent. The rich stucco and paint in the tomb of the Caetennii (right) contrasts strikingly with the austere and almost stark exteriors of these 'house-tombs', which were discovered under St Peter's in 1939–40. (18)

Classicism: the statuesque figures from the famous Villa of the Mysteries at Pompeii (left) represent the earlier tradition in Roman painting – self-contained and finished products of a self-sufficient and perfected society. The scene probably depicts the Dionysiac initiation of a bride-to-be. In this section a child reads the ceremonial rules between two matrons, one sitting, the other standing. In the centre a woman ritually washes her hands, while on the right is Silenus playing a lyre. (19)

Impressionism: from the 1st century AD onwards another style of painting grew up which, by deliberate sketchiness and incompleteness, sought to convey the wider, spiritual implications of an episode or scene. In the well-known Trojan Horse painting (below left), also from Pompeii, the four almost corpse-like figures splashed in the foreground point to the tragedy which all their efforts are only hastening; while the long-robed, torch-bearing figures caught in a lurid light, the shadowy forms of the warriors which appear above their heads and, in the background, the bare outline of the doomed city, convey essentially the same message. (20)

Christian Impressionism: it was the second style which the earliest Christian painters adopted. The figures of the pursuing Egyptians from the fresco of the Crossing of the Red Sea in the catacomb of the Via Latina (below) provide a striking parallel. (21)

A mystagogue addressing his followers, the apotheosis of an Emperor, or a camouflaged Ascension? Whatever the subject of the vault-fresco in the tomb of Marcus Clodius Hermes (left), in it the spiritualization of the human form reaches its extreme. The followers, their heads mere blobs, their figures elongated streaks, give the impression of a mass of people united in straining upward towards a common goal. (22)

Human heads, painted in the most accomplished impressionist technique, have been discovered in the Campanian city of Stabiae, south of Pompeii (above). The features are suggested rather than delineated. Parts of the face are highlighted, while the rest is in shadow. The eyes are pools of darkness, the hair wispish. Everything points to something beyond, with which the spirit is in communion. (23)

A wider range of meaning than could be conveyed by the Greek ideal of physical perfection was demanded by artists of Imperial times. They turned to allegory and symbolism, hinting at truths beyond the senses. There was a growing conviction that the forces of evil and death could be vanquished, could be 'swallowed up in victory'. It is this conviction that accounts for the frequency of representations of the Labours of Hercules (above) or of battles of Greeks against Amazons or Romans against barbarians (below) on Roman funerary monuments of the period. (24, 25)

'To everything there is a season, and a time to every purpose under the heaven: a time to be born and a time to die ...' The 'season' sarcophagus (above) takes comfort, in death, from the endless cycle of eternity. Shown are the figures of winter with high laced boots and crowned with reeds, and spring crowned with flowers. Right: another image of the happy after-life, the pastoral paradise, here on the sarcophagus of Julius Achilleus, one-time gladiatorial trainer and civil servant. Naturally, this theme was frequently borrowed by the Christians. (26, 28)

Personal immortality was to be won by faithful performance of one's earthly duties. Above: a cloth-merchant of Trier records his working life on his tomb, now known as the Igel monument. (27)

Death, the violent sundering of the soul from the body, and the journey of the former to the other world, were symbolized in Roman funerary art by scenes of abduction – the Rape of Europa by Jupiter, of the Leucippidae by the Dioscuri, of Ganymede by the eagle, or of Persephone by Pluto. The mosaic of the Rape of Europa (left) comes from a Roman villa at Lullingstone, Kent, England. (29)

Rebirth from the grave to immortal life as the fruit of victory over death is implied by renderings of another of Hercules' exploits, his reclaiming of the dead Alcestis from Hades (above), on a relief from Celeia, Yugoslavia. A gentler passage to the other world is sometimes shown, in representations of the journey of the soul across the sea to the Isles of the Blest. Borne on the backs of Tritons, sea-Centaurs, dolphins and other kindly sea-beasts, the soul appears as a Cupid or a Nereid. (31)

The delights of the happy dead are symbolized on the mosaic in Bishop Theodore's cathedral at Aquileia by boating and fishing Cupids (left), another pagan motif taken over by the Christians. Right: from the same mosaic, a more specifically Christian theme, Jonah lying under the gourd, was taken by the Early Christians as a prefiguration of rest in Paradise. Even here pagan influence is not lacking: Jonah is shown in the pose in which Endymion had been depicted many times. (30, 32)

The sufferings of this world were not diminished by hopes of a happy after-life, and even those hopes (outside Christianity and the mystery religions) were slim. During the 2nd and 3rd centuries AD, when Rome was faced with relentless pressure on the northern frontier together with internal crises, official Roman art seems increasingly aware of tragedy. Whereas the defeated barbarians of Trajan's Column show a certain repose in death, those on the Column of Marcus Aurelius are contorted and agonized. The rain god (below), from the same Column, actually commemorates a miraculous deliverance of the Roman army, but appears as a figure of doom, as he broods huge and menacing above the piled-up bodies of dead soldiers and of dead and dying horses, with water dripping from his hair, beard, wings, arms and finger-tips, a haunting and terrifying symbol. (33)

TREBONIANUS GALLUS

GALLIENUS

Stress, strain, fear and brutality are marked in the portraits of the Emperors of the 3rd century. **Trebonianus Gallus** (251–3) had a disastrous reign, as might be inferred from the deep furrows on his forehead (far left): the Persians overran Mesopotamia, the Goths, temporarily bought off, re-entered Moesia, and plague was rampant. He was finally murdered by his troops. Even the idealism of the portrait of **Gallienus** (left) cannot conceal the prevailing hardness of the age. He had a relatively successful career (253–68), crushing numerous revolts and winning a brilliant victory over the Goths, until he fell victim to his own staff. Coarse-featured and cruel-eyed, **Balbinus** (below, left) was dragged from the palace and murdered by the Praetorian Guard after having reigned for only three months (238). The shifty opportunist character of **Philip the Arabian** (244–9), allegedly the son of a notorious Arab brigand and later claimed as the first Christian Emperor, is well caught in this portrait (below, right). Finally, in the time of the Tetrarchs, there developed what can only be described as a real cult of Imperial ugliness (right). (34–38)

TWO TETRARCHS

BALBINUS

PHILIP THE ARABIAN

'Maiestas Augusti': alongside the realistic Imperial portraiture of the 3rd century another trend is discernible, a trend which looks up to the Emperor as above the troubles of ordinary people and as the focus of their hopes. On the Column of Marcus Aurelius, on the Arches of Septimus Severus at Rome and Leptis, on the Arch of Constantine and the Obelisk of Theodosius I and, finally, on a *missorium* in Madrid (left) the Emperor (Theodosius) appears in a rigidly frontal pose which anticipates Byzantium, looking straight out of the scene in which he is nominally engaged as if to give salvation to the spectator and to receive his homage. Beside him are his sons Valentinianus II and Arcadius. (39)

'Maiestas Christi': what the pagan Roman world had been looking for in the person of a divine Emperor, it found in that of an imperial divinity. One of the most impressive presentations of Christ as Ruler, *Pantocrator*, is in the apse mosaic of Santa Pudenziana, Rome, where he dominates the scene flanked by apostles, personifications of the Evangelists (the beasts) and the Jewish and Gentile Churches (the female figures). The background is based on Christian buildings in Jerusalem. (40)

ARCHITECTURE AND ART IN THE GRAECO-ROMAN WORLD

31 BC–AD 390

JOCELYN M.C. TOYNBEE

ARCHITECTURE

Rome's continuity with Classical and Hellenistic Greece cannot seriously be questioned, so far as concerns trabeated architecture, that is buildings with horizontal entablatures above their columns. Of this the outstanding representative is, of course, the Greek temple, a basically post and lintel structure using one or other of the three famous Orders, and with all its decorative features – columns, architrave, sculptured frieze and pediments – worn on its exterior. Roman-age architects did, indeed, introduce new elements, both constructional and ornamental, into this type of building. For example, the 2nd-century AD so-called Temple of Bacchus at Baalbek in the Lebanon[1] is internally of an architectural and sculptural elaboration unparalleled in any Classical Greek or Hellenistic shrine. But, by and large, throughout the history of the Graeco-Roman temple in Imperial times an accepted tradition ran on unbroken to the end. There was, however, another, dominating style of Roman architecture that was completely untraditional and revolutionary – the new style of building, mainly for roofing and walling, that emerged under the late Republic and stamped its unmistakable character on the Rome of the Empire and on the many Romes-in-miniature of Italy and of the western provinces.

Stone arches and stone and brick vaults and domes were by no means unknown in the Hellenistic-Roman East. In Italy stone vaults and circular tombs with stone, corbelled, domical roofs had been made by the Etruscans: stone-cut arches in bridges and aqueducts and stone barrel-vaults were built by the Romans from the 3rd century BC onwards. What revolutionized those architectural forms was the discovery and exploitation in Italy under Roman auspices of the vast possibilities of concrete construction – that is, of stone- or brick-faced walls and vaults and tile-faced domes whose immensely strong cores were composed of an aggregate of lumps of stone, broken bricks, tiles, and so forth mixed in mortar, to which in central Italy was added pozzolana, a local volcanic substance of especially effective binding quality. The result was a veritable transformation of architecture as the ancient world had known it hitherto – a turning outside-in, so that it was the composition of a building's interior, not its external look, that was all-important. The new technique could involve the covering, when necessary, of enormous spans; and its essential aim was to contain and organize volumes of space within the uncrackable shells that it provided.[2]

Concrete construction could serve a very wide variety of purposes and express many facets of the Roman scene. It could produce city-defences, the substructures of amphitheatres and theatres, the walls of rows of shops, and, as can be seen most spectacularly in Rome and Ostia, the walls and ceilings of lofty blocks of domestic flats. But its most significant achievement was covered halls, large or small, for secular, quasi-religious, or religious uses. Among the most familiar examples of large secular structures of this type are the main rooms of public baths (*thermae*) – dressing-room (*apodyterium*), cold room (*frigidarium*), warm room (*tepidarium*) and hot room (*caldarium*). At Pompeii in the Stabian, Forum, and Central Baths (pre-AD 79) all these rooms have concrete p 180 vaulting, sometimes covered internally with very fine figured (16) stucco-work. Of the colossal *thermae* in Rome those of Caracalla *f 9* (AD 211–7) have a vast rectangular hall as the pivot of the whole complex – probably the *apodyterium*. It measures internally about 170 by 82 feet and its concrete vaulted roof was supported by eight piers ranged in two parallel rows and connected by eight arches: of its once elaborate internal decoration some remarkable figured capitals survive. Very similar in build is the central rectangular hall of the Baths of Diocletian (AD 298–305/6), measuring about p 174 (2) 200 by 80 feet. Its vaulted roof rests on eight piers linked by arches; and its internal fifty-feet-high columns of grey granite are ornamental rather than structural in function. All the walls and vaults of both of these great thermal complexes were covered externally with stucco imitating unadorned marble blocks with heavily drafted joints. The contrast between austere exterior and exuberant interior, which all the rooms of these *thermae* must originally have offered, is peculiarly blatant in the case of a provincial bathing establishment, probably dating from the 3rd century AD, the so-called Hunting Baths at Leptis Magna in p 177 Tripolitania. There starkly plain domes and semi-domes and (10) barrel-vaults of Nissen-hut-like severity, all of concrete, mask externally interiors whose walls, vaults, and floors are gay with brightly coloured figure-scenes in painting and mosaic and with elegantly worked non-figured floral and geometric patterns in the same media.

Setting for a god

A half-secular, half-religious character may be accorded to the large concrete-domed or concrete-vaulted state rooms in the palaces of Rome, in as much as it was there that the Emperor, a personage in some sense divine or endowed, in part at least, with the qualities and functions of godhead, appeared ceremonially before his subjects. Such is the domed octagonal entrance salon or pavilion which is the most spacious apartment in the portion of Nero's Golden House (*Domus Aurea*) on the Esquiline Hill *f 1* (*c.* AD 64) still surviving, and it was possibly once the palace's centre-piece. It has five small rectangular chambers leading off it radially, and in the apex of its domical vault there is a wide circular opening. Through this *oculus* a dramatic flood of sunshine would

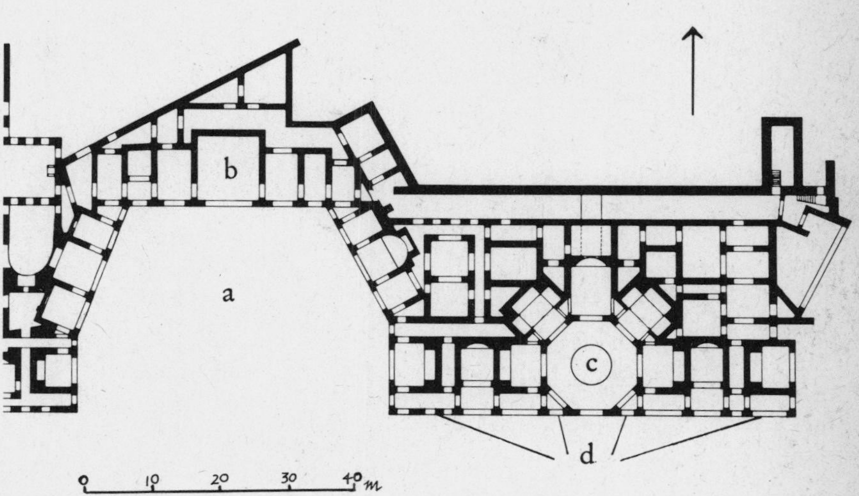

Nero's 'Golden House' in Rome, approached by a courtyard (a) and a reception room (b), had as its centre-piece an octagonal audience-hall (c), partly lit by a colonnade (d) and partly by an aperture in the roof. (1)

have lighted up the figure of the ruler and his entourage and also the room's internal decoration, which, to judge by what has been discovered in other rooms of the Golden House, very probably consisted of mosaics on the vault and of painted and gilded stucco-work and marble revetments on the walls. In the official portion
f 2 of Domitian's palace on the Palatine (*Domus Flavia*), begun *c.* AD 90, three large state apartments, all probably once barrel-vaulted in concrete, would appear to have been consciously designed to enhance the *mystique* of the Emperor's person. All are rectangular in shape and each has, at the end opposite the entrance, an apse in which the Imperial presence could be manifested, on occasion in actuality and permanently in image, at the focal point of the chamber's long axis. These rooms are (to use the names assigned to them in modern times) the *basilica* or judgment-hall and the *aula regia* or reception-hall, to the north of the great central peristyle, and, to the south of it, the *triclinium* or banqueting-hall. The *basilica* is very likely to have had two internal colonnades, although no traces of the original columns have survived. The walls of the *aula regia* were, like its floor, sheathed in coloured and patterned marbles and adorned with a series of niches (*aediculae*) each flanked by ornamental columns resting on low projecting bases. Each of the side walls of the *triclinium* consisted of six great piers with wide doors and windows between them giving access to large decorative fountains (*nymphaea*) with enclosing-walls beyond.[3]

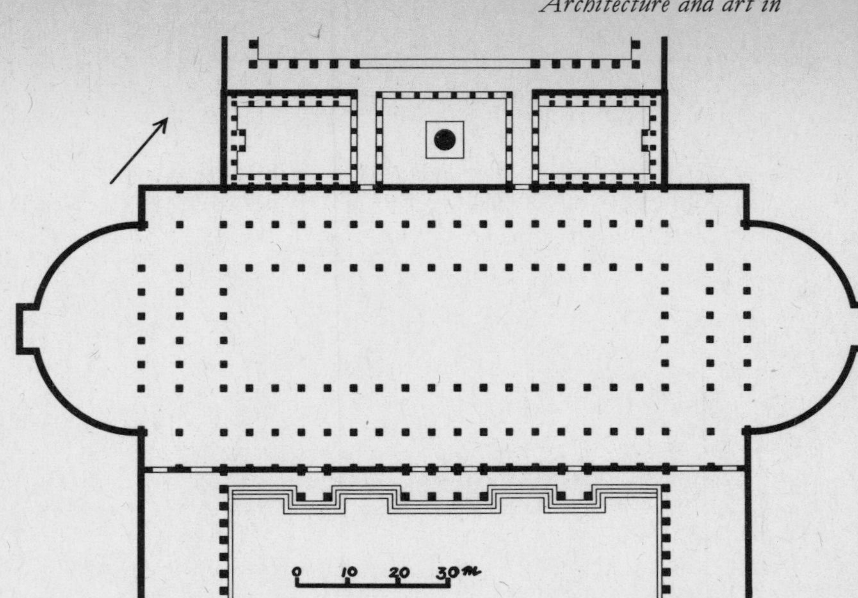

Roman civic basilicae were of two main types, with the entrance and the magistrate's seat facing it either on the short or on the long sides. Some examples of this latter 'Vitruvian' type have apses at each end, as in the Basilica Ulpia. (3)

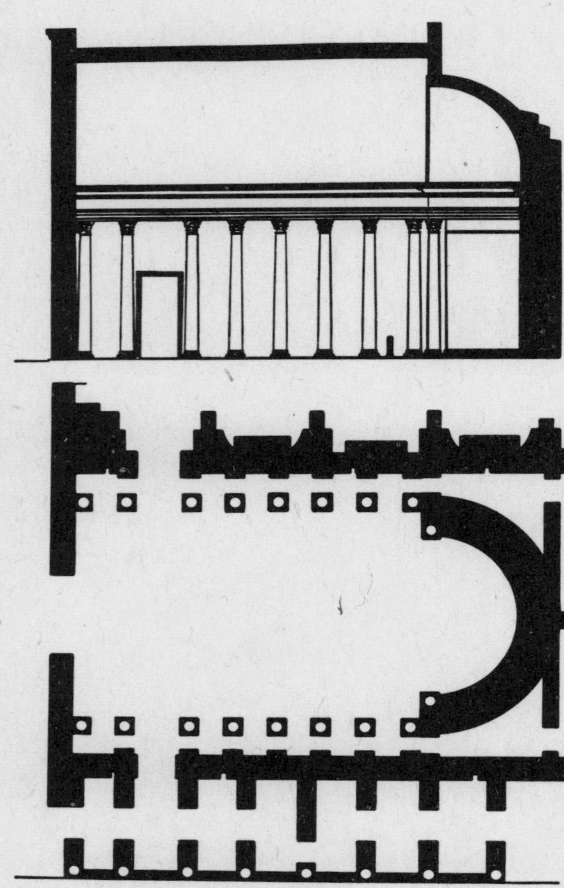

Domitian's palace on the Palatine included three rooms – a reception room, a banqueting-hall and a basilica (above) – all with an apse at one end which concentrated attention on the god-like ruler. (2)

The audience-hall was, naturally, also a distinctive feature of late-Roman palaces, whose owners were surrounded by even larger suites and by an even more elaborate courtly ritual than were their predecessors of the 1st century AD. Such a hall, now known from its substructures only, measuring about 102 by 36 feet and approached through a colonnaded forecourt, a porch, and a concrete-domed vestibule, formed the centre-piece of the southern half of Diocletian's palace at Split on the Dalmatian coast (*c.* AD 306). This hall is without an apse and is likely to have had, not a concrete-vaulted, but a timber-pitched, roof.[4] Slightly later, and built by Constantine at Trier (Augusta Trevirorum) on the Moselle, when that city became the seat of one of the centrifugal Imperial resi-
dences under the late Empire, is the so-called *aula palatina* or palace p 176
audience-hall – a building whose brick-faced concrete walls have survived virtually intact up to their original height through the centuries. It measures about 180 by 90 feet and has an apse at one end; and the walls of its long sides and apse are pierced by windows in two tiers, with perfectly plain, strengthening pilasters between them. A wooden gallery may have run round the building beneath each tier of windows.[5] The roof was pitched and was probably of timber. Inside there are no colonnades and nothing remains of the original decoration of the hall's walls and floor (which was hollow and heated)[6] or of its other arrangements, apart from niches for statues in the apse wall. This apse, which is separated by a huge 'triumphal arch' from the rest of the room and has a floor on a higher level, would have enshrined the Imperial throne.

The town halls of antiquity

The audience-hall at Trier is now popularly known as the *basilica*, a term also so used, as we have seen (above), for one of the state apartments of the *Domus Flavia*. The word is, of course, a Greek adjective meaning 'royal'; and in Roman times and in the western half of the ancient world it was applied to rooms or halls of varied kinds and purposes, of which the best known are the great halls attached to the civic centres of Rome and of Italian and western-provincial cities – halls in which justice was administered and commercial business transacted. This last class of *basilica* first appears in the West at the beginning of the 2nd century BC with the now-vanished *Basilica Porcia*, the earliest extant example, of a few years later, being the *Basilica Aemilia*, also in the Roman Forum.

These civic *basilicae*, which are oblong structures divided by internal colonnades into 'nave' and 'aisles', fall into two main types. In one type the main entrance is in one short side, with the presiding official's seat (*tribunal*) in the centre of the other short side, which could be either straight or apsed, *e.g.* Pompeii, Roman Corinth, Leptis Magna (early-Imperial *basilica*).[7] The second type has the main entrance in one of the long sides and sometimes a rectangular projection for the *tribunal* at the centre of the other long side, *e.g.* Fanum in North-East Italy, Cosa in Etruria, Sabrata in Tripolitania:[8] in other examples of this type there is no such central projection, but each of the short sides forms an apse, *e.g.* the *Basilica Ulpia* in Trajan's Forum in Rome, the Severan (early-3rd- f 3
century AD) *basilica* at Leptis Magna.

The last-mentioned building is particularly well preserved, for p 176
its austere retaining-walls of large limestone blocks, once crowned by a pitched and timber roof, still stand to an impressive height. Many of the columns of the internal colonnades with their huge Corinthian caps survive, as do also the two pairs of tall square pilasters that flank either apse. These pilasters are very ornately p 177

carved in the two-dimensional, black and white, lace-like technique characteristic of the period, with Bacchic and Herculean scenes and figures and with foreparts of animals springing from the hearts of flowers, all inset like medallions in vertical running scrolls of vine and acanthus. Another relatively well-preserved civic *basilica* is 174–5 Maxentius' *Basilica Nova* built in brick-faced concrete at the begin- (4–5) ning of the 4th century AD to the east of the Roman Forum. Its original main entrance is in its straight eastern short side and its corresponding western short side is apsed. The 'nave' is separated from the 'aisles' by six massive piers supporting arches, while the 'aisles' are divided into six 'side-chapels' by cross-walls, each of which is pierced by an arch. The 'nave' had a clerestory and both 'nave' and 'aisles' were vaulted. From what remains of the boldly designed coffering of those vaults we may surmise that the inside was once magnificently adorned. Constantine made a new entrance in the centre of the southern long side and threw out a second apse on the northern long side opposite.

How the Greek word 'royal' came to be attached to these civic buildings in the West is one of the minor puzzles of Roman architectural history. No comparable civic buildings called by this name are known (apart from those in some Roman colonies) in the Greek-speaking provinces, where the term only appears much later to designate a Christian church. It could be that the Roman Republican structures took their name from colonnaded throne-

Furthermore, the Augustan architectural writer Vitruvius, in one of the chapters of his *De architectura* that deal with domestic building,[9] describes what were virtually the little palaces of Roman *nobiles* who served the state as holders of public office and for whom there had to be provided, not only *vestibula regalia,* but also *basilicae* 'arranged with all the magnificence of public buildings because in their houses public deliberations and private trials and law-suits are often transacted'. For house-*basilicae* of this kind in domestic complexes there is also the evidence of archaeology. In the west wing of the Roman 'palace' (whether of a local native dynast or of an important Roman civil servant from Italy is as yet unknown) recently excavated at Fishbourne near Chichester and dating from the late-1st century AD there is a large, apsed basilican room with a bench running round the inside of the apse and a polychrome mosaic on the floor: it was approached from the entrance-hall in the east wing, exactly opposite, by a ceremonial path, with flower-beds on either side of it, that crossed the 'palace's' central garden.[10] In the vast 4th-century villa unearthed near Piazza f 4 Armerina in central Sicily – a villa that possibly belonged to an Emperor, more probably to a high-ranking official in the Imperial service or even to a private multimillionaire – an enormous apsed room is approached from the central peristyle across a corridor. Neither here nor in the Fishbourne hall are there traces of internal colonnades.

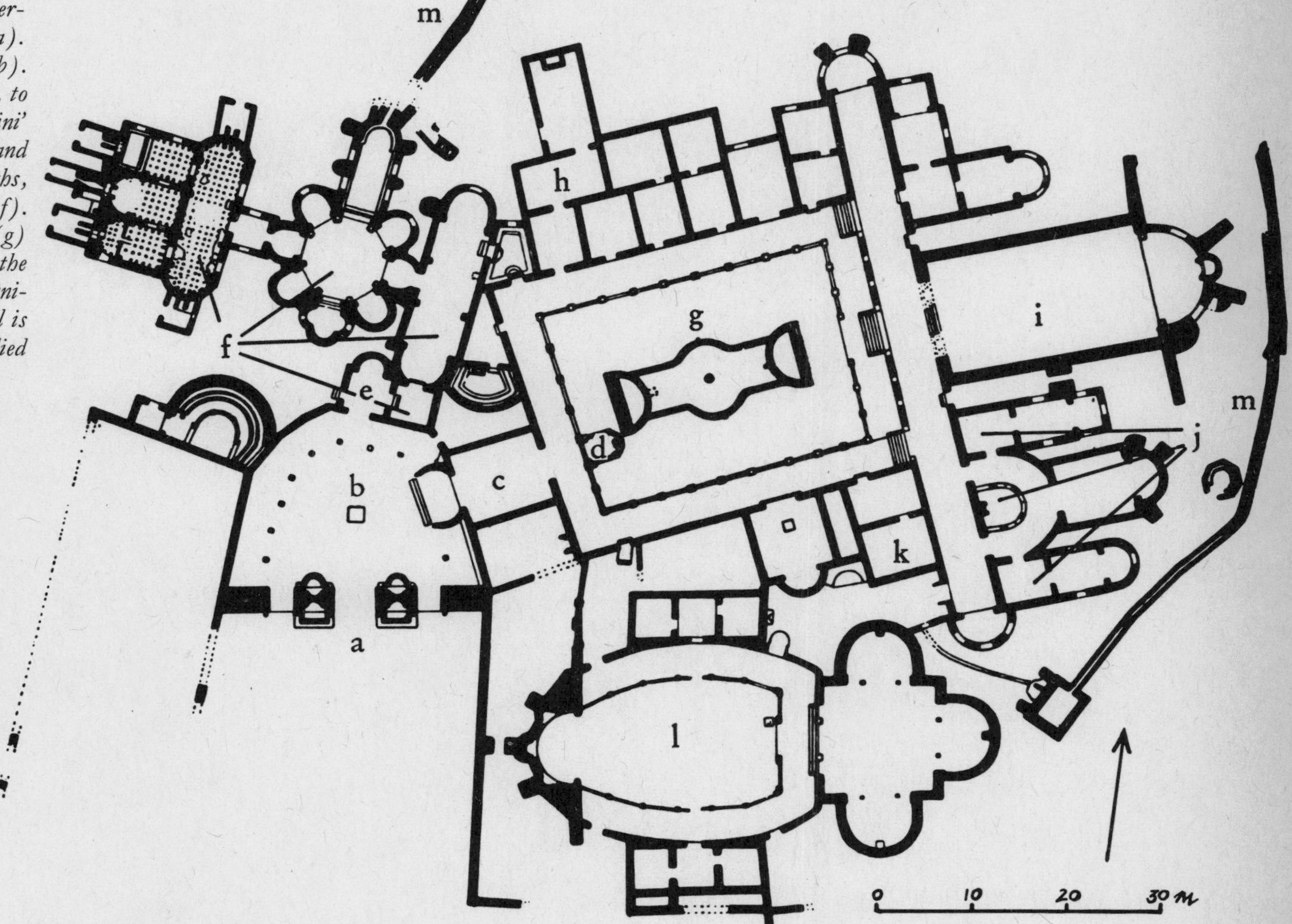

The large villa near Piazza Armerina in Sicily was approached at (a). One came first upon an atrium (b). The living apartments are at (j), to the north-east of the famous 'Bikini' mosaic (k), and a court (l) and triconch hall. A complex of baths, including a latrine (e), is at (f). To the north of the peristyle court (g) is a fountain (h), to the west the Imperial shrine (d) and a muniment room (c). The audience-hall is at (i). Two aqueducts (m) supplied the villa with water. (4)

or audience-rooms of contemporary Hellenistic kings, although no Hellenistic palace incorporating such a hall has so far come to light; and in the Roman buildings it was a magistrate, not a ruler, who 'gave audience'. The essential 'royal' factors in the West would have been the colonnades inside and the official seat at a focal point. Moreover, reception-rooms displaying two or more of the basic features of the civic *basilica* – oblong shape, internal colonnades, and an apse or other form of accommodation for the seat of the presiding personage – were, as has been shown (p. 194), part of the palace architecture of the Roman Emperors, much of whose court practice and ideology was derived from that of the Hellenistic monarchies.

Refuge from the world

Of the application of the term *basilica* to a hall used for strictly religious purposes we have one specific instance. This is the *Basilica Hilariana*, an underground place of worship on the Caelian Hill in Rome, frequented by the College of *Dendrophori* ('Branch-bearers'), 'clergy' of the mystery-cult of the Magna Mater which had been brought to the capital from Asia Minor.[11] The site of this shrine was discovered and its antechamber excavated, but of the shape and arrangements of the room itself nothing is known. On the other hand, there has been a full investigation of another subterranean hall of a very definitely basilican character, found just outside the Porta Maggiore on the south-eastern outskirts of p 174 (3)

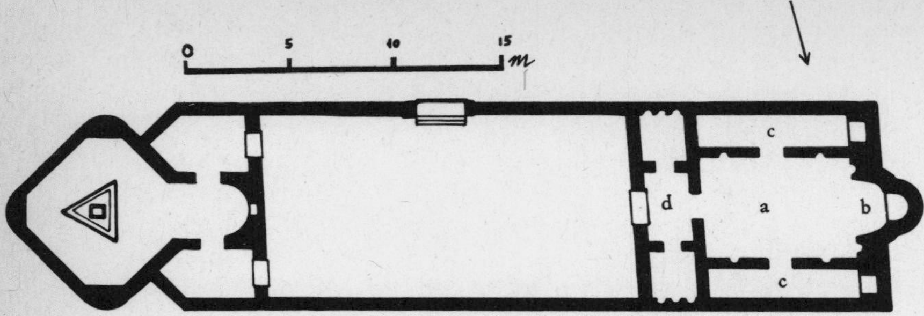

The shrine of the Syrian Goddess in Rome had a 'nave' (a), 'aisles' (c), apse (b) and 'narthex' (d), all preceded by a great courtyard. (5)

Rome. This hall measures about 40 by 30 feet, has an apse at one end and a small square 'narthex' at the other end, and is divided into 'nave' and 'aisles' by two rows of rectangular piers. For the walls and piers, trenches and pits had been dug, into which concrete was poured; and, when this had set, the earth within the walls was cleared away and the whole place was roofed with concrete vaults, barrel-vaults for 'nave' and 'aisles' and a half-dome in the apse. Inside, apse, walls, and piers are richly adorned with stucco reliefs of very fine quality and in a style that can be dated to the 1st century AD. The scene in the half-dome seems to represent a ritual death and rebirth under the guise of Sappho's leap into the sea from the Leucadian Rock to gain the further shore, where Apollo waits to receive her. Despite a recent attempt to interpret this hall as a 'summer-house',[12] there can be little doubt that it was the meeting-place of some religious community whose goal was most probably the attainment of after-life happiness.

Such, certainly, was the goal of the devotees of the Syrian
f 5 Goddess, whose shrine on the Aventine Hill in Rome is basilican, with apse, 'nave', 'aisles', and 'narthex'.[13] It was also the goal of the worshippers of the Persian god Mithras. Temples of Mithras are also essentially basilican, with a 'nave' and 'aisles', the latter often filled with raised benches, on which the faithful reclined at a sacred meal, and a 'narthex'. Some Mithraea are equipped with a rectangular or curved apse, in which the cult-image was displayed, at the short end opposite the door. There are at least two Mithraea known, both with an apse opposite the entrance, in which colonnades divided 'nave' from 'aisles' – that at Lambaesis in Algeria, which had two rows of four piers each;[14] and that brought to light in 1954 beside the Walbrook in the City of London, where there are two rows of seven columns each along the 'nave'.[15] Both of these buildings were probably lighted by clerestory windows in the walls of the 'nave', which rose above those of the 'aisles'; and both would have had a half-dome in the apse, while the roofs of 'nave' and 'aisles' would have been of timber, pitched in the case of the 'nave' and sloping penthouse-wise in that of the 'aisles'. No traces of wall-paintings or of mosaic-work on walls or floor exist in these two buildings; but, to judge from the amount of sculpture found in the London and other Mithraea and from Mithraea in Italy and
p 252 elsewhere with brilliantly painted walls and fine mosaic pavements,
(50) the plain outsides would have masked handsomely adorned insides. The point of a Mithraeum, as of all mystery-shrines, was, in fact, to be an enclosed interior in which the worshippers and their art and ritual would be securely hidden from the outer world.

The 'outside-in' style of architecture

Other religious buildings, non-basilican, but constructed in the new concrete technique and combining an austere, box-like outward aspect with lavish adornment inside, are the house-tombs or mausolea, rectangular or circular. Of the rectangular variety, ranged in blocks and rows along the streets and lanes of 'cities of the dead' (*necropoleis*), some of the most striking examples are those on Isola Sacra, north of Ostia, belonging to the middle-class inhabitants of the town of Portus Augusti,[16] and those revealed in
f 6 1939–40 under St Peter's in Rome and associated with the same kind of bourgeois *milieu*. Barrel-vaulted on Isola Sacra and cross-vaulted on the Vatican, these tombs have walls that are faced externally with neat, plain brickwork only occasionally relieved by pictorial panels of marble, terracotta, or mosaic, by entablatures and façade-windows with moulded terracotta and intarsia features, and by the terracotta capitals of shallow brick pilasters spaced along the façades or set at the corners. But such restrained external embellishments pale before the gaudy, sometimes almost riotous, effects of colour, modelling, and carving within. The walls are p 181
lined with small, square niches for cremation-urns and long, (18)
arched recesses for inhumations in sarcophagi, many of them elaborately sculptured, while the spaces between these burial-places are filled with figured and floral polychrome frescos and with figured and geometric painted stuccoes. Brightly coloured stucco coffering covers some of the vaulted ceilings: other ceilings bear frescos; and on many of the floors there are mosaic pavements, black-and-white and polychrome, not infrequently including figure-scenes. Here again, all the resources of artistry are concentrated on the inside, to please the departed, who were conceived of as in some sense dwelling in the tomb, and to cheer the survivors when they assembled to commemorate their dead.

The large round, brick and concrete building, now known as the p 179
Church of Santa Costanza, was constructed in the early-4th century (14, 1
in a cemetery area on the Via Nomentana at a short distance to the north-east of Rome's ancient circuit of walls. After Constantine's conversion it was certainly used as the mausoleum of his two nominally Christian daughters, Constantina and Helena. But the

These 'house-tombs' were discovered under St Peter's in 1939–40. An austere exterior decoration, consisting mainly of architectural motifs, contrasts strikingly with their bright interiors (see plate 18). (6)

p 180 (17) surviving early-4th-century vault-mosaics are completely 'neutral' in content, without any trace of direct Christian influence: Renaissance drawings of lost dome-mosaics with biblical themes are counterbalanced by other drawings and descriptions of mosaics of a Bacchic character; and the place may have been originally a pagan building to which the Christian scenes were slightly later additions. Such was certainly the round Church of St George at Salonika[17] and perhaps San Stefano Rotondo on the Caelian Hill in Rome.[18] As a circular mausoleum, Santa Costanza is the direct descendent of such great gasometer-like masonry cylinders as the
p 139 (66) Mausoleum of Hadrian (Castel Sant' Angelo) and the Mausoleum of Augustus in Rome and the Augustan tombs of private persons to be found to the south of the capital – Caecilia Metella's on the Via Appia, Marcus Plautius Silvanus' near Tivoli, and Lucius Munatius Plancus' at Gaeta. Its originality lies in the fact that its hemispherical dome rests on a drum borne on an arcade of twelve pairs of columns placed radially to the circumference. The wall of the drum rises with clerestory windows above the roof of the barrel-vaulted ambulatory which runs round the lower part of the building and gives access to the main central space below the dome through arches that link the pairs of columns. In the thickness of the ambulatory's solid outer wall are contrived three large and twelve small niches, some curved, others rectangular, the large ones, at least, no doubt intended for burials in handsome sarcophagi. To judge by what remains of its original mosaic decoration on the ambulatory vault, the inside of this mausoleum was as ornamental as its outside was severe.

No religious building exemplifies more magnificently the new Roman architectural style, according to which the whole *raison d'être* of an outside is to serve as a container for an inside, than does
p 178–9 (11–13) Hadrian's Pantheon – well characterized as 'perhaps the first major monument to be composed entirely as an interior'.[19] The temple comprises three main parts, of which the first, a porch of granite columns supporting marble entablatures and a marble pediment, represents a concession to the old traditional trabeated style and serves only to enhance the daring of the major and essential portion behind it, namely the immense rotunda, 182 feet in diameter and 142 feet high from its floor to the opening (*oculus*) in the apex of its dome. An intermediate rectangular block of brick-faced concrete links the porch with the rotunda, of which both cylinder and dome are again of brick-faced concrete – the former probably once coated with plain stucco and lacking all relief apart from the three simple cornices that girdle it and divide it into three broad bands, the latter formerly sheathed in gilded tiles. Inside all is ornament. Below the spring of the dome there are two zones of purely decorative architectural motifs, the zone on ground level consisting of a continuous series of seven marble-lined niches, alternately curved and rectangular, cut in the thickness of the wall and screened by a marble entablature that is carried round on marble columns and pilasters, the upper zone made up of alternating panels and shallow gabled niches, also all in marble. The under-surface of the dome is formed of huge, once gilded concrete coffers set in five concentric circles and diminishing in size as they approach the open apex, through which the sunlight, striking down in an enormous beam, moves mysteriously across the vast imprisoned space below.

A mirror of the heavenly kingdom

It should now be evident what this highly selective sketch of Roman buildings dating from the late-1st century BC to the 4th century AD is attempting to achieve. The selection has been made to demonstrate that in the architecture of the pagan Empire there existed a wide variety of forms which structurally, and in some cases also ideologically, provided models for the Christian Church as soon as she ceased to be content to celebrate the Eucharist in an ordinary dwelling-room, otherwise used for mundane domestic purposes, and required for her worship, first, rooms that were set apart in houses or house-complexes and were specially adapted for the liturgy, later, independent churches, small or large. All the halls, whether built in concrete or in stone, that have been reviewed in these pages, from those in the great public *thermae* to the Pantheon, are essentially interiors, most of them presenting externally an austere, impassive, almost forbidding aspect to the world without, as though to safeguard and accentuate by way of contrast the wealth of artistry and of activity within. All, whether secular, quasi-religious, or religious, were enclosed places of assembly, *ecclesiae*; all, even the privately- or Imperially-owned family mausolea, served a communal and social function; and some of them directed the gaze of those who entered them along their main axis to a distant focal point, whether personage or object.

We have only to compare the earliest known churches with their pagan counterparts in order to realize how much material lay ready to the hands of the first Christian builders. In the only pre-Constantinian house-church whose plan has survived complete, that, dating from the first half of the 3rd century, at Dura Europus f 7
on the Euphrates, two adjacent chambers were thrown together to form a long assembly-room with a low platform at one end of it (in another room in the house a quite elaborate baptistery was installed); while a literary text records that in the 3rd century a certain Theophilus, one of the foremost and richest citizens of

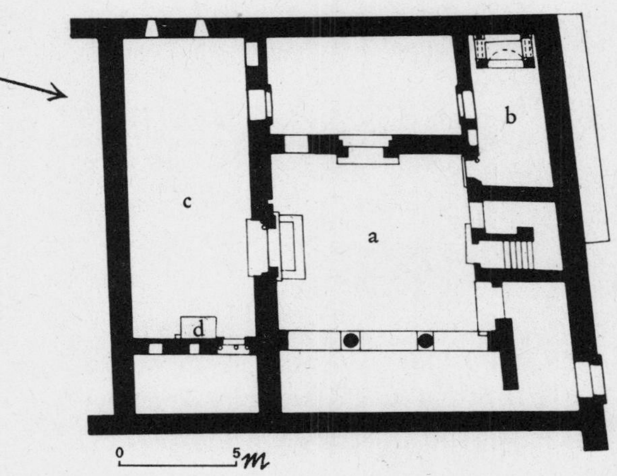

On the ground floor of the Dura Europus house-church, two rooms were thrown together to form a place of assembly (c) with a low platform (d). The baptistery is at (b); (a) is a courtyard. (7)

Antioch-on-the-Orontes, 'consecrated as a church (*ecclesiae nomine*) the great *basilica* of his house (*domus suae ingens basilica*)'.[20] The parallel with pagan palace and domestic *basilicae* and audience-halls is obvious. Also based on small *basilicae* were the small apsed *memoriae* (memorial shrines) and *martyria* (martyr-shrines) of the Christian communities, such as those at Salonae near Split;[21] and there is also a little evidence for small rectangular apseless *memoriae* and *martyria* on the pagan model (p. 196). Small independent, apsed basilican churches of the 4th and 5th centuries, such as the little building found beneath the present Church of St Severin at Cologne,[22] the church (with baptistery attached) within the walls of the Roman fort at Zurzach (Tenedo) in Northern Switzerland,[23] and the tiny church (if church it really is) near the civic centre of f 8

This tiny basilica at Silchester, probably a church, consisted of nave (a), apse (b), aisles (c), narthex (d) and two rudimentary transepts (e). (8)

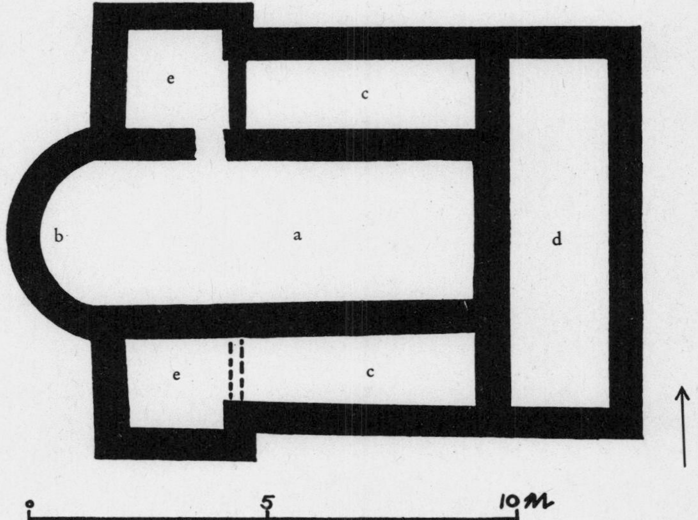

The central hall of the Baths of Caracalla, Rome, *measured about 170 by 82 feet and was only part of this vast complex, measuring 750 by 380 feet. Its concrete vaulted roof was supported by eight piers ranged in two parallel rows connected by eight arches. (9)*

Silchester (Calleva Atrebatum) in Hampshire – all of these could easily be mistaken, on the score of their ground-plans, for pagan mystery-temples (p. 195–6).

f 10 When Constantine made his great foundations – Old St Peter's and the Lateran in Rome, the *Basilica Apostolorum* on the Via Appia just to the south of Rome, the Church of the Holy Sepulchre in Jerusalem, and the Church of the Nativity at Bethlehem – and inaugurated the whole line of monumental, independent Christian *basilicae* – characterized by forecourt, internal colonnades separating nave from aisles, pitched roof with clerestory, and an apse near or in which (except in the Lateran and the *Basilica Apostolorum*) a holy place marked the focal point[24] – it was doubtless from the large bath-halls, from the palace audience-halls, and from the internally colonnaded civic *basilicae*, as well as from the big Christian house-*basilicae* of the 3rd century, that his architects drew many of their ideas for what were, however, *qua* churches, basically original creations. To assess the part played by the palace audience-hall, in particular, in the evolution of the Christian *basilica* we have only to set side by side pictures of the hall at Trier (p. 194) and the 5th-
176 century Church of Santa Sabina on the Aventine Hill in Rome:
7, 8) they are almost twin buildings externally. The suitability of bath-
f 9 halls, audience-halls, and civic *basilicae* for adaptation for Christian
4 (2) worship is attested by the fact the main hall of the Baths of Diocle-
6 (7) tian (p. 193), the audience-hall at Trier, and the Severan *basilica* at
6 (6) Leptis Magna (p. 194–5) were all at various dates turned into churches; and there are other instances of such transformations.
f 1 Finally, it is in halls of the type of the octagonal pavilion in Nero's
(66) Golden House (p. 193), in round mausolea (p. 196–7), and in a
78–9 great circular temple such as the Pantheon (p. 197) that we find
–13) the pagan prototypes of the centrally-planned, domed churches, polygonal or rectangular in outline – San Vitale at Ravenna, SS. Sergius and Bacchus and Santa Sophia in Constantinople, and many a lesser church in Syria.[25]

The wealth and talent lavished on the inside decoration of these outwardly plain early churches – from the unsophisticated mural
270 paintings in the baptistery of the Dura house-church to the apse-
, 20) mosaic and twisted marble columns, elegantly carved with vine-scrolls and Cupids, in Old St Peter's and on again to the glorious 4th- to 6th-century wall- and vault-mosaics of St George at Salonika, of San Lorenzo at Milan, and of the Ravenna *basilicae* and baptisteries – lie outside our present scope, but represent the Christian flowering of the 'outside-in' style of Roman architecture. A Christian church is essentially a mirror of the heavenly kingdom, with whose worship its worship is one. The thing that matters to the Christian is what goes on inside the building and how its interior can be made to express most perfectly the sublime nature of that activity. To pass from a simple, unadorned exterior into a world of beauty of colour, form, and liturgy is a symbolic act that was particularly meaningful to the Early Christian communities.

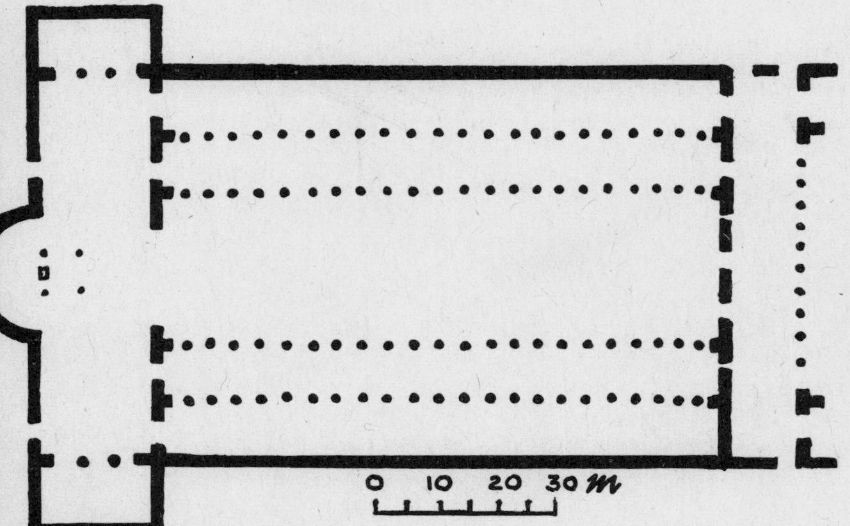

Constantine's monumental basilican foundations like St Peter's in Rome are characterized by a forecourt and internal colonnades. A holy place, such as a saint's tomb, often marks the focal point in or near the apse. (10)

ART

Impressionism

Among the most famous of Roman-age mural paintings is the p 182
frieze, which most probably depicts the Dionysiac initiation of a (19)
bride-to-be, in the so-called Villa of the Mysteries on the outskirts of Pompeii. It was executed about the middle of the 1st century BC; but whether it was copied from some lost late-Hellenic or early-Hellenistic picture, or represents, taken as a whole, the more or less original creation of the painter whom the householder employed, is a question that we cannot yet answer through lack of evidence. None of the Greek masterpieces described by ancient writers has survived and practically no monumental paintings of any kind dating from pre-Imperial times outside Italy are known. For us the essential fact about the almost life-size figures in this frieze, whatever their origin may be, is that they are wholly classical in the strict and proper meaning of that term – statuesque, self-contained, finished in every detail, exquisitely and neatly rounded off. They are, in fact, the products of a closed, perfected, and self-sufficient world.

How completely different from the Villa of the Mysteries frieze p 182–3
is another painting from Pompeii, this time presenting a Roman, (20)
Virgilian subject – the entry of the Wooden Horse into Troy – and undoubtedly created in Italy. This is one of the most striking examples that we have in ancient art of the impressionistic style, where the artist aims no longer at attaining perfection of colour, form, and detail, but at producing by means of vivid contrasts of light and shade and by deliberate sketchiness and incompleteness an effect or impression which conveys to the beholder the wider implications of the episode. For instance, the four dead-white, almost corpse-like men splashed in in the foreground, leaning backwards as they strain to pull towards them the enormous horse, point beyond the scene itself to the tragedy to which all their efforts are but tending. No less eloquent of imminent disaster are the rows of Trojan spectators in the background – long-robed, torch-bearing figures in front, caught by a lurid light, and behind them, and with heads and shoulders just appearing above those figures' heads, the dim and shadowy forms of the warriors. Still further in the distance are the pale-violet coloured walls and towers of the doomed city, seen as through a haze in the barest outline.[26]

This device for achieving the impression of a crowd that is larger than the eye can see by raising the heads of the figures behind above those in front appears in Roman art in media other than painting. In sculpture we find it in groups of soldiers on two reliefs in Rome, one in the Villa Borghese, the other on the Arch of Constantine, both of which once formed part of a great Trajanic
frieze.[27] It occurs again in miniature on a bronze coin of Hadrian, *f 11*
where the reverse-type shows the Emperor addressing from a platform an assembly of citizens. The device may be said to reach its crescendo in a 9th-century Christian mosaic, that in the semi-dome of the Church of Santa Maria in Domnica on the Caelian Hill in Rome, where the heavenly host, in number past counting, is suggested by tier upon tier of haloes.[28]

To return to painting – discoveries at the Campanian city of Stabiae, some miles south of Pompeii, but overwhelmed by the same disaster of AD 79, have revealed a whole series of impressionistic studies of the human head. There is to be seen neither the p 185
naturalistic style of late-Hellenic and early-Hellenistic renderings (23)
nor the chronicling, photographic 'verism' of late-Hellenistic and Roman Republican portraits. It would be almost true to say that at Stabiae the features are less delineated than indicated or suggested. Parts of a face are highlighted while the rest is all in shadow; the eyes are sometimes deep pools of darkness; the hair is untidy and wispish. Everything points to incompleteness, to something outside, with which the spirit that the face veils is in communion.

The economy of detail which is the hallmark of Roman impressionistic painting is nowhere more evident than in a fresco of late-2nd or early-3rd-century AD date in the interior of one of the house-tombs brought to light beneath the Church of San Sebastiano on the Via Appia south of Rome. From the inscription on the tomb's façade it is known as that of Marcus Clodius Hermes; and the
picture in question is framed by a straight-sided octagon within a p 184
concave-sided outer one. The scene is dominated by a large, (22)

summarily drawn male figure, wearing a short tunic, a flying cloak, and possibly a cap or helmet, holding in his left hand a long rod or spear, and seemingly floating in the air. He extends his right hand as though addressing, or bidding farewell to, a crowd of figures on a much smaller scale who stand below him. In these figures, sketchy spiritualization of the human form reaches its extreme: the heads are mere blobs; the attenuated, elongated trunks are little more than tapering streaks; and the feet are hardly shown at all. The effect is of a mass of people united by a common upward straining towards a goal above them. Is this the apotheosis of an Emperor or hero? Or could it be, in the light of the probably Christian paintings on the outside of the tomb, a camouflaged Ascension? The spectators do, at any rate, seem to be being stretched, like elastic, out of themselves to the world beyond them into which the floating man will vanish.

Christian or not, the tomb of Hermes painting's closest links are with the unequivocally Christian frescos in the catacombs of p 183 (21) Rome. There, too, in the rendering of scenes from the Old and New Testaments and of such symbolic figures as the Pastor Bonus and Orans, all is cut down to the minimum – to the bare essentials of the story or symbol, with few, if any, picturesque accessories. Granted that in the catacombs the impressionistic, sketchy style may be partly accounted for by the fact that the painting had to be done by torch- or lamp-light and that the best artists could not be afforded, still the aim was the same as in the pagan paintings that have been surveyed, namely to focus the spectator's mind on ideas that are wider in their range than the scenes themselves.[29]

An impressionistic device for suggesting a large crowd was to raise the heads of those behind above those in front, as on this coin where Hadrian addresses an assembly of citizens. (11)

Allegory

We have now seen how in Roman-age painting, and to some extent also in works in other media, style and technique can convey an impression of a larger scene and even of a different world beyond the limits of the picture that is actually presented. When we turn to the content of Imperial art, particularly of its tomb-art, but also of some paintings and mosaics in domestic contexts, we find the same principle at work: it is not the surface-meaning of an episode from mythology or human life that is important, but its value as an allegory of an event, an achievement, or a state in an order of existence unperceived by the senses.

The violent sundering at death of soul and body and the former's journey to the other world are pictured on carved sarcophagi, on grave-reliefs, and in paintings and mosaics on the walls and floors of tombs, in the decoration of mystery-shrines, and even on mosaic p 188 (29) f 12 paintings in houses, by scenes of rape or carrying-off – for example, the Rape of Europa by Jupiter,[30] of the Leucippidae by the Dioscuri,[31] of Ganymede by the Eagle,[32] of Persephone by Pluto.[33] A gentler passage to the after-life is reflected in a wide variety of renderings on sarcophagi of the journey of the soul across the ocean to the Blessed Isles. Souls in the guise of Cupids or Nereids are borne across the waves on the backs of Tritons, sea-Centaurs, dolphins, and kindly sea-beasts of many breeds. Sometimes the portrait or portraits of the dead are carried in a shell by Tritons, or in the narrow frieze along the lid of a sarcophagus sea-beasts converge from either side upon the central inscription panel for the name of the deceased – coming to bear him or her away.[34] Shorthand versions of the voyage appear in the form of dolphins or masks of Oceanus carved on sarcophagi or gravestones, painted on the walls of tombs, or worked in mosaic on their floors.

Such scenes of the happy homecoming of the dead were but one way of expressing the ever-deepening conviction of the great mass of people in Roman Imperial times that the terror and power of death could be conquered and that a life richer and more blessed than the life experienced here was attainable hereafter. Death could, in fact, be 'swallowed up in victory' and turned into a means of triumph. Hence the persistent representation in Roman tomb-art in all media, but particularly on carved sarcophagi, of figures of Victory,[35] of trophies of arms, of battle-scenes of Greeks against Amazons[36] or of Romans against barbarians, which stand for the struggle with, and the triumph over, evil and death, as do also the p 186 (25) frequent hunting-scenes where lions, boars, bears, and other ravening beasts are vanquished.[37] Hence, too, the popularity on funerary monuments of Hercules' Labours as allegories of the overthrow of the forces of destruction, in the shape of beasts and p 186 (24) monsters, by those of good.

Rebirth from the grave to immortal life as the fruit of victory over death is implied by the renderings of another of Hercules' p 189 (31) exploits, his reclaiming of the dead Alcestis from Hades. Moreover, personal immortality could, it was believed, be earned in this life both by the faithful performance of earthly work and duties and by cultural accomplishments. Just as the soul, on trial after death, of Cornelia, wife of Lucius Aemilius Paullus, censor in 22 BC, catalogues her virtues and good works in the address to her husband composed for her by Propertius;[38] so the genre-scenes from daily life on countless examples of funerary art have more than merely commemorative or biographical connotations. On the Igel monument, near Trier, scenes from the business activities of the p 187 (27) Secundini family, which owned the tomb, are featured along with the 'Labours' of Perseus and Achilles and the apotheosis of Hercules. In the new, partly Christian, partly pagan, catacomb on the Via Latina there is a painting of an instruction-class for medical students in what must have been a doctor's burial-place; and a painting of a steward doing accounts with an underling occurs in p 208 Tomb G in the Vatican necropolis.[39] A whole series of sarcophagi shows episodes from the lives of generals, statesmen, merchants, p 159 (27) philosophers, poets, musicians, and even of specially gifted children. Other sarcophagi carry figures of the Muses, devotion to whom in this life merited bliss hereafter.[40]

The Isles of the Blessed

A favourite image in Roman picture-language of after-life happiness is the Bacchic paradise. Bacchus, the most popular of 'saviour-gods' in the Graeco-Roman world of the first three centuries of the Christian era, is depicted on numerous sarcophagi as riding in triumph in a chariot drawn by felines, with a revelling crowd of Satyrs, Silenuses, and Maenads in his train;[41] or he stands, half-drunk and leaning on his *thyrsus* (staff), attended by a whole company, or by a small selection, of similar revelling personages.[42] Or the god himself may be absent from the *thiasos* (revel-rout) of his followers.[43] Another common theme on sarcophagi is that of the finding by Bacchus of the sleeping Ariadne on the island of Naxos – an allegory of the soul's awakening from the sleep of death to mystic marriage with its god.[44] It may, moreover, very well be that the marriage-scenes figured on not a few sarcophagi allude, not only to the earthly weddings of the husbands and wives buried in them or to belief that married love survives the grave, but also to this mystic union of the soul with the divinity after death.[45]

Also on sarcophagi revelling and sometimes drunken children – Cupids and Psyches and winged or wingless *Amorini* – symbolize p 186 (26) other-world beautitude.[46] Personifications of the Four Seasons on

A mosaic from St Peter's necropolis of the carrying off of Persephone (almost completely effaced) by Pluto symbolizes the sundering of the soul from the body at death. Pluto's quadriga is preceded by Mercury, conductor of souls. The flowers below were being gathered by Persephone and her companions. (12)

sarcophagi and grave-reliefs, in tomb-paintings and on tomb-mosaics represent either the endless cycle of eternity or all the blessings and delights of the happy dead under the guise of flowers (Spring), corn (Summer), grapes (Autumn), and edible birds and animals (Winter). Yet a further image is the pastoral paradise, such
p 187 as that on the 3rd-century sarcophagus of one Julius Achilleus,
(28) who had been, so the inscription tells us, no farmer, but an official of the chief gladiatorial training school in Rome and, later, on the staff of one of the great bureaux in the Imperial civil service. But the carving on his coffin represents scenes from peasant life within the gated precinct of a farm – the herding of horses, cattle, sheep, and goats, the milking of goats, and various works of husbandry.

Two other 3rd-century sarcophagi depict the Christian version of Achilleus' pastoral paradise;[47] and in view of the indubitably allegorical, non-literal implications of all the renderings of episodes from mythology and daily life that have been considered here, it is no surprise to find pagan motifs and figures of the same kinds employed as allegories of Christian teaching. Bellerophon slaying the Chimaera, denoting the conquest of evil, appears on the same mosaic as what is almost certainly a bust of Christ, with the Chi-Rho
73 (1) monogram behind the head, in a 4th-century villa at Hinton St Mary in Dorset. Bacchic masks and figures and masks of Oceanus occur in the Roman catacombs.[48] Groups of boating and fishing
188–9 Cupids, symbols of bliss in paradise, and the story of Jonah's
30, 32) resurrection form one continuous picture on the mosaic floor of the 4th-century cathedral at Aquileia in North-east Italy, where personifications of the Seasons likewise appear. In the Vatican necropolis a 3rd-century AD pagan hunt-sarcophagus was equipped with a Christian inscription and was reused for Christian burial.[49] These are but samples of a widespread phenomenon of Early Christian practice. Just as heroes and episodes from the Old Testament feature in art as types of Christ and of New Testament events, so pagan heroes and their exploits could be rendered as foreshadowing the Gospel. The gentile world could claim, if with lesser right than the Jewish, to have had its *praeparatio Evangelii.*

Anguish and ugliness

The diffusion throughout the Empire of this mainly optimistic view of man's destiny after death did not bring with it insensitiveness to the tragedies and horrors of life in this world. Indeed, from about AD 160 to the end of the 3rd century, when the ancient world was passing through a time of acute crisis, these afflictions would appear to have been felt more sharply than they ever had been before, to judge by the reflection of them in the sculpture of the period – in reliefs depicting warfare and in portraits.

In the reliefs of Trajan's Column, carved in the early years of the 2nd century AD and recording that Emperor's two wars against the Dacians, one can observe a genuine awareness on the part of Rome of the pathos of the 'noble savage's' defeat and death.[50] Even the prostrate bodies of the slain foe show a certain dignity, repose, and peacefulness. On the reliefs of the Antonine Column, on the other hand, carved at the end of the 2nd century AD to commemorate Marcus Aurelius' German and Sarmatian wars, a very different spirit can be detected.[51] The fallen bodies of the enemy are far more violently contorted; the expressions on the faces of those barbarians who still fight on or are already vanquished are more desperate and agonized; the stocky, sometimes almost puppet-like figures of the Roman soldiers display a greater callousness and ruthlessness in capturing, wounding, or despatching their opponents. The persistent, relentless pressure on the northern frontiers of the Empire has changed the Roman attitude. Even the figure
of the Rain-god, who actually brings longed-for relief to the p 190
thirst-stricken Roman army, becomes a haunting symbol of (33)
impending doom as he broods in gigantic proportions, with extended, dripping arms and wings, above the piled-up bodies of dead soldiers and of dead or dying horses.

The same preoccupation with the anguish of war confronts us on some of the late-2nd- and early-3rd-century AD sarcophagi with battle-scenes that have been interpreted as allegories of the struggle with evil and the conquest of death (p. 200).[52] On the front of these pieces every inch of the surface available for sculpting is crammed, tapestry-like, with tangled masses of combatants rising in tier above tier from the lower to the upper limit of the field. Figures of Romans, barbarians, and horses, some of them rendered in the boldest foreshortening, writhe in and out, upwards and downwards. Postures are tortured, expressions are grim and agonized, no refinement of cruelty is spared. All this is particularly vividly p 186 (25) portrayed on the Ludovisi piece. There we see a Roman soldier gripping a barbarian by the neck and chin: is he going to force open his victim's mouth and tear his tongue out? Another Roman grasps a bearded foe by the hair as he lifts his sword for the final blow. Other barbarians forced to the ground glare upwards in pain and despair. A young, beardless one, falling mortally wounded from his horse, opens his mouth as he yells with rage and anguish. This is ancient war in its most ghastly form.

The strain, stress, fear, and brutality engendered by the troubles of the 3rd century AD have stamped themselves unmistakably upon the sculptural portraits of successive Emperors. Of such a type are p 191 (37) the likenesses of Balbinus (238), coarse-featured and cruel-eyed; of the frightened and distinctly sinister Gordian III (238–44);[53] of p 191 (38) the scowling Philip the Arabian (244–9), with brow and cheeks gashed by furrows – traits that appear again with no less intensity p 335 (8) on the portraits of Trajan Decius (249–51) and even more disturb- p 190 (34, 35) ingly on those of Trebonianus Gallus (251–3). Even the idealism consciously adopted for the likenesses of Gallienus (253–68) cannot conceal the pervading atmosphere of dread and hardness; and, with the portraits of Claudius Gothicus (268–70), Tacitus (275–6), and Probus (276–82), inscrutable relentlessness comes to a climax.[54] Finally, at the end of the 3rd century and in the opening years of the 4th, in the period of the Tetrarchies, the terrors of the times are mirrored in what can only be described as a real cult of ugliness in p 191 (36) Imperial iconography – in the porphyry groups of the twin Augusti and twin Caesars at Venice and in the Vatican and in a bust at Cairo. This is the art of people who have lost their faith in civilization.

Maiestas Augusti

But Imperial figures did not always make such unprepossessing and repugnant appearances as this during the period that ran from *c.* AD 160 to the early decades of the 4th century. It was, indeed, to the Emperor that the anxious and bewildered peoples of the Roman world looked up as to one who stood, to some extent at least, above the troubles of their own lives, as to one who could help and save them, not in the after-life, but here and now by reason of a power that was more than merely human. This feeling for the ruler is tellingly reflected in historical, and occasionally in funerary, reliefs. On the Antonine Column, when Marcus Aurelius is shown in a scene of *adlocutio* or harangue to his troops, he does not stand in profile looking at the men whom he addresses, as Trajan does in similar situations on his Column; Marcus is rendered in a strictly frontal pose, raised high above his audience, over whose heads he is gazing – not at them, but at the living viewer, then and now. He is, as it were, lifted right out of the conflict on to another plane, while the soldiers massed below look up to him for supernatural aid.[55] Precisely the same type of representation of the Emperor's *adlocutio* is to be found among the episodes from Septimius Severus' Eastern wars that are carved in relief on his Arch in the Roman Forum.[56] On another much humbler Arch of Septimius in Rome, the one dedicated to him in the Forum Boarium by the silversmiths (*argentarii*) and cattle-dealers (*boarii*), he and his Empress are depicted as sacrificing at a tripod placed between them. Yet they pay no attention to the ritual act that they are supposed to be performing, but stand facing, and gazing out at, the spectator as if to receive his veneration and homage.[57]

Still more striking in this use of frontality to enhance the Emperor's god-like dignity are some of the reliefs carved on the great four-way Arch that was erected in Septimius' honour at his birth-place, Leptis Magna. One frieze-shaped panel from the attic of the Arch presents the Emperor's triumphal entry into his native city after his eastern victories.[58] The procession is advancing from left to right and is being watched by a row of citizens standing to the front in the background. Their frontality is logical enough; and so is that of the boy who leads the horses of the chariot and of the bearded man who accompanies him, since, while walking to the right, they are turning round to observe the chariot's progress. Of the main cortège the four horses, and the side and wheel of the chariot are all in profile: so is the cavalcade of horsemen, shown in two superimposed tiers, who follow the chariot at the left-hand end of the panel. But the carved breastwork of the chariot appears in full; and above it the central Imperial group of Septimius and his two sons is revealed in a rigidly frontal posture; all three are looking straight out of the picture at the viewer. It is as if a cult-relief had been suddenly inserted for adoration into the place that should have been occupied by the chariot's passengers. There is a world of difference between this group of figures and the corresponding one carved, *c.* AD 80, in the scene of Titus' Jewish triumph on his Arch in Rome.[59] There the chariot is emerging out of the background and turning to the spectator's left; and, although the torsos of the Emperor and the Victory who crowns him are largely frontal, his face and extended right arm are in profile, following the direction in which the procession is moving.

No post-Severan historical reliefs of the 3rd century AD have survived; but in the centre of the upper part of the battle-scene on the Ludovisi sarcophagus (above), probably the coffin of an Emperor, the mounted figure of the general-Emperor, while participating in the struggle, is at the same time detached from its agonies. His head and torso are twisted round to face the viewer and he stretches out his right arm and hand in a gesture of encouragement and 'salvation'. But it is in two historical reliefs of the early-4th century on Constantine's Arch in Rome that *maiestas Augusti* first appears in a kind of 'stage-set' as a divine epiphany among a crowd of mortals. These long, narrow friezes depict Constantine's address to the citizens of Rome and his distribution of largesse to them after his defeat of his rival Maxentius at the Milvian Bridge.[60] In both cases the figure of the Emperor is completely central to the scene and completely frontal, in the first case standing on the Rostra, in the second case seated on a lofty pedestal. His figure is also presented on a larger scale than are the figures of the populace, massed on either side, whose attention is riveted upon him as they listen to his words and hold out their hands to receive his bounty. In the scene of largesse the bearers of two lighted torches flank the Emperor and his entourage. In these Constantinian friezes both concept and composition are essentially the same as in Theodosian works of the end of the 4th century – the epiphanies of the Emperor and his sons in the royal box carved in relief on the base of the Obelisk in the hippodrome of Constantinople,[61] and the vision of him enthroned with his sons beneath an elaborate architectural canopy on the round silver dish (*missorium*) p 192 (39) in Madrid.

What the pagan or secular Roman world, from Marcus Aurelius' generation to Theodosius' was looking for in these scenes of *maiestas Augusti* it discovered in *maiestas Christi*, in the exaltation of the God-Man, fully divine and fully human, Saviour in the next world and in this, as presented on the 5th-century sarcophagi of Ravenna[62] and in the apse-mosaics of 4th-, 5th- and 6th-century churches – for instance, Old St Peter's[63] and Santa Pudenziana in p 192 (40) Rome and San Vitale at Ravenna.[64]

VIII

ORDEALS OF THE MIND

GREEK PHILOSOPHY
FROM THE AGE OF CICERO TO PLOTINUS

A. HILARY ARMSTRONG

'Far be it from us to suppose that God abhors in us that by virtue of which he has made us superior to other animals.'

ST AUGUSTINE

'O Philosophy, the ruler of life! thou seekest out virtue and expellest vice! what should we be, what would human life be without thee?' To Cicero, as to all intellectuals and thinkers of the ancient world, philosophy was an all-embracing activity, teaching a man about himself, the world and the Divine, telling him how to live rightly, and moreover moving him to action. What the ancient meant by philosophy we should be more inclined to call ideology, for by subscribing to a philosophical doctrine he was committing himself morally – and even spiritually – in a way that has little in common with the academic discipline that is called philosophy today. When Christianity emerged upon the intellectual scene of the Roman Empire, therefore, it was natural for the Christians to present their beliefs as the only true philosophy. The distinction between philsophy and theology was not established in Christendom until the Middle Ages.

In iconography, it was the type of the philosopher as an ascetic sage (made popular by the Cynics and early Stoics) which caught the imagination of the Mediterranean world. The one opposite, from the Villa of Boscoreale near Pompeii, wears the woolen cloak of the Cynics, the original beggar-philosophers, whose way of life was adopted to some extent by the more austere members of other schools. (1)

The philosopher, the 'man of the Muses', who by meditation on spiritual values attains immortality, is frequently found on pagan sarcophagi. Above: two philosophers with Muses and a tragic mask. (2)

A beard and a concentrated gaze became the hallmarks of philosophers. The marble fragment (above, left) shows two with scrolls, accompanied by a pupil (?). The bronze philosopher (above, right) holds a codex. (3, 4)

'Pleasure is the goal' proclaims the cup (above) showing Epicurus and Zeno as skeletons. The pig recalls Horace's 'sleek hog from Epicurus' sty'. But the true Epicurean was deeply religious. (5)

Sun, moon and star gods figured in later Stoic and Platonist 'cosmic theology'. Above, on this dish: the sun and moon, preceded by the Morning and Evening Stars; below: earth, sea, water deities and the Seasons. To the right is the *genius saeculi* in a zodiac frame, supported by Atlas, and a snake-entwined obelisk. In the chariot: Cybele and Attis, surrounded by Corybantes. (6)

Sandals and a simple woolen mantle were further attributes. The sixth philosopher (above), from Ravenna, is a Christian philosopher. (7)

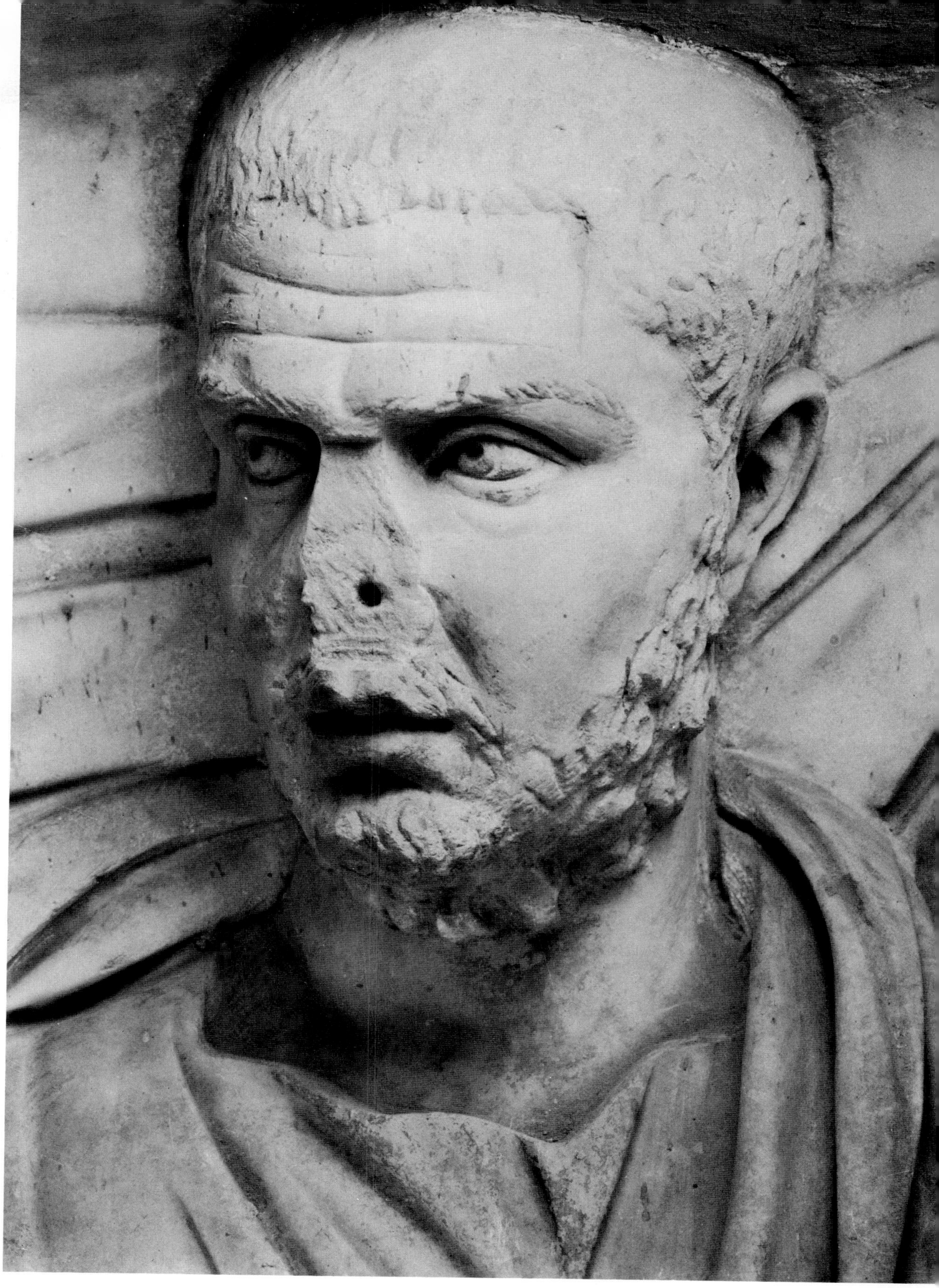

The Platonists, after a period of scepticism, in which they claimed to be following Socrates as portrayed in Plato's early dialogues, were finally led back to dogmatic teaching in the 1st century BC by Antiochus of Ascalon. The Middle Platonist school embraced a variety of thinkers of whom the best known was that most attractive of intelligent amateur philosophers, Plutarch. Strongly influenced by the Pythagorean revival, they developed Plato's thought in a more theistic direction. Chief among their doctrines was a belief in a transcendent supreme God; and Plato's Ideas come to be spoken of as thoughts in God's mind. Both views were to receive further development in Neoplatonism.

However it was Plotinus who brought lasting fame to the late Platonism. His thought charged with an intense religious experience, he preached a philosophy in which we are woken up to a knowledge of ourselves and our place in reality, and brought back to the transcendent source of all things. This portrait figure on a sarcophagus is identified by some scholars as being Plotinus. (8)

Philosophy in the ancient world could include all kinds of physical and biological science, and there was sometimes a close connection between philosophy and medicine. The Sceptic Sextus Empiricus was a physician, and the greatest ancient medical writer, Galen, had strong philosophical interests. The fresco from the catacomb of the Via Latina (above) probably represents a medical class. The doctor is the central figure, accompanied by a bearded assistant and pupils, one of whom demonstrates on a subject. (9)

GREEK PHILOSOPHY FROM THE AGE OF CICERO TO PLOTINUS

A. HILARY ARMSTRONG

THE AGE in which Cicero studied Greek philosophy and transmitted what he found interesting and important in it to the polite Roman world of his time, and to later Latin-reading generations, was the 1st century BC, and this was one of the great turning points in the history of European thought. The two centuries or so after the death of Alexander the Great had been one of the most sceptical, critical and rationalist periods in that history. But now, in the age of Cicero, there appears in the two most important philosophical schools, Stoicism and the Platonic Academy, the beginning of a new kind of other-worldly religious philosophy which came eventually to dominate the thought of educated men in the Roman Empire from the 2nd century AD onwards and formed the intellectual background for the first beginnings of Christian thought.

To appreciate the importance of this change it is necessary to understand what philosophy meant to most men of the ancient world who took any serious interest in it. It was not just one intellectual discipline among many others, highly specialized and of interest almost exclusively to its professional practitioners, and perhaps not providing even them with the principles by which they lived their lives. It was a completely all-embracing activity, engaging heart and will as well as mind (to use an anachronistic and rather artificial division which the ancients would hardly have understood). The object was to teach men the whole truth about themselves, the world and the Divine (whatever that might turn out to be), and thus to show them how they ought to live, and not only to show them but to move them to make a real effort to live rightly. It was a kind of philosophy which had a very strong ethical emphasis and an extremely close connection with religion, so much so that it was perfectly natural for the Early Christians to present their developing theology (as we should call it) as the only true philosophy: the present sharp distinction between theology and philosophy was not fully established in the western Christian world till a thousand years after the period with which we are dealing, and has never been clearly made in eastern Christianity. There were of course in our period, besides cultivated amateurs of philosophy like Cicero and popular philosophical preachers like Dio Chrysostom or Maximus of Tyre, plenty of serious professional philosophers, giving courses of lectures, often highly technical and specialized, on the doctrines of the school to which they professed adherence, discussing more or less acrimoniously the ideas of their professional colleagues, and, increasingly as time went on, commenting on the great classical texts of Greek philosophy, the works of Plato and Aristotle. But the professionals were at least as much concerned as the amateurs and the popular preachers were with encouraging and helping their hearers to live the philosophical life, with its austere morality and increasingly deep religious concern.

Before discussing the changes which took place in the 1st century BC in the two schools of most importance for the future, Stoicism and Platonism, it will be as well to look briefly at what was 208 (9) happening in the others. The Peripatetic school (the school of Aristotle) never exercised a very wide-ranging influence. In the time between the death of Aristotle and the beginning of our period it had developed strong interests in all sorts of specialist empirical knowledge (what we should call science and history), and this had pushed metaphysical speculation rather into the background. In so far as the Peripatetic school preserved any interest in general philosophical questions, its members tended to a much more exclusively this-worldly, naturalistic and materialistic (in a quite modern sense) view of reality than that of their founder Aristotle. But in the 1st century BC the school made one very notable contribution to the development of the religious metaphysics and psychology of late antiquity. This was the publication, about 40 BC, by a Peripatetic philosopher, Andronicus of Rhodes, who became head of the school, of a great edition of the lectures which Aristotle had delivered in the school and which, it seems, had not been generally available before. This belated publication of Aristotle's lectures effectively pushed out of circulation his earlier, more popular, and in some cases more Platonic works, which had been widely read up to this time, so that the complete works of Aristotle which we now have are the lecture-courses which were included in the edition of Andronicus. This made Aristotle's mature thought available to later Greek philosophers, with the result that we find a large Aristotelian component in most later Platonism. The members of the school increasingly devoted themselves to commenting on the works of their founder, and some of their commentaries, notably those of the great Peripatetic commentator Alexander of Aphrodisias (early-3rd century AD), had a considerable influence on the Neoplatonism of Plotinus.

The Epicureans were unaffected by the changes of the 1st century p 206 (5) BC. They continued imperturbably to maintain the doctrine of their master Epicurus, which was, in inadequate summary, the following. The peace of mind which is man's true pleasure and real good can only be secured by a firm faith in certain great truths and by a strong pursuit of a certain line of conduct. The truths were that the universe is a chance structure of atoms, that the gods, though they exist and can be contemplated by philosophers, cannot and do not govern the world or interfere in any way with human life, and that death is the end and is nothing to be afraid of. In the field of action, peace of mind was to be attained by cutting desires to the natural minimum and living an austere withdrawn life in the company of like-minded friends. The Epicureans were still offering a vigorous opposition to the dominant religious and philosophical tendencies in the 2nd century AD, when an Epicurean citizen of Oenoanda in Lycia, Diogenes, set up in his native place a great inscription on stone, most of which survives, expounding Epicurean doctrine. But the Epicureans had never been more than a relatively small minority, and at some time between the 2nd and the late-4th centuries AD, the school quietly died out.

A perfectly good and wise gas

Stoicism in the 1st century BC continued to maintain its basic p 206 (5) doctrines and view of the world without essential change. It saw the universe as a single living organism, permeated and governed in every detail by a material God who had produced it out of his own substance and, according to most forms of the doctrine, would periodically reabsorb it into himself and then reproduce it exactly the same, and so on for ever through an endless series of cycles. This material God was an 'intelligent fiery breath', a sort of perfectly good and wise gas. All the active, formative, structuring elements in the universe were parts of this divine substance and the passive inert element which was formed and structured was a modification of it, so that God and the universe could be simply identified. Hence the universe was the best of all possible universes, which is why the only possible future was one of exact cyclic repetition: there was no room for change or progress, because everything, being God, was already as good as it could be. Man's soul was a part of the divine fire, and what he had to do was to live virtuously according to the divinity within him, which was nature or reason, regarding all else as indifferent: rather paradoxically in view of their identification of man's soul and everything else with the divinity, the Stoics thought that man had the power not to do this, and that the vast majority of men did not in fact do so.

Stoic pantheism did not at all, as it might logically have done, lead to a totally permissive morality in which all sorts of human behaviour are accepted as varying manifestations of the divine in man. It produced a thoroughly puritanical and exclusive, though in its older forms completely this-worldly, morality of the impassive fulfilment of rationally apprehended obligations. In this way alone could man realize his true divinity. Only sages did so, and there were very few sages, if there were any at all.

These basic doctrines, as has been said, persisted through the 1st century BC without essential change. But the great geographer, historian and philosopher Poseidonius of Apamea in Syria, whose lectures Cicero heard at Rhodes, was a Stoic who, without abandoning Stoicism, seems to have introduced into his version of it some elements from the thought of Plato, whom he greatly admired. Unfortunately none of the works of Poseidonius have survived and we know very much less about his teaching than we should like to, though modern scholars have speculated about it extensively, and with a good deal of creative imagination. But Poseidonius' somewhat Platonized Stoicism does appear to have played an important part in the formation of a kind of religious philosophy which was very widespread from the 1st century BC onwards among educated men, and which had a deep influence on Neoplatonism and on the minds and imaginations of Christians for many centuries after the end of the ancient period; perhaps to some extent it still continues to influence them, often unconsciously, today.

p 206–7 (6) This is what may be called the cosmic religion or cosmic theology. In it the universe is still seen, as in the older Stoicism, as a divine living organism and man as a being whose true rational self is part of the divine fire which governs and animates the world. But the influence of Platonism results in the introduction of elements of dualism, transcendence and other-worldliness which were absent from the older Stoic world-picture. The divine fire is now thought of as mainly concentrated in the Upper Cosmos, the region of the heavenly bodies. As in nearly all ancient astronomical systems, these bodies are believed to circle the earth in vast orbits. The earth lies in the centre, a mere point in size compared to the great fiery bodies of the heavens, surrounded by its dark misty lower atmosphere. Beyond this, and beginning with the sphere of the moon, the regions of intense and splendid fiery light, where the living and divine globes of sun and moon and stars circle in their everlasting dance, stretch out to the outermost sphere of heaven. This great structure of the universe is conceived in most forms of the cosmic religion, as it was already by Aristotle, to be everlasting, without beginning or end, though Poseidonius himself returned to the older Stoic doctrine, abandoned by some of his predecessors, that it was periodically reabsorbed by the Divine Fire (the 'conflagration') and was then re-created. The eternity of the world was one of the great points of controversy between Christians and later pagans, another being of course the divinity of the heavenly bodies.

Purification and release

As will be easily seen, this system is geocentric in the sense that the earth is in the middle, but by no means geocentric or man-centred in its scale of values. The earth is not only insignificantly small in comparison with the heavenly bodies. It is the darkest, dampest and dirtiest place in the universe, full of corruption and decay. The very ancient Greek opposition between the hot, dry, bright, active, male, good, divine principle and the cold, moist, dark, passive, female, evil principle is clearly apparent in the cosmic religion. And though man's highest part, his ruling principle or rational self, is a divine thing and part of the sacred fire that has descended from the Upper Cosmos, his earthly life and concerns are insignificant and vile, and the divine fire in him is clogged and contaminated by the passions which are added to his soul in the darker regions below the moon. The morality, therefore, which goes with this cosmic theology is a dualistic one of purification and escape. Man's object must be to purify his soul of the contaminations of this lower region by living virtuously and rationally (the two are synonymous) and eventually, after death and whatever subsequent further purification is needed, to escape to his true home in the Upper Cosmos.

In this whole way of thinking there is a curious kind of materialistic, intracosmic, other-worldliness whose influence seems to have persisted long after the world-picture to which it belongs had been formally abandoned. For the believer in the cosmic religion, God was literally 'up there' and 'out there', and human fulfilment was a matter of purging away the dark-damp-passionate and becoming all bright-dry-rational and so going up to God. There are still people who seem to think about or imagine the spiritual and moral life instinctively in terms rather like these, though they certainly do not consciously believe in the ancient astronomy and the theology which goes with it. Further, it was quite easy to fit a Platonic or Aristotelian transcendent immaterial deity, responsible for the form, order and motion of the divine universe and only accessible through it, into this world-picture, and this was quite often done – naturally enough, as important elements in the cosmic theology go back to Plato and Aristotle themselves. But, when this was done, inevitably the transcendent spiritual God would tend to be thought of as being transcendent in the sense of being up and outside, beyond and above the universe and physically remote. This tendency to a false understanding of transcendence could be overcome, as we shall see when we come to consider the thought of Plotinus; but it was very widespread in the thought of the early Roman Empire, and it has influenced a good deal of Christian thinking since.

The later Stoics of the Roman Empire, except for Seneca sometimes, show little influence of the Platonized Stoicism of Poseidonius. Their greatest teacher, Epictetus (about AD 50–130), was a conservative who maintained the doctrines of the older Stoicism. But they were all primarily moralists, not deeply interested in other parts of the dogmas of their school, but concerned to promote the Stoic life according to nature and reason, with its indifference to all else but virtue and its passionate devotion to the all-pervading divinity of which we are parts. Epictetus preaches this finely, in all its narrowness, rigidity and hard nobility. But the most attractive book which this later Stoicism has left us is the 'spiritual journal' or record of his daily self-examination written by the philosopher-emperor Marcus Aurelius Antoninus, who ruled the Roman Empire from AD 161 to 180. It is a record, addressed to himself and possibly not intended for publication, which shows, perhaps better than anything else in ancient literature, what philosophy as a way of life could mean to the men who followed it. It is a melancholy book on the whole, expressing here and there a rather morbid self-disgust. But it is the record of a most humane and sensitive man, full of a deep loyalty to, and acceptance of, the divine whole of which he felt himself to be a part and the divine reason which permeated and ordered it, the book of a man who in a strong practical sense felt himself to be a citizen of the city of the universe, the city of God.

They knew only that they did not know

The change which came over the school of Plato, the Academy, in the 1st century BC was a good deal more radical than the mild and partial Platonizing of Stoicism. For some two centuries before the age of Cicero, the Academy had been maintaining a sceptical position which its members saw as a development of the agnosticism of Socrates as portrayed in Plato's earlier dialogues, the Socrates who only knew that he did not know. The school conducted a formidable attack on all forms of dogmatism, especially the naïve and extreme dogmatism of the Stoics, with the object of producing a complete suspense of judgement, which they saw as the only satisfactory intellectual state. In this they stood very close to another independent contemporary school, the Sceptics properly so-called, whose position was still being vigorously maintained in the 2nd century AD by some tough-minded empirical medical men, p 208 (of whom the most important was Sextus Empiricus. However, the founder of the Sceptics, Pyrrho (about 360–270 BC), seems to have been closer to the general pattern of ancient philosophy than the

Academics or later Sceptics, in that philosophy was for him a way of life, and the only way of life which would bring happiness. The sceptical suspense of judgement and inability to make any definite statement about anything was for him the only means of attaining the imperturbable peace of mind which – he agreed with Stoics and Epicureans – was the highest human good and the aim of all philosophy.

There is a slight suggestion of the oriental sage about Pyrrho (he is said to have met Indian holy men while accompanying Alexander the Great's expedition to the East). But the sceptical Academics and later Sceptics were thinkers of a thoroughly Western, and indeed modern Western, type. Their way of philosophizing comes closer to modern English academic philosophy than anything else in the ancient world, and they and the Peripatetics are almost the only ancient philosophers whom one can imagine being happy in the intellectual climate of a modern English or North American university. This formidably sceptical tradition of criticism of the dogmatic philosophers had its effect on the development of later Platonism. It did nothing to shake the self-confidence of the Epicureans, and its effects on Stoicism, in so far as it had any, seem to have been limited and passing. But it probably contributed something to the deep conviction of later Platonists that God is unknowable and that no statement we can make about him is really adequate, a conviction which has had a great deal of influence on later Christian thought. The sceptical tradition also helped to lead the more sophisticated Platonists, particularly Plotinus, to abandon the old naïve presentation of God's action in forming and ordering the world as analogous to a craftsman's action in planning and executing a job of work – an analogy which appears to have satisfied Plato.

The return to metaphysics

The man who led the Academy back from scepticism to dogmatic teaching was Antiochus of Ascalon, another of the distinguished Greek philosophers whose lectures Cicero heard. He seems to have been even more open to the ideas of other schools than Poseidonius, to have started the idea, prevalent among a great many, though not all, later Platonists that Plato and Aristotle agreed in all important matters; and not only to have been influenced in his own thought by Stoicism but to have held that Platonism and Stoicism were in essentials the same philosophy. Later Platonism on the whole follows Antiochus' lead in being a philosophy of synthesis, in which ideas deriving from all the great schools except the Epicurean are discernible, though the attitude of individual Platonists to Aristotle and the Stoics varies very much (they are pretty consistently more hostile to Stoicism than Antiochus appears to have been, though often deeply influenced by Stoic teaching, in particular its moral teaching). Unfortunately, as with Poseidonius, we are not very well informed about the teaching of Antiochus. Modern scholars have speculated about it extensively on the basis of such evidence as there is, but have by no means arrived at agreement. However, it seems clear that it was the movement which Antiochus (and other contemporary revivers of Platonism and Pythagoreanism whose names we do not know) inaugurated that led to the distinctive type of later Platonism whose outlines begin to become clear to us in the 1st century AD.

Our earliest witness to this 'Middle Platonist' way of thinking is Philo the Jew of Alexandria, an older contemporary of St Paul. Philo is a figure of great importance in the history of European thought. He was a devout Jew who had received a Greek philosophical education and used it to interpret the Jewish Scriptures (in their Greek translation, the Septuagint) in a way which seemed to him to make philosophical sense and to commend their teaching, so interpreted, to his Greek-educated contemporaries. By doing this he opened the path which Christian thinkers were to follow from the 2nd century AD onwards. The Christians were deeply influenced by his way of interpreting the Scriptures and reading Greek philosophy into them. He is the ancestor of Hellenized Christianity in both its Greek-speaking, Eastern, and its Latin-speaking, Western form (St Ambrose in particular in the West owes a great deal to him). Philo's influence was on Christianity (which he never knew anything about) and not on later Judaism: rabbinical Judaism is in strong reaction against the sort of Hellenization of which Philo is the greatest example, and the mediaeval Jewish philosophers did not know his work. As a witness to contemporary pagan Greek thought he has to be used with care. For all his Hellenism, he remained a good Jew, and his theism is basically that of the Bible rather than that of contemporary Platonists. But by comparing his thought with that of later pagan Platonists with no Jewish contacts we can see that some important features of Middle Platonism were already apparent in the Greek thought of his time.

The Middle Platonists of the period from the late-1st century to the early-3rd century AD are a very varied group. There are rhetoricians interested in philosophy, Apuleius and Maximus of Tyre. There is the attractive, if not very profound, Plutarch, a philosophical amateur in the best sense, a man of wide-ranging curiosity, extensive reading, and deep and sane piety. And there are numbers of professional philosophers, like Albinus and Atticus, many of them little more than names to us, engaged in lecturing, commenting and writing on philosophical topics. They also show considerable differences in the degree to which their thought is influenced by that of the other great schools. Most show some influence of Stoicism, though they tend to be officially anti-Stoic. Some, like Albinus, are deeply influenced by Aristotelianism, but there is also a strongly anti-Aristotelian tendency represented by Atticus.

An important influence was that of the Pythagorean revival. This began in the 1st century BC and its influence is already apparent in Philo. The two schools, Pythagoreans and Platonists, were closely related and they interacted on each other continually, so that it is not always easy to determine to which of the two groups an individual philosopher should be regarded as belonging. This is natural enough, as Plato's own thought had a considerable Pythagorean element in it, especially in his later years when he was (according to Aristotle: there is very little trace of these doctrines in the Dialogues) much preoccupied with numbers and the principles of numbers, the One and the Indefinite Two, which he regarded as the ultimate principles of all reality. The later, post-Platonic Pythagoreans maintained this doctrine of the two opposite principles of reality, but reduced the duality in the nature of things to an ultimate unity either by placing a supreme One above the One which was coupled with its indefinite opposite in the generation of number, or by making the One produce its opposite, a kind of indefinite quantity which it then limited and formed into number by a sort of self-contraction.

It is in these Pythagorean systems that the absolutely transcendent One as first principle of reality, which was of such great importance, as we shall see, in the thought of Plotinus and his successors, appears for the first time. It is especially clear in the system of Moderatus of Gades (1st century AD), whose thought shows striking similarities with that of Plotinus, as does that of a later Pythagorean, Numenius of Apamea (2nd century AD), whom Plotinus was accused of plagiarizing – unjustly, for the differences between the two thinkers are as great as the resemblances.

The supreme God

In spite of the variety of types to be found among the Middle Platonist philosophers and the variety of influences to which they were subjected, there is a certain degree of unity in Middle Platonist speculation which makes some general statements about it possible (though the variations are more numerous than can be indicated here, and sometimes important, and there is a good deal of inconsistency and incoherence which general statements are bound to conceal). This later Platonism was much more clearly and firmly theistic than the thought of Plato himself, as far as we can judge from the Dialogues and from the scanty and obscure evidence about his oral teaching. At the head of the Middle Platonist system stands a supreme God, who is the highest Intelligence and is also sometimes called the One or Good. A most important development, which had a great influence on later thought, is that the Platonic Ideas, the eternal Forms or patterns which according to Plato are the archetypal models and causes of all that exists in our world, are now said to be God's thoughts. They exist eternally in his mind and are the plan or pattern on which he makes the world. Philo already accepts this doctrine: its origins, in spite of a great deal of speculation by modern scholars, remain obscure. But it seems possible that it originated in the sort of Platonized Stoicism which we have associated with the name of Poseidonius. Wherever it began, the doctrine of the Ideas as God's thoughts is an essential part of pagan and Christian Platonism from the 1st century BC onwards.

The transcendence of this supreme God is very much stressed in later Platonism. Sometimes, notably in the thought of Albinus, the influence of Aristotle's conception of the completely detached, self-thinking Divine Mind is evident. There are already traces of the 'negative theology' which we shall meet fully developed in Plotinus, in which God is said to be 'not this', 'not that', the implication being that he is the Wholly Other, beyond anything which we can think or imagine. In the simpler and less sophisticated forms of Middle Platonism there is a hierarchy of subordinate gods and spirits (*daemones*) between the supreme God and the world and ourselves. Some of the spirits, those who act as intermediaries and messengers between gods and men, are good; but others are evil, demons in fact in the Christian sense, and these provide a convenient explanation for the uglier, crueller, primitively crude rites of traditional pagan religion, which are held to be directed to them, not really to the gods. The more professional philosophers accept the hierarchy of gods and spirits; but some of them also introduce a division, of great importance later in Neoplatonism, between the Supreme Mind or God and a Second Mind, inferior to and dependent on the First. In Numenius the First God is purely contemplative and it is the Second who forms and directs the world: the Soul of the World (all Platonists believed that the physical universe was an ensouled living being) is the Third God. However, in spite of this stratification of spiritual being and insistence on the transcendence of the Supreme, it would be a mistake to think that for Middle Platonists God is always ineffably remote. In Plutarch and Atticus in particular, we meet a simple pious theism, in which God cares for the world and for men and directs all things to a good end by his providence.

The Middle Platonists generally, but not always, think of the physical universe as eternal, without beginning or end. Their explanations of the evils in it tend to be dualistic; evil is due either to the disorderly and corrupting influence of a pre-existing matter, coeternal with and not derived from God, or to an evil soul, again coeternal with God and not dependent on him. Their conception of man is also dualistic in a different sense, in the manner of Plato's *Phaedo*. He is very much a spirit using an earthly body, and his object is to escape from it and to return after purification to his true home in the spiritual world. The morality which they taught was generally an austere (though not inhumanely ascetic) one, often strongly influenced by Stoicism.

The first Christian thinkers, on the whole, found this Platonist philosophical theism the most congenial of the available philosophies, though the very anti-philosophical Tertullian found no difficulty in thinking of God and the soul as material in the Stoic manner, and Christian morality, like Platonist morality, was (and sometimes still is) deeply affected by Stoicism. But it was Platonic theism, as taken over, adapted to the Christian faith, and developed by St Justin, the Alexandrians Clement and Origen, and the Fathers of the Church of the 4th and 5th centuries, which became the foundation of traditional Christian philosophy and theology in both East and West. More about its capture of and its effects on the minds of Christians will be found elsewhere in this volume.

Platonism and Plotinus

p 207 (8) This later Platonism was transformed and given a new vigour in the 3rd century AD by Plotinus, the one great philosopher of our period and one of the greatest and most influential in the whole history of European thought. From his time until the end of the teaching of philosophy by pagan Greeks in the 6th century AD there was only one kind of philosophy which counted for anything, and this was Platonism in the form which he gave it, with various later pagan and Christian developments and modifications. Plotinus' influence, sometimes direct, more often indirect, continued through the Middle Ages and the Renaissance, and it is still sometimes perceptible in some philosophers and theologians of our own time. The reasons for Plotinus' decisive influence on the philosophy of succeeding centuries are that he was a considerably more powerful and coherent thinker than any of his predecessors (as far as we can tell from our fragmentary knowledge of them) and that his thought was dominated and charged with a peculiar intensity by religious experience of a very high quality.

Plotinus lived from AD 204/5 to 270. We are well informed about his life, as his disciple and literary executor, Porphyry, wrote a biography of him, which he prefixed to his great edition of his master's writings, the *Enneads*: it is printed in all modern editions and translations of Plotinus' works. It is our most complete picture of a professional philosopher of later antiquity, and a very attractive one. It shows a man who lived to the full the philosophy which he taught, and whose other-worldliness did not mean inaccessibility or inhumanity or lack of concern for the well-being of his friends in this world. We learn from it that Plotinus studied philosophy at Alexandria with the mysterious Ammonius 'Saccas', who had also, probably, been the master of the great Christian thinker Origen. It seems likely from the quality of his two great pupils that Ammonius was a remarkable person. Porphyry's account suggests that his influence on Plotinus went deep. But he wrote nothing, and the attempts of modern scholars to reconstruct his thought go so far beyond the very inadequate ancient evidence that they cannot be regarded as successful. After eleven years with Ammonius, Plotinus joined the expedition of Gordian III against Persia in the hope of getting to know something of the philosophy of the Persians and Indians. But Gordian was murdered in Mesopotamia and Plotinus escaped with difficulty to Antioch and afterwards went to Rome. He never met any Persian or Indian thinkers, and there seems to be no good reason for assuming any Indian influence on his philosophy, though there are some striking similarities. It was at Rome that he did all his teaching and writing, but there is nothing Western or Latin about him (except perhaps his name). His thought is completely Greek. In his later years, at least, in Rome, he was a man of considerable social standing with many senatorial followers and admirers, and he was a personal friend of the Emperor Gallienus and his wife. But it does not appear that he exercised, or wished to exercise, any political influence. The political side of Plato's thought hardly seems to have interested him at all. This is true of all the later Platonists of whom we know anything, though it seems likely that there were others who were more interested in political philosophy. Some traces of their ideas may survive in the work of the great Muslim philosopher al-Fārābī.

Negative theology

Philosophy for Plotinus is the way in which we are woken up to a knowledge of our true self and its eternal place in divine reality and are brought back to union with the transcendent source of all things, the One or Good. It is a process of self-discovery in which we find that we are not just isolated selves but are living and contemplative parts of a divine world, in which the part is the whole, because it knows the whole. Moreover we are carried on beyond our realized contemplative universality in the everlasting return of the divine whole to union with its origin. This origin Plotinus calls the One or Good, though he knows very well that these, like all names, are inadequate. The One is really beyond the reach of words or thought. He is experienceable rather than in any ordinary sense knowable. (Though the words for One and Good are neuter in Greek, Plotinus more often than not uses the masculine, not the neuter, pronoun, in referring to the principle which he so names, so my use of 'He' here and in what follows is legitimate Plotinian usage.)

He – the One or the Good – is wholly other than all the realities and values which He creates and is absolutely beyond all determination and limitation (this is what Plotinus intends to indicate by the name 'One'). He cannot be said to know Himself because this would imply a sort of minimum duality between knowing subject and known object and so would imply a degree of internal division or limitation. He cannot even be said to be, since being for Plotinus is always being something, some one particular, definite, limited, describable thing, and the One is absolutely unlimited and so indescribable. But in spite of these extreme negations, on which he often insists, Plotinus does not experience or present the One as a mere negation or as an unconscious formless nothing-in-particular. He is more real than the beings we can know or speak of, more awake and aware than mind at the height of its intuitive self-knowledge. He is a life more intense than any life we know. He is the creator of all value and the goal of all desire (this is what the name 'Good' is intended to point to).

Plotinus finds the language of personality inadequate, like all language, in speaking about the One: but he seems to find it at least less inadequate than impersonal language which would present the supreme reality as an abstraction or a 'thing', a dead passive object, or an unconscious force. As the One has a self-awareness that is higher than intellect, so He has a spontaneity, beyond necessity and freedom of choice, that is higher than will. Plotinus speaks of Him as love of Himself and father of all, though he certainly never thinks of Him as a loving father concerned with and caring for His creatures. And our final encounter and union with Him is at least more like a personal encounter and a union of lovers than it is like the discovery and taking possession of an infinitely valuable object or the passing of a drop of water into the boundless ocean. Just because the One is so wholly other than all things, we are not separated from Him by any spatial distance or limitation. Plotinus has an extremely vivid sense of the inadequacy and misleadingness of spatial language in speaking of spiritual realities. The One for him is not 'out there' or 'up there', but is most intimately present in ourselves. Though Plotinus accepts the basic dogmas of the cosmic religion, the supremacy of fire among material things, the eternity of the world and the divinity of the heavenly bodies, there is none of the false transcendence of the cosmic religion in his way of thinking about the One or the other great divine realities.

Plotinus is fond of speaking about the production of these other realities, Intellect and Soul, in terms of the radiation of light from the sun or heat from fire, a radiation which leaves the source unchanged and undiminished. This 'emanation' language seems to
06–7 (6) derive from the Platonized Stoicism I mentioned earlier in this chapter, in which it was used quite literally to describe the radiation of man's fiery intellectual principle from the sun, the source of divine fire. In Plotinus it is only a metaphor, and one which should not be misunderstood as meaning that the whole process of creation is a sort of automatic, unconscious outflow. He certainly always insists that the production of the lower realities in no way affects the source. The One does not plan out reality and then decide to create it. The production of everything is eternal, without willing or planning or choice or care for what is created. It cannot be conceived that it should not happen, because good is always productive and creative and the Supreme Good supremely productive and creative. Whether he is thinking about divine or human action, Plotinus always ranks immediate, spontaneous, unselfconscious creativity above carefully thought-out plans deliberately carried out. His ideal man is one who always does the right thing immediately, as a direct expression of his inward goodness, without having to think about it or being selfconsciously aware that he is doing the right thing. And he rejects as absurd and objectionable the idea of God as Architect of the Universe, looking at a pre-existing plan and deciding to carry it out and putting his decision into execution – an idea which seems to have been reasonably satisfactory to Plato and to have satisfied most pagan and Christian theists in Plotinus' time, as it still does some in ours. But though the production of all things by the One does not in any way affect the One, is entirely un-deliberate, and cannot be conceived of as not happening, it is also entirely spontaneous, not a sort of automatic reflex action but more like an instantaneous explosion of free creativity. The One for Plotinus is not bound by any sort of necessity or law of nature, internal or external. He is prior to necessity, and establishes it in creating.

Intellect and soul

The first great derived reality which proceeds from the One is Intellect. Plotinus distinguishes two phases in its timeless generation. It springs eternally from the One as an unformed life, a 'sight not yet seeing' and, as it springs, it eternally turns back upon the One in contemplation, is filled with content and becomes Intellect and the totality of real being. The impulse for its turning back in contemplation is the love which the One gives it in producing it as life, and this love not only makes it contemplate the One but eternally carries it beyond contemplation to mystical union, so that it is always both Intellect knowing and Intellect in love, Intellect sober and Intellect drunk. It is held back from total reabsorption into the One by a sort of self-assertion, a will to separate existence, which Plotinus sometimes regards as an imperfection. In its normal contemplation, Intellect cannot receive the One in His absolute unformed and unbounded unity and simplicity. It 'breaks this up', Plotinus says, or 'makes it many', and so, under the impulse of the One, establishes itself as a complex reality, a one-in-many, as perfectly unified as anything which is not the One can be.

This complex reality of Intellect is the world of Forms or Ideas. These are, as in Plato, the eternal archetypes of the things we know in this world, but in other ways they are very different from the Platonic Ideas. They are awake and alive, not just things to be thought about but thinking minds. Intellect is a community of living intelligences, each of which knows, and so in a sense is, the whole of which it is a part: there is no spatial separation or delimitation of parts in the spiritual world. This world of intelligible reality is not a structure of lifeless abstractions, but 'boiling with life', full of light and colour and the richest, though not infinite, variety (the number of the Forms was finite for Plotinus, though not for his pupil Amelius: but he sometimes says that there are Forms or Ideas of individuals).

Plotinus' great visionary descriptions of Intellect are written under the pressure of a religious experience as intense as that which underlies his doctrine of the One, an experience of unity with the living All, clearly felt as distinct from that of unity with the transcendent One. With this experience there comes a clearer realization than is to be found in Plotinus' predecessors of the characteristics of a purely intuitive and immediate thinking which is really identical with its object, and this transforms the doctrine of the Ideas in the mind of God which Plotinus inherited from his Middle Platonist predecessors, as his experience of the final mystical union transforms the Pythagorean doctrine of the transcendent One.

At our highest we can live on the level of Intellect and be carried back by its return in love to the One. But we properly belong to the next great derived reality or hypostasis, Soul, which is produced by Intellect as Intellect is produced by the One. Soul, however, stands much closer to Intellect than Intellect does to the One, and the spheres of the two overlap to some extent. Even when Plotinus separates them most sharply, he holds that Soul at its highest (and this includes our souls) is raised to the level of Intellect and is continually illuminated by its light. But the characteristic and distinctive activity of Soul is not intuitive but discursive thinking, reasoning from premises to conclusions. There is a restless element in it which makes it want to separate and divide, to have one thought after another instead of a single timeless contemplation (this Plotinus sometimes sees as an illegitimate self-assertion). So Soul establishes itself in a process of thought and a succession of thoughts, and in so doing brings time into being, and subjects to time the material universe which it forms, orders and animates. It is Soul, not directly Intellect, which is the maker of the material world; but it makes it by imaging in it the Forms which it receives from Intellect, and of course with the power which springs from the One. The material universe of Plotinus is very much the material universe of Platonized Stoicism. It is a single organic p 206–7 (6)
living being, with a hierarchical ordering of its parts in which fire and light occupy the outer and nobler spheres and are closest by their nature to spiritual being. But spiritual being is not for Plotinus outside or up above the universe. Soul, Intellect and the One are intimately and immediately present everywhere because they are not in space at all.

It is important to notice that the World-Soul which animates the physical universe is not identical with Universal Soul, and that our souls are not parts of it or derived from it. It is our elder sister, not our mother. Man's relationship to the physical universe and its spiritual principle is intimate but independent. Plotinus distinguishes between a higher World-Soul which administers the universe and a more immanent and body-bound Lower Soul or Nature which is the immediate principle of life and form for bodies. The material universe is good as a whole and in its parts because it is the work of a good divine Soul, and the Forms in it, which give it such limited reality as it has, are images or expressions of those in Soul which derive in their turn from Intellect. Plotinus defends its goodness passionately against the Gnostics, and holds that if we do not value it properly we cannot rise beyond it to the higher spiritual world which is its archetype and our true home. But it is none the less immeasurably inferior to the world of Intellect: its sharp spatial separations, and the continual conflicts and changes of the region below the moon, though brought into a wonderful order by the providence of the higher powers, make it a very second-rate universe by comparison with the glory of that changeless unity-in-diversity of superabundant life. It is no better than it is, partly because the Forms in it are the lowest and weakest images or expressions of the original Forms in Intellect, and partly because matter, which is what underlies it, though derived ultimately from the higher realities, is a principle of opposition to them, an absolute negativity and formlessness which, though it is a dark emptiness with no character of its own, somehow imparts something of its empty negation to the things which participate in it.

The 'middle part'

The range of Soul in Plotinus is very wide, from the light of Intellect to the darkness of matter, and man, who is essentially Soul, can live consciously on any level within that range. He is a complex being. His true, eternal self is a Higher Soul, living on the level of Intellect and continually illumined by it, which does not sin or suffer and remains essentially free and unhampered in its thinking activities by the body and its world, into which it does not 'come down'. That element in this Higher Soul, however, which is most characteristically 'ourself', the 'middle part' whose activity is discursive reasoning, can have its attention distracted from Intellect and be drawn into an egoistic self-isolation and materialistic obsession with the petty affairs of its disturbing and hampering individual earthly body. (The beings of the Upper Cosmos, the living divine heavenly bodies, are in no way disturbed or hampered by their fiery bodies, which Plotinus thinks of as wholly good and in no way an impediment to the activity of soul.) However, the human Higher Soul remains essentially detached from and independent of the body and its earthly life. What 'comes down' and joins with the bodily organism to form the 'joint' or 'composite' being is only an irradiation from the higher self, an image or expression of it on the lower level. It is this composite being, the 'other man', distinct from the 'man within' or true self, which sins and suffers and is emotionally disturbed, and in general is the subject of what we normally regard as human experience. It is this too which undergoes the successive reincarnations and the punishments in the underworld between earthly lives in which Plotinus, as a good Platonist, believed.

The less important, though absolutely necessary, part of the task of philosophy according to Plotinus is the disciplining and ordering of the lower self so that it shall be the least possible hindrance to the activity of the higher self. Its more important function is to train and direct the attention of the higher self so that it shall live as far as possible wholly in the light of Intellect, in unbroken contemplation of the higher realities. The right relationship of the two selves and the necessary control of the lower is brought about by a moderate and humane asceticism and by the vigorous practice of the individual and social virtues. Plotinus thought that a philosopher should renounce property and worldly ambition and withdraw from public life, but he did not believe that he should ever neglect his real duties to his friends and neighbours. He practised what he preached and gave a great deal of disinterested service to those around him as arbitrator in disputes, adviser in practical problems, and kindly and businesslike guardian to the orphan children of his friends. He was a vegetarian, but he is not greatly interested in details of ascetic diet or regimen. His sexual morals were austere enough, and he had a particular dislike of philosophical paederasty. But, again, he is not particularly interested in the subject, and has none of the neurotic obsession with chastity that is to be found in some Christians, ancient and modern.

A vision of the good

In the process of wakening the soul and directing its attention back to the true eternal world which is its home, an important part is played by the beauty of nature and art, the contemplation of which can lead our mind back to the intelligible beauty. Plotinus, unlike Plato, puts art on a level with nature as a way back to the intelligible world. The artist has direct access to the Forms in the intelligible world, and is not, as Plato thought, a mere copyist of the things in the world of the senses. It is in so far as it reflects the living unity and completeness of the intelligible form that a work of art is beautiful; and what makes beauty attractive and stirs our love for it is the radiance of the life which comes from beyond the world of Forms, from the Good. But though perceptible beauty plays its part in arousing our love for the intelligible, the main work of making us understand who we really are and where we really belong must be done by philosophy. This is for Plotinus not just a way of solving intellectual problems, though problems as they arise must be honestly faced and solved, nor is its object simply the production of an all-embracing logically coherent pattern of relations between concepts, though logical coherence must be attained as far as possible. But the principal purpose of philosophy is to make us see, and in contemplation to unite ourselves to, the eternal realities to whose world we find, in this contemplation, that we belong.

Philosophy is the way back to God through complete self-realization. It is in fact for Plotinus religion, and the whole of religion. External rites and material sacraments can have no importance for him, for the body cannot affect the soul, and there is no room in his thought for a divine revelation which might require special symbolic communication. Nor is there any room for methods of prayer and techniques of meditation. Philosophy is prayer, in the sense of 'lifting up the heart and mind to God', and any other kind of prayer is for him a magical activity unworthy of the serious attention of the philosopher.

There seems to be in the thought of Plotinus no alternative route to God for non-philosophers. In the thought of those later pagan Neoplatonists who followed Iamblichus, a high place is given to theurgic rites as means to a union with the divine which philosophy could not effect. But this is alien to the way of thinking of the founder of Neoplatonism. Plotinus' view is that by the practice of philosophy we realize our true nature and place in the world of Intellect, in a sense by our own efforts: though we must remember that for Plotinus all that we have and are is given by the Good, and what we are given is a dynamic being 'homed' on its origin, driven on in its return by the love which comes from the Good and illumined by the light of Intellect, which is always there for us if we will turn towards it and use it. In the world of Intellect we are raised to union with the Good, not by any automatic process or at our own will and pleasure, but when He 'comes' or manifests Himself. The soul suddenly 'takes light' and becomes that light which it sees. It shares, for a moment, the eternal union, in love, of Intellect with the One. This supreme experience is no more describable than the Good is describable. Plotinus tries to indicate or point to it, but says that only those who have shared it can really understand what he is talking about. The Good remains what He always is, the Wholly Other, distinct from all else, even from the Intellect which is eternally united with him, but the soul, while it sees and is united, has no awareness of distinction from Him.

This account of the philosophy of Plotinus is very sketchy and inadequate, and needs to be supplemented by a great deal of further reading, preferably in the works of Plotinus himself, of which good English translations are available. But it may serve to give some idea of a kind of thought whose influence on the Christian thinkers of succeeding generations was very great indeed. In the West Ambrose and Augustine, and in the East the Cappadocian Fathers, were deeply influenced by Plotinus; and the very influential Christian thinker who wrote under the pseudonym of 'Dionysius the Areopagite' owed much to the later pagan Neoplatonism, best represented for us by Proclus. Through these, and many others, the influence of Neoplatonism passed into the Christianity of the Middle Ages, and beyond – though it is also true that this philosophical religion, so remote from Christianity in some ways though so close to it in others, has sometimes provided European minds with an alternative to Christianity and has offered a continuing challenge to Christian orthodoxy, especially in its narrower and more rigid forms.

IX
THE SON OF MAN

JESUS IN THE CONTEXT OF HISTORY

DAVID FLUSSER

'Think not that I am come to destroy the Law, or the prophets: I am not come to destroy, but to fulfil.'

'GOSPEL ACCORDING TO ST MATTHEW'

Jesus of Nazareth
was born during the reign of Augustus and died during that of Tiberius. As a Jew, he fully accepted the Jewish Law. The community that he founded, comparable in some ways to a group such as the Essenes, saw itself as a movement of reform and fulfilment within Judaism, not as a secession from it; and it always called itself the 'new Israel'. Most of Jesus' ethical precepts, and even the forms in which he expressed them, can be paralleled in rabbinical teachings, and the earliest Christians were devout worshippers at the Temple. But, as happened in the case of the extremist Jewish religious groups, he and his followers came into conflict with the Roman authorities, and he was executed for sedition.

Information about the life of Jesus is remarkably full, though it comes entirely from writers who accepted him as the son of God. The earliest sources are the letters of St Paul and the Acts of the Apostles. Paul is comparatively uninterested in the earthly life of Jesus, stressing above all his continuing spiritual presence. The first biographical accounts – the Gospels – date from between AD 70 and AD 100. That of St Mark is probably the oldest. The Evangelists were addressing a primarily non-Jewish public, and the period when they wrote (just after the disastrous Jewish War of AD 66–70) was one during which anti-Jewish feeling was rife throughout the eastern Roman Empire. They are accordingly at pains to emphasize the differences between Jesus' doctrines and those of orthodox Judaism; to show the Jews as hostile to him and responsible for his death, and the Roman authorities as impartial but weak. Elements that have more in common with mystery religions than with Jewish beliefs (the birth of a god from an earthly mother and divine father; his redemptive sacrifice and a meal at which he is symbolically eaten; personal salvation through initiation, etc.) became incorporated into the evolving liturgy and theology, though admittedly they were also creeping into Judaism itself. The plain historical fact of Jesus' existence was, however, always central to the new faith, and in this it differed from all the mystery-cults. Instead of a non-historical and purely mythical figure, Christianity offered a man who had lived and died at a specific time and place.

Relics claiming to be associated with the life of Jesus have been known and venerated from early times, but only one has a serious claim to be considered genuine. This is the so-called Holy Shroud of Turin – a strip of linen about twelve feet long, bearing the impression of the back and front of a man. Not only can the head, trunk, and limbs be easily recognized but it is marked on the face, hands, side and feet with dark stains that may be blood. The face itself (opposite) is unnervingly convincing and tragic. Against its authenticity are the facts that there is no record of its existence before 1356, and that in 1389 a man is obscurely recorded as having confessed that he painted it. In its favour is an impressive array of evidence from several scientific disciplines. The image is made in *negative* (the reproduction shown here is the 'positive' of the face from a photographic negative, not what is actually seen on the shroud) – a process a mediaeval forger is unlikely to have known about and used. It has also been found that the image *could* have been produced on a cloth soaked in aloes by contact with a recently dead corpse of which the sweat contained concentrated urea; and that such sweat is secreted by a body in intense physical pain. Moreover, the weave of the cloth (herringbone or 'twill' weave) was common in the East during the time of Jesus but unknown in the West until after the 14th century. Lastly, the dark stains thought to be blood correspond exactly with the real wounds of a crucified man, including nails through the wrists, not the palms (a historical detail unknown until modern times). Stimulated by the Shroud, a great deal of medical research has been carried out, and while much tends strikingly to support its authenticity, nothing has so far been produced conclusively to disprove it. The question therefore remains open until direct physical tests are allowed. (1)

Nazareth, looking south-east. (2)

Bethlehem, looking west. (3)

Jesus' home was the province of Galilee, north of Judaea, though according to St Luke and St Matthew he was actually born at Bethlehem (left), the birthplace of David and the town from which the Messiah was prophesied to come. His childhood and early life were spent at Nazareth (far left), which was always spoken of as his native place. On returning from his baptism in the Jordan 'he came to Nazareth, where he had been brought up; and, as his custom was, he went into the synagogue on the sabbath day and stood up for to read'. But the citizens of Nazareth 'were filled with wrath, rose up and thrust him out of the city'. He went to Capernaum on the Sea of Galilee. 'No prophet is accepted in his own country.'

Right: the Sea of Galilee, where four of the Disciples (Peter, Andrew, James and John) were fishermen. All round its shores are places associated with Jesus' ministry. The Sermon on the Mount is said by tradition to have been preached on the hill in the foreground.

Below: Galilee in springtime. This is the most fertile part of Palestine, contrasting sharply with the desert in the south and east. Many of Jesus' parables and similes from rural life were no doubt suggested by such a background. During his lifetime it was ruled, not by the Roman prefect of Judaea, but by Herod Antipas (son of Herod the Great), a puppet-king, but one who shared the religion of his subjects. (2–5)

The Sea of Galilee, from the Mount of Beatitudes. (5)

The Galilaean countryside. (4)

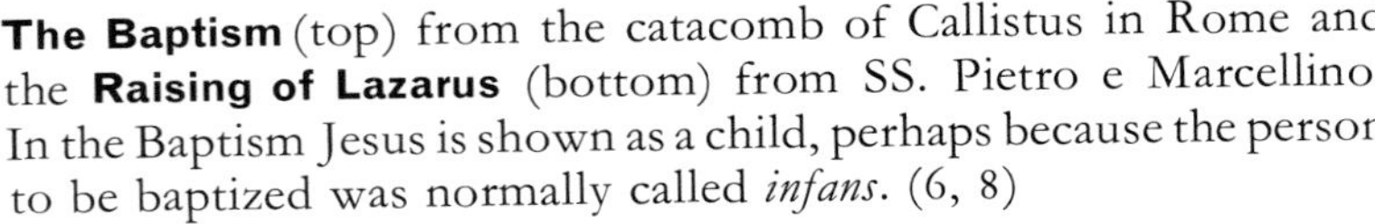

The Baptism (top) from the catacomb of Callistus in Rome and the **Raising of Lazarus** (bottom) from SS. Pietro e Marcellino. In the Baptism Jesus is shown as a child, perhaps because the person to be baptized was normally called *infans*. (6, 8)

The Woman at the Well (top) from the catacomb of Callistus, and the **Woman with the issue of blood** (bottom) from that of SS. Pietro e Marcellino. At this period, the miracles promising eternal life were stressed, not the suffering of the Passion. (7, 9)

The Gospel story was not put into pictorial form, so far as we know, until the late-2nd century AD at the earliest. The first representations of Jesus' life come from Roman catacombs. A whole new iconography had to be invented – the familiar repertoire of art for the next 1500 years – with scenes ranging from the Annunciation to the Ascension. After the time of Constantine such scenes were also displayed on small ivory plaques and boxes. Some of the oldest are shown on these two pages. Below left: Jesus preaching, with a row of small upturned faces before him. Centre: the turning of the water into wine during the Wedding at Cana—'Jesus saith unto them, Fill the waterpots with water. And they filled them up to the brim. And he saith unto them, Draw out now, and bear unto the governor of the feast'; here a servant pours water into the pots while the Virgin stands watching. The miracle was interpreted allegorically to mean both the transformation of the individual soul by Christ and the replacement of the old faith by the new. Below right: the miracle of the Loaves and Fishes—'And they say unto him, We have here but five loaves and two fishes. And he said, Bring them hither to me. And he commanded the multitude to sit down on the grass, and took the five loaves and the two fishes, and looking up to heaven, he blessed, and brake, and gave the loaves to his disciples, and the disciples to the multitude. And they did all eat and were filled: and they took up of the fragments that remained twelve baskets full.' (10–12)

The healed paralytic, from the catacomb of Callistus: 'That ye may know that the Son of Man hath power on earth to forgive sins, (then saith he to the sick of the palsy) Arise, take up thy bed and go unto thine house. And he arose and departed to his house.' (13)

The healing of the leper and of the blind; these miracles were interpreted as signs of Jesus' power of eternal salvation. Leprosy and blindness were seen as symbols of sin, even if not (as is often implied by his words of healing) actually caused by it. (14, 15)

'Behold we go up to Jerusalem; and the Son of Man shall be betrayed unto the chief priests and unto the scribes, and they shall condemn him to death.' Jerusalem is a hill town, dominating the stony country of Judaea (above, with the city in the distance). In the time of Jesus it was customary for Jews to visit Jerusalem for the Passover festival, as he and the disciples were doing. The circumstances of his Entry into Jerusalem and his clash with the Temple authorities are presented in varying versions by the Gospel writers, but it is clear that, in the tense political atmosphere that prevailed, the priests, and later Pilate, took these events to be potentially dangerous, and some of his own supporters hailed him as the successor of David. (16)

'Then was Jesus led up of the spirit into the wilderness.' The desert country (above) to the east of Jerusalem and bordering on the Dead Sea was frequently the setting of Jewish religious experience. It was there that the prophets and mystics went to receive divine guidance; and it was there that John the Baptist had preached his inspired message. (17)

'A sepulchre which was hewn out of the rock.' The tomb in which Jesus' body was laid is traditionally that under the Church of the Holy Sepulchre. There is, however, another possible site of the same period, known as the Garden Tomb (right). Its bare, unaltered state makes it powerfully evocative of the Gospel accounts of Jesus' burial. (18)

Pontius Pilate governed Judaea for Rome from AD 26 to 36. His name has been known from literary sources (the Gospels, Josephus, Philo) but until recently there was no physical relic of his life. Now a fragment of inscribed stone has come to light at Caesarea (1961) reading 'TIBERIEVM ... [PO]NTIVS PILATVS [PRAEF]-ECTVS IVDAE[AE]'. It records the dedication by Pilate of a 'Tiberieum', a building in honour of the Emperor Tiberius; and proves that his title was 'prefect', not 'procurator'. (19)

The Passion was for long avoided as a subject for religious art. There is only one catacomb painting that seems to refer to it – the Crowning with Thorns (possibly the Flagellation) in the catacomb of Praetextatus, dating from the 3rd century (top right). Among the earliest connected series of pictures showing the Passion are those on a 5th-century ivory pyxis, of which two panels are shown here (right). In the central picture, Pilate washes his hands, Jesus carries the Cross and Peter denies him. In the lower picture, Judas hangs himself and Jesus is crucified, with Mary and St John on the left, and the Centurion, on the right, recognizing him as the Son of God. (21, 22, 23)

Where Jesus was condemned and scourged has been a subject of debate. St John calls the place 'Lithostrotos' or 'the Pavement'; and Christian tradition locates it in the Roman fortress of Antonia where the stone floor (below) still shows the marks made by Roman soldiers for the games that they played. (20)

JESUS IN THE CONTEXT OF HISTORY

DAVID FLUSSER

THE MAIN AIMS of this contribution are, first, to show what Jesus' place was among the various trends of the Judaism of his time and, second, to estimate the impact on Christianity of his teachings and of his life and death.

According to the Christian tradition (Mark vi 3, Matt. xiii 55), p 218 (2) it was stated, as being a matter of common knowledge, by Jesus' contemporaries in his home town Nazareth in Galilee, that he was the son of a carpenter there, and he perhaps became a carpenter himself. In Jewish society in Jesus' day, carpenters were reputed to be learned, and, although Jesus did not receive the academic title 'rabbi', he acquired a considerable amount of Jewish learning. He was extremely well versed in the Hebrew Bible and in the traditional interpretation of it; he was familiar with Jewish ethical and religious teaching; and he was able to observe the manifold legal prescriptions involved in the Mosaic Law and in Jewish oral tradition.

In the time of Jesus, Jews lived, learned, and faithfully practised their religion, and their daily life was largely governed by religious precepts. This form of life was natural to Jesus and his contemporaries. Jesus did not seek to abrogate or even to reform the p 310 (*f 1*) Jewish Law. According to Paul, for whom the Jewish Law became a serious problem, Jesus was 'born under the Law to purchase freedom for the subjects of the Law' (Gal. iv 4–5); he 'became a servant to the circumcised in order to prove God's honesty by fulfilling His promises to the fathers' (Rom. xv 8). The evidence in the synoptic first three Gospels confirms these statements.

Jesus and the Pharisees

Some Church Fathers tried to define Jesus' attitude towards the Law by assuming that he observed the written Law but opposed the oral Law of the Pharisees. This was the position of the Sadducees, but Jesus had nothing in common with this rationalistic conservative movement. The Early Fathers and the modern scholars who have held this view have based their opinion mainly upon the passage about the washing of hands (Mark vii 1–23). There (Mark vii 8) Jesus says to the Pharisees: 'You neglect the commandment of God in order to maintain the tradition of men.' But in Jesus' time the washing of hands before meals was not considered to be one of the requirements of the oral Law; it was not even obligatory; it was merely voluntary. According to the Pharisees themselves (Mark vii 5), this custom was simply a 'tradition of elders', it was not part of either the written or the oral Law. Moreover, it was not Jesus himself, but only 'some of his disciples', who neglected the custom.

The passage about the washing of hands does not justify the assumption that Jesus opposed the Jewish legal practice of his time; but, by the 3rd century, Origen understood it as signifying the rejection of Jewish dietary laws by Jesus. The overwhelming majority of modern translators thoughtlessly accept Origen's interpretation when they take Mark vii 19b to mean: 'Thus he (Jesus) declared all foods clean' – although the Greek original can hardly be read in this sense.

When we compare Jesus' words and actions in the synoptic Gospels with the rabbinical prescriptions of his time, it becomes clear that, even in his most revolutionary actions, he never transgressed the bounds of the contemporary interpretation of the Mosaic Law. Although it was forbidden to cure non-dangerous illnesses on the Sabbath by physical means, it was permitted to cure them by words, and this is what Jesus did. Jesus' saying that 'the Sabbath was made for the sake of man and not man for the Sabbath' (Mark ii 27) has a close parallel in rabbinical literature. Moreover, the occasion on which this statement was made is the only instance in the synoptic Gospels of Jesus' violating the Sabbath: it was forbidden to pluck ears of corn on the Sabbath. According to Luke (vi 1), Jesus' disciples 'were plucking ears of corn, rubbing them in their hands, and eating them'. However, a newly discovered Jewish-Christian text, and also the so-called *Diatessaron*, do not say that they were plucking them; according to both these texts the disciples only rubbed the ears in their hands on the Sabbath. Most rabbis did not even permit this, but a Galilaean rabbi opposed them. Thus the only violation of the Sabbath (and this by the disciples and not by Jesus) in the synoptic Gospels is evidently the fruit of a misunderstanding on the part of the Greek translator: the original tradition did not speak about plucking ears of corn on the Sabbath but only about rubbing them, an act which was not universally forbidden.

These questions may seem trivial, yet they are important, because Jesus' attitude towards the Mosaic Law was decisive from two historical points of view – for the understanding of Jesus as a Jew of his time and, in the second place, for the effects of his teaching on the Christian Church. There was a real tension between Jesus and the local 'orthodoxy' in Galilaean villages, but such tension occurs in all religious communities; charismatic personalities, although they often have opinions which differ from those of the institutional authorities, are not necessarily schismatics or heretics. Jesus was crucified by the Romans as a rebel after his clash with the Sadducaean temple authorities in Jerusalem; the Pharisees are not even mentioned in the synoptic Gospels as a party to the so-called trial of Jesus. They had no real cause to hate him so profoundly as to seek to have him put to death. All the motifs of Jesus' famous invective against the Pharisees in Matthew xxiii are also found in rabbinical literature. Both in Jesus' diatribe and in the self-criticism of the rabbis the central polemical motif is the description of the Pharisees as being prone to hypocrisy. Jesus says that 'they make up heavy loads and lay them on men's shoulders, but they will not stir a finger to remove them' (Matt. xxiii 4). In the Talmud we read about five types of Pharisaic hypocrisy: the first is to 'lay the commandments upon men's shoulders' (J. Berakhoth 14b). The indictment of the Pharisees for hypocrisy is naturally stronger in the Essene literature than in Jesus' words, because the Essenes opposed the Pharisaic doctrine itself. Although not a member of the Pharisaic community, Jesus approved of the Pharisaic understanding of the Law:

> The doctors of the Law and the Pharisees sit in the chair of p 80 (2) Moses; therefore do what they tell you; pay attention to their words. But do not follow their deeds; for they say one thing and do another (Matt. xxiii 2–3).

Pharisaic theology and legal attitudes were those of contemporary non-sectarian Judaism, and this was their strength. Jesus would not disagree with them.

Jesus adhered to the standard Judaism of his time, and from this point of view it is natural that his disciples, and after them the Jewish Christian community, should have lived according to the Law. Nevertheless, the mistaken evaluation of Jesus' criticisms of local bigotry as reservations about Judaism itself, or as an actual repudiation of it, later became a fruitful source of error for Christianity. The necessary condition for this 'anti-legalistic' interpretation of Jesus' words was the fact that Christianity became p 285–92 (1–20) a religion for gentiles. In contrast to Judaism and to the religions of other Asian countries, from Persia eastwards, the Graeco-Roman civilization was not based upon a ritualistic system of precepts and prohibitions. Thus the conquest of the Western world by Christianity was only possible if the new religion abandoned the ritualistic way of life. This step was made possible by the develop- p 301–8 (1–17) ment of a new Christian theology whose most outstanding exponent was, as is well known, the Apostle Paul. In the apostolic and sub-apostolic period the Christian Church's rejection of the Jewish Law was mostly based upon Christology: the death of the Lord was, so to say, the death of Jewish legal obligations. It was only later on, from the 3rd century onwards, that the Church Fathers found in Jesus' criticism of the institutional bigotry of his opponents an important argument for Christian freedom from Jewish ritual. Although such a reinterpretation of Jesus' position is historically untenable, the exaggeration of the polemical note in Jesus' sayings by Christian theologians led to important achievements in Western ethics.

The Golden Rule

The specific moral character of Jesus' teaching – which, as we have seen, has often been misinterpreted as being opposed to the Judaism of his time – is in truth not as exceptional as one might suppose. The ancient rabbis did not feel a tension between their punctilious occupation with ritual and legal casuistry and their sublime moral and theological message; in this they were similar to the Indian sages. For example, Rabbi Akiba was not only a great expert in Jewish Law but was also the man who said that the essential message of the Mosaic Law is that one should love one's neighbour. As we know, this was also Jesus' opinion (Matt. xxii 39). Again, Jesus said: 'Whatever you wish that men would do to you, do so to them, for this is the Law and the prophets' (Matt. vii 12). This precept, the so-called Golden Rule, had already been declared by the Jewish sage Hillel (*c.* 20 BC) to be the essence of Judaism. Hillel was the founder of one of the two most important rabbinical schools – the other was that of Shammai. Both schools were Pharisaic.

It would be a mistake to think of the Judaism of Jesus' time as being identical with the religion of the Old Testament or as being a mere development of the ancient faith of Israel. New questions arose and new religious problems had to be solved. The simple biblical ethics could no longer satisfy more modern and sophisticated minds, and the social structure of the Ancient Near East no longer existed. A more subtle and more highly differentiated approach to moral and theological problems was needed. The human condition itself had now become more problematic.

One of the central problems of the Old Testament was the righteousness of God: how can He be righteous if good men suffer and the wicked are often happy? In Jesus' day the righteousness of man became a problem. Is the traditional strict division of mankind into the righteous and sinners tenable if no man is totally sinful and if none can achieve complete righteousness? Even if in this life the righteous were to receive recompense from heaven and the wicked their due punishment, would this be consistent with God's goodness and mercy? If man knows that recompense from God awaits him for his good deeds, can his actions be dictated by a high morality? Even as early as the beginning of the 2nd century BC a Jewish sage had said: 'Be not like slaves who serve the master on condition of receiving remuneration, but be like slaves who serve the master not on condition of receiving a remuneration' (Sayings of the Fathers, Pirkei Aboth 1, 3). According to this saying, heavenly recompense and punishment are certain, but people have to act as if they did not know. This saying shows how high the standard of Jewish ethical reflection was at that time. It is natural that in such an atmosphere an elaborate casuistic approach to ethical problems should develop: it became clear that a slight trespass can easily lead to a heavy sin; that a man who seemed to be righteous could in reality be a great sinner; and that a wicked man could be saved by one truly great deed. This new discriminating moral attitude can be well illustrated by its oldest witness, a passage (Ecclesiasticus xxvii 30–xxviii 7) from the book of Jesus ben Sira (*floruit* 185 BC):

> Wrath and anger, these also are abominations
>   And a sinful man clingeth to them,
> He that taketh vengeance shall find vengeance from the Lord,
>   And his sins (God) will surely keep (in memory).
> Forgive thy neighbour the injury (done to thee),
>   And then, when thou prayest, thy sins will be forgiven.
> Man cherisheth anger against another,
>   And doth he seek healing from God?
> On a man like himself he hath no mercy;
>   And doth he make supplication for his own sins?
> He, being flesh, nourisheth wrath;
>   Who will make atonement for his sins?
> Remember thy last end, and cease from enmity;
>   (Remember) corruption and death and abide in the commandments.
> Remember the commandments and be not wroth with thy neighbour.
>   And (remember) the covenant of the Most High and overlook ignorance.

All the motifs which occur here are characteristic of the new sensitivity in the Judaism of Jesus' day, whose *theologoumena* Jesus accepted and developed. Through the Gospels they became an inseparable part of Christianity. The new approach to moral theology in Judaism caused ideological controversies in Pharisaic circles. We have seen that love of one's neighbour was regarded as being the sum total of the Mosaic Law. We have also seen a rabbi teaching that man should perform God's will without taking into account any divine reward. Certain Pharisaic circles came to the conclusion that it is better to love God unconditionally than to be God-fearing, because the fear of God includes fear of His punishment. There were 'Pharisees of love' who opposed the 'Pharisees of fear' on the ground that these stood for a lower standard than theirs. Jesus saw in the love of God and one's neighbour the two 'great rules in the Law', on which the whole Law depends (Matt. xxii 36–40), and, according to the Gospels (Mark xii 32–4; Luke x 25–8), he was conforming, in this point, to the teaching of the Pharisees. Jesus added an important corollary to the theses of his Jewish predecessors. The Judaism of his time, or at any rate certain circles in it, forbade people to hate their enemies and required them to behave in the same way towards sinners as towards the righteous. Jesus called for love even of one's enemies and even of sinners. This demand of Jesus was evidently too radical for the young Church. In the New Testament love of one's enemies is mentioned only in Jesus' teaching in the synoptic Gospels. The requirement that one should love the sinner became know later through the synoptic Gospels, but it was not always practised by Christians.

A lowly spirit and a humble mind

In the Old Testament the religion of Israel was already a message about a God who is both righteous and merciful. Socially unfortunate persons and groups are specially cherished by God, and the community is under an obligation to protect them. According to the Bible, the God of Israel does not like powerful men and physical force. He likes the poor and the meek: 'the meek shall inherit the p 219 (
earth'. The consequence of this religious attitude was that meek- p 221 (
ness, humility, and even poverty began to be seen by Judaism as positive human qualities. This development has already started in certain parts of the Old Testament. In the inter-testamental period 'a lowly spirit and a humble mind' (Pirkei Aboth 5, 19) became important positive religious values and 'a haughty spirit and a proud mind' were marks of fatal wickedness. Many believed that it is better to suffer persecution than to be a persecutor. Naturally this moral approach was especially widespread in those Pharisaic circles that saw the whole meaning of Judaism in the love of one's neighbour and in an unconditional love of God. Through Jesus, among other channels, this attitude became one of the most important formative elements of Christianity.

It was not only Pharisaic circles that arrived at a 'pietistic' approach to a human being's relations with God and with his fellow men. A similar development also occurred in a community
p 84–6 that was the second source of Jesus' teaching, namely in Essenism,
(11–17) which is now well known through the Dead Sea Scrolls. The Essene doctrine of double predestination clearly influenced the Pauline and Johannine theology of election; it was revived in a new
p 316 ideological context by Augustine; and it was finally accepted by
(f 4) both Luther and Calvin. Jesus could not accept this theology, but he was deeply influenced by the social doctrines of the Essenes, which were in many points similar to the Pharisaic demand for humility, but were even more radical than this. The main difference was that the Pharisees did not dream about social revolution and, although they were inclined to recognize the spiritual value of poverty, they did not see it as a positive human and religious value, whereas the Essenes saw themselves as the 'paupers of salvation', elected by God to inherit the earth.

This ideology of poverty led the Essenes to despise wealth as a dangerous power which leads man astray from God. The rabbis, on the other hand, did not stress this danger and often saw in wealth a sign of divine favour. Jesus accepted the Essene position without accepting its full revolutionary implications. He thought that it is difficult for a rich man to be saved, and he warned his disciples:

> No one can serve two masters; for either he will hate the one and love the other; or he will be devoted to the one and will despise the other. You cannot serve God and mammon (Matt. vi 24).

As in the Essene view, the praise of poverty was linked, in Jesus' message, with an appreciation of meekness, humility, and the
p 219 (5) acceptance of persecution. The spirit of the Beatitudes is practically
p 221 (12) the Essene spirit, and the first three Beatitudes even have important parallels in the Dead Sea Scrolls. The author of the Essene Thanksgiving Scroll (18, 14–15) thanks God:

> . . . for having appointed me in Thy truth a messenger of the peace of Thy goodness, to proclaim to the *meek* the multitude of Thy mercies, and let them *that are of contrite spirit* hear salvation from an everlasting source, and for them *that mourn* everlasting joy.

Jesus' first three Beatitudes are addressed to the *poor in spirit*, to the *meek*, and to *them that mourn* (Matt. v 3–5). Moreover, 'poor in spirit' is one of the terms by which the members of the Dead Sea sect described themselves.

Jesus' Beatitudes are a hymn of hope for the future. A similar hope is expressed in a passage from the *Testaments of the Twelve Patriarchs*, a Jewish work, with Christian interpolations, which has many affinities with the Dead Sea Scrolls. According to the *Testament of Judah* (25, 4–5), in the eschatological future:

> Those who have died in grief shall arise in joy, and those who have been poor . . . shall be made rich, and those who were hungry shall be filled, and those who have been weak shall be strong, and those who were put to death for the Lord's sake shall awake to life. And the harts of Jacob shall run in joyfulness, and the eagles of Israel shall fly in gladness; but the ungodly shall lament and the sinners shall weep, and all the peoples shall glorify the Lord for ever.

The affinity between this text and both the Beatitudes and the Woes of Jesus (Luke vi 24–5) is clear enough.

The *Testaments of the Patriarchs* and the so-called 'Two Ways', which form the first six chapters of the early Christian *Didache*, are the two Jewish sources which are the most closely akin to Jesus' moral teaching. Like Jesus' message, they are inspired by Essene doctrines, but they are not strictly Essene. They too are far from the Essene exclusiveness of election and – with the exception of the *Testament of Asher* – instead of an ideology of hatred of sinners they preach, as do some Pharisaic circles and Jesus, the love of God and one's neighbour. But, like Jesus and unlike the Pharisees, they stress the religious ideals of poverty and simplicity of heart: at this point both the *Testaments of the Patriarchs* and the 'Two Ways' in the *Didache* are close to the Essene spirit. Thus it would appear that

In Jesus' lifetime, Palestine was divided into three units: the Tetrarchy of Galilee with Peraea; Ituraea (Bashan); and Judaea, Samaria and Idumaea, until AD 6/7 under Archelaus, subsequently under Roman governors. (1)

these two Jewish sources originated in semi-Essene circles which were influenced by the attitude of the 'Pharisees of Love'. It also seems very probable that the Essene *theologoumena* came to Jesus in a modified form from the fringes of Essenism, and not from Essene orthodoxy. We know of only one man who was close to the Essenes but opposed their sectarian claims: this was John the Baptist. Thus we can suppose that motifs common to Jesus and p 220 (6)
the Essenes are a fruit of the Baptist's influence upon Jesus.

'Philanthropy' and the agapaistic spirit

From the historical point of view the most important fact is that through Jesus' words, as well as through other channels, a special kind of Jewish thought made a central formative impact on European society. This is especially true of that kind of Jewish religious and moral thought which was common both to the Essenes and to certain Pharisaic circles. It is interesting to note that in most cases Christianity accepted from Jesus those ideas which had existed in Judaism before him: the points at which he departs from Judaism and makes an original contribution were evidently not recognized or were too difficult to accept. We have already seen that, even in the New Testament, the love of one's enemy appears only in the words of Jesus himself, and, if this sublime achievement of Jesus became known to Christians later, it has actually been followed only by outstanding individuals and not by Christians in the mass. The demand, which often wins intellectual acceptance but is not commonly followed by Christians, is that one should not repay evil with evil; this idea can sometimes be found in Essene literature, and it plays an important part in the *Testaments of the Patriarchs*. It was also common in 'pietistic' Pharisaic circles.

Besides accepting poverty as a positive value, the Christians saw in humility a typical Christian virtue. Clement of Rome (end of the 1st century) saw Jesus as the teacher of humbleness of mind: if the Lord humbled himself, he shall be in this an example for those who come under the yoke of his grace (*First Clement* 13, 2; 16, 1–2; 17; see also Ignatius of Antioch *Epistle to the Ephesians* 10, 3). It is important to realize that the Greek word translated here and in many passages in the New Testament and in the Septuagint as 'humble' has, in Greek, the connotation of 'abject' or 'abased' and is 'a word which nearly all pagan authors . . . employ as a term of contempt' (E. R. Dodds *The Greeks and the Irrational* p. 215). Julian the Apostate even thought that the Christians had adopted the term because they had misunderstood a passage in Plato.

This example is only one of many pieces of evidence that bring out the difference between the ethos of pagan antiquity and the Jewish–Christian spirit. Graeco–Roman culture and civilization and Jewish ethics in their Christian shape became the two roots of European thought. The first is well known, but the importance of the second ought also to be stressed. Humanism is based upon these two sources, and it seems that the Jewish–Christian heritage pre-
p 205–8 vails in it, although the impact of Greek philosophy certainly must
(1–9) not be neglected. It could be maintained that this identification with the poor, the humble, the simple, and the persecuted constitutes only a plebeian ethos which gives no answers to important social problems. The government of subjects could never be based upon a morality such as this. What can a king or a government learn from the precepts of Jesus, who said:

> The kings of the Gentiles exercise lordship over them; and those in authority over them are called benefactors. But not so with you; rather let the greatest among you become as the youngest and the leader as one who serves (Luke xxii 25).

The Emperor Julian was perfectly right when, apropos of Jesus' words: 'Sell your possessions and give to the poor; provide yourselves with purses that do not grow old' (Luke xii 33 has 'give alms'), he affirmed that, if this 'political precept' were to be followed, no city, no nation, no house could endure.

The government of a Christian state could never be organized exclusively according to the teaching of Jesus and the Apostles. The practice of the Greeks and the Romans and the Old Testament was always indispensable for Christian statesmanship. But kindness to one's neighbour, based upon love and not only, as the Greeks preferred, upon rational philosophical understanding, also has positive merits. Compassion towards the outcast and sympathy with the persecuted created a social conscience and led to reforms, revolutionary movements, and revolutions, which were not always bad. And the positive valuation of simplicity of heart could sometimes overcome intellectual pride. History has shown that the detached wisdom of the Greeks and the order of the Roman state can lead to a heartless society and to imperialistic oppression and aggression. It became clear that the Greek ideal of *philanthropia* is not as effective as active love of one's neighbour. Thus the Jewish heritage in Christianity has had a very beneficial influence upon mankind.

Even as early as the middle of the 2nd century the spread of Christianity was seen as being a threat to the established order. A rabbi at that time expressed a feeling which was evidently widespread, when he said that one of the eschatological plagues will be that 'the (Roman) Kingdom will pass over to Christianity' (Mishnah, Sotah 9, 15); and later this nightmare became a political reality. One
p 342–4 of the irresistible forces which brought about the victory of
(28–34) Christianity was its new morality. Its social attitude was different from the pagan ethos, and it was therefore attractive to large masses of the population. We have seen that this ethical position came to Christianity from certain Jewish circles. Most of these ideas were made known to Christians through the teaching of Jesus, but sometimes they influenced Christianity independently of Jesus,
e.g. through Paul. The importance of these achievements for p 310
humanity is evident. (*f 1*)

'Conceived by the Holy Ghost'

It was not only Jesus' teachings but also his life and his real or p 220–1
supposed view of what he was that left their imprint upon human (6–15)
history. Christology is not a pagan invention of the Hellenistic *f 1*
Christian communities. This becomes clear from the Book of Revelation, where the main motifs of fully developed Christology are already present. The author of the book, John of Patmos, has nothing in common with Paul. He was a Hebrew-speaking Jew for whom it was difficult to write in Greek. No Greek influence can be found in his book. His spiritual and probably also his historical home was the Jewish mother church at Jerusalem. His Christology, which is one of the main themes of his book, reflects the beliefs of a section of the Palestinian Jewish Christian community. On this point Jewish Christians did not by any means present a united front. We know that groups which were later regarded by the Church as being heretical stressed the prophetic aspect of Jesus;
and his role as the Messiah and his resurrection did not play a p 223
great part in their system. This view can sometimes be detected in (18)
the older strata of the synoptic Gospels. In the Gospel according to St Mark, even in its present form, the resurrection is not recorded and, in the short description of it in Matthew (xxviii 16–20), we read that, when the disciples saw the resurrected Lord, 'they worshipped him, but some doubted'. The doubters did not include Peter and Jesus' brother James, the future leaders of the mother church: the resurrected Lord appeared to both (I Cor. xv 5–7).

On the question whether Jesus was the Messiah, the differences between the various Jewish Christian groups possibly reflect an uncertainty about the attitude of Jesus himself. Even during his lifetime some people had hoped that he was the Messiah – the inscription on the Cross proves this definitely. Certainly Jesus saw himself as a prophet, and this belief of his found expression not only in the New Testament but also in later Jewish Christian sects. He evidently never used the term Messiah when speaking about himself or when proclaiming the coming of the Son of Man, probably because politics were too deeply involved in this title. But he must surely have seen himself as being more than a herald of the Kingdom of Heaven and more than a healer and wonder-worker. Before the discovery of the Dead Sea Scrolls we did not have any authentic utterances of charismatic Jewish leaders of Jesus' time. We can now study the Thanksgiving Scroll, a collection of hymns composed by an Essene leader – some scholars think by the Teacher of Righteousness himself, who was the founder of the sect. Here we may observe in another Jewish religious personality in antiquity, besides Jesus, a sublime realization of his own high place in the divine economy of the world. The author of the Essene Thanksgiving Scroll says about himself (4, 27–9):

> Through me Thou hast illuminated the faces of many and Thou hast become mighty infinitely; for Thou hast made known to me Thy wondrous mysteries and by Thy wondrous secret Thou hast wrought mightily with me; and Thou hast wrought wonders in the presence of many for the sake of Thy glory and to make known Thy mighty works unto all the living.

With these words we may compare the poem of Jesus which was, as is shown by its form, composed in the style of Essene hymnology:

> I thank thee, Father, Lord of heaven and earth, for hiding these things from the learned and wise and revealing them to the simple. Yes, Father, such was Thy choice. Everything is entrusted to me by my Father; and no one knows the Son but the Father and no one knows the Father but the Son and those to whom the Son may choose to reveal Him . . . (Matt. xi 25–30).

Here Jesus formulates his claim to be the sole repository and mediator of the divine mysteries expressing the relation between Father and Son. He claims to be God's son in other authentic sayings too. In the rabbinical literature, charismatic wonder-workers of Jesus' time are described as having access to God as a beloved son has it to his father. As we have seen, and as can be proved from other sayings, sonship also involved, for Jesus, his task as a prophetic revealer of the will of his heavenly Father. As is well known, the unity between the Father and the Son soon became one of the central points of the Christian faith. Later (I believe), but as early as the Gospels according to Matthew and Luke, Jesus became a literal son of God, without an earthly father. It was only p 306–7 (12, 14–15) when this concept came to be understood in terms of the unity of the Father and the Son that it became a part of trinitarian doctrine. My belief is that originally stories about Jesus' divine birth were p 264 (3) 'mythical' explanations of Jesus' view of himself as being the beloved son of his Father in Heaven. Even the pagan parallels to the story of Jesus' birth never implied that the hero or the historical personality was a god or that he was identical with his divine father.

'Born of the Virgin Mary'

The idea that a man can be begotten of God without an earthly father seems to us today to be so far from Judaism that it could have developed only in pagan Christianity. The concept is surely at odds with strict Jewish monotheism; but it was not foreign to more mythologically-minded Jewish circles in antiquity. The Jewish philosopher and theologian Philo of Alexandria asserts that:

> the persons . . . such as Abraham, Isaac, Jacob, and Moses . . . are not represented by him [*i.e.* by Moses in the Pentateuch] as knowing women . . . For he (Moses) shows us Sarah conceiving at the time when God visited her in her solitude [Gen. xxi 1], but when she brings forth it is not to the Author of their visitation, but to . . . Abraham. And even clearer is Moses' teaching of Leah that God opened her womb [Gen. xxix 31]. Now to open the womb belongs to the husband. Yet when she conceived she brought forth not to God . . ., but to . . . Jacob . . . Again Isaac . . . besought God, and through the power of Him who was thus besought . . . Rebecca became pregnant [Gen. xxv 21]. And without supplication or entreaty did Moses, when he took Zipporah . . ., find her pregnant through no mortal agency [Ex. ii 22] (*On the Cherubim* 40–47).

According to the Jewish Pseudepigrapha, a similar suspicion also arose about the birth of Noah. The nature of the new-born baby was unlike man's nature. His father, Lamech, became afraid and did not believe that his son was sprung from him: for he was in the likeness of the angels of heaven. He turned to his wife, making her swear by the Most High that she would tell him the whole truth, without lies. Although she swore that the seed and the conception and the fruit were his, he became calm only when he was assured by his grandfather Enoch, the heavenly scribe, that Noah was really his son (*Book of Enoch* chapter 106; Genesis Apocryphon from Qumran, column 2).

The most important parallel to Jesus' miraculous nativity is to be found in the *Book of the Secrets of Enoch* (the so-called 'Slavonic Enoch'). Some scholars have thought that this book was composed by a Christian, and this is also the opinion of the most recent editor, A. Vaillant (Paris 1952), though his own edition has proved that there were no Christian interpolations in the original version. The strange story of the supernatural birth of the biblical Melchizedek, contained in this book, is as follows: When Noah's brother, Nir, was priest of God, his wife conceived from the Word of God. The angry husband wanted to repudiate her, but at that very moment his wife died. The child left the womb of his mother, complete in his body and blessing the Lord with the seal of priesthood upon his breast. Then Nir and his brother recognized that the child was born from the Lord. Later, the Archangel Michael took Melchizedek up to Paradise lest he suffer during the deluge; for he will be Melchizedek 'a priest for ever'.

The last words are a quotation from Psalm cx: 'The Lord has sworn and will not change His mind; you are a priest for ever, after the order of Melchizedek.' The phrase, translated in the Septuagint as 'after the order', indicates that the psalm is addressed to some person unknown, but the words are not quite clear from the linguistic point of view. Some commentators have thought that in this psalm God is speaking to Melchizedek himself, and this has given rise to the Jewish tradition which is manifest, *inter alia*, in Hebrews vii 3: 'Melchizedek is a priest for ever; he has neither a beginning of his days nor an end of his life, but continues to be a priest permanently'. This was also the opinion of the author of the *Book of the Secrets of Enoch*.

We can also understand how a Jewish tradition arose that Melchizedek was born without an earthly father. The same psalm contains a difficult verse (verse 3) which is translated in the Septuagint: 'From the womb, before the morning star, I have begotten thee.' The Greek translator was right: the enigmatic Hebrew text of Psalm cx 3 reflects the Ancient Near Eastern belief that the ruler is symbolically the son of God, a belief that is also reflected in the famous words of Psalm ii: 'You are my son, today I have begotten you.' If the mythologically-minded reader starts with the assumption that, in Psalm cx, God is addressing Himself to Melchizedek, and if he takes the verse literally, he may come to the conclusion that 'the Word of God has created' Melchizedek in the womb of his mother (*The Book of the Secrets of Enoch* ed. Vaillant p. 81).

The mysterious personality of Melchizedek, as described in Genesis xiv and referred to in Psalm cx, became a magnet for irrational tendencies in post-biblical Judaism. An important fragment from the Dead Sea Scrolls even forecasts the coming of f 2 Melchizedek as the Heavenly Judge in the Last Judgement. The origin of this idea is not difficult to explain if one takes Psalm cx as being addressed to Melchizedek himself. As has been mentioned, the Psalm speaks about a 'priest for ever'. This could be understood to imply that Melchizedek is an eternal being: 'he has

An important fragment found in the eleventh cave at Qumran appears to attribute divinity to the Old Testament priest Melchizedek. In lines 9 and 10 (line 1 is missing), the author interprets Psalm lxxxii 1, 'God (Eloihim) has taken His place in the divine council; in the midst of gods He will hold judgement', as referring to Melchizedek. Line 25 ends by saying, 'Your God, that is . . .'. Unfortunately the manuscript breaks off here, but scholars believe that the missing word is 'Melchizedek', and that originally this line contained an explicit statement of his divinity. (2)

neither a beginning of his days nor an end of his life, but continues to be a priest permanently' (Hebr. vii 3). Melchizedek grew to mythical proportions: immortal like Enoch, Elijah, and, according to some views, Moses himself. The immortal Melchizedek could become the eschatological judge, especially if we bear in mind the fact that Psalm cx begins with the words: 'The Lord says to my lord: "Sit at My right hand till I make your enemies your footstool."' The men of Qumran took sitting on the right hand of the Lord to mean sitting in judgement, in keeping with verses 5 and 6 of the same psalm: 'The Lord is at your right hand: he will shatter kings on the Day of His Wrath. He will execute judgement among the nations. . . .'

If the Essenes interpreted Psalm cx as referring to Melchizedek, they could also relate Psalm lxxxii to him. This psalm, which also speaks of God's judgement, begins with the words: 'God (Elohim) has taken His place in the divine council; in the midst of gods He will hold judgement.' The author of the new Essene text took the word *Elohim* (God) as referring to Melchizedek. This does not necessarily imply that the Essenes credited Melchizedek with being of a divine nature, since the word 'Elohim' could also be interpreted as referring to a judge; but there is some ambiguity in this strange interpretation. Towards the end of the fragment the Essene author interprets in his own way Isaiah lii 7: '. . . who says to Zion: "Your God is king."' Zion is interpreted as 'those who establish the covenant', *i.e.* the Essene community. The use of the term Zion or Jerusalem as a symbol for the Christian Church is to be found already in the New Testament (Gal. iv 26; Hebr. xii 22). The text then continues: 'Your God, that is. . . .' Unfortunately the fragment ends abruptly here, but scholars are justified in conjecturing that, here too, our author interpreted the word 'Your God' as applying to Melchizedek; he is thought of as being the eschatological ruler of the Essene Church.

Thus Melchizedek, though human, is also a supernatural being with a sort of mythical biography: according to an apocryphal book he was begotten in his mother's womb by the Word of God; he was immortal, a 'priest for ever', and at the End of Days he will be the eschatological heavenly judge. In the Bible he is twice called 'God', and he will be king in the New Jerusalem, which is a symbol for the Essene Community. The Dead Sea Scrolls are Essene and the *Book of the Secrets of Enoch* is a Jewish work. The mythical motifs relating to Melchizedek were developed from Old Testament sources. Hence the example of Melchizedek proves that the time was ripe for the birth of Christianity, not in the Hellenistic world and certainly not in the pagan world, but in the Land of Israel, where Jesus and his first disciples lived.

'And sitteth on the right hand of God'

According to the Essene fragment, the Last Judgement will take place on high and Melchizedek will be assisted by all the celestial powers. '"Belial and the spirits of his lot" will then be judged, . . . and Melchizedek will vindicate God's judgements.' He will not only pass judgement but will also execute it. At this time he will separate the righteous, who are his lot and heritage, from the wicked, both human and demonic. Melchizedek appears here in a very similar role to that of the Son of Man of the Ethiopic *Book of*
f 3 *Enoch* and of the Gospels:

> When the Son of Man comes in his glory, and all the angels with him, then he will sit on his glorious throne. Before him will be gathered all the nations, and he will separate them one from the other as a shepherd separates the sheep from the goats, and he will place the sheep at his right hand, but the goats at his left . . . And they will go away into eternal punishment, but the righteous into eternal life (Matt. xxv 31–46).

In the New Testament the first verse of Psalm cx is applied to Jesus. In the synoptic Gospels it is twice quoted by Jesus: in Matthew xxii 44 (and parallels) with reference to the Messiah; and in a *logion* (Luke xxii 69 and parallels) which is Jesus' answer to the question of the High Priest, whether he is the Messiah. Jesus answered: 'From now on, the Son of Man shall be seated at the right hand of the Power.' The authenticity of the first saying may perhaps be doubted, but it is extremely difficult to doubt the authenticity of Jesus' answer to the High Priest; and this would hardly make sense unless we assume that Jesus identified himself with the Son of Man. I believe that Jesus did make this identification, at least in the end. His lofty conception of what he was comes out in his claim to be the beloved son of his heavenly Father, and thus he could also identify himself with the figure of the Son of Man. As far as is known, he refused to accept explicitly the title of Messiah, but his aversion from this can be explained by the title's political content. However, Jesus' conception of what he was is not only an historical, but also, in a sense, a literary problem: although I myself believe that he had a 'messianic self-consciousness', there is a decided possibility that he never identified himself with the Saviour. Even in the text of the synoptic Gospels he is never represented as claiming to be the Saviour, and he always refers to the 'Son of Man' in the third person.

The question of Jesus' conception of what he was is manifestly very important *per se*, but it is not decisive in connection with our inquiry, since our purpose here is to trace the Jewish roots of Christology in relation, direct or indirect, with the life and the person of Jesus of Nazareth, and to show that, in principle, the Christian conception of Christ did not originate in paganism, though it could be accepted without any great difficulty by the pagan world because there were parallel ideas there. In my belief, this conception originated in the mythologizing Jewish atmosphere for which there is evidence in apocalyptic circles, in other Jewish apocrypha, and to some extent in rabbinical literature and in Jewish mysticism.

In all Jewish sources the eschatological figure of the Son of Man is always delineated in the same few sharp lines. Although he is a human being, he is also supernatural. He is the eschatological judge of the cosmos: sitting on high upon the throne of God's Glory, he will judge all mankind and will divide, with the help of the heavenly hosts, the righteous from the sinners. He will also execute the sentence. The vision of the Son of Man was already known to the author of the Book of Daniel (vii 7–27); but here his appearance is somehow changed in order to adapt him to a new meaning. In Daniel he became a collective symbol for the Saints of the Most High, for Israel or the elect. Therefore, although 'thrones were placed' and judgement took place, the Son of Man who came 'with the clouds of heaven' did not himself judge, but to him was given the everlasting dominion over the world.

In the Book of Daniel, the Son of Man became the symbol of a collective group. As we have seen, the eschatological functions attributed to the biblical Melchizedek in an Essene fragment are identical with those of the Son of Man in other sources. In the *Book of Enoch* the Son of Man is once – evidently in a later edition – the heavenly scribe, Enoch himself (chapter 71), and he is twice identified with the Messiah (48, 10; 52, 4). According to the *Testament of Abraham*, the Son of Man – in Hebrew *Ben Adam*, literally 'the Son of Adam' – is Abel. He will be the eschatological judge because it is the will of God that mankind shall be judged by a man.

Although it is not absolutely certain that Jesus identified the Son of Man with the Messiah, this seems highly probable. It was of central importance for the development of the Christian faith that Jesus not only used the title of Son of Man for the Saviour, but also described him in the way in which others conceived of the Son of Man. For Jesus too, the Son of Man is the heavenly judge, sitting on the glorious throne of God on high in the company of angels. The concept of the Son of Man is the highest, most godlike concept of the Saviour that ancient Judaism ever knew. He is the direct representative of God; he, so to speak, reflects the Glory of God. In virtue of being this, he is, according to the *Book of Enoch*, pre-existent; and this concept is sometimes also hinted at in speculations about the Messiah in the rabbinical literature. This was the way by which the idea that the Saviour is identical with the Word by which God created the universe established itself in Christianity. The identification is not peculiarly Christian. It is possible that it is not to be found in Jewish sources; to see in a human Saviour an incarnation of God's Glory might make him too divine to be acceptable to Jews. Yet, before the discovery of
the Essene fragment, we could not have imagined that the eschato- *f 2*
logical judge could be designated by the title 'God' even in an unorthodox Jewish scripture.

Christ seated in judgement appears on this 6th-century ivory, probably originating in Syria. Melchizedek again provides the Jewish precedent, and his role in the new Essene fragment is very close to that of the Son of Man in the Gospels. (3)

A name which is above every name

One of the characteristics of post-biblical Judaism was the importance of hypostatic titles of God. This development was the result of the emphasis in Judaism on God's transcendence. It was practically forbidden to pronounce His biblical name and, instead of naming God, Jews used to speak of the Wisdom, the Spirit, the Word, the Power, or the Glory. But these titles could also be understood as a reflection of God in the world, as the immanence of the transcendent God, and consequently it was impossible in Judaism to speak of more than one hypostasis, and the hypostatic terms were interchangeable. This was also the situation in early p 306–7 (12, 14–15) Christianity; it was only later, when the doctrine of the Trinity developed, that it became impossible for Christians to identify the Spirit with the Word, since the Word became a term for the Son, and the Holy Spirit became the third person of the Holy Trinity. This was not so at the beginning: Paul could still say that Christ is the Spirit. A plurality of hypostases, as a system of emanations or as p 319–22 (1–10) persons engaged in a cosmic drama, is characteristic of the Gnostic attitude and also of the Jewish mysticism of the Middle Ages and of modern times.

The use of hypostatic terms was already extensive in the 2nd century BC, and it is not only typical of rabbinical Judaism but is also to be found in Hellenistic Judaism, in the Wisdom of Solomon, for instance, and in the writings of Philo of Alexandria. When Philo speaks of the Logos, the Word of God, his inspiration comes primarily from Palestinian Judaism and not from the Greek p 206–7 (5, 6) philosophy of Heraclitus and the Stoics. All the Jewish hypostatic terms occur in the New Testament. Thus it seems very unlikely that the term 'Logos', which is actually less important in the New Testament than it might appear to be, will have been derived by Christianity from the works of Philo. In the Christian literature of the apostolic and sub-apostolic period which was produced in Hellenistic Christian communities (*e.g.* the Pauline corpus), the hypostatic terms and conceptions were derived from Hellenistic Judaism or else directly, through the mother church, from Palestinian Jewry.

The various terms, such as the Wisdom, the Spirit, the Word, the Power and the Glory can describe God himself, his attributes, and his immanence. This ambiguity was dangerous for Jewish (and Christian) monotheism, as is demonstrated by the rise of Gnosticism, but it was fruitful for Christology, and this from the very beginning. This was not an exclusively Christian achievement, as can be shown by citing one example. Even as early as the beginning of the 2nd century BC the pre-existent Wisdom of God – as it appears in the biblical Book of Proverbs – was identified with the Mosaic Law, which was also conceived of as being pre-existent. The oldest evidence for this concept is the book of Jesus ben Sira (Ecclesiasticus). In this book (xxiv 3) the Wisdom, which is the personified Law of Moses, says *inter alia*: 'I came forth from the mouth of the Most High, and covered the Earth like a mist.' This means that God's Wisdom, which is His pre-existent divine Law, is also His creative Word, which issued from His mouth; and His Spirit, which 'was moving over the face of the waters' (Gen. i 2).

If such an identification of some of the hypostases with the eternal Law was possible in Judaism, we can understand how, in as early a stratum of Christian literature as the New Testament itself, all Jewish hypostatic titles of God are named – for instance, Christ sits on the right of the Power, Glory or Greatness – and how Christ himself, being the pre-existent Son of Man, could be invested with all the Jewish titles of God's immanence – 'the Word' being only one of them. Although, as has already been noted, the designations of the Saviour have nothing typically Christological about them, the identification of Christ with God's immanence enhances the superhuman aspect of Christ's nature and makes him a reflection of God: the union between the Father and the Son is unique and almost complete. Through the identification of the pre-existent Son of Man with the Word, Christ acquired a prehistory before the incarnation: through Him the world was created.

It is evident that Christian teaching about the Father and the Son departs from its Jewish premises. It may be based partly upon what Jesus himself thought that he was: he saw in himself the beloved son of his heavenly Father and probably he went so far as

'It is expedient for us that one man should die for the people.' Caiaphas' remark points to a long tradition in Judaism of expiatory martyrdoms. This scene from the Santa Sabina doors, dating from c. AD 430, is one of the earliest renderings of the Crucifixion. The Crosses are reticently omitted. (4)

to identify himself with the Son of Man. This is the highest conception of the Saviour that was known in ancient Judaism. The Son of Man is the pre-existent divine judge, sitting in heaven on the glorious throne of God. In Christian doctrine the Saviour was identified with the immanence of God. Being the Word, Christ was the instrument through which God created the universe. Even the later idea that Jesus was born through the Holy Spirit, without an earthly father, has parallels in Jewish sources.

It is possible that this last concept is hinted at in as early a Christian work as the Book of Revelation (xii), where John of Patmos speaks about the woman who gave birth to a male child. But, even granting that this suggestion is no more than a conjecture, there is no doubt that all the other important Christological concepts of the Church appear in this book: Jesus is the Davidic Messiah, the future king of the nations, and he will rule them with a rod of iron; he is the Son of Man and God's Word and His son; he was dead and was resurrected; he 'has freed us from our sins by his blood and made us a kingdom, priests to his God and Father' (i 5–6). His expiatory death is a sacrifice: he is the Lamb who was slain and by his blood he ransomed for God men of every tribe and tongue and people and nation (v 9).

As a lamb to the slaughter

As has been noted, there is no indication of any Hellenistic influence upon the Book of Revelation, and it even seems likely that the old suggestion that the book is in opposition to or in tension with Pauline Christianity is not without ground. Thus the Christology of the Book of Revelation seems to have its roots in Jewish Christianity. This also seems very probable in itself, because, as we have tried to show, the most important motifs in the
p 222 Church's conception of Christ already existed independently in
(16) pre-Christian Judaism. The same is also true of the expiatory
p 223–4 death of Jesus. A critical reading of the Gospels raises doubts
(18–23) about whether Jesus himself thought of his imminent death as
265 (6) being an expiation for the sins of his people; but the idea that
f 4 martyrdom is a vicarious suffering for Israel was widespread
among the Jewish people. Two quotations will suffice. The Second Book of Maccabees contains the famous description of the martyrdom of the seven brothers and their mother. According to this passage, the youngest brother said before his death:

> I, like my brothers, give up body and life for the laws of our fathers, appealing to God to show mercy to our nation . . . and through me and my brothers to bring to an end the wrath of the Almighty which has justly fallen on our whole nation (II Macc. vii 37–8).

In this passage, martyrdom is regarded as being not only an expiatory death but also a punishment for the sins of the nation. The martyrdom of a father and his seven sons as described in another Jewish book, the *Assumption of Moses* (chapter 9), reveals another aspect of this concept. In a time of religious persecution the man says to his sons:

> Now, therefore, my sons, hear me: for observe and know that neither did our fathers nor their forefathers tempt God, so as to transgress his commands. And you know that this is our strength and thus we will do. Let us fast for the space of three days and on the fourth let us go into a cave which is in the field and let us die rather than transgress the commands of the Lord of lords, the God of our fathers. For, if we do this and die, our blood will be avenged before the Lord.

The martyrdom itself is left undescribed, partly because the author regards it as being an eschatological event. Immediately after the father's words there follows a lyrical description of the future heavenly bliss: 'And then His kingdom will appear throughout all His creation, and then Satan will be no more and sorrow will depart with him . . .' Thus, according to the *Assumption of Moses*, the consequence of the martyrdom of the father and his saintly sons will be the revelation of the Kingdom of Heaven.

From these two quotations and from other Jewish sources we can see how important the idea of the expiatory function of martyrdom was in Judaism. But it should be also observed that the motif of the martyrdom of the Saviour is not to be found in ancient

Christ's Resurrection and Ascension had precursors in the stories of Melchizedek, Elijah and Enoch among others. In this scene from the Santa Sabina doors, Elisha takes Elijah's mantle, while two peasants are respectively amazed and terrified. (5)

Judaism. The historical fact that there was a man who was thought to be, or who thought himself to be, the Messiah, that this man suffered martyrdom, and that his followers did not abandon this belief after the catastrophy but, on the contrary, were actually fortified in their hope by the appearance of the resurrected Saviour – all this was of central importance for the Christian faith. Thus the Messianic motifs, originating in Jesus' view of what he was and in his teaching and in other Jewish sources, were fused into a unity with the Jewish concept of the expiatory force of martyrdom. The pre-existent divine being, incarnated by the will of his Heavenly Father, became the Davidic Messiah of Israel, died for our sins, arose from the dead, is sitting on the right hand of God, and will be the eschatological judge of the universe.

'The third day he rose again'

The nearest parallel to Christology is the faith of the disciples of John the Baptist. John speaks about a mighty one who 'will clear his threshing floor and gather his wheat into the granary, but the chaff he will burn with unquenchable fire' (Matt. iii 12). This is clearly the typology of the Son of Man. Evidently John did not identify himself with the mighty one, but his disciples saw in him the Messiah. John the Baptist was of priestly origin and he could therefore be held to be, not the Davidic, but the Aaronic, Messiah. In his lifetime many saw in him the prophet Elijah. According to the Bible, Elijah did not die, but was taken up into heaven and will return at the End of Days. If John the Baptist was Elijah, then he was virtually immortal, and it would be very improbable that his death at the hands of Herod Antipas would be the definitive end of his life. Although his body was laid in a tomb by his disciples (Mark vi 29), he was believed to have been raised from the dead (Mark vi 14).

It is therefore possible that, when the disciples saw the resurrected Jesus, their sight was, so to speak, sharpened by the knowledge that previously John the Baptist too had been raised from the dead. But, even if this suggestion may appear to be too rationalistic, we have to remember that a belief in immortal men and in ascensions was not as alien to ancient Judaism as it is to modern ideas. We have already mentioned Melchizedek and Elijah; we have also to remember the biblical Enoch; and the list can be enlarged. What is important is the Christological function of this belief in the resurrection and ascension of Jesus. By his ascension 'God has highly exalted him and bestowed on him the name which is above every name' (Phil. ii 9): the divine Lord returned to his Father. The resurrection could be conceived of as being Jesus' bounden victory over death and sin.

Thus the Jewish prophet from Galilee became the object of a cosmic drama which could bring salvation to the pious spectators. As has been explained, there were two roots from which this drama grew up: the first was Jesus' conception of himself as being the Son, his message about the coming of the Son of Man, and other Jewish mythical and Messianic doctrines; the other root was Jesus' tragic death, interpreted in terms of Jewish concepts of martyrdom. When we consider Jesus' death on the Cross from the standpoint of the history of mankind, we cannot but acknowledge its decisive importance for the genesis and development of Christianity. It is evident that Jesus' personal tragedy became the very centre of Christian teaching: this was the indispensable condition for the kindling of the faith of which Jesus became the object. If the martyr is at the same time the Messiah, then his expiatory death has a cosmic importance. His death becomes the fulfilment of the Law and the Prophets:

> Thus it is written that the Christ should suffer and on the third day rise from the dead and that repentance and forgiveness of sins should be preached in his name to all nations (Luke xxiv 46–7).

His expiatory death fulfilled the purpose of the incarnation of the pre-existent Son of Man. The resurrection restored him to his proper place on high at the side of his Father.

Jesus' tragic death also won for Jewish moral teaching, which entered Christianity through Jesus himself as well as through other channels, a new place in the new religion. It came to be associated with Christology: the Christian must not resist wicked men,

> Because Christ also suffered for you, leaving you an example, that you should follow in his steps . . . When he was reviled, he did not revile in return; when he suffered, he did not threaten; but he trusted to him who judges justly (I Peter ii 21–4).

The Christian must be humble because Jesus humbled himself. If, for the Jews as well as for Jesus himself, the love of one's neighbour was the sum total of the Law, this precept now became both an old and a new commandment, because, by sending His Son to his death to atone for human sins, God revealed His love of sinners.

The Jewish component of Christian faith and ethics has often been underestimated, because the Jewish sources are manifold, are in many cases not easily accessible, and are in some points difficult to understand. However, it is not our task to stress this point. Our aim has been simply to bring out the overwhelming direct and indirect importance of the person of Jesus in the context of the history of Christianity.

X

PAGANISM'S DEATH STRUGGLE

RELIGIONS IN COMPETITION WITH CHRISTIANITY

M.J. VERMASEREN

'What does it matter by what system of knowledge each of us seeks the truth? It is not by one single path that we arrive at so great a secret.'

SYMMACHUS 'THIRD RELATIO'

Christianity was not alone
in offering an alternative to the conventional pagan religion, nor was it altogether alone in the kind of alternative that it offered. The need for a faith that would have a new moral basis, that could promise individual salvation and make meaningful the most profound personal experiences, was universally felt. Hence the popularity of these so-called 'mystery' religions which were for several centuries Christianity's rivals. They all originated in the Near East: the cult of Mithras in Iran, that of Cybele in Asia Minor, those of the various Baals in Syria and of Isis in Egypt.

The worship of Isis goes far back in Egyptian history. Married to her brother Osiris, Isis was to see him murdered and hewn into fourteen pieces by another brother Seth, 'the god of confusion'. After many wanderings she reassembled all the pieces and restored Osiris to life. The myth lays the same stress on death and resurrection that was to recur in Christianity, and something of the same combination of the human and the divine. This Coptic fresco from Karganis in Egypt dates from the 3rd century AD. It shows Isis suckling her son Harpocrates. The parallel with the Madonna and Child of Christian iconography is too obvious to need comment, and in fact such paintings may well have influenced Early Christian art. Harpocrates was the god of silence. His finger in front of his mouth indicates the secret nature of the cult, which by this time had changed from a purely Egyptian state religion to the deeply personal faith of many devotees throughout the Empire. Augustus and Tiberius had to take strenuous measures to counter this 'orientalizing' influence in Italy. (1)

'King of Upper and Lower Egypt', the mighty figure of Osiris was worshipped from the earliest times. In this 26th-Dynasty (635–525 BC) bronze (right), he is represented as a mummy wearing the *uraeus*-crown of Upper Egypt and carrying a crook and a flail. (2)

When the Romans came to Egypt, Isis was already the supreme figure of the cult, and her worship had spread to other parts of the Near East. In AD 38 a temple ('Iseum') was built for her in the Campus Martius in Rome, attracting a large following especially among the upper classes. The marble relief shown below probably came from this building. It shows an Isiac procession, with, from left to right: a young priestess holding a *sistrum* (rattle) and a *simpulum* (ladle), a shaven-headed priest carrying a vessel of holy Nile water in his covered hands, another priest wearing a falcon head-dress and reading from a scroll, and a priestess with a lotus in her hair carrying the *uraeus*-snake and *situla* (bucket). (3)

'Voluntary death' (below centre), one of the ceremonies undergone by the Isiac *mystes*, is illustrated in a mosaic found at Antioch. The initiate at the gates of Hades is reassured by Isis' outstretched hand, while Hermes, conductor of souls, touches him with his staff. (5)

The Temple of Isis in Rome appears on a coin of Vespasian (below right) of AD 71. Five steps lead up to the entrance. Through the door the cult statue of Isis can be seen. She is flanked by hieratic Egyptian standing figures and seated sphinxes. In the pediment, Isis-Sothis holding a *sistrum* rides the dog Sirius. (7)

A stone fragment (below far right) showing the seated Osiris is part of a granite slab imported from Lower Egypt and built into the Iseum of Rome. (8)

A masked priest (right) dances before the Temple of Isis: a wall-painting from Herculaneum. The temple has been decorated with branches. In front of it stands an altar. The other figures play the double pipe, beat the drum, rattle the *sistrum* or kneel in adoration before the priest, who may represent Osiris. (6)

Serapis, the corn-god, was introduced by the first Hellenistic ruler of Egypt, Ptolemy I (323–285 BC), who wished to reform the bull-cult of Osiris-Apis and blend it with Greek elements. Serapis, in this version of the myth, became the husband of Isis. His cult-image (below: head from the Mithraeum of Santa Prisca in Rome) clearly shows his Hellenistic origins, with his Zeus-like face crowned by the *modius*, a basket filled with fruit and decorated with olive branches. (4)

S
C

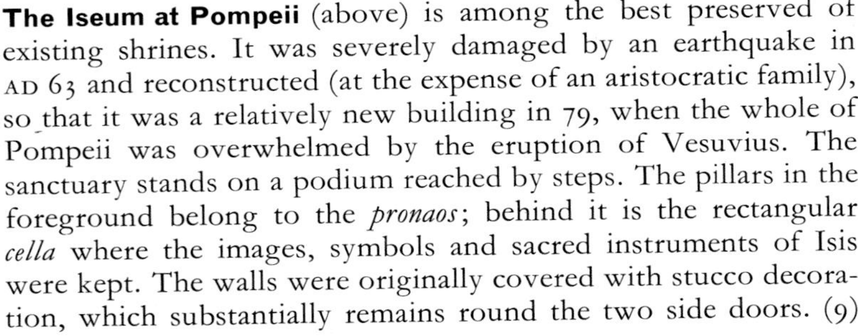

The Iseum at Pompeii (above) is among the best preserved of existing shrines. It was severely damaged by an earthquake in AD 63 and reconstructed (at the expense of an aristocratic family), so that it was a relatively new building in 79, when the whole of Pompeii was overwhelmed by the eruption of Vesuvius. The sanctuary stands on a podium reached by steps. The pillars in the foreground belong to the *pronaos*; behind it is the rectangular *cella* where the images, symbols and sacred instruments of Isis were kept. The walls were originally covered with stucco decoration, which substantially remains round the two side doors. (9)

Before the shrine of the goddess flanked (as in the Vespasian coin) by sphinxes, a shaven priest holds a vase, wrapped in his cloak, for the veneration of the worshippers. What the vase contains is a subject of debate: probably sacred Nile water. This fresco is also at Herculaneum. Beside the high priest stands a priestess, holding *sistrum* and *situla*, and a negro priest with *sistrum*. The men in the centre foreground are also probably priests. The altar, on which a fire burns, has four 'horns', like that of Pompeii. On each side rows of chanting worshippers watch the ceremony, and four beautiful black and white birds – ibises, sacred to Isis – give the scene an exotic touch of their native Egypt. (10)

The cult of the Syrian gods, introduced into Rome about the 1st century AD, comprised a crowd of rival gods all claiming to be supreme. Each was the lord of one of the Syrian cities: Adonis of Byblos, Atargatis (a goddess) of Bambyce, and various Jupiters. Jupiter Dolichenus, with his conical cap, is seen (above) standing on a bull, a double axe in one hand, lightning in the other. Opposite him stands his consort Juno on a hind, carrying a staff and a mirror. Between them is a burning altar surmounted by an eagle and by busts of Serapis and Isis. The figures in the upper corners are the Dioscuri Castor and Pollux. (11)

Jupiter Dolichenus had a temple in Rome (model below). The main room, with the altar against the far wall, had a mosaic floor and benches. In front of it was another apsed room with four niches; behind it a room with a basin. (12)

A young mystery god entwined by a snake (below) was found in the Syrian sanctuary on the Janiculum, Rome, and shows Egyptian influence. As is seen in the relief above, the Syrian gods were associated with the Isis cult. (13)

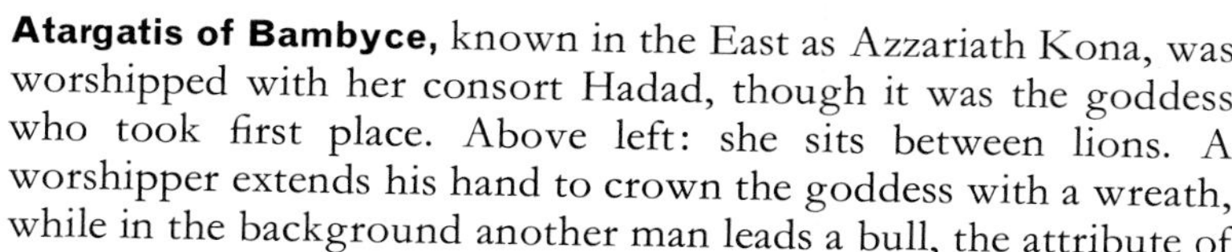

Atargatis of Bambyce, known in the East as Azzariath Kona, was worshipped with her consort Hadad, though it was the goddess who took first place. Above left: she sits between lions. A worshipper extends his hand to crown the goddess with a wreath, while in the background another man leads a bull, the attribute of Hadad. Centre: Hadad between bulls, holding (like Jupiter in the relief opposite) a double axe and with lightning engraved on the background. Right: a marble statuette, also from the Janiculum site, probably representing Atargatis entwined by the snake. The Egyptian influence is again marked. (14, 15, 16)

'To the most holy sun, Tiberius Claudius Felix, Claudia Helpis and their son Tiberius Claudius Alypus made this sacred dedication.' The altar (below) was dedicated to the sun god by Syrian emigrés from Palmyra in Rome. (17)

Inscribed in Greek and in Palmyrene Aramaic, this Roman altar is dedicated to the Palmyrene sun god Malachbel and moon god Aglibol (note the crescent behind his shoulders). In the centre there is a cypress tree. (18)

The boy-emperor Elagabalus, hereditary priest of Elagabal, sun god of Emesa, caused a revolution in Roman religion by deposing Jupiter and installing his own god in Rome. Elagabal was worshipped in Syria in the form of a large black meteorite. The two lower coins (left) show his temple at Emesa. Elagabalus brought this stone to Rome (commemorated in the top coin) and built a temple for it on the Palatine. The god's reign was a brief as the Emperor's. Elagabalus was murdered in a palace revolution in 222 at the age of 18, and Jupiter resumed his supremacy. (19, 20, 21)

In far-away Britain Jupiter Dolichenus had his following, probably mostly soldiers. This fragment of a jar found in Northamptonshire, which shows a deity wearing a conical cap and brandishing a double axe (*cf.* plate 11), probably represents Dolichenus. (23)

Sacrificing to the Palmyrene gods: a famous fresco from Dura Europus. The gods of Palmyra, Malachbel and Aglibol, had won adherents in Rome as early as the 1st century AD. Malachbel was the more powerful and popular. At the end of the 3rd century Aurelian, aided, he believed, by the local sun god, defeated the Queen of Palmyra, Zenobia. A new temple was built in Rome and the religion of *Sol Invictus* became officially established. (24)

The triad of Jupiter-Baal, Venus-Atargatis and Mercury-Semeios was worshipped in the splendid sanctuary of Baalbek, or Heliopolis, 'City of the sun' (left). A portico led through a six-sided vestibule to a square court, beyond which stood the great temple itself. To the left is the Temple of Bacchus. (22)

The great Earth-Mother had been worshipped since remote antiquity. In the mountains of Asia Minor she was given the name of Cybele, and it was in this Phrygian form that she entered the Greek pantheon. By the 5th century BC she was being represented in a way that became traditional (left) seated on the throne between two lions. (25)

Cybele was brought to Rome after a consultation of the Sybilline Books had revealed that the Romans would only defeat Hannibal with her help. A mission was sent to King Attalus of Pergamum, and in 204 BC her cult statue, or another sacred black stone, arrived in the capital. This relief (below) shows her seated between lions on a ship, the prow of which ends in a *thyrsus* staff. (26)

A high-priest of the cult of Cybele, an *archigallus*, reclines (below) on a marble funerary couch. He wears a tiara on his head and a bracelet on his right wrist, and holds a pine-branch, which was the symbol of Attis. At his feet, there is a mystic casket and a snake. (27)

The young lover Attis figured in the myth of Cybele in Asia Minor but was at first omitted in the Greek and Roman versions. He was said to have aroused Cybele's fury by falling in love with a nymph; he became melancholy (right: a Roman stucco relief of the 1st century AD), fell into a frenzy, emasculated himself and died. The idea of resurrection seems to have been added later, when Attis is portrayed (below) as a dancing winged god, symbol of the renewal of life in nature. (29, 30)

Cybele on her lion-flanked throne with Hermes and Attis: a terracotta lamp from Rome. (28)

The Temple of Cybele on the Palatine, as rebuilt in the Augustan period, is shown in this relief (right) surrounded by worshippers. The pediment sculpture should be especially noted. A crown on a throne symbolizes the goddess. It is flanked by two reclining figures, each with one arm resting on a tambourine, one of the musical instruments of the cult. In each corner are lions with their heads above baskets. The acroteria of the temple are decorated with statues of Kuretes – Cretans who were entrusted with the education of Zeus by Rhea, a figure analogous to Cybele. (31)

Between Christianity and the mystery religions the parallels were many and complex. Some have already been noted in reference to Isis. The Syrian sun-cult, *Sol Invictus*, also had its effect. Constantine was reputed to have had a miraculous vision of the sun-disk overlaid by the Cross, and Early Christian writers, as we shall see in another chapter, took over some of its imagery. But it was with Mithraism that the parallels were most striking.

Mithras' investiture of Sol after the bull-slaying (above) was compared to the baptism of Christ (above right); while Mithras' making rain by shooting an arrow at the sky was seen as an analogue of Moses bringing forth water from the rock (opposite top). (32, 33, 36, 37)

The Mithraic meal was compared by Christian writers to the Eucharist. After slaying the bull, Mithras and Sol ritually dined off its body (right). The Mithraists partook of a symbolic meal in commemoration of this, and it seems that by the Christian era bread and wine had in fact replaced the meat and blood. Although there is nothing to suggest that the Mithraists identified Mithras with the bull, or regarded the food as symbolic of his body, the ceremony clearly has something in common with the Early Christian 'love feast'. Far right: one of the earliest representations of such a scene, from the catacomb of SS. Pietro e Marcellino. (34, 38)

Mithras' ascension and return to the realm of light aided by Sol (right) is an obvious parallel to Elijah's ascent to heaven in a chariot (far right), and was noted as such by Early Christian writers. (35, 39)

AGAPE·MISC
NOBIS

The Mithras cycle, represented in many Mithraea, may be compared to the iconographic cycle that grew up among Christians, stretching from Creation to the Day of Judgement. The Mithraic story too began with Creation, but the scenes thereafter did not follow a fixed order. Four of them have been shown on the previous page. The other important ones are illustrated here. **Saturn and Jupiter** (left, top) first ruled the world; here Saturn hands over a thunderbolt, Jupiter a staff. **Mithras was born** (left, second from top) from a rock, holding a globe and dagger. **Hunting the bull** (right, above) he is accompanied by the lion and the snake. In the struggle, **Mithras rides the bull** (left, third from top). After catching it, **Mithras carries the bull** to a cave (below, left). **The bull-slaying** (right, centre) was the central episode of the myth: note in this relief the dog and snake; two figures called Cautes and Cautopates holding torches respectively upward and downward; Sol and Luna; and a raven who is a messenger from Sol. The bull's tail ends in ears of corn, indicating the fertility aspect of the cult. **The ritual meal** between Mithras and Sol, shown also in plate 34, is represented (below) on a cup. It is served by Mithraists; also present are a lion, a raven and a cock. (40–46)

Spiritual progress in Mithraism was represented as a ladder (far right). Seven grades, each under the protection of a planet, led through the elements (bottom: water symbolized by a vase, air by the helmets of the Dioscuri, and fire by an altar, off the picture) to paradise (top: the flowers). They were: 'Raven', under Mercury (*caduceus* and flask of lustral water); 'Mystic Bride', under Venus (diadem and lamp); 'Soldier', under Mars (spear, helmet and wallet); 'Lion', under Jupiter (fire-shovel, *sistrum* and thunderbolt); 'Perses', under the moon (sword, scythe and crescent); 'Heliodromus', under the sun (radiate crown, torch and whip); 'Pater', under Saturn (spear, helmet, sickle and dish). (49)

The lion-headed god of infinite time (right) shows the mixture of Hellenistic and oriental influences in Mithraism. His four arms and four wings recall the four winds. His devouring lion's head is a symbol of fire. On his breast is an eye, on his stomach and knees are lions' heads. (47)

Mithraea normally consist of a long room with benches down the side and an altar at one end, with a representation of Mithras slaying the bull. In that of Santa Prisca (below) he is accompanied by Oceanus. (48)

The central mystery of Mithraism – the slaying of the bull – eludes final explanation. The most that can be said is that it certainly had to do with the burgeoning of new vegetative life: the snake which licks the bull's blood probably symbolizes the earth which will be fertilized by the blood, and the bull's tail (as in the relief on the previous page) sometimes ends in ears of corn. On the spiritual plane, Mithras' deed is designed to ensure immortality. In this fresco in the Mithraeum under Santa Maria di Capua Vetere (above), the familiar elements are present – the dog and the snake, Cautes and Cautopates, Sol and Luna, and the raven. Mithras' relation with Sol is also emphasized by one of the rays of Sol's radiate crown shooting in the direction of Mithras. (50)

In his native Persia Mithras had been a fairly minor figure fighting on the side of Ahura-Mazda, the God of Light. Even in classical times his connexion with Zoroastrianism had not been forgotten. This figure of a *magus* (left) with cane and scroll from the Dura Europus Mithraeum is probably the *pater* of the community. (51)

RELIGIONS IN COMPETITION WITH CHRISTIANITY

M. J. VERMASEREN

CULTS AND CREEDS from the East – particularly from Asia Minor and Egypt – had been introduced into Greece before the Hellenistic period. With the deeper contact between Greek and Asiatic cultures brought about by Alexander and his successors, the Diadochi, many of them took root all over the Mediterranean world: the cult of Mithras from Iran, of Cybele and Attis from Phrygia, of Osiris and Isis from Egypt, and of Jupiter Dolichenus from Syria. Each carried its own foreign characteristics with it, and they continued to spread under the Roman Empire. Some – for example the cults of Mithras and Cybele – were tolerated by the state from the beginning. Others – for example the cult of Isis – met with opposition in the first half of the 1st century AD. The cults were favoured by some of the more important Roman families, while soldiers and traders from the East built temples and erected altars to their own deities in the farthest corners of the Empire. One can sometimes trace the spread of the various cults from city to city, follow-
132–3 ing the Imperial roads, and it is possible to recognize the artistic
0–46) schools who worked for them, especially in Rome itself. All of
them except the cult of Mithras included both official public ceremonies and more private meetings that were not open to ordinary people. In cases where only *mystae* (*i.e.* initiates) were admitted we can legitimately speak of 'mystery-cults', or secret societies with special initiations.

It was against a background created by these oriental cults that the Christians founded their own communities. It is necessary to study these other cults in order to show what Christianity shared with them and how it differed.

Mithraism

f 1 In Iran the god Mithra was originally a helper of the supreme deity of all Goodness. According to the Iranian Scripture, the Avesta, the Wise Lord, Ahura-Mazda or Ohrmuzd, who is the God of the Light, fights an everlasting battle against Ahriman, the Lord of Evil and Darkness. In this dualism Mithra fights at the side of Ahura-Mazda and on the side of the truth; he protects treaties, houses, plants and cattle. He is the mighty warrior who gives victory to soldiers. Eventually, but only in a remote future, Ahura-Mazda and his true helpers will be victorious over the army of Ahriman, and then a new era will dawn.

The cult of Mithra was established among Indo-Iranian tribes; we find his name and his functions in both the Avesta and the Rigvedic hymns. In the Avesta there is even a special song in his honour (Yašt 10) which, according to Ilya Gershevitch, is to be dated to the second half of the 5th century BC; but it is clear that the god's worship was already widely diffused in the pre-Avestan period (early-14th century BC), although we still have no information about a mystery-cult at this time such as existed in the Roman period. F. Cumont supposed that the transformation of a special cult in the East into a secret cult in the western world was due to the Magians, oriental priests who came to Western Asia in the course of the expansion of the Iranian Empire. During this period the Mithra cult will have been strongly influenced by Babylonian astrological theories. However, there is no archaeological evidence to confirm the hypothesis of the existence of organized Mithraic temples in Asia Minor.

In the West Mithra was called Mithras and, according to
26 (3) Plutarch, the Romans first encountered him in Pompey's campaign
against the Cilician pirates in 67 BC. Yet the first mention of the
famous artistic group of Mithras as bull-slayer is in the poet p 250
Statius (*c.* AD 80). It is to be noted that in Pompeii, which was (45)
destroyed in AD 79, no trace of Mithras has been discovered. There p 251
is thus a gap of some centuries in our exact knowledge of this (48)
mysterious god. We have much archaeological evidence about p 252
Mithras in the western world but little in the way of documents. (50)
Clearly there are certain connections between the Iranian Mithra and the Roman Mithras, but these must not be overemphasized. To give one example, monuments of Mithras *tauroktonos* have been discovered in hundreds of places in the Roman Empire, but in the Avestan writings there is not one single direct testimony to the story of Mithras killing the bull. In order to lay bare the mysteries of Mithras it therefore seems better to start from the authentic data in the Roman Mithraic temples, which in the last few years have also yielded some texts, and then to consider how to connect these results with the surrounding Mithraic world and Mithras' origins.

The life cycle of Mithras

The temples of Mithras are in general subterranean and small. They p 251
are designed for restricted groups from which women were (48)
excluded. They are vaulted, the vault being a symbol of the celestial sky. There is a central corridor flanked on each side by raised benches, on which the initiates reclined as they followed the ceremonies. Against the rear wall there is a picture or relief of
Mithras killing the bull (these may be painted, carved in marble, p 250
or moulded in stucco). This is the principal scene in the visual (45)
presentation of Mithraism. In Italy, and even more commonly in p 251
the German and Danubian provinces, this scene is surrounded by (48)
presentations of other deeds of the god and/or by presentations p 252
of some other mythological stories that found their way into (50)
Mithraism. Sometimes the back of the main relief carries a separate
scene, usually depicting Mithras' sacred meal with the Sun-god p 248
(Helios-Sol). The cycle seems to run as follows (though the (34)
various scenes do not have a fixed order): p 250

(1) Creation of the cosmos. (46)

(2) Reign of Saturn-Kronos, who is often represented as p 250
holding a sickle. (40)

(3) The war of Jupiter against the Giants.

(4) Jupiter enthroned among the other Olympians.

(5) The birth of Mithras. This scene also occurs on some p 250
monuments by itself and must therefore be one of the more (41)
important events in the story of this god. He is born from a rock (*petra genetrix*), which is another symbol of Heaven. He himself is a sun god; the light of the sun streams from the celestial vault. He is represented as a child or sometimes already as an adult. He carries a torch and a knife or a dagger. His birthplace is occasionally connected with a spring (*fons perennis*). In two monuments which show Orphic influence the young god is born from an egg and is assimilated to Phanes. The birthday (*natalis invicti*) of the God was celebrated each year on December 25th after the winter *solsticium*. The god's life begins with a miracle, and, like the Greek Herakles, Mithras is destined to accomplish other miraculous deeds, though this not without labour. In this way his earthly life serves as an example for his devotees.

(6) Mithras kneeling or sitting on a rock and shooting an arrow p 249
in the direction of a rock or of the clouds. This scene also occurs (36)
by itself on some monuments. In front of the rock two persons are catching in both hands, and drinking, water which is pouring forth

from heaven. This water-miracle seems to suppose a period of
dryness from which the God now delivers mankind.
p 250 (7) Preparation for the bull-slaying. Mithras is hunting the bull
(44) and after many struggles succeeds in catching it. There are succes-
p 250 sive scenes of the bull in a house, in a boat and in a meadow, and
(42) of Mithras riding the bull.
p 250 (8) After catching the bull Mithras carries it on his shoulders
(43) towards a cave (*transitus dei* or Mithras *taurophoros*).

(9) The scene of Mithras *tauroktonos* in the central part (see below).

p 248 (10) Treaty between Mithras and Sol. Sometimes Sol kneels
(32) before Mithras and a sort of investiture is taking place. The Iranian
god is giving Sol an accolade. Sometimes the two deities are
standing on either side of an altar and are shaking hands; the treaty
is also ratified by giving blood. On a relief from Ptuj in Yugoslavia
a raven is shown picking little pieces of meat from a spit during
the ceremony.
p 248 (11) A sacred meal of the two deities in a cave. There are many
(34) representations of this scene by itself, which shows its importance
p 250 in the cult.
(46) (12) Sol standing in a *biga* or *quadriga* helps Mithras to ascend.
p 248 Both now leave the earth and return to the realm of light.
(35) In all these scenes Mithras wears oriental dress (tiara, long
trousers or *anaxyrides, tunica* and mantle). Though he is a sun god,
p 252 he is only exceptionally shown as radiate. His dress is often red,
(50) whereas the bull is white. Two scenes are of the greatest importance: the bull-slaying and the sacred meal. The first scene of the
two, the *tauroktonos* scene, has up till now found no convincing
explanation (there are various objections to the theories of Lom-
mel). On the monuments Mithras is killing the bull, which he
presses to the ground with his knees. The expression on his face
shows that he is killing the animal against his will. He seems to be
in some relation with Sol, who is depicted in the top left-hand
p 252 corner and at whom he is looking over his shoulder. Sometimes
(50) one of the rays of Sol's radiate crown shoots in the direction of
p 250 Mithras. There is a raven, usually carved on the edge of the rocky
(45) cave, who is a messenger from the region of Sol. On the top right
hand corner of the relief there is a corresponding figure of Luna.
Sol and Luna represent the waxing and waning light. Mithras
himself, who was especially venerated on the 16th of the month,
is also portrayed as the solar light of the noontide of each day. This
symbolism is accentuated by two standing figures who wear the
same dress as Mithras and who hold a flaming torch respectively
upwards and downwards. Their names are Cautes and Cautopates,
which in recent times have been interpreted as epithets of Mithras
himself. A late text of the 4th century AD says that these two torchbearers form a trinity with Mithras.

A dog and a snake are licking the blood from the bull's wound.
The dog is Mithras' helper and the snake is probably a symbol of
the earth, which will be fertilized by the blood. The presence of a
fertilizing power is, indeed, also proved by the fact that the bull's
p 250 tail sometimes ends in ears of corn; and a scorpion which clasps the
(45) bull's testicles seems to want to corrupt the seed. There is an
element of dualism in the conception of Mithras as bull-slayer;
but the conception of the consequences of his deed is optimistic.
The material result is the burgeoning of new vegetative life from
the bull; the spiritual result is the obtainment of the after-life. This
p 251 becomes apparent in a line of verse recently discovered in the Santa
(48) Prisca Mithraeum on the Aventine and dated to AD 202:

Et nos servasti eternali sanguine fuso
(And you saved us by having shed the eternal blood).

p 248 This line is closely related to the other most important religious
(34) ceremony, the sacred meal. In the representations of this scene on
p 250 the monuments, Mithras and Sol are sometimes the only partici-
(46) pants; but there are also monuments on which the gods, their
representatives and their followers are all shown together. The
gods are reclining and they are drinking the bull's blood and eating
its body. In the Santa Prisca Mithraeum this scene is painted on
the left-hand wall next to the cult niche, and in front of it there is
a raised podium on which the two highest initiates (*Pater* and
Heliodromus) reclined and played the roles of the deities who had
originally set the pattern. The newly discovered verses in Santa
Prisca and evidence in the Mithraeum at Dura Europos indicate
that bread and wine had replaced the meat and blood. Some
Christian authors even compared the Mithraic meal with the
Christian Eucharist. But this evidence is late, and there is really p 249
nothing to suggest that Mithras was identified with the bull, or in (38)
other words that in killing the bull he sacrificed himself for
Mankind. It is certain, however, that the Mithraists believed that
the practice of eating the meat or bread and drinking the blood or
wine was favoured by the god and was ensuring them a happy
after-life. In this way the bull-slaying and the sacred meal influence
each other. From the outset the purpose of Mithras' birth and
deeds was to save Mankind from the realm of darkness and
confusion.

The Christian authors compared another Mithraic ceremony p 248
with Christian baptism. It seems that the worshippers of Mithras – (32–3)
like the initiates into the Isiac mysteries – underwent a purification
through all four elements, and through baptism – as in Christianity p 249
– they were purified from sin. The Mithraic water-miracle was (36–7)
compared to that of Moses, and Mithras' ascent to Heaven together p 248–
with Sol, upon completion of his exploits, was compared to the (35, 39
ascent of Elijah in Christian art. It is a pity that we are able to do no
more than set out these comparisons; we have no evidence for the
exact extent of the correlations between Mithraism and Christianity.
In the case of the water miracle, one of the verses in the Santa Prisca
Mithraeum runs:

Fons concluse petris, qui geminos aluisti nectare fratres
(Rock-bound spring that fed the twin brothers with nectar).

The two brothers, *i.e.* Cautes and Cautopates, the companions of Mithras and his two substitutes, are fed with *nectar*, *i.e.* with the drink of the gods which gives eternal life. Analogously the actual members of the Mithraic community, the *fratres*, receive from the god the eternal food in the form of the heavenly water and the bull's blood (*eternali sanguine*).

The eternal battle between Good and Evil, which is part of the
Iranian tradition and which was later taken over by Gnosticism
and Manicheanism, is also displayed in some representations of
Mithras as a hunter (*e.g.* at Dieburg, Rückingen, Dura Europos). p 250
The god, accompanied by his faithful animals, such as the lion (44)
and the dog, is hunting other animals who seem to be friends of
the Evil One. The god Mithras is always defending Goodness,
which shows itself in virtue, might, heroism, righteousness,
treaties, and general morality. Those who are his faithful followers
and *socii* do as he did. It is only by following his divine example
that they can be sure of attaining eternal life. A relief from Dieburg
in Germany demonstrates that Stoicism influenced the cult of
Mithras. Mithras is now compared with Phaethon, who in his
downfall symbolizes the final *conflagratio* of the cosmos. A verse in
the Santa Prisca sanctuary also alludes to this event, which will
take place at the end of time:

Accipe thuricremos pater accipe sancte leones
per quos thura damus per quos consumimur ipsi

(Accept, o Holy Father, accept the incense-burning Lions
Through whom we offer the incense, through whom we ourselves are purified).

The Mithraist believed that his spiritual principle came down
into the world from the sun. As it passed through the spheres of the
seven planets, this principle was laden with various non-spiritual
qualities from which during his life-time the true Mithraist tried to
free himself. In so doing he started upon his return to the light.
There are therefore seven grades symbolizing this return, seven p 251
steps in the initiation, which are like the steps of a ladder. At the (49)
same time as he ascends this ladder he passes through the four
elements, and with each step he comes nearer to his god. These
seven grades of initiation, each of which is under the protection of
one of the seven planets and which have special symbols, are:
Raven (Mercury) – Mystic bride (Venus) – Soldier (Mars) – Lion
(Jupiter) – *Perses* (Moon) – *Heliodromus* (Sun) – *Pater* (Saturn). The
highest grades of *Pater* and *Heliodromus* are the earthly representatives of Mithras and Sol. They were the leading persons in the
Mithraic community.

Like most of Mithraism these theories did not have their origin in Iran but were undoubtedly introduced in Hellenistic times when the cult was transformed into a mystery-cult (see above, p. 253). p 251 (47) The god of infinite time, called a monster by Jerome, is likewise a mixture of Hellenistic influences. He is shown with a human body but with a devouring lion's head (the symbol of fire), with four wings (the directions of the winds), and often entwined by a snake decorated with the signs of the Zodiac.

These mysteries, with their ceremonies of baptism and a sacred meal, with their high standard of morality, with their creed of redemption and salvation and with the strong personal feelings towards the god which they involved, were destined to become as fervent a cult as the new Christianity, which in the same way sprang from both the oriental and the western world. The Christian authors themselves manifestly recognize some similarities; but the fact that in Mithraism only men were admitted brings its followers into a rather closer relation to Manicheanism and the Gnostic sects. This hypothesis can only be proved definitely when more Mithraic texts are discovered. Then we shall know the exact extent to which these various sects met and influenced each other.

This intense head of Mithras, found in London in 1954, comes from a group in which the god performed the elemental act of sacrifice, and so brought life out of death for mankind. (1)

Cybele and Attis

In the mountains of Asia Minor, and also in the Greek world, there existed from remote antiquity a mighty goddess. In the Mediterranean world she was πότνια θηρῶν (*potnia thērōn*), mistress of the beasts, especially of the fiercest animals such as the lion and the panther. Laroche and Will have recently tried to discover her origins, and have traced similarities and connections between the Asiatic and the Greek goddess. Their researches seem to show that in Asia Minor as well as in Crete she was regarded as the goddess who gives life to mankind, animals and vegetation, and who after death takes this life back into her divine womb. She was the divine Earth Mother: even in the Neolithic period she was represented (*e.g.* at Çatal Hüyük) in the act of giving birth and also as a goddess of death, accompanied by a bird of prey or supported by two leopards. This ancient Goddess seems to correspond to the Phrygian Κυβέλη, Κυβήβη, Κυβήκη or Κύβηλις of whom frequent traces begin to appear even as early as the 2nd millennium BC in various Anatolian sites, among others Boğazköy and Kargamiš. In later times Pessinus, the modern Balahisar, became the most important centre of her worship.

Mother of gods and men

This Phrygian goddess was known to Greece in the Archaic period, although the Greeks also worshipped specifically Greek derivations from the original Earth Mother (Rhea, Demeter). One of the principal sites in the spread of her influence in the western world was Cyme in Asia Minor; other places where the Orient transmitted the goddess to the West were Miletus, Smyrna and Clazomenae. The Phrygian mother was assimilated to the Great Mother who presided over several mountains; she also became the Mother of the Gods (Μήτηρ θεῶν *mētēr theōn*) and was connected with Kronos and with Zeus. She was now represented by varied but well-defined artistic types, which seem to have been established long before the end of the 5th century BC – the date at which Agoracritus of Paros gave the goddess her classical form in his great statue of her sitting between two lions with a whelp in her p 246–7 (25–6, 28) lap. This type is the most common one and is later found throughout the Roman Empire. Of equal antiquity is the type of the goddess standing between two lions springing up at her but tamed by her mighty hands. When Cybele is seated on a throne, as in Anatolian and Athenian reliefs, she is often flanked either by a young man and an older man or else by a young man and a girl. It is clear that the younger person, who is a servant and holds a jug in his right hand, represents Hermes. p 247 (28) The girl, who usually holds a torch in each hand, seems to be Hekate. The interpretation of the bearded man is more difficult, but he is probably Zeus. It is remarkable that this figure, which may represent the *paredros* of the goddess, occurs only on reliefs from the Ionian coast (Smyrna and Magnesia) and that it was not transmitted to the later Hellenistic period. In some reliefs, however, such as that found in Lebadea in Boeotia (2nd century AD), Cybele is the true Mother of the Gods, enthroned in front of the gods, who are here shown in pairs. Among these gods there are sometimes also three Kuretes near her. They commemorate the Cretan Rhea who brought Zeus into the Dictean cave, where he was nursed by the nymphs and by the goat Amaltheia. Dionysiac elements are to be seen in the Pans and dancing Maenads, and reliefs from Eleusis and Athens also show the goddess in friendly relations with Demeter. Both goddesses wear the same dress, *polos*, long tunic and mantle, both have a *tympanum* and a *patera* in their hands, but Cybele is distinguished by being accompanied by a lion. She often wears a turreted crown, and in Roman times, as for example in the pediment of her temple on p 247 (31) the Palatine, this was even used as a symbol for the goddess.

p 247 (28–30) It is clear that the goddess was connected with a young lover, Attis, in the legends of Asia Minor; but Attis is found only exceptionally on the older monuments. It is difficult to be sure of the exact date at which Attis was introduced into the Cybele cult. The Greeks in their worship of Cybele generally omitted Attis, who is constrained to emasculate himself in the service of the deity. However, he appears once among the reliefs at Massilia (Marseilles) which were imported from Asia Minor in the 6th century BC. On a relief from the Piraeus, now in Berlin, which probably dates from the 4th century BC, he is seated on a rock, and a goddess Agdistis, who is identified with Cybele, approaches him holding a jug in her right hand. It is evident that the Greeks, who disliked the Iranian Mithra killing the bull, equally had a horror of the emasculated Attis.

The Hannibalic crisis

The Romans also thought of Cybele and Attis as being specifically Asiatic deities. It was only after their intervention in the affairs of Asia Minor that the Roman Senate passed a special motion for the introduction of Cybele and her priests into the capital. Undoubtedly the prime movers in this were certain aristocratic Roman families that claimed a Trojan origin and were proud of being descended from comrades of Aeneas who were held to have come to Italy with him, (though the goddess did not come from Troy but, according to different traditions, either from Pessinus or from Pergamum). The reason for this move was the desperate situation in 213 BC, when it looked as if Hannibal was going to be victorious in the Second Punic War. Even in the Forum and on the Capitol the people were imploring foreign gods to help them (Livy XXV 1, 6ff.) and the senators, who were men of sound judgement, were forced to act. A consultation of the Sibylline Books elicited that the enemy could be expelled and conquered when the Mother of Ida was transferred from Pessinus to Rome (Livy XXIX 10, 4).

In 205 BC a Roman embassy was sent to King Attalus of Pergamum, and it seems that it was he who handed over the goddess, embodied in a sacred black stone, to the Roman People. (Some
p 246 (26) monuments display a statue of the goddess seated on the ship that is being towed miraculously by a priestess, Claudia Quinta.) The cult statue arrived in Rome on April 4th, 204 BC. It was housed initially in the Temple of Victory, but on April 10th, 191 BC, a new temple for the goddess was dedicated to her on the Palatine next to the primitive huts on the Germalus. Official festivities in honour of the Magna Mater (Μήτηρ μεγάλη *mētēr megalē*) were instituted. They were to be held from the 4th till the 10th of April each year (the *Megalensia*). For use in these ceremonies a small theatre was built in front of the temple. The original building has not survived, although the excavations of Pietro Romanelli have revealed a partial rebuilding dating from the years 110–109 BC and a restoration dating from the Augustan period after a second fire. However, a relief dating from the time of the Emperor Claudius, which is part of the Ara Pietatis and is now in the Villa Medici, depicts the
p 247 (31) façade of the temple: the steps and six Corinthian columns supporting the pediment, and the entrance door. In the pediment there is a throne on which is placed the mural (battlemented) crown of Cybele. On either side there is a reclining figure with one arm resting on a tambourine, and in each corner a lion with his head above a basket. The acroteria of the temple are decorated with statues of Kuretes.

In the legends woven round the entry of the goddess into the capital there is no mention of her male associate Attis. This must mean that when his cult was introduced on the Palatine it was kept in the background and was restricted to the precincts of the temple. We know that much later, during the reign of Claudius, Attis the lover of Cybele became more popular and gained official recognition. In Asia Minor, on the other hand, it appears that Attis was highly appreciated from the 6th century BC onward, and here various legends about his life grew up.

According to Herodotus (I 34–45), Attis (or Atys) was the son of Croesus, King of Lydia, and was killed by Adrastus, son of the Phrygian King Gordius, during a hunting party. This Lydian version differs widely from the story current in the temple-state of Pessinus, which has been transmitted by both Pausanias and Arnobius. In the Phrygian version there is a long saga recounting the antecedents of Attis' miraculous birth. There is a mountain, Agdus, which took the shape of Rhea. Father Zeus did not succeed in having intercourse with the goddess, and he lost his semen on the rock. In the tenth month the mountain brought Agdistis, a bisexual being, into the world. Agdistis was violent and furious; so the gods decided to forestall any possible danger from this hermaphrodite. The wine god Dionysus mixed wine with the water of the spring where Agdistis quenched his thirst, and, when the monster was sunk in a deep sleep after having taken the mixture, Dionysus tied his genitals to a tree with ropes. Upon awakening, Agdistis emasculated himself. From the blood of the wound a tree arose which bore fruit. Nana, daughter of a king (or of the River Sangarius), took some of the fruit and put it in her lap. The virgin now became pregnant and her father tried to kill her, but the Great Mother saved her. She also saved the baby – Attis – when Sangarius gave the order to expose him. He was fed by a goat and was brought up among shepherds. Some texts relate that, like Agdistis, he was bisexual, but he is commonly described as a handsome young man.

We must not forget that in this intricate story Agdistis, and Nana too, are ultimately identical with the Earth Mother herself. Thus Attis is born from a virgin mother. He is sometimes represented as sitting on his mother's lap; he also sometimes appears as Attis *pastor,* seated among his flock and playing the syrinx. In the classical authors, however, he is a hunter and son of a king. It is related that he contracted a marriage with the daughter of the King of Pessinus, or that he fell in love with the nymph Sagaritis, daughter of Sangarius. The goddess punished Attis severely for this misdemeanour, since she had saved him at his birth and later
p 247 (30) on had made him her inseparable lover. He fell into a frenzy, emasculated himself with a stone under a tree, and so died. This episode is represented on several monuments. The texts do not expressly tell us that Attis came to life again: Jupiter is able to grant to the sorrowing Cybele only that his hair shall grow for ever and that his little finger shall be ever in motion; hence Ovid tells us that he was metamorphosized into a pine tree. However, scenes of the emasculated Attis dancing indicate that the idea of resurrec- p 247 (29)
tion was added to the legend later. At the same time, Attis was portrayed as a god and became a symbol of the renewal of life in nature.

It is difficult to decide what belongs to the myth and what belongs to the cult, but there are certainly many marked similarities between myth and cult. The priests of Attis, the Galli, were until the time of Claudius of oriental origin; they were often eunuchs and they imitated Attis in their behaviour. The myth is also reflected in their festivities, which were held in the month of March. These important ceremonies in honour of Cybele and Attis were reorganized in the reign of Claudius, although we know of them only from later authorities. They preceded the already official festival of the *Megalensia* in April during which *ludi* were celebrated in the theatre and in the Circus Maximus and the upper classes offered a meal to the other citizens.

A holy fortnight

The order of events is recorded in the calendar of Philocalus for the year AD 354:

(1) March 15th: *canna intrat*. The *collegium* of the *cannephori* brought bunches of reeds from the River Almo to the temple on the Palatine. The nature of this rite is uncertain. The only explanation of it which we have is that given by John Lydus (*De Mensibus* IV 39), who wrote in the 6th century AD. According to him the rite was designed to ensure fertility for the coming year. During this ceremony the reed-bearers and the *archigallus*, the high priest, p 246
sacrificed a bull six years old ὑπὲρ τῶν ἐν τοῖς ὄρεσιν ἀγρῶν (*hyper tōn* (27)
en tois oresin agrōn), for the wild beasts in the mountains. The initiates abstained from certain foods, among others bread, since corn is the symbol of Attis.

(2) March 22nd: *arbor intrat*. Now the *collegium* of the *dendrophori* goes to the sacred forest and one of them cuts down a pine tree, the symbol of Attis. These tree-bearers bring the pine, which represents the corpse, in a procession to the Palatine and they adorn it with the symbols of Attis. Among these are musical instruments, and an Attis-like figurine is shown on a monument from Ostia. There follows the ritual of mourning and lamentation.

(3) March 24th: *Sanguem* or *Sanguis*. The Galli imitated Attis on this day by being castrated; others who were already completely initiated now scourged and wounded themselves, the blood being regarded as a fertilizing power, as in the Attis legend. On the same day the pine tree was brought into the innermost part of the temple and remained there till the next year.

(4) March 25th: *Hilaria*. Most scholars agree that this feast, which is only known from later evidence, was celebrated in honour of the resurrection of Attis (Firmicus Maternus *De Errore Profanarum Religionum 3*: *quem paulo ante sepelierant revixisse iactarunt*) or of the awakening of nature. One indication of this is the fact that on March 25th the day is for the first time longer than the night. Figurines of a dancing winged Attis may also point in the same p 247
direction. On the other hand P. Lambrechts is of the opinion that (29)
the *Hilaria* did not belong to the original festivals of the Magna Mater at Rome but were introduced only later. According to this theory the joy of the initiates has reference not to Attis but to the goddess, whose cult statue is about to be purified from the blood of the Galli. On this view the *Hilaria* are simply a preliminary festival for the *Lavatio*.

(5) March 26th: *Requietio*. Day of rest.

(6) March 27th: *Lavatio*. The statue of the goddess, together with the cult objects, is brought on a carriage to the River Almo outside the Porta Capena in order to be purified. The silver statue is described as having, in place of a head, the original black stone brought to Rome from Pergamum (or from Pessinus). The explanation of this ceremony depends upon that of the *Hilaria*. According to the resurrection theory, the *Lavatio* is most probably a purification after the *hieros gamos* with the awakened Attis; on the alternative theory, it is a purification of the statue after the *dies sanguinis*.

L. Cornelius Scipio Orfitus dedicated this altar in AD *295 to the 'Magna deum Mater' and to Attis. Below the inscription, which also mentions a 'taurobolium' and a 'criobolium', is a tiara and a staff. (2)*

(7) March 28th: *Initium Caiani.* The ceremonies of this day took place in the Phrygianum on the Vatican hill adjoining the circus of Caius Caesar 'Caligula' (hence the name).

In this temple on the Vatican a special ceremony was performed, particularly in the 4th century AD, although epigraphical evidence shows that it also took place at an earlier date at other places in the
f 2 Roman Empire. This rite was called *taurobolium*; and, according to the Christian poet Prudentius (*Peristphanon* lines 1006–50), it
p 246 (27) consisted in sprinkling the high priest (*archigallus*) with the blood of a bull. The bull was slaughtered on planks above a pit in which the priest was standing. After the aspersion he showed himself to the faithful, and they adored him because he had now been purified. According to inscriptions the *taurobolium* was sometimes replaced by the sacrifice of a ram (*criobolium*).

R. Duthoy has shown that the addition of the idea of purification in the 4th century AD was the final stage of an evolution in the conception of the rite. At the end of the same century we also find inscriptions speaking of a purification of the faithful through the *taurobolium* either for a period of twenty years or, in one exceptional case (*Corpus Inscriptionum Latinarum* VI 510), for ever (*in aeternum renatus*). At this time rebirth probably meant purification from sin, a preparation for a happy after-life. But in inscriptions of an earlier period, especially after the reform of the cult by Antoninus Pius, the ceremony is said to be performed *pro salute* of the Emperor. When the act is performed on behalf of an individual, his birthday is sometimes expressly mentioned. Some scholars interpret the word *natalicium* as meaning the day of initiation, but this is by no means certain.

Another interesting ceremony, performed specifically in connection with Attis, is known from a sacred formula transmitted by two Christian authors, Clement of Alexandria (*Protrepticus* II 15, 3) writing in the 2nd century, and Firmicus Maternus (*De Err. Prof. Rel.* 28, 1), writing in the 4th century. Clement gives the formula in Greek:

> ἐκ τυμπάνου ἔφαγον· ἐκ κυμβάλου ἐπίον·
> ἐκερνοφόρησα· ὑπο τὸν παστὸν ὑπέδυν
> (*ek tympanou ephagon; ek kymbalou epion; ekernophorēsa; hypo ton paston hypedyn*).

Clement therefore notes four consecutive acts, which he calls the 'symbols' of the initiation (τὰ σύμβολα τῆς μυήσεως *ta symbola tēs myēseōs*): 'I ate from the *tympanum*; I drank from the *cymbalum*; I carried the *cernus*; I went into the *pastos*.' Firmicus gives the formula in both Greek and Latin, but the two versions do not agree with each other completely. In the Greek version the man who is now in the interior of the temple says: ἐκ τυμπάνου βέβρωκα· ἐκ κυμβάλου πέπωκα· γέγονα μύστης Ἄττεως (*ek tympanou bebrōka; ek kymbalou pepōka; gegona mystēs Atteōs*). But the Latin text runs: *de tympano manducavi, de cymbalo bibi, et religionis secreta perdidici.* So Firmicus mentions three acts, the first two agreeing with those mentioned by Clement, the last differing: 'I ate from the *tympanum*; I drank from the *cymbalum*; I became an initiate of Attis (I learned fully the secrets of religion).'

What is eaten and drunk from the tambourine and the cymbal, the musical instruments of the cult, is not revealed. The texts mention only a sacred meal in a symbolic and in a restricted form respectively. According to Clement, the *mystes* carried the *cernus*, a vessel known from the Eleusinian mysteries but also used in the *taurobolium* ceremony. In this, the *cernus* contained either the *vires, i.e.* the testicles, of the slaughtered bull (*cf.* the *castratio* of the Galli), or the bull's blood. Entry into the *pastos* is suggestive of the interior of the temple, mentioned by Firmicus. Παστός means either bridal chamber, a bridal bed or an embroidered bed curtain. Hence most scholars explain this text as an allusion to a sacred marriage, *i.e.* unification with the deity, which, according to Clement, is the culminating act of the ceremony. According to Firmicus, however, the culmination is the fact that the *mystes* now becomes an initiate of Attis or that he is now in possession of a secret knowledge of the mysteries. Firmicus also mentions that the *mystes* is now *moriturus*, about to die, and this may mean either that he has undergone a preliminary voluntary death, as in the p 238–9
Isiac and Mithraic mysteries, or else that he is already an old man. (5)
Thanks to his initiation, and consequent unification, during his life-time, the *mystes* will be sure of recognizing his guiding deity in the after-life.

The Egyptian mysteries

In Egypt, where even the script was holy and where in religion it was the mysterious relationship between life on earth and life in the hereafter that overshadowed everything else, the myth of Osiris was current from the earliest times. In the age of the 18th p 238 (2)
dynasty (1580–1314 BC) there was already a special hymn in honour of the god, and we have information about his cult from a still earlier period. According to the Pyramid Texts, the divine couple Geb (earth) and Nut (the goddess of heaven) brought forth Osiris, the elder Horus or Harueris, Typhon or Seth, Isis and Nephthys on five consecutive days of the month of August. These are all members of a pantheon, consisting of nine deities, which was created by the priests of Heliopolis. Osiris became king of Upper and Lower Egypt and was paired with his sister Isis. But he was to be murdered by his brother Seth, the 'god of confusion'.

In the same saga the goddess Nut reassembles Osiris' limbs; Isis and her sister Nephthys go in search of their brother lamenting and crying, and with the aid of Re, the sun god, whose real name is known only to Isis, Osiris comes to life again. Harueris, who is p 237 (1)
now identified with Horus the son of Osiris and Isis, avenges his father in a terrible battle, and the story ends with a new period of Osiris' reign. As her name implies, Isis is also connected with the 'throne', *i.e.* with the royal power. In the older tradition Seth is, in some versions, married to Nephthys and, in throwing his brother 'down on his side', he is helped by Thoth. In some versions Osiris is succeeded by Horus, the future ruler on earth. Osiris is the god who manifests himself in vegetation and hence is connected with the inundation of the Nile. He also – and this aspect is most important – becomes king of the realm of death, though in the solar system of the priests at Heliopolis he also becomes king of heaven.

The priestess of Isis wears a fringed mantle gathered by a knot at the breast over a long tunic. The 'situla' and 'sistrum' are well-founded restorations. (3)

There are also certain festivals in honour of Osiris during which his death and resurrection were commemorated in a sacred drama. These celebrations were public and were therefore not mysteries in the strict sense. Like her consort Osiris, Isis played the part of the fertilizing power. Herodotus (II 40, 42) observed that this couple were the most fervently adored of all gods in Egypt.

It is not until the beginning of the 2nd century AD that the story of Osiris and Isis is told in its most complete form. Plutarch's version in his *De Iside et Osiride* (*cf.* also the splendid commentary by T. Hopfner) differs in certain respects from that of the Pyramid Texts, and Plutarch also gives more details.

(1) The body of Osiris is hewn into fourteen pieces, which are buried by Isis. This is the reason why Osiris' tomb is found in several places in Egypt.

(2) There now follow many details of the wanderings of Isis before she finds Osiris' corpse. Like Demeter, she had to become the servant of a royal family, and she seeks to give immortality to the royal child that is her charge.

(3) It is not Osiris' mother Nut, but Isis, who awakens the god to life again.

(4) In this version Thoth aids Isis, not Seth.

The rise of Isis

During the many centuries of the duration of the cult there was an evolution in the myth, and certain features also vary as between different cities. The goddess Isis gradually became the more important figure, and her cult spread outside her own country. In 333/2 BC the Athenians gave permission for a sanctuary to be built in her honour in the Piraeus, but the great expansion started during the reign of Ptolemy I (323–285 BC). As the successor of Alexander the Great, Ptolemy sought to reconcile the native Egyptian and the Greek genius; he therefore enlisted the aid of an Egyptian and an Eleusinian priest, Manetho and Timotheus, for reforming the cult of the Osiris-ized bull Apis at Memphis. The name of the god
p 238 (4) Sarapis is derived from the combination Osor-Hapi, that is of the god of the underworld and the deified bull. The Greek artist Bryaxis created the classical form of the cult-statue in which the hybrid nature of the god is clearly expressed. The god is seated on a throne and his bearded face resembles that of Zeus and Asklepios. As a god of vegetation he wears on his head a *modius*, a basket filled with fruit and decorated with olive branches. He has a sceptre in his left hand and his sovereignty over the underworld is indicated by the three-headed Cerberus at his side. The statue was adorned with precious stones and many hundreds of copies have been found all over the Mediterranean world.

In two exhaustive studies, Frazer has demonstrated that the upper classes in Egypt favoured the cult, that a splendid temple was soon built for Sarapis on the Rhacotis Hill in Alexandria and that, of the variant traditions of the origins of the cult in Tacitus *Histories* IV 83–4 and Plutarch *De Isid. et Osir.* 28, the tradition which holds that the cult arose in Memphis is the most probable. At the same time the Ptolemies constructed a large sanctuary for Isis on Philae Island in the Nile above Syene. Sarapis and Isis are now the divine couple and their son is Harpocrates. The p 237 (1)
latter, who is identified with Horus, is shown with his finger in front of or in his mouth and is thus the symbol of silence and secrets. This means that in the Hellenistic period the cult of Isis and Sarapis was transformed into a mystery-cult. The exact date of this transformation is unknown.

The cult spread throughout the Aegean area, partly through the influence of the Ptolemies but mainly through traders, mercenaries, priests and travellers (Frazer). In the 3rd century BC a private individual, hailing from Memphis, introduced the cult of Sarapis to Delos. There were societies of Sarapiastai, who held communal banquets in honour of their god. In his cult there are also θεραπευταί (*therapeutai*), societies of the faithful, equipped with priests (ἱερεῖς *hiereis*), torchbearers (δαδοῦχοι *dadouchoi*), temple attendants (ζάκοροι *zakoroi*), interpreters of dreams (ὀνειροκρίται *oneirokritai*) and p 240–1
singers of hymns (ἀρεταλόγοι *aretalogoi*). We hear too of κάτοχοι (9)
(*katochoi*), *i.e.* persons cloistered in the sacred precinct of the temple in some Serapea ('Sarapis' became 'Serapis' in Latin).

By the time when the Romans came into contact with Egypt Isis was already supreme. In the various hymns dedicated to her and mentioning her attributes, the goddess is given all possible epithets. In these aretalogies there is a general tendency towards monotheism. Isis is assimilated to the principal goddesses of other countries; she gives wealth to, and is queen of, the other deities. She is the common queen of heaven, of the underworld, of the earth and the sea (*Isis regina*). Like Sarapis, she is credited with having a health-giving power. She is πολύμορφος (*polymorphos* 'multiform') and πολυώνυμος (*polyōnymos, myrionyma,* the goddess with a multitude – a myriad – of names); she is the present, the past and the future, or in other words Tyche ('Fortune'). No wonder that the worship of this mighty goddess spread to Italy as early as the 2nd century BC (*e.g.* to Puteoli and to Pompeii).

From 58 to 48 BC the Senate tried to expel the Egyptian cults, and Augustus and Tiberius followed the same policy, since in their time too the political atmosphere at Rome was, in general, hostile to Egypt. But from the time of Caligula and Nero onwards the cults of Egypt began to spread over the whole Empire, and Isea especially were built in large numbers. In AD 38 the large Iseum p 239
and Serapeum was built on the Campus Martius in Rome. During (7–8)
the same period the worship of the goddess penetrated into the Imperial palace on the Palatine, and in the 3rd century AD a second Serapeum was built on the Quirinal.

Only a few of these temples of Isis in the Roman Empire have been studied in detail. The one at Pompeii, founded by an aristo- p 241
cratic family, is well known. The sanctuary consists of a rectangular (10)
area surrounded by a peristyle of 25 columns. Inside this area there is a temple with six altars and another building with decorations in stucco, which may be a *megaron* (sanctuary). Adjoining the temple there are two large and five small rooms. The two large rooms have been identified with the *ecclesiasterion* (the room for the mysteries), and the *sacrarium* (the room for the rites of initiation). As can be p 239
seen from the famous frescos of cult scenes found at Herculaneum, p 240–
the whole feeling of these temples is Egyptian. (9)

In the course of the year there were festivals with processions, p 238
not only inside these sanctuaries but also in the public streets. On

March 5th the rite of the *navigium Isidis* reopened the sailing season, which had closed in the previous November. Apuleius, in his *Metamorphoses* (*i.e. The Golden Ass* XI 8–17), gives a detailed description of the carnival-like procession during this ceremony. A ship dedicated to Isis was launched, and the procession halted at certain places where *pausarii* displayed the holy objects to be worshipped by the people. The drama of Isis and Osiris was performed from October 26th to November 3rd: the acts were the lamentations of Isis and her wanderings; the finding (*inventio*) of Osiris' body; its reassemblage with the aid of Anubis; and finally the *hilaria* after the resurrection (εὑρήκαμεν· συγχαίρομεν *heurēkamen; synchairomen* ('we have found him, we rejoice together'). The people
239 (6) must have been impressed by the Egyptian rites (*sacra Aegyptia*)
p 240–1 and by the priests in their black garments (μελανηφόροι *melanēphoroi*)
(9) with their shaven heads. The *hymnodi* accompanied their songs with the rattling of the *sistrum*, and the holy water of the Nile was specially venerated.

However, the real mysteries were reserved for performance in the innermost parts of the temple. The initiation ceremony was secret. Sometimes the initiate was summoned by Isis herself to become a *mystes* of the goddess. In the inscriptions there are frequent mentions of the words *ex visu, ex monitu* (from a vision, from an intimation), and this was the way in which the deity ordered the neophyte to come into a close personal relation with her and to become her slave in the sacred sacrifice. For the Isiac mysteries we have the testimony of Apuleius. Writing in the 2nd century AD, he describes the initiation of 'Lucius', who is really himself. The initiation is performed in three consecutive stages. Apuleius gives more details than any earlier source, but it seems that not even his revelations can satisfy modern scholarship, since the most diverse theories have been based upon what he has written.

Lucius experienced feelings of the most profound happiness as he gradually approached the goddess. He had been changed into an ass and was looking for help in this disastrous situation. Lo, Isis promised him deliverance. The first miracle took place during the procession on the occasion of the *navigium Isidis* in the harbour of Cenchreae. After eating roses he changed back into a human being. He was convinced that it was only the goddess who had been able to help him, and from that day on he spent his time within the precincts of the temple and passed many hours in contemplation of her statue.

During this period Lucius was preparing himself for the first initiation, the date of which had, however, to be fixed by the goddess herself. Finally, after a period of abstinence from forbidden food (*cibis profanis ac nefariis*), the hour of initiation arrived. His guide was a high priest (*sacerdos primarius*) bearing the name of Mithras. After a purification and a fresh period of ten days' abstinence from meat and wine, Lucius was dressed in a linen garment and was brought into the inner recesses of the sanctuary:

> *Accessi confinium mortis et calcato Proserpinae limine per omnia vectus elementa remeavi, nocte media vidi solem candido coruscantem lumine, deos inferos et deos superos accessi coram et adoravi de proxumo.*
>
> I approached the very gates of death and set one foot on Proserpine's threshold, yet was permitted to return, rapt through all the elements. At midnight I saw the sun shining as if it were noon; I entered the presence of the gods of the underworld and the gods of the upperworld, stood near and worshipped them (translation by Robert Graves in the Penguin Classics).

238–9 Lucius underwent a voluntary death and a new birth as Helios.
(5) The latter event is spoken of in the following lines of the story. Lucius, dressed as the sun, is shown to the crowd. 'That day was the happiest of my initiation, and I celebrated it as my birthday.' After Lucius had been in the hands of a blind fortune, Isis now becomes the true Fortune for him; he is converted to a definitely new life of purity.

Yet Isis summoned him to a second initiation into the mysteries of Osiris, 'the supreme Father of the Gods':

> I made all preparations, spent another ten days without eating meat, and submitted to having my head completely shaved, after which I was admitted to the nocturnal orgies of the Great God and became his illuminate (translation by Robert Graves).

In a third initiation Lucius had a vision of Osiris himself, the *deus deum magnorum potior et potiorum summus et summorum maximus et maximorum regnator Osiris*: 'God more powerful than the great gods, and chief of the more powerful gods, and greatest of the chief gods and ruler of the greatest gods, Osiris'. Lucius finally became a member of the *collegium* of the *pastophori* (the 'shrine-bearers') and a temple councillor.

The Syrian cults

As the contacts between Syria and Rome became closer, the Syrian cults began to spread throughout the Roman Empire, although in many cases the Syrian deities came to the capital not direct but via the Greeks. The cults were sometimes even favoured by the Emperors. Nero is said (Suetonius *Nero* 56) to have been a devotee p 335 (5)
of the Syrian Goddess for a certain period, and later the Syrian influence at the court of Septimius Severus and his immediate successors made the various Baals become very popular at Rome. The most important cult was that of the Syrian sun god. Towards the end of the 3rd century, during the reign of Aurelian (AD 270–5), this cult began to dominate all the rest.

It is generally accepted that the monotheistic tendency of these cults was what chiefly attracted the Romans to them. Each of the Lords of the various Syrian cities tried to become the one supreme Lord of Heaven, but none of them succeeded. These Baals were brought to the West by traders, by the army, and by the common people. It is noteworthy that most of the sanctuaries of Syrian Gods in Rome were situated in close proximity to the Tiber. It was only in some exceptional cases that these Syrian cults were represented as mystery-religions. The myth of Adonis, the beautiful young Lord of Byblos, was eminently suitable for a mystery-religion, but Adonis influenced the Romans only slightly. The Adonaea mentioned on the marble city-plan of Rome are probably not connected with his cult, as they have been thought to have been by some scholars.

A much more important part was played at Rome by the cult of Atargatis from Bambyce (Hierapolis), who came to the West p 243
together with her consort Hadad. The goddess was the leading (14–16)
member of this partnership; she was the Dea Syria *par excellence*. During the reign of Alexander Severus a separate temple was built in her honour in Rome, possibly in Trans Tiberim. Lucian's detailed description of her temple and worship in Hierapolis (Περὶ τῆς Συρίης Θεοῦ, written in the 2nd century AD) informs us that she was identified with other great goddesses such as Isis and Cybele. She was the fertilizing power of nature and at the same time the queen of heaven. On the monuments she is accompanied by two lions. Hadad, who was originally a thunder god and later on a sun god, is accompanied by two bulls. Lucian (*ibid.* XXXI) mentions that both statues were made of gold and that both deities were mounted on animals. Another parallel with Cybele is that, during the processions, the priests of the cult of Atargatis wounded themselves and collected money. The sacred prostitution in her temple in Syria was not to be found in the West.

Versions of Jupiter

In the other Syrian cults it was the god and not the goddess who played the more important role. These gods were generally the local protectors of a city and were originally fertility gods, and hence they were called Jupiter Damascenus, Jupiter Heliopolitanus, Jupiter Dolichenus, and so on. Later on they tended each to become the supreme god, and they were accordingly identified with the sun. They were often also weather gods, and they became the Lords of Heaven.

Jupiter Heliopolitanus, the ancestral god of Heliopolis, formed a trinity with Venus-Atargatis and their son Mercury-Semeios. Their most famous temple was at Baalbek, and it has been excavated. p 244–5
The building of it was started under the Seleucids, it was enlarged (22)
during the reign of Antoninus Pius (AD 138–61), and it was finally *f* 4
completed by his successors. The temple-complex consists of the propylaea, a hexagonal court surrounded by columns, a large square court with Corinthian porticos on three sides, and finally the temple proper of the triad. Next to this temple there was another

smaller sanctuary dedicated to Bacchus. It must be assumed that in this temple there was a *telesterium*, *i.e.* a room for initiation into the cult.

The main temple is also known from coins struck in the 3rd century AD. Macrobius, who was writing *c.* AD 400, has described the cult statue of Jupiter Heliopolitanus (*Saturnalia* I 23, 12):

> It is in fact a golden statue of beardless aspect, standing like a charioteer with a whip in its raised right hand, a thunderbolt and corn-ears in its left – attributes which all indicate the combined power of Jupiter and the sun (translation by A. B. Cook).

This statue was still in existence in the 6th century AD, and many copies of it are known in both bronze and marble. Some of them show the planets of the week or just the three royal planets, Mars, Jupiter and Mercury, on the God's clothing – the *ependytes*, a sort of cuirass (for the three royal planets, see also the decoration on the tomb of King Antiochus of Commagene on the Nemrud-Dagh). Oracles were given by Apollo in the temple of Hadad and Atargatis at Hierapolis. At Heliopolis Jupiter himself foretold the
p 335 (6) future. The oracle given to the Emperor Trajan when passing
through Baalbek during his campaign against Parthia shortly before his death (AD 117) became famous.

Archaeological finds have revealed that the Syrian cult was introduced into Rome even as early as the 1st century AD. A sanctuary which was officially recognized by the state was built in the Antonine period on the Janiculum in Trans Tiberim in honour of the Heliopolitan triad. This temple shows traces of work of various later periods, and this clearly demonstrates that the cult was most popular in the 2nd and 3rd centuries AD. Besides a cult for public worshippers there was also a secret mystery-cult. The temple had an east-west orientation, and in its final stage (4th century AD) it was divided into a central court with two adjacent rooms. The western part of the building consisted of three rooms of equal size for the worship of the Heliopolitan triad. A human skull was found in the central room and a triangular altar dedicated by a certain Doryphorus *pater*. This title possibly points to Mithraic influence. During the reigns of Marcus Aurelius and Commodus the most important person in the temple was a Syrian, M. Antoninus Gaionas. In the inscriptions he is said to have been a *cistiber* and a *deipnokritēs*. The latter title indicates that he presided over the sacred meals in the mysteries. The eastern part of the sanctuary seems to have been reserved for the secret part of the cult. Here there is a polygonal room and another room in which a triangular grave was found. Opposite the grave there is a niche in which a black statue, said to be that of a Pharaoh, was placed. The Egyptian influence is probably to be explained by the hypothesis that the statue really represents Osiris. However, the grave itself contained a gilt-bronze statue of an unknown male deity who has many affinities with the time god, since his body is entwined, seven times round, by a snake, which lays its head upon that of the god. The god is portrayed as a beardless youth in a hieratic attitude, but he wears an unusual dress, with a cap made from a single piece of material. It is possible that this statue is also meant to represent Osiris as a sun god who is identified with the son of Hadad and Atargatis and who in the mysteries was expected to awake after a period of sleep.

The most popular, in the Roman Empire, of all the Syrian cults p 242
was, however, that of Jupiter Dolichenus. He is often found in (11)
places where Mithraism had prepared the way. He originated at p 245
Doliche near the foot of the Antitaurus range, *ubi ferrum nascitur* (23)
('where iron is born'). On the monuments he is shown in association with a bull, and he brandishes the double axe and lightning – in fact he is a weather god who has become a sun god as well. On the many monuments known to us he is sometimes presented in military dress and standing upon a bull, with his *paredros* Juno, who is usually standing upon a hind. The goddess plays the less important role of the two. The presence of the twin Dioscuri, Castor and Pollux, who also often appear in his company, testifies to the eternal cosmic character of the supreme god, since the twins are the symbols of the two hemispheres. Sol and Luna often occur on Dolichenean reliefs too. The reliefs are sometimes triangular. Unlike the Mithraea, the Dolichena do not have a regular ground plan and there was a certain amount of freedom in the making of
the design. In Rome the largest sanctuary of Dolichenus was the p 242
one on the Aventine. The inscriptions also mention *triclinia* and (12)
cenatoria, provided, no doubt, for sacred meals of the devotees, who were organized in a *collegium* of *fratres*, as the Mithraists were. The occurrence of Isis and Serapis on Dolichenean monuments also shows that there was some Egyptian influence.

There are only a few mentions, in the West, of the gods of p 243
Palmyra. The most important of them are the two gods Malakbel (17–18)
and Aglibol, representing respectively the sun and the moon. p 245
There was a votive relief in Rome in honour of both deities as early (24)
as the 1st century AD. Malakbel was the more popular of the two, since he was the god who, as sun god, was the symbol of the ever renewing and resurrecting power.

At the beginning of the 3rd century AD Elagabalus, who was p 244
already the priest of the sun god of his native city Emesa, tried to (19–21)
establish his favourite in Rome as the sole sun god there, but he did not succeed. However, later in the same century the Emperor Aurelian, who had subdued the mighty state of Palmyra to Rome during the reign of Queen Zenobia, again introduced into Rome a Syrian sun god and built a large temple for him in the
capital. This *deus sol invictus* (divine unconquered sun) did succeed p 243
in becoming the chief sun god, although in a Roman and not in an (17)
Eastern form, and he absorbed the various tendencies toward sun-worship in the Roman Empire. Under Aurelian's successors, including Constantine, all this was to become involved in politics.

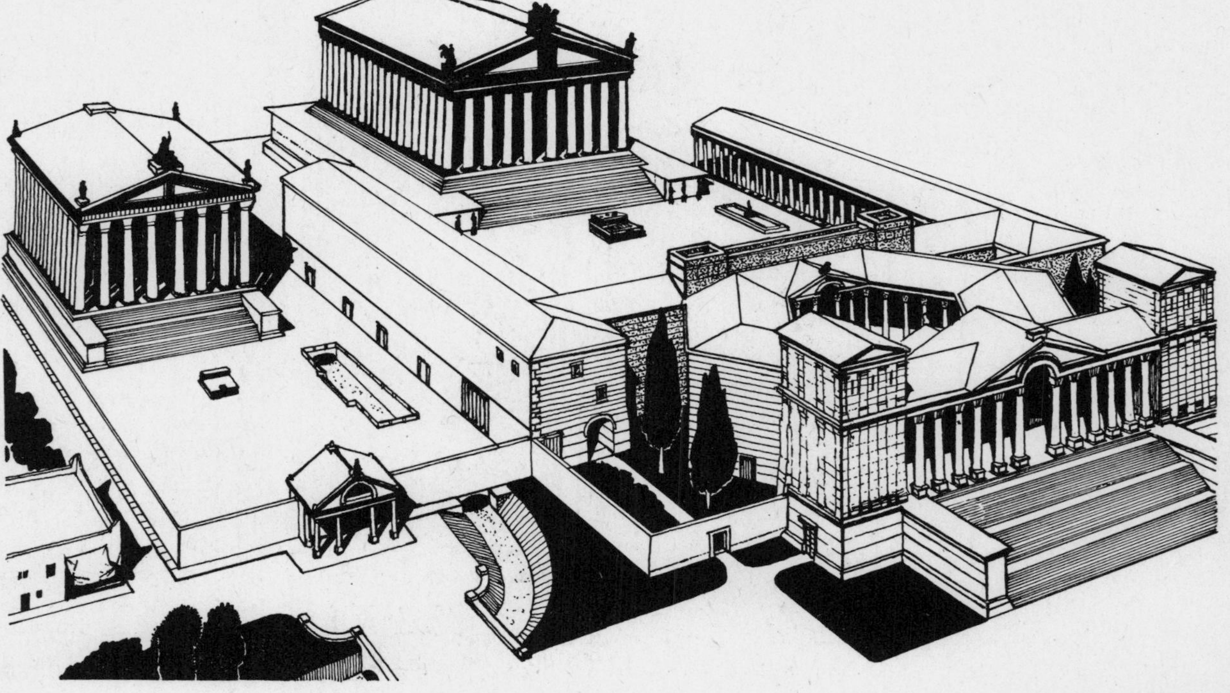

The Temple of Jupiter Heliopolitanus at Baalbek, seen in plate 22, was approached through a propylaea, a hexagonal columned court, and a large rectangular court with Corinthian porticos on three sides. To the left is the 'Temple of Bacchus'. (4)

XI

'THAT THE SCRIPTURE MIGHT BE FULFILLED'

CHRISTIANITY AS A JEWISH SECT

JEAN DANIÉLOU

'I have learned from written documents that,
until the siege of the Jews under Hadrian,
there had been in Jerusalem a succession of fifteen bishops,
all of whom are said to have been Hebrews of ancient stock.
In fact, the entire church of Jerusalem
consisted at that time of practising Hebrews.'

EUSEBIUS 'ECCLESIASTICAL HISTORY IV'

Primitive Christianity,
like the early history of Israel and Judah, has a form and structure very different from our conventional picture of it. In both cases the reason is the same: retrospective editing of historical texts by the victorious party. The conceptual framework of the New Testament writers led them to present history as a successful launching of Christianity upon the Graeco-Roman world after a little local difficulty, stemming from a handful of conservative 'Judaizers', and easily settled. In fact the documents contained in the New Testament relate mainly to the 'Hellenist' party. Until AD 70, when its centre at Jerusalem was destroyed, a Jewish form of Christianity was dominant, and the Hellenizing tendencies represented by Paul were followed only by a minority.

The Judaeo-Christian and 'pagano-Christian' Churches differed sharply from each other. In the former, Jewish religious regulations, such as circumcision, were still held to be obligatory, and the faith was expressed less in theological and metaphysical formulae than by a symbolic system of mystic letters and numbers, secret rites and signs, and esoteric names and doctrines. In recent years a number of relics of the Judaeo-Christians have been recovered in Palestine, some of which are shown on the following pages. They reveal that many Early Christian images, which are usually thought to be the legacy of Hellenistic Christianity, in fact derive from Judaeo-Christian milieux. Two examples are the martyr's crown of palm, which derives from those offered at the Feast of Tabernacles; while the Cross was linked in Judaeo-Christian minds with the ancient Jewish symbols of the plough and the axe, as several discoveries have recently confirmed.

Judaeo-Christianity had no future and has died out completely, so much so that its history and the relevant mentality are only now being painfully pieced together. The 'Church of the Circumcision', originally an equal partner, has vanished, leaving the field to the 'Church of the Gentiles'. Personifications of the two Churches are seen here, in the mosaics from the Church of Santa Sabina in Rome. (1, 2)

CLESIAEXCIR
UMCISIONE

ECLESIAEX
GENTIBUS

Jesus was a Jew, and he was punctilious in observing Jewish ritual, claiming that he had not come to destroy the Law and the prophets, but to fulfil them. Like other Jewish boys, he was presented in the Temple forty days after he was born, and he was received there by Simeon and Anna (above); on the steps of the Temple, which incidentally is shown as the pagan Temple of Roma Aeterna, are the two doves which were the parents' traditional offering. And throughout his life he was able to fulfil the requirements of the oral and written Law (for the apparent exceptions, see Chapter IX).

Much later, his work completed, he was seen as the 'star out of Jacob' which Balaam had foretold (left: Balaam and the star from the catacomb of Priscilla). It appears that this identification first arose in Judaeo-Christian circles at Damascus: the curiously reiterated association of Damascus with the prophecy in Christian *testimonia* provides confirmation. In exile at or near Damascus after 63 BC, the Zadokites had encountered strong opposition from the Magi. Their Judaeo-Christian successors claimed Balaam as a Magus and Christ as the fulfilment of his prophecy, just as at Athens Paul diplomatically appealed to Greek literature. (3, 4)

Despite his reverence for tradition, Jesus frequently found himself in conflict with the traditional Jewish authorities. His mission has much in common with reformist Jewish sects of the time, and two incidents in particular, the Cleansing of the Temple (above) and the Entry into Jerusalem (right), are redolent of Zealot ideology. However, despite the undoubted presence of Zealots among Jesus' disciples, his actions appear to have been free from the violence characteristic of this politico-religious sect. (5, 6)

Apocalyptic thought is the distinguishing characteristic of Judaeo-Christians. Angelology was their special study, and much attention was paid to passages where angels are mentioned. Interest centred on the opening chapters of Genesis. Below: God placing the Cherubim 'at the east of the Garden of Eden' from a 17th-century copy of the 5th-century Cotton Genesis, burnt in the 18th century, which probably originated in Syria. Left: a Byzantine version of the Archangel Michael who, together with Gabriel, Uriel and Raphael, is one of the angels most frequently mentioned. The inscription, no doubt continued on the other leaf, reads: 'Receive these gifts, and having learnt the reason. . . .' (7, 8)

Deriving from Babylonian modes of thought, angels provided a convenient means of covering up Israel's polytheistic past, though at the cost of some terminological confusion. Abraham's three visitors under the oak at Mamre, variously termed 'angels' and 'men', and later seen as a prefiguration of the doctrine of the Trinity, were probably originally Yahweh and two other deities. (9)

In Eastern thought, unlike Western, the Cross was not regarded primarily as a symbol of the Passion. In virtue of its material, it was a symbol of power – a sceptre or rod, while, in virtue of its form, it symbolized the radiation of the action of Christ throughout the cosmos. Sometimes the cross is combined with Christ's body (as on the gold plaque from the Crimea on p. 290). On this Coptic textile (right), the cosmos may be represented by the dark circle. The five white marks on the horizontal arm of the cross stand for the Five Wounds. (10)

The Coptic Church may have derived from Judaeo-Christian missions, although its origins remain obscure. Certainly Paul never reached Egypt, and the presence in Africa of large Jewish communities suggests that the earliest missionary activity there may have been Judaeo-Christian. Below: a Coptic Ascension. (11)

Condemned wholesale as heresy by Western theologians, Judaeo-Christianity was in fact articulated into several distinct branches, Millenarianism, Encratism, Ebionism, etc. Right: inscriptions relating to millenarian beliefs. They include, from left to right, the sign for 1000, the palm branch or Tree of Life, linked with millenarian themes in the Old Testament, and the harp of David to draw souls to the Kingdom of Heaven. The Greek letters each have a complex symbolic meaning. However Judaeo-Christianity had its own heterodoxy, *viz*. Gnosticism, which in turn became the first great pagano-Christian heresy. (12)

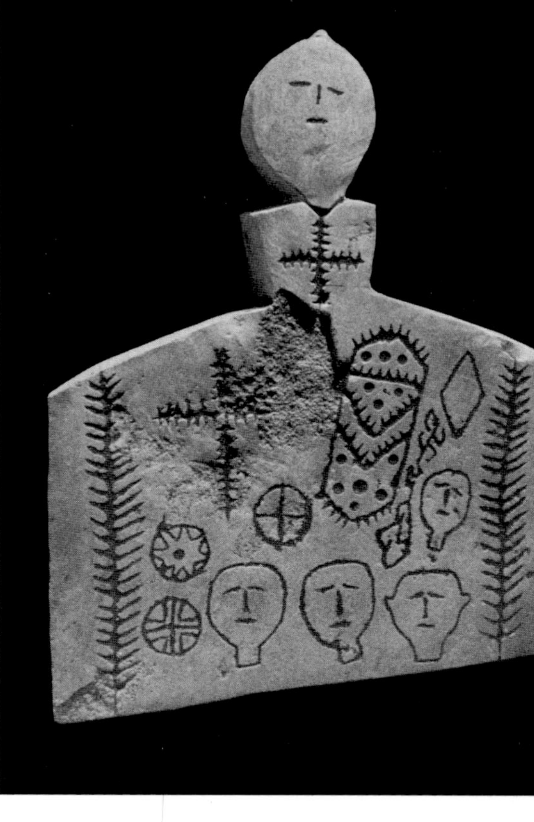

The Archontics were a Judaeo-Christian Gnostic sect existing in Palestine and Armenia about the middle of the 4th century. They believed in seven heavens each ruled by a prince (*archōn*), the seventh by Sabaoth, god of the Jews and father of the devil. Centre, far left: the ladder of heaven. In the eighth heaven dwells the supreme Mother of Light. Souls are the food of the princes, who cannot live without them. Having reached Knowledge (*gnōsis*), the soul flies to each heaven, petitions its prince, and finally reaches the supreme Mother. 'They deny the resurrection of the body,' says Epiphanius, 'admitting only that of the soul; they condemn baptism and reject participation in the Holy Mysteries as something introduced by the tyrant Sabaoth.'

Their funeral stelae, discovered recently in Hebron, have various shapes – statuettes, crosses, *scala cosmica*, cosmic rectangle – and, with certain variations such as the seven-stepped cosmic ladder, seem in the main to follow the common vocabulary of Judaeo-Christian symbolism.

The omnipresent Cross is the dominant motif in Judaeo-Christian art. Justin says, 'Nothing in the world can exist or make a whole without this sign,' and the Judaeo-Christians saw it everywhere – in the man, plant, axe, plough, serpent, star, square, triangle and even circle. In its original, Judaeo-Christian, form, the Cross did not signify only the Passion. As the last letter of the Hebrew alphabet, it was the Name of Yahweh, or Christ, and, traced as a 'seal' (*sphragis*) on the forehead, it signified that the believer belonged to him.

Note also: Centre far left: the *scala cosmica* with symbols of the heavens, including a rosette, palm branch and cross; at the top, two hills stand for the supreme Mother; below her is one of the princes flanked by two Cherubim; below that, an anchorite's hut bearing an image of the deceased; a bent sword; mythical animals; fifteen dots are receptacles for the elements. Centre left: two notched crosses. Centre right: this statuette bears the *sphragis* on head and shoulders (not visible in our picture); a bird perhaps standing for Christ; mystic letters; at the bottom a key and the Greek letter S (C) for Saviour. Centre far right: note the mystic flask. Below far left: three phalli symbolize the life-giving power of the Cross. Below left: the ten faces surmounted by a notched cross are probably funerary portraits of the deceased. Below right: the incised figure on the cross bears three of the eighteen dots on its body. (13–19)

The eastern half of the Mediterranean largely sets the geographical bounds of Judaeo-Christianity. On this page some of the surviving Christian monuments from this area appear. They show some oriental features, as well as those derived from Graeco-Roman iconography. Chief among such monuments is the house-church at Dura Europus – completely Eastern in plan and the only house-church to survive in anything like its original state. Most of its unsophisticated frescos differ in subject matter from contemporary Western art and, as regards style, display the 'Parthian' predilection for frontal heads. Left: the naturalistic Good Shepherd from the lunette above the baptismal font is also a Western motif. (20)

Five women the total number mentioned in the *Diatessaron* – approach the Holy Sepulchre (below, left), which is shown as a Roman sarcophagus (only two of the women, and traces of a third, now remain). They stand in an oriental, rigidly frontal, pose, and carry torches, the flames black to indicate that they are dimmed by the light of the angel (the star), who bade the women: 'Be not affrighted: Ye seek Jesus of Nazareth, which was crucified: he is risen; he is not here; behold the place where they laid him.' (21)

The Cross on this 5th-century church pavement at Shavey Zion (above right) is flanked by pomegranates, symbols of eternal life (*cf.* the Hinton St Mary mosaic on p. 173, which may show Christ similarly flanked). Below are three chevrons, standing for Golgotha, and two stylized fish. It was eventually thought unsuitable to place the Cross on the floor, where it might be trodden upon, and the practice was forbidden by an Imperial decree of AD 427. (22)

The fish as a Christian symbol is usually thought to derive from the Greek word for fish (*ichthys*), an acrostic of 'Jesus Christ, Son of God, Saviour'. However there may also be a Jewish derivation: the living water, which was a figure of God, was thought to contain living creatures, or fish. 'These waters that issue forth . . . shall go into the sea . . . and the waters shall be healed. And every living creature that creepeth whithersoever the torrent shall come shall live; and there shall be fishes in abundance' (Ezekiel xlvii 8–10). Fish and a basket of bread (below, right) come from the church at Tabge, founded on the supposed site of the miracle of loaves and fishes. The same objects serve as Eucharistic motifs in the Roman catacombs. (23)

'When I consider Thy heavens, the work of Thy fingers, the moon and the stars which Thou hast ordained. . . .' The sun, moon and stars, the zodiac and the seasons on this synagogue mosaic from Beth Alpha (right) symbolized the divinely governed order of nature. The zodiac also symbolized the twelve patriarchs, who were themselves assimilated to stars. This becomes clear from a passage in Philo: 'The twelve gems [on the high priest's breastplate] are figures of the zodiac. They are the symbol of the twelve patriarchs, with the object of making them stars and as it were giving each its own constellation.' The zodiac is attested in synagogues as early as the 4th century AD, but that at Beth Alpha appears to be influenced by the mosaic, superior to it in style, in the monastery of the Lady Mary at Bethshean (below right), and so must be dated after AD 569. The chariot of the sun in the central roundel recalls Elijah's chariot, symbol of the soul's ascent to God. (24, 25)

The twelve months together with the sun and the moon from Bethshean (right). It is not known when the custom began in the East of using the Roman names of the months and transliterating them into Greek. (25)

'There is one only true prophet and we, the twelve apostles, proclaim his word. It is he who is "the acceptable year", and we, the apostles, are the twelve months' (*Clementine Recognitions* IV 37). The Christians brought the development of the zodiac-months-patriarchs equation to its culmination, transferring it from the floor to the dome, which was particularly suited to this subject, in the baptisteries of the Orthodox and Arians at Ravenna. The Arian mosaic (above) is a rationalized version of the Orthodox. It is controversial how far it reflects their divergences in doctrine. The main differences are that the apostles process towards the *hetoimasia* (preparation of the throne), while Christ is beardless. A personification of the River Jordan accompanies the scene. (26)

The Church plays a remarkable role in Judaeo-Christian literature, and one of the images expressing the mystery of her grandeur was the vine, whose antiquity is attested by its appearance on Jewish coins (above). A Judaeo-Christian mosaic from Nebo in Transjordan (right) reveals why the Santa Costanza mosaics (below) were acceptable to the Christians too when they adapted the building. As Hippolytus says, 'The spiritual vine was the Saviour. The shoots and vine branches are his saints, those who believe in him. The bunches of grapes are his martyrs; the trees which are joined with the vine show forth the Passion; the vintagers are the angels; the baskets full of grapes are the Apostles; the winepress is the Church; and the wine is the power of the Holy Spirit.' (27–9)

CHRISTIANITY AS A JEWISH SECT

JEAN DANIÉLOU

THE OFFICIAL documents which tell us about the origins of Christianity – the writings of the New Testament – were written in Greek and are connected with Hellenistic Christianity. This has been a long-persisting obstacle to the recognition that Christianity, which arose in a Semitic milieu, was, to start with, deeply involved both sociologically and culturally in the Jewish world. The rediscovery of this Jewish Christianity is one of the achievements of recent scholarship; it was made possible by the combined effect of a number of discoveries concerning both the Jewish culture of that p 84–5 age – illustrated by the Qumran manuscripts – and the Judaeo– (11–16) Christian culture – illustrated by the manuscripts found at Nag Hammadi and by the Judaeo–Christian inscriptions in Palestine.

The pioneer scholars were each concerned with a particular aspect of the problem. S. G. F. Brandon[1] and Bo Reicke[2] placed Early Christianity in the context of the anti-Roman agitation of the Zealots. Herbert Braun studied its links with the Essene movement.[3] H.-J. Schoeps identified it with Ebionism.[4] Marcel Simon defined Judaeo–Christianity by its adherence to ritual observances.[5] I characterized it as a particular kind of culture, the apocalyptic kind.[6] These approaches are all valid,[7] and help to arrive at a description of the full complexity of Judaeo–Christianity, a complexity which reflects that of contemporary Judaism.

Points of departure

p 264–5 Christianity belonged to the Jewish world because its founder did: (3–6) born of a Jewish mother, Jesus spoke Hebrew and Aramaic like all Jews at the time. He was circumcised on the eighth day after his birth, observed the Sabbath, and went to worship in the Temple; he was well versed in the Jewish Scriptures and he used the rabbinical method of teaching, as Gerhardsson has shown.[8] The difficulty lies in locating him in the complex currents of the Judaism of his time. The Gospels make it clear that he ran into a collision with the Sadducaean aristocrats, who stood for a compromise with the Romans who were in occupation; but he also opposed the Pharisees; he reproved them for their casuistry and their compromises. The movement which he created round himself had affinities with the radical reformist movements of the Zealots and the Zadokites, yet was independent of them.

The essential characteristic of the Zealots, whose ideals were both religious and military, was their implacable determination to liberate the Holy Land from the yoke of a pagan occupation. Josephus' picture of them does them less than justice. There are some indications that Jesus shared this ambition; there were Zealots among his disciples, and some dramatic acts of his that are p 265 reported in the Gospels, such as the cleansing of the Temple and (5, 6) the triumphal entry into Jerusalem, are counterparts of Zealot demonstrations. Brandon is no doubt right in saying that Mark, and the other evangelists after him, writing, as they were, for a Roman audience, had every reason to play down Jesus' sympathy for the revolt against Rome, rather than to underline it.[9] All the same, Jesus' possible sympathy for the Zealots stopped short of action. In his activities there was none of the violence that was characteristic of theirs.

Points in common with the Zadokite movement are more striking. Jesus shared with them the fundamental idea that the end of the world was at hand, and like them he interpreted Old Testament prophecies in that sense. However, granting that the context is in truth the same, Braun has convincingly shown that the attitudes were different.[10] For the Zadokites, reform meant a stricter observance of the Law; for Jesus it meant going beyond the Law. The Zadokites' movement was separatist. They held that the Temple had been profaned. Jesus addressed his message to all, and went to worship in the Temple like the majority of the Jews. The p 80–81 Zadokites saw 'the Last Things' through the eyes of Ezekiel: the (2–9) people of Israel were to achieve a state of ritual sanctity and were to be installed in a purified terrestrial Jerusalem, world without end. The goal of Jesus' vision was the everlasting Kingdom of God, preceded by the resurrection – a kingdom to which all are called.

What is certain is that the context of Jesus' preaching is to be found in these reformist movements. He never attacked them, as he did attack the Sadducees and the Pharisees; and this is why the Zadokites are never mentioned. We have to start from these movements if we are to understand his activity by locating it in its place in history. It went far beyond these movements in its universalism and in its radicalism, but it presupposes their existence. This explains the difficulty that Early Christianity found in extricating itself from this political and religious context and in bringing out, to the full, the implications of Jesus' teaching.

The conflict between official Judaism and the reformist Jewish movements is the framework within which the trial and death of p 224 Jesus must be envisaged. They end the first phase of the history of (19–23) Judaeo–Christianity, which is the ministry of Jesus himself. The next phase opens when, after his resurrection, the little group of apostles which he had gathered round himself begins to organize itself. They saw in the resurrection of Jesus 'the Last Things' proclaimed by the prophets of Israel, and therefore they called upon all Jews to recognize this epoch-making event. They regarded themselves as being the true Israel, the community of the New Testament. Actually, they ran into a collision with a persistent hostility on the part of official Judaism, as represented by both the Sadducees and the Pharisees. In consequence they were no more than a minority group, on a par with the other Jewish dissenting sects, but they continued to be a Jewish sect all the same. They continued to be faithful observers of the Law and of the worship in the Temple.

This situation did not create any problems as long as the Christian community consisted solely of Jews; but very soon the question arose of the attitude to be adopted towards converts from the pagan world. A very early practice, which was sanctioned in the year 49 by the Council of Jerusalem, was to exempt pagan converts from circumcision and from all Jewish observances except the so-called 'precepts given to Noah', but many Judaeo–Christians refused to countenance this concession. Moreover, a more radical current of opinion, represented by Paul, held that even the Judaeo– p 310 Christians themselves were not bound by the rules of ritual purity (*f1*) and that, in particular, they could sit at table with uncircumcised Christians. This is the significance of the incident at Antioch in the same year 49. Paul regarded circumcision, the Sabbath, and the worship in the Temple as being obsolete from now on, even for Jews. Christianity had to liberate itself from its religious and political ties with Judaism if it was to open its doors to the gentiles.

In the political and religious climate of the rising tide of Jewish revolt against Rome, Paul's attitude was bound to seem treasonable to the Judaeo–Christians, since these remained loyal Israelites. We find this in later Judaeo–Christian literature: in the writings of

Pseudo-Clement, Paul is 'the enemy', and the Judaeo–Christian document used by the Tabhbit Dalà accuses Paul of tactical duplicity.[11] From this date onwards a rift began to open between Judaeo–Christians and pagano-Christians, and this rift was never re-closed. But the essential fact for us, a fact which Brandon has emphasized, is that until the year 70 the Judaeo–Christian wing of the Church was the majority and Paul remained isolated.

The Christian Caliphate

In the first place, this is true of Jerusalem. At a very early stage, opposing tendencies came to light there. As early as the years 35–6, 'the Hellenists' – a group for whom the author of the Acts makes no secret of his sympathy – went into action against 'the Hebrews', *i.e.* the Judaeo–Christians who observed the Law. One of the distinctive marks of 'the Hellenists' was their rejection of the worship in the Temple. In this point they were akin to the Essenes and were precursors of Pauline radicalism. But they ran into a collision with the hostility of the Jewish authorities. Their leader, Stephen, was stoned to death and 'the Hellenists' had to leave Jerusalem for Samaria and Antioch. Thus Christianity in Jerusalem remained in the hands of the Judaeo–Christians, whose loyalty to the Law earned them the sympathy of the Jewish authorities.

The undisputed head of the 'Hebrew' Christian community was James, the brother of the Lord. Side by side with the Apostles, p 273 (26) James was the most important personality in the Christian community at Jerusalem. When Paul went to Jerusalem in the year 41 he saw Peter and James; at the council in the year 49, James was the only speaker besides Peter. We must take some account of Eusebius' statement that 'Peter, James, and John did not reserve for themselves the leadership of the local church of Jerusalem; they chose James the Just to be bishop' (*Ecclesiastical History* II 1, 3). The Apostles regarded themselves as being responsible for the universal Church, but placed the local churches in the care of prominent men (*First Clement* 44, 3), to whom they delegated their powers. For instance, Peter, during his lifetime, entrusted the church of Rome to Linus and Anacletus according to Rufinus.

We should not be wrong in seeing in James the founder of Judaeo–Christianity who, as such, remained deliberately committed to Judaism, in confrontation with Pauline Christianity. James' role is consequently the leading one in all Judaeo–Christian literature. According to the *Gospel of the Hebrews*, which is the product of a Judaeo–Christian community in Egypt, it was to James that the risen Christ first appeared. Clement, in his *Hypotyposeis*, is transmitting an Egyptian Judaeo–Christian tradition when he places James, side by side with John and Peter, among the recipients of the *gnōsis* of the risen Christ. The *Clementine Recognitions*, the *Second Apocalypse of James* (discovered at Nag Hammadi), a comment of Hegesippus preserved by Eusebius, the Edessan *Gospel of Thomas* – these authorities all agree in making James the outstanding figure in the Judaeo–Christian Church. Moreover, James was a typical Judaeo–Christian in his assiduous attendance at the Temple and in his taking of the vow of a Nazerite.

James was, of course, 'a brother of the Lord'. One of the most curious features of the church at Jerusalem is the position that was held in it by Jesus' family. James' successor was Simeon, the son of Cleopas, a cousin of the Lord (*Ecc. Hist.* III 11; and Eusebius quotes from Hegesippus the statement that 'those who were called the brothers of the Saviour governed the entire church, in virtue of their being martyrs and relatives of the Lord' (*Ecc. Hist.* III 32, 5–6). It would seem to be very much in line with Semitic customs that Jesus' family should have assumed this position in the Judaeo-Christian community. Stauffer calls it 'the Caliphate'.[12] This dynasticism is likewise to be found in the Zealot movement, and later in Islam. The importance of Jesus' family has been overlooked by a number of commentators: they have regarded the Apostolic preaching as being the sole source of the Gospels, whereas in truth the Gospels have a second source – particularly for the gospels of Jesus' childhood and genealogy – in the archives of his family.

There can be no doubt that the oldest documents of Christian literature, which have not got beyond being simply Christian exegeses of the Jewish Bible, are products of these Judaeo–Christians, who were at home with both the Jewish and Christian orthodoxy. We find in Barnabas, Justin Martyr, Clement of Alexandria and Irenaeus fragments of *midrashim* of Exodus and Ezra, Isaiah, Jeremiah, and Ezekiel, which are counterparts of the rabbinical *midrashim* of the same period. We also find *targumim* where the text of the Scripture itself is both translated and interpreted, and where there is no division between Scripture and oral tradition. Rabbinical exegesis and, in the case in point, that of Qumran especially, has its Christian analogue in the *pesher* in which the commentary on a prophetic versicle takes the form of demonstrating its fulfilment in actual events. Some of these exegeses go back to Christ himself.

Judaeo–Christianity maintained its supremacy in the church in Jerusalem and in Palestine until the last Jewish revolt was crushed p 75 (*f 6*) by Hadrian. Eusebius writes:

> I have learned from written documents that, until the siege of the Jews under Hadrian, there had been in Jerusalem a succession of fifteen bishops, all of whom are said to have been Hebrews of ancient stock. In fact, the entire church of Jerusalem consisted at that time of practising Hebrews (*Ecc. Hist.* IV 5, 2).

Eusebius calls them 'the bishops of the circumcision' (*Ecc. Hist.* IV 5, 3). In Hadrian's time, Jerusalem became a Greek city and, from then on, its church was governed by Greeks. Groups of Judaeo–Christians did survive, however, particularly at Hebron and at Nazareth. They remained especially attached to the places that played a part in Jesus' family tradition, until these places were rediscovered, as they were in the 4th century, by the pagano-Christians. The Judaeo–Christians' places of worship, funerary p 268–9 (12–19) steles, and liturgical formulae have been brought to light recently by Fathers Testa and Bagatti.[13] But the Judaeo–Christians were now cut off from the official church of Jerusalem and were regarded as being Judaizers, so they eventually died out.

Missions to the Jews

It was not only in Jerusalem and in Palestine that Judaeo–Christianity was dominant during the first century of the Church. Everywhere the Judaeo–Christian mission seems to have developed before the Pauline mission; this is the explanation of the repeated references to conflict in Paul's Epistles. He met the same opponents everywhere – in Galatia, at Corinth, at Colossae, at Rome, at Antioch. By putting together the facts given in the Pauline Epistles and the information supplied by the archaic non-canonical Christian literature we can form some idea of the expansion of Judaeo–Christianity. The Christian missionaries – on the evidence of Paul's Epistles themselves – preached in the first instance to the Jews in synagogues. The earliest Christian communities therefore consisted everywhere of Judaeo–Christians. It was not till later that communities of pagan converts took shape. The coexistence of these two communities was one of the fundamental problems which confronted Christianity before the year 70.

The principal centres of the Judaeo–Christian church are known. The coast of Palestine and Syria, from Gaza to Antioch, seems to have been the first field of Peter's missionary activity, on the evidence of the Acts of the Apostles and the Clementine literature. The Acts testify to Peter's links with the Judaeo–Christian community at Antioch. For Asia Minor, the Epistle to the Galatians and the Epistle to the Colossians bear witness to the existence of practising Judaeo–Christians there. Furthermore, Papias testifies that in Phrygia a Millenarianist form of Judaeo–Christianity p 268 (12) persisted until the end of the 2nd century. In Greece, I Corinthians reveals a confrontation between the Pauline community, a community attached to Peter, and another, which was more self-consciously Judaeo–Christian and was attached to Apollos. That Rome was an important centre of Judaeo–Christianity is indicated by the very archaic liturgy preserved in the *Epistle of Clement* and by the catechetic traditions preserved in the *Shepherd of Hermas*. Both Suetonius and Tacitus took the Christian community to be a Jewish sect. Paul may have been the victim of these Judaeo–Christians in Rome, as Cullmann has suggested.[14]

We have no direct information on the origins of Christianity in Africa, but the importance of the Jewish community there suggests that the earliest Christian missionary activity in Africa was Judaeo–Christian. It is possible, as Braun has shown,[15] that local Christians may have used the Jewish translation of the Bible into Latin.

The decoration on this Coptic textile suggests an abstracted human body with raised hands. In the centre of the medallion, which may represent the head, is a cross. (*1*)

p 292 African Christianity appears to be the result of a synthesis of the
(20) Semitic and the Latin spirit; hence its robust originality in contrast
to Roman Christianity, which bore the stamp of Hellenism. The
p 267 origins of the Egyptian Church are equally obscure; but one thing
(10, 11) is certain: Egypt lay outside the field of Paul's mission. Brandon[16]
p 288–9 and Hornschuh[17] give convincing reasons for seeing in the
(6–10) Egyptian Church the product of a Judaeo-Christian mission. The
Gospel of the Hebrews and the traditions recorded by Clement of Alexandria derive from this original Judaeo-Christianity in Egypt, which antedates the emergence of Alexandrian Christianity with its Hellenistic inspiration.

The Judaeo-Christian communities in the Mediterranean area constituted the main body of the Church until the year 70. During this period, pagano-Christianity continued to be a minority form of the religion, and its legitimacy continued to be contested. The
p 54–7 Jewish War and the fall of Jerusalem in the year 70 reversed the
(21–8) situation. The Jews were now discredited throughout the Empire,
and the Christians tended to draw away from them. The Hellenistic Christian communities gained the upper hand. Paul triumphed posthumously: Christianity disengaged itself socially and politically from Judaism, and became a third force. All the same, until the year 140 and until the repression of the last Jewish revolt, Judaeo-Christianity continued to be dominant culturally. This was the great age of Judaeo-Christian literature. In Jerusalem the family of Jesus retained its authority. As late as about the year 140 Justin Martyr mentions the existence of circumcised Christians.

So far we have considered the expansion of the Judaeo-Christian mission in the Mediterranean. But there was another area, the regions to the east of Palestine, which was a preserve of this mission and which later enjoyed a special position because it had not been touched by the mission of Paul. The Judaeo-Christian origin of the Church there is all the more certain because the local language in general use was Aramaic, the language of the Judaeo-Christians of Jerusalem. The Acts of the Apostles naturally tell us nothing about the preaching of Christianity in these regions, except for the story of the baptism of Queen Candace's eunuch, who was an Arab. We can, however, catch glimpses from later traditions. These must be carefully sifted, but they do preserve some authentic historical elements, in spite of the misrepresentation of the true picture in the Western version of it.

The first region which concerns us is Transjordan. Here we find first Judaeo-Christians from Jerusalem, who had taken refuge in Pella even before 70. Pella was the birthplace of the 2nd-century apologist Aristo, who was a Jew in race and culture. Judaeo-Christian emigration certainly increased with the Hellenization of Palestine after the year 140. These Judaeo-Christian emigrants lost touch very soon with the Great Church; they are Epiphanius' 'Nazarenes', who, he tells us, observed the Sabbath and practised circumcision. Their gospel was written in the Hebrew alphabet. Fragments of it have come down to us through St Jerome, and these fragments show that it was independent of our Greek Gospels. The fact that it is quoted in Tatian's *Diatessaron*, in the *Gospel of Thomas*, in Ephrem, and in the works of Macarius shows that this Gospel was current throughout the area of the Judaeo-Christian mission.[18]

Other more curious groups existed in Transjordan and in Syria. Irenaeus mentions the Ebionites, who were strict Judaeo-Christians but who, in addition, took daily baths for purification, used unleavened bread and water for the Eucharist (rejecting wine), held a dualist doctrine, and saw in Christ the true prophet, aided by an archangel. The Judaism of these Judaeo-Christians was closely akin to that of the Zadokites. To identify them with the Judaeo-Christians of Jerusalem, as Schoeps does, is as erroneous as it is to make them into Gnostics. The baptist form of Judaeo-Christianity was also represented by the Elkasaïtes.

The Christianity which developed in Osrhoëne and Adiabene was certainly also a product of the Judaeo-Christian mission. Though the legend, reported by Eusebius, that Christ himself had sent missionaries to King Abgar of Edessa is based in reality on the
conversion of a different Abgar at the end of the 2nd century, it is *f 2*
nonetheless true that the tradition that the region of Edessa had been evangelized by the Apostle Thomas has some foundation in historical fact. The earliest documents we have on Edessan Christianity – namely the *Gospel of Thomas*, the *Song of the Pearl* contained in the *Acts of Thomas*, and the *Odes of Solomon* – go back, in part, to the end of the 1st century and display the characteristic features of Judaeo-Christianity. One of the marks of Syriac Judaeo-Christianity is its asceticism, and this remained strongly
pronounced until the 4th century. But the curious work of Bar- *f 7*
desanes, dating from the end of the 2nd century, indicates that there were variant forms of Judaeo-Christianity in Edessa itself.[19] Beyond Edessa, Christianity penetrated into Adiabene, where there was an important Jewish community, and no doubt reached India very soon, since Pantaenus, writing in the mid-2nd century, asserts that he found in India a gospel in a Hebrew script.

Abgar of Edessa, the first Christian king. (*2*)

Gnōsis

In our survey of the area covered by Judaeo-Christianity during the first Christian century, running from the year 40 to the year 140, we have observed incidentally the astonishing variety of its forms. This variety corresponds to a large extent to the varieties that are to be found in contemporary Judaism. There was the rabbinical Christianity of Jerusalem, with its attachment to the
Temple, its *targumim*, and its *midrashim*; there was the Millenarianist p 268
Christianity of Phrygia; there was the Hellenistic Judaeo- (12)
Christianity of Clement of Rome; there was the Encratite Judaism of the Edessians; and there was the baptist Judaeo-Christianity of the Ebionites. All these diverse types of Early Christianity have been clearly distinguished by W. Bauer.[20] Sometimes they co-existed in the same region: we have already seen the 'Hebrews' and the 'Hellenists' coexisting in Jerusalem. Rome had Judaeo-Christians of both Greek and Semitic culture, a phenomenon that has its counterpart in the Jewish communities at Rome which we know from their cemeteries. At Edessa the milieux which produced the *Gospel of Thomas*, the *Odes of Solomon*, Tatian, and Bardesanes were all different from each other.

These different manifestations of Christianity were not understood by the western heresiologists. These, from Justin Martyr and Irenaeus onwards, judged them in terms of Pauline Christian orthodoxy, which, by their day, had triumphed. Millenarianism, Encratism, and Ebionism were regarded in these Western Christian milieux as being heresies; but this was a retrospective application of a later norm to the period which concerns us. Judaeo-Christianity was not, however, exempt from heterodoxy in the p 268–9 strict sense of the word. I am referring to Gnosticism. There have (13–19) been wide differences of opinion about the basis of this movement, which played so large a role from the 2nd to the 4th century. Too often it has been merely identified with the existence of a *gnōsis*, which is a standard feature of Judaeo-Christianity to which we shall return. Some scholars have seen in it a doctrine of Hellenistic origin – a popular form of Platonic dualism. Connections have been seen with Egyptian religion, with Iranian dualism, and with Babylonian astrology. The discovery at Nag Hammadi of genuine Gnostic documents has shown that the essence of these is derived from a Jewish milieu.[21]

In so far as Gnosticism has a doctrine, this consists in a revolt against Yahweh, the god of Israel, and against the creation which is his handiwork and the Law which is his commandment. Yahweh, Gnostics held, was an inferior demiurge, the creator of a world that was a failure. *Gnōsis* is, for the Gnostics, the revelation of the true god and the possibility of a return to him by breaking with the world and with the Law. This radical dualism, in which the stellar universe itself is held to be demonic, is bound up with a particular historical situation, namely a crisis of the Jewish spirit which, after a period of intense eschatological expectation, had met in the end with an unparalleled historical catastrophe. This Jewish reaction quickly communicated itself to Judaeo-Christians, who set the god revealed by Jesus Christ in the same radical opposition to the God of Israel.

Ancient historians are thus no doubt right in following Simon and Menander, who trace the origins of Gnosticism back to a heterodox Jewish community at Samaria. Satornilus gave Gnosticism its definitive shape at Antioch at the end of the 1st century. The oldest documents found at Nag Hammadi – the *Apocrypha of John*, the *Apocalypse of Adam*, and the *Book of the Great Seth* – are evidence of this barely Christianized Jewish Gnosticism. In the middle of the 2nd century, Gnosticism found its great masters in Egypt with the advent of Basilides and Valentinus, who spread the p 319–22 movement throughout the Mediterranean world. However, from (1–10) Antioch Gnosticism also spread eastward, and there, with the advent of Mani in the 3rd century, it achieved an extraordinary expansion.

Thus since the beginning of our era Judaism, together with its unconventional versions, has been the crucible of the great universalist religions of modern times – rabbinical Judaism, Christianity, Manicheanism, and Islam.

Apocalyptic and Judaeo-Christianity

Now that we have set out the early history and geography of Judaeo-Christianity, we have to bring out its distinctive features. First of all, the term 'Judaeo-Christianity' can be used either in a narrower or in a broader sense. It can be confined to the church of Jerusalem, which was composed of circumcised Christians governed by Jesus' family. This is what Schoeps does when he restricts the use of the term 'Judaeo-Christian' to the Ebionites, in whom he sees – though this is disputable – the heirs of the church of Jerusalem. This usage is, however, obviously too narrow. An alternative is to use the term 'Judaeo-Christians' to mean Christians who remained faithful to Jewish observances: the Sabbath, circumcision, the worship in the Temple. This definition is perfectly p 80–81 acceptable. It corresponds fairly closely to the original Judaeo- (2–9) Christianity, represented by the opponents of Paul. This flourished until about the year 140. But at a very early stage the observance of 'Jewish' customs came to be regarded, even in Semitic circles, as being incompatible with the Christian faith. The *Epistle of Barnabas*, the Letters of Ignatius of Antioch, and the works of Justin Martyr are directed not only against Jews, but also against 'Judaizing' Christians. Judaeo-Christianity that remained faithful to Jewish ritual did in fact survive for a long time among small groups, as Marcel Simon has shown, but very soon it became marginal to the Church.

A third criterion is the geographical and linguistic one. Judaeo-Christianity can be equated with Aramaic-speaking Eastern Christianity, whether Syrian, Transjordanian, or Arabian. However,

Angels, their kinds and functions, were deeply studied in Judaeo-Christian thought. On this 6th-century ivory, probably from Syria, two bear gifts to a draped cross. (3)

'With twain he covered his face, and with twain he covered his feet, and with twain he did fly.' This seraph is on a 6th-century liturgical fan found near Aleppo. (4)

Mystic meanings of the Cross are common in Eastern thought. In the four rods and eight branches on these Coptic textiles one can perhaps see the Apostles. (*5, 6*)

the term used in this sense is not accurate, and it would be better to use Gregory Dix' phrase and to speak of Syriac Christianity.[22]

There is one more way of defining Judaeo-Christianity which is not incompatible with any of the interpretations given above, but which is wider than them all. The term can be used to describe a form of Christianity whose liturgical, theological, and ascetic structure has been borrowed from the Jewish milieu in which Christianity itself first appeared. In terms of this usage there have been Judaeo-Christians who have rejected Jewish observances. This is the definition that I have adopted in my *Théologie du judéo-christianisme*, and it is the one that I follow in this present chapter.

We have today enough Judaeo-Christian documents, orthodox or heterodox, to give us an idea of this Judaeo-Christian culture. In some cases these documents are Christian revisions of Jewish writings, such as the *Testaments of the Twelve Patriarchs*; in some cases they are fragments of exegesis, which survive especially in the *Epistle of Barnabas*, and which derive, as we have seen, from the methods of rabbinical exegesis; in some cases our documents are hymns like the *Psalms of Solomon*, which are akin to the Hodayoth of Qumran, or they are apocalypses like the *Apocalypse of Peter* and the *Apocalypse of James*. Some of these works are composite: the *Ascension of Isaiah* includes a martyrdom, an apocalypse, and visions; the *Epistle of the Eleven Apostles* contains a testament and a catechism as well as an apocalypse; in the *Epistle of Barnabas* there are an exegetic tract and a moral catechism; in the *Shepherd of Hermas* we find visions, a moral catechism, and again an apocalypse. Some works belong to Christian literary genres – gospels, acts, epistles – but this with a strong Jewish flavour.

The most characteristic feature of Judaeo-Christian culture is its concern with the apocalypse; this is not only a literary genre; it impregnates the totality of thought. It is to be found particularly in
p 266 the exegesis of the beginning of Genesis. Apocalyptic is essentially
(8) a revelation of the secrets of the heavenly world, with its topo-
p 266–7 graphy and its inhabitants. Angelology plays a prominent part in it.
(7–11) In this sense apocalyptic is a *gnōsis*, and has the esoteric character
f 3, 4 that the word *'gnōsis'* implies. There was a Jewish *gnōsis*, especially among the Zadokites; there was a Judaeo-Christian *gnōsis*, of which Gnosticism was the heterodox form. Apocalyptic is also a theology of history, involving a strict doctrine of predestination, according to which the events of history have been recorded in the heavenly books since the beginning of time and can thus be foreknown by men of vision. The vision extends over the whole of history, but the interest is concentrated on 'the Last Things'.

'The Moabites and Ammonites filling the Church'

This apocalyptic framework, which Judaeo-Christianity shared with contemporary Judaism, was the setting for Judaeo-Christian theology. The Trinity was expressed in categories derived from angelology; the Incarnation was presented as the hidden descent
of the Well-Beloved through the seven heavens and their angels; p 268
Christ's descent into Hell and ascension convey the mystery of (13)
salvation in terms of Jewish religious cosmology. The Cross is, in p 267
virtue of its material, a sign of power – a sceptre or a rod – while, (10)
in virtue of its form, it symbolizes the radiation of the action of *f 1, 4, 5*
Christ throughout the cosmos. In the Gnostic system, as already in the Epistle to the Ephesians and in Revelation, the Church is held to have been pre-existent in the mind of God. Finally, Christ is to reign on Earth for a millennium before the Last Judgement and the coming of the new world.

There are striking features in the structure of the Church itself.
It is governed by a college of twelve elders, among whom one is p 272–3
pre-eminent. This dispensation is documented in the Clementine (24–6)
writings and is presupposed in the Letters of Ignatius of Antioch, who compares the Elders with the Senate of the Apostles. This system seems to have been preserved for a long time in the Egyptian Church. Initiation was in three stages: baptism by fire or by exorcism, baptism by water, and baptism by the Holy Spirit, accompanied by anointing and coronation. Rites relating to death were highly developed, as we know from plaques found in ossuaries. The death and resurrection of Christ were commemorated on Nizan 14, the day of the Jewish Passover, in accordance with Quartodeciman usage. The Judaeo-Christian Church had strong ascetic tendencies, particularly in Syria, where ascetics and virgins were privileged members of the community.

During the 3rd century Judaeo-Christianity retained a high degree of vitality in an area extending from Transjordan to Mesopotamia. Polemics against 'Judaizers' show that it survived in the West as well. In Palestine the official Church was Greek from the time of Hadrian onwards, but Judaeo-Christianity maintained a clandestine existence there too. Cut off from the official Church, and most highly developed among the populace, Judaeo-Christianity in Palestine verged on superstition in certain features, particularly in the prominence of the cult of the dead. All the same, the community also included cultivated members. Origen records interesting traditions that had been communicated to him by Judaeo-Christians whom he met when he was living at Caesarea in Palestine. The community in Jerusalem centred on the Judaeo-Christian synagogue of the Cenacle, on Mount Zion.

In Transjordan the most important centre was Bosra (Bostra), in Auranitis, which was at its peak under the Severi. The Emperor Philip the Arabian, who was certainly a Christian, came from this region. The Bishop of Bosra between 240 and 254, Beryllus, was accused of holding heretical opinions, which were in fact doctrines of Judaeo-Christian theology. At Bosra a synod was convened in which Origen took part. When in 248 a new council met in Arabia, to decide whether the soul survives the death of the body, there
was a confrontation between the Semitic and the Christian con- p 82–3
ception of the nature of man. This question was the subject of a (10)
further debate – the text has recently been discovered at Toura – between Origen and a bishop named Heraclides. It may be the community at Bosra which is described in the *Didascalia of the Apostles*, a work of the mid-4th century. The spirit of this work is shot through with Judaism, yet at the same time the writer warns his readers against being tempted by Judaism. The Judaeo-Christian community here presents itself as still belonging sociologically to the Jewish milieu.

The Christian communities in Transjordan were not solely of Jewish origin. Here, as in Palestine, there were Christians of Greek origin as well. In addition to these groups, a particularly interesting category is that of the Semitic tribes – Moabites, Ammonites, and Edomites – who are so often mentioned in the Old Testament, where their lineage is traced back to Lot, Esau, and Ishmael. Christianity was preached to these tribes by Judaeo-Christians, and at the end of the 3rd century we are told by Eusebius that they had been converted. Commenting on references to Moab and Edom in Psalm lix 10, he writes that 'those who travel through the Arabian region can observe for themselves the fulfilment of these prophecies when they see the Moabites and Ammonites filling the Church of God'. In the 4th century, Aetheria visited the sanctuaries which they had dedicated to their biblical ancestors, St Melchizedek, St Lot, and St Job.

In Coele Syria too a great part of the preaching of Christianity was done by Judaeo-Christians. At Beroea (Aleppo) Jerome found a Judaeo-Christian gospel in Hebrew, and one of the oldest works in Syriac is an apology, wrongly attributed to Melito of Sardis, whose author was a Judaeo-Christian from Mabbug-Hierapolis. It was also in a Judaeo-Christian milieu in Coele Syria, about the year 160, that the *Grundschrift* underlying the Pseudo-Clementine writings[23] was composed. Again we have archaeological evidence p 270–1 (20–21) for the presence of Judaeo-Christianity at Dura Europos, in the church and the baptistery there. The subject-matter and the style of the frescos are completely different from any of the same date in the West. The Judaeo-Christian inspiration fuses here with Parthian culture, as had already happened in the works of Bardesanes. At the end of the century the short-lived Kingdom of Palmyra produced the curious figure of Paul of Samosata. Installed as bishop of Antioch, he introduced there oriental usages, in particular an antiphonal psalmody in which the verses were chanted alternately by a choir of men and a choir of women. This is reminiscent of Jewish customs described by Philo in his treatise *On the Therapeutae*.

The birthplace of antiphony

The most vital centre of Semitic Christianity was Osrhoëne. Here the tradition established by Bardesanes was maintained by his son Harmodios. It was no doubt in Osrhoëne that antiphonal singing originated, before spreading throughout the Christian world. In the sphere of asceticism, Syriac Christianity had distinctive features in which Messalianism originated. The *Acts of Thomas* and the Pseudo-Clementine *Treatise on Virginity* provide evidence f 7 of an ascetic ideal which regarded celibacy as being the normal state for Christians. In this environment the custom of spiritual marriages, between a virgin and an ascetic, developed – a custom which John Chrysostom still had to combat at the end of the 4th century. Whether this Encratism is typically Semitic, or whether it came from Egyptian Christianity, as Quispel holds, it is certainly characteristic of Syriac Christianity in the 3rd century.[24]

Eastward, Christianity continued to develop round Nisibis and, beyond the Tigris, in Adiabene round Arbela and round the episcopal see of Seleucia-Ctesiphon in Babylonia. We know from the *Book of Local Laws* that there were Christians in Media and in Bactria. Mani appears to have met Christians in India. These p 320 (5) were the regions in which Manicheanism took its rise eventually in the 4th century. Its founder, Mani, seems originally to have belonged, like his father Palek, to a baptist sect that had a close affinity with the Mandaeans. Later on, Mani came into contact with members of various religious groups – Zoroastrians, Brahmans, Jews, and also Christians. Though his dualist and syncretistic doctrine is opposed to Christianity, it has nevertheless adopted a number of features borrowed from Judaeo-Christianity. The *Psalms of Thomas*, of which a part is Judaeo-Christian, provide important evidence on this point.

In the 3rd century the expansion of both Judaeo-Christianity and Manicheanism ran into opposition from a new dynasty, the p 336 (11) Sassanids. The Emperor Shapur I conducted victorious campaigns against the Roman Empire, and extended his power over the entire region to the east of the Euphrates, including Osrhoëne. Shapur re-established Zoroastrianism, the ancient religion of Iran, and restored the authority of the Magi. Mani, who was related to the Arsacids and who partook of their syncretism, was put to death in the year 277 under Bahram I, Shapur's successor. Some of the Osrhoënian Christians were deported to Babylonia, a move which incidentally reinforced Christianity in Seleucia-Ctesiphon. But the political insulation of oriental Christendom to the east of the Euphrates from the West accentuated the estrangement between the Judaeo-Christian churches of the East and the Western churches.

Though originally Judaeo-Christianity had been coextensive with the whole Church, and though it continued to be a power till about the year 140, in the West it rapidly forfeited its supremacy to

The monastic life, characteristic of Syriac Christianity, is represented by the monk holding a cross on this 4th-century hexagonal glass bottle from Syria. On either side of him are two palm branches. (7)

Pauline Christianity, which succeeded in severing its ties with Judaism. From the end of the 2nd century onwards, Judaeo-Christians were regarded as being heretics. It is they who are censured under the names Ebionites, Quartodecimans, Encratites, Millenarianists, or, more commonly, Judaizers. Cut off, as they were, from the Great Church, they very soon died out in the West. But their survival in the East can be traced from the 3rd to the 4th century, particularly in Palestine, Arabia, Transjordan, Syria, and Mesopotamia. Some were absorbed by Islam, which is itself in some ways an heir of Judaeo-Christianity; others adopted the orthodoxy of the Great Church, while retaining their Semitic culture, and something of their influence survives in the churches of Ethiopia, Syria, and Chaldaea.

There remains one final question: does Judaeo-Christianity have any future? St Paul saw, with profound insight, that Christianity had to extricate itself from its Jewish matrix if it was to achieve universality and not remain a Jewish sect. But, now that Christianity has achieved that universality, the terms of the question have been changed and indeed reversed. Christianity's current problem is actually the deficiency of its Judaic expression, which is one of the necessary aspects of its universality. Here again Paul's dialectic seems prophetic. Now that the gentiles have entered the Church, the possibility of the Church's growing a Judaeo-Christian branch presents itself again. There is nothing to prevent the establishment of Christian communities formed of converts from Judaism, for whom the liturgical language would be Hebrew. There is not even any reason why circumcised Jews should not profess faith in Christ: this, after all, is what the Apostles were and is what they did. The problem which we have been examining is not only of historical interest but is also a living reality today.

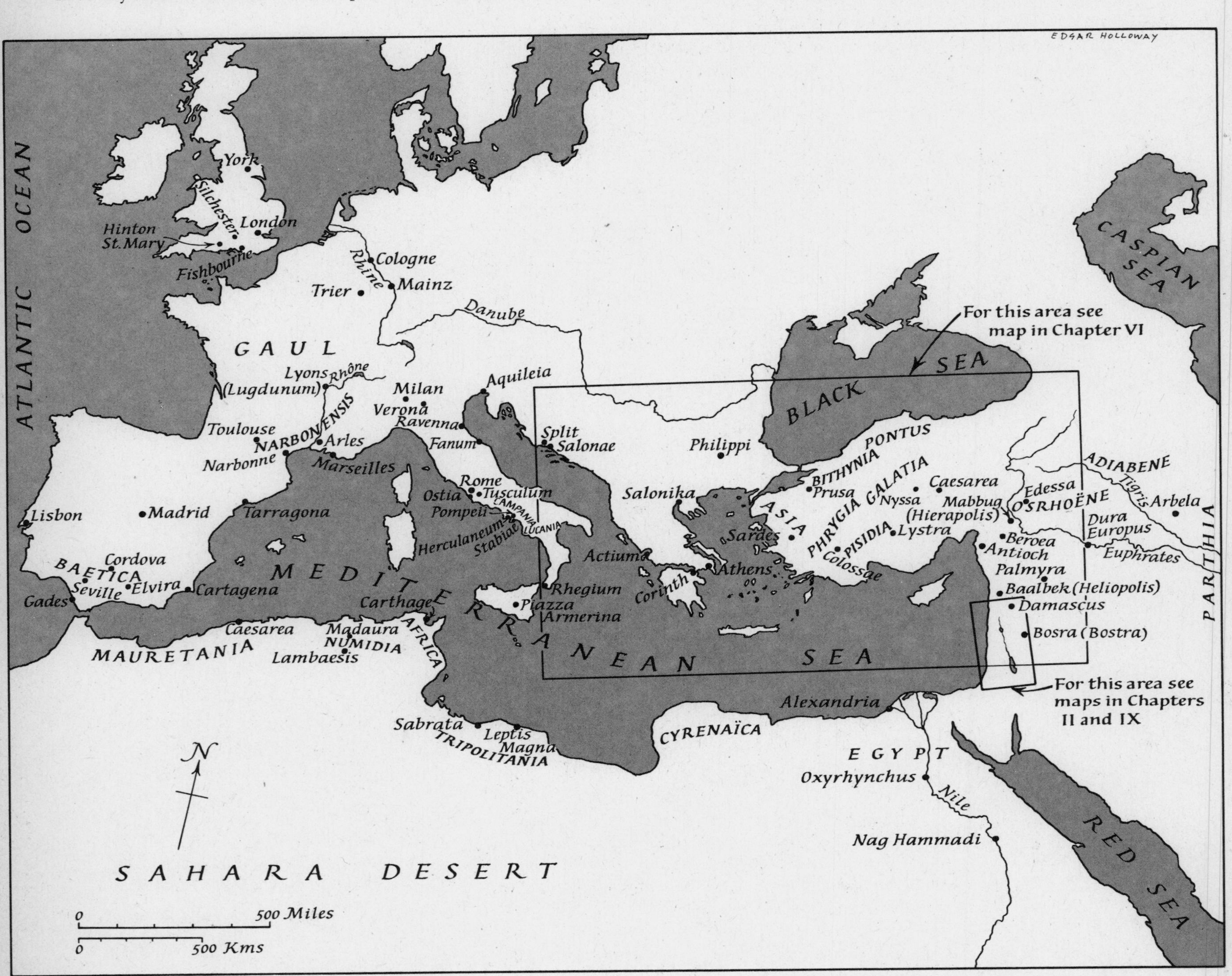

The Roman Empire in Early Christian times. (8)

XII
THE WORD GOES FORTH

CHRISTIANITY AS
A MISSIONARY RELIGION

JEAN DANIÉLOU

'Our people [the Jews] seem to have been abandoned by God, and now true belief is increasing among those who thought that they were already religious.'

'SECOND CLEMENT'

The spread of Christianity
from the Jewish world which gave it birth, until it became the universal religion of the whole Mediterranean region, had three historical stages. It was with Pentecost (right) that the mission of the Church began. As the disciples were gathered in Jerusalem, 'suddenly there came a sound from heaven as of a rushing mighty wind, and it filled the house where they were sitting. And there appeared unto them cloven tongues like as of fire, and it sat upon each of them'. They were all filled with the Holy Ghost, and began to speak in other languages, with the result that 'Parthians, and Medes, and Elamites, and the dwellers in Mesopotamia, and in Judaea, and Cappadocia, in Pontus, and Asia, Phrygia, and Pamphylia, in Egypt and in the parts of Libya about Cyrene, and strangers of Rome, Jews and proselytes, Cretes and Arabians' were added to the Church.

The second stage was the mission of St Paul to the gentiles. Beginning, like other Judaeo-Christian missionaries, by preaching in the synagogues, Paul was to find that his message had more impact on non-Jews. He became the 'apostle of the gentiles' and was condemned to life-long conflict with the conservative authorities at Jerusalem, who favoured the imposition of Jewish observances on gentile converts. In the event, it was Paul's more catholic conception of Christianity which triumphed; and Judaeo-Christianity steadily faded away.

The final engagement of Christianity in the Graeco-Roman world and its disengagement from Judaism dates roughly from the period between the two Jewish revolts of AD 66–70 and 312–5. Taking their cue from St Paul, who was himself steeped in the blend of Jewish and Greek culture developed in Hellenistic Judaism, the first Christian apologists evolved, not a different way of life, but a different way of living the common Graeco-Roman life. Their success was absolute. As Western civilization grew out of Graeco-Roman civilization, it was the Christian version of Graeco-Roman civilization which for many centuries became, at least nominally, the common Western way of life.

The illustration shown here, from the Rabula Codex of AD 586, is the earliest surviving representation of Pentecost. The Virgin Mary stands in the centre, with six apostles on each side. Above her the dove of the Holy Ghost descends, and over each head are the 'cloven tongues like as of fire' mentioned by the author of Acts. (1)

Scenes from the life of St Paul are portrayed on this 4th-century diptych (left). Top: he disputes with pagan philosophers, possibly including Dionysius the Areopagite on the left. Centre: in Malta, after his shipwreck, he shakes the viper from his wrist into the fire, to the amazement of the populace. The figure in a clasped cloak is probably Publius, later his host, whose father, on the right, St Paul cured of a wasting disease. Below: Publius' father on the right, and another man on the left, present two invalids. (2)

The familiar myths known since childhood to every Greek and Roman, were used by Early Christian preachers as vivid symbols of the doctrines of the new religion, while they were, at the same time, ridiculed for their immoral elements. Hercules overcoming monsters suggested Christ overcoming the forces of evil (above left: Hercules and the Hydra). Another example is the pairing of the lawgivers Moses and Minos; while the musician David recalls Orpheus with his lyre (see p. 302–3). (3)

Christ as Good Shepherd appears together with Hermes, conductor of souls, in the catacomb of San Sebastiano (above). Below: Odysseus bound to the mast of his ship when passing the haunts of the Sirens was compared to Christ or to the true believer. As Clement says: 'Let us then shun custom . . . as the Sirens of legend. Sail past the song; it works death. Only resolve, and thou hast vanquished destruction; bound to the wood of the cross, thou shalt live freed from all corruption.' (4, 5).

The Coptic Church, born out of a controversy in the 5th century, in which the doctrine of the two natures of Christ was involved, represents the most vital of early artistic trends outside the Western tradition. Although some Western elements are present, such as the flying angel (above), descended from Roman Victories, the predominant influence is the native Egyptian (below left: the bird-soul (*rha*) on a Christian tombstone). Below right: a Copt holding a cross. (6–8)

As the Greeks, and all those familiar with Greek seafaring imagery, saw the Cross in the anchor or the yard-arm of a ship, so the Copts saw the Cross in the traditional Egyptian hieroglyph meaning life, the *ankh* (above). In Latin, this was known as the *crux ansata*, the cross with a handle. Mystic meanings of the Cross are common in Eastern thought: it is sometimes combined with the body of Christ (*cf.* plate 12); and a similar identification may have been read into the Egyptian sign. (9)

The wide-eyed Madonna (left), so different from the usual Western image, formed part of a 6th-century Annunciation. Coptic church sculpture was mostly of wood, but much has survived, thanks to the dryness of the climate. It was frequently painted, and traces of the colours can still be seen here. (10)

Across Europe the new faith left many traces of its progress. The barbarian invaders of the 5th and 6th centuries, who destroyed most of the records of the Romano-Christian churches, were in their turn converted, reproducing Christian motifs in their own bizarre styles.

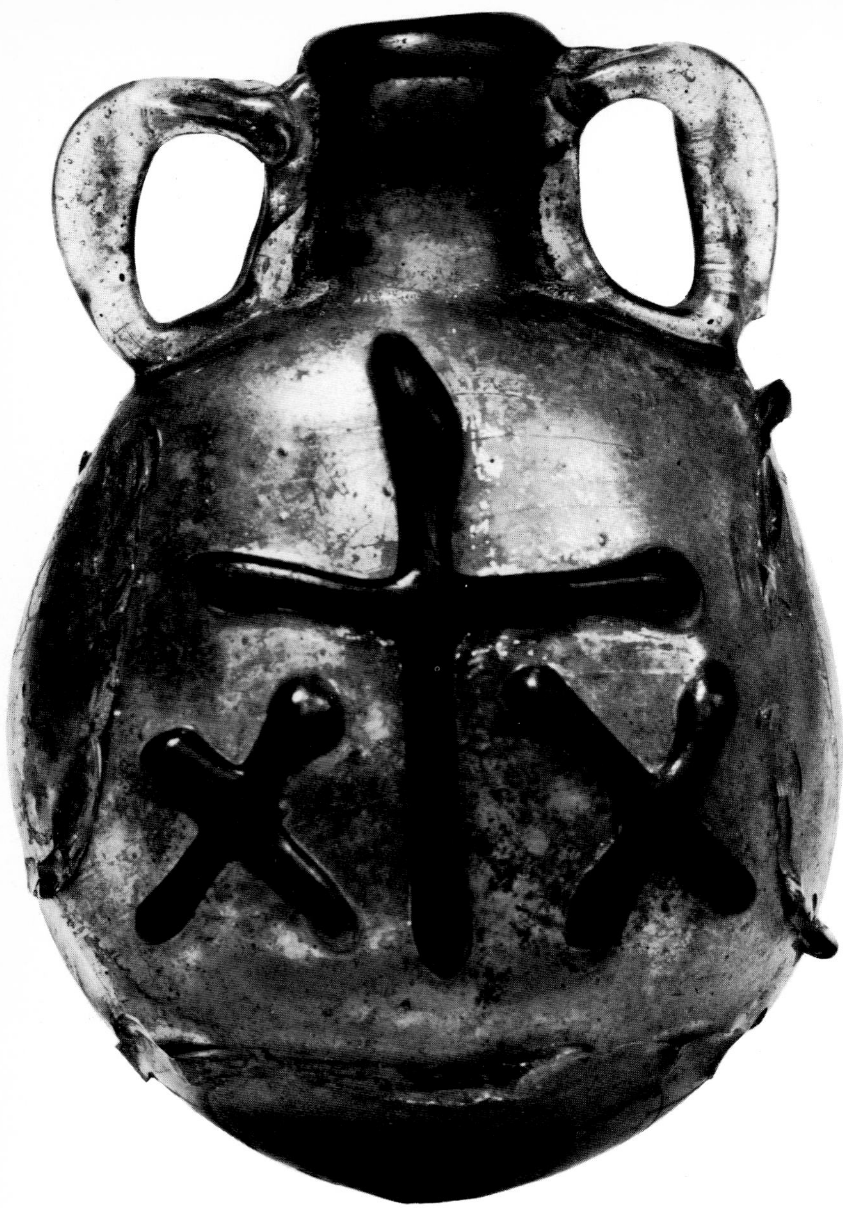

Rome: found in the catacombs, this 4th-century glass flask, shown here twice actual size, is decorated with three applied crosses, those of the two thieves being diagonal, St Andrew's crosses. (11)

From the Crimea comes this gold medallion. The decoration, which is deeply engraved on the reverse, appears to be a Crucifixion. The crucified man's body is combined with the cross. (12)

England: Alpha and Omega, the first and last letters of the Greek alphabet, symbolized Christ, 'the beginning and the ending'. They appear with the Chi-Rho on this spoon, which forms part of the Mildenhall treasure discovered in Suffolk in 1946. (13)

From Germany comes the tombstone of Leontius, an eight- or nine-year-old child (the numeral is unclear). The Alpha and Omega are suspended from the arms of a Latin (upright) Chi-Rho, flanked by two doves, symbols of peace. (14)

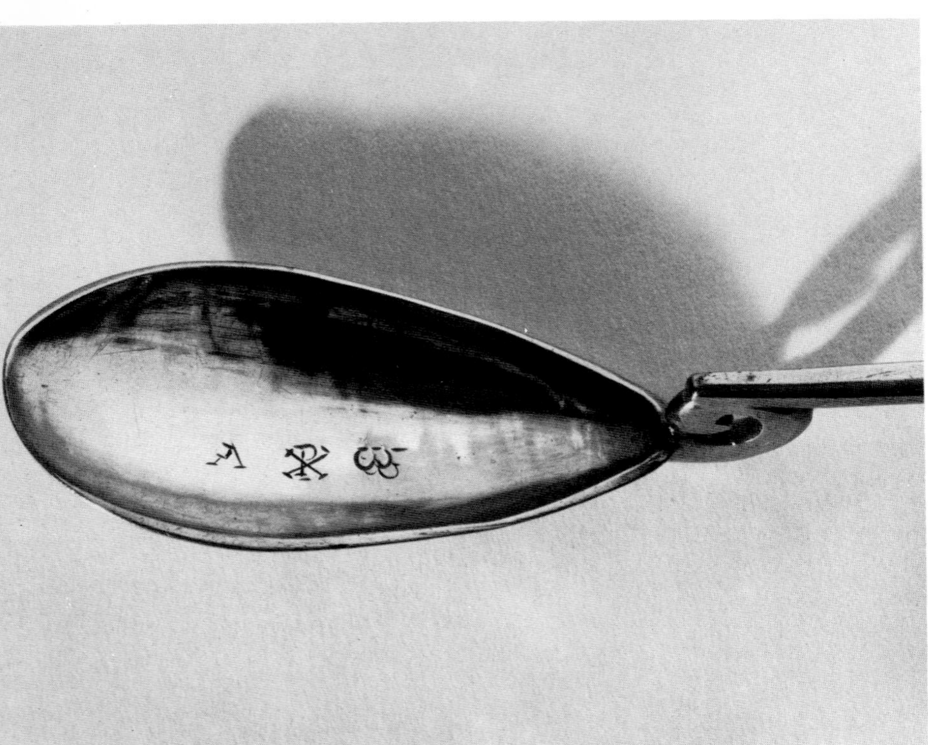

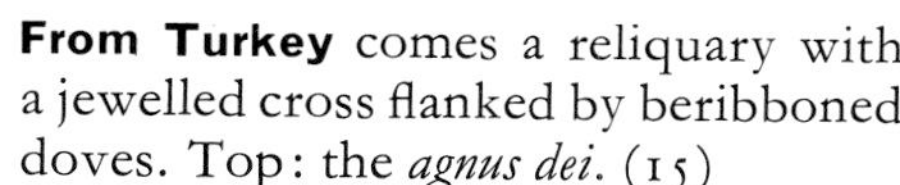

From Turkey comes a reliquary with a jewelled cross flanked by beribboned doves. Top: the *agnus dei*. (15)

From Spain comes a Visigothic sarcophagus, showing the Chi-Rho. The workmanship is rough and the meaning of the figures uncertain. (18)

France: imagery from the East gives the key to much that is puzzling in Frankish iconography. The Alpha and Omega suspended from the Cross was a common motif. It also appears on the tombstone of Bishop Boethius of Carpentras (above), which is particularly interesting in that the artist, not understanding his model, has copied it from the wrong side, so that the Greek letters are reversed. (16)

Ireland: the 6th-century cross at Carndonagh is decorated with a Crucifixion (?) and Celtic designs. (17)

Cyprus: St Sergius or St Bacchus on a bowl. He wears the collar of the Imperial bodyguard; his cloak has a patch of different colour. (19)

Latin Christianity came from Africa, it has often been said. Certainly the first major literary works in Latin were written in Africa, notably those of Tertullian. The strength and originality of African Christianity is probably due to its being a synthesis of the Semitic and the Latin culture. This 6th-century mosaic of Daniel and the lions comes from Sfax, 150 miles south-east of Tertullian's home town, Carthage. Daniel, between pine trees, wearing a cloak and Phrygian cap, is of the oriental type, *i.e.* clothed, orientals having a horror of nudity. The mosaic is close in style to the 3rd-century Jewish paintings at Dura Europus. (20)

CHRISTIANITY AS A MISSIONARY RELIGION

JEAN DANIÉLOU

THE TRANSMISSION of the religion of Christ from the Jewish world, within which it made its first appearance, to the pagan world is the great revolution which occupies the 1st and 2nd centuries. This was the natural outcome of the very nature of the Christian message, which is not the religious expression of a culture, as were the great pagan religions, and is not the election by God of one people for an historic mission, as was Judaism, but is the proclamation to all mankind of the advent of the 'Last Things'. However, the recognition of this universalism, the break with the Jewish social and cultural context, and the expression of Christianity in new forms taken from Hellenistic culture were all gradual processes. We must first describe these early stages, then we shall look at the expansion of Christianity in the Graeco-Roman world, until the moment when, by Constantine's doing, it becomes the religion of the Empire.

The ministry of Jesus did not extend beyond the frontiers of Israel, and it was almost exclusively addressed to Jews. Moreover, Jesus' work was confined to laying the foundations of the Christian
p 285 mission; he was not a missionary himself. It is with Pentecost that
(1) the mission of the Church begins. The miracle of the tongues is obviously meant to bring out the universality of the Christian message; the list of peoples enumerated refers us back to the table in Genesis ix in which the Jewish nation is only one among many. All the same it is obvious that the non-Jews, or Gentiles, who came as pilgrims to Jerusalem were what was known as 'God-fearers', *i.e.* non-Jewish converts to Judaism. The first Christian preaching was therefore not addressed to outright pagans. At this point it is essential to recall a fact that Marcel Simon has pointed out.[1] Before the Christian mission there had been a Jewish mission, but this mission had more effect in spreading the Jewish religion among non-Jews than in incorporating new recruits in the ranks of the Chosen People by the rite of circumcision.

In fact the problem of the conversion of pagans to Christianity presented itself only gradually. It seems to have been minimal during the first decade of the Church's existence, since it was essentially to Jews and proselytes that the Christian missionaries addressed themselves. The question became important only when Paul and Barnabas were sent to Asia Minor in the year 48. Their methods were no different from those of other Judaeo-Christian missionaries: they preached in the synagogues. But, as it happened, their preaching had a greater impact on the pagans than it had on the Jews. This was the case at Pisidian Antioch, at Lystra, and at Iconium. They made converts, and this aroused the jealousy of the Jews, who mobilized the local authorities or roused the populace against them (Acts xiii 50; xiv 2 and 9). At Lystra Paul introduced a new type of preaching, in which he declared that all nations – not only Jews – are called to the salvation given in Jesus Christ.

Circumcised and uncircumcised

This admission of pagans into the Church was to create serious problems. Paul did not require them to conform to the Jewish observances, particularly not to the rite of circumcision. In Antioch this seemed normal, but the Judaeo-Christians of Jerusalem protested. The question was brought before the Apostles and Elders at Jerusalem in the year 49 and was settled by a decision which was in fact a compromise: pagan converts need not be circumcised, but Jewish converts remained bound by the Law. On the other hand, pagans had to observe most of the other 'Noachic' (pre-Mosaic) rules: they had to refrain from eating the flesh of animals that had been sacrificed to idols or that had been slaughtered by strangling, and they had to perform sexual purifications. But the tension remained. At the end of the same year, Peter and Paul were present simultaneously at Antioch. Peter felt bound not to share the meals of pagan converts, since these were still tainted with ritual impurity; Paul reproached him vigorously for this. Peter seems to have adhered strictly to the decisions of the Council of Jerusalem, whereas Paul saw in them only a compromise. This is shown by Paul's line on the question of meat sacrificed to idols in his First Epistle to the Corinthians – a line which is radically different from John's Revelation ii 14 and 20. Paul was going to be in continued conflict with the Judaeo-Christians until his death, as all the Epistles show. His triumph was posthumous.[2]

Paul justified his personal practice in his Epistles: God is the God of the pagans as well as of the Jews (Romans iii 29); all alike are sinners and are saved only by faith (Romans iii 21); circumcision or noncircumcision are immaterial; 'there are no longer either Jews or Greeks' (Galatians iii 28). This did not mean that the Law had no role, but its role was one of preparation: it was a tutor (Galatians iv 2). Now the old régime had been superseded. Paul's assertion is primarily theological: faith alone can save, and this faith is offered to all. This is the permanent basis of Christian universalism and missionary duty. But it also means that Christianity must break its constricting Jewish bonds. It is in no way tied to Semitic culture; Judaeo-Christianity is only one branch of the new religion. Christianity must involve itself with Hellenistic civilization, as well as with other non-Jewish cultures.

This second aspect of Christianity is implied in Paul's message. To what extent did he make it effective? It would be erroneously premature to see in Paul the influence of Greek philosophy and rhetoric which was to appear in the Apologists. But it would also be erroneous to interpret Paul in terms of a purely Hebraic culture. Paul's background is Hellenistic Judaism, and his Bible is the Septuagint.[3] Now Hellenistic Judaism had already established a relation between biblical revelation and Greek culture, for the Septuagint is a theological interpretation of the Hebrew Bible for use by Greeks. Paul is in this tradition. He is the creator of the Christian Greek; but the Christian Greek was himself the heir of the biblical Greek, and thus it was through Hellenistic Judaism that Christianity and Hellenism met. It was gradually, as more converts came in from Hellenism, that the Christian Greeks abandoned their original Semitic affiliations and came directly into contact with Hellenism.

Thus the idea of a Christianity extricated from Judaism was already conceived of by Paul, but there seems not to have been any great expansion before the year 70. We have seen Paul converting pagans in Asia Minor during his first journey. After the Council of Jerusalem a second mission brought him to Greece. At Beroea, 'of honourable women which were Greeks, and of men, not a few' were converted (Acts xvii 12). At Athens, Acts mentions the conversion of Dionysius the Areopagite and of a woman called Damaris (xvii 34); at Corinth, Paul, faced with the hostility of the Jewish community, concentrated entirely on spreading the Gospel among the pagans (Acts xviii 6). During a third voyage, he ran into opposition at Ephesus from manufacturers of idols (Acts xix 23–41). This is the earliest evidence for an anti-Christian reaction among pagans and is therefore an indication that the process of conversion had become an important movement. The reference to 'saints of Caesar's household' (Philippians iv 22) shows that there were ex-pagan Christians in Rome. All the same, the Epistles show that during Paul's lifetime the Judaeo-Christian element was still dominant in the Church. Furthermore, Paul's mission was confined to Syria, Asia Minor, Greece, and Rome. p 290–1 (11, 13, 19) It is difficult to ascertain whether there were Christian missions to pagans elsewhere, before the year 70. We have seen that in Egypt, in Osrhoëne and in Adiabene only Judaeo-Christians were found at this date.

The break with Judaism

The period extending roughly from 70 to 135 marks Christianity's break with its Jewish origins, and the spread of pagan Christianity. In Domitian's reign the Christian community was still implicated in the reaction against the Jews, but, as Tacitus and Pliny testify, this was the moment at which Christianity became a distinct entity which created special problems for the Roman authorities. The basic documents for the Christian mission in this period are the Gospels. They are a presentation of Christ to the Graeco-Roman world. Already in the Gospel according to St Mark Christ is clearly and deliberately dissociated from the Jewish revolt, and his loyalty to Rome is stressed[4] – a point that is made even more strongly in the Gospel according to St Luke. The Acts of the Apostles describe the progress of the Gospel from Jerusalem to Rome, and give prominence to pagan conversions, such as that of Queen Candace's eunuch and of the centurion Cornelius. The Gospel according to St John emphasizes still more strongly the hostility of the Jews towards Christ and it reacts against the vestiges of Messianism in the Asian Christian communities. The Gospels were a highly effective instrument for the propagation of Christianity. Fragments of the Gospel according to St John, dating from the beginning of the 2nd century, have been found in Egypt and in the mid-2nd century the pagan Celsus was aware of this Gospel's existence.

The break with Judaism, which is the hallmark of this period, reveals itself in such writings as the Epistle of Barnabas and the letters of Ignatius of Antioch. In some cases it takes the form of a complete rejection of the Old Testament. This is what we find in p 319–22 (1–10) the then vigorously developing movement of Gnosticism. The essence of Gnosticism is the rejection of the God of Israel. He is regarded as an inferior demiurge, and his creation and his Law are rejected with him. Gnosticism is an extreme version of the Pauline tendency. Its principal exponents are Satornilus and Carpocrates in Syria, Marcion in Asia Minor, and Basilides in Egypt. One must distinguish the Gnosticism that is a total rejection of the Jewish God and of Judaism, from the *gnōsis* that is simply a search for higher religious knowledge and that is found in this period among Judaeo-Christians as well as among ex-pagan converts.[5] The importance of Gnosticism can be measured by the importance of the literature to which it gave rise (a substantial portion of this has been discovered at Nag Hammadi), and by the refutations of it in the following period from Justin, Irenaeus, and Tertullian. It is noteworthy that the Christian writers of this period, orthodox and Gnostic alike, come for the most part from a Judaeo-Christian background. Their ideology is anti-Jewish but their culture is still Semitic.

The final extrication of Christianity from its Jewish origins and its decisive engagement in a dialogue with the Hellenistic culture p 139 (65) date from the reigns of Antoninus Pius (138–161), Marcus Aurelius (161–180), and Commodus (180–193). The circumstances were particularly favourable. The Graeco-Roman world of that age was particularly open-minded and liberal-minded. It was interested in religious and philosophical doctrines. The traditional schools of philosophy were transmitting the teachings of the great p 205–8 (1–9) masters. The Platonists had Gaius and Albinus, Taurus and Atticus; the Aristotelians had Alexander of Aphrodisias; the Stoics had Fronto. Lectures on philosophy were fashionable – lectures such as those given by Maximus of Tyre and by Dio of Prusa (Dio Chrysostom). Medicine flowered in Galen, astronomy in Ptolemy. At the same time eastern religions were spreading through the Empire. This was the age of mystagogues like Apollonius of Tyana, of the Chaldaean Oracles and of the Hermetic writings. Some souls, for instance Numenius, combined the philosophic tradition with these currents of mysticism. Everywhere there was an atmosphere of intellectual freedom, in contrast to the severity of the preceding period, represented by Plutarch and Seneca. Lucian represents the new age, and his ruthless criticism is directed against traditional myths as well as the new religions, against the philosophers as well as the rhetoricians.

Apologia

This was the world that confronted Christianity and constrained it to define itself. This task of definition was performed in the 'Apologetic' writings – a set of works which, though superficially diverse, all have the common purpose of presenting Christianity to the pagan world. This is the body of specifically missionary literature, which derives its inspiration from three sources: early Christian preaching, Jewish missionary literature and Greek philosophical hortatory works[6] (part of the Aristotle's *Apologia* survives). The most important of Christian Apologists is Justin Martyr, with his treatises *On Monarchy* and *On the Soul*, his *Addresses to the Greeks*, his two *Apologiae*, and his *Dialogue with Trypho*. There is also the treatise addressed to Autolycus by Theophilus, bishop of Antioch, Tatian's *Address to the Greeks*, the *Apologia* of Athenagoras, the *Epistle to Diognetus*, and the *Protrepticus* of Clement of Alexandria. Only a fragment survives of the *Apologia* of Melito of Sardis. Eusebius mentions the *Address to the Greeks* of Apollinaris of Hierapolis and Miltiades' *Apologia*. In spite of differences in detail, these works present a common attitude and we must now identify its main features.

This attitude is in the first place an attack on Hellenism both as popular paganism and as learned philosophy. Criticism of the former is directed primarily against the myths, and here Christian writers could take their cue from pagan writers such as Lucian. They seized this opening. Justin Martyr, Theophilus, Athenagoras, Clement and above all Tatian delighted in exposing the ridiculous and immoral elements in Greek mythology. They are fully *au fait* with the allegorical interpretations of it. They also criticize idolatrous cults, the manufacture of idols, sacrifices, garlands of flowers and incense. This attack struck at the very foundations of Graeco-Roman society, based, as this was, on family religion and civic religion. In Justin Martyr's and Tatian's eyes these cults were directed to the demons, who duped men into worshipping them. Emperor-worship was singled out for special criticism: it was p 139 (62, 64) essential to demonstrate that this cult was not an indispensable expression of civic loyalty and that Christians were model citizens. Clement denounced not only the official religions but also the mystery cults. One further aspect of pagan society came in for p 237–5 (1–51) violent attack, namely pagan morals: prostitution and abortion, p 152–3 (13, 15) theatre and circus, social injustice. Here the Apologists were following in the steps of St Paul.

The Apologists did not confine their attacks to popular paganism; they also criticized the contemporary systems of philosophy. Their first move was to make personal attacks on the philosophers' characters: Tatian collected all the scandalous stories about them that he could find. The next targets are contradictions in their writings which reveal the lack of certitude in their thought. Originality is dearer to the philosophers than truth. These general criticisms were followed up by specific criticisms of each system. Plato believed in the transmigration of souls; Aristotle held mistaken views on the immortality of the soul and on Providence; the Stoics had a materialistic idea of God; the Epicureans recognized the reality of nothing but chance. These accusations were directed mainly against the great traditional systems as these were taught in the institutes, but they are also directed partly against contemporary philosophies attributed to the major systems. Justin Martyr attacks Platonism in the 'Middle' form represented by Albinus or Atticus, and at the beginning of his *Dialogue* he describes the contemporary Aristotelians.

'Consider it well'

In their confrontation with the illusions and errors of paganism, the Apologists present Christianity, not as a new religion, but as the true religion. Justin Martyr appeals to the intellect (*logos*) of those who love wisdom (philosophy): 'If this doctrine seems to you to be in conformity with reason and truth, consider it well' (*First Apologia* 68, 1). The first point in the Christian message is the nature of the true God. He is 'unique, eternal, invisible', in the words of Athenagoras (*Supplicatio* 10). God transcends the whole of the universe, which is his creation. He cannot be known by the human intellect. He has a Word and a Spirit, through whom he acts in the world. He created human beings in order to associate them with his own life by the Resurrection, but only the just will participate in eternal life. This is the religion that was given to Man at the beginning of time, but human beings have been deceived by the demons into turning away from it. This is why the Son of God came to destroy the demons' power and to establish the true religion for ever.

The main objective in the teaching of the Apologists was to demonstrate that the Christian message is in conformity with reason and truth. Justin Martyr appeals without hesitation to the testimony of the philosophers, and Tertullian to the consensus of mankind. The point is that in spite of the influence of the demons truth has not been entirely corrupted in pagan hearts. This truth, which they have known only in a fragmentary and corrupt form, is revealed to them fully in Christianity. Therefore there cannot be different kinds of religion. There has always been only one truth. 'The doctrine of Plato' is not foreign to that of Christ, though it is not entirely similar to it. 'Everything good that the philosophers have taught belongs to us Christians' (*Second Apologia* 13, 2–4). Thus from the beginning of the world there has been the same struggle between the Word and the demons. There has never been any other truth than Christian truth. Christianity *is* the truth, and everything else is error. Why did God permit the demons' activity? Because, says Justin Martyr, Man's free will has to be put to the test: 'there would be no merit if there was no possibility of making the choice between two different paths' (*Second Apologia* 7, 5–6).[7] One can now see how, for the Apologists, the relation between Christianity, religion, and philosophy presents itself. There can be no question of these being different realities. Christianity is the true religion and the true philosophy. Pagans had had a partial knowledge of these, and this knowledge derived from two sources. On the one hand the true religion is the original religion, and the history of philosophy and religion is one of decay. Justin Martyr and Clement here avail themselves of the ideas of Antiochus of Ascalon and Poseidonius of Apamea. Contemporary philosophies were merely debasements of the teachings of the great founders of religions: Orpheus, Zoroaster, the Buddha. But Justin and Clement go still farther back in time. Judaism is the oldest religion (this made it vital for them to demonstrate the chronological priority of Moses over Orpheus and Zoroaster), and it was the Jewish prophets who had been the most faithful guardians of the original revelation. But, they argued, contemporary Judaism was a falsification of the religion of the sages. Ultimately both Jewish prophets and Greek sages testified to the original religion.[8]

Alongside of this explanation there was another, which did not, however, exclude the first. The action of the Word of God, contradicted by the demons' action until the defeat of these by Christ, had operated continuously throughout the history of mankind. The Word 'sowed' truths in the human soul:

> Christ is the first-born of God, his Word, in whom all men participate. Those men who have lived in accordance with the Logos are Christians, though they may have been reckoned as being atheists. Examples among the Greeks are Socrates, Heraclitus and their like, and among the barbarians Abraham, Ananiah, Azariah, Misaël, Elijah and the rest (*First Apologia* 46, 1–4).

This is because 'the seed of the Logos is planted in all mankind' (*Second Apologia* 8, 1). Besides the conflict of good and evil, there is within each human being a struggle between the Word's activity and the demons'. The Apologists raised the question of the conflict between truth and falsehood both in the objective realm of the historical philosophies and religions and in the subjective realm of human conscience.

In what sense did the Apologists identify Christian revelation with the true philosophy? This is the ultimate question which the policy of identification raises. Some writers, such as Harnack and

'Alexamenos worships his god,' proclaims this anti-Christian Greek graffito found on the Palatine, showing a crucified man with an ass's head. (1)

de Faye, have held that the Apologists were reducing revelation to the level of rational truth – were transforming it, in fact, into philosophy. Actually, as Holth[9] and Hydahl[10] have demonstrated the contrary would be closer to the truth. As Justin Martyr and Clement see it, truth is one. This is the truth that is fully present in Christianity. It was given to Man in the very beginning. The philosophies and the religions are debasements of it, produced by the activity of the demons. The Incarnation and Resurrection of Christ have restored this truth. It cannot be apprehended by Man out of his own resources. The Word and the Spirit introduced mankind to it originally, and they are reintroducing to it those pagans who accept the Gospel.

A new type of Christian

In the mid-2nd century the source of the recruitment of Christianity changed. Up till then the Church had consisted mainly of Jews or proselytes converted to Judaism. This source of recruitment gradually dried up. Christians now came mainly from pagan backgrounds. On this point we have the evidence of Justin Martyr (*First Apologia* 53) and that of *Second Clement*, a homily dating from the mid-2nd century: 'Our people [the Jews] seems to have been abandoned by God, and now true belief is increasing among those who thought they were already religious' (*Second Clement* 3). Justin Martyr, too, testifies that 'there are now believers of all races, barbarians and Greeks, nomads and those who live in tents, whatever they may be called' (*Dialogue* 117). Christians are now recruited from all backgrounds. Already in the time of Trajan, Pliny testified that in Bithynia Christianity had developed even in the villages and the countryside, and had come to include 'converts of all ages and all ranks' (*Letters to Trajan* 96–7). Justin Martyr notes the same fact. There are now Christians both among the élites and among the people (*Second Apologia* 10). During this period intellectual pagans began to take umbrage at this development and to react against it. Christians were accused of undermining traditional beliefs and thus endangering the political structure based on these beliefs. They were also accused of practising immoral rites: p 337 cannibalistic feasts, incestuous unions, the worship of an ass's head (13) – a caricature of the Christian liturgies. We find this in Fronto, *f1* Antoninus Pius' and Marcus Aurelius' instructor in history. We p 139 find it in Lucian's *Life of Peregrinus*; in Crescens, the Cynic philo- (65) sopher who denounced Lucian; in Celsus, who has given us the first systematic refutation of Christianity; and in the Emperor Marcus Aurelius himself. Christianity had now bored its way into pagan society, and pagan society now saw Christianity as a threat and began to organize against it.

At the end of this period and during the early-3rd century a new type of Christian took shape. His manners, culture and thought were entirely Greek. He had been taught to read and been given a start in literature by the *grammaticus*, taught the art of public speaking by the *rhetor*, taught to think by the philosopher; but at

The anchor was a disguised Cross. The Greek inscription reads, 'Fish (ichthys, i.e. Jesus Christ, Son of God, Saviour) of the living.' The Latin inscriptions are conventional pagan funerary formulae. (2)

the same time he was a Christian. His Christianity will now find expression in terms of the Hellenistic forms of sensitivity and intellectualism. This represents a new stage of missionary expansion as compared with the age of the Apologists. These had demonstrated that, as a vision of the universe, Christianity amounted to an original doctrine that was opposed to Hellenism, though Hellenism did contain some values which Christians had no reason to reject. We shall see Origen, who had been born in a Christian milieu, become a student of the Platonist Ammonius Saccas because he realized that Christianity needed the weapons of Greek culture for waging its war with the paganism of the intellectuals. It was on this level that there was a meeting between Christianity and Hellenism – not a syncretism but the expression of the Christian faith in a Greek form. Christianity was permeating the entire gamut of civilization, which is, of course, the normal development of missionary work.

This permeation was to be achieved in all fields – on the level of imagination to start with. Greek children were brought up on the *Iliad* and the *Odyssey* as Jewish children were on Genesis and Exodus. When Greek children were converted to Christianity, their imagination remained Greek. Christian themes suggested and awakened familiar images and took the impress of their style. Clement of Alexandria provides us with numerous examples of this: the daughters of Jethro by the well of Midian recall Nausicaa making her expedition to the clothes-washing beach (*Stromateis* IV 19, 123, 1); Lot's wife changed into a pillar of salt evokes a recollection of Niobe turned to stone (*Strom.* II 14, 61); Moses is p 302–3 (4, 7) paired with Minos, the musician David recalls Orpheus with his lute.[11] Odysseus fastened to the mast became the symbol of Christ p 286–7 (5) *f2* fastened to the Cross. A ship suggested the Church, blown by the wind of the Spirit towards the port of salvation. Thus a whole range of seafaring imagery, foreign to Jewish culture, developed p 286 (3) in Christianity.[12] Hercules overcoming the monster suggested Christ overcoming the forces of evil.[13] The pseudo-Justinian writings and the *Banquet* of Methodius of Olympus provide typical illustrations of these transpositions, and they are, of course, to be found in the first examples of Christian art, which date from this period. The sleeping Jonah is portrayed as Endymion, and David p 287 (4) as Orpheus. Christ, in the catacomb of San Sebastiano is accompanied by Hermes.

Problems of presentation

This parallelism between Greek myths and biblical stories raised an important question – the question of allegory. Cultivated Greeks of the 2nd century did not take Homer's stories as being historical; they gave the stories a symbolic meaning. The gods of Homer could embody physical realities: thus Hephaistos was fire, Hera air, Poseidon the sea. Others – particularly the Pythagoreans and Stoics – saw in the Homeric tales allegories of vices and virtues. The *De Antro Nympharum* of the Neoplatonic philosopher Porphyry is a remarkable example of this, dating from the 3rd century. Christian symbolism, on the other hand, was of a quite different order; it was based on typology, which saw in the (historical) events of the Old Testament (historical) prefigurations of the history of the Church. Justin Martyr's *Dialogue* and Irenaeus' *Adversus Haereses* are invaluable documents of this typological way of thinking.[14]

In the minds of the Alexandrians Clement and Origen, Christian typology was influenced by allegory. This was partly due to Philo, who had 'allegorized' the Old Testament on Stoic lines. Thus Christian allegory is one of the forms of the Hellenistic expression of Christianity.[15]

A second aspect of the Hellenization of Christianity is the philosophical one. Here one must be precise. On the one hand, as we have seen, the Apologists had presented Christianity as the true philosophy and, in virtue of its being this, they had contrasted it with the Greek philosophies in point of their content. Now the problem was different; it was a problem of experimentation, by Christianity, in the use of categories borrowed from Greek philosophy and adapted to express the Christian mystery. For this purpose, Greek philosophy provided a remarkable instrument, one which made it possible to make the Biblical raw material explicit with greater rigour. Thus the Apologists already used favourite expressions of Middle Platonism to describe God as unbegotten, ineffable, incomprehensible, always consistent with himself, and immutable. We find Justin Martyr seeking to express the theology of the Word by drawing a contrast between the inner Word and the prefigured Word.[16] The circumlocutionary term 'delimitation' is used to designate what was later to be called 'person'. At this stage a whole series of expressions came into use – 'essence', 'hypostasis', 'subject', etc. – which were to become the vocabulary of classic theology.

There are also now signs of a growing concern to present the truths of the faith coherently. This concern is the Christian expression of a desire for synthesis which was one of the characteristics of the spirit of the age.[17] This concern is scarcely noticeable in the Apologists. It makes its appearance with Valentinus and his disciples, particularly Ptolemy and Heraclion. The *Treatise on the Three Natures* which has been discovered at Nag Hammadi, and which is the work of Valentinus' school, is one of the earliest known theological syntheses. The theology of the Valentinian school is related to Gnostic radicalism. We find a similar preoccupation in Clement of Alexandria. He did not set out his system in a comprehensive fashion, but he gives us the key to his method. It is a question of advancing from simple faith to *gnōsis* by demonstrating the connection between the truths and the fundamental principles of the revelation.[18] The really great synthesis is Origen's. It amounts to a general effort to explain the whole economy of the creation by starting from the love of God and the freedom of Man. All spirits have pre-existed on a footing of complete equality. The different levels of creation result from the use made by the spirits of their freedom of choice. The love of God will restore them to their original perfection through voluntary conversion.[19]

'Not different from other men'

Finally there is the third realm in which Hellenistic Christianity manifested itself – the realm of morals. Here again there was a specifically Christian code of morals based on hope and charity, humility and chastity. But the way of life within which this moral code was to be given expression was the way of Hellenistic society. There came to be a Christian style of dressing and eating, of playing games, and going to the theatre. Hellenistic Christians could be distinguished from their pagan contemporaries, not by their living of a different life, but by their way of living the same life. Thus the *Epistle to Diognetus* says:

> Christians are not different from other men in their accent or in their language or in their clothing: they follow local customs of eating and living. They marry like everybody else, they have children, but they do not practise the exposure of new-born babes.

This is one of the features in which Christian universalism was in opposition to Jewish particularism. The Jews had their own special customs: circumcision, dietary laws, the sabbath rest. The Christians had nothing like this. They adopted every custom of the country they lived in, as long as it was compatible with their beliefs. More accurately, they were nationals who Christianized the national way of life.

There were, of course, difficulties. During this period there were conflicts between uncompromising tendencies and more liberal ones. In Judaeo-Christianity there was a strong ascetic tendency which frowned on marriage, a tendency that was still to be found in Valentinus, Tatian, and Montanus. The bishop Dionysius of Corinth and the writer Clement of Alexandria opposed this, and without minimizing the importance of virginity defended the legitimacy of marriage. Professions also presented problems: here again rigorists like Tertullian and Hippolytus considered that a Christian could not be a soldier. Business entailed profit, so Apollonius rejected it. The most difficult questions arose over professions which might seem to involve complicity with idolatry – the sculptor, the *grammaticus*, the actor.

An invaluable document on all these matters is Clement's *Pedagogue*, in which we can catch a glimpse of the everyday life of a 3rd-century Christian in Alexandria. For him the ethics of the Gospels are the true humanism, just as the tenets of the Gospels are the true philosophy. But these Gospel ethics must be freed from Jewish observances and must be practised in the context of ordinary Greek life.[20]

Latin Christianity and Africa

So far we have spoken of Christian expansion in the Hellenistic world, but the word 'expansion' must not be taken in a geographical sense. It is true that, since the Apostolic age, Christianity had spread round the perimeter of the Mediterranean basin. Many of the writers whom we have cited – Valentinus, Justin Martyr, p 290 (11) Tatian, Hippolytus, Irenaeus – lived in Rome for at least part of their lives. All the same, it is also a fact that in the 2nd century Christianity was confined to speakers of Greek. Most of the Christian writers in the West were of eastern origin. Justin Martyr p 291 (15) was a Samaritan, Tatian a Syrian, Valentinus an Egyptian, Irenaeus an Asian. In the first phase of its expansion Christianity had hardly 288–9 (6–10) spread beyond Jewish circles; in its second wave of expansion its range was practically confined to Greek-speaking milieux. Even the Latin or African converts, such as Tertullian, came from urban milieux where Greek was the language of culture. Apparently the evangelization of the uncultivated masses of the population of the rural hinterland had not yet seriously begun in Africa or in Rome. It was in the 3rd century that Christianity and the specifically Latin tradition eventually met.

p 292 (20) It has often been said that Latin Christianity came from Africa. It was certainly in Africa that its earliest major literary works appeared, but there seem to have been some Latin-speaking Roman Christians as early as the 2nd century. This is indicated by the presence, in the *Shepherd of Hermas*, of Latin Christian words translated into Greek.[21] As early as that there were Latin translations of the Old Testament, particularly of the Psalms. Possibly these Christian translations had been preceded by Jewish ones.[22] In any case certain Greek words had been translated in Rome at a very early date, in particular the *Epistle of Clement*, which was of particular interest to the Roman community.

Nevertheless in Rome, that most cosmopolitan of cities, Greek continued to be the most common language of the Church until the mid-3rd century, when the first Roman Christian writer to write in Latin, Novatian, appeared. On the other hand, at the very beginning of the 3rd century Latin Christian works of genius were produced in Africa, namely Tertullian's. Even before that, the *Acts of the Scillitan Martyrs*, which date from the year 180, were written in Latin. They speak of the *libri et epistulae Pauli*, which seems to imply the existence of a Latin translation of the Bible. Thus Latin Christianity did exist in Africa by the end of the 2nd century.

It is to Tertullian that Latin Christianity in Africa owed its distinctive form. Tertullian knew Greek, had even written in Greek, and had a wide knowledge of both pagan and Christian Greek literature. He certainly knew the Asian Christian writers, Irenaeus, Melito and Miltiades, and he made use of Justin Martyr and Theophilus. In this respect he was to be an intermediary between Hellenistic and Latin Christianity. But, though he owes much to these writers, his own work is original and typically Latin. He borrowed from the popular Christian Latin idiom, which seems to have been already developed by then and to have become differentiated from classical Latin – hence his highly concrete vocabulary. A lawyer by profession, he introduced into Latin theology legalistic concepts which were destined to persist there. He was the first to use such words as *culpa*, *meritum* and *satisfacere*. He was familiar with classical Latin literature; the influence of Lucretius has been detected in his work; but he lacked the Ciceronian classicism of his Roman contemporary Minucius Felix. In philosophy Tertullian was familiar with the Middle Platonism that was represented in late-2nd-century Africa by Apuleius;[23] but Tertullian was more deeply influenced by Stoicism, which with its materialistic outlook was closer to his own concrete-minded temperament. This, then, is the date of the appearance of some of the features that are characteristic of Latin, in contrast to Greek, Christianity.

In the mid-3rd century the Western Church became completely Latin. The acts of the African councils convened by Cyprian in Carthage were recorded in Latin. Cyprian himself had been a *rhetor*, and wrote a more classical Latin than Tertullian's. Africa is indubitably the correct location of the poet Commodian, considering the unmistakably African Christian character of his extremely concrete interpretation of Scripture and of his apocalyptic view of history. At Rome Novatian, who eventually broke with the bishop of Rome, Cornelius, wrote his treatise *On the Trinity* in Latin.

The Western Church gradually assumed a distinctive character, with its own language, art and style. Even its problems were different from those of the Eastern Church: while the latter were doctrinal, those of the Western Church were disciplinary. Here the most serious controversy that arose was over the attitude to be taken towards the *lapsi*, *i.e.* those Christians who had recanted during the persecutions. The rigorous line taken by Novatian and Cyprian was countered, once more, by the more tolerant attitude of the bishop of Rome. They were again in opposition over the validity of baptisms administered by heretics. In such matters the Eastern Church was content to tolerate differences. From this time onwards the desire to organize and unify was characteristic of Latin Christendom.

The Christians come into power

By the second half of the 3rd century Christianity's peaceful conquest of the Roman Empire was complete. For instance, there is evidence for the existence of Christian communities in Britain: p 290 (13) London and York were represented by bishops at the Council of Arles in 314. In Gaul the biggest concentration of Christians was p 291 (16) still along the Mediterranean coast, but there were also Christians in all the major centres of population. In Spain thirty-three p 291 (18) churches were represented at the Council of Elvira (held at an early date in the 4th century). The entire North African coast had been p 292 (20) evangelized. The Synod convened at Carthage in the year 256 was attended by eighty-seven African bishops. In the Balkans, Christi- p 290 (12) anity had spread to the northern limits, and was developing considerably in what are now Croatia and Hungary.

Christianity spread through all social classes. The masses were being won over, and the increase in numbers was so great that in towns it had evidently become difficult to hold the local Christian community together by keeping it centred on the bishop. Districts had to be sub-divided, particularly in the suburbs, and priests appointed to them. This was the origin of the Roman *tituli*. In the countryside evangelization lagged behind, but groups of Christians were forming. In Africa and in Italy bishoprics were being multiplied. In the neighbourhood of Rome, many country towns had their own bishops, and in Asia Minor during this period there were *chōrepiskopoi*, *i.e.* village bishops, who were regarded as being of lower rank. The more usual way of solving the problem in the countryside was the way taken in the towns: the number of parishes served by priests was multiplied.

As the Christian Church increased in numbers, Christianity won over the ruling classes. It is wrong to say that these were converted only after the official adoption of Christianity as the religion of the Roman state: the trend was already marked in the period under review. Eusebius observes that, under the Emperors who reigned in the second half of the 3rd century, there were some Christian provincial governors. There were numerous Christians in the Imperial Household, and even in the Imperial family. Inscriptions show that there were Christians holding office in the municipal *curiae*. Anatolius, the bishop of Laodicea, had previously been a member of the senate of Alexandria. Domnus, bishop of Antioch, had previously been a high-ranking officer in the army. The Emperor appointed a Christian, Dorotheus, to the post of manager of the purple dye works at Tyre. Gregory and Athenodorus, two bishops of Pontus, came from senatorial families, and so did Basil and Gregory of Nyssa.

Christianity also made its mark in the realm of thought. Origen had given an immense impetus to theology and exegesis; and the Didaskalion of Alexandria, which he had founded, subsequently produced such remarkable men as Theognostos and Pierios. But Origen's most important legacy to the East was a generation of distinguished bishops who were his pupils. Dionysius of Alexandria had been director of the Didaskalion before becoming bishop, and his theology of the Word, based on that of Origen, provoked a controversy between him and Dionysius of Rome. At (Palestinian) Caesarea, where Origen had taught, Pamphilus maintained the Origenist tradition. Caesarea was the *alma mater* of Eusebius, who stood for a modified version of Origenism. Bishop Theotecnus (*c.* 260) was a disciple of Origen, and so were the great apostles of Cappadocia and Pontus, Firmilian of (Cappadocian) Caesarea and Gregory Thaumaturgus.

Another centre of high Christian culture was Antioch, where the tradition differed from Alexandria's in being more literary. Antioch produced a great exegete in Lucian of Antioch. Here the work of Origen aroused strong reactions, illustrated by Methodius of Olympus' treatise *On the Resurrection*. The great doctrinal controversies were beginning to take shape.

This development of Christianity in all fields was bound to create tensions in a society whose framework was still fundamentally pagan, and this tension manifested itself concretely at all levels. For Christians to hold public office created problems, since p 341 (23) magistrates normally had to perform ritual acts. In some cases the Emperor would excuse provincial governors from such participation; in other cases, conversely, Christian magistrates were forbidden to attend church during their term of office. But problems also presented themselves at the popular level. All collective activities – theatre, circus, official visits – entailed sacrifices to the tutelary gods of the cities, and the Christians' refusal to take part in these public exercises relegated them to the fringe of urban life. Family life and education presented analogous problems, and the councils held during this period had to legislate on all these delicate situations.

The blood of the martyrs

Confronted, as it now was, with the rising tide of Christianity, the pagan Empire at first resorted to force as a means of defence, and the second half of the 3rd century was the age of the great persecutions. Earlier persecutions had been local, and had been due to Christians' lack of legal status. Now the Emperors themselves took p 335 (8) the initiative. In the year 250 the Emperor Decius sought to promote Roman unity by ordering all citizens to take part in a general sacrifice. Many Christians fell away, but nevertheless there p 349 (*f4*) were a number of martyrs including Fabian, bishop of Rome, and the Roman priest Hippolytus. Cyprian of Carthage and Dionysius of p 344 (31) Alexandria avoided arrest by decamping, but Origen was arrested and tortured.

p 336 (11) Persecution was resumed in 257 under Valerian, but this time for different reasons. Dionysius makes Macrianus, the finance minister, responsible for the decision, and he interprets it as an attempt to raise funds. Incidentally, this is an indication that p 338–9 (15–21) ecclesiastical property had now become an important asset and that the Church now had its quota of wealthy aristocrats. This, however, was not the only motive for the persecution of the year 257. There were also religious motives which were not so much concerned with the defence of traditional religion but were principally inspired by a new pagan mysticism that was animated by a passionate hatred of Christianity. This was the date of the Neoplatonist Porphyry's treatise *Against the Christians*, and the same hatred of Christianity was manifested by Hierocles, the governor of Egypt. It was to reappear in the 4th century with the Emperor Julian, who was a disciple of the Neoplatonic philosopher Iamblichus. This was the final form of pagan opposition.

Between 260 and 303 the Church enjoyed a time of peace. Gallienus, Valerian's son, restored the confiscated property of the p 190 (35) Church and re-licensed Christian worship. This was an important act; for, while it did not make Christianity a *religio licita*, it amounted to *de facto* recognition. Now for the first time Christians had legal status. Furthermore, the judicial competence of bishops was recognized in matters of church administration. When Paul, bishop of Samosata, appealed against his deposition to Aurelian, the Emperor referred the decision to the bishops in communion with the church of Rome. This was tantamount to a recognition of the existence of a legitimate ecclesiastical authority.

This time of peace was cut short in 303 by a final persecution which was the most terrible of all and was the culminating confrontation between Christianity and the pagan Empire. The special character of this persecution was due to the transformation which the Empire itself was then undergoing. The Empire was in the midst of a terrible crisis. From outside it was threatened by the p 336 (12) Persians in the East and the barbarians in the North, and from within by economic crisis and political anarchy. To cope with this p 350 (*f5*) situation, Diocletian imposed an iron discipline:

> The new Empire presents itself to us as a new totalitarian state in, alas, the most modern sense of the word. The would-be absolute authority of the sovereign was exercised through a scientifically organized administrative machine. . . . The Lower Empire was an oppressive police state which lowered menacingly over everyone.[24]

This political system was not *per se* anti-Christian; in fact it was maintained under the Christian Emperors of the 4th century. But under Diocletian it allied itself with pagan mysticism, and this made a conflict inevitable.

Between February 303 and February 304 Diocletian published four edicts against the Christians, which struck like strokes of lightning: interdiction of worship, seizure of churches, arrest of heads of churches, and obligation to sacrifice to the gods. Christians who held out were put to death with refinements of cruelty un- p 340– (25, 26 exampled in earlier persecutions. Others were deported in vast numbers to the mines, the concentration camps of the Roman world. The law was not enforced everywhere with the same vigour, and the West in particular was less affected. Constantius Chlorus, the father of Constantine the Great, promulgated only the first edict, p 344 (33, 34 and that with circumspection. In Italy and Africa the persecution was brief. But in the East it was more severe, and Eusebius has given us the history of the martyrs of Palestine. The persecution was maintained until 312 under Diocletian's successor, Galerius. The Church had never been so profoundly stricken.

Actually, however – and this is what matters here – it was the Church that emerged triumphant from this ordeal of violence. The martyrs' courage revealed the vitality of Christianity, and it was paganism which had to yield, a paganism which no longer corresponded either to popular feeling or to the thought of the élite. Far from halting the spread of Christianity, persecution gave it a new vigour. Even after the Peace of the Church, even in a Christian Empire, the memory of the martyrs kept alive the memory of the triumph over persecution. This climate of heroism was maintained by the impetus of the monastic movement. The last persecutions, those of Decius, Valerian and Diocletian, were the supreme effort of the pagan world to halt Christianity's expansion. They incurred the retribution of defeat. Mediterranean civilization had become a Christian civilization, and Constantine merely set the seal on an accomplished fact when he put the Empire on a Christian basis. This was the terminal date of the missionary era of the Early Church, and Christianity now had only to complete and confirm its triumph. The era of Mediterranean Christianity had begun.

XIII

THE PHILOSOPHY THAT FAITH INSPIRED

GREEK PHILOSOPHY IN PHILO AND THE CHURCH FATHERS

HARRY A. WOLFSON

'Either Christians are now philosophers, or philosophers had already been Christians.'

MINUCIUS FELIX 'OCTAVIUS'

'The wisdom of man'—philosophy, 'the wisdom which the Greeks seek after' – was contrasted by St Paul with 'the wisdom of God' – truth gained from revelation. Yet as Christianity became part of the Hellenistic world the two grew together into a new discipline: theology. That was the achievement of the Greek and Latin Fathers. For them, philosophy too came from God, though not in so direct a way as the Law to the Jews. They found the same truths in the philosophers and the Scriptures and they took over many technical philosophical terms in order to define and defend the concepts of the new faith – terms like 'substance', 'essence', 'hypostasis'.

The controversy over the Eucharist, for instance, was one that could only have arisen in the context of Greek philosophy, and its eventual solution in terms of 'substance' and 'accidents' depends wholly on Aristotelian theory. Earlier disputes focused on how far the bread and wine were to be regarded as symbolic, the champions of the 'real presence' gaining ground, though Augustine seems to have leaned towards the opposite view. The fact that it was the central mystery of the Church, however, was never doubted from the very earliest times. This mosaic of the early-4th century shows a theme that has been called 'The Victory of the Eucharist'. An angel holds a laurel wreath and palm branch over a basket of bread and chalice of wine (the latter almost obliterated). It is part of the pavement of the former cathedral of Aquileia, and marked the position of a portable wooden altar. The damage to the right hand corner occurred when the altar was reconstructed in the late-5th century; it was crudely repaired in ancient times (1)

'Philosophy especially was given to the Greeks as a covenant peculiar to them,' wrote Philo. Such an approach made it easy to see both the pagan philosopher as divinely inspired and Christ himself as the True Philosopher. The two reliefs (right) make this point vividly. One is the sarcophagus of a philosopher, believed by some historians to be none other than Plotinus. He sits reading from a scroll with two women pupils and an older man listening. The bearded figures at the sides are probably other philosophers, and on the extreme right is part of a sundial.

The other panel (centre), from an ivory casket of the 4th century, shows Christ teaching the Apostles. The scene clearly looks back to the earlier model, and was no doubt meant as an explicit reference. (2,3)

The allegorical method of expounding pagan myths, as distinguished from the allegorical method of expounding Scriptural texts, was taken over by Christian teachers from the pagans themselves, who had also used it in giving moral meanings to old stories. Bellerophon (opposite, left) slaying the Chimaera (a hybrid of lion, goat and snake) became a 'type' of Christ defeating the powers of evil: 'the Devil, as a roaring lion, walketh about, seeking whom he may devour'. Similarly Apollo, the Sun God, was identified with Christ, 'the Sun of Righteousness', both in a hymn of Clement's and in the vault mosaic (opposite right) of a Christian tomb. (5,6)

Orpheus the musician, who charmed the beasts and stopped rivers by his playing, was the 'type' of King David, the singer of the Psalms, or (in virtue of his mission to Hades to rescue Eurydice from the dead) of Christ. This 4th-century ivory pyxis (right) may or may not be Christian, but the sarcophagus (opposite) certainly is, for Christ-Orpheus is shown with a sheep between his feet and a dove by his right shoulder. (4,7)

Christ riding the chariot of the Sun, from the Necropolis of St Peter's, Rome. (6)

Bellerophon slaying the Chimaera, from an ivory plaque that is probably Christian. (5)

The exposition of Scriptural texts in a Christian sense by the allegorical method began with St Paul, who Christianized a certain method of interpretation current in Judaism. To this Pauline method of allegorical interpretation, which sought in the Old Testament adumbrations of the advent and life of Christ, was later added a philosophical kind of allegorical interpretation, and this was extended and applied also to the New Testament and to the doctrines which the Church drew from it.

The Crossing of the Red Sea prefigured baptism. 'All were under the cloud,' wrote St Paul, 'and all passed through the sea and all were baptized unto Moses in the cloud and in the sea.' The image was taken up by Tertullian, Ambrose and others. This ambitious 4th-century mosaic (left) is in Santa Maria Maggiore, Rome. (8)

Jonah's three days in the belly of the whale were taken to refer to the three days between Christ's death and resurrection. The fresco shown here, from the catacomb of the Giordani, Rome, dates from the 4th century. (9)

Moses striking the rock to bring water to the Israelites in the desert anticipated Christ's promise: 'Whosoever drinketh of the water that I shall give him shall never thirst; but the water that I give him shall be in him a well of water springing up into everlasting life.' (10)

Noah saved man from physical drowning, as Christ was to save him from the waters of spiritual death. This picture comes from an early Christian illuminated manuscript, the Vienna Genesis. (11)

The incomprehensible mysteries of the Trinity (Three in One) and the Incarnation (God becoming Man) were two vital fields where philosophical techniques, mostly Aristotelian in origin, were used to reconcile the seeming paradoxes of revelation.

'Three persons, one substance' was the formula finally adopted by the Fathers to describe the Trinity. The earliest representation in art is on the so-called 'dogmatic' sarcophagus (above), where all three persons, identical bearded figures, take part in the creation of Eve. The Son appears for a second time on the right, as a young man walking with Adam. (12)

The Incarnation united two natures —human and divine—in the single person of Christ. Several of the early theological disputes centred on the question of how the two natures were related, and this is reflected to some extent in the iconography. The Christ-child, for instance, could be seen either as a divine figure, as in the mosaic on the far right where he sits on a jewelled throne and is attended by Holy Wisdom, or as a human baby playing on his mother's lap (right – the 13th century mosaic is thought to follow a 5th century original). It was the second approach that became more usual, though artists strove to suggest his divinity through gesture and expression. (13, 16)

'And lo! three men stood by him; and when he saw them he ran to meet them from the tent door and bowed himself towards the ground.' Abraham's three mysterious guests in Genesis xviii were interpreted by the Early Church as prefiguring the Trinity. This mosaic is in Santa Maria Maggiore, Rome. (14)

Three concentric circles on a mosaic beneath one of the arches in the baptistery of Albenga, Italy, probably refer to the triple immersion in the name of the Father, the Son and the Holy Ghost. The Chi-Rho symbol and the Alpha and Omega are similarly repeated three times. The twelve doves represent the Apostles. (15)

To establish true doctrine was the task of the Early Fathers, and it was their conclusions that swayed the series of great councils beginning with that of Nicaea in 325, when the orthodox Creed was hammered out amid bitter controversy. The mosaic panel shown here, from the north hall of the former cathedral at Aquileia, shows a local Christian, Cyriacus, who is wished life in the inscription above, as a ram, *i.e.* one of the flock of Christ. Its proximity in the same mosaic to images of the fight against heresy (shown in the next chapter) may indicate that Cyriacus was active in the struggle with Arianism. (17)

GREEK PHILOSOPHY IN PHILO AND THE CHURCH FATHERS

HARRY A. WOLFSON

SCRIPTURE AND PHILOSOPHY[1]

When, at about the middle of the 2nd century AD, philosophically trained gentiles began to flock to Christianity – invariably, as they confess, by becoming acquainted with the teachings of Scripture – they formed a conception of the relation between philosophy and Scripture like that which about a century earlier was formed by the scripturally trained Philo on his becoming acquainted with the teachings of the philosophers. Philosophy and Scripture were held by them to contain two kinds of wisdom. One is that which Paul calls the 'wisdom of men'[2] or the wisdom 'which the Greeks seek after'.[3] The other is that which, again, Paul calls 'the wisdom of God'[4] and which, speaking of the particular gospel of his preaching, he describes as coming to him 'through the revelation of Jesus Christ',[5] but which the Fathers of the Church, if they were to speak of the matters dealt with by them in their own preachings, would describe as coming to them through the revelation of the two Testaments; for to all of them, as to Irenaeus, 'both Testaments are the revelations of one and the same Householder'.[6] Like Philo, they could not help observing striking similarities between some of the humanly discovered wisdom and the divinely revealed wisdom, such, for instance, as between the teachings of the philosophers and the teachings of the prophets about the unity of God, between their respective denunciations of the worship of images, between their respective condemnations of certain evil religious practices, and between their respective preoccupations with the problem of the righteous or virtuous conduct of men.[7]

p 302 (2, 3) *f 1*

These striking similarities seemed to the Fathers, as they did to Philo, to require an explanation. The explanation which they formally advanced, like the explanation which is informally suggested by Philo in various places in his works, is based upon the assumption that the similarities of the philosophic teachings to the prophetic teachings are also in some indirect way of divine origin. This single explanation is presented by the Fathers in three different forms. Sometimes they say that these similarities are borrowings on the part of the philosophers from the Scripture; sometimes they describe them as the discoveries of the philosophers by that power of reasoning which has been implanted in them by God; but sometimes they variously express themselves to the effect that philosophy is God's special gift to the Greeks by way of human reason as Scripture is to the Jews by way of direct revelation. In Philo the view that philosophy, like Scripture, was a special gift of God is indirectly suggested in two statements. In one of these he describes the Law as the words 'which God showers from . . . heaven'[8] and in the other he says that 'it is heaven which has showered philosophy upon us'.[9] Among the Church Fathers this is hinted at by Justin Martyr in his description of philosophy as that which 'is sent down to us',[10] but Clement of Alexandria – who in one passage, reflecting Philo's statement, only says that philosophy has come down 'from God to men . . . in the same way in which showers fall down on the good land'[11] – says in another passage that 'philosophy . . . was a schoolmaster to bring the Hellenic mind to Christ, as the Law was to bring the Hebrews';[12] and in still another passage, having in mind the description of the Law as a covenant between God and Israel,[13] he says that 'philosophy especially was given to the Greeks as a covenant peculiar to them'.[14]

The belief in the divine origin of Scripture, which implies a belief in its completeness and perfection, led the Fathers, as it had led Philo, to the further belief that, in addition to the obviously striking similarities between the teachings of philosophy and Scripture, many more of the teachings of philosophy, which human reason and experience have found to be true, must have their similarities in the teaching of Scripture. Conditions of life made it necessary for the Fathers, as they did for Philo, to put this further belief of theirs to practical use. For in the Roman world the Christians were exposed to all the charges and accusations which had been levelled previously against the Hellenistic Jews, especially the charge of atheism, which was evoked by the Christian continuation of the Hellenistic Jewish attack upon polytheism, idolatry, and the various forms of heathen worship. If their rejection of the Law had exempted them from the ridicule heaped upon the Jews for their observance of the rite of circumcision and the dietary laws and the Sabbath, the particular form of their religious organization and the particular mode of their religious propaganda brought upon them new accusations, such as infanticide, cannibalism, incest, and disloyalty to the state.[15] Following the kind of defence that had already been developed among the Hellenistic Jews, the Fathers tried to show that in their attack upon polytheism and idolatry and the various forms of heathen worship they were merely following in the footsteps of the best pagan philosophers and that their doctrines, though outlandish, were in agreement with the teachings found in philosophy.

And so the Fathers of the Church, like Philo before them, entered upon their systematic undertaking to show how, behind the homely language in which Scripture likes to express itself, there are hidden the teachings of the philosophers couched in the obscure technical terms coined in their Academy, Lyceum, and Porch. When opponents among the Fathers quoted, against their attempt to philosophize Scripture, Paul's warning against being spoiled 'through philosophy and vain deceit',[16] they argued that the warning was only against the use of that kind of philosophy which is vain deceit but not against true philosophy, which conforms, or can be made to conform, with the teaching of Scripture.[17] The method used by the Fathers, and before them by Philo, in their common effort to invest the language of Scripture with meanings other than its literal meaning, is described by them as being allegorical.

p 206 (5–8)

The so-called 'typological allegory'

Now it happens that, before Philo and the Church Fathers, a similar allegorical interpretation of texts had been used by various Greek philosophers with reference to the mythologies in Homer and Hesiod. One would therefore naturally expect the existence of some relation between the earlier and the later uses of this method of interpretation. What that relation actually was may be determined by three sets of facts.

p 302–3 (4–7)

First, in Greek philosophy, as far as written records are concerned, the term 'allegorical' as a description of the philosophical interpretation of mythology occurs for the first time in the work of a certain Stoic named Heraclitus,[18] who is supposed to have been a contemporary of Philo's. Before him this method was described by Theagenes of Rhegium as 'physical and ethical'[19] and by Plato and Xenophon as the 'underlying meaning' (ὑπόνοια *hyponoia*).[20] In Philo, the combined terms 'physical and ethical' and the Greek term for 'underlying meaning' and various grammatical forms of the term 'allegory' are all used as a description of his non-literal interpretation of scriptural texts to which he gives philo-

St Paul began the allegorical interpretation of Old Testament texts in a Christian sense. This 3rd-century fresco from the hypogeum of the Aurelii is thought to be the earliest representation of him. (1)

sophical meanings. In addition, Philo uses, as a description of his non-literal interpretation, a number of other terms, some of which occur in Heraclitus either in combination with the term allegory or in the sense of allegory; but, among those other terms used by Philo are included the terms 'type' (τύπος *typos*) and 'shadow' (σκιά *skia*) and 'parable' (παραβολή *parabolē*),[21] none of which occurs in Heraclitus in any connection with allegory. There are also in Philo non-literal interpretations of scriptural texts in which the new meanings given by him are not philosophical but rather those common in the non-literal Midrashic interpretations used by the rabbis, among which there is his use once or twice of that particular kind of Midrashic interpretation which may be described as predictive, that is, as predicting some future event. The antiquity of this kind of Midrashic interpretation is attested by its use in the recently discovered Dead Sea Scrolls.

Second, in Christianity, the non-literal interpretation of scriptural texts designated by the term allegorical did not begin with the Church Fathers. It began with Paul. But with Paul the non-literal allegorical interpretations of scriptural texts are not of the philosophical kind; they are all of the Midrashic kind, and mainly of that Midrashic kind of interpretation which we have described as predictive. Then also, in addition to his use of the term 'allegory',[22] Paul uses, like Philo, the terms 'type'[23] and 'shadow'.[24] It is on the basis of his use of the term 'type' that students of Christianity refer to Paul's predictive kind of interpretation as typological allegory and regard it as an innovation introduced by Paul. Moreover, in the Epistle to the Hebrews, which is traditionally attributed to Paul, the Midrashic kind of predictive interpretation is described not only by the Philonic term 'shadow'[25] but also by the Philonic term 'parable'.[26]

Third, the first occurrence in the Church Fathers of non-literal interpretations of scriptural texts was of texts of the Old Testament, and the interpretations used were all of the Midrashic predictive kind, like that used by Paul. In Barnabas this is described by the term 'type', used by Paul and Philo, and in Justin Martyr it is described not only by the term 'type' but also by the term 'parable', used in the Epistle to the Hebrews and in Philo, and, in addition, by the terms 'symbol' (σύμβολον *symbolon*) and 'tropology' (τροπολογία *tropologia*), both of which are used by Philo, the latter term in its adjectival form 'tropical' (τροπική *tropikē*). The first to introduce non-literal interpretations of the philosophical kind in its application to texts of both the Old and the New Testament is Clement of Alexandria. From that time on, the philosophical kind of interpretation is used by the Fathers alongside of the Midrashic kind of predictive interpretation, the so-called 'typological allegory'. The terms used by them as descriptions of both these kinds of non-literal interpretations are, besides a few new terms, all terms used by Philo, to whom also some of their non-literal interpretation of Old Testament texts can be traced.[27]

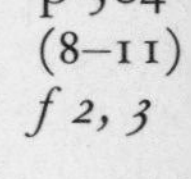
p 304–(8–11) *f 2, 3*

From all this it may be gathered that the allegorical interpretation did not come to the Fathers directly from Greek philosophy; it came to them from Philo, partly through the Pauline writings, though in the course of its use by them it came into direct contact with the allegorical method, as used in Greek philosophy, and was affected by it.

The handmaid of theology

Their common belief that the wisdom of Scripture was directly revealed by God in contrast to the wisdom of philosophy which was the product of human reason, though not without the help and foresight of God, led both Philo and the Fathers to the principle of the subordination of philosophy to Scripture or, as it came to be known, the subordination of reason to faith. Scripture, in their view, contained certain beliefs which, though rationally undemonstrable, are fundamental, and to these philosophy, whenever it happened to disagree with them, had to yield. Now, in Greek philosophy, the view that there was a subordinate relationship between the encyclical studies and philosophy, in the limited sense that the former were serviceable and useful to the latter, had been expressed by the application to them respectively of the terms 'handmaids' (θεράπαιναι *therapainai*) and 'mistress' (δέσποινα *despoina*).[28] With this in the back of his mind, Philo, in his allegorical interpretation of the story of Sarah and Hagar, takes Hagar, the handmaid, to symbolize the encyclical studies, and Sarah, the mistress, to symbolize wisdom, which he uses in the sense of Scripture. Philo thus concludes: 'Just as encyclical culture is the handmaid (δούλη *doulē* = θεραπαινίς *therapainis*) of philosophy, so also is philosophy the handmaid of wisdom.'[29] The same allegorical interpretation of the story of Sarah and Hagar is reproduced by Clement of Alexandria in a passage in which he mentions Philo. Thus, quoting the verse in which Abraham says to Sarah: 'Behold, thy maid is in thy hand; deal with her as it pleases thee,'[30] he interprets it allegorically: 'I embrace worldly culture as a younger maid and as a handmaid (θεραπαινίδα *therapainida*), but thy knowledge I honour and reverence as a full-grown mistress (δέσποιναν *despoinan*).'[31] Again, like Philo, Clement says: 'As the encyclical branches of study contribute to philosophy, which is their mistress (δέσποινα *despoina*), so also philosophy itself co-operates for the acquisition of wisdom. . . . Wisdom is therefore the mistress (κυρία *kyria*) of philosophy, as philosophy is of preparatory culture.'[32] Following Philo or Clement of Alexandria, the same allegorical interpretation of the story of Sarah and Hagar and the same ancillary conception of the relation of philosophy to Scripture is reproduced in various forms by other Fathers. John of Damascus, after alluding to that ancillary conception in his statement that 'it is fitting for the queen to be served by certain handmaids (ἅβραις *habrais*)', goes on to say: 'Let us, therefore, accept the (philosophers') sayings in so far as they serve the truth, but reject the impiety' that is in them.[33]

The ancillary relationship of philosophy to Scripture, or of reason to faith, thus had for Philo and the Fathers two different meanings, corresponding to two different kinds of scriptural teachings with which philosophy was to be brought into relation. First, with regard to scriptural teachings with which philosophy was in agreement, it meant that philosophy was to be used in the explanation and the justification of those teachings for the benefit of those who stood in need of such explanations and justifications. Second, with regard to those scriptural teachings with which philosophy was in disagreement, it meant that philosophy had to be rejected.

Of these two meanings, the second, referring as it does to scriptural teachings which were in conflict with philosophy, was accepted by the Fathers without any qualification. But in regard to the first meaning, referring as it does to scriptural teachings which could be rationally supported by philosophy, the question arose whether mere faith in those teachings was sufficient without the use of rational philosophic support.

In answer to this question, three views appeared among the Fathers. To some of them, of whom Tertullian was the spokesman, simple faith was self-sufficient. To others, of whom Origen was the spokesman, simple faith was inferior to rationalized faith. To still others, of whom Clement of Alexandria was the spokesman, simple faith and rationalized faith were equal. The last view found support in the philosophic use of the term 'faith' as a technical epistemological term. It happens that in a number of passages Aristotle uses the term 'faith' (πίστις *pistis*) as a designation both of undemonstrated immediate knowledge and of demonstrated derivative knowledge; and Simplicius, long after the time of Clement of Alexandria, is evidently following an old Peripatetic tradition when, in commenting on Aristotle's statement that 'anyone syllogizing may believe',[34] he says: 'Faith is twofold, the one without demonstration . . . the other after demonstration.'[35] Now some of the Aristotelian passages in which the term 'faith' is used in those two senses are quoted by Clement in several passages of his *Stromateis*. Then, in one passage, reflecting all these passages, he says that (1) 'faith in God' is 'obedience to the commandments', but that (2) 'demonstration . . . produces scientific faith (ἐπιστημονικὴ πίστις *epistēmonikē pistis*) which becomes "knowledge" (γνῶσις *gnōsis*)',[36] or, as he says in another place, 'knowledge is a sure and strong demonstration of what is received by faith'.[37]

This, then, was the common attitude of Philo and the Fathers toward philosophy. How that attitude manifested itself in their actual use of philosophy in their interpretation of Scripture may be illustrated by an analysis (1) of their common use of the Platonic Theory of Ideas in their respective treatments of their common belief in a Logos, and (2) of the Fathers' use of philosophy in their treatment of the ramifications of their particular conception of the Logos into the Christian doctrines of the Trinity and the Incarnation.

THE LOGOS AND THE PLATONIC IDEAS[38]

Philo, who, on the basis of Scripture supplemented by Jewish tradition, believed that, before the creation of the world, God created certain incorporeal things after the pattern of which He subsequently created corporeal things in this created world, identified this belief of his with the Platonic Theory of Ideas. But in Plato he found contradictory statements with regard to the origin of the Ideas. In some of these statements the Ideas are described as uncreated and coeternal with God; in others they are described as created by God; and in still others the language used lends itself to the interpretation that they are mere thoughts of God. Harmonizing these conflicting statements, Philo arrived at a view according to which the Ideas had existed from eternity as thoughts of God; but that, when God was about to create the world, He created the Ideas as incorporeal patterns for the corporeal things of which the world was to consist. Then in Plato he found that the incorporeal Ideas were integrated into what Plato calls an 'intelligible animal', in contrast to the corporeal world which he calls the 'visible animal'.[39] To Philo, however, who, unlike Plato, did not believe that the corporeal world possessed a soul, the term 'animal' did not seem to be an appropriate description of it. He therefore changed the term 'animal' in both descriptions to the term 'world', and thus the contrast between the integrated Ideas and the corporeal world became a contrast between the 'intelligible world' and the 'visible world'. Then, also, Philo found in Aristotle a reference to a saying, evidently of some Platonists, that 'the thinking soul' is 'the place of Forms',[40] that is, of Ideas. Under the combined influence of two precedents – on the one hand the Greek use of the term *logos*, meaning, literally, 'word', in the sense of what Aristotle calls here 'the thinking soul' and in the sense of Plato's statement that all animals and plants and inanimate substances 'are created by a *logos* [that is, a reason] and a divine knowledge which comes from God',[41] and on the other hand the scriptural statement (Psalm xxxiii 6 in the Septuagint version) that 'by the *logos* of the Lord the heavens were established'[42] – Philo came to describe the Logos as the place of the intelligible world of Ideas by which the world was created.

The Logos, together with the intelligible world of Ideas within it, thus had, for Philo, two stages of existence; first, as existing within God and hence identical with Him; second, as a real being which came into existence by an act of creation. That, according to Philo, the Logos, together with the intelligible world of Ideas within it, entered upon its second stage of existence by an act of creation, like that by which the visible world came into existence, may be gathered from Philo's description of the Logos as 'older (πρεσβύτερος *presbyteros*) than all things which were the objects of creation',[43] and likewise from his description of the intelligible world as being 'older' in comparison with the visible world as being 'younger' (νεώτερος *neōteros*).[44] Now the terms 'older' and 'younger' are evidently used here by Philo in the same sense in which they are used by Plato in his description of the universal soul as being not 'younger' (νεωτέρα *neōtera*) than the world but rather 'older' (πρεσβυτέρα *presbytera*) than it.[45] But this description by Plato of the universal soul and the world as being respectively older and younger makes a comparison between two created things, since, for Plato, the universal soul, like the world, is created. Consequently, when Philo describes the Logos as being 'older' than all created things and the intelligible world as being 'older' than the 'younger' visible world, the implication is that, for him, the Logos as well as the intelligible world is created in the sense in which the visible world and all things in it are said to be created. Accordingly, Philo's description of the Logos as 'the firstborn son' of God[46] is to be taken as having carried, for him, the same sense as his description of righteous human beings as 'sons of God'.[47] Philo is using the phrase, not in the sense of being begotten of God but rather in the sense of being created by God. Therefore when Philo says of the Logos that it is 'neither uncreated as God is nor created as you are'[48] he means by this that, though the Logos was created like all created beings, still, as an incorporeal being, its creation was not like that of man, who was created, as Scripture says, out of dust from the earth.[49]

Since the Logos is said by Philo, in the passage just quoted, to be not uncreated, as God is, the Logos cannot be called God. Accordingly, when Philo himself happens to interpret the term 'God' in Genesis xxxi 13 as referring to the Logos, he hastens to explain that this does not mean that there are 'two Gods'; for, as he goes on to say, 'He that is truly God is one, but those that are improperly so called are more than one.'[50] And so also, when Philo himself happens to describe the Logos as 'a second God'[51] or as 'second to God',[52] this description of the Logos means simply that it is 'divine' (θεῖος *theios*), which is Philo's usual description of the Logos.[53]

In the beginning was the Word

Among the Fathers, speculation about the Logos hinged upon the word *Logos* in the Prologue to the Gospel according to St John, where it is used as a designation of the pre-existent Christ who subsequently became flesh and where it is described as 'the only begotten from the Father'[54] and as 'God'.[55] Whatever these two descriptions of the Logos may have meant originally when used by John, the Church Fathers, from the earliest times, beginning with those Fathers described as Apostolic, took them to mean literally that the Logos was begotten or generated out of the essence of God and that it was God in the sense that the Father, its begetter, was God. Somewhat later, however, beginning with those philosophizing Fathers called Apologists, two questions arose with regard to this Johannine Logos. First, while all of them believed that the Logos as a real being was not created by God but was generated out of His essence, the question arose among them as to when that generation had taken place. Second, the Fathers somehow came to believe that the Logos of John, like the Logos of Philo, was some kind of version of the Platonic Theory of Ideas, and so the question arose among them as to whether the implication of the Johannine Logos-ized version of that theory, namely, that the Ideas were generated together with the Logos out of the essence of God, represented the Theory of Ideas as originally conceived of by Plato.

The first question – the question when the generation of the Logos had taken place – gave rise to two theories. The first of these two theories to arise was a two-stages theory of existence like that held by Philo, except that the entrance of the Logos upon its second stage of existence, when it became a real being after it had been from eternity a thought of God's, was effected, not by its being created by God, but by its being generated from His essence. The exponents of this theory were such Greek Fathers as Justin Martyr, Tatian, Athenagoras, Theophilus, Hippolytus, and Clement of Alexandria, and such Latin Fathers as Tertullian, Novatian, Lactantius, and, much later, Zeno of Verona. This theory's opposite was a single-stage theory of existence known as that of eternal generation. This was introduced, for different reasons, by Irenaeus and Origen, and it is this single-stage theory that was tacitly recognized as the established Christian belief, though the two-stages theory was never formally anathematized and hence was never branded as being heretical. As representative examples of the manner in which the two-stages theory of existence was presented by its adherents among the Fathers, we may quote two brief statements, one written in Greek by Theophilus and the other written in Latin by Tertullian. As presented by Theophilus, it reads that 'before anything came into being', the Logos was God's 'own mind and thought . . . but, when God wished to make all that He determined on, He begot the Logos as something uttered, "the firstborn of all creation"'.[56] As presented by Tertullian, the theory reads that, 'before all things God was alone', though not without that Reason or Logos 'which He had in Himself';[57] but, 'as soon as God willed to produce' the world, 'He first brought forth the Logos itself'.[58]

When exactly the Platonic Ideas were read into the Johannine Logos is not clear. Justin Martyr says that, before he became a Christian, the Platonic 'conception of incorporeals quite overpowered me and the contemplation of Ideas furnished my mind with wings',[59] but he does not tell us whether, after his conversion to Christianity, he abandoned his belief in Platonic Ideas altogether or whether he has only given them another interpretation. About twenty-five years later, Athenagoras, referring to the Logos during its first stage of existence, says that 'the Son of God is the Logos of the Father in Idea and in operation, for after the pattern of Him and through Him were all things made'; but, then, referring to the Logos during the second stage of its existence, he says that 'He came forth to be the Idea and operating power of all material things'.[60]

Athenagoras does not tell us how his conception of the Ideas is related to that of Plato. His contemporary Irenaeus, however, makes it clear that his Logos-ized Theory of the Ideas was unlike that of Plato. Plato's Theory of Ideas in their integration is represented by Irenaeus as a belief in the existence of a 'pattern' (*exemplum*) by the side of matter and God, and this, he says, is the basis of the Gnostic theory of aeons. Both of these theories he rejects. His own view is that God 'receives from Himself the pattern (*exemplum*) and form (*figurationem*) of those things which are made',[61] by which he means that the Ideas come from God Himself; for they are contained in the Logos, and the Logos, according to Irenaeus, is eternally generated from the essence of God. Similarly Tertullian makes the Platonic Theory of Ideas the source of the Gnostic theory of aeons, both of which he rejects. As for his own conception of Ideas Tertullian starts out by saying that the Latin term *sensus*, 'mind' or 'thought', means the same as the Greek term *Logos* and the Latin term *sermo*.[62] He then goes on to say:

> As soon as God willed to bring forth . . . the things which He, together with His . . . Logos, had devised within Himself, He first brought forth the Logos itself . . . in order that all things might be made through that through which they had been planned and devised, yea, and already made, in so far as they were in the mind of God (*in dei sensu*).[63]

From this it may be inferred that the Ideas, which are said by Tertullian to have existed 'in the mind of God', existed in the Logos of God.

Plato Philonized and Johannized

While Irenaeus and Tertullian regarded the Johannine Logos-ized Theory of Ideas as something different from the Theory of Ideas as conceived by Plato himself, Clement of Alexandria and Augustine regarded them as being the same. *f 4*

Clement's view with regard to the relation of the Johannine Logos-ized Theory of Ideas to the Platonic Theory of Ideas may be gathered from the following passages.

In one passage,[64] Clement makes three statements. First, on the basis of a quotation from John, he identifies John's 'Logos' with 'truth'. Second, on the basis of a quotation from the *Phaedrus*, he shows that Plato identified 'truth' with 'an Idea', that is to say, with the totality of Ideas. Third, 'an Idea', Clement says, is that which 'the Barbarians have termed the Logos of God', by which, as it can be shown, he means that the Jews, as represented by Philo, have defined the Logos as being the totality of Ideas. Here then we have an identification of the Logos-ized Theory of Ideas of John with that of Philo, and the identification of both of these with the Platonic Theory of Ideas.

In another passage,[65] after ascribing to 'the Barbarian philosophy' what is known to us as the Philonic contrast between 'the intelligible world' and 'the sensible world' and also as the Philonic interpretation of the account of the first day of creation as referring to the creation of 'the intelligible world', Clement says: 'Does not Plato hence appear to have left the Ideas of living creatures in the intelligible world, and to make intelligible objects into sensible species according to their genera?' Here then we have a suggestion that Plato's account of creation in the *Timaeus* is based on the Book of Genesis, the interpretation of which by Philo was accepted by Clement as its true meaning.

The Crossing of the Red Sea, a classical prefiguration of baptism, is found on many sarcophagi which may have been influenced by the relief of the Battle of the Milvian Bridge on the Arch of Constantine (see p. 342–3). (2)

In still another passage,[66] the Philonic statement that God is 'the incorporeal dwelling-place (χώρα *chōra*) of incorporeal Ideas'[67] (reproduced by Clement in the formula that God is 'the dwelling-place of Ideas'), is attributed by Clement to Plato, who, Clement says, 'has learned from Moses that He was a place (τόπος *topos*) which contained all things'. The Moses to whom Clement traces the view which he attributes to Plato is really Philo, who interpreted the term 'place' in the verse 'and he saw the place afar off'[68] as referring to God,[69] explaining that God is called place 'by reason of His containing all things'.[70]

Thus Clement of Alexandria first identifies both the Johannine and the Philonic Logos-ized Theories of Ideas with the Platonic Theory of Ideas and then shows how the Platonic Theory of Ideas was derived from the teachings of Moses as interpreted by Philo.

Augustine, at one time, tried to prove the existence of an intelligible world beyond the world of sense from Jesus' saying: 'My kingdom is not of this world.'[71] When later he retracted this interpretation of the verse, he still argued for the existence of an intelligible world of Ideas within the Logos, which to him was eternally generated from the essence of God.[72] This conception of a Logos-ized Theory of Ideas is constantly treated by Augustine as if it were the same as the original Platonic theory. In one place he gives direct expression to this view, and that is in his *Commentary on John*, where he says, without any qualification, that 'in the books of the philosophers' it is also to be found 'that God has an only begotten Son, by whom all things are'.[73]

THE TRINITY AND PHILOSOPHY[74]

Philo, as we have seen,[75] after interpreting the term God in a certain scriptural verse as referring to the Logos, hastened to explain that this does not imply the existence of 'two Gods', arguing that 'He who is truly God is one', so that, whenever he himself happens to apply the term God to the Logos, he uses it loosely in the sense of divine. In the light of this, when the Fathers insisted that the Logos is God in the true sense of the term God, the implication was that there were two Gods. And so, when the Nicene Creed started with the affirmation of a belief 'in one God' and then went on to affirm that the Logos, to whom it refers as 'the Son of God' and the 'only-begotten', is 'God of God', there was a simultaneous affirmation of a belief in one God and of a belief in two Gods, or rather of a belief in one God who was two Gods. Moreover, when the Holy Spirit, who in Justin Martyr is described only as that whom 'we worship and adore',[76] was ultimately declared to be God, the simultaneous affirmation became that of a belief in one God and of a belief in three Gods, or, again, rather of a belief in one God who was three Gods. How to explain and to justify such a conception of a triune deity became a matter of discussion among the Fathers from Justin Martyr to John of Damascus. To all these philosophically trained Fathers this conception of a triune deity seemed to be in violation of what came to be called the Law of Contradiction, which, as formulated by Aristotle in terms that he attributes to Heraclitus, reads: 'It is impossible for contrary attributes to belong at the same time to the same subject.'[77]

p 306–7 (12, 14–15)

Two attempts at solving the problem were made in the course of its history, one by denying the reality of the Logos and the Holy Spirit and the other by denying their Godhood. The first solution had at least eight successive sponsors. One of them, Sabellius, is said to have maintained that 'Father and Son are the same'[78] and that the terms Father and Son and Holy Spirit are merely actions (ἐνέργειαι *energeiai*) or names (ὀνομασίαι *onomasiai*) and are to be compared to 'the light and the heat and the circular form in the sun'.[79] The second solution, offered by Arius, was in effect a return to the Philonic view[80] that the Logos, as well as the Holy Spirit, was not generated from the essence of God but rather was created by God, and that therefore, like anything created by God, it was not God. Both these solutions were anathematized and were branded as heretical.

Most of the Fathers, however, adhering as they did to the established Christian belief in a triune God, tried to defend this belief. Their defence of it consisted primarily in the assertion that the two doctrines, Generation and Trinity, are two ineffable and incomprehensible mysteries, which are not subject to any of the criteria of human reason. Still, while not attempting to probe into the rationality of these mysteries, they tried to explain them and to make them intelligible and to clear them of the most obvious objections, and this they did by the use of philosophic terminology and philosophic concepts. Here are a few examples.

First, wishing to express their opposition to those who claimed that Father and Son and Holy Spirit are only names, they argued that these members of the Trinity are distinguished from each other 'in number' (ἀριθμῷ *arithmō*) and not 'in name only'.[81] What they meant to say is that each member of the Trinity is what Aristotle would call a real individual being (τὸ ἄτομον *to atomon*); for a real individual being is described by Aristotle as being 'one in number' (ἓν ἀριθμῷ *hen arithmō*).[82]

Second, in order to explain how, on the basis of their belief that the Logos was generated out of the essence of God, they were justified in believing that it is God, they drew upon Aristotle's statement that 'it is the most natural function of all living things . . . to reproduce their species, animal producing animal and plant plant',[83] as also 'man begets man' (another quotation from p 308 (17) Aristotle).[84] Thus Augustine, in his argument against the Arian theologian Maximinus, quotes Aristotle's statement that 'man p 322 (10) begets man', with his own addition 'and dog dog', and he then challenges his opponent as follows: 'For you see that a corruptible creature can beget an offspring like itself, and yet you believe that God, the Father almighty, could not beget His only-begotten Son except with a nature of an inferior kind.'[85]

Third, in their attempt to show that, while the conception of a triune God is a mystery which cannot be solved by human reason, it is still free of the charge of its being a violation of what Aristotle could have called the Law of Contradiction, the Fathers try to show that even philosophers sometimes allow the simultaneous description of a thing as being both one and many. In this connection they draw upon Aristotle's enumeration of various ways in which things which are many may legitimately be called one without any violation of the Law of Contradiction. Two of these ways are especially selected by the Fathers as useful for their purpose. One is that which Aristotle describes as the unity of species or of genus, illustrated by the example of several distinct human beings who may be described as being one because of their belonging to the same species man or to the same genus animal.[86] Thus Basil explains that the three members of the Trinity, each of them God, may be said to be one God, in the same way as 'Peter, Andrew, John, and James' are said to be 'one man'[87] or 'one animal'.[88] The other way is that which Aristotle calls the unity of substratum, illustrated by the example of oil and wine which may be described as one because of their common 'substratum' (ὑποκείμενον *hypokeimenon*), which is water.[89] Thus, according to Augustine, the three members of the Trinity, each of them God, may be said to be one God, in the same way as we say of three golden statues: 'three statues, one gold'.[90]

In search of a philosophical nomenclature

Having thus explained how philosophically the three members of the Trinity, despite their each being God, may still be described as one God, the Fathers began to look in the stockpile of philosophic terminology for two good technical terms, of which one would be used as a designation of the reality of the distinctness of each member of the Trinity as an individual and the other would be used as a designation of their underlying common unity. The first two Fathers who dealt with this problem, Origen in Greek and Tertullian in Latin, experimented with various terms.

As a designation of the reality of the distinctness of each member of the Trinity as an individual, the following Greek terms were suggested by Origen:

1. πρᾶγμα (*pragma*),[91] 'thing', evidently based upon a statement by Aristotle in which the Greek term for 'thing' is contrasted with the Greek term for 'name'.[92]

2. οὐσία (*ousia*),[93] which is usually translated either literally as 'essence' or conventionally as 'substance'. This term *ousia*, according to Aristotle, may be used either in the sense of 'primary *ousia*', that is, 'individual', or in the sense of 'secondary *ousia*', that is, 'species' or 'genus'.[94] Here it is quite evidently used by Origen in the sense of 'primary *ousia*'.

3. ὑποκείμενον, *hypokeimenon*. In Aristotle, as we have seen, this term is used in the sense of 'substratum'. Origen, however, says that the Son is distinct from the Father 'according to *ousia* and *hypokeimenon*',[95] which shows that he uses it in the sense of 'primary *ousia*' and 'individual'. This use of the term may have been suggested to him by a passage in Aristotle in which the term ὑποκείμενα (*hypokeimena*) is contrasted with the term καθόλου (*katholou*), 'universal'.[96]

4. ὑπόστασις, *hypostasis*. In a passage in which Origen criticizes those whom he at first describes as maintaining that the Father and the Son are 'one . . . in *hypokeimenon*', he then repeats the same criticism by describing them as denying that the Father and the Son are 'different . . . according to *hypostases*'.[97] This shows that he uses the term *hypostasis*, as he uses the term *hypokeimenon*, in the sense of 'individual' and 'primary *ousia*'. That such a use of the term *hypostasis* was already known by the time of Origen may be inferred from a passage in Hippolytus in which, evidently drawing upon some older source, he describes Aristotle's terms 'individual' and 'primary *ousia*' by the expression 'hypostatic *ousia*' (οὐσία ὑποστατική).[98]

In Latin, Tertullian suggests the following terms:

1. *res*,[99] which is a literal translation of the Greek πρᾶγμα (*pragma*).

2. *substantia*,[100] which may be used here either as an etymological translation of the Greek ὑπόστασις (*hypostasis*) or as a conventionalized translation of the Greek οὐσία (*ousia*). In either case, it is used here by Tertullian in the sense of 'primary *ousia*'.

3. *persona*,[101] which has its counterpart in the corresponding Greek term used by Tertullian's contemporary Hippolytus.[102] This term has no technical philosophic background. But both in Latin and in Greek it has the meaning of 'individual'.

As a designation of the underlying common unity of the three persons of the Trinity, Origen uses again the term *ousia*.[103] In this case he undoubtedly uses it in the sense of 'secondary *ousia*', that is, species or genus. Similarly, Tertullian uses again the term *substantia*,[104] as a translation of either *hypostasis* or *ousia*, but in either case it is in the sense of 'secondary *ousia*'. It is quite possible, however, that, if employed here as a translation of *hypostasis*, it might be used in the sense of 'substratum', to which the term *hypostasis* lends itself and in which sense it is used later in the Nicene Creed.

Ultimately, in Greek, the Cappadocians adopted the formula μία οὐσία, τρεῖς ὑποστάσεις (*mia ousia, treis hypostaseis*), of which, says Augustine, the Latin translation should be *una essentia vel substantia, tres personae*, and not *una essentia, tres substantiae*. Augustine's objection to the latter rendering was on the ground, as he says, that 'with us it is the already established usage that by *essentia* we understand the same thing that is understood by *substantia*'.[105] Augustine's *essentia vel substantia*, it may be remarked, reflects, in reverse order, the terms used in the phrase *ex alia substantia aut essentia* in the Latin translation of the Greek phrase ἐξ ἑτέρας ὑποστάσεως ἢ οὐσίας (*ex heteras hypostaseōs ē ousias*) in the Nicene Creed, where, as here by Augustine, these two terms are used in the sense of 'substratum'.

THE INCARNATION AND PHILOSOPHY[106]

In both Philo and John, the Logos is said to be that through which p 306–7 (12–13, 16) God created the world. In Philo, however, at the creation of the world the Logos is said to have been caused by God to become immanent in the world and to be used by God as that through which He operates the laws of nature in it. In its immanence the Logos is thus described by Philo as 'extending itself from the midst [of the world] to its utmost bounds';[107] as being 'such a bond of the universe as nothing can break',[108] as being that which 'holds together and administers all things',[109] and as being 'the ruler and steersman of all'.[110] It is to be remarked that some of the terms used by Philo in describing his immanent Logos are used by Plato and by the Stoics in describing their respective world souls.

So also the Fathers – evidently taking John's statement that the Logos 'was in the world',[111] which follows his earlier statement that 'all things were made through' the Logos,[112] to mean that, after the creation of the world, the Logos became immanent in it – conceived of this Johannine immanent Logos as that through which God operates His laws of nature in the world. The Fathers thus apply to this immanent Logos the following descriptions: God 'set in order all things through him';[113] through the Logos, the world 'is set in order and kept in being';[114] the Logos 'is called the governing principle because he rules and is master of all things fashioned by him';[115] the Logos 'orders all things in accordance with the Father's will and holds the helm of the universe in the best way'.[116]

For Philo the career of the Logos comes to an end on its becoming immanent in the world. For the Fathers, however, its career does not end there. For them, about 3760 years and three months after the creation of the world, if we combine the traditional date for the Christian era with the traditional Jewish date for the era of creation, or 5500 years after the creation, if we follow the calculation current among the Church Fathers, or 4004 years after creation, if we follow the chronology of Archbishop Ussher, Jesus was born and thereby the Logos entered a new stage of existence. In John that new stage of existence is described by the statement: 'And the Logos became flesh.'[117] In other parts of the New Testament, however, the pre-existent Christ whom John calls Logos is described

The three youths of Babylon, Shadrach, Meshach and Abednego, who defied the order to bow down to Nebuchadnezzar's golden statue, being saved from the 'burning fiery furnace', were a prefiguration of divine redemption. (3)

as having 'a body' prepared for him[118] or as 'becoming in the likeness of men'[119] and as 'being found in fashion as a man'.[120] This enfleshment, that is, incarnation (σάρκωσις *sarkōsis*) or embodiment (ἐνσωμάτωσις *ensōmatōsis*) or humanation (ἐνανθρώπησις *enanthrōpēsis*) of the Logos, like its Generation and the Trinity, was declared by the Fathers to be an ineffable and incomprehensible mystery. Still, under a complexity of influences again, like the mystery of the Generation of the Logos and the mystery of the Trinity, it was presented and explained and justified by the use of philosophic terminology and philosophic concepts and reasoning.

This complexity of influences falls into three parts.

First, in Philo, the relation of the immanent Logos to the body of the world is described in terms of an analogy with the relation of the soul to the body in man. Thus, having in mind his own interpretation of the phrase 'garments (χιτῶνας *chitōnas*) of skin' in Genesis iii 21 to mean the body in which the soul abides, and interpreting the term 'garments' (ἱμάτια *himatia*) in Leviticus xxi 10 to mean the world in which the immanent Logos abides,[121] Philo compares the relation of the immanent Logos to the world to the relation of the soul to the body.[122] Then, also, having in mind the term 'houses' used in the Book of Job (iv 19) as a description of human bodies in their relation to human souls, Philo describes man's body as 'house',[123] and he similarly describes the world in its relation to God, who abides in it through the immanent Logos, as 'house'[124] and 'temple'.[125] So also, in Paul, the human body in its relation to the soul is described as 'house'[126] and as 'tabernacle';[127] and, in John, the Logos, which became flesh, is said to have 'tabernacled among us'[128] and the body of Jesus in which the Logos is incarnate is described as 'temple'.[129]

Second, in Aristotle, the soul is contrasted with the body as form is with matter,[130] and form and matter are each described as an *ousia* or a nature.[131] Accordingly in the language of Aristotle soul and body could be described as two *ousiai* or two natures. Similarly, Philo contrasts God, whom he describes as a 'simple nature',[132] with man who, he says, is made up of many things, among them 'soul and body', and this implies that soul and body are two natures.

Third, according to Aristotle, soul and body, though each an *ousia* and a nature, are 'one'[133] and so also any given man, though consisting of a soul and a body, is to be described as a 'primary *ousia*'[134] and as an 'individual'[135] and as 'one in number'[136] – terms which, as we have seen, are used by the Fathers as the equivalent of the terms 'person' and *hypostasis*.[137] The question raised by Aristotle – why soul and body are one[138] and hence why man is one[139] – is answered by Aristotle himself in his own comparison of the relation between soul and body with the relation between matter and form. In discussing the relation of form to matter, Aristotle says in one place that the form is the source from which a thing derives its individuality and its name, so that a thing whose matter is bronze and whose form is statue is called statue.[140] So also, in the case of soul in its relation to body, Aristotle says in another place that it is 'the intellectual element' in man that 'is generally thought to be a man's real self'.[141] The same view is re-echoed by Philo in his statement that 'the mind in each of us is rightfully and in the true sense the man'.[142] It is re-echoed again later by Plotinus in his statements that 'the soul of man is man'[143] or 'the soul of man is man himself'[144] or 'the real man coincides with the rational soul'.[145]

And the Word became flesh

With all these precedents in the back of their minds, all the Fathers, however else they may differ with regard to the relation of the incarnate Logos to that in which it is incarnate, agree in comparing that relation to the relation of soul to body. They all describe that in which the Logos is incarnate by various Greek or Latin terms which mean 'house' or 'tabernacle' or 'temple' or 'garment'.[146]

But, as we have seen, that in which the Logos was incarnate is described in the New Testament as being 'flesh' or 'body' and as being 'man'. Now man, whom philosophers define as a rational animal, possesses a soul which they describe as rational. Accordingly, the Fathers were divided on the question as to whether that in which the Logos was incarnate was a man who possessed a rational soul or only a body which was without a soul.

The view commonly held by the Fathers was that that in which the Logos was incarnate was a man endowed with a rational soul. Since it was generally assumed that the relation of the Logos to the man in Jesus was analogous to the relation of the soul to the body in man, and since philosophically the soul and body in man constituted two natures or two *ousiai*, Jesus is said to possess two natures or two *ousiai*, corresponding to the Logos and to the humanity in him. Then, also, since man, though consisting of two natures, is one individual or person, so also Jesus, though consisting of two natures, is one person; and, since that which makes man one person is his soul, so also that which makes Jesus one person is the Logos in him.

As illustrations of how all this is expressed by the Fathers, we may quote a few representative statements. The analogy of soul and body is exemplified in a statement of Augustine's, which reads: 'The Son of God, who is the Logos of God, has man, as soul has body. . . . What is man? A rational soul having a body. What is Christ? The Logos of God having man.'[147] The doctrine of the two

This fresco in the Lateran library is the earliest known representation of St Augustine. It dates from about AD 600. (4)

ousiai or natures appears in Melito of Sardis when he describes the 'God' and the 'perfect man' in Jesus as being 'two *ousiai*'.[148] Origen refers to the divine and the human in Jesus as being 'the nature of that deity' and 'that human nature'.[149] Tertullian, using the Latin *substantia* for the Greek *ousia*, says of Jesus that he has 'two substances' or 'two natures'.[150] The doctrine of the one person appears in Augustine when he says: 'Just as soul is united to the body in unity of person so as to constitute man, so in the same way is God united to man in unity of person so as to constitute Christ.'[151]

A dissenting view was advanced in the latter part of the 4th century by Apollinaris. On purely theological grounds, he started with the belief that that in which the Logos was incarnate could not be a complete man possessing a rational soul.[152] It had to be a body. At first, it is reported, he believed that the body had neither a rational nor an irrational soul, but then he changed his mind and maintained that the body had no rational soul but had an irrational soul. This change of mind may be explained as being due to a change in his philosophic position on a problem with regard to man's irrational soul.[153] According to Aristotle and the Stoics, and also Plato in all but one of his dialogues, the so-called irrational soul in man is only a faculty of his soul, so that his body is without an irrational soul. It is this view which Apollinaris at first followed. According to Plato in the *Timaeus* and Philo in his interpretation of the account of the creation of man in Genesis ii 7, the irrational soul of man is part of his body, together with which it was created, though, according to Philo, it is also united with man's rational soul and is part thereof.[154] This is the view that Apollinaris adopted on second thoughts. Since, according to Apollinaris, Jesus had no rational soul, he had no human nature; there was in him only a divine nature, corresponding to the Logos in him.

The difference of opinion on the question whether Jesus had two natures or one nature produced the two positions known as Dyophysitism and Monophysitism, and it led logically to a difference of opinion on the question whether Jesus had two wills or one will, which produced the two positions known as Dyotheletism and Monotheletism. Those who believed that Jesus had two natures believed also that he had two wills, whereas those who believed that Jesus had only one nature believed also that he had only one will.

Among the Dyophysites, however, there was one, Pyrrhus of Alexandria, who, in spite of his belief that Jesus had two natures, maintained that he had only one will, the divine will. He debated on this subject with Maximus Confessor.[155] Among the arguments by which Pyrrhus supported his view there was one in which, having in mind statements by Aristotle to the effect that action in accordance with one's nature may be described as necessary[156] and hence as compulsory[157] and involuntary,[158] he started out by saying that 'what is natural is entirely necessary', and on the basis of this he went on to argue that, if, as it is claimed, there must be two wills in Jesus to correspond to his two natures, then these wills will each be natural, and, being natural, they will be necessary and compulsory, and thus Jesus would act without freedom of the will. Maximus' refutation of this argument may be restated as follows: Aristotle, in one of the statements which Pyrrhus had in mind,[159] does indeed say that necessity applies to action according to one's own nature, but immediately after that he himself adds that 'of the products of (man's) reason some are never due to . . . necessity'. On the basis of this, Maximus concludes that, inasmuch as Jesus had only a rational soul, the corresponding nature and will of which were, as was maintained by those who believed in two natures and two wills, always in harmony with the nature and will of the Logos in him, his actions in accordance with these two natures and wills in him were not performed by necessity, and hence not by compulsion. They were completely free.

The Christian Fathers as selective philosophers

This is how Philo and the Fathers used philosophy in the discussion of their common belief in a Logos, and how the Fathers used it in the discussion of the Trinity and the Incarnation; and this, one may find, is also how they used philosophy in the discussion of their common or particular conceptions of all the various scriptural teachings, ranging from the creation of the world to its future in the end of days. In all these attempts of theirs to apply philosophy to problems arising from scriptural teaching, one will find that the Fathers as well as Philo did not approach their task as partisans of any of the various schools of Greek philosophy. Their speculations on all such problems did not turn on contrasts between the different systems within philosophy; they turned only on a contrast between Scripture and philosophy. Within philosophy itself there were, for them, only doctrines which were in agreement with Scripture and doctrines which were in disagreement with Scripture, though on certain doctrines they found that some philosophers were in agreement with Scripture more often than others. In battling among themselves, the Fathers did not battle as followers of certain opposing schools of Greek philosophy; they battled only as advocates of opposing interpretations of Scripture. Their opposing interpretations of Scripture, however, were sometimes influenced by philosophic considerations or were supported by philosophic arguments, and it is in this way, therefore, that the Fathers are found occasionally to have aligned themselves with certain philosophic attitudes on certain particular problems. But it would be altogether wrong historically to arrange the Fathers into groups, to dress them up in the uniforms of the Academy and the Lyceum and the Porch, to march them under the school banners of Plato and Aristotle and the Stoics, and to make them sing the schools' respective school songs.

XIV

RIVAL THEOLOGIES

GNOSTICISM, MARCION, ORIGEN

ROBERT M. GRANT

'I admonish you to take nothing but Christian nourishment; shun alien pastures, for there is heresy.'

IGNATIUS OF ANTIOCH 'EPISTLE TO THE TRALLIANS'

Competing beliefs,
characteristic of the later pagan world, also gave rise to bitter divisions within the Christian Church. As Christian doctrine evolved, it managed to incorporate much of the thought and experience of other sects, as we have seen in previous chapters. For a time, therefore, while the basic dogmas were still being hammered out, it was possible for many adherents of pre-Christian religions to adopt Christianity nominally, interpreting it in senses that fitted their own philosophies. The history of the Early Church is a series of confrontations between such rival interpretations, and, with each decision, one group would be excluded from the Church. The losers were branded by the name of heretics, though in these early times the distinction between a dissident Christian and a member of another religion having something in common with Christianity is not easy to draw. The Gnostics, for instance, tried to adapt the Christian idea of a Saviour God to their own dualistic universe – a universe governed by forces of Light and Darkness, Good and Evil. At that date there was no official dogma on these points, and, since what later became Christian orthodoxy was largely forged under the impact of Gnosticism, it might be doubted whether the Gnostics can strictly be called heretics. But they were united in thinking that the creator god of the Old Testament was an inferior being, totally separate from Christ, and that only they had the secret saving knowledge (*gnōsis*). Gnostics took pains to conceal what this knowledge was, and their doctrine is therefore still largely mysterious.

However remote these beliefs seem from Christian orthodoxy, the Gnostics regarded themselves as Christians and are related to conventional Christianity by two facts. First, they began the systematic exegesis of the New Testament, although it must be admitted that their interpretations are often far-fetched. Second, their dualist theology, a blend of Jewish angelology and Platonic cosmology, was the sort of intellectual backing that Christianity required if it was to enter the Graeco-Roman world on equal terms. Origen was influenced by the Gnostics and, although Origen himself was not regarded as being absolutely above reproach, many of his ideas passed into the growing body of Christian doctrine.

There are in Rome some catacombs which contain examples of common Christian imagery as well as scenes which have no Christian parallels, and which make one suspect that those catacombs were used by heterodox sects. Such is the hypogeum of the Aurelii. It contains a Fall, a Creation of Adam, a Good Shepherd, and also the scene opposite. The type of the Good Shepherd addressing a flock of sheep has no known parallel. It must therefore be regarded as a portrayal, not of Christ, but of the mystical holy shepherd. (1)

Two Gnostic amulets from the same container (above), one silver and one gold, were found in Egypt. (2, 3, 4)

An unknown supreme being was the real god of the Gnostics in the systems of their greatest teachers, Valentinus, Marcion and Basilides. Further spirits were created as emanations of this supreme deity. Some of the lower angels are seen on the right.

The arcosolium of Vibia, part of a Christian catacomb, was used by a sect known as Sabazians, as its dedication indicates. Inside there are three scenes: Vibia, the deceased, carried off by Pluto, the judgement of Vibia, and (below right) the introduction of Vibia to a celestial banquet of the *bonorum iudicio iudicati*, 'those judged by the judgement of good men'. The strikingly large amphora at the right recalls another in the Cava della Rosa, used by Valentinians.

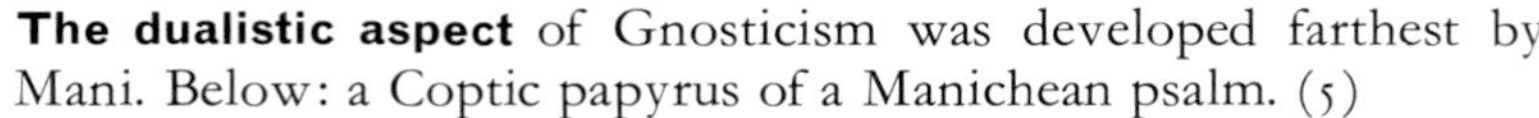

The dualistic aspect of Gnosticism was developed farthest by Mani. Below: a Coptic papyrus of a Manichean psalm. (5)

The cock-headed demon Jao who had figured in various Gnostic systems appears on this gem (above) found in Italy. (7)

The female deity (above) is again found in Gnostic systems. She is probably flanked by the Dioscuri, Castor and Pollux. (8)

The introduction of Vibia by Mercury to the celestial banquet (below). She is shown again seated at the table. (6)

Strange scenes involving griffins and a man with a cock's head in a 4th-century mosaic discovered at Brading in the Isle of Wight are thought to be connected with a Gnostic sect. Animal and bird masks were worn as ritual disguises and occur frequently on Gnostic gems (*cf.* plate 7). The building on the hill, approached by a staircase or by a ladder, would appear to be a temple which the griffins are guarding. (9)

The fight against heresy is probably symbolized in this mosaic of a cock attacking a tortoise (right). It is on the floor of part of the Early Christian cathedral of Aquileia; the section next to it, showing the ram as the type of the true believer, has been reproduced on p. 308. The amphora above the combatants is the prize. The tortoise was a conventional symbol of evil. This scene occurs again in another part of the cathedral, and, although its precise significance is now lost, it clearly had an important meaning for Christians of the time. (10)

GNOSTICISM, MARCION, ORIGEN

ROBERT M. GRANT

EARLY CHRISTIANITY is often thought of as having been a movement unified by devotion to past tradition, by experience of present persecution, and by vivid expectation of the future reign of God. Christians, it is assumed, must have been of one mind in a common faith and hope, expressed in works of love. Such an impression is modified, however, as soon as we look carefully at the letters of Paul in the New Testament or at the writings of the early Apostolic Fathers. The atmosphere is thick with controversy; competing views, political as well as religious, constantly come to expression. By the middle of the 2nd century AD the surviving Christian literature is almost entirely controversial. The major writings attack Gnosticism or express Gnostic ideas – or else they defend Christians from accusations made by the populace or the Roman state.

At the beginning of the 2nd century AD the most prominent figures among Christians can be called representatives of the 'establishment', whether or not it was as firmly established as they liked to think. Such men were Clement of Rome, Ignatius of Antioch and Polycarp of Smyrna. During the subsequent century and a half some 'establishment' writers were certainly important, men like Justin, Theophilus of Antioch, Irenaeus of Lyons, and
p 342–3 Cyprian of Carthage. What is even more remarkable is the number
(31) of prominent individuals who for one reason or another were in conflict with what was coming to be regarded as orthodoxy. The great Gnostic teachers Basilides, Marcion, and Valentinus regarded themselves as Christians even though Justin and Irenaeus attacked them. Indeed, Tertullian goes so far as to say that Valentinus became a heretic when he failed to win an episcopal election. Justin's own pupil, Tatian, an insistent advocate of compulsory universal asceticism, founded a sect of his own.

At Alexandria both Clement and Origen, in different ways, upheld the idea of a Christianity superior to its ordinary formulation. It is not surprising that the latter was excommunicated by his bishop, although both teachers were protected by Alexander of Jerusalem, who had studied in the Alexandrian school. At Rome Hippolytus militantly criticized not only the various Gnostic groups but also two successive popes, whom he found deficient in orthodoxy, intelligence, and morality. Similarly at Carthage, Tertullian, no martyr himself, was eager to lead others to martyrdom and extreme asceticism. Dissatisfied with the conventional Christianity which he had at first vehemently defended, he became an enthusiastic devotee of the 'spiritual' movement known as Montanism and in his last writings denounced ordinary Christians and their bishops.

All these men, the principal Christian theologians of the early-3rd century AD, offered alternatives to conventional Christianity. They had predecessors in Old Testament times and later. The Old Testament prophets arose within the setting of the Hebrew tradi-
p 310 tion which they criticized; they deeply influenced it and their
(f1) writings were preserved by the priests. The Apostle Paul changed the shape of primitive Christianity, while his letters came to constitute a major section of the New Testament. Similarly the Church later made use of many of the insights of Clement, Origen, Hippolytus, and Tertullian, even though the orthodoxy of these men was questioned either during their own time or later.

It need hardly be said that none of them viewed himself as unorthodox. Indeed, Clement was himself a presbyter and thought that the orders of Christian ministers had angelic archetypes. Origen could view his own ministry as prophetic, but he was ordained by bishops in Palestine. Hippolytus was sure that Zephyrinus of Rome was an avaricious, illiterate fool, led astray by his even worse subordinate and then successor, Callistus, but that he himself, as a significant person attacked by nobodies, was following in the footsteps of the Apostle Paul. Tertullian supposed that he was maintaining the teaching of Jesus and the apostles against those who had perverted it.

Only one of these men was opposed in principle to the organized religion to which, in one way or another, all offered alternatives, and testimonies from all but Clement show that they deeply respected the Roman see, long the centre of traditional life and thought. Tertullian's early work contains an ultra-Roman vindication of tradition, and his later reference to the pope as *pontifex maximus* (the name for the pagan Roman high priest) reflects the depth of his disillusionment. Hippolytus himself taught in Rome and insisted that Roman bishops up to the time of Zephyrinus taught the orthodox faith. In a letter, Origen said that he once visited Rome because he had 'prayed to see the most ancient church
of the Romans', and many years later he wrote a defence of his p 349
orthodoxy to Fabian of Rome. *(f4)*

In spite of loyalty to tradition, however, these men drastically reinterpreted it. In this respect they were not unlike the Gnostics whom they all bitterly opposed. The origins of their independent attitude thus go back to the early years of the 2nd century AD and are to be found within Gnostic circles.

'Spiritual beings'

By the middle of the 2nd century AD we possess clear evidence for the existence of groups within Christianity whose ideas, roughly in agreement with one another, were regarded as offensive by those who apparently represented the majority. Although only some of them seem to have styled themselves 'Gnostics', in modern usage the term 'Gnostic' is conventionally and conveniently used to cover all of them. All alike believed that they possessed a secret saving knowledge or 'Gnosis' by means of which they were duly saved; and all alike believed that this knowledge was superior to the 'faith' of the ordinary Christians. Some called themselves 'spiritual beings' as contrasted with the merely 'psychic' Christians, possessing soul but not divine spirit. From the Pauline Epistles it is fairly clear that such invidious comparisons were being made during the early-1st century AD, at least at Corinth, although the specifically Gnostic theological ideas do not yet appear. These theological ideas were generally based on an intense hostility toward the world and toward human life in it – one might almost speak of self-hatred – and therefore a rejection of the creator-god of the Old Testament, who made the world and thought that it was good. The only real god of the Gnostics was the unknown supreme being, who was not a creator at all. The world came into existence only because of some kind of error or rebellion in the spheres of 'aeons' far from the world and almost equally far from the unknown god. Man as consisting of body and soul owes his existence to powers vastly inferior to the supreme being, although, since these powers were feebly trying to imitate the supreme god, this god, who is good, sent to man a spark of his own fire; this spark is the divine spirit in man and is the only part of man capable of salvation.
Salvation is return to the unknown god above, and it is achieved p 320
either through rites and semi-magical formulae or through the (2–4)
knowledge which is itself salvation. Toward the end of the 2nd *f2*

century AD Irenaeus of Lyons describes the divergent views of two Gnostic schools. One made use of a baptismal anointing with oil and water and various formulae. The other explicitly rejected such rites and held that 'the mystery of the ineffable and invisible power cannot be performed by means of visible and perishable created things'. In their view, 'knowledge (*gnōsis*) is the redemption of the man within'. Obviously this divergence resembles the conflict, found in many other religions, between ritualists and spiritual interpreters.

The Gnostics not only knew what the human situation was, but also how it had come to be what it was. To be sure, Irenaeus could contrast the variety of their explanations with the unity of the Catholic story of creation, solidly based on a rather literal interpretation of the Old Testament. In general, however, they started from the highest being, the unknown god, and explained that
p 321 inferior beings had originated by means of a series of emanations
(7 8) in pairs from him (sometimes they also began with a pair). After
f 1, 5, 6 a dozen or so pairs of 'syzygies' had emanated from above and the 'Plerōma' or totality of spiritual being had come into existence, the last of the spiritual beings, known as Sophia (Wisdom), 'experienced passion without the embrace of her *confrère* Thelēsis (Will)'. Her passion was the desire to comprehend the magnitude of the Father above, and in consequence of it she gave birth to a shapeless substance; thus primal matter originated. In the Valentinian system there is another, lower Sophia, given the Hebrew name 'Achamoth', who after her mother's return to the aeons above gave birth to actual matter and to the creator of the actual world; he and his angels made the existing world.

We need not enter into the complex details of the Valentinian story in order to see that it is essentially a systematized mixture of Jewish angelology and Platonic cosmology, developed in a sharply dualistic direction. It would appear that on this foundation the Valentinians erected a superstructure in which the cosmic Christ was active both within the Plerōma and in the work of redemption.

Sex and syzygies

What consequences did this kind of world-view have for the daily lives of the Valentinians? They were critical, not to say condescending, toward the moral strivings of ordinary Christians. 'For us,' says Irenaeus, 'they declare that good works are necessary; otherwise we cannot be saved.' The Gnostic way, however, was quite different. The Valentinians were 'spiritual' not in consequence of actions but 'by nature'; they would certainly be saved under all circumstances. In their view there were three classes of men – a point they tried to confirm from the frequent mentions of three persons in Jesus' parables – and they themselves constituted the highest class. Merely 'material' men, incapable of religious or Gnostic insight, could not possibly be saved; 'psychic Christians' could be saved only if they became Gnostics; and of course the Gnostics were the 'spiritual' men. To be a Gnostic involved continuous meditation on the mystery of the spiritual 'syzygy':

In order to protect themselves against the demons, the Gnostics considered it important to know their names. Chnoubis is the radiate serpent. (*1*)

> Whoever is in the world and does not love his wife so that he unites with her is not 'of the truth' and will not reach the truth; whoever is from the world and unites with his wife is not 'of the truth' and will not reach the truth because he has united with his wife with sexual desire.

This passage, with its allusions to Johannine language, reflects the Valentinian ambivalence toward sex. On the one hand, sex is good in so far as it is related to the syzygies above; on the other, it is bad because worldly. The Valentinians compared themselves to gold immersed in mud but not harmed by it. Admittedly, however, straightforward approval of sexual intercourse, even within marriage, is hard to find in early Christian literature.

Irenaeus also found that the Valentinians were far from respecting the traditional Christian dietary regulations (as expressed in Acts xv and I Corinthians viii–x):

> They eat meats sacrificed to idols without discrimination [doubtless relying on I Corinthians x 25–7], regarding themselves as unharmed by them; they are voluntarily the first to attend every gentile festival in honour of the idols, and some of them do not even abstain from the murderous spectacle of fights with wild animals and gladiators.

This is to say that on the one hand the Valentinians developed a 'spiritual' doctrine far more exalted than that of most Christians, who were brought up with the Old Testament, while on the other hand they seem to have conformed to the ordinary practices of pagan society without question. Other Gnostic groups went even farther. The followers of the Alexandrian Basilides, for example, insisted that 'one must not "confess" [either in church or before Roman judges] the one who was crucified, but the one who came in the form of a man and was thought to be crucified and was called Jesus'. The result of confessing the crucified one would be coming under the power of the inferior angels who made human bodies, whereas if one denied the crucified Jesus one would be free from them. Others said one should deny with the mouth but not with the heart. Some Gnostics actually went so far as to pronounce curses against Jesus. Naturally they encountered little difficulty with the Roman state, though Christian martyrs detested them.

We have already spoken of the Gnostics' ambivalence in relation to sex, but we should add that this ambivalence is found in regard to other matters. The world was made by an inferior if not evil god. What attitude was one to adopt toward it? Some Gnostics advocated extreme asceticism. The Syrian Saturninus, for example, held that marriage and generation came from Satan and therefore were to be rejected. Many of his followers also rejected the eating of meat. Another Syrian, Tatian, called marriage nothing but 'corruption' and 'fornication'. Apparently, however, there were more Gnostics who insisted upon a kind of compulsory, if not compulsive, promiscuity which was supposed to demonstrate their freedom from the angels who made the world and laid down the rules of conventional morality. According to the Carpocratians, actions are good or evil only in the light of human opinion. The true Gnostic must experience everything; only thus can he escape further imprisonment in the body. The Cainites insisted that only Judas Iscariot knew the true mystery of the betrayal. With him as their patron saint, so to speak, they could go on to argue that 'perfect knowledge' was simply to do 'everything' without fear. (Is it possible that they quoted I John iv 18, 'perfect love casts out fear'?)

Reading between the lines

We may wonder how the adherents of these systems could relate themselves to conventional Christianity. Certainly they did so, for otherwise Christian writers would not have treated them as heretics. The answer seems to lie principally in the realm of biblical exegesis. As far as our evidence shows, the Gnostics were the first systematic exegetes of the New Testament books. While most of them firmly rejected the Old Testament as the self-revelation of an inferior god, they found considerable support for their views by means of subtle, non-historical interpretations of various isolated verses in the New Testament books. We have already seen

The serpent appears as an amulet on this 3rd-century magical papyrus in the British Museum. (*2*)

that they found three classes of men in the parables of Jesus – for example, in the three measures of meal (Matt. xiii 33). The fact that the Plerōma contained thirty aeons was proved from the Saviour's age according to Luke iii 23 and the total number of hours involved in the parable of the labourers in the vineyard (Matt. xx 2–16).

Their method is clear enough when we consider the fact that the Valentinians found the twelfth aeon, the suffering Sophia, in the story of the woman who had suffered hemorrhages for twelve years (Mark v 25) and in that of Jairus' daughter, twelve years old (Mark v 42). The Gnostics believed, as confirmed allegorizers, that nothing in scripture could lack spiritual meaning. All of it was a letter addressed to them and written, so to speak, in invisible ink. Why was it said that the woman had suffered for twelve years? What was to be made of the verse about Jairus' daughter: 'and the girl immediately arose and walked, *for* she was twelve years old'? Gnostic exegetes alone were capable of penetrating such mysteries.

Not all Gnostic exegesis was as foolish as it seems from these examples. Indeed, anticipating the work of many New Testament critics, some of them differentiated what was spoken by the spiritual Christ from what was said by the human Jesus.

The significant letters of the Valentinian Ptolemaeus, addressed to a woman named Flora – perhaps a symbol for the Roman Church – are intended to bring order out of the current chaos in Old Testament exegesis. Just what is the status of the law of Moses? Ptolemaeus chooses a middle path between ascribing it to God the Father and assigning it to the devil. It is not from the Father because it had to be completed by the Saviour; it is not from the devil because it was directed against injustice. Relying on the Saviour's teaching, Ptolemaeus derives the law from three different sources: (1) from God himself, for example forbidding divorce; (2) from Moses, permitting divorce; and (3) from the elders of the Jewish people. The first kind of law – alone valid – is also divisible into three: (a) the pure legislation (the Decalogue); (b) the part mixed with wrong and injustice, which the Saviour abolished; and (c) the prefigurative, symbolical part, which the Saviour transposed. This part consists of the ceremonial law. Since neither the supreme God nor the devil gave this law, it must come from the
p 320 (7) *f 5* Demiurge, the inferior creator known to Valentinian theology.

In Ptolemaeus' opinion his classification could be proved from the words of the Saviour and from the apostolic tradition which the Valentinians had received through a succession of teachers. The Valentinian theologian Theodotus used the same method in dealing with the teaching of Jesus itself. It is (a) prefigurative and mysterious, (b) parabolic and enigmatic, and (c) clear and straightforward. The third part consisted of doctrines which Jesus delivered in private to his disciples (*cf.* Mark iv 11–12, 33–4).

Here we encounter a characteristically Gnostic idea. There is an esoteric tradition secretly transmitted from one apostle or another p 319 (1)
and known only to Gnostics. According to Clement of Alexandria, the Valentinians appealed to the authority of a certain Theodas, a companion of Paul, just as the followers of Basilides referred to Glaucias, an interpreter of Peter. (More 'orthodox' Christians said that Peter's interpreter was Mark, author of the Gospel.) Other sects made other choices. Clement himself, as a rather Gnostic Christian, spoke of an inner group consisting of James, John, Peter and Paul. We find a similiar emphasis in the opening lines of the *Gospel of Thomas*: 'These are the secret words which the living Jesus spoke and Didymus Judas Thomas wrote down.' *Thomas* goes on to make clear that they have a Gnostic import. 'And he said, Whoever finds the interpretation of these words will not taste death.' Here, as among the other spiritualizing Gnostics, knowledge is salvation. According to a famous passage quoted by Clement, the knowledge consists of who we were, what we became, where we were, where we have have been thrown down,

Gnostic influence is seen in this Venetian alchemical manuscript which shows the cosmos as a snake. The inscription reads: 'The one is the all.' (*3*)

toward what we are hastening, from what we are redeemed, and what generation and regeneration are. Most of these questions were being asked by ordinary Christian converts. The Gnostic element lies in the answers, given in the Gnostic myth with its picture of the Saviour as the one who helps us escape from the world and return to our true native land above.

Voices from the desert

The *Gospel of Thomas*, which we have just mentioned, is perhaps the most significant document among nearly fifty books discovered about 1947 at Nag Hammadi in Egypt. These books constituted a Gnostic library, written in Coptic and copied in the 4th century AD for preservation against confiscation by Church and state. When it was found, it could be seen that the famous 'Sayings of Jesus' found at Oxyrhynchus in 1897 and 1903 really belonged to a 3rd-century AD Greek version of the same book. *Thomas* contains about 114 sayings, parables, and dialogues ascribed to Jesus and his disciples. More than half of them find parallels in the synoptic gospels, and this fact has stirred up a vigorous debate. Are these sayings in *Thomas* taken from our synoptic gospels? Or do they go back to oral traditions conceivably just as old as those underlying the other gospels? Or is the situation a mixed one, with materials partly from books and partly from traditions?

In any event, the traditions have obviously been highly developed. The second saying, for example, reads thus:

> If those who draw you on say to you, 'Behold the kingdom is in the heaven,' then the birds of the heaven will be there before you. If they say to you, 'It is in the sea,' then the fishes will be there before you. But the kingdom is within you [*cf.* Luke xvii 21] and outside you. When you know yourselves, then you will be known . . .

The idea that God is present in the heaven and in the deep is clearly expressed in the Old Testament (*e.g.* Psalm cxxxix 8–9), but according to this saying the kingdom cannot be localized at all. It consists of the self-knowledge recommended by the Delphic oracle, but this self-knowledge is described in the terms used by Paul in speaking of God's knowledge of him (I Cor. xxii 12; Gal. iv 9).

The self and its knowledge are primary for *Thomas*, and the external rites of religion are entirely secondary. Saying 5 represents the disciples as asking Jesus, 'Do you want us to fast? And how shall we pray, give alms, and practise dietary observances?' The answer comes only in Saying 14:

> When you fast you will beget sin for yourselves, and when you pray you will be condemned, and when you give alms, you will do evil to your spirits. And when you go away into any land and wander in the regions and they receive you, eat what they set before you, heal the sick among them. For what goes into your mouth will not defile you, but what comes out of your mouth, that will defile you.

The starting-point of this answer seems to lie in the synoptic tradition that the disciples of Jesus did not fast (*cf.* Mark ii 18). It is also somehow related to Matthew's Sermon on the Mount, in which Jesus instructs his disciples to give alms only in secret, to pray only in secret, and to fast only in secret (Matt. vi 1–18). The combination of 'eat what they set before you' with 'heal the sick' occurs only in Luke x 8–9. And the statements about defilement are paralleled in Mark vii 18–20. It would appear that at this point, at least, *Thomas* has taken themes from our synoptic gospels and has made them more radically Gnostic. His doctrine is sharply opposed to the general practices of 2nd-century Christianity.

In *Thomas* there are also more strictly Gnostic teachings, such as the pantheistic doctrine expressed in Saying 77:

> I am the Light which is over all of them; I am the All; the All has gone out from me and the All has reached me. Split wood, I am there; take up the stone, and you will find me there.

There are echoes of traditions also found in the apocryphal gospels of the Hebrews and the Egyptians, as well as '*agrapha*', sayings of Jesus transmitted orally by early Christians but not recorded, as far as we know, in other gospels. In other words, the *Gospel of Thomas* is a compendium of all sorts of 'sayings of Jesus', given a special 'twist' by the context in which they are now placed. This context is basically Gnostic.

Among the Nag Hammadi documents there is also a so-called *Gospel of Philip*, not really a gospel but a jumbled (intentionally?) collection of Gnostic doctrines essentially Valentinian in origin; there is a *Gospel of Truth*, on the borderline – like other Valentinian documents – between Valentinianism and more orthodox Christian writings. There are no fewer than three copies of the *Apocryphon* (secret book) *of John*, known to Irenaeus at Lyons about AD 180 and used in heretical groups as late as the 8th century AD. This treatise, preserved also in a 4th-century Berlin papyrus, is especially important because it allows us a glimpse of the way in which Gnostic treatises were developed. It would appear that Irenaeus knew nothing of its ascription to John or of the 'apostolic' framework in which it is set; he could hardly have refrained from criticizing such 'blasphemy' had he encountered it, although it occurs in all four Coptic versions. Two of the versions contain lengthy lists of the parts of the body and the Gnostic angels responsible for each, to a total of 360 or 365. At the end of these lists the reader is referred to a *Book of Zoroaster* which was used by followers of the Gnostic teacher Prodicus and was vigorously attacked as a forgery by Porphyry and other Neoplatonists. In the development of the *Apocryphon* we see the same tendency as in *Thomas*, toward the combination of diverse sources into a Gnostic, syncretistic whole.

The *Apocryphon of John* is in large measure a commentary on the Book of Genesis, reinterpreted by treating the creator as ignorant and malevolent. Genesis does not mean what Moses said but has a hidden meaning known only by Gnostic revelation. At this point, in spite of all the difficulties presented by the Old Testament, Christians believed that they had to reject Gnosticism. The evil in the world was not due to its creator.

Marcion, renovator of the faith

There had been Christians in Bithynia and Pontus, on the south shore of the Black Sea, for several generations before Marcion, owner of a coastal trader or two, decided to leave Pontus and come to Rome in about the year AD 137. Conceivably his father was a local Christian bishop, as later heresiologists tell us. In any case, he himself was a convinced, even militant Christian, and it appears that he had been deeply affected by the Jewish messianic revolt against Rome which had shaken the East between AD 132 and 135. This revolt, led by a certain Simon bar Koziba and promoted by the famous rabbinical teacher Akiba, had resulted, according to the historian Dio Cassius, in the death of no fewer than 580,000 Jews. It had involved the persecution of Palestinian Christians who refused to recognize Bar Koziba as 'Bar Kokhba', 'son of the star' – the star of Numbers xxiv 17, a prediction of Jewish victory. It had ended with the destruction of Jerusalem and the creation, on the site, of a new Roman city named Aelia Capitolina. The influence of traditional Jewish Christianity was practically terminated; in Aelia the Christian bishops were now gentiles, not Jews.

In these circumstances it was not surprising that Marcion, as a gentile Christian, should try to create a new form of Christianity free from its ties with Judaism and, indeed, with its own past. In his view Christianity was essentially new. It was not based on the Old Testament revelation, which had been given by an inferior creator-god who was merely just, not the good Father of Jesus. Indeed, the basic tenets of the Old Testament were in contradiction with the teaching of Jesus. Marcion wrote an elaborate treatise, entitled *Antitheses*, in which he set forth the discrepancies between Jesus' words and those of the prophets. The *Antitheses* began with a proclamation of the absolute uniqueness of the gospel: 'O miracle upon miracle, ecstasy, power, and wonder it is, that one can say nothing about it, nor think about it, nor compare it with anything.' One could not, therefore, compare it with the Old Testament. Jesus was not the son of either Joseph or Mary; he spoke of his 'mother' as 'those who hear the word of God and do it' (Luke viii 21). He actually came down from heaven in the fifteenth year of Tiberius Caesar – as a spirit bringing salvation. He taught against the law and the prophets (Luke iv 22) and by touching a leper he broke the law (Luke iv 40). Other passages in Luke were interpreted in the same way.

The catacomb of Trebius Iustus has a Good Shepherd on its ceiling, but also other unorthodox scenes including the one shown here, which appears to hark back to the pagan concept of grave goods. (*4*)

One of Marcion's favourite texts was Luke v 36–7:

> No one tears a piece from a new garment and puts it upon an old garment; if he does, he will tear the new, and the piece from the new will not match the old. And no one puts new wine into old wineskins; if he does, the new wine will burst the skins and it will be spilled, and the skins will be destroyed.

According to Epiphanius, writing more than two centuries later but using old sources, Roman presbyters attempted to tell him that the old wineskins were the hearts of the Pharisees and Scribes (as the context might suggest); unfortunately they added that the old garment meant Judas, grown old in avarice, who could not be patched on to the garment of the apostles. Conceivably Marcion viewed their mention of Judas' avarice as a dig at himself, for he had been in a position to give the Church a large sum of money when he arrived in Rome. Whether this be so or not, he is said to have replied, 'I will rend your church and cast division into it for ever.'

It is odd that his break with the Roman presbyters apparently did not come until he had been in Rome for seven years. Presumably during that period the theological confusion of Roman Christians was such that his clear-cut views appealed to many. Since we know that they were reading the rather peculiar document known as the *Shepherd of Hermas,* a work deeply influenced by Jewish apocalyptic ideas but containing no mention of Jesus, the situation may well have been one in which any systematic theology could have flourished.

According to Hippolytus, Marcion, while in Rome, came under the influence of a Gnostic teacher named Cerdon, who already taught that the just god proclaimed by the law and the prophets was not the good Father of Jesus. The activities of Cerdon also reflect the doctrinal chaos of Roman Christianity at the time. He would often come to the Christian assembly and confess the common faith but would then teach his own doctrines in secret. After a series of such waverings he was finally condemned and withdrew from the congregation. It is not certain, however, that Cerdon really taught Marcion anything. The pronounced individual stamp of Marcion's teaching seems to make it all of one piece. Furthermore, it is likely that since, as Irenaeus tells us, Polycarp of Smyrna addressed Marcion personally as 'firstborn of Satan', his views were already firmly heterodox as he passed through Smyrna on his way to Rome.

A higher criticism

Marcion was not only a theologian but also a critic of the New Testament books. As Irenaeus puts it, he

> circumcised the Gospel according to Luke, taking out everything about the generation of the Lord as well as many of the Lord's words in which he is most clearly described as acknowledging the Creator of this universe as his Father.

In addition

> he cut up the letters of the Apostle Paul, taking out whatever the Apostle clearly said about the God who made the world (since he is the father of our Lord Jesus Christ) and whatever the Apostle taught with reference to the prophets who predicted the coming of the Lord.

This is to say that in Marcion's view there was an authentic *Gospel* just as there was an authentic *Apostle*, and he gave these titles to the two books in which he presented the original texts.

The idea that an authentic theology underlies commonly accepted texts is to be found in the writings of two of Marcion's non-Christian contemporaries. Both Plutarch and Philo of Byblos held that ancient oriental theology had been corrupted by the interpolations made either by poets or by priests. This is essentially Marcion's view. In his opinion there was an authentic gospel which Jesus proclaimed. This gospel was altered by the apostles, who when preaching among Jews could not proclaim a god other than the one in whom the Jews believed. In other words, the original gospel was corrupted for apologetic purposes in the earliest days of Christianity. It was restored by means of another revelation, this time to the Apostle Paul – who, as Galatians proves, was frequently in conflict with the Jerusalem apostles. 'Paul alone knew the truth.' Unfortunately his letters too were later interpolated so that they do not set forth the pristine, or repristinated, gospel in all its purity. The task of the Marcionite exegete is therefore to begin with certain key passages such as those in which Paul said that his gospel was the only one there was ('my gospel', Rom. ii 16, xvi 25; no other II Cor. xi 4, Gal. i 6–9) or argued with Peter (Gal. ii 14–16). In the light of these passages he can determine what the interpolations are. This kind of analytical process lay at the base of Marcion's exegetical work. Unlike other Gnostics, he had no myth secretly transmitted from the apostles; and no other Gnostic groups used his method, as far as we know.

Should one then regard Marcion as a Gnostic at all? Certainly he was no ordinary Gnostic. His literary method proves that. On the other hand, his treatment of the Old Testament is shared with Gnostics, and so is his description of the supreme God as unknown and to be contrasted with the inferior creator who announced the coming of a warrior Messiah. Like ascetic-minded Gnostics, he rejected marriage.

To treat him as simply a Gnostic does less than justice to his strong emphasis on the Pauline themes of faith and grace. Indeed, Adolf Harnack once claimed that, among 2nd-century Christians, only Marcion understood Paul, though he had to add that Marcion misunderstood him. Marcion was not simply a Gnostic; he was a Christian reformer, eager to restore 'the lost radiance of the gospel' in a time when Christian theology – as we know it from documents contemporary with him – was practically without leadership.

Marcion's movement did not succeed, either in his own time or later. Many of the arguments used against it seem to be based merely on conservative traditionalism, and can hardly have convinced anyone not a traditionalist. The basic difficulties, however, were both historical and theological. First, historically his reconstructions of the original documents are rather unconvincing. In regard to Luke especially, it can be shown that what he omitted is stylistically the same as what he kept, and also it can be explained as negating his basic theological outlook. Second, his theology with its two gods is not in harmony with the teaching of either Jesus or Paul (in spite of Paul's unguarded dualism in II Cor. iv 4), both of whom regarded the one God as the God of the Old Testament.

It has been claimed that Marcion was really responsible for the canon of the New Testament, which did not exist before his time but is reflected in writings directed against him. Such a claim is somewhat exaggerated, for New Testament books were already regarded as scripture by Gnostics before his time, whether or not these writers reflected commonly held ideas.

The demiurge Jao is shown as a monstrous being with the head of a cock (cf. plates 7 and 9). (*5*)

A holy eunuch

Origen of Alexandria was a man who stood within the Church but constantly looked outside. Born and brought up a Christian, he never seems to have doubted that Christianity was true, but he spent most of his sixty-nine years in trying to interpret the meaning of Christian truth in terms comprehensible to educated men. In this regard he was following, on a higher level, the path already mapped out by the Greek apologists of the 2nd century AD and by Clement, who, unlike Origen, had been head of a private Christian school at Alexandria. Even in his youth Origen had memorized the scriptures and had shown such proficiency in teaching converts that Demetrius, bishop of Alexandria, made him head of the diocesan school.

We may wonder a bit about his zeal when we hear of his urging his father, in prison as a Christian, to become a martyr, and when we learn that he would have joined his father had not his mother hidden his clothes. It is also likely that a few years afterwards he underwent castration in order to be free from criticism in his dealings with Christian women; since we hear of this episode from his admirers it is not likely to have been invented by his enemies. Certainly he was a devotee of the most arduous asceticism, which he definitely regarded as superior to married life. He devoted himself single-mindedly to the work of the Christian teacher and was able to produce his many writings only because of the aid provided for him by a rich Alexandrian Christian named Ambrose.

Origen's physical asceticism was accompanied by a certain mental asceticism which led him, quite early, to abandon his studies of Greek philosophy and turn primarily to the study of the Scriptures. In spite of this movement away from Graeco-Roman culture, he never abandoned the basic ideas which he had acquired as a student of Ammonius Saccas, the teacher of the Neoplatonist p 207
Plotinus. (8)

According to Plotinus' disciple Porphyry, Ammonius himself was born a Christian but was converted to philosophy, while Origen took the opposite course. Educated in Greek learning, he came to be fascinated by Christianity, although he continued to employ the ideas of Plato and other philosophers. (As Eusebius points out, Porphyry does not seem to know anything about Origen's early life.) This much is true in Porphyry's account: though Origen sold his library of Greek literature and gave up this kind of teaching, the influence of philosophy on his thought is very clear not only from fragments of his lost *Miscellanies* but also from the structure and content of his treatise *On First Principles* and from the ideas and references provided in his late apology *Against Celsus*. Though he stopped teaching the course of preliminary studies in the Christian school – the 'encyclia' or *liberales artes* – he assigned them to his pupil Heraclas, later head of the school and then bishop of Alexandria.

'That I can't believe'

Origen was concerned not only with philosophy but especially with biblical interpretation. The work *On First Principles* begins with a discussion of God and the world but culminates in a careful and elaborate statement about the nature and necessity of allegorical exegesis. Following Philo, the Stoics, and earlier Christians at Alexandria, Origen insists that many biblical texts are absurd or immoral if taken literally. He reinterprets them in the light of his Neoplatonic Christian theology. In dealing with the St John's Gospel, for example, he notes that the cleansing of the temple is p 265
placed early in Jesus' ministry by John but late by the other (5)
evangelists. He concludes that the evangelists were describing a real temple in Jerusalem but did not intend to write historically about God, since God cannot be confined to particular times or places. Many other biblical narratives and statements have only a symbolical meaning, which can be found by means of ingenious spiritual exegesis.

In Origen's view the Bible is misunderstood by Jews who take it literally, by heretics who reject the unity of God, and by 'the simpler' Christian believers who simply do not think. The highest understanding involves knowing that Scripture speaks of God and his only Son and their interrelations, of the causes and effects of the Incarnation, of other spiritual beings, and of the origin of the world and of evil. Since the Bible does not seem to speak only of these matters, we must conclude that God planned it thus in order to encourage thought. If everything were clear we might assume that the only meaning is the literal one. For this reason God placed what may be called stumbling blocks in it, although where the historical corresponds with the mystical meaning it could be allowed to stand. In general, however, the letter as such is useless. How could there be 'days' before the sun was created? Was there a real garden of Eden in which God walked and looked for Adam? Much of the Old Testament legislation, taken literally, is ridiculous or immoral. Thus far Origen has dealt only with the writings ascribed to Moses, which had often been allegorized in Hellenistic Judaism.

The novelty of his treatment lies in his extension of it to the apostolic writings. Where is there a 'high mountain' from which all the kingdoms on earth could be seen (Matt. iv 8)? How could one greet no one on the road? Why would one turn the right cheek? Why pluck out the right eye (Matt. v 39) when both, presumably, offended? All this shows that the meaning of the gospels cannot be the literal one, although Origen feels he must say that there is more true history than 'bare spiritual explanation', and both the Decalogue and some of the Sermon on the Mount are permanently valid.

Underneath Origen's statements there is a rather rigid rhetorical-grammatical structure. For his purposes the Bible consists of history and law. History can be subdivided into authentic history, myth, and fiction, and for him neither myth nor fiction can be treated literally. Among examples of authentic history he refers to Jerusalem, the metropolis of the Jews, where Solomon built a temple. This point is significant, because in the *Commentary on John* he makes clear that the only historical fact about the cleansing story is that there was a temple in Jerusalem. As for laws, they too can be subdivided into genuine legislation and commandments either irrational or impossible. It is irrational to command men not to eat such birds as vultures, which they would not eat anyway. We have already cited 'impossible' commandments from the gospels.

This scheme is rather attractive, but, apart from Origen's philosophical-theological presuppositions, it leads not to the idea of a hidden spiritual revelation but to the break-up of the whole Bible. To be sure, most readers actually do thus break it up, at least implicitly, but the rigidity of his classifications stands in the way of an historical understanding – in which he was not interested. He would have agreed with the statement of the Stoic allegorizer called Heraclitus: 'The myths [of Homer] are sacrilegious unless they are understood allegorically.'

From his *Commentary on John* it is clear that he shared Heraclitus' view:

> We now have to transform the 'sensible' gospel into an intellectual and spiritual one; for what would the narrative of the 'sensible' gospel amount to, if it were not developed to a spiritual one? It would be of little account or none. Anyone can read it and assure himself of the facts it tells – nothing more. But our whole energy is now to be directed to the deep things of the meaning of the gospel and to search out the truth that is in it when divested of analogies.

The gospel, he says, is really Jesus himself. But what he means by Jesus is the Jesus who is understood in Origen's theology. 'I wonder at the stupidity of the general run of Christians in this matter.' They do not adequately analyze the true nature of the Word. 'They do not adequately allow him any independent hypostasis nor are they clear about his essence.'

This kind of biblical interpretation, along with Origen's incessant criticisms of other Christians, goes far to explain his difficulties at Alexandria and his conflict with the aged traditionalist bishop Demetrius. In addition, Demetrius may have been aware, as Origen himself perhaps was not, how close it was to some of the views already set forth by Gnostic teachers. For example, Origen's ideas about the preaching of the apostles are remarkably close to those of Marcion. Both began with the same data; both drew conclusions in much the same way. We have already seen that Marcion regarded the apostles as knowing the true nature of Jesus but misinterpreting it for their hearers.

Bes Pantheos, the Egyptian god of recreation, was taken over by Gnosticism. He is represented as a grotesque dwarf, with large head, goggle eyes, shaggy beard and tail, and with a large crown of feathers on his head. (*6*)

To justify the ways of God to men

In the preface to his systematic theology, *De Principiis,* Origen says that in their preaching the apostles set forth the essentials of the Christian faith but did not provide any rational proof of it; the articles of faith were simply stated (*quia sint*) without any analysis of modes (*quomodo sint*) or origins (*unde sint*). That is to say that they discussed existence rather than essence. They left many questions open for future discussion, and such discussion is what Origen himself was determined to provide. He did so by making a distinction between what he explicitly taught (*dogmata*) and the questions which he investigated and discussed. This kind of statement can be taken in two ways. Either Origen was insisting upon the provisional character of his statements, as most scholars have claimed, or he was actually concealing some of his own systematic conclusions from public view – as Clement had earlier concealed some of his ideas. This interpretation has been maintained by F. H. Kettler in a recent study (*Der ursprüngliche Sinn der Dogmatik des Origenes* Berlin 1966), and at most points it seems convincing.

This means, then, not only that Origen's basic ideas were in part different from those of other Christians but also that he was well aware of the difference.

According to Origen, the first preaching of the apostles had to do with the life of a 'great and wonderful man' who performed astonishing miracles. This simply said that he did and taught such and such. In this kind of preaching the idea of Christ remained concealed within and under the name of Jesus. It was merely preliminary and led onward to the perfect preaching and understanding of who he was. The preaching thus corresponded with the double nature of Christ as human and divine; indeed Origen frequently speaks of 'the supposedly human Jesus'.

In part this distinction was intended to explain how the various gospel sayings could all have been expressed by the same person. For Origen, the 'supposedly human Jesus' said, 'I am the Resurrection and the Life,' although actually these words were uttered by the Logos incarnate, not by the man who died. Interestingly enough, the same problem had been faced by the Valentinian exegete Theodotus, who had stated that 'Jesus was different from the elements [psychic and material] which he assumed', and in consequence the spiritual Jesus had said, 'I am the Life' or 'I am the Truth' or 'I and the Father are one.' Theodotus had also pointed out that in the passion predictions (*e.g.* Mark viii 31) 'he seems to be speaking about someone else'. Both the Valentinians and Origen were confronting the problems posed by the rather incoherent Christological statements of the gospels. Both were trying to solve them systematically.

One might suppose that the allegorical method would have freed Origen from the need for an accurate text of the Greek Bible. Actually, however, such a text was all the more necessary because it provided the foundation for the allegorizations. He therefore devoted himself to the creation of the *Hexapla* in six columns, showing both what the Septuagint (the Greek version used by the churches) did say and also what it should have said at points where other versions contained either more or fewer words. In his many sermons and commentaries on the books of the Bible he studied the meanings of individual words and the nature of literary forms. He was also concerned with the canon of the Bible and laid some emphasis on literary criticism for determining the origins of individual books. At this point, however, he set a high value on traditional acceptance and usage, for it was necessary to have a commonly accepted base of inspired books on which to build interpretations to be shared with other Christians.

Consultant heresiologist

From AD 204 to 231, Origen spent most of his time at Alexandria, even though he once visited Rome and on another occasion was provided with a military escort for a journey to Arabia, the occasion being a theological colloquium with the Roman governor there. In 231 the situation at Alexandria finally blew up. Demetrius, who had been bishop for nearly forty years and had originally appointed Origen head of the catechetical school, had been willing to allow a large measure of freedom to the brilliant teacher, though he had recalled him from Palestine when he preached in churches there. Now Origen was invited to Athens as a consultant on heresy, and he accepted the invitation, apparently without the bishop's consent. On his way he stopped at Caesarea in Palestine, where his admirer Theotecnus ordained him presbyter, with the approval of Alexander of Jerusalem. He passed through Ephesus and spent some time at Athens before returning eastward to Antioch, where the Emperor Alexander Severus' mother Mammaea had asked him to confer with her. At Antioch a heretical teacher had already attacked him, relying on notes he had taken at Ephesus and had circulated in the form of a 'disputation' between himself and Origen. Origen demanded that the book be produced so that by its style and content it could be proved false. The heretic refused to meet the challenge.

Meanwhile at Alexandria Demetrius was deeply troubled by Origen's ordination and by the reports of his teaching, as well as by the fact that Origen was a eunuch and should not have been ordained. It is not clear whether or not Origen returned to Alexandria. In any event, a synod of bishops and presbyters banished him from the city. He was neither to live nor to teach there, and he soon joined his friends and protectors at Caesarea. Soon Demetrius convoked another synod, this time consisting of himself and some Egyptian bishops – all of whom owed allegiance to him – and deposed Origen from the presbyterate. This decision was easier to express than to enforce. Though it was ratified by synods at Rome and elsewhere, it was not confirmed by bishops in the eastern churches controlled by Origen's admirers. The churches of Achaïa, Phoenicia, Palestine, and Arabia refused to accept it.

In a letter to friends at Alexandria, Origen described his encounter with the heretical teacher at Antioch, insisted that his teaching was being misrepresented, and denounced Demetrius and the other clerics who had 'vainly' excommunicated him. He compared himself with the Old Testament prophets who had rightly denounced the shepherds, elders, priests, and princes of the people. Resuming work on the St John's Gospel – although, as he complained, without the stenographers supplied at Alexandria – he stated that God had brought him out of the land of Egypt. After his departure, 'the enemy redoubled his violence through writings truly alien to the gospel, and raised against us all the winds of wickedness in Egypt'. God had now quenched the fiery darts of the enemy, presumably with the support of the Palestinian bishops.

The Church of Caesarea was obviously the promised land, and, although Origen continued to travel about the eastern world, acting as arbiter and judge in theological controversies, he was never to return to Egypt. Demetrius' death was doubtless hastened by the crisis, but his successor Heraclas made no effort to recall him, his former colleague. Origen's insistence on Heraclas' concern for Greek philosophy may not have been viewed with favour. In any case, Heraclas was doubtless trying to restore the lost unity of the church.

During the persecution under Decius (AD 249–51) Origen was p 335 imprisoned and tortured, apparently at Caesarea, and while in (8) prison he received a letter on martyrdom from his pupil Dionysius, now bishop of Alexandria. A few years later he died at Tyre and was buried there. If he wrote two works ascribed to him by the Neoplatonist Porphyry, he must have composed them at this time. They bore the titles *On demons* and *That the King* [presumably God] *is the only Creator*. Not preserved by Christians, they may have reflected a movement toward philosophical discussion which was unwelcome in Church circles.

We should not suppose that Origen was occupied exclusively with theological scholarship. During the brief reign of the pro-Christian Emperor Philip (AD 244–9), he addressed letters to him p 191 and to the Empress Severa; he also defended his own orthodoxy in (38) letters to Fabian of Rome and many other bishops, evidently seek- p 349 ing for revocation of the earlier decisions of synods. According to *(f 4)* Jerome, he 'repented of having written such things and assigned the blame for his rashness to Ambrose because he had published works written for private use'. This explanation is neither convincing nor generous. Ambrose had devoted much of his time and fortune to the furtherance of Origen's writing. The complaint that he left Origen nothing in his will is mentioned by Jerome and comes, one would suppose, from Origen himself; but there may not have been much to leave.

From such biographical details we gain an impression of a man who, though deeply devoted to Church and scholarship, was often torn between the two and was no less emotional than the bishop Demetrius, who is criticized on this ground by Eusebius.

Alternatives and assimilation

The ideas of Origen flourished in eastern Christianity for many centuries, and, though several Christian leaders at the end of the 4th century AD denounced him (we may mention Epiphanius and Jerome), there were always men devoted to his memory and to aspects of his method. In the West a similar situation obtained in regard to the thought of Hippolytus and, especially, Tertullian. Clement was not so influential; his contribution was less easy to assimilate. Through both Clement and Origen some of the insights of Philo and the Gnostics were mediated to later, more 'orthodox' Christians. Without the work of the Gnostics and the Alexandrians no genuinely philosophical theology could have arisen within Christianity, and it could not have entered into communication with the intellectual groups from which it later derived much of its strength.

With the passage of time what came to be viewed as the exaggerations of men like Origen and Tertullian were modified, and the ideas of these fathers of Eastern and Western theology were reinterpreted by subsequent theologians. Without their efforts to create new and fresh interpretations of the gospel, however, Christianity would have remained a purely traditional sect, clinging to its memories of the past and never launching out on the open sea of the Graeco-Roman world.

XV
THE PERSECUTIONS

CHRISTIANITY'S ENCOUNTER WITH
THE ROMAN IMPERIAL GOVERNMENT

G. E. M. DE STE. CROIX

'I am God's wheat, and I am ground by the teeth of wild beasts, to be found pure bread of Christ.'

IGNATIUS OF ANTIOCH 'EPISTLE TO THE ROMANS'

'The blood of the martyrs is seed,' wrote Tertullian; 'the more you mow us down, the more we grow.' It was a perceptive truth as well as a challenge. The persecutions to which the Early Church was subjected during the first three centuries of its existence form an essential part of its history. Too intermittent and unsustained to succeed in stamping it out, they were violent enough to weld believers into tightly organized bodies and to give them a fierce determination which in the end equalled that of their enemies.

Christians were persecuted for a variety of reasons – some springing from policy, some from misunderstanding, some from a real fear that opposition to the Roman religion meant danger to the state. There were fanatics on both sides, but the bulk of pagans would no doubt have echoed the deputy prefect of Egypt who in 257 asked Dionysius of Alexandria, in honest bewilderment: 'Who prevents you from worshipping this god of yours also, if he is a god, along with the natural gods?'

When persecution did flare up it was made horrifying by the cruelty that was a normal part of Roman life. The agonies suffered by the Christians were the same as those suffered by any enemy of Rome, and the arenas where they died had seen the deaths of countless victims in less inspired causes. Most famous of such arenas, identified by persistent tradition as the site of martyrdom, is the Colosseum at Rome. Certainly execution by being thrown to the beasts is known to have occurred at Rome, and the Colosseum would be the most natural location, although it has been shown that the occurrence of Christian martyrdoms there cannot actually be proved. The building was begun by Vespasian on the site of part of Nero's 'Golden House', inaugurated by Titus in AD 80, but only finally completed in AD 217 after the great fire, when the upper story, hitherto of wood, was replaced by the present one in stone. It is elliptical in shape, measuring 620 by 513 ft, the arena 287 by 180 ft, and approximately 160 ft to the top of the outer wall. This is of four stories, three arcaded with attached Doric, Ionic and Corinthian orders, the top solid with Corinthian pilasters and windows. Its capacity is now estimated at about 50,000; the ancient Roman estimates which vary from 80,000 to 100,000 are clearly exaggerated.

The seats of the spectators rose above the arena and separated from it by a high wall. They were divided into several sections *(maeniana)* by passageways round the amphitheatre. The lowest section, known as the *podium*, was for state officials, the next for the wealthy or nobles and those above for the rest of the populace. Apparently seats were always reserved: they are usually carefully numbered, and tickets of clay bearing the seat number have been found. The seats were supported on walls running radially to the exterior, between which the exit stairs were most ingeniously arranged so that the enormous crowds could flow evenly to the exit arches which surrounded the ground story. In addition, vaulted corridors ran round the outside; the arcaded exterior was therefore a necessary and logical expression of the construction. (1)

Roman religion was almost literally the Roman ruling class at its devotions. It was a public observance, rather than a matter of individual conscience and belief. Men and women who were adherents of one of the eastern mystery religions could without moral discomfort attend the public religious ceremonies in honour of the traditional gods. To the Christian – as to the Jew – it was idolatry, a concept barely intelligible to the average pagan. As part of the Roman policy of not interfering with the traditional religious practices of peoples coming under their rule, the Jews were excused from participating in these ceremonies. The Christians, on the other hand, were seen as a new group actively influencing Roman citizens in an anti-Roman direction.

A typical ceremony, the *suovetaurilia*, sacrifice of a bull, a ram and a pig to Mars, is shown in this relief (below). The priest, who may be the Emperor Domitian, throws on an altar grains of incense taken from a box held by an assistant. The two laurel trees and two altars may allude to Divus Vespasianus and Divus Titus. (2)

The Altar of Peace (below) makes clear the way in which the state was identified with the gods. Its long frieze of figures in relief shows all the notables of Rome, the Imperial family, consuls, senators and officials, going in procession to sacrifice. (3)

Emperor and High Priest were – logically – the same man. Here Augustus (below) assumes the role of Pontifex Maximus, indicated by the toga drawn over the head. Augustus did much to promote the state cults during his long rule after Actium. (4)

Nero (54–68) blamed Christians for the great fire of Rome in AD 64. (5)

Trajan (98–117) persecuted Christians only if they came to his notice. (6)

Marcus Aurelius' reign (161–180) saw sporadic local persecution. (7)

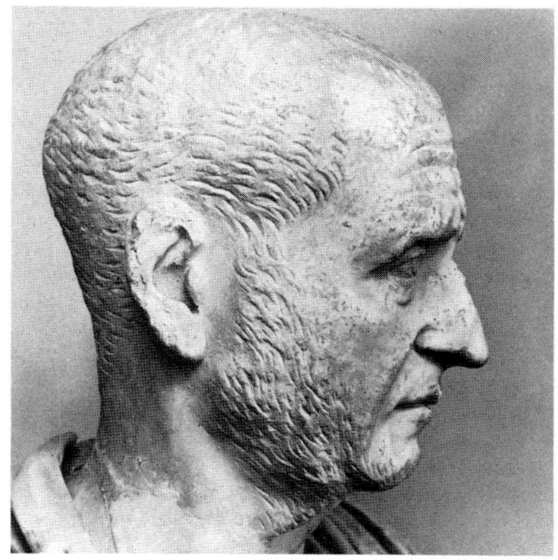

Decius (249–251) ordered a universal act of sacrifice. (8)

'It is this worship,' cried the pagan aristocrat Symmachus, after the Christian Emperor Gratian had removed the Altar of Victory from the Senate House in the 4th century, 'which subdued the world to Rome's law. It is these rites which kept Hannibal from the walls.' Right: Victory from the Arch of the Severi at Leptis Magna. (9)

The Stoic Emperor, Marcus Aurelius (below), sacrifices in front of the temple of Jupiter, Juno and Minerva, on the Capitol. He was consistently hostile to Christianity, which threatened the ideology of the state. (10)

Valerian's persecution of 257–9 was virtually over before he was defeated and captured by the Sassanian King Shapur I in 260, an event commemorated in this relief at Naqsh-i-Rustem. It was interpreted as a divine judgement by the Christians. Valerian is shown kneeling before his captor. His son Gallienus restored their property and churches, out of indifference rather than conviction, and the Church enjoyed a time of relative peace.

During Valerian's persecution many of the most famous Christian martyrs, including St Sixtus and St Lawrence, had been killed. But the period of tranquillity that followed saw the building of house churches and martyria, many of which have been illustrated in earlier chapters. (11)

The last persecution opened in 303, under Diocletian and Maximian. Each 'Augustus' was assisted by his 'Caesar'. Galerius was Diocletian's Caesar in the East, Constantius Chlorus was Maximian's in the West. This was the famous 'tetrarchy' represented in the porphyry group now placed next to St Mark's in Venice.

Diocletian is the third from the left. He established the tetrarchy and, egged on by Galerius, he started the last and greatest persecution of the Christians. Both acts indeed had a common purpose: to strengthen the Empire. Christian services were forbidden, churches destroyed, books and church property confiscated. But the Church itself was too firmly rooted to be eradicated. By 305 it was clear that the attempt had failed, although anti-Christian action went on until 313. (12)

'Take, eat, this is my body.' These words which instituted the Eucharist were misunderstood (perhaps maliciously) by the pagan enemies of the Church and led to wild accusations of cannibalism, just as the love feasts of the Christians were used to bolster charges of sexual licence. In reality, as unprejudiced observers like Pliny knew, all that they did was 'to gather together for a communal and simple repast'. The meal shown here (above) comes from the catacomb of Priscilla. Such meals, represented in several places in the catacombs, had reference to several ideas: the Celestial Banquet; the funeral meal; the Eucharist; perhaps also the Wedding at Cana. (13)

The 'Underground Church' meeting in secret in the catacombs has been shown to be largely a product of romantic imagination. The catacombs were cemeteries following Jewish models, and the normal places of worship were house-churches of which only one has survived, at Dura Europus. The catacombs did, however, contain chapels, and Christians probably did assemble there in times of persecution to honour their dead. This gallery (right) is in the catacomb under the Church of Sant' Agnese; coffins were placed lengthwise in the recesses of the wall. (14)

Church property was seized during the Great Persecution (303–313), and severe penalties visited upon those who concealed it. Detailed records survive of a raid at Cirta in Numidia, on May 19th, 303, in which not only books, plate and lamps were confiscated but also 82 women's tunics, 38 veils and 47 pairs of women's boots.

The Scriptures were naturally the chief items sought by the authorities. By the 4th century the codex – the bound book – was coming to replace the papyrus roll. A papyrus fragment (left) contains verses 1–11 of the Epistle to the Hebrews, Chapter 12. The codex (below) is the most complete of the early codices, the Codex Sinaiticus, dating from the 4th century. (15, 16)

Prized ivory bookcovers telling the story of Christ's life must have been among the treasures of early churches. This 4th-century example is later than the persecutions but is still classical in style. In the centre stands the lamb in the wreath of victory – victory over death. On top, between the symbols of St Matthew and St Luke, is the Nativity. On the left, the Annunciation, the Magi and the Baptism. Right, Mary and the star, Christ and the Doctors and the Entry into Jerusalem. Below, between portraits of the two evangelists, is one of the few representations in Early Christian art of the Massacre of the Innocents. (19)

Four bronze lamps that once hung in the churches of the Early Christians employ a variety of symbolic shapes. Above: Christ and St Peter in the boat. Far left: Moses striking the rock, a symbol (as we have seen) of Christ bringing the water of life. Centre: a griffin (the forces of evil) with the Chi-Rho monogram on its side. Left: the fish, the sign of Christ because the letters of the Greek word *Ichthys* stand for Jesus Christ Son of God Saviour. (17, 18, 20, 21)

The making of a martyr: prosecution began with a trial before a Roman magistrate. The standard charge was simply 'being a Christian', *nomen Christianum*, and was normally brought by a private accuser, who if he failed laid himself open to the counter-charge of 'malicious prosecution'. This Pompeiian fresco (above) is a caricature, but gives a good idea of the appearance of a Roman trial. Here the magistrate sits with two assessors. The fresco is also interesting in representing the Judgement of Solomon – evidence for Jewish influence in Italy at a comparatively early date. (22)

Death in the arena was one of the penalties that followed a verdict of guilty. Condemned prisoners were pitted against wild animals, as in the mosaic (above) from Zliten in Tunisia, as part of specially organized festivities or 'games'. A more normal, if less spectacular, method of execution was beheading, of which a unique representation survives (above right) in a Roman house under SS. Giovanni e Paolo. Many more Christians died of disease and hunger in filthy overcrowded dungeons. Others perished in the mines, the concentration camps of the ancient world. Martyrdom, however, was considered to be a direct passport to Paradise – hence the large numbers of 'voluntary martyrs' who at one time embarrassed sections of the Church. (25, 26)

If he denied that he was a Christian, the defendant was invited to prove it by sacrificing to the gods or offering a pinch of incense on an altar. The ceremony would have looked much like this scene from Dura Europus, where a tribune sacrifices to the Palmyrene gods. (23)

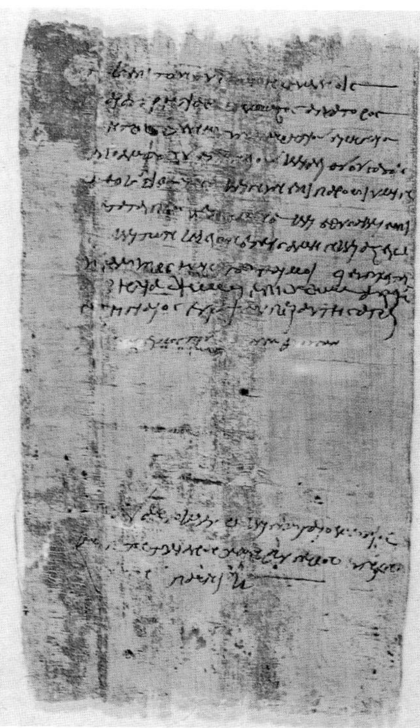

A certificate was evidence for the sacrifice prescribed by Decius. One is shown here: 'I have in your presence and in accordance with the command, made sacrifice and libation. . . . I, Aurelia Demos, have presented this declaration. I, Aurelius Irenaeus, wrote for her as she is illiterate.' (24)

The martyr's crown won veneration from the beginning. Another fresco from SS. Giovanni e Paolo (right) shows two worshippers kneeling at the martyr's feet. The parted curtains indicate that he is in Paradise. (27)

The final victory of the Church came when Constantine and Licinius issued their edict of toleration in 313 ('Edict of Milan'). Out of the chaos of the tetrarchy four figures had emerged by 313, Constantine and Licinius, who were sympathetic to Christianity, and Maxentius, son of Maximian, and Maximinus Daia, a kinsman of Galerius. The victory of Christianity was sealed by Constantine's defeat of Maxentius at the Battle of the Milvian Bridge in Rome. Christianity gradually became the official religion of the Empire.

The Battle of the Milvian Bridge (below), seen here in the relief on the Arch of Constantine, made Constantine ruler of much of the western part of the Roman world, and was hailed by Christians as the triumph of their faith. Constantine had cleverly enlisted their support by his adoption of the Chi-Rho as his emblem and by his story of his vision with the words HOC VINCE ('By this conquer'). The Chi-Rho had, however, already been used as a ligature in both pagan and Christian contexts. (28)

Christ as Victor is the theme of this sarcophagus (right) dating from soon after Constantine's death, *c.* 350. In the centre is Christ's monogram combined with the cross and the wreath. The soldiers at the foot, who show that this is the Resurrection scene, sit in the traditional posture of defeated barbarians in Imperial reliefs. On the left stands Christ, no longer crowned with thorns but with the laurel wreath, and Simon of Cyrene carrying the cross. On the right, Christ calmly converses with Pilate, who turns away, while a servant brings the basin in which he will wash his hands. (30)

The martyr's memory was cherished by preserving relics and building memorial churches. Bottom left: two bishops carry a casket containing relics of a martyr (perhaps Euphemia of Chalcedon) in solemn procession to a newly-built church. Bottom centre: the memorial church of Cyprian near Carthage begun shortly after 313. Bottom right: the martyrion of Babylas at Kaoussiye near Antioch, built before 387 in the form of a cross. (29, 31, 32)

'A day bright and radiant', in the words of the church historian Eusebius, brought victory to Constantine and to Christianity. Constantine himself, an enigmatic figure (seen, right, in a fine bronze now in Belgrade), was more cautious. He stopped the persecutions, but in doing so he was careful not to repudiate other religions. In his edicts and letters he tends to use phrases which would not offend pagans, such as 'the Deity enthroned in heaven'; and similar phraseology ('the influence of the godhead') appears on the triumphal arch (below) which the Senate set up in his honour beside the Colosseum. The sculpture on the arch includes no Christian themes and in fact was for the most part hastily assembled from older pagan monuments. Constantine assumed the official duties of *pontifex maximus* of the old religion, and confirmed the privileges of its priests. In the market place of his new capital he placed the chariot of the Sun God, surmounted by the cross. He took the monogram of Christ, the Chi-Rho, as his standard, but referred to it only as 'this salutary token of strength'.

But if Constantine acted and spoke warily, most Christians felt no such hesitation. They built huge new basilican churches, filling them with rich offerings and works of art. Free from persecution, they soon became persecutors themselves. 'Wild beasts are not such enemies to mankind,' wrote the 4th-century pagan historian Ammianus Marcellinus, 'as are most Christians in their deadly hatred of one another.' (33, 34)

CHRISTIANITY'S ENCOUNTER WITH THE ROMAN IMPERIAL GOVERNMENT

G.E.M. DE STE. CROIX

IN DEALING with a much disputed historical problem, where the evidence is puzzling and at first sight contradictory, it is a good principle to begin with a careful scrutiny of the best and clearest evidence. In the case of Christianity's encounter with the Roman Imperial government there can be no doubt what that evidence is: the famous letters exchanged between Pliny the Younger and the
p 335 (6) Emperor Trajan, relating to the persecution Pliny was conducting in Pontus (on the southern shore of the Black Sea) in the year AD 110 or just after.

The background must be quickly sketched in first. Jesus had been tried and sentenced as a political criminal by the Roman governor of Judaea, Pontius Pilate (whose title, by the way, is now known to have been not *procurator* but *praefectus Iudaeae*). Pilate's first question to Jesus, corresponding to our 'Do you plead guilty or not guilty?', was, 'Are you the King of the Jews?'; and the notice on the Cross, given in all four Gospels, confirms that he was accused and convicted for allegedly giving himself that title – for being a Resistance leader, to use modern terminology. That they actually worshipped so dangerous and undesirable a figure would anyway have made the Christians suspect in Roman eyes, although one may feel that by itself it need not necessarily have led to the suppression of Christianity.

For the first phase of the relations of the Christians with the Roman Imperial administration we are entirely dependent upon the Acts of the Apostles, which regards persecution as being caused almost entirely by the hostility of the Jews. The Roman authorities either profess complete indifference to the religious squabbles between Jews and Christians, as did Annius Gallio, the proconsul of Achaïa (and brother of the great Seneca), who 'drove the Jews from the judgment seat' when they accused Paul before him on a religious charge; or else they actually protect the Christians, as did Claudius Lysias, the military tribune at Jerusalem, who went to considerable trouble to prevent Paul from being lynched by the Jews and to get him out of Jerusalem to Caesarea under escort. The fact that Acts has the propagandist purpose of depicting the Christians as the victims of Jewish vindictiveness, while the Roman officials either maintain a benevolent neutrality or intervene in favour of the Christians, need not make us distrust its general picture, which rings true at most points where it can be tested. But Acts ends in the most tantalizing way, without telling us the result of the process against Paul to which its last eight chapters are devoted. (This need not surprise us, if Paul was indeed martyred at Rome, as tradition has it, for it would have been highly embarrassing to the author of such a work to have to record an Imperial condemnation of a leading Christian missionary.)

The decisive change in the attitude of the Roman government to Christianity may have come in AD 64 (just after the narrative of Acts closes), with the great fire at Rome. For the connection
335 (5) *f 6* between the fire and a severe persecution by Nero at Rome, of which tradition makes Peter and Paul the most distinguished victims, we are dependent upon a single passage in Tacitus (*Annals* xv 44), where unfortunately we are faced, as Professor Beaujeu has recently put it, with 'extreme conciseness, equivocal language, ambiguous structure, uncertainty even in establishing the text'. Skating lightly over this episode until we have got on to firmer ground, after considering the Pliny-Trajan correspondence, we need only record the fact that Christians were almost certainly martyred at Rome during the reign of Nero (AD 54–68); and we can safely use the evidence of the Apocalypse to conclude that at some time or times during the second half of the 1st century AD, presumably in the reign of Nero or Domitian, Christians were also martyred in Asia Minor. But the facts are unclear, and it is only with Pliny that we come out of the mists.

The Pliny-Trajan correspondence

The more one studies the two letters of Pliny and Trajan, the more one admires their clarity and conciseness. With them the mould sets, as it were, and we can see persecution taking the precise shape it will long retain. Pliny tells Trajan that he has never been present at any trials of Christians, and he is uncertain 'for what offence or to what extent it is customary to punish or to investigate' in these cases. His purpose in writing the letter is to ask Trajan some questions about how he ought to proceed. He lists his uncertainties, which are three. The first, whether he ought to take into account the age of the accused, was rightly ignored by Trajan. This was precisely the kind of thing about which a provincial governor was given a complete discretion and was expected to exercise it; and we have later evidence that other governors sometimes did and sometimes did not spare an accused Christian of tender years. Pliny's other two uncertainties are whether penitent apostates from Christianity could be pardoned, and whether he is to punish 'for the Name itself' (just for being a Christian, that is to say), even if no *flagitia* are alleged, or 'for the *flagitia* associated with being a Christian'. (The term *flagitia* signifies crimes of a particularly unpleasant or disgraceful nature, such as the cannibalism and incest p 337 (13) with which the early Christians were so often charged – 'abominations' would be a fair translation.)

On a superficial reading of Trajan's brief reply (less than one-fifth the length of Pliny's letter) it may seem that he does not specifically answer the last question. In fact he does answer it decisively, by implication: persecution is to be for the Name, not the *flagitia*. As we shall see, there was a vitally important difference. Trajan, in replying as he did, was very probably confirming standard practice and certainly giving Pliny the answer he desired.

First, we must consider an important legal technicality. Although the contrary is sometimes asserted, there is absolutely no doubt, from the technical language used by both Pliny and Trajan, that the standard charge against a Christian was already the Name (the *nomen Christianum*), just 'being a Christian'. Pliny refers to 'those who were *charged* before me *with being Christians*', and the only question he says he asked them was 'whether they *were* Christians'. (The latter is an important point: a Roman judge always began by asking the accused whether he admitted the charge; so if Pliny asked the accused, 'Are you Christians?', the charge must have been one of 'being Christians'.) And Trajan in his reply speaks of 'those who had been *accused* before you *as Christians*', and goes on to say that anyone who '*denies he is a Christian*' and proves it is to go free. One cannot get round that evidence, and of course there is plenty more from later trials. The origin and the implications of persecution for the Name will be considered presently. All we need do now is simply to note that it had come to be recognized, not later than the early years of the 2nd century AD, that if an individual were prosecuted in due form before a Roman magistrate on the p 341 (22) ground that he was a Christian, and if he refused to recant, he could be punished with death. The procedure, by *cognitio extra ordinem* (already, in spite of its name, the standard procedure for the punishment of most crimes), was not mere 'police action' but a judicial trial (*iurisdictio*) in the full sense, even if a contrary appearance is sometimes produced by the fact that a confession of Christianity, amounting to a plea of 'Guilty' to the charge, might be immediately followed by sentence, without even the calling of witnesses.

Now in spite of his expressions of uncertainty to Trajan, Pliny had not just sat scratching his head: he had in fact taken action, indeed very drastic action. The clue to the solution of all the main problems of this correspondence is the recognition that Pliny in effect divides his Christians into three quite distinct classes, whom we may call for convenience Confessors, Deniers and Apostates. The first, the Confessors, admitted they were Christians and stuck to it even when warned that they would suffer for it. The second class, the outright Deniers, said they were not *and never had been* Christians at all. The third class, the Apostates, admitted they had once been Christians but claimed they had already given up Christianity. (There were also three chronological stages in the affair, and three different procedures by which the accusation of being Christians had arisen; and both these sets of distinctions correspond precisely with our three classes of accused. One may suspect that Pliny has oversimplified, and that in practice the situation was not quite so tidy; but that need not concern us here.)

Confessors, Deniers and Apostates

The Confessors had been formally denounced as Christians in proper form by 'delators' (*delatores*, who were not mere informers but actually conducted the prosecution themselves). Pliny asked them three times over, 'Are you Christians?', threatening them with punishment if they persisted; and then he ordered them off to execution – or, if they were Roman citizens, sent them off to be tried in Rome.

The Deniers, who had been the subject of an anonymous denunciation but asserted they had never been Christians, Pliny released, upon their invoking the gods, offering wine and incense to the Emperor's statue, and reviling Christ. 'It is said,' Pliny adds, 'that genuine Christians cannot be made to do any of these things.' It is convenient, if not strictly correct, to refer to what the Deniers did as 'sacrificing': the cult act most usually prescribed in these cases was some form of sacrificing to the gods or the Emperor.

The Apostates, who appear only in the third and final stage, are the people with whom Pliny's letter is really concerned. They had been denounced by an informer (*index*): this was a half-way stage between formal prosecution by a *delator* and anonymous denunciation. Pliny need not have acted on this information, but he did: he summoned the accused before him. They said they had been Christians but had ceased to be so, some for two years, others for up to twenty. All of them did what the Deniers had already done: they 'sacrificed', by doing reverence to Trajan's statue and the images of the gods, and they cursed Christ. In their case alone Pliny reveals that he had investigated the nature of the Christian cult, which he found (rather to his surprise, perhaps) to be quite harmless, if degradingly superstitious in character. Even when he had two women slaves among the accused put to the torture, he got nothing incriminating out of them. 'I found only,' he says, 'a depraved superstition carried to extreme lengths.'

But Pliny did not release these Apostates immediately they had sacrificed, as he had released the Deniers. He says he had adjourned the trial, and he is now referring the matter to Trajan. Why did he think that Trajan might want him to treat Apostates differently from Deniers, who had never been Christians at all? The answer is that only in connection with the Apostates did the question of *flagitia* arise. Pliny had begun by persecuting for the Name, without enquiring into *flagitia*. With the Deniers no question of *flagitia* arose if one accepted their assertion that they had never been Christians at all, as Pliny was prepared to do. But the Apostates *had once been Christians*. Might it not be necessary, therefore, to punish them for the *flagitia* which (as all the world knew) were involved in the practice of Christianity? Ah, but Pliny had now discovered that adherence to Christianity did not necessarily involve *flagitia*. He was in a quandary. The question now was: were Christians to be punished for the Name *only*, or for the *flagitia*?

The difference was vital:

(1) Punishment for the Name alone (a) would be inflicted for the mere confession of Christianity, without evidence of any other crime; but (b) could be avoided altogether by denial *or apostasy*, demonstrated by the performance of pagan cult acts.

(2) Punishment for the *flagitia* (a) would involve an inquisition into their nature, with witnesses and evidence produced, but (b) presumably, if *flagitia* were discovered, or plausibly invented, the guilty could not escape by merely apostatizing from Christianity.

It should be obvious that steadfast Christians (Confessors) might greatly prefer the second alternative, punishment for *flagitia* only – if this course were adopted, they would presumably have to be set free if no *flagitia* were proved. But for Deniers and Apostates, of course, including those prepared to apostatize at their trial, the former alternative, persecution for the Name, was infinitely preferable, because then there would be simply no case against them: they would merely sacrifice and be set free. And it is the Apostates Pliny is really thinking about. He *had* dealt with the Confessors: he had cut off their heads. He *had* dealt with the Deniers: he had set them free when they sacrificed. Evidently he was persuaded that this was the customary procedure, as no doubt it was. For all he knew, Trajan might order something different. But his question to Trajan comes only when he has disposed of the Confessors and Deniers and is now confronted (according to his own statement) only with Apostates. He might have to deal again at some future time with the other two classes, and he is asking for a general directive; but it is the Apostates he is primarily interested in. Sensibly enough, he wants to be allowed (this is an important point) to *encourage apostasy* by offering a free pardon to Apostates. Expressing his gratification at the good effects his persecution has

In De Rossi's engraving of the papal burial vault in the catacomb of Callistus as he found it in 1854, one can pick out fragments of the epitaphs of the Popes Anterus, Lucius and Eutychian, of the word 'episkopos' (bishop) and of the memorial tablet set up by Pope Damasus a hundred years after their deaths. (1)

The epitaph of the martyrs Simplicius and Faustinus is touchingly simple: 'XP. The martyrs Simplicius and Faustinus who suffered death in the River Tiber and have been laid to rest in the cemetery of Generosa "super Philippi".' (2)

already had in helping to restore the traditional religion, he ends with the words, 'From this it is easy to infer what a large number of people could be reformed if an opportunity were provided for repentance.'

Trajan says a great deal in his admirably terse reply. While declining to lay down a cut-and-dried rule applicable to every case (no doubt because he wanted to preserve the discretion always granted to provincial governors), he does define some principles which were to govern the treatment of Christians for a long time to come. He makes it clear, for good and all, that those who are convicted of being Christians are to be 'punished': this would p 340–1 (25, 26) normally involve death by decapitation, but the magistrate trying the case (normally a provincial governor) might see fit to prescribe some lesser penalty or some more unpleasant form of death. But the Emperor makes three important provisos which worked in favour of the Christians and helped to mitigate the severity of persecution. First, Christians are not to be sought out (*conquirendi non sunt*). Secondly, proceedings must be conducted by formal delation – a qualification which discouraged frivolous or baseless accusations, for an unsuccessful delator might become liable in his turn to an action for *calumnia* (malicious prosecution). In particular, no notice is to be taken of anonymous accusations, 'for this kind of thing creates the worst sort of precedent and is out of keeping with the spirit of our age'. And thirdly, responding to Pliny's evident desire to be allowed to treat Apostates exactly the same as Deniers, Trajan rules that 'Anyone who denies he is a Christian, and proves it by making supplication to our gods, is to obtain pardon on the score of his repentance, however suspect his past conduct may have been' – the last words driving home the point that persecution is for the Name only, that even Apostates need fear no enquiry into *flagitia*.

Now Trajan is here authorizing a course of action in relation to the suppression of a 'foreign superstition' which is radically different from any adopted previously by the Roman government in relation to other such 'superstitions'. In the past, action had never been taken against foreign religions except when they gave social or moral or political offence. The adherents of no other religion were ever punished for simply professing the superstition: they were punished for the specific crimes (or undesirable acts) they were alleged to have committed – for the *flagitia*, never the *nomen*. (The clearest and best known example is the suppression of the Bacchic cult in Italy in 186 BC.) And in other respects the persecution of the Christians was similarly unique in Roman criminal law: in particular, the only punishable offence was not *having been* a Christian, but *being and remaining* a Christian, with the opportunity (available to no other criminals) of obtaining a free pardon by sacrificing, right up to the moment of sentence.

Pax Deorum

Why did the Romans, by prosecuting Christians for the Name alone, treat Christianity so differently from all other religions and indeed from all other crimes? Surely because the Christians were recalcitrant 'atheists', who rejected and despised all forms of Graeco-Roman religion and refused to participate in pagan cult – p 334–5 (2–10) and thereby would endanger the *pax deorum*, the proper harmonious relationship between gods and men, and tend to bring down on the whole community the wrath of the gods on whose goodwill the prosperity of the State depended. As late as AD 384, when Christianity had captured the seats of power, and paganism was fighting a last rearguard action, the great pagan aristocrat Symmachus, pleading for the restoration to the Senate House of the altar of Victoria, the goddess who personified the irresistible might of p 335 (9) Rome, could still declare, as generations of Romans had done before him, that when religion – the old traditional religion – is slighted, the whole state suffers: famine and disaster follow. He makes Rome herself admonish the Christian Emperor: 'It is this worship which has subdued the world to my laws. It is these religious rites which drove Hannibal from my walls, the Senones from the Capitol.' That was always the Roman attitude. Persecution for the Name may have been sparked off first by the conviction of many Christians as incendiaries and malefactors during the great fire at Rome in AD 64, but this is by no means certain. As soon as Christianity became recognizably distinct from Judaism, the Christians' refusal to acknowledge state and civic cults and family worship would have made them appear a gang of undesirables, deserving punishment because they utterly rejected an essential element in the Roman 'way of life' and thereby imperilled the very foundations of the community and showed themselves to be enemies of the state. (The Jews were equally 'atheists'; but they could be excused, as the Christians could not, because they were practising, as all men should, their ancestral religion, admittedly older than Rome itself.) We must not, however, suppose that there had been a 'general law' in the form of an Imperial edict proscribing Christianity: this theory, once held by many ecclesiastical historians, has never been countenanced by specialists in Roman law and public administration and is now totally discredited.

One very important feature of the trial of Christians was 'the p 341 (23) sacrifice test', as it may be called – which, before it was applied to Christians, had been used by the Greeks of Antioch during a pogrom, as a method of exposing Jews. According to his own account, Pliny did not order (or even invite) Confessors to sacrifice; it was the Deniers and (by Trajan's decision) the Apostates who were *invited* to sacrifice in order to prove their sincerity – they did not need to be *ordered* to do so; they would have been only too pleased to be allowed to demonstrate the truth of their plea. But by degrees the sacrifice test came to play quite a different role, and what had been a privilege for Pliny's Deniers and Apostates became a sinister threat to the steadfast Christian Confessor. As judicial torture during the 2nd and 3rd centuries AD became a standard part of the trial of anyone except a member of the privileged upper classes, any magistrate who wanted (as did the great majority) to make Apostates and not Martyrs might say to the accused Christian Confessor, 'I don't want to have to cut off your head. Sacrifice, and I'll let you go. Just drop a few grains of incense on the fire by the altar. If you won't, I'll torture you.' And now, the keener the magistrate is to avoid executing the Christian, the more savagely he is likely to torture him. Of course he could execute him, if he wanted to, as soon as he had confessed to being a Christian; but it looks as if the use of torture became the standard practice. And here we may note yet another feature distinguishing trials of Christians (as Tertullian emphasized) from all other Roman criminal processes: the accused was tortured not to make him confess or admit something, but to make him 'deny'.

The emphasis placed upon sacrificing (in the loose sense of performing some pagan cult act) in accounts of Christian martyrdoms from Pliny onwards is itself a proof that the really objectionable feature of Christianity in Roman eyes was its exclusiveness, its rejection of all other forms of religion. One single act of religious conformity was enough to set an accused Christian free without punishment. 'Those who do not profess the Roman religion,' said the proconsul of Africa to Cyprian at his trial in AD 257, 'must not refuse to take part in Roman religious ceremonies.' This happens to be the proconsul's version of a recent specific Imperial decree requiring Christian clergy to conform to pagan cult; but it was something which any Roman magistrate might say to any accused Christian at any time. The exclusiveness of Christian Confessors puzzled and exasperated the pagans. As the deputy prefect of Egypt said to Dionysius, bishop of Alexandria, also in AD 257, 'Who prevents you from worshipping this god of yours also, if he is a god, along with the natural gods?' That was how any pagan would feel. One wonders why the Christians were never tempted to rely on II Kings v 18–19, where Naaman asks for pardon should he bow himself, with his master the King of Syria, in the temple of Rimmon, and the prophet Elisha makes an evidently acquiescent reply.

The Christians to the lions

The Christian apologists of the 2nd and 3rd centuries AD make it very clear that it was above all when popular superstitions were aroused by some great calamity like a plague or a famine that a desire for scapegoats was most likely to find satisfaction in Christian blood. As Tertullian says,

> The pagans suppose that the Christians are the cause of every public disaster. If the Tiber overflows or the Nile doesn't, if there is a drought or an earthquake, a famine or a pestilence, at once the cry goes up, 'The Christians to the lions.'

Sometimes there were lynchings. It is impossible to make even a rough guess at the total number of martyrs, or to estimate the frequency of persecution; but the rule that Christians could be attacked only by formal delation and were not to be sought out probably ensured that persecution was seldom severe except at times of public disaster. From at least Trajan's time onwards the Roman authorities must have felt they had established a very reasonable method for dealing with these 'atheists'. Until the 4th century AD very few of them were members of the governing class, and with luck their activities would not be conspicuous or important enough to arouse the wrath of the gods and bring down vengeance on the community; but, if it did, delators would soon be forthcoming, and the Christians would be suppressed.

It is interesting to find that there is good evidence of Christians sharing the outlook of their pagan contemporaries to the extent of feeling that the religious misbehaviour of individuals might bring down divine punishment not merely upon the individuals concerned but upon at least the immediate communities and even perhaps the Empire as a whole – and its rulers. This evidence extends from Early Christian times right down into the late Empire. Old Polycarp, who was said to have known the Apostles personally, used to tell a story, reported by both Irenaeus and Eusebius, of how the Apostle John, entering the baths at Ephesus, caught sight of the notable heretic Cerinthus inside, and immediately rushed out, shouting, 'Away, lest the very baths collapse, for within is Cerinthus the enemy of the truth.' A letter of the Emperor
p 344 Constantine written in the winter of AD 313–4 shows his very real
(33, 34) anxiety that if he, as Emperor, fails to suppress religious strife such as the Donatist schism, he may be held personally responsible by God and punished himself, with the whole Empire which the celestial will has entrusted to his care. An Imperial Constitution of AD 438, directed against Jews, Samaritans, heretics and pagans, blames these religious dissidents for the recent droughts and frosts and failures of the harvest. Many similar examples might be quoted.

A Roman magistrate was expected to keep the area under his control peaceful and undisturbed; and, if there was a general movement of popular opinion demanding the blood of the Christians, he would have little reason to deny 'legitimate' satisfaction to it, and thereby invite riots and lynchings. Pilate acted as any prudent Roman governor would have done when all the local notables unanimously demanded the blood of a low-class agitator. Governors before whom Christians were denounced at times when public animosity was running high would rarely have any motive for saving an accused Christian – though Tertullian does mention four African proconsuls who had gone out of their way to do so.

It was certainly the individual provincial governor (the only man in the province with the power to pass a death sentence) who played the major role in deciding the fate of Christians, rather than the Emperor. It soon became a theme of Christian propaganda that it was only under 'bad Emperors' like Nero and Domitian that Christians were persecuted, while under 'good Emperors' they were protected; but this is quite false, and in any event the Emperor would rarely be involved.

Nor is it correct in any sense to say, as so many have done, that the Christians were persecuted 'because they refused to worship the Emperor'. The Imperial Cult plays only a very minor role in the persecutions. Much more often the cult act prescribed is sacrificing to the gods (sometimes specifically *for* the Emperor); and when the act does directly concern the Emperor it is more likely than not to be an oath by his Genius, which a steadfast Christian would refuse to swear, although it did not actually involve an attribution of deity to the Emperor.

Another misconception about the persecutions which is sometimes encountered is that the Christian churches were attacked as illegal associations (*collegia illicita*). But the attacks were not against the organized Christian bodies: it was individual Christians who were prosecuted, and there is no actual record that legal action was ever taken against them *as* members of *collegia illicita*, although it is probably true that it could have been.

Certificates and compromise

For nearly a century and a half after Pliny's day the situation of the Christians remained substantially as it was left by him and Trajan. A new phase opened in AD 250 (a time of political chaos and barbarian invasion), with the first of the three general persecutions,
that of the Emperor Decius – which, incidentally, was preceded by p 335 (
a violent anti-Christian riot at Alexandria, the last major spontaneous popular outbreak against Christianity of which we have knowledge anywhere, apart perhaps from riots in a few individual cities where there was a particularly enthusiastic cult of a local deity, such as Marnas at Gaza. The edict of Decius simply ordered everyone in the Empire to sacrifice to the gods by a particular day, and to obtain a certificate that he had done so. (The sands of Egypt
have preserved to this day more than forty of these certificates.) p 341
In so far as it was actively enforced (as to some extent in some areas (24)
it evidently was), it would represent an abandonment of Trajan's principle, *conquirendi non sunt*, for Christians would be forced to expose themselves by their refusal to sacrifice; but except in this one respect there was no abandonment of the traditional policy. In the past, subject to the discretion of the magistrate concerned, any Christian who was prosecuted was liable to the death penalty unless he sacrificed. The only difference now (of course it was an important one) was that all Christians, in theory, were to be put to the test. The government, it must be emphasized, was interested in only one thing: procuring a single act of outward conformity. It made no attempt (as Diocletian and to a lesser extent Valerian did later) to suppress the practice of the Christian religion. The motive of the Decian persecution has been admirably expressed by the late Norman Baynes: 'Roman greatness had ever been dependent on the favour of the divine powers – on the maintenance of the *pax deorum*. Now that the Empire was threatened with unexampled perils, how could success be more surely guaranteed than by a massive demonstration of an Empire's loyalty?'

The persecution did not last long: the force of it was soon spent, and all danger was removed by the death of Decius on the Danube frontier in the late summer of AD 251. Our detailed evidence is virtually confined to Africa and Alexandria, although we have scattered bits of reliable information and a quantity of less trustworthy material for other areas, including Italy and Spain. A considerable number of Christian Confessors must have been imprisoned, and many of them tortured (as Origen was, for example),

The epitaph of Pope Pontian, who died a martyr's death in 235 in the mines of Sardinia, was discovered along with those of other martyred popes in the papal burial vault. The letters MR for 'martyr' were added at the end of the century. (3)

but protracted imprisonment – a rare thing in the ancient world –
f 4 seems to have been more common than outright execution. Fabian,
P 343 Babylas and Alexander, the bishops of Rome, Antioch and
(32) Jerusalem, suffered for their faith, Fabian being executed and Babylas and Alexander dying in prison; but apparently not one of the scores of bishops of Africa perished. In Spain (where two bishops apostatized), Gaul and some other provinces there is no reliable evidence of martyrdoms at all, although of course this does not necessarily mean that there were none. In the great city of Alexandria, where there must by now have been thousands of Christians, a letter of Dionysius the bishop records exactly nineteen martyrs most of them evidently very humble folk. Not more than half a dozen names are known from Rome, and not all of them are well attested. For over a year no successor was appointed to Fabian, the martyred bishop. This has been quoted as proof of the severity of the persecution at Rome, but it was more probably due to the temporary collapse of the Roman church, in which we know there were many apostates. The election of Fabian's successor produced a violent schism in the church of Rome, led by Novatian, whose sect survived until the 7th century AD; and a minor schism, led by Novatus and Felicissimus, also occurred in the African church: here there was evidently a large number of apostates, for the language used by Cyprian their bishop shows that as soon as the edict of Decius was published, very many Christians rushed forward and sacrificed openly in order to clear themselves of all suspicion.

In default of evidence about the number of martyrs and the proportion of apostates, there has been a tendency to resort to 'must-have-been's'. The edict of Decius ordered everyone to sacrifice, and the penalty for disobedience was – or could be – death. Those who are eager to strengthen the credit of the Christian Church have naturally assumed that there 'must have been' a whole host of martyrs, while those who have contrary inclinations have pointed to the remarkable absence of good evidence for more than a handful of martyrdoms and have insisted that the great majority of Christians 'must have been' apostates. There is no reason to

Pope Fabian ruled the Roman church from 236 to 250, when he fell in the Decian persecution. His epitaph reads: 'Phabianos epi(skopos) m(arty)r' Fabian, bishop and martyr. The letters MR were again added at the end of the century. (4)

adopt either of these extreme views. An examination of the detailed and clear evidence afforded by the letters of Cyprian and his disciplinary treatise, *On the Lapsed*, enables us to draw two important conclusions about the course of the persecution.

The first, which applies to the whole Empire, is that Christians must not be thought of as divided into apostates and martyrs, or even apostates and confessors: in between the two extremes there was a substantial third group referred to many times by Cyprian as the *stantes* or *consistentes*, who were not arrested or called upon to make any public confession of their faith but had at least run the risk of punishment by failing to sacrifice by the appointed day, and might charitably be assumed (as Cyprian maintains) to be ready to confess their faith should they be apprehended. Cyprian would have these people treated as potential confessors: he very reasonably says that the confessors proper had made a public and they a private confession. We have no information as to what steps were taken to discover those who had no certificates, and it seems unlikely that any systematic procedure was adopted. (We know from a letter of Dionysius of Alexandria that in that city – and therefore, presumably, in at least some if not all other provincial capitals and perhaps a good many other towns – there was some kind of public roll-call; but this formed part of the procedure for organizing the sacrifices and was not a subsequent check.) Cyprian himself and many of his clergy were in this category: they took to flight and hid themselves until the persecution was over – a course of conduct which did not pass without censure.

The second conclusion will necessitate our drawing a distinction between the western and eastern parts of the Empire – the Latin-speaking and Greek-speaking churches. It is that very large numbers of Christians who did not in fact sacrifice managed by bribing officials to secure certificates (*libelli*) stating falsely that they had done so. In the West these people – *libellatici* as they were called – were deemed to have apostatized, but their offence was treated as a much more venial one than sacrificing itself: Cyprian insists that it is a less grave sin than, for instance, adultery. These *libellatici* were accepted back into the Church on very easy terms; the *sacrificati* and *turificati*, who had actually sacrificed or offered incense, were only readmitted on proof of penitence and after a long period of probation. (Until now it had apparently been usual to exclude apostates irrevocably. The new procedure shocked the diehards, and the Novatian schism and some of the difficulties Cyprian experienced were due to their intransigent refusal to readmit the *lapsi* and let bygones be bygones.)

In the East, however, we never hear a word about *libellatici* or about the purchase of exemption from the obligation to sacrifice – a fact which too many historians have ignored. It is true that we have very little evidence about the course of the Decian persecution in the East, apart from the information given to us by some letters of Dionysius of Alexandria (reproduced in Eusebius' *Ecclesiastical History*), hardly extending beyond that city. There is, however, very good reason to suppose that the absence of any concern about *libellatici* in the East is not due merely to the nature of our sources, but is a real fact. The explanation must be that in the East the purchase of exemptions did take place, but was not regarded as sinful, so that those who had obtained false certificates by bribery or otherwise were not regarded as apostates in any sense. There are two pieces of evidence for this conclusion, one negative and one positive. First, there is the complete absence from the eastern part of the Empire of all those complaints about the purchase of certificates which figure so prominently in the West during the next few years. And, secondly, there is an explicit piece of evidence in the *Canonical Letter* written at Easter AD 306 by Peter, bishop of Alexandria during the earlier part of the Great Persecution. The famous Fourth Edict of the Great Persecution, issued in AD 304, was a general order to sacrifice, in terms very similar to those of the edict of Decius. And Peter's Twelfth Canon specifically declares that those who purchased immunity from this decree are not to be blamed, for they sustained a loss of money in order to save their souls. Canon 13 similarly exculpates those who left everything and fled. If that was the attitude in the East during the Great Persecution, we can safely assume that the situation was the same in the persecution of Decius, and that eastern *libellatici* were not considered to have lapsed in any sense.

Divine judgement

In the half-century after the death of Decius in AD 251 there was one brief and limited 'general persecution': that of the unfortunate Emperor Valerian in AD 257–9. This was different in character from its predecessor: it represents a stage intermediate between the Decian and the Great Persecution. In AD 257 the government attempted for the first time to interfere directly with the collective practice of Christian worship. Christians could still worship their own God as much as they wanted to in private (note the remark of the deputy prefect of Egypt to Dionysius, quoted above), but
p 337 they were forbidden to assemble together for common worship
(14) and might not enter their cemeteries, where religious services were frequently conducted. Furthermore, all bishops, priests and perhaps deacons (but not the minor clergy and laity) were ordered to sacrifice to the gods, on pain of exile. A year later, in AD 258, a more severe edict was issued: the higher clergy who had not sacrificed were to be executed; laymen belonging to the senatorial or equestrian orders who persisted in the profession of Christianity were to be deprived of their dignities and their property, and if they still refused to recant they too were to be put to death; and Christian *Caesariani* (the non-military members of the Imperial civil service, mainly Imperial freedmen) were to be sent in chains to work on the
p 342–3 Emperor's estates. Under the second edict there must have been
(31) numerous executions, among the martyrs being Cyprian of Carthage; but it is quite impossible to give any estimate of the total number who perished.

The persecution died down in AD 259, and in 260 Valerian received what the Christians interpreted as a divine judgment: he
p 336 was defeated and captured by the Persians, who kept him a prisoner
(11) until he died. Valerian's son and successor, Gallienus, immediately issued edicts and rescripts granting toleration to the Christians. What the legal position of Christianity was from now until the beginning of the Great Persecution in AD 303 is still a matter of dispute; but it seems probable that if an accuser was forthcoming and the magistrate who tried the case was willing to receive the accusation, a Christian who refused to sacrifice might still be punished with death, although in practice this rarely happened, because it was known that most of the Emperors were not in favour of it, and after the middle of the 3rd century AD, as the Christians became more numerous and less exclusive and secretive, far less impulse towards persecution came from below, from the ordinary inhabitants of the Empire.

The Great Persecution

p 336 The Great Persecution which opened early in AD 303 was the most
(12) severe test with which the Christian churches had been faced, at
f 5 any rate in the eastern part of the Empire, where it went on for some ten years. In the West the persecution was very much milder, for there it lasted only about two years and the only edict which was promulgated (or at any rate actively enforced) was the first,
p 338–9 the main points of which were the destruction of churches and
(15–21) prohibition of services and an order to hand over all sacred books and church property. The less rigorous eastern churches seem not to have regarded the handing over (*traditio*) of even the Scriptures as a religious offence, but in the West it was treated as a major sin, and the *traditores* were considered to be apostates. There were martyrdoms, especially in Africa, of those who refused to commit *traditio* or who continued to hold services; but there cannot have been very many of these. The number of martyrs in the East may have been large, but our only complete figures are those given by Eusebius for Palestine, where there were rather less than a hundred. In many of these cases we are given particulars of arrest and trial; and here an interesting feature emerges which we very often encounter in the history of the persecutions from the mid-2nd century AD onwards: the willingness and indeed the active desire of many ardent Christians to expose themselves unnecessarily to martyrdom. Some of these are 'voluntary martyrs' in the full sense, bringing death upon themselves by deliberate acts, sometimes of a provocative nature (tearing down persecuting edicts, smashing images, interrupting a provincial governor while sacrificing, and even assaulting him), while others at least go out of their way to draw attention to themselves, if only by ministering openly to

Diocletian persecuted the Christians until he retired in 305 to his vast palace at Split. (5)

arrested confessors. Of the fourteen Palestinian martyrs whom Eusebius records as suffering before the abdication of Diocletian in May AD 305, no less than eight were volunteers and two drew attention to themselves, leaving only four at the most whose arrest was not due to their own deliberate act – four in over two years, in a province in which Christians seem to have been quite numerous. It is often said that voluntary martyrdom was confined mainly to heretical sects like the Montanists; but the detailed evidence does not support this assertion. The ecclesiastical authorities, in their wisdom, did all they could to discourage these rash acts, for two good reasons: volunteers might be betrayed by their own unsuspected weakness, and, even worse, they might bring down added pagan animosity upon their own communities. But voluntary martyrdom remained much more prevalent even among the orthodox than has been generally realized. In fact
Christianity was above all *a religion of martyrdom*. The martyrs were p 341
the Christian heroes, and the 'baptism of blood' was regarded as a (27)
direct passport to Paradise. We do not know how and when voluntary martyrdom began; but there were Jewish precedents for it, and its incidence seems to have increased rather than diminished as time went on, with a climax during the Great Persecution.

The failure of persecution had become evident even before the
victory of Constantine and Licinius; and Galerius and Maximinus, p 342–3
the two Emperors who were most active in the Great Persecution, (28)
both abandoned it just before they died, in AD 311 and 313 respectively.

Doubtless Professor Vogt is right in saying that 'the martyrdoms of the Roman persecutions belong to the history of freedom'. There are some splendid pleas for complete freedom and toleration in religious matters made by Christians, especially Tertullian and Lactantius, during the period of persecution; and the document which more than any other signalizes the abandonment of persecution, the so-called 'Edict of Milan' (issued by the Emperors Constantine and Licinius in AD 313), repeatedly affirms in the most emphatic terms that liberty of religion ought to be complete and unrestricted. 'It is a human right,' said Tertullian, early in the 3rd century AD, 'a privilege of nature, that everyone should worship as he pleases.' Lactantius, nearly a hundred years later, is even more eloquent:

> Religion should be defended not by killing but by dying. . . . For nothing is so much a matter of freewill as religion. . . . The right principle is to defend religion by patience or by death. . . . Sacrificing to the gods, when it is done against a man's will, is a curse. . . . We, on the contrary, although our God is the God of all men, whether they like it or not, do not require that anyone should be compelled to worship him, nor are we angry if a man does not do so. . . . We leave vengeance to God.

And, in his Epitome of the work known as the *Divinae Institutiones* from which the statements just quoted have been drawn, Lactantius says, 'It is religion alone in which freedom has planted her dwelling. For beyond everything else it is a question of freewill.'

The first inquisitors?

Matters were rather different, however, once the Christians had p 343
finally turned the tables on their enemies. Pleas for toleration now (30)
come almost exclusively from pagans, from heretics (or schisma-

tics, like the Donatists) who are being persecuted by the Catholics, or from the Catholics when they are being persecuted by heretics or schismatics. The surviving writer who has the most unblemished record in this respect is the great pagan historian, Ammianus Marcellinus. In one fierce sentence Ammianus has concentrated the resentment he felt against the Christians for the implacable way in which they persecuted each other – Catholics, heretics and schismatics, Athanasians, Arians and Donatists: there was little to choose between them in this respect. Ammianus has just described how the pagan Emperor Julian used to summon the bishops of the rival sects to the palace, and politely exhort them to lay aside their discords and each to pursue his own religion without concern. 'Listen to me,' the Emperor would thunder at them, reminding them that he had obliged even the barbarous Alamanni and Franks to do that. But they paid no regard. Julian knew they would not, of course, and Ammianus evidently thought he was acting deliberately, so that the freedom given to all the sects might increase their internal divisions and prevent them from acting as one against him. And then in ten blistering words Ammianus frames his indictment of the Christians for persecuting each other with such animosity: Julian knew from experience, he says, 'that wild beasts are not such enemies to mankind as are most Christians in their deadly hatred of one another'. Elsewhere Ammianus gives a good idea of the sort of thing he had in mind: in a single day in AD 366, during the faction fights between the supporters of the
f 1 rival popes Damasus and Ursinus, no less than 137 corpses were left on the floor of a Christian basilica in Rome.

Other pagans spoke eloquently in favour of toleration, now that the most they could hope for was to be among its beneficiaries. The most justly famous of all these pleas for toleration, emanating from paganism in its twilight period, is the *Third Relatio* of Symmachus, which has already been quoted above. Champion of the old religion as he was, Symmachus knew he could not afford to overplay his hand, and he pleads only for tolerance:

> Everything is full of God. We all look up to the same stars; the same heaven is above us all; the same universe surrounds every one of us. What does it matter by what system of knowledge each of us seeks the truth? It is not by one single path that we arrive at so great a secret.

The plea was vain, and within a few years paganism, which had already been attacked at many points, was being persecuted officially and actively. The decrees of the Emperors were supplemented by spontaneous action by Christian enthusiasts. There were attacks on temples and statues by Christian fanatics, especially monks, and in AD 415 the pagan philosopher Hypatia, friend and teacher of the distinguished Christian bishop Synesius of Cyrene, was literally torn to pieces at Alexandria by a frenzied Christian mob. A series of laws in the 5th and 6th centuries attacked pagans personally, debarring them from various forms of public employment and so forth, rendering them incapable of making wills or receiving inheritances or giving evidence in court; and Justinian finally ordered all pagans to be baptized on pain of exile and confiscation of property. It is often said that Imperial laws such as this were probably not enforced in practice, but this ignores evidence such as the 6th-century inscription from Sardis which shows a number of pagans being punished as such, one at least with ten years' enforced service in a hospital.

The persecution of heretics and schismatics was a good deal more relentless than that of pagans. The title in the *Theodosian Code* which deals with heretics (16, 5) contains no less than sixty-six laws issued between 326 and 435, and we can add many more of the 5th and 6th centuries. This policy met with almost universal approval, and protests against Imperial severity were rare. Christians of all kinds, orthodox as well as heretics, were quick to denounce persecution only when they themselves were at the receiving end. As Professor A. H. M. Jones has said:

> The Donatists originally appealed to Constantine to settle their quarrel with the Catholics: it was only when the verdict went finally against them that they evolved the doctrine that the Church ought to be independent of the state. . . . Athanasius, Hilary and the homoousian party in the West enunciated a similar doctrine and put forward pleas for religious liberty when Constantius II was lending his support to their adversaries. They had raised no protest when Constantine had ejected their rivals, and they said nothing about religious freedom when Gratian and Theodosius I banned all beliefs but their own.

It was Augustine who, in the words of his latest biographer, Mr Peter Brown, 'wrote the only full justification, in the history of the Early Church, of the right of the state to suppress non-Catholics'; and for this reason Augustine has been described by one of his greatest admirers, Dr van der Meer, as 'the true father of the Inquisition'. Although he was at first opposed to the legal coercion of his Donatist opponents and never actually countenanced the use of the death penalty for heresy alone, he finally discovered that, where persuasion failed, persecution could be very effective; and he set himself to justify it, in his characteristic way, by supplying scriptural precedents from the Old Testament and even in the end appealing to the parable of the Great Supper in St Luke's Gospel, with perverse ingenuity interpreting the order to the servant to 'go out into the highways and hedges and compel them to come in' as a justification of the forcible suppression of heresy and schism. In a famous sermon delivered at Caesarea in Mauretania, in which he declared that there was no salvation to be had outside the Catholic Church, Augustine explicitly said, 'I persecute openly because I am a son of the Church.' It was his membership of the Church which fortified Augustine in his determination to resort to persecution when persuasion failed. Indeed, should not the persecution of heresy be considered a duty? – since successful coercion could save the heretic from eternal damnation and was therefore (as we might say) in his own best interests. To execute the heretic, however, was to send him straight to perdition. The death penalty, therefore, which lay judges often did not scruple to inflict, ought not to be used. At least the argument was logical.

This 2nd-century aedicula found under St Peter's in excavations during and after the Second World War is almost certainly the traditional shrine of St Peter. Whether it marks the actual burial place is more conjectural. (6)

NOTES TO THE TEXT

I
The Mediterranean world's age of agony

1. 'Syria' is a convenient label for the section of the 'Fertile Crescent' between Egypt and Babylonia. It is used here in this neutral geographical sense, without any cultural or political implications. The Greeks called this region 'Syria' because it had been incorporated politically in the Assyrian Empire's Neobabylonian successor-state, and the whole former domain of the Neobabylonian Empire was officially styled 'Ashuria' by the Persian Imperial government, after the Neobabylonian Empire had been conquered and annexed by it. The Greeks called Southern Syria 'Palestine' after the Philistines who settled on the Gaza Strip in the 13th- and 12th-century BC *Völkerwanderung*.

II
A clash of ideologies

1. Daniel xi 14.
2. *Commentarium in Danielem* 9, 13–14 (Migne *Patrologia Latina* XXV 562).
3. Josephus *Antiquitates Judaicae* ed. B. Niese, Berlin 1892 XII 219–36; 239ff.
4. *Ibid.* XII 138–44.
5. *Ibid.* XII 145–6.
6. E. Bikerman *Revue des études Juives* vol. 100 Paris 1935 p. 4ff.
7. Josephus *AJ* XII 160ff.
8. Joseph the tax-farmer and, even more, his son Hyrcanus were eminent representatives of the type of the Hellenized Jew in the Judaea of the 3rd century BC. *Cf.* Josephus *AJ* XII 186ff.; 230ff.
9. See A. Schalit *Annual of the Swedish Theological Institute (ASTI)* vol. I Leiden 1962 p. 123ff.; and the forthcoming book *König Herodes* Berlin 1969 p. 519ff.
10. J. Ma'aser Sheni ('Second Tithe') 5, 9. It is significant that the Jerusalem Talmud mentions 'colleagues' (Haberim), *i.e.* people organized in 'associations', in conjunction with the poor of Jerusalem. Although it is true that the passage is late, there is no doubt that the information conveyed in it is much earlier, *i.e.* at least of an early Maccabaean date, so that the actual situation in Judaea at that time is well reflected in it.
11. II Macc. iii 11.
12. *Ibid.* iii 4ff.; iv 1ff.
13. Josephus *AJ* XII 236.
14. For a discussion of Antiochus' Hellenizing tendencies, see V. Tchericover *Hellenistic Civilization and the Jews* Philadelphia and Jerusalem 1959 p. 178f.; p. 471 note 4.
15. I Macc. i 10ff.; II Macc. iv 9; Josephus *AJ* XII 239–41.
16. I Macc. i 15; Josephus *AJ* XII 241.
17. II Macc. iv 34–5.
18. *Ibid.* iv 39–42.
19. B. Niese *Geschichte der griechischen und makedonischen Staaten* Gotha 1893; reprint Darmstadt 1963 vol. 3 p. 175f.
20. For the various theories of the causes of Antiochus' persecution of the Jewish religion, see Tchericover *op. cit.* p. 175ff. The most famous and most controversial theory is that propounded by E. Bickermann in his book *Der Gott der Makkabäer* Berlin 1937.
21. I Macc. i 54, 59; II Macc. vi 1–9; Josephus *AJ* XII 253.
22. I Macc. ii 41.
23. *Ibid.* iv 36–59; Josephus *AJ* XII 316–25. See also F.-M. Abel *Histoire de la Palestine depuis la conquête d'Alexandre jusqu'à l'invasion arabe* Paris 1952 vol. I p. 134ff.
24. A most interesting case of such a clash between a group of returning exiled Jews who tried to settle in the region of Samaria and were driven away by hostile local inhabitants, in all probability Samaritans who may themselves have been of Ephraimitic stock, has been preserved in the (albeit late) scholion to the Fastscroll (Megillath Tha'anith' of Marcheshwan 25. Although the scholion is of a much later date than the Fastscroll, it contains some valuable information which also holds good for the above case. See Hans Lichtenstein 'Die Fastenrolle' in *Hebrew Union College Annual* vol. 8–9 Cincinnati 1931–2 p. 289f.; *cf.* also A. Schalit in the forthcoming *Concordance to Josephus* Leiden 1968 supplement I p. 130ff.
25. Josephus *AJ* XIII 255–6; *De Bello Judaico* I 63.
26. Josephus *AJ* XIII 275–81; *BJ* I 64–5.
27. Josephus *AJ* XIII 314–18. Josephus is the only source in which Aristobulus' kingship is mentioned. But it can be proved even from Josephus himself that his information is devoid of all historical value. On this problem, see my forthcoming book *König Herodes* p. 743f.
28. The problem has been discussed in many articles, especially by Samuel Klein. See also the valuable suggestions made by Y. M. Grintz in his excellent work on the Book of Judith (Hebrew) Jerusalem 1957.
29. Josephus *AJ* XII 257–8; *BJ* I 63.
30. A. H. M. Jones *The Cities of the Eastern Roman Provinces* Oxford 1937 p. 256–7. Jones' remark on Gerasa (p. 454 note 39) is in my opinion unfounded. Εσσα in *AJ* XIII 393 for Γερασα in *BJ* I 104 is nothing but a mutilated Γερε(α)σα ([ΓΕΡ]ΕΣΣΑ=ΓΕΡΑΣΑ).
31. Jones *op. cit.* p. 252.
32. Jones *op. cit.* p. 242.
33. Jones *op. cit.* p. 257. A general survey of the conquests made by the Hasmonaeans is given by Josephus *AJ* XIII 395–7. Compare also the parallel list in *AJ* XIV 18. For a detailed study on these two mutilated lists, see Schalit *Eretz Israel* (Hebrew) Jerusalem 1951 vol. I p. 104ff.
34. Jones *op. cit.* p. 257.
35. For the whole problem, compare Hans Lewy 'Ein Rechtsstreit um den Boden Palästinas im Altertum' in *Monatsschrift für Geschichte und*

Wissenschaft des Judentums vol. 77 Breslau 1933 p. 84–99; 172–80.
36. For a detailed discussion see Schalit *König Herodes* p. 524ff.
37. Josephus *BJ* I 67; see also *AJ* XIII 296.
38. Josephus *BJ* I 88–98; *AJ* XIII 372–83.
39. Josephus *AJ* XIV 75–6; *BJ* I 155–7 gives a list (perhaps not complete) of cities liberated by Pompey. In *AJ* XIV 88 and *BJ* I 166 he gives a list of cities rebuilt by Gabinius.
40. *Cf.* Schalit *König Herodes* p. 14.
41. Josephus *AJ* XIV 91; *BJ* I 170.
42. *Cf.* Schalit *Roman Administration in Palestine* (Hebrew) Jerusalem 1937 p. 32ff.
43. Josephus *AJ* XIV 137; 143–4. For the territorial innovations and taxes in Judaea ordered by Caesar in 47 BC, see especially *AJ* XIV 202–10. For all problems connected with the orders given by Caesar in Judaea, see Schalit *König Herodes* p. 753ff.; 777ff.
44. Josephus *AJ* XIV 489–90; XV 8–10.
45. See Schalit *König Herodes* p. 97; 691f.
46. Josephus *AJ* XV 366.
47. Josephus *AJ* XVI 38–40. Herod's views on Roman rule are reflected in the speech delivered by Nicolaus of Damascus in Ephesus (14 BC) before M. Vipsanius Agrippa and Herod. *Cf.* Josephus *AJ* XVI 31–57. For a full discussion see Schalit *op. cit.* p. 426ff.
48. E. Schürer *Geschichte des jüdischen Volkes im Zeitalter Jesu Christi* 4th ed. Leipzig 1907 vol. 2 p. 43 and note 69; D. Sourdel *Les Cultes du Hauran à l'époque romaine* Paris 1952 p. 21; *cf.* W. Dittenberger *Orientis Graeci inscriptiones selectae* supplement to *Sylloge Inscriptionum Graecarum* 2nd ed. Leipzig 1903 no. 415.
49. Compare Schalit *op. cit.* p. 450ff. Compare also the same author's forthcoming article in *ASTI* vol. 6 Leiden 1968.
50. On the other hand it is possible that Claudius' decision regarding the young Agrippa may have been influenced by persons like Marsus, the governor of Syria, in the Emperor's inner circle. For the tenseness of the relations between Agrippa I and Marsus, see Josephus *AJ* XIX 326; 340–2; 363.
51. Tacitus *Histories* V 10: *augebat iras quod soli Iudaei non cessissent.*
52. Josephus *BJ* VI 329.
53. Sulpicius Severus *Chronica* II 30.
54. Were Jesus of Nazareth's activities part of this movement? Such an opinion was expressed over thirty years ago by R. Eisler in his exciting book on the Messianic movement in Judaea entitled *Jesous Basileus ou Basileusas* Heidelberg 1929–30, 2 vols. Eisler's daring thesis has, however, been rejected by scholars. It is indeed very difficult to accept such a solution of the problem. The personality of the historical Jesus is covered with so many layers of various traditions and tendencies (*cf.* for example P. Winter *On the Trial of Jesus* Berlin 1961) that it is a formidable undertaking, in our present state of knowledge, to try to penetrate to the historical kernel of the problem. What appears beyond all doubt is the Messianic claim attached to Jesus' personality by his followers, but not necessarily by himself. The nature of this 'Messianism' is indeed an open question. As for the Qumran sect and its connections with the Sicarian movement, the whole discussion lacks firm ground.
55. For the history of the Bar Kokhba war, see the detailed account by S. Yeivin *The Bar Kokhba War* (Hebrew) 2nd ed. Jerusalem 1952.
56. Jones *op. cit.* p. 363; Sir George Hill *A History of Cyprus* vol. I Cambridge 1949 p. 241–3, citing a fragment of Appian in *Fragmenta Historicorum Graecorum* VI p. 65; Dio Cassius LXVIII 32 with the corresponding passage of Xiphilinus; Eusebius *Ecclesiastical History* IV 2; Eusebius *Chronicle* (Armenian) ed. A. Schoene, Berlin 1875 vol. 2 p. 164; Jerome *ibid.* p. 165; Orosius VII 12, 6–8. See also H. I. Bell 'Anti-Semitism in Alexandria' in *Journal of Roman Studies* vol. 31 London 1941 p. 15–16; A. Fuks 'Aspects of the Jewish Revolt in AD 115–7' in *J.R.S.* vol. 51, 1961 p. 98–104.
57. Jones *op. cit.* p. 363.
58. Hill *loc. cit.*
59. See note 55.

VI
'The world's great age'

1. Thus the usual terminology; but this is at present under discussion. According to the recent study by C. Saumagne 'Le droit latin et les cités romaines sous l'Empire' in *Publications de l'Institut de Droit romaine* vol. 22 Paris 1965, the word *municipium* refers most appropriately to that type of community in the province which had the 'Latin Right', and where full Roman citizenship was obtained by undertaking local *honores* or filling the office of decurion.
2. On this, see especially Sir Ronald Syme *Colonial Élites, Rome, Spain and the Americas* London 1958, and the recent study by Barbara Levick *Roman Colonization in Southern Asia Minor* Oxford 1967.
3. There has been a lively debate about the meaning of the Greek word *sōma* ('body'). See F. de Visscher *Les Édits d'Auguste decouverts à Cyrène* Louvain 1940, and *Nouvelles Études de Droit* Milan 1949. In the opinion of the writer too much doubt has been thrown on the meaning of *sōma* as 'community'.
4. See L. Robert on the inscriptions of Aphrodisias in *L'Antiquité Classique* vol. 35 Paris 1966.
5. The allusion in Josephus *Antiquitates Judaicae* XIX is confirmed by Suetonius *Caligula* 58: *pueri nobiles ex Asia.*
6. See his *Carrières procuratoriennes* Paris 1960.

VII
Away from sheer beauty

1. D. M. Robinson and Hoyningen-Huene *Baalbek/Palmyra* New York 1946 plates on p. 50, 51.
2. For a very detailed and stimulating study of concrete architecture in general under the early Empire, see W. L. MacDonald *The Architecture of the Roman Empire i: an Introductory Study* New Haven and London 1965.
3. The large apsidal room in Hadrian's villa near Tivoli, adjacent to the round 'teatro marittimo' and often called the 'Sala dei Filosofi' or 'Library' may have been a throne-room. See S. Aurigemma *La Villa Adriana* Tivoli 1953 p. 16 fig. 3.
4. D. S. Robertson *A Handbook of Greek and Roman Architecture* 2nd ed. Cambridge 1943 p. 317 fig. 135, p. 319.
5. *Trierer Zeitschrift* vol. 18 Trier 1949 p. 170–93: see especially fig. 11 on p. 190.
6. *Germania* vol. 34 Leipzig 1955 p. 200–210.
7. *Papers of the British School at Rome* vol. 22 London 1954 p. 73 fig. 2.
8. *Ibid.* p. 72 fig. 1.
9. VI 5, 2.
10. *Antiquaries Journal* vol. 44 London 1964 p. 5 pl. 8b; vol. 45, 1965 p. 7 fig. 1 and pl. 2; vol. 46, 1966 p. 33–4 fig. 4; vol. 47, 1967 p. 55–8 fig. 2 and pl. 7.
11. *Corpus Inscriptionum Latinarum* Berlin 1863 vol. 6 no. 306973; E. Nash *Pictorial Dictionary of Ancient Rome* London 1968 p. 183–5.
12. *Festschrift E. von Mercklin* Waldsassen 1964 p. 90–105.
13. *Journal of the British Archaeological Association* series 3 vol. 16 London 1953 p. 8 fig. 4.
14. *Académie des Inscriptions et Belles-Lettres: Comptes Rendus* Paris 1954 p. 269–78 fig. 1.
15. *Recent Archaeological Excavations in Britain* ed. R. L. S. Bruce-Mitford, London 1956 p. 139–42 pls. 16, 17 (conjectural restorations); W. F. Grimes *The Excavations of Roman and Mediaeval London* London 1968 figs. 24, 25 (ground plans).
16. G. Calza *La necropoli del Porto di Roma nell'Isola Sacra* Rome 1940.
17. J. G. Davies *The Origin and Development of Early Christian Church Architecture* London 1952 pl. 9 (exterior).
18. F. W. Volbach *Early Christian Art* London 1961 pl. 28 (exterior).
19. J. B. Ward Perkins *The Italian Element in Late Roman and Early Mediaeval Architecture* London 1947 p. 7.
20. Pseudo-Clement *Recognitions* X 71.
21. E. Dyggve *History of Salonitan Christianity* Oslo 1951 fig. 4, 13–15.
22. *Journal of the British Archaeological Association* series 3 vol. 16 1953 pl. 1 fig. 2a.
23. *Ur-Schweiz* vol. 19 Basle 1955 p. 65–96.
24. *Papers of the British School at Rome* vol. 22, 1954 p. 86 fig. 4. For the *Basilica Apostolorum*, see F. Tolotti *Memoria degli Apostoli in Catacumbas* Rome 1953.
25. Davies *op. cit.* p. 56–73.
26. A Maiuri *Roman Painting* Geneva 1953 colour plate on p. 75.
27. E. Strong *La scultura romana* Florence 1923 vol. 1 figs. 91, 94.
28. G. Matthiae *Le chiese di Roma del iv al x secolo* Bologna 1962 fig. 175.
29. J. Wilpert *Die Malereien der Katakomben Roms* Freiburg-im-Breisgau 1903.
30. *E.g.* grave-monuments at Celeia, Yugoslavia: J. Klemenc *Rimske Izkopanine v Sempetru* Ljubljana 1961 pls. 34, 35.
31. *E.g.* sarcophagi: J. M. C. Toynbee *The Hadrianic School* Cambridge 1934 pl. 40 figs. 3, 4; K. Lehmann-Hartleben and E. C. Olsen *Dionysiac Sarcophagi in Baltimore* New York 1942 fig. 11; stucco relief; *Monumenti Antichi dei Lincei* vol. 31 Rome 1926 pl. 21 fig. 1 (underground basilica near the Porta Maggiore, Rome).
32. *E.g.* stucco relief: *ibid.* pl. 21 fig. 2; floor mosaic: S. Lysons *Reliquiae Romano-Britannicae* London 1817 vol. 3 pls. 5, 7–9 (Roman villa at Bignor, Sussex).
33. *E.g.* sarcophagi: C. Robert *Die antiken Sarkophagreliefs* Berlin 1919 vol. 3, 3 pls. 119–31; floor mosaics: *American Journal of Archaeology* vol. 51 Boston, Mass. 1947 pl. 70 (Tomb I in St Peter's necropolis, Rome); wall painting: S. Reinach *Répertoire de peintures grecques et romaines* Paris 1922 p. 18 no. 6 (Tomb of Vibia on the Via Appia near Rome with inscription *abreptio Vibies et descensio*).
34. A. Rumpf *Die Meerwesen auf den antiken Sarkophagreliefs* Berlin 1939; J. M. C. Toynbee and J. B. Ward Perkins *The Shrine of St Peter and the Vatican Excavations* London 1956 pl. 28.
35. *E.g.* sarcophagi: Lehmann-Hartleben and Olsen *op. cit.* fig. 27.
36. *E.g.* sarcophagi: P. G. Hamberg *Studies in Roman Imperial Art* Uppsala 1945 pls. 42, 43.
37. *E.g.* sarcophagi: Strong *op. cit.* vol. 2 (1926) p. 58; M. Guarducci *Cristo e San Pietro: un documento precostantiniano della necropoli vaticana* Rome 1953 fig. 9.
38. IV 11.
39. Toynbee and Ward Perkins *op. cit.* pl. 16.
40. M. Wegner *Die Musensarkophage* Berlin 1966. For culture and intellectual life in general as passports to immortality, see F. Cumont *Recherches sur le symbolisme funéraire des Romains* Paris 1942 chapter 4.
41. *E.g.* Lehmann-Hartleben and Olsen *op. cit.* figs. 7, 8, 39.
42. *E.g. ibid.* fig. 42; Toynbee and Ward Perkins *op. cit.* pls. 26–8.
43. *E.g.* Lehmann-Hartleben and Olsen *op. cit.* fig. 30.
44. *E.g. ibid.* figs. 9, 10, 42; Toynbee and Ward Perkins *op. cit.* pl. 22.
45. *E.g.* Strong *op. cit.* pl. 56.
46. *E.g.* Toynbee *op. cit.* pls. 51–4.
47. F. Gerke *Die christlichen Sarkophage der vorkonstantinischen Zeit* Berlin 1940 pl. 3 fig. 1; pl. 4 fig. 1.
48. Wilpert *op. cit.* pls. 8, 134a; G. B. de Rossi *Roma sotterranea* Rome 1867 vol. 2 pl. 18 fig. 1.
49. See note 37.
50. K. Lehmann-Hartleben *Die Trajanssäule* Berlin 1926; P. Romanelli *La colonna traiana* Rome 1942.
51. P. Romanelli *La colonna antonina* Rome 1942; G. Becatti *La colonna di Marco Aurelio* Milan 1957.
52. Hamberg *op. cit.* pls. 40, 41, 44.
53. B. M. Felletti-Maj *Iconografia romana imperiale da Severo Alessandro a M. Aurelio Carino 222–85 d.C.* Rome 1958 pl. 21 figs. 66–8.
54. Felletti-Maj *op. cit.* pl. 51 figs. 171–4; pl. 54 figs. 187–8; pl. 56 figs. 193–6.
55. See note 51.
56. R. Brilliant *The Arch of Septimus Severus in the Roman Forum* Rome 1967 pls. 67–8, 77, 87.
57. D. E. L. Haynes and P. E. D. Hirst *Porta Argentariorum* London 1939 pl. 6.
58. D. E. Strong *Roman Imperial Sculpture* London 1961 pl. 117.
59. *Ibid.* pl. 59.
60. A. Giuliano *Arco di Costantino* Milan 1955 figs. 34–5.
61. Volbach *op. cit.* pls. 54–5.
62. *Ibid.* pls. 176–7.
63. E. Kirschbaum *The Tombs of St. Peter and St. Paul* London 1959 pl. 32.
64. Volbach *op. cit.* pl. 158.

XI
'That the Scripture might be fulfilled'

1. *The Fall of Jerusalem and the Christian Church* London 1951; *Jesus and the Zealots* Manchester 1967.
2. *Diakonie, Festfreude und Zelos* Uppsala 1951.
3. *Qumran und das Neue Testament* Tübingen 1966. See also J. Daniélou *The Dead Sea Scrolls and Primitive Christianity* New York 1958; and *The Scrolls and the New Testament* ed. K. Stendahl, London 1958.
4. *Theologie und Geschichte des Judenchristentums* Tübingen 1949.
5. *Verus Israël* 2nd ed. Paris 1964.
6. J. Daniélou *The Theology of Jewish Christianity* London 1964.
7. See *Aspects du judéo-christianism* Paris 1965.
8. *Memory and Manuscript* Uppsala 1961 p. 171–81.
9. *Jesus and the Zealots* p. 309–10.
10. H. Braun *op. cit.* vol. 2 p. 85–9.
11. See Schlomo Pines *The Jewish Christians of the Early Centuries according to a New Source* Jerusalem 1966.
12. 'Zum Khalifat der Jacobus' in *Zeitschrift für Religions- und Geistes-*

geschichte vol. 4 Marburg 1952 p. 193–214.

13. See E. Testa *Il simbolismo degli Giudei-Cristiani* Jerusalem 1962; also B. Bagatti *L'Église de la circoncision* Jerusalem 1965.
14. *Saint Pierre* Paris 1952.
15. *Deus Christianorum. Recherches sur le vocabulaire doctrinal de Tertullien* Paris 1962 p. 12, 14.
16. *The Fall of Jerusalem and the Christian Church* p. 217–48.
17. *Studien zur Epistula Apostolorum* Berlin 1965 p. 99–116.
18. See G. Quispel *Makarius, das Thomas-evangelium und das Lied von der Perle* Leiden 1967.
19. See H. J. W. Drijvers *Bardaisan of Edessa* Assen 1966.
20. *Rechtgläubigkeit und Ketzerei im ältesten Christentum* 2nd ed. with an introduction by Georg Strecker, Tübingen 1964.
21. See R. M. Grant *Gnosticism and Early Christianity* New York 1939.
22. *Greek and Jew* London 1953.
23. See G. Strecker *Das Judenchristentum in den Pseudoklementinen* Berlin 1958.
24. *Op. cit.* p. 109–12.

XII
The Word goes forth

1. *Verus Israël* Paris 1948.
2. See J. Daniélou and H.-I. Marrou *Nouvelle histoire de l'Église* Paris 1963 p. 59–69.
3. See E. Langerbeck *Aufsätze der Gnosis* Göttingen 1967.
4. See S. G. F. Brandon *Jesus and the Zealots* Manchester 1967.
5. See J. Daniélou 'Judéo-christianisme et Gnose' in *Aspects du judéo-christianism* Paris 1965 p. 139–66.
6. See J. Daniélou *Message évangélique et culture hellénistique* Paris 1961 p. 13–16.
7. *Ibid.* p. 34–9.
8. See N. Hyldahl *Philosophie und Christentum. Eine Interpretation der Einleitung zum Dialog Justins* Copenhagen 1966 p. 227–53.
9. 'Logos Spermatikos, Christianity and Ancient Philosophy according to St Justin's Apologies' in *Studia Theologica* vol. 12 Lund 1958 p. 110–168.
10. *Op. cit.* p. 256–95.
11. See J. Daniélou *Message* p. 73–101.
12. See H. Rahner *Griechische Mythen in Christlicher Deutung* Zurich 1945 p. 365–84.
13. M. Simon *Hercule et le christianisme* Paris n.d. p. 75–125.
14. See J. Daniélou *Sacramentum futuri, Essai sur les origines de la typologie biblique* Paris 1950.
15. See J. Pépin *Mythe et Allégorie. Les origines grecques et les contestations judéo-chretiennes* Paris 1958.
16. See C. Andresen 'Justin und der Mittlere Platonismus' in *Zeitschrift für die neutestamentalische Wissenschaft* vol. 44 Berlin 1952 p. 157–93.
17. See H. Jonas *Gnosis und Spätantike Geist* Göttingen 1954 vol. 2.
18. See A. Méhat *Études sur les Stromates de Clément d'Alexandrie* Paris 1966.
19. See J. Daniélou *Origène* Paris 1950 p. 222–35; also F. H. Keller *Der ursprüngliche Sinn der Dogmatik des Origenes* Berlin 1966.
20. See J. Daniélou and H.-I. Marrou *op. cit.* p. 206–15.
21. See C. Mohrmann *Études sur le latin des chrétiens* Rome 1958 vol. I p. 52–4.
22. See R. Braun *Deus Christianorum, Recherches sur le vocabulaire dogmatique de Tertullien* Paris 1962.
23. See J.-H. Waszink *Tertulliani De Anima* Amsterdam 1947 p. 41–4.
24. See J. Daniélou and H.-I. Marrou *op. cit.* p. 168.

XIII
The philosophy that faith inspired

1. *Cf.* my *Philo* 4th ed. Cambridge Mass. 1968 vol. I p. 2–199; and *The Philosophy of the Church Fathers* 2nd ed. Cambridge Mass. vol. I p. 1–140.
2. I Cor. ii 5.
3. I Cor. i 22.
4. I Cor. i 21, 24.
5. Gal. i 12.
6. *Adversus Haereses* IV 9, 1.
7. *Cf. Philo* vol. I p. 17–19.
8. *Legum Allegoria* III 56, 162.
9. *Specialibus Legibus* III 34, 185.
10. *Dialogus* 2.
11. *Stromateis* I 7 (*Patrologia Graeca* VIII 732B).
12. *Ibid.* I 5 (717D).
13. Deut. v 2.
14. *Strom.* VI 8 (*PG* IX 288C).
15. Tertullian *Apologeticus* chapters 1, 4, 5, 7 and 20.
16. Col. ii 8.
17. Origen *Contra Celsum* I *Praefatio* 5; Augustine *Confessions* VIII 2, 3.
18. Heraclitus *Quaestiones Homericae* ed. F. Oelmann, Leipzig 1910.
19. *Cf.* H. Diels *Die Fragmente der Vorsokratiker* 5th ed. Berlin 1922, 8 Theagenes 2.
20. Xenophon *Symposium* 3, 6; Plato *Republic* II 378D.
21. *Cf. Church Fathers* vol. I p. 30–1.
22. Gal. iv 24.
23. Rom. v 14; I Cor. x 11.
24. Col. ii 16–17.
25. Heb. x 1.
26. Heb. ix 9.
27. *Cf. Church Fathers* vol. I p. 43–72.
28. H. F. von Arnim *Stoicorum Veterum Fragmenta* Leipzig 1903–5 vol. I 349–50.
29. *De Congressu* 14, 78–80.
30. Gen. xvi 6.
31. *Strom.* I 5 (*PG* VIII 725B).
32. *Ibid.* (721B–724A).
33. *Dialectica* I (*PG* XCIV 532B).
34. *De Caelo* I 2, 269b 13–14.
35. *Simplicius in De Caelo* ed. I. L. Heiberg, Berlin 1894 p. 55: 11, 3–4.
36. *Strom.* II 11 (*PG* VIII 985A), but see note 4 *ad. loc.*, and Stahlin's edition of the *Stromateis* Leipzig 1906 p. 139: 11, 5–6.
37. *Ibid.* VII 10 (*PG* IX 481A).
38. *Cf. Philo* vol. I p. 200–294; *Church Fathers* vol. I p. 192–286; and my *Religious Philosophy* Cambridge, Mass. 1961 p. 27–49.
39. *Timaeus* 39E and 30D.
40. *De Anima* III 4, 429a, 27–8.
41. *Sophist* 265C.
42. In the Septuagint version this is Psalm xxxii.
43. *De Migratione* 1, 6.
44. *De Opificio* 4, 16.
45. *Timaeus* 34C.
46. *De Agricultura* 12, 51.
47. *De Confusione* 28, 145.
48. *Quis Heres* 42, 206.
49. Gen. ii 7.
50. *De Somniis* I 39, 227–9.
51. *Quaestiones in Genesin* II 62.
52. *Leg. All.* II 21, 86.
53. *De Abrahamo* 41, 244 and *passim.*
54. John i 14.
55. John i 1.
56. *Ad Autolycum* II 22.
57. *Adversus Praxeam* 5.
58. *Ibid.* 6.
59. *Ibid.* 2.
60. *Supplicatio* 10.
61. *Adv. Haer.* II 16, 3.
62. *Adv. Praxeam* 5.
63. *Ibid.* 6.
64. *Strom.* V 3 (*PG* IX 32B–33A).
65. *Ibid.* V 14 (137A).
66. *Ibid.* V 11 (112A).
67. *Cf. De Cherubim* 14, 49.
68. Gen. xxii 4.
69. *De Somniis* I 11, 64.
70. *Ibid.* 65.
71. John xviii in *De Ordine* I 11, 32.
72. *Retractiones* I 3, 2.
73. *In Joannis Evangelium* 2, 4.
74. *Cf. Church Fathers* vol. I p. 287–363.
75. *Cf.* above at notes 50–53.
76. *First Apologia* 6.
77. *Metaphysics* IV 3, 1005b 26–7.
78. Athanasius *Fourth Oratio Contra Arianos* 2 (*PG* XXVI 469C).
79. Epiphanius *Adversus Haereses Panarium* Heresy 62 (*PG* XLI 1052B).
80. *Cf. Religious Philosophy* p. 126–46.
81. *Dialogus* 128.
82. *Categories* 2, 1b 6–7.
83. *De Anima* II 4, 415a 26–9.
84. *Met.* VII 7, 1032a 25.
85. *Contra Maximinum* II 6.
86. *Met.* V 6, 1016a 32–3, combined with 1016b 31–2, and *Cat.* 3, 1b 10–15 and 5, 2a 14–19.
87. *Epistula* 38, 1 (*PG* XXXII 325B); *cf.* 38, 3 (328A).
88. *Epistula* 236, 6 (884A).
89. *Met.* V 6, 1016a 17–24.
90. *De Trinitate* VII 6, 11 (*Patrologia Latina* XLII 994).
91. *Contra Celsum* VIII 12 (*PG* XI 1533C).
92. *Sophistical Refutations* 17, 175a 8–9.
93. *De Oratione* 15 (*PG* XI 465A).
94. *Cat.* 5, 3b 10–18.
95. *De Oratione loc. cit.*
96. *Met.* I 2, 982a 21–3.
97. *In Joannem* X 21 (*PG* XIV 376B).
98. *Refutatio Omnium Haeresium* ed. P. Wendland, Berlin 1918 VII 18, 1–2.
99. *Adv. Praxeam* 7.
100. *Ibid.*
101. *Ibid.*
102. *Contra Haeresin Noeti* 7 and 14.
103. *In Joannem* 10, 21 (*PG* XIV 376B).
104. *Apol.* 21 (*PL* I 399A).
105. *De Trinitate* V 8, 10–19.
106. *Cf. Church Fathers* vol. I p. 364–493.
107. *De Plantatione* 2, 9.
108. *Ibid.*
109. *Vita Mosis* II 26, 133.
110. *De Cherub.* 11, 36; *De Migratione* 1, 6.
111. John i 10.
112. John i 3.
113. Justin Martyr *Second Apologia* 6.
114. Athenagoras *Supplicatio* 10.
115. Theophilus *Ad Autolycum* II 10.
116. Clement of Alexandria *Strom.* VII 2 (*PG* IX 408B).
117. John i 14.
118. Heb. x 5; *cf.* Col. ii 9.
119. Phil. ii 7.
120. Phil. ii 28.
121. *Quaest. in Gen.* I 53; *cf. Philo* vol. I p. 118.
122. *De Fuga* 20, 122.
123. *De Somniis* I 20, 122.
124. *De Posteritate* 2, 5.
125. *Spec. Leg.* I 12, 66.
126. II Cor. v 1.
127. *Ibid. Cf.* Wisdom of Solomon ix 15 and Plato Axiochus 366A.
128. John i 14.
129. John ii 23.
130. *De Anima* II 1, 412a 16–20.
131. *Met.* V 4, 1015a 7–13.
132. *Leg. All.* II 1, 1.
133. *De Anima* II 1, 410b 6.
134. *Cat.* 5, 2a 11–13.
135. *Ibid.* 2, 1b 6.
136. *Ibid.* 6–7.
137. *Cf.* above at notes 32 and 91–102.
138. *Met.* XII 10, 1075b 34–6.
139. *Ibid.* VIII 5, 1045a 14.
140. *Ibid.* VII 10, 1035a 7–9.
141. *Nicomachaean Ethics* IX 4, 1166a 16–17.
142. *Quis Heres* 48, 231.
143. *Ennead* III 5, 5.
144. *Ibid.* IV 7, 1.
145. *Ibid.* I 1, 7.
146. *Cf. Church Fathers* vol. I p. 367–9.
147. *In Joannis Evangelium* 19, 15; *cf. Epistula* 137, 3, 11.
148. *Fragmenta* 7 (*PG* V 1221A).
149. *De Principiis* I 2, 1.
150. *De Carne Christi* 5.
151. *Epistula* 137, 3, 11.
152. *Cf. Religious Philosophy* p. 147–9.
153. *Cf. ibid.* p. 149–53.
154. *Cf. Philo* vol. I p. 386–7, and *Leg. All.* I 12, 32.
155. *Cf. Church Fathers* vol. I p. 484–6.
156. *Posterior Analytics* II 11, 94b 37–95a 1.
157. *Met.* V 5, 1015a 29.
158. *Eth. Nic.* III 1, 1109b 35.
159. *Anal. Post.* II 11, 95a 3–5.

SELECT BIBLIOGRAPHY

II
A clash of ideologies

F.-M. ABEL *Histoire de la Palestine* Paris 1952 vol. 1.

W. F. ALBRIGHT *From the Stone Age to Christianity* 2nd ed. Baltimore 1946.

V. APTOWITZER *Parteipolitik der Hasmonäerzeit* Vienna 1927.

L. BAECK *The Pharisees and Other Essays* New York 1947.

E. BEVAN *Jerusalem under the High Priests* reprint, London 1940.

E. BIKERMAN 'The Historical Foundations of Post-Biblical Judaism' in L. Finkelstein ed. *The Jews* New York 1949 vol. 1 p. 70ff.

L. FINKELSTEIN *The Pharisees, the Sociological Background of their Faith* New York 1938, 2 vols.

C. GUIGNEBERT *The Jewish World in the Time of Jesus* London 1939, translated from the French, Paris 1935.

S. B. HOENIG *The Great Sanhedrin* Philadelphia 1953.

J. JEREMIAS *Jerusalem zur Zeit Jesu* 3rd ed. Göttingen 1962.

III
A divided faith

G. BAUMBACH 'The Zealots' in *Bibel und Liturgie* vol. 41 Klosterneuburg 1968 p. 2–25 is a successful attempt to define the politics of the individual Jewish resistance groups against Rome.

M. BURROWS *The Dead Sea Scrolls* London 1956, is a discussion of the problems raised by the Dead Sea Scrolls and their religious-historical significance.

W. R. FARMER *Maccabees, Zealots and Josephus* 2nd ed. New York 1958 is a study of the development of the national movement in Jewish Palestine from the time of the Maccabaean war to the uprisings against Rome.

L. FINKELSTEIN *The Pharisees* 3rd ed. Philadelphia 1962, 2 vols. deals with the origins, teachings and social function of Pharisaism.

R. T. HERFORD *The Pharisees* London 1924 is a popular and well-known landmark with a strong bias in favour of the Pharisees.

J. MAIER *Die Texte vom Toten Meer* Munich 1960, 2 vols. is the best annotated translation of the Dead Sea Scrolls.

G. F. MOORE *Judaism in the First Centuries of the Christian Era* 8th ed. Cambridge, Mass. 1958 is a first-class description of Judaic teachings and spiritual currents in the period given in the title.

J. PARKES *The Foundations of Judaism and Christianity* Chicago 1960 is a brief and easily comprehensible description of Judaism in the late-Old Testament and early-New Testament period, as well as of the spiritual currents prevalent at that time.

H. H. ROWLEY *The Relevance of Apocalyptic* 2nd ed. London 1947 is a good description of apocalyptic and the literature concerning it.

K. SCHUBERT *The Dead Sea Community* London 1959 deals with the Dead Sea Scrolls and their religious-historical significance for Judaism and Christianity.

K. SCHUBERT 'Die jüdischen Religionsparteien im Zeitalter Jesu' in K. Schubert ed. *Der historische Jesus und der Christus unseres Glaubens* Vienna 1962 p. 15–101.

E. SCHÜRER *Geschichte des jüdischen Volkes im Zeitalter Jesu Christi* Hildesheim 1964 (a new edition of the Leipzig 1901–9 edition) is a very good account of the mundane, cultural and religious history of the Jews in Palestine and the Diaspora at the time of Jesus.

V. TCHERIKOVER *Hellenistic Civilization and the Jews* Philadelphia 1959 is a remarkable description of the political and cultural differences between Judaism and Hellenism.

R. DE VAUX *L'Archéologie et les manuscrits de la Mer Morte* London 1961 is a description of the excavations at Khirbet Qumran and their importance for the interpretation of the Dead Sea Scrolls.

IV
A taste for things Greek

E. R. BEVAN *The House of Seleucus* London 1902 and A. Bouché-Leclerq *Histoire des Seleucides* Paris 1913–14 are still the standard works on the Seleucid kingdom. These works deal mainly with political history.

E. R. BEVAN *Jerusalem under the High Priests* London 1904 is an excellent book on Hellenism and the Jews. By the same author there are two chapters in the *Cambridge Ancient History* vol. 8 chapter 16 'Syria and the Jews' and vol. 9 chapter 9 'The Jews'.

A. H. M. JONES *The Greek City from Alexander to Justinian* Oxford 1940 deals with the foundation of Greek colonies in the Levant from the reign of Alexander onwards, and with the Hellenization of the native communities.

A. H. M. JONES *The Cities of the Eastern Roman Provinces* Oxford 1937 (revised ed. in the press) chapter 10 describes the development of Greek cities of Syria and Palestine.

A. H. M. JONES *The Herods of Judaea* 2nd ed. Oxford 1967 is a popular book on the Herodian period.

A. MOMIGLIANO 'Herod of Judaea' in *Cambridge Ancient History* vol. 10 chapter 11.

M. ROSTOVTZEFF 'Syria and the East' in *Cambridge Ancient History* vol. 7 chapter 5 deals more with the social and economic history.

W. W. TARN *Hellenistic Civilization* 3rd ed., revised by the author and G. T. Griffith, London 1952 is an excellent short book on the Hellenistic age in general. It has notes giving references to the original authorities and modern books, and a bibliography of general works.

V
The Empire of Rome

There is no satisfactory single book in any language on the Imperial administration, and most of the great monographs are now somewhat antiquated.

F. F. ABBOT AND A. C. JOHNSON *Municipal Administration in the Roman Empire* Princeton 1926 is most useful, but does not sufficiently distinguish the variant systems in different areas.

J. CROOK *Consilium Principis* Cambridge 1955 deals with the Imperial cabinet.

A. H. M. JONES *The Greek City* Oxford 1940 is a detailed study of municipal government: part 3 'Internal Politics'; part 4 'The Civic Services'.

H. LAST 'The Principate and the Administration' in *Cambridge Ancient History* vol. 11 chapter 10, and 'Rome and the Empire' *ibid.* chapter 11 are still the best general survey.

A. N. SHERWIN-WHITE *Roman Society and Roman Law in the New Testament* Oxford 1963 chapter 1 deals with the powers of governors.

A. N. SHERWIN-WHITE *The Roman Citizenship* Oxford 1939 parts 2 and 3 deals with the extension of Roman privileges to provincials, and their reactions.

G. H. STEVENSON 'The Imperial Administration' in *Cambridge Ancient History* vol. 10 chapter 7, and 'The Army and Navy' *ibid.* chapter 8 deals with the system of the early Empire.

G. H. STEVENSON *Roman Provincial Administration till the Age of the Antonines* 2nd ed. Oxford 1949 is somewhat brief.

VI
'The world's great age'

J. CARCOPINO *Daily Life in Ancient Rome* Harmondsworth 1962 is a very lively and erudite treatment of life in the capital, its building problems, its spectacles, etc.

T. FRANK ed. *An Economic Survey of Ancient Rome* Paterson N.J. 1959 is a collection with commentary of the principal sources for the history of economic life in the various parts of the Empire. This work has many contributors, and is arranged thus: part 1, Rome and Italy of the Republic, by T. Frank; part 2, Roman Egypt, by A. C. Johnson; part 3, Britain, Spain, Sicily and Gaul, by R. C. Collingwood, J. J. van Nostrand, V. M. Scramuzza and A. Grenier respectively; part 4, Africa, Syria, Greece and Asia Minor, by R. M. Haywood, F. M. Heichelheim, J. A. O. Larsen and T. R. S. Broughton respectively; part 5, Rome and Italy of the Empire, by T. Frank (posthumous).

L. FRIEDLAENDER *Darstellungen aus der Sittengeschichte Roms in der Zeit von Augustus bis zum Ausgang der Antoninen*, revised by G. Wissowa, Leipzig 1920–3, 4 vols. English translation *Roman Life and Manners under the Early Empire* London 1908–13. This work can always be recommended for a general description, taken from literary and other sources, of life under the Empire.

J.-G. GAGÉ *Les Classes sociales dans l'Empire romain* Paris 1964 sets out the classes, divided into the early and late Empire, with chapters on 'the 3rd-century crisis'.

P. GRIMAL *The Civilization of Rome* London 1963 deals with various aspects, practical and otherwise, with excellent illustrations.

J. J. HATT *La Gaule romaine* Paris 1959 deals with the effects, social and otherwise, of the Roman domination on one region of the Empire with an aboriginal culture, namely Gaul.

A. H. M. JONES *The Cities of the Eastern Roman Provinces* Oxford 1937 (reprint in the press) deals with the same subject in the eastern provinces.

C. JULLIAN *Historie de la Gaule* Paris 1908 vols. 5 and 6 also deals with Gaul from this point of view.

D. MAGIE *Roman Rule in Asia Minor* Princeton N.J. 1950, 2 vols. also deals with the social effects in Asia Minor.

H.-I. MARROU *Historie de l'Education dans l'Antiquité* Paris 1935 deals with educational institutions.

PAULY-WISSOWA *Real-Encyclopädie für Altertumswissenschaft* describes the careers of the aristocracy, arranged by families. The problems of 'prosopography' are of great importance for this subject. 'Prosopography' is the identification and study of the biographies of innumerable persons with senatorial and equestrian careers, known through inscriptions in the form of a *cursus honorum*, or more rarely through literary sources. The *Prosopographia imperii Romani* (letters down to the time of Julius Caesar with short commentaries in Latin) is being republished.

H. G. PFLAUM *Les Carrières procuratoriennes* Paris 1960, 4 vols. is very useful and up-to-date on the grades of equestrian offices. See also the series of studies on the composition of the Senate by Lambrechts, Barbieri, etc.

M. ROSTOVTZEFF *The Social and Economic History of the Roman Empire* Oxford 1957, 2 vols. remains the best general treatment, original and powerful.

VII
Away from sheer beauty

Pagan Rome

L. CREMA *L'architettura romana* Turin 1959.

A. FROVA *L'arte di Roma e del mondo romano* Turin 1962.

G. M. A. HANFMANN *Roman Art* London 1964.

H. KÄHLER *Rome and her Empire* London 1963.

W. L. MACDONALD *The Architecture of the Roman Empire* New Haven and London 1965

A. MAIURI *Roman Painting* Geneva 1953.

D. S. ROBERTSON *Handbook of Greek and Roman Architecture* 2nd ed. Cambridge 1943.

D. E. STRONG *Roman Imperial Sculpture* London 1961.

J. M. C. TOYNBEE *The Art of the Romans* London 1965.

R. E. M. WHEELER *Roman Art and Architecture* London 1964.

Romano-Christian

P. DU BOURGET *La peinture paléochrétienne* Paris and Amsterdam 1965.

J. G. DAVIES *The Origin and Development of Early Christian Church Architecture* London 1952.

A. GRABAR *The Beginnings of Christian Art* London 1967.

R. KRAUTHEIMER *Early Christian and Byzantine Architecture* Harmondsworth 1965.

F. VAN DER MEER AND C. MOHRMANN *Atlas of the Early Christian World* London 1958.

F. VAN DER MEER *Early Christian Art* London 1967.

H. P. L'ORANGE AND P. J. NORDHAGEN *Mosaics from Antiquity to the Early Middle Ages* London 1966.

W. F. VOLBACH AND M. HIRMER *Early Christian Art* London 1961.

J. WILPERT *Die Malereien der Katakomben Roms* Freiburg-im-Breisgau 1901.

VIII
Ordeals of the mind

General

A. H. ARMSTRONG ed. *The Cambridge History of Later Greek and Early Mediaeval Philosophy* Cambridge 1967; reprint 1969.

A. H. ARMSTRONG *An Introduction to Ancient Philosophy* 4th ed. revised, with a critical introduction by the author, London 1965.

Entretiens Hardt vol. 3 *Recherches sur la Tradition Platonicienne* Vandoeuvres-Geneva 1957 is a collection of papers and discussions in English, French and German.

Plotinus

A. H. ARMSTRONG *Plotinus* Loeb Classical Series, London and Cambridge, Mass. 1966– (in progress; vols. 1–3 published) is a Greek text and English translation with notes.

A. H. ARMSTRONG *Plotinus* London 1953, New York 1962 consists of selections in translation.

S. MACKENNA *Plotinus, The Enneads* 3rd ed., revised by B. S. Page, London 1962 is a complete English translation.

Books on Plotinus

Entretiens Hardt vol. 5 *Les Sources de Plotin* Vandoeuvres-Geneva 1960 is a collection of papers and discussions on Plotinus in English, French, German and Italian.

W. R. INGE *The Philosophy of Plotinus* 3rd ed. London 1929; reprint 1948, 2 vols.

J. M. RIST *Eros and Psyche: Studies in Plato, Plotinus and Origen* Toronto 1964.

J. M. RIST *Plotinus: The Road to Reality* Cambridge 1967.

IX
The Son of Man

J. P. AUDET 'Affinités littéraires et doctrinaires du "Manuel de discipline"' in *Revue Biblique* vol. 59 Paris 1952 p. 219–38 gives the philological proof that the first six chapters (the 'Two Ways') of the famous *Didache* are an ancient Jewish treatise connected with Essenism.

F. M. BRAUN 'Les Testaments des XII Patriarches' in *Revue Biblique* vol. 67 Paris 1960 p. 516–49 is the best article on the *Testaments of the Twelve Patriarchs* since the discovery of the Dead Sea Scrolls.

A. BUECHLER *Types of Jewish Palestinian Piety from 70 BCE to 70 CE* London 1922 and *Studies in Sin and Atonement* London 1928 are the best introduction to the spiritual atmosphere of rabbinical Judaism in the time of Jesus. See also D. Flusser 'A New Sensitivity in Judaism and the Christian Message' in *Harvard Theological Review* vol. 61 Cambridge, Mass. 1968 p. 107–17.

R. EPPEL *Le piétisme juif dans Les Testaments des Douze Patriarches* Paris 1930 is still important for the religiosity of the *Testaments*.

D. FLUSSER 'Blessed are the Poor in Spirit' in *Israel Exploration Journal* vol. 10 Jerusalem 1960 p. 1–12 deals with the relationship of Jesus' Beatitudes to the Dead Sea Scrolls.

D. FLUSSER *Jesus in Selbstzeugnissen und Bilddokumenten* Hamburg 1968 p. 89–102 deals with the problem of Jesus' self-consciousness.

M. D. HOOKER *Jesus and the Servant* London 1959 is an important contribution on the Suffering Servant in Isaiah and the New Testament

M. B. VAN IERSEL *Der Sohn in den synoptischen Jesusworten* Leiden 1961 deals with Jesus' Sonship.

M. DE JONGE and A. S. VAN DER WOUDE have published and discussed the Melchizedek fragment in *New Testament Studies* vol. 12 London 1966 p. 301–26. See also D. Flusser 'Melchizedek and the Son of Man' in *Christian News from Israel* Jerusalem 1966 p. 23–9.

E. LOHSE *Märtyter und Gottesknecht* Göttingen 1955 deals with expiation by means of suffering and death.

S. MOWINKEL *He That Cometh* Oxford 1956 deals with the concept of the Son of Man in Judaism. See also E. Sjöberg *Der Menschensohn im äthiopischen Henochbuch* Lund 1946, and M. Stone 'The Concept of the Messiah in IV Ezra' in *Religions in Antiquity, Essays in Memory of E. R. Goodenough* Leiden 1968 p. 295–312.

K. STENDAHL 'Hate, Non-retaliation and Love' in *Harvard Theological Review* vol. 55 Cambridge, Mass. 1962 p. 343–55 deals with some very important moral aspects in the *Testaments of the Twelve Patriarchs*, the Dead Sea Scrolls and Christianity.

X
Paganism's death struggle

General

F. CUMONT *Les religions orientales dans le paganisme romain* 4th ed. Paris 1929.

A. J. FESTUGIÈRE *Personal Religion among the Greeks* Berkeley 1954.

F. C. GRANT *Hellenistic Religions: The Age of Syncretism* New York 1953.

M. P. NILSSON *Geschichte der Griechischen Religion* Munich 1950 vol. 2 'Die hellenistische und römische Zeit'.

A. D. NOCK *Conversion* Oxford 1933.

R. PETTAZZONI *I Misteri* Bologna 1924.

K. PRÜMM *Religionsgeschichtliches Handbuch für den Raum der altchristlichen Umwelt* Rome 1954.

Mithraism

F. CUMONT *Textes et Monuments relatifs aux Mystères de Mithra* Brussels 1896–8, 2 vols.

F. CUMONT *Die Mysterien des Mithra* 3rd ed. Leipzig 1923.

M. J. VERMASEREN *Corpus Inscriptionum et Monumentorum Religionis Mithricae* Hague 1956–60.

M. J. VERMASEREN *Mithras, Geschichte eines Kultes* Stuttgart 1965.

Cybele and Attis

R. DUTTOY *The Taurobolium* Leyden 1969.

H. GRAILLOT *Le culte de Cybèle* Paris 1912.

H. HEPDING *Attis, seine Mythen und sein Kult* Grieszen 1903.

P. LAMBRECHTS 'Les fetes "phrygiennes" de Cybèle et d'Attis. in *Bulletin de l'Institut historique belge de Rome* vol. 27 Rome 1952 p. 141–70.

M. J. VERMASEREN *The Legend of Attis in Greek and Roman Art* Leyden 1966.

The Egyptian Mysteries

H. I. BELL *Cults and Creeds in Graeco-Roman Egypt* Liverpool 1957.

P. M. FRASER 'Two studies on the Cult of Sarapis in the Hellenistic World' in *Opuscula Atheniensia* vol. 3 Lund 1960 p. 1–54.

P. M. FRASER 'Current Problems Concerning the Early History of the Cult of Sarapis' in *Opuscula Atheniensia* vol. 7 Lund 1967 p. 23–42.

T. HOPFNER *Plutarch über Isis und Osiris* Prague 1940; reprint 1967, 2 vols.

G. LAFAYE *Les divinités d'Alexandrie hors de l'Égypte* Paris 1884.

The Syrian Cults

W. ATALLAH *Adonis dans la littérature et l'art grecs* Paris 1966.

R. DU MESNIL DU BUISSON *Les tessères et les monnaies de Palmyre* Paris 1962.

O. EISSFELDT *Tempel und Kulte syrischer Städte in hellenistisch-romischer Zeit* Leipzig 1941.

P. MERLAT *Jupiter Dolichenus* Paris 1960.

P. S. RONZEVALLE *Jupiter Héliopolitain* Beirut 1937.

XI and XII
'That the Scripture might be fulfilled'

The Word goes forth

B. BAGATTI *L'Église de la circoncision* Jerusalem 1965 deals with the later history of the Judaeo-Christian community at Jerusalem. It contains many sources which are not, however, always treated sufficiently critically.

W. BAUER *Rechtglaübigkeit und Ketzerei im ältesten Christentum* 2nd ed., with an introduction by G. Strecker, Tübingen 1964 is always valuable on the various tendencies within Judaeo-Christianity.

S. G. F. BRANDON *Jesus and the Zealots* Manchester 1967 is the best work on the relation of Judaeo-Christianity to the Zealots.

H. BRAUN *Qumran und das Neue Testament* Tübingen 1966, 2 vols. is the methodical and critical study on the relations between the Essene and the Christian texts.

J. DANIÉLOU *The Theology of Jewish Christianity* London 1964 is the only treatment of the doctrines and customs of the Judaeo-Christians in their entirety. For their methods of exegesis, it should be supplemented by J. Daniélou *Etudes d'exégèse judéo-chrétienne* Paris 1966.

EUSEBIUS *Ecclesiastical History* I–III is the principal source for the Judaeo-Christian community at Jerusalem.

R. M. GRANT *Gnosticism and Early Christianity* New York 1959 is the best exposition of the Jewish sources of Gnosticism.

M. HORNSCHUH *Studien zur Epistula Apostolorum* Berlin 1965 p. 99–116 deals with the Judaeo-Christian community in Egypt.

G. QUISPEL *Makarius, das Thomasevangelium und das Lied von der Perle* Leiden 1967 p. 5–9 deals with the Judaeo-Christian community in Osrhoëne.

M. SIMON *Les sectes juives au temps du Christ* Paris 1958 is the best treatment of the relations between Christianity and the Jewish sects in general.

M. SIMON *Verus Israël*, revised edition, Paris 1964 appendix on p. 477–512 is the best treatment of the various definitions of Judaeo-Christianity.

E. STAUFFER 'Zum Khalifat des Jacobus' in *Zeitschrift für Religions- und Geistesgeschichte* vol. 4 Marburg 1952 p. 193–214 deals with the place of Jesus' family in the Judaeo-Christian community at Jerusalem.

XIII
The philosophy that faith inspired

This chapter is based exclusively upon my *Philo: Foundations of Religious Philosophy in Judaism, Christianity, and Islam* Cambridge, Mass. 1947; 4th ed. revised, 1968, 2 vols.; *The Philosophy of the Church Fathers* Cambridge, Mass. 1956; 2nd ed. revised, 1964 vol. 1; and *Religious Philosophy* Cambridge, Mass. 1961, to which specific references are given in the notes. The following annotated bibliography, confined to works in English or English translation, and dealing only with topics covered in this chapter, was prepared by Professor George H. Williams, Hollis Professor of Divinity at Harvard University.

Scripture and philosophy

C. BIGGS *The Christian Platonists of Alexandria* Oxford 1886 p. 57–8 and 134–51 discusses allegory in Clement of Alexandria and Origen.

H. CHADWICK 'Philo and the Beginnings of Christian Thought' in A. H. Armstrong ed. *The Cambridge History of Later Greek and Early Mediaeval Philosophy* Cambridge 1967 part 2 p. 137–92 deals with the confluence of Scripture and Greek philosophy in Philo and with the subsequent problems in Christian thought through Origen.

J. DANIÉLOU *The Theology of Jewish Christianity* Paris 1958; London and Chicago 1964 chapter 3 deals with Jewish Christian exegesis.

J. DANIÉLOU *From Shadows to Reality: Studies in the Biblical Typology of the Fathers* (Paris 1950 as *Sacramentum Futuri*) London and Westminster, Md. 1960 traces the application throughout the Patristic era of five selected Old Testament figures from Adam to Joshua.

R. M. GRANT *The Letter and the Spirit* London 1957 traces allegorical methods in the Hellenistic tradition, in Philo, and in Christian usage (mostly Greek) through Clement of Alexandria and Origen.

J. N. D. KELLY *Early Christian Doctrines* London 1958; 4th printing 1968 chapters 2 and 3 deals with Scripture, typology and allegory.

The Logos and the Platonic Ideas

C. BIGGS *op. cit.* pp. 15–26 deals with the Logos in Philo and the Church Fathers.

C. H. DODD *The Interpretation of the Fourth Gospel* Cambridge 1953; paperback ed. 1968 section 1,3 deals with Philo on the Logos.

J. LEBRETON *History of the Dogma of the Trinity, from its Origins to the Council of Nicaea* Paris 1910; English translation from the 8th French ed. London 1939 traces the pre-Christian philosophical use of the Logos.

R. MCL. WILSON *The Gnostic Problem: A Study of the Relations between Hellenistic Judaism and the Gnostic Heresy* London 1950 deals with Philo's Logos in a special context.

Trinity, Incarnarion and philosophy

C. BIGGS *op. cit.* p. 51–75 and 162–92.

J. F. BETHUNE-BAKER *Early History of Christian Doctrine* London 1903; 7th ed. 1942 p. 197–300.

J. DANIÉLOU *Jewish Christianity* chapter 4 'The Trinity and Angelology'.

R. M. GRANT *The Early Christian Doctrine of God* Charlottesville 1966 limits its six chapters to Triadology and the patristic proofs thereof.

A. GRILLMEIER *Christ in the Christian Tradition, from the Apostolic Age to Chalcedon (451)* London 1965 is a much amplified version of his magisterial historical essay in *Das Konzil von Chalkedon* Würzburg 1951.

J. N. D. KELLY *op. cit. passim.*

J. LEBRETON *op. cit. passim.*

G. L. PRESTIGE *God in Patristic Thought* London and Toronto 1936, drawing upon the author's earlier philological and theological research in connection with the Lexicon of Patristic Greek, deals systematically and genetically with Triadology and Christology.

XIV
Rival theologies

W. BAUER *Rechtgläubigkeit und Ketzerei im ältesten Christentum* Tübingen 1934; reprint 1964 and H. E. W. Turner *The Pattern of Christian Truth* London 1954 contain general discussions of the problems of 'orthodoxy' and 'heresy'. Bauer exaggerates the antiquity and importance of 'heresy'; Turner defends the existence of a 'main stream'.

G. W. BUTTERWORTH *Origen on First Principles* London 1936; paperback New York 1966 is an English translation of this work.

H. CHADWICK *Origen: Contra Celsum* Cambridge 1953; reprint 1965 is a translation of the *Contra Celsum*.

J. DANIÉLOU *Origen* London and New York 1955 is a recent study of Origen.

R. M. GRANT ed. *Gnosticism: an Anthology* London 1961 contains translations of Gnostic documents.

R. M. GRANT *The Earliest Lives of Jesus* London 1961 discusses the attitudes of the Gnostics and Origen toward the gospels.

R. P. C. HANSON *Allegory and Event* London 1959 is another recent study of Origen.

A. HARNACK *Marcion: das Evangelium vom fremden Gott* Leipzig 1924 assembles the ancient sources for Marcion.

XV
The persecutions

N. H. BAYNES *Cambridge Ancient History* 1939 vol. 12 pp. 789–95 gives a very detailed bibliography to 1939.

EUSEBIUS *Ecclesiastical History* is by far the most important literary source. There is a good English translation and commentary by H. J. Lawlor and J. E. L. Oulton, *Eusebius, Ecclesiastical History* London 1927–8, 2 vols.

W. H. C. FREND *Martyrdom and Persecution in the Early Church* London 1965 is the one major work on the subject in English—a very stimulating book, but see the reviews in *Journal of Roman Studies* vol. 56 London 1966 p. 231–6 and *Journal of Theological Studies* vol. 18 London 1967 p. 217–21.

A. H. M. JONES *The Later Roman Empire* Oxford 1964 vol. 2 p. 938–56 deals with the persecutions by Christians of pagans, Jews, heretics and schismatics.

E. KNOPF AND G. KRÜGER *Ausgewählte Märtyrerakten*, 4th ed. by G. Ruhbach, Tübingen 1965 p. vi–xi and 130–44 contains good general bibliographies (arranged under headings) of modern works on the persecutions and subjects connected therewith.

J. MOREAU *La persécution du Christianisme dans l'empire romain* Paris 1956 is the best short book on the persecutions—better still in the German translation, *Die Christenverfolgung im römischen Reich*, of 1961, which, unlike the French original, gives references to ancient sources and modern works.

PLINY *Epistulae* X 96–7 are the relevant letters of Pliny and Trajan. The only good English translation is by B. Radice, *The Letters of the Younger Pliny* Harmondsworth 1963 p. 293–5. See also the commentary in A. N. Sherwin-White *The Letters of Pliny* Oxford 1966 p. 691–712.

G. E. M. DE STE. CROIX 'Why were the Early Christians Persecuted?' in *Past and Present* vol. 26 London 1963 p. 1–38; *cf.* vol. 27, 1964 p. 23–33; and 'Aspects of the Great Persecution' in *Harvard Theological Review* vol. 47 Cambridge, Mass. 1954 p. 75–113 give full references to the ancient sources and the modern literature on most of the subjects discussed in this chapter.

J. STEVENSON *A New Eusebius* London 1957 (and reprints) contains a valuable collection of source-material in English translation on the Early Church to AD 337 (including the persecutions).

LIST AND SOURCES OF ILLUSTRATIONS

The page on which an illustration appears is shown by the first set of numerals, its plate or figure number by the second, figures being distinguished by italics. Sources of photographs are given in italics.

I
The Mediterranean world's age of agony

II
A clash of ideologies

after AD 135. Israel National Museum. *Françoise Foliot*

38. Southern Italy: tombstone with Menorah and Hebrew inscription. *Archaeological Museum of Bari*

39. Alexandria: bronze lamp with handle in form of Menorah. Coll. Mme M. S. Schloessinger, New York. *Françoise Foliot*

40. Rome: graffito with Menorah and ritual objects, from the Jewish catacomb of Vigna Rondanini; *c.* AD 300. *Benedettine di Priscilla*

41. Rome: sarcophagus with Menorah flanked by Victories and figures of the Seasons, from the catacomb of Vigna Rondanini; *c.* AD 300. Museo delle Terme. *Mansell*

42. Hamman Lif, Tunisia: detail of pavement from synagogue of Naro; 4th century AD. *Courtesy Brooklyn Museum*

64 43. Dura Europus: synagogue fresco showing the Ark of the Covenant; before AD 256. National Museum, Damascus. Courtesy Bollingen Foundation. *Fred Anderegg*

67 *1.* Araq el-Emir: reconstruction of castle of the Tobiads; 2nd century BC. After H. C. Butler *Ancient Architecture in Syria*. *Trevor Hodgson*

69 *2.* Map of Palestine, showing Maccabaean conquests. *Edgar Holloway*

72 *3.* Jerusalem: the 'Theodotos inscription'; Herodian period. Israel National Museum. *Trevor Hodgson*

73 *4.* Si'a: reconstruction of Temple of Zeus Baalshamin, with statue of Herod the Great. After M. de Vogüé *Syrie Centrale: Architecture Civile et Religieuse*

74 *5.* Coin of Agrippa I; 'year 2', *i.e.* AD 38/9. British Museum. *Trevor Hodgson*

75 *6.* Coin of Hadrian ploughing the line of the walls of Aelia Capitolina; AD 135 (?). *Trevor Hodgson*

III

A divided faith

79 1. Dura Europus: synagogue fresco showing the Temple and Aaron; before AD 256. National Museum, Damascus. Courtesy Bollingen Foundation. *Fred Anderegg*

80–1 2. Chorazin: 'seat of Moses'; 3rd century AD. *Courtesy Israel Department of Antiquities and Museums*

3. Jerusalem: ossuary of Simon 'who built the Temple'; Herodian period. Israel National Museum. *Ronald Sheridan*

4. Dura Europus: synagogue fresco, the closed Temple; before AD 256. *Courtesy Directorate General of Antiquities, Damascus*

5. Capernaum: Ark of the Covenant on a limestone synagogue frieze; 2nd–3rd century AD. *Custodia di Terra Sancta*

6. Jerusalem: the 'Wailing Wall'; some blocks of Herodian period. *Courtesy Israel Government Press Office*

7. Jerusalem: ossuary of Nicanor 'who made the doors', *i.e.* of Herod's Temple; Herodian period. *British Museum*

8. Jerusalem: inscription forbidding gentiles to enter the Temple; Herodian period. Archaeological Museum, Istanbul. *Courtesy Israel Department of Antiquities and Museums*

9. Jerusalem: detail of the Temple, from the reconstruction model of ancient Jerusalem by M. and E. Avi-Yonah. *Ronald Sheridan*

82–3 10. Dura Europus: synagogue fresco of Ezekiel's vision in the valley of the dry bones; before AD 256. National Museum, Damascus. Courtesy Bollingen Foundation. *Fred Anderegg*

84–5 11. Khirbet Qumran: the Manual of Discipline; before AD 68. *Israel National Museum*

12. Khirbet Qumran: tables; before AD 68. *Courtesy John Allegro*

13. Khirbet Qumran: the Isaiah scroll; before AD 68. *Courtesy Professor John C. Trever*

14. Khirbet Qumran: jar containing scroll, from cave 1; before AD 68. *British Museum*

15. Khirbet Qumran: inkwell and potsherd with Hebrew alphabet; before AD 68. *Courtesy John Allegro*

16. Khirbet Qumran: the Copper Scroll; before AD 68. *Courtesy John Allegro*

86 17. Khirbet Qumran: view of the Essene monastery, showing a group of cisterns; 8th century BC–AD 68. Copyright Daily Telegraph. *Graham Findlayson*

18. Khirbet Qumran: caves 4 and 5. Copyright Daily Telegraph. *Graham Findlayson*

89 *1.* Beth Shearim: graffito of psyches; after AD 135. *Trevor Hodgson*

90 *2.* Reconstruction of Herod's Temple. After M. de Vogüé *Le Temple à Jerusalem*

93 *3.* Coin of the Second Revolt, with façade of the Temple and the Ark of the Covenant; AD 133. British Museum. *Trevor Hodgson*

95 *4.* Plan of the 'monastery' at Khirbet Qumran. After R. de Vaux *L'Archéologie et les manuscripts de la Mer Morte*. *Paula Brown*

97 *5.* Dilepton of Mattathias Antigonus (enlarged), with Menorah and Table of Shewbread; 40–37 BC. British Museum. *Trevor Hodgson*

IV

A taste for things Greek

101 1. Homs (Emesa): the silver 'Aleppo mask' of a helmet; 1st century AD. Courtesy Syrian Department of Antiquities and Museums. *British Museum*

102–3 2. Stater of Mallus, with Demeter: *c.* 375 BC. Staatlichen Munzkabinetts, Berlin. *Max Hirmer*

3. Stater of Soli, with bunch of grapes and owl; *c.* 350 BC. British Museum. *John Freeman*

4. Stater of Tarsus, with girl playing knucklebones; *c.* 400–380 BC. Private Coll. *Max Hirmer*

5. Pompeii: the 'Alexander mosaic', from the House of the Faun; 4th–1st century BC. National Museum, Naples. *Alfredo Foglia*

6. Herculaneum: bronze bust of Seleucus I; before AD 79. National Museum, Naples. *Mansell*

7. Egypt: marble mask of Ptolemy I; Hellenistic. *Ny Carlsberg Glyptothek*

104–5 8. Sidon: black basalt sarcophagus of King Tabuit; 6th century BC. Courtesy Archaeological Museum, Istanbul. *Avni Toraman*

9. Sidon: marble 'Lycian' sarcophagus; 4th century BC. Courtesy Archaeological Museum, Istanbul. *Avni Toraman*

10. Sidon: marble 'Satrap' sarcophagus; 5th century BC. Courtesy Archaeological Museum, Istanbul. *Avni Toraman*

11. Sidon: marble 'Mourning Women' sarcophagus of King Abdastart I; 4th century BC. Courtesy Archaeological Museum, Istanbul. *Avni Toraman*

12. Sidon: marble 'Alexander' sarcophagus, probably of Abdalonymus; 4th–3rd century BC. Courtesy Archaeological Museum, Istanbul. *Avni Toraman*

106–7. 13. Marissa: wall-painting with hunting scene, from the hypogeum of Sesmaios; 3rd century BC. After J. P. Peters and H. Thiersch *Painted Tombs of the Necropolis of Marissa*

14–16. Faiyum: terracotta figurine and clay vases; 4th century BC. *Courtesy Allard Pierson Museum, Amsterdam*

17. Sidon: tomb-painting of a Greek mercenary; 3rd–2nd century BC. Courtesy Archaeological Museum, Istanbul. *Haluk Doganbey*

18. Faiyum: mummy of Artemidorus; 2nd century AD. *British Museum*

108–9 19. Dodona: bronze statue of Zeus; *c.* 470 BC. *Staatliche Museen, Berlin*

20. Ras Shamrah: stele of Hadad, the Canaanite Baal; 2nd millennium BC. *Louvre*

21. Anzio (?): Apollo Belvedere; 2nd century AD. Vatican Museums. *Mansell*

22. Egypt: limestone statuette of Reshef; 20th–26th Dynasty (*c.* 1000–525 BC). *Metropolitan Museum, New York*

23. Farnese Hercules; 1st century BC. National Museum, Naples. *Mansell*

24. Melkart, from the stele of Bar-Hadad. *Courtesy Syrian Department of Antiquities and Museums*

25. Selinus: detail of limestone relief with the death of Actaeon, from the metopes of the Temple of Hera; *c.* 460 BC. National Museum, Palermo. *Mansell*

26. Tunisia: stele of Tanit (?). *Bardo Museum*

27. Medici Venus; Roman copy of 3rd-century BC original. Uffici, Florence. *Mansell*

28. Amathus: detail of a sarcophagus with Astarte; 6th century BC. *Metropolitan Museum, New York*

110–1 29. Amman (Philadelphia): the acropolis and the theatre; 1st century AD. *Adolfo Tomeucci*

30. Jerash (Gerasa): the northern theatre; 1st century AD. *Roger Wood*

31. Palmyra: Temple of Baal Samin; 1st century AD. *Adolfo Tomeucci*

32. Jerash (Gerasa): the forum, from the acropolis; 1st century AD. *Adolfo Tomeucci*

112–3 33. Boscoreale: silver dish with personification of Alexandria; 3rd century BC–1st century AD. Louvre. *Giraudon*

34. Dura Europus: personification of Palmyra, from the Temple of the Palmyrene Gods (reconstruction); 3rd century AD. Yale University Art Gallery. *Bradford Welles*

35. Marble copy of Eutychides' bronze of Antioch on the Orontes; Roman. Vatican Museums. *Mansell*

36. Dura Europus: gypsum cult-relief with Zeus Baalshamin, from the Temple of the Gadde; 'year 470', *i.e.* AD 158–9. Yale University Art Gallery. *Bradford Welles*

37. Palmyra: the colonnaded main street; 1st century AD. *Courtesy Professor A. H. M. Jones*

38. Dura Europus: aerial view; 280 BC–AD 256. *Courtesy French Institute of Archaeology, Beirut*

114–5 39, 40. Antioch: mosaic with street scenes; 5th century AD. Museum of Antiquities, Antioch. After A. Grabar *Byzantium*

41. Tabge: Nilotic mosaic from the Church of the Multiplication of Loaves and Fishes; 5th century AD. *Courtesy Unesco*

42. Edessa: the 'Funerary Couch' mosaic; AD 277/8. Transcription by Mrs Seton Lloyd. Courtesy Professor J. B. Segal. *Thames & Hudson Archives*

43. Antioch: mosaic with good-luck symbols; 5th century AD. Museum of Antiquities, Antioch. *Roger Wood*

116 44. Dura Europus: bas-relief of Zeus Kyrios; 'year 343', *i.e.* AD 32. Yale University Art Gallery. *Bradford Welles*

118 *1.* Attica: painting of a merchant-ship, from a black-figure cup; *c.* 540 BC. British Museum. *Jon D. Wilsher*

119 *2.* Palmyra: bust of Aqmat, daughter of Hagago; 2nd century AD. British Museum. *Trevor Hodgson*

121 *3.* Alexandria: stele of Shiatby; 4th century BC. Alexandria Museum. *Trevor Hodgson*

V

The Empire of Rome

125 1. Rome: the 'Barberini Roma'; 4th century AD. Museo Nazionale Romano. After J. Wilpert *Die Römischen Mosaiken und Malereien*

126–7. 2. Denarius with portrait of Julius Caesar; 44 BC. Cabinet des Médailles, Paris. *Editions Arthaud*

3. Rome: marble bust of Pompey; *c.* 48 BC. *Ny Carlsberg Glyptothek*

4. Denarius probably minted by Lucullus when he was Sulla's quaestor; *c.* 82–80 BC. British Museum. *John Freeman*

5. Detail from coin of Nero, with closed Temple of Janus; AD 65 (?). *Fototeca Unione*

6. Rome: detail of Mother Earth, symbolizing peace and plenty, from the Ara Pacis; 13–9 BC. *Mansell*

7–14. Rome: personifications of provinces, from the Temple of Hadrian; AD 145. Palazzo dei Conservatori. *Fototeca Unione*

15–24. Coins of Trajan and Hadrian with personifications of provinces; 2nd century AD. British Museum. *John Freeman*

25. Rome: statue of Augustus from Prima Porta; *c.* 20–17 BC or later. Vatican Museums. *Mansell*

128–9 26. Carthage: mosaic showing the estate of the *colonus* Julius; 4th century AD. *Bardo Museum*

27. Saint Romain en Gal (Colonia Iulia Vienna): detail of the sacrifice to Ceres, from a mosaic pictorial calendar; Imperial period. Louvre. *Giraudon*

28. Zliten: detail of mosaic with threshing scene; 1st century AD. Castello Museum, Tripoli. *Roger Wood*

29. Zliten: detail of Autumn, from mosaic of the seasons; 4th century AD (some date it earlier). Castello Museum, Tripoli. *Roger Wood*

30. Sousse (Hadrumentum): detail of mosaic showing race-horses in N. Africa; Imperial period. Bardo Museum. *Roger Wood*

31. Zliten: detail of mosaic with oxen ploughing; 1st century AD. Castello Museum, Tripoli. *Roger Wood*

130–1 32. Rome: interior of Diocletian's senate-house; late-3rd century AD. *Gabinetto Fotografico Nazionale*

33. Graveson: detail showing magistrates' seat, from the stele of C. Otacilius Oppianus; 1st century AD. *Musée Calvet, Avignon*

34. Rome: relief representing the purse of the *viator ad aerarium* (treasury official). Vatican Museums. *John Freeman*

35. Denarius of the quaestors L. Calpurnius Piso and Q. Servilius Caepia; 100 BC. British Museum. *John Freeman*

36. Denarius of Q. Cassius commemorating the trial of the Vestals in 113 BC; 58 BC. British Museum. *John Freeman*

37. Denarius of P. Porcius Laeca with the inscription Provoco ('I appeal'); *c.* 90 BC. (?). British Museum. *John Freeman*

38. Rome: detail of a relief found beneath the Palazzo della Cancellaria, with personifications of the Senate and the People; 1st century AD. Vatican Museums. *German Archaeological Institute*

39. Rome: detail of Augustus with the two consuls of the year 13 BC (?), from the Ara Pacis; 13–9 BC. *Mansell*

132–3 40. Wadi Mojib, Jordan: Roman milestones on the Via Traiana; 2nd century AD. *Adolfo Tomeucci*

VI
'The world's great age'

VII
Away from sheer beauty

VIII
Ordeals of the mind

IX
The Son of Man

X
Paganism's death struggle

XI
'That the Scripture might be fulfilled'

XII
The Word goes forth

XIII
The philosophy that faith inspired

XIV
Rival theologies

XV
The persecutions

The letters 'a' and 'b' after page references indicate the left-hand and right-hand columns respectively on the page. Page numbers in *italic* indicate illustrations.

INDEX